SCJD Exam with J2SE 5

Second Edition

Andrew Monkhouse and Terry Camerlengo

Apress®

SCJD Exam with J2SE 5, Second Edition

Copyright © 2006 by Andrew Monkhouse and Terry Camerlengo

ISBN (pbk): 1-59059-516-5

Printed and bound in the United States of America 9 8 7 6 5 4 3 2 1

Lead Editor: Jason Gilmore
Technical Reviewer: Jim Yingst
Editorial Board: Steve Anglin, Dan Appleman, Ewan Buckingham, Gary Cornell, Tony Davis,
    Jason Gilmore, Jonathan Hassell, Chris Mills, Dominic Shakeshaft, Jim Sumser
Project Manager: Beth Christmas
Copy Edit Manager: Nicole LeClerc
Copy Editor: Liz Welch
Assistant Production Director: Kari Brooks-Copony
Production Editor: Lori Bring
Compositor: Dina Quan
Proofreader: Elizabeth Berry
Indexer: John Collin
Artist: Kinetic Publishing Services, LLC
Cover Designer: Kurt Krames
Manufacturing Director: Tom Debolski

Distributed to the book trade worldwide by Springer-Verlag New York, Inc., 233 Spring Street, 6th Floor, New York, NY 10013. Phone 1-800-SPRINGER, fax 201-348-4505, e-mail orders-ny@springer-sbm.com, or visit http://www.springeronline.com.

For information on translations, please contact Apress directly at 2560 Ninth Street, Suite 219, Berkeley, CA 94710. Phone 510-549-5930, fax 510-549-5939, e-mail info@apress.com, or visit http://www.apress.com.

The source code for this book is available to readers at http://www.apress.com in the Source Code section. You will need to answer questions pertaining to this book in order to successfully download the code.

Contents at a Glance

PART 1 ▪▪▪ Introduction and General Development Considerations

PART 2 ▪▪▪ Implementing a J2SE Project

PART 3 ▪▪▪ Wrap-Up

Contents

PART 1 ■■■ Introduction and General Development Considerations

PART 2 ▪▪▪ Implementing a J2SE Project

PART 3 ▦▦▦ **Wrap-Up**

About the Authors

 **ANDREW MONKHOUSE** is a moderator on the JavaRanch web site, currently moderating the SCJD and SCJA forums.

Andrew has passed SCJP 1.2, SCJP 1.4, SCJD, SCWCD, SCBCD, and Part I of SCEA. He has been working with computers for too long (his first program was written on mark-sense cards, which are similar to punch cards).

Andrew has worked in a number of positions from programmer, to architect and IT manager, working on VMS, Unix, Macintosh, and Microsoft operating systems. He's built back-end, middleware, and front-end solutions for a variety of industries. Andrew is an Australian at heart, although he is frequently in other countries for work purposes.

 **TERRY CAMERLENGO** has over 9 years of software engineering experience from numerous corporations, including Fortune 500s and dot-coms. He is experienced in all phases of the software life cyle, with a focus on object-oriented technologies such as Java, C#, C++, and .NET. His expertise includes front-end web design, server-side enterprise development, and relational database modeling and development. Terry holds both Sun and Microsoft certifications, and graduated with a degree in computer science and philosophy from Ohio State University. Currently Terry works for Ohio State University's James Cancer Center in the Biomedical Informatics department as a senior developer and research specialist and is pursuing advanced studies in computational biology.

About the Technical Reviewer

JIM YINGST studied engineering physics at the University of Arizona, but after graduating he got sucked into the IT job market instead because, well, it seemed like a good idea at the time. He now roams the West helping tech companies find solutions to their IT problems.

Jim is a sheriff (administrator) and longtime contributor at www.javaranch.com, where his duties include answering Java questions, redirecting off-topic posts, and dealing with troublesome Australians.

He seems to spend most of his free time obsessively visiting bookstores. On rare occasions he actually reads the stuff he buys, mostly science fiction. The rest of the time he's probably listening to obscure progressive rock bands or finding new Thai restaurants. Jim lives in Boulder, Colorado.

Acknowledgments

We would like to thank the following people:

- Mehran (Max) Habibi, who did so much work on the first edition and in getting this edition started, as well as introducing us to each other and to the Apress staff

- Our technical editor Jim Yingst, who not only verified our writing but made so many wonderful suggestions

- The fantastic staff at Apress for working with us on this project, and taking our raw work and producing a polished publication

- Each other

Without the help of all these people, this book would not be anywhere near as good as it is. We would also like to thank family, friends, and colleagues who put up with our bouncing between being totally unsociable when there were deadlines to meet, and desperately trying to catch up with everyone in the quiet times.

Andrew Monkhouse and Terry Camerlengo

Introduction

The Sun Certified Developer for the Java 2 Platform assignment offers a unique opportunity for Java developers to put their Java skills to practical use without requiring any specific development or runtime environment. The assignment also provides a great learning environment as many different APIs can be used, and many alternative solutions can be provided. This book introduces many of the concepts you will need to know in order to pass the SCJD assignment.

Many developers are a little daunted by the scope of the assignment, as it covers everything from a back-end database, a server application, a front-end application, API documentation, and user documention. This book covers each section in detail, helping you gradually build up your knowledge of each topic while working toward a sample project. This book will also introduce you to the new features of JDK 5, providing contextual usage of the new APIs and features within our sample project.

The Sun assignment deliberately does not specify an operating system platform or development environment to be used—all that is needed is a computer capable of running a current version of the JDK. Throughout this book we have used JDK 5 on Windows 2000. Since this book introduces JDK 5 features, and uses them throughout our sample project, you will need JDK 5 to run our sample applications; however, the sample application is not dependent on Windows 2000.

We hope you enjoy this book, and we look forward to hearing that you passed and any comments you may have on this book. You can contact both authors at scjd@apress.com.

PART 1

Introduction and General Development Considerations

CHAPTER 1

■ ■ ■

Introduction

Welcome to *The Sun Certified Java Developer Exam with J2SE 5, Second Edition*. By taking advantage of the new features of J2SE 5, passing the Sun Certified Java Developer (SCJD) exam is easier than ever before. Features such as generics, the enhanced for loop, autoboxing and unboxing of primitives, the new concurrency classes, and other new capabilities offer developers a richer and more robust tool set than ever before. This book and the accompanying sample project will help you acquire the understanding necessary to pass the SCJD examination while learning the finer points of the J2SE Development Kit (JDK 5). If you have been meaning to take the SCJD exam or you are ready to further explore the mysteries of Java, you have found the right book.

The best way to learn a new skill is to use it. This is true in tennis, pottery, and yes, programming. With that principle firmly in mind, this book helps you learn about J2SE 5 while detailing the strategies, skills, and information needed to pass the SCJD exam. Sun Microsystems designed the SCJD exam to be a realistic example of what a professional Java developer can expect to encounter in the real world. The SCJD exam covers a large portion of J2SE, including Remote Method Invocation (RMI), threading, file input/output (I/O), and Swing.

The sample project, Denny's DVDs (introduced in Chapter 3), is designed to explore the same concepts that the SCJD exam does. Unlike on the SCJD exam, however, the underlying concepts are explained in detail. When you have finished this book, you will have learned the skills necessary to take and pass Sun's exam.

The two major topics discussed in this chapter are

- Finding out how to download and take the SCJD exam

- Understanding the goals of this book

J2SE 5

J2SE 5 is a major update, designed to improve ease of development, increase scalability, provide for additional monitoring and manageability, and enhance the Java desktop clients. While J2SE 5 offers a slew of new and exciting features, this book focuses on bread-and-butter topics such as threading, RMI, Swing, sockets, exception chaining, logging, and serialization. Once you understand the foundations, everything else follows naturally.

The SCJD Exam

The SCJD certification is a comprehensive test used by Sun to verify the skills of advanced Java programmers. It is generally considered a strong benchmark of competence. This book focuses on the features of J2SE 5 that are relevant to this exam. Adequate preparation is essential to pass the exam. Due to its difficulty, the opportunity to take the SCJD exam is only available to programmers who have already passed the Sun Certified Java Programmer (SCJP) exam. Fortunately, this book explains the concepts you need to know to pass the SCJD exam.

■**Note** Three Sun Certified Java Programmer exams are currently available: one for certification on each of the J2SE 1.2, J2SE 1.4, or J2SE 5.0 platforms, respectively. While the questions for each of these certifications differ slightly (for example, the J2SE 1.2 exam has Abstract Windowing Toolkit [AWT] questions), you only need to be certified in any one of these three certifications in order to be eligible for the SCJD certification.

The Certification Process

The SCJD certification process consists of two parts. The first part is an assignment consisting of a custom-designed sample project with a sample data file, an interface to be implemented, and specific requirements. You complete the assignment and return it for grading. Information on how to register for the assignment and download the assignment instructions and data file are presented in the next section of this chapter.

When you have completed the assignment and returned it for grading, you move on to the second part of the certification process, which is a written test designed to confirm that you wrote the assignment you submitted, and to investigate the understanding that led to the design and implementation decisions made during the first part of the exam. You may take up to 90 minutes to complete the written exam; however, since there are currently only four questions on the exam, you should find that you have more than enough time to complete it.

It is not possible to have notes or material with you for that exam. As such, it is best to take the written exam as soon as possible after you have submitted your assignment, while all the details are still fresh in your mind. Both sections are graded at once, even though the coding section is collected first. This means that the second exam will ask generic questions rather than specific ones about your individual project. You need a holistic understanding to pass both parts of the SCJD exam.

■**Caution** The assignment you submit will not be passed to an assessor for grading until *after* you have completed the essay exam. If you do not take the essay exam, you will not receive any warning that your assignment is not being assessed—it will just sit in limbo until you finally do take the essay exam.

The goal of the SCJD exam is to validate your understanding of the most important Java skills, including threading, RMI, sockets, serialization, file I/O, and Swing. Each assignment project can be unique, testing these features to different degrees. For example, while you must write a server capable of handling concurrent requests, the interface provided might change which classes you allow multiple threads to run on. Or your requirements could call for strict search requirements versus more general searching ability. This book gathers together everything you need to know about all the relevant topics and integrates in the relevant changes in J2SE 5.

Sun also requires you to use a current JDK (one that has not been superseded by a newer JDK by more than 18 months) for developing your solution, ensuring that candidates stay current with the latest features of the JDK. A list of release dates may be found at `http://java.sun.com/j2se/codenames.html`.

Downloading the Assignment

You can register for the assignment and examination by visiting `http://www.sun.com/training/certification/java/java_devj2se.html` in the United States. Many other countries also allow online registration—you can view contact details at `http://www.sun.com/training/world_training.html`. After paying for the assignment, you will receive an e-mail from Sun telling you exactly how to download the Java archive (JAR) files that contain the assignment instructions. Receiving this e-mail may take a few days, or it may happen that same day. As soon as you receive the JAR files, make a couple of copies and store them safely. It is very expensive to get a second copy of the assignment to match the subject of this section.

■**Tip** The Sun Education web site lists the web address where you may download your assignment. You may be able to download your assignment before you have received an e-mail specifying that your account has been configured for downloading.

Documentation and Questions

You are probably going to have questions regarding the requirements of the exam. Generally, Sun will not answer these questions. This may be because they want to see how well you can choose between different solutions (and describe why you made your decisions). It may be because they are trying to emulate real-world conditions where the client is not always willing to communicate. It may even be because answering questions for each test applicant is an untenable task. In any case, it is very important that you articulate your questions and deal with them in the documentation you must create as part of your assignment deliverables. If nothing else, you should document your assumptions and choices. For more help, we suggest using the excellent resources available at JavaRanch (`http://www.javaranch.com`) and the various helpful Java certification groups on Yahoo.

Chapter 2 provides good suggestions on how to work with Javadoc-style comments and offers some industry best practices. Don't use outlandish naming conventions or even Hungarian notation. If possible, use whatever style the material itself uses. As far as the SCJD exam is concerned, Sun really wants you to color inside the lines.

Who Should Read This Book

This book is for the working Java professional who needs an introduction to J2SE 5 and has an eye toward learning the material needed to pass the Sun Certified Java Developer exam. The SCJD exam gives programmers a slice of what they can expect on a real-world assignment, and you have to be ready for that challenge. A developer who has passed, or could pass, the Sun Certified Java Programmer (SCJP) exam will feel at home here. A developer with less than six months of experience should probably supplement this book with some of the excellent Java books available from Apress or other publishers.

This book describes in detail many features of the JDK, some of which have been part of standard Java for many years, and some of which have only been introduced in JDK 5. The only assumption we have made in this book is that the reader will be familiar enough with Java to pass the SCJP exam—so we do not need to spend time explaining the basics of the language (for example, the difference between an int and a long). However, we do go into details of changes to the language, so candidates who have not yet learned the JDK 5 language enhancements can discover them here.

About This Book

This book addresses the SCJD certification, which is one of several Java certification exams offered by Sun Microsystems. The SCJD and SCEA (Sun Certified Enterprise Architect) certificates require candidates to complete projects, whereas the other certifications only require theory-based exams in which the candidate typically has multichoice questions to answer. As far as programming goes, the SCJD exam is the most challenging of the exams that Sun offers, and that is precisely why it is the focus of this book.

This book is divided into three parts. Part 1 focuses on general development considerations and outlines a sample project. Part 2 teaches necessary concepts from the ground up, while facilitating both understanding and implementation. Part 3 concludes the book with a discussion of design and implementation decisions made and possible alternative paths.

A sample project is provided that offers challenges similar to those you'll find on the SCJD exam while introducing and taking advantage of the relevant new features of J2SE 5. Each topic related to the exam is explained in detail, and trade-offs are considered. Where appropriate, parallel development paths are explored and implemented.

Where applicable, chapters briefly discuss the design patterns being used and offer a brief explanation of those patterns. We strongly encourage you to purchase or download some pattern resources. Various web sites offer insightful tutorials, including the Sun site (http://www.sun.com) and TheServerSide.com (http://www.theserverside.com). There are also various excellent books on the topic, including *Head First Design Patterns*, by Elisabeth Freeman, Eric Freeman, Bert Bates, and Kathy Sierra (O'Reilly, 2004).

Throughout this book, we present numerous examples that aid in the development of a real-world Java application. Each chapter contributes directly to this application by addressing a critical topic such as threading, Swing, or networking. The text explores questions that naturally arise in these topics and explains how the challenges can be met. More important, the trade-offs and implications of these choices are discussed.

- Chapter 1, "Introduction." This chapter is a general introduction provided to help you decide if this book meets your needs. It lays out the structure of the educational program to follow, introduces the goals of the exam, and focuses the technology discussions to follow.

- Chapter 2, "Project Analysis and Design." This chapter details basic project considerations such as directory structure, package development, coding conventions, ReadMe files, and general approaches to starting a project for the SCJD exam.

- Chapter 3, "Project Overview." This chapter introduces the sample project, Denny's DVDs. This application requires that you develop classes to access a file in a database-like manner, build a Swing user interface, and design a networking layer. It is important to read this chapter carefully because it helps to define exactly what the project is trying to accomplish.

- Chapter 4, "Threading." This chapter starts from scratch and helps guide you to a clear understanding of threads. You will also learn about the `Runnable` interface, the `Thread` class, locks, synchronization, waiting, sleeping, notification of one or all waiting threads, the constraints of using threads with Swing, deadlocks, and thread scheduling. We will then move on to the new scheduling package of J2SE 5, and demonstrate how this can make threading easier. The focus is on the threading material you need to know in order to earn your Java developer certification.

- Chapter 5, "The DvdDatabase Class." This chapter demonstrates how to create a class that will meet the requirements of our sample project and implement a specified interface. We will use the Façade, Value Object, and Adapter patterns to simplify the code.

- Chapter 6, "Networking with RMI." This chapter provides an introduction to distributed computing. You will learn about RMI and how to utilize it when building your clients and servers.

- Chapter 7, "Networking with Sockets." This chapter provides an introduction to an alternative method of developing distributed computing. You will learn about sockets, and the pros and cons of working with sockets instead of RMI. Chapter 7 also briefly discusses security, serialization, the Command and Proxy patterns, and the sample project.

- Chapter 8, "The Graphical User Interfaces." This chapter provides an introduction to Swing. It is designed for Java programmers who have little to no Swing experience. The chapter assumes you are starting from scratch and quickly explains the fundamentals of how Swing works, what the MVC pattern is, how events are handled, how `JTables` work, and how all the pieces fit together.

- Chapter 9, "Project Wrap-Up." This chapter gives us a chance to examine the project in hindsight. We apply finishing touches and organize our JAR files. We also review the decisions made and the trade-offs involved, and prepare the project for submission.

The source code for the project, as well as various helpful diagrams and documents, can be obtained from the Source Code section of `http://www.apress.com`.

Setting Up the J2SE 5 JDK and Environmental Variables

Setting up the J2SE 5 JDK is very straightforward. Sun provides extensive documentation on how to do so for the various platforms, so we will not rehash all of that material.

Information on downloading and configuring the J2SE 5 JDK is available at `http://java.sun.com/j2se`.

Summary

In this chapter, we presented a broad overview of the Sun Certified Java Developer (SCJD) exam, as well as strategies you can use to meet your goal of passing the exam. We identified the areas that the exam covers, discussed the test itself, and offered some suggestions on taking it. We also provided a breakdown of the topics discussed in this book, integrated in the relevant J2SE 5 material.

With this information, you have already begun to prepare for the exam.

Congratulations! With about four weeks spent covering the issues set forth in this book, you should be able to take and pass the SCJD exam. In general, you should expect to spend a week on each of the four major topics: threading, Swing, networking, and the user interface. Of course, this will vary depending on your personal background. You now have a sense of what to expect. Good luck, study hard, and e-mail us at `scjd@apress.com` when you pass the exam.

FAQs

Q Am I ready to take the SCJD exam?

A If you have passed, or could pass, the Sun Certified Java Programmer (SCJP) exam, you are ready to prepare for the SCJD exam. There is no time limit on completing the assignment, so you could purchase it and learn as you work through the book and assignment simultaneously. However, be aware that there is a time limit on the exam voucher, and some Sun offices require you to purchase both the assignment and the exam voucher simultaneously.

Q Will this book help me if I am preparing for the Sun Certified Java Programmer (SCJP) exam?

A Using this book in conjunction with a book covering the SCJP topics may help your understanding of the topics; however, we do not recommend that this book be used as reference material for SCJP candidates. Although several of the topics required for SCJP certification are covered in this book in detail, many required topics are either not covered or are used without explanation on the assumption that their usage is well known. In addition, this book covers many topics that are not required for the SCJP.

Q I'm having some difficulty setting up my environment. Where should I turn for help?

A Look to the Sun Microsystems Java web site (`http://java.sun.com/j2se`) and follow their documentation exactly. If that doesn't work, contact Sun directly.

Q What topics does this book discuss?

A This book discusses and explains RMI, threading, Swing, networking, assertions, exception chaining, and logging.

Q How much does the SCJD exam cost?

A The exam costs roughly US$400. This price is, of course, subject to change at Sun's discretion.

Q I've lost my exam—what should I do?

A Try downloading the exam from Sun's site again. If that doesn't work, contact Sun directly.

CHAPTER 2

∎∎∎

Project Analysis and Design

This chapter introduces project issues that are common to all software projects, discussing them in relation to this book's sample project and the Sun assignment that you need to complete to become a Sun Certified Java Developer. In particular, the following topics will be covered:

- Planning the beginning stages of the SCJD exam

- Organizing the layout of your project

- Documenting projects

- Becoming familiar with industry-standard principles on source code formatting and Javadoc, and incorporating these principles from the onset of project development

- Using Java packages to group code based on functional similarities

- Learning common development practices, including using assertions and logging

This chapter does not attempt to forge a new road, but rather leads down the well-worn paths of Java standards, such as coding conventions, Javadoc usage, and packaging concepts. Some of these tools are necessary in order to pass the SCJD exam, and all should be used every day by a Java developer.

By using these standards from the beginning, you will be well on your way to reaching your goal of being a certified Java 2 developer.

Implementing a Project

It is very tempting to start a project by jumping right into code. Doing so is fun and grants an immediate sense of progress. However, this approach often has significant drawbacks. Beginning a project without proper planning may tie the project to unspoken assumptions, cause you to overlook critical information, or introduce design flaws that manifest as the project progresses.

Generally, it is best to start by confirming requirements, designing data flow, and sketching a prototype of the graphical user interface (GUI) layout. After this step comes the design.

■**Note** Many different development methodologies are used in varying degrees in the software industry. Some of the commonly used design approaches are the Iterative Process, the Rational Unified Process, the Boehm Spiral Model, and XP (Extreme Programming). In this book, we are using another common model: the Waterfall Model. As its name implies, this design model requires that development be an ongoing process, with one version of software based on a previous version, and so on. In addition, requirements are determined before project design and development begin in this model. The SCJD exam allows unlimited time to complete the project, and it requires that you work as a single developer. Both of these special criteria set forth in the SCJD exam fit perfectly into the Waterfall methodology.

Design is a fluid process that is grounded by coding. The best way to begin a project design is to explore the technical challenges ahead by coding a little, designing a little, and coding some more. In this respect, project design becomes an iterative process. Some suggested principles follow.

Getting Started

As a first step, spend a little time verifying your understanding of the requirements. Read the material several times and scrutinize its contents. Explore the logical breakdown of functionality and document your assumptions. Make sure that you note the umbrella activities that encompass several different variations under a given topic. This often helps with the package structure design. For example, it might make sense to have a GUI package that is responsible for visual presentation.

Gathering Requirements

Requirements are functions of a project that the client wants in the system you are creating. The requirements should detail everything that the system is required to do. Our suggestion is to ask questions. Better yet, ask a lot of questions. Write down the questions before you formulate answers, and ensure that they make sense. For the sake of clarity, phrase them differently and ask them again. It is probably best to be thought a little slow at the beginning of a project than to be proven careless at the end.

Confirm all assumptions either in writing or as a GUI layout. Of course, on this project, you are not going to be able to ask anyone your questions, but that should not prevent you from articulating potential issues and project risks. As a matter of fact, it should encourage you to formulate questions to organize your thoughts.

■**Note** Chapter 3 introduces some example use cases derived from project requirements. Chapter 8 presents a full example of dealing with use cases and their translation to project functionality.

Prototyping the GUI

When you begin prototyping the GUI portion of the project, draw out simple layouts of the various command windows with pencil and paper. This activity will help you acquire a sense of what the user needs to see before you decide how the interface will work internally. This is often a crucial step in reconciling user expectations with the reality imposed by the system implementation. Chapter 8 presents examples of GUI prototyping and the interface layout process.

We recommend that you prototype the GUI using pencil and paper at this stage, rather than directly on the computer. Coding directly on computer runs the following risks:

- The design that you thought was so good, and that you spent so much time on, might be rejected by your sample testers (see the sidebar, "Sample Testers"), resulting in wasted time.

- You will almost certainly require more time to prototype a GUI on the computer compared with sketching the GUI layout on paper. We recommend you show your prototype to some sample testers (see the sidebar), and if they have recommendations for change (or, worst case, reject your prototype) there will be less time wasted if your prototype is only a penciled sketch.

- If you have a penciled sketch of your GUI, you can discuss it with your sample testers anywhere, regardless of whether there is a computer handy. And any changes they suggest can be incorporated in a few seconds.

- If you have spent a large amount of time coding your prototype, there is a natural resistance to changing it, which might result in you rejecting some otherwise excellent ideas from your sample users.

- You may get frustrated with implementation details long before a prototype is in place, and as a result you may sacrifice a good design for something that is easier to develop, and, accordingly a lower score for your GUI.

- If you code the GUI now, you may end up with something that you believe is very nice, but which you later find your users don't like. Once again, you run the risk of having to start from scratch.

▓**Note** In Chapter 8 we will be developing the GUIs for our sample project, and as part of this we will be showing some rough sketches of alternate screen layouts we might use for our project.

SAMPLE TESTERS

It is a truism that programmers write programs for programmers. That is, for any given assignment, we as programmers will tend to write a program that *we believe* is very logical but that most nonprogrammers will find difficult to use. This effect happens in all professions, and some professions employ staff simply to work on aesthetics—for example, some car manufacturers hire staff whose only job is to ensure that the car will look good to the final consumer.

We need to do something similar if we want to write GUI applications that the end users (in the case of the Sun assignment, the assignment assessor) will like and accordingly, approve (in the case of the Sun assignment, award full marks). Having end-user approval is extremely important—otherwise we end up in a never-ending cycle of making one change after another to the GUI. We need someone who is (preferably) not a programmer who can look at our prototype and our final application, and tell us what needs to be changed to make them feel like it is a great application, and not just a mediocre one.

These are our sample testers. They could be your spouse, your significant other, your mother, or the office secretary. They are the people who are likely to spot some feature that they consider standard, but that you have managed to leave out. And they are the ones who are likely to look at your application and tell you that something is in the wrong place. And when it comes to testing the final application, they are the ones who are likely to do the things you were not expecting—trying to open two applications at once, or trying to reduce the size of your application screen below the size you thought anyone would use.

The people to try to avoid are other programmers—they are the people who are most likely to not mention some feature because they don't like that particular feature themselves. Furthermore, they may ignore a usability issue because they are used to working around issues in others' programs.

So see if you can think of some sample testers, take your rough sketches of screens to them, and ask them what they think. Then listen to their comments, and go back and make any necessary modifications.

If possible, take some samples of totally different screens to your sample testers—give them a choice of what sort of interface they would like to work with. They will feel that they have more involvement, and they will often feel that they can suggest more modifications to one of your sample layouts since it has not yet been finalized.

Using Accepted Design Patterns

Failing to follow conventions is rarely worth the development time. Worse, it may cause you to fail Sun's exam. Worst of all, in the real world it will attract the hatred of programmers who will have to maintain the cryptic code that ensues.

While it is possible, and often clever, to implement custom solutions to general problems, you should resist the temptation to do so for this project and Sun's exam. In real life, however, custom solutions are occasionally faster and cheaper than general solutions. For example, a custom method that sorts the elements of an array may be faster than the methods that are built into the Arrays class.

Since this book's focus is not software design patterns, there are many design patterns that we cannot cover in this book. We strongly recommend that you read up on these yourself, as you will use them in your development career. The most widely recognized book on the subject is *Design Patterns* by Erich Gamma, Richard Helm, Ralph Johnson, and John Vlissides (Addison-Wesley Professional, 1995). This is commonly referred to as the "Gang of Four," or GOF, book. You may find that this is not the easiest book to read, so you may wish to investigate some of the alternatives such as "Head First Design Patterns" by Elisabeth Freeman, Eric Freeman, Bert Bates, and Kathy Sierra (O'Reilly, 2004), the Portland Pattern Repository at `http://c2.com/ppr/index.html`, or the Wikipedia entries for design patterns starting at `http://en.wikipedia.org/wiki/Design_pattern_(computer_science)`. Sun's J2EE design patterns at `http://java.sun.com/blueprints/patterns/` are also very useful, but you should be aware that they are J2EE-centric, and may describe patterns in a form that may not seem to make sense for this assignment.

Documenting Design Decisions

Document the choices that you make during the development process. Write down the various decisions you make and the reasons you make them. For example, if you decide to use an `ArrayList` instead of a `Vector` for an internal data structure, document the fact the `ArrayList`s are not synchronized and thus were chosen because they are a more lightweight data structure. There is no need to go overboard with this type of documentation, so be mindful to use common sense. This sort of documentation is a crucial tool in debugging and performance tuning, and it also serves as an excellent source for anyone who needs to understand the code.

Whatever you do, don't leave documenting your design decisions until the end of the project. If you wait until after you have completed coding before beginning this document, not only will you have to remember why you chose a particular option, but you will also have to remember that you had other options in the first place! For example, if you decided at the start of the assignment that you were going to use a custom dialog box, at the end of the assignment you might have forgotten that you had originally also considered having an editable cell on the main window.

It is quite possible that by the time you get to the end of the assignment, you may find that your design decisions document is huge—minor decisions can be removed to reduce the size of the document.

■**Tip** You might want to use bullet points to describe your design decisions. Not only will this reduce the amount you write, but also they are easier to remember when it comes time for the exam. This is especially useful for candidates for whom English is not their first language—you will not have to be so concerned about how good your spelling is or how well you have formed your sentences.

For instance, we might document a few decisions like so:

- Sockets used instead of RMI—allows complete control over threads

- `RandomAccessFile` used instead of separate `DataInputStream` and `DataOutputStream` classes—allows for random access to the file

Testing

You should begin testing by writing a unit test client for each class, or you can use a testing tool such as JUnit (`http://www.junit.org/`) to automatically generate test clients. When you design a custom test, it is best to write the test class before implementing the methods to be tested.

We recommend that you design tests that cover the conditions set forth in a project's written requirements before beginning the development process. Under these conditions, if a class provides the functionality detailed in the project requirements without failing the prewritten tests, then the test can be considered a success. Additional functionality beyond what is required is unnecessary. Writing test cases before coding deliverable classes will prevent the overzealous programmer from dwelling on functionality that is not required.

As your project develops, you may find yourself adding to, or changing, methods within the class. Be sure to update test clients accordingly as the project classes evolve. It is generally recommended that test cases should never be deleted—once the test has been written, it provides valuable confirmation that basic functionality still works if you modify your deliverable classes.

■Note A unit test simply tests a unit (usually a class) that you have written. If your class has a setDvdName(String dvdName) method, then your unit test should call it, preferably with the various kinds of input it can expect. You should do this for every method. Unit testing is not required for the exam, but we strongly recommend it as a sanity test. Of course, you should not send your unit tests or their results to Sun.

When the application is ready for system testing, recruit some volunteers to help. It is generally best to avoid system-testing your own code—use an unsympathetic and unbiased eye to look over the system. When you design the system test, it is a good idea to work with the client. If this is not possible (as it is not in this project), then use the requirements gathered at the beginning of the project.

■Note A system test simply tests how the various units (usually classes) fit together. For example, your client class might need to call your DVD class's setDvdName(String dvdName) method. Even though you know the client and the DVD class both work correctly from the unit test, you don't know if they work well together. For example, there might be a network problem or the client class might store DVD names as an array of characters, where the DVD class uses String. System testing enables you to make sure that all of your classes play nicely together.

Organizing a Project

One of the first tasks in any software project is determining a sound organization for all related project materials. An organizational paradigm, in this case, is a directory structure aimed at organizing all files associated with the project. It is extremely difficult to decide such matters later in the development process and attempt a retrofit. You should decide upon a directory structure early in the project planning stage. A typical project directory structure follows. Sun does not dictate a directory structure for the development of the SCJD assignment; however, on some assignments they do specify some top-level directories to be used in the submission. The directory structure in Table 2-1 acts as a suggested organizational foundation for the assignment. We use the structure detailed in Table 2-1 throughout this book's example application project.

Table 2-1. *Suggested Directory Structure*

Subdirectory	Recommended Use
src\	Contains all of the .java source files written during the course of the project.
classes\	Contains all compiled class files and any packaged JAR files. The classpath will point to this directory when we are running our application.
bkp\	A directory to hold any files needed for backup.
tst\	Contains all of the .java source files written for unit-testing the project.
tmp\	A "hold anything" directory for temporary storage.
log\	A directory to store all logged output.
doc\	Holds all documentation, including Javadocs, end-user documentation, and design decisions documentation.

High-Level Documentation

In addition to completing the code portion of the test, to pass the SCJD exam you must author and submit several forms of documentation. At the time of writing, the following documentation is required:

- Javadoc documentation (discussed in depth later in this chapter).

- A plain text file named version.txt.

- User instructions—unless the user instructions are built into your application and available while the application is running.

- A design decisions document. The design decisions document is discussed in detail in the following section.

The version.txt file must contain an explanation of the following items:

- The version of the JDK used for development

- The development platform

This book uses JDK version 5 and Microsoft Windows 2000.

▓**Caution** There are currently several different Sun assignments in use, and instructions may vary between assignments. Sun may also release assignments in the future with other minor differences in the instructions. While the information in this book will be generally applicable to any current assignment, you must take care to read the instructions you have received from Sun carefully, and ensure that you follow them.

WHAT EXTRA FILES SHOULD YOU INCLUDE IN SUBMISSIONS?

We often see questions from candidates asking whether they should include their test cases and/or their class diagrams in their submission.

Our general recommendation is not to include anything that you have not been asked for. The latest instructions from Sun include a comment that you will not be given extra marks for anything you do outside of the requirements, so you are not going to gain anything by providing the assessor with these extra files. However, it is unfortunately possible that in providing these files you may inadvertently lower your score simply by making a mistake that the assessor notices in a file that you didn't need to provide.

The one time we might consider changing this general recommendation is where the additional files make it much simpler to understand your submission. A class diagram might be one such example (however, the assignment is simple enough that if you need a class diagram to understand the submission, then you have probably overcomplicated your solution).

User directions are essential. After all, if you do not explain to the client how to use the application, then the application is rendered useless. As a result, you should take great care when writing these instructions. The only safe assumption you as the developer can make is that the end user has no experience with this particular application. Every step, no matter how minute, must be detailed in the instructions. After you list the instructions, test their clarity by handing them off to unsuspecting friends (preferably nonprogrammers). If they can follow the instructions, then the instructions are adequate.

■**Caution** The current assignment instructions specify that the instructions you write may be placed in a specific directory or may be available online. This directive has caused confusion in the past, as some candidates have felt that this might mean that this requires them to run a web server—but this is not the case. Sun only requires that the assessor have access to the instructions, which can be achieved if the instructions are in the required directory, or alternatively can be called up from within your application (for example, pressing the F1 key in Microsoft Word will bring up "online help" even if you do not have an Internet connection).

Design Decisions Document

Throughout the SCJD exam, certain design and implementation choices are already dictated by Sun. One example is that the exam requires the use of the JTable Swing component. Other choices, however, are left up to you, the test taker, to decide. For instance, you may choose to implement a networking layer that uses RMI, or you may take a different approach that is built upon sockets. Each implementation has advantages and disadvantages. You must be certain to document your choices because it is necessary to defend these design decisions to the individual who will ultimately decide if your test submission passes or fails.

For the SCJD exam, clearly document your design choices in a design decisions document. This document should contain examples of specific decisions, such as your choice of design pattern or the use of one technology over another. Circumstances may also arise in which design decisions were made based on unclear functional requirements. If this situation does occur, raise the issue as a design decision and document all the assumptions you made to deal with the problem. Be certain to complete the design decisions document, because it is the only chance the test allows you to defend your submitted project.

▓**Tip** It is worth noting that in the Sun assignment, as with projects in real life, there are sometimes several solutions to any given problem. It is also possible that for *every* possible solution there will be reasons why that particular solution is not optimal. You should not spend too much time trying to find the "one perfect solution"—it may not exist. Sun has deliberately left enough vagueness in the assignment instructions that there are very few areas where candidates have limited choices. In all other cases, it does not matter so much what choice is made, but it does matter how you came to your choice, which should be detailed in your design decisions document.

Java Coding Conventions

One of the common goals in our industry is the ability to hand over the project to someone else—let them do any maintenance in the future, as you won't be available (you will be working on more exciting projects and going on vacation).

To meet this goal, the code we write needs to be formatted in such a way that you can hand it over to somebody else, and they will happily accept it. It will not do your reputation any good if you hand over the code, and the other person throws it all away as being incomprehensible. In the same way, it would not do us any good if we did not organize this book into chapters, paragraphs, and sentences—if you can't read this book, you won't learn much from it.

The developers of Java, C, and C++ deliberately avoided forcing coders to follow a specific coding convention—there are syntactical requirements, but as long as you meet them, the code can appear on a printed page any way you like it to. For instance, consider the following code snippet:

```java
public class MyTest {
    public static void main(String[] args) {
        System.out.println("Hello");
    }
}
```

That code is interpreted by the Java compiler in exactly the same way as

```java
public
class
MyTest{public static void main(String
z[]){System.out.println("Hello");}}
```

You'll undoubtedly agree that the first format is far more readable than the second.

While it is easy to agree that a code-formatting style should be followed, it is less easy to agree on the code-formatting style itself. For example, often one person prefers to have the brace ({) at the end of an existing line; another prefers to have the brace on its own line. Both coders can have compelling arguments for their particular style, but realistically only one style should be followed on any given project.

In the workplace, management will usually specify which particular style must be used. For this book, and for the SCJD assignment, we recommend you use the Sun Code Conventions for the Java Programming Language, which you can download at `http://java.sun.com/docs/codeconv/`. Sun has specified 11 areas where they believe coding guidelines are needed, and these can be grouped into the following major categories: naming conventions, file layout, source code format, and comment format. We introduce each of these categories next.

Naming Conventions

The Sun Code Conventions specify different naming conventions for packages, classes and interfaces, methods, variables, and constants.

For all of the naming conventions, you should try to avoid using abbreviations, except where the abbreviation is more commonly recognized than the complete word. At the same time, you should try not to make your names too long, or they will quickly become tedious to read and write. Consider the variable names shown in Table 2-2.

Table 2-2. *Variable Naming Examples*

Contents	Good Variable Name	Poor Variable Name
The balance of an account	`accountBalance`	`usersCurrentAccountBalance` (too long) `ab` (not a common abbreviation; doesn't mean much)
HTML editor class	`HtmlEditor`	`HyperTextMarkupLanguageEditor` ("HTML" is a common abbreviation, so using it will enhance the readability of this class name)

Package Naming Conventions

Package names start with your fully qualified domain name, written in lowercase and in reverse. So if you worked for a company with the domain name `example.com`, then your package names should start with the same name in reverse (`com.example`).

From that point on, you would follow your company's naming conventions. A sample naming convention might be to use the project name, followed by a conceptual grouping of classes. For instance, as we are working on the SCJD project, which contains a GUI client, we could have a combined package name of `com.sun.edu.scjd.gui` (for simplicity though, we have used the base package name of `sampleproject` throughout our project, and the GUI code is therefore in package `sampleproject.gui`).

■**Tip** In the real assignment, Sun will typically specify a package name for at least one class. Therefore, you do not need to be concerned that you do not have an existing domain name that you can use as your base package name.

Class and Interface Naming Conventions

Class and interface names should always start with a capital letter, and should be a noun (they should describe an object, not an action on the object). For example, "Book" might be used as the name of the class containing information about a book.

It is common to combine two or more nouns or an adjective and a noun together to form the class name, in which case CamelCase is used (the first letter of each word is capitalized, producing the undulating pattern associated with camels). For example, "SocketFactory" might be used as the name of a class that creates socket connections.

■**Tip** You should try to have only one responsibility for each class. For instance, a class that is responsible for creating an RMI connection to a server should not also be responsible for displaying data to the end user. If you can maintain "one responsibility per class," you will find it easier to name your classes. This provides a major benefit later when it is time to modify or maintain your classes—the separation of responsibilities and clear class names makes it much easier to determine which classes need to be modified.

Method Naming Conventions

Method names should always start with a lowercase letter, and should begin with a verb (they should describe an action on the object). For example, within our DVD class, the method name getLeadActor indicates that we can call this method to get the name of the lead actor for the DVD.

It is very common to combine several words to give more information on what the method does. For instance, using the method name getLeadActor makes it far more explicit when *using* this method that we are specifically retrieving the lead actor's name (and not the name of some other person associated with this DVD). As can be seen in this example, CamelCase is used when combining words.

Variable Naming Conventions

Variable names should always start with a lowercase letter, should be short, and should describe what data is stored in the variable. For example, within our DVD class, the variable name leadActor would contain the names of the lead actor of the film on DVD.

Again, it is very common to combine several words to provide more information on what the variable does. As you can see in this example, CamelCase is used when combining words.

■**Note** The Sun Coding Conventions specify that you should apply the same naming convention to all instance, class, and local variables. Be aware that you may see code written by other coders where instance or class variables are signified by an underscore or some other special mark. Another way to achieve the same effect is by using the convention variable when referring to a local variable, this.variable when referring to an instance variable, and Class.variable when referring to a class variable. Doing so makes it explicit which type of variable you are referring to.

Constant Naming Conventions

Constants are always written in all capital letters, with individual words separated by under-scores. An example might be the constant DIRECTOR_LENGTH, which would be set to the maximum size of the director's name stored in our database.

File Layout

A Java class or interface always consists of the following standard layout:

1. Beginning comments

2. Package and import statements

3. Class or interface declarations

The Sun Code Conventions state that two blank lines should appear between each of these major sections. That is, there should be two blank lines between the beginning comments and the package statement. Similarly, there should be two blank lines between the import state-ments and the class or interface declarations. In all other cases where a blank line will help readability (say, between method declarations), you would normally only have a single blank line. A simple example is shown in the following code snippet:

```
1  /*
2   * HelloWorld.java    version 1.0.0    date 2005-06-20
3   * Copyright © Andrew Monkhouse & Terry Camerlengo 2005
4   *
5   * This is a version of the hello world program
6   * The beginning comment, has two blank lines following it
7   */
8
9
10 package com.example.javaExamples;
11
12 import java.util.Date;
13
14
15 public class HelloWorld {
16     public static void main(String[] args) {
17         sayHello();
18     }
19
20     public static void sayHello() {
21         System.out.println("Hello, world at " + new Date() + "\n");
22     }
23 }
```

As shown here, there are two blank lines between each of the major sections: lines 8 and 9 separate the beginning comments from the package and import statements, and lines 13 and

14 separate the import statements from the class declaration. In all other cases, only a single blank line is used to separate minor sections: line 11 separates the package statement from the first import statement, and line 19 separates the contructor and method declarations.

Beginning Comments

Beginning comments are separate from Javadoc comments and, as such, are often not understood by Java programmers. The beginning comments contain some of the same information as the Javadoc comment for the class, but there are a couple of major differences: the information is provided in one standard place, and very specific information is listed. While the Javadoc comments might contain a superset of the same information as the beginning comments, there is no specific line number the information will appear on, and the desired information may be buried among API documentation. Beginning comments contain the following:

- Class name

- Version information (might be automatically filled in by your revision control system)

- Creation/modification date (might be automatically filled in by your revision control system)

- Author/last modifier (might be automatically filled in by your revision control system)

The entire comments block is a C type comment, not a Javadoc comment—that is, the comment block starts with /* and not /**.

Package and Import Statements

Following the beginning comments, you put your package statement, a blank line, and then your import statements, as shown in lines 10–12 of the preceding code example.

Although the Sun Coding Conventions document does not specify whether you should list every class or include the entire package, one common usage is to list individual classes in a package until there are three classes listed in a single package. After that, it is common to import the entire package.

Likewise, the Sun Coding Conventions do not specify whether import statements should be in any particular order. Worrying about such details is probably going beyond the scope of the requirements (and may cause your colleagues to look at you in a funny way). Many developers tend to keep them in alphabetical order, but don't get too concerned about this.

■**Tip** Many integrated development environments (IDEs) have some of the following features: automatic addition of missing import statements; automatic removal of unused import statements; and automatic refactoring of too many or too few imports in a given package. While these features can help improve your coding speed in your real job, we recommend you switch these features off while working on the SCJD assignment. One of the problems with using some of the IDE "features" is that it can become difficult to determine what has gone wrong if something does go wrong—if you learn to work with import statements manually for the SCJD assignment, you are more likely to be able to handle any issues later in life.

It is common practice to include a blank line between an import of standard J2SE packages, standard J2EE packages, external packages, and internal packages.

Class or Interface Declarations

The Sun Coding Conventions specify that a class or interface declaration should contain some or all of the following elements in the specified order:

- Class/interface Javadoc comments

- Class/interface statement

- Class variables

- Instance variables

- Constructors

- Methods

Variables should be sorted according to accessibility, from most accessible (public) through to least accessible (private). For example:

```
public class VariableOrderExample {
    public int aVariableModifiableByAnyOtherClass;
    public String anotherPublicVariable;
    // protected variables appear after public variables
    protected int protectedVariable;
    // now list the variables with default access
    Character defaultAccessVariable;
    // finally list the variables with private access
    private int noOtherClassCanSeeMe;
}
```

■**Tip** Although the location of constants is not specified by the Sun Coding Conventions, common usage is to list them prior to the class variables.

Methods, on the other hand, should be grouped by functionality rather than scope. This means you should put a common private method close to the public methods that call it.

Source Code Formatting

While you write your code, you should maintain a consistent approach to the following style issues:

- Indentation

- Line lengths/wrapping

- Spacing

- Statement formatting

- Variable declaration formatting

Most of these formatting rules have been designed so that people reading your code can do so using the IDE, editor, screen resolution, and so forth of their choice. If you were to choose a nonstandard formatting convention, then others may find your code hard to read.

■Caution Do not ever forget that you will be submitting your source code to an unknown assessor for review. You really need to write your code so that it is a pleasure for them to assess. This also applies in your real job—you should always be writing code that your coworkers are happy to use.

Indentation

The Sun Coding Conventions contain the following indentation requirement: "Four spaces should be used as the unit of indentation. The exact construction of the indentation (spaces vs. tabs) is unspecified. Tabs must be set exactly every 8 spaces (not 4)" (Sun Coding Conventions, `http://java.sun.com/docs/codeconv/html/CodeConventions.doc3.html`, 1999).

This description seems to cause a great deal of confusion when first read, so an example is in order:

```
1  public class IndentationExample {
2      /* this line is indented once */
3      public IndentationExample() {
4          /* this line is indented twice */
5      }
6  }
```

Lines 2, 3, and 5 all have one indentation, so you should prefix them with four spaces. Line 4 has two indentations, so you *should* prefix them with eight spaces. However, eight spaces are also equivalent to a tab, so you *could* use a tab instead of the eight spaces for line 4. To avoid confusion, we recommend that you use eight spaces instead of a tab.

■Tip Many IDEs and editors give you the option to insert a specified number of spaces whenever you press the Tab key (and even handle backspacing over the indentation/reformatting entire blocks of code). We recommend you check whether your IDE/editor provides this functionality and turn it on when available.

Line Lengths/Wrapping

As mentioned earlier, you cannot know what sort of an editor or what screen size your assessor will be using. Limiting line lengths to 80 characters will ensure that your code should be readable in most cases.

Lines that are longer than 80 characters should be broken after a comma or before an operator whenever possible. The second (and subsequent lines) should be indented to the beginning of the expression on the previous line, or eight spaces. For example:

```
int i = myMethod(longNamedVariable1, longNamedVariable2,
                 longNamedVariable3, longNamedVariable4);
```

Line wrapping for if, for, and while statements generally uses the eight-space indentation rule rather than the beginning of the expression, since using the beginning of the expression can cause confusion with the line that follows, which will be indented four characters. The following example shows both the preferred and nonpreferred way of breaking if statements:

```
// nonpreferred way
if (myMethod(longNamedVariable1, longNamedVariable2,
    longNamedVariable3, longNamedVariable4)) {
    // code starts here - see how confusing this is ?
    doSomething();
}

// preferred way
if (myMethod(longNamedVariable1, longNamedVariable2,
        longNamedVariable3, longNamedVariable4)) {
    // code starts here - now we can see the difference between
    // the condition and the code to be run within the condition
    doSomething();
}
```

In cases where you have multiple levels of code in one line, for example, calling a method and using the result as a parameter to another method call, it is preferable to break the line at the higher level—keep the call to the external method on one line where possible. For example:

```
int i = myMethod(variable1,
                 callToAnotherMethod(variable1, variable2),
                 (variable1 + variable2));
```

In such cases as this last example, you should consider whether your code would be more readable and understandable if you were to refactor it. For example, you could

- Move the external procedure call to a separate line.

- Move the calculation in parentheses to a separate line.

- Make both modifications.

Consider how much easier the following code might be to read and maintain:

```
int dbValue = callToAnotherMethod(variable1, variable2);
int calculated = variable1 + variable2;
int i = myMethod(variable1, dbValue, calculated);
```

Once you get beyond your third or fourth level of indentation, you may find that these rules are hard to follow. This is often also an indication that your code may be difficult to follow, and you should think about whether you could move some of the indented code into a separate method.

Spacing

Spacing is intended to make code easier to read, but too much of it can have the opposite effect and make the code harder to read and maintain. In general, you should put one space between a keyword and a parenthesis, after commas, between expressions in `for` statements, after casts, and around all binary operators. Examples of these are shown in Table 2-3.

Table 2-3. *Spacing Examples*

Rule	Example
Space between keyword and parenthesis	`while (true)`
Space after commas	`myMethod(variable1, variable2);`
Space between expressions	`for (expression1; expression2; expression3) {`
Space after casts	`int i = (int) aLongValue;`
Space after binary operators	`a = b + c;`
	`c = 5 * 10;`

Statement Formatting

Most of the statement-formatting rules simply follow on from the rules we have already discussed.

Most programmers have a preferred method of writing compound statements—for example, where to place braces, and whether braces are optional. Rather than leaving this for endless debate, Sun has specified that braces must be used to enclose statements as part of a control structure—even if only one statement is used in the control structure. For instance, even if there is only one line of code to be executed following an `if` statement, it must still be enclosed in braces, as shown here:

```
if (variable == someValue) {
    doSomething();
}
```

As you can see, the statement between braces should be indented one indentation level (four spaces), and the closing brace should start on its own line at the original indentation level.

Tip Many tools are available that you can use to help you confirm that the code you have written confirms to the Sun coding standards. One such tool is Checkstyle (`http://checkstyle.sourceforge.net/`)—it integrates neatly into many popular IDEs, and supports many different coding styles, not just Sun's. A good style checker will provide you with a report on what it believes needs to be changed, after which you can manually verify each item.

Caution Try to avoid using automatic code reformatters for this assignment. Occasionally they will reformat your code in a manner allowed by the coding conventions but contrary to the way you (or the assessor) would want to see it. Unfortunately, once this has been done, it is hard to undo, and most automatic formatting tools do not provide an easy way to review the changes before accepting or denying them.

Variable Declaration Formatting

Variables should be declared one per line, preferably with comments following the declaration where applicable.

The Sun Coding Conventions state that you may separate variable names from their types by either a space or by tabs. Unfortunately, using multiple tabs can result in you spending too much time reformatting code when you add a new variable later, so we recommend you always conform to a single space between the type and the name of the variable.

Where possible, variables should be initialized when they are first declared. Furthermore, variables should be declared near the start of the smallest enclosing brace that provides the necessary scope. You should not wait to declare a variable until just before you use it.

Formatting of Comments Within the Code

Two forms of comments are allowed within Java source code: documentation comments (Javadoc comments) and implementation comments (all other comments).

Javadoc comments will be covered in more detail in the section on Javadoc later in this chapter; for now, suffice it to say that Javadoc comments are designed to create API documentation that another programmer can use to learn how to use your class and its associated constants, methods, (and possibly) variables without looking at your source code. Since Javadoc comments are designed to be used by external programmers, they should explain conceptually how your code works as a whole—they should never get into implementation details.

Implementation comments, on the other hand, are supposed to give hints to programmers (or the assessors) who are looking at your code as to what is happening.

Caution Do not go overboard with adding implementation comments to your code. If you are using good names for your classes, methods, and variables, your code will be generally self-documenting. In such cases, adding too many comments is self-defeating—the comments distract from the code and quickly fall out of date.

Implementation comments come in two flavors: the block comment (enclosed between /* and */ tags), and comments that start with the tag // and continue until the end of the line.

When adding a single comment line, or adding a comment to the end of a line of code, we recommend that you use the // comment delimiter, as shown in the following examples:

```
// this is an example of a comment using a single line of text
doSomething();        // this is an example of a comment at the end of a line
```

When a comment won't fit on a single line of text, use block comments, as shown here:

```
/*
 * This comment explains why the following code must be used instead of a more
 * "intuitive" way. As it takes more than one line, it is in a block comment.
 */
```

Try to avoid using block comments to comment out lines of code—you should use // comments instead. Using block comments to comment out lines of code makes it very hard for other programmers to determine which code is in use and which has been commented out. Comments that start on a line by themselves should always be indented to the same level as the code they apply to.

Suggested Coding Conventions for New Features in JDK 5

The Sun Coding Conventions have not yet been updated to reflect the additions in JDK 5. In this section, we will give a brief explanation of some of the new features, and demonstrate the coding convention as typified in the JDK 5 API, Sun sample code, and the Java Specification Request (JSR) that specified the new feature.

▪Note Before starting JDK 5, Sun asked the Java developers what features they would like to see in the new version. All requests were considered, and users were allowed to vote for those features they considered most valuable. A JSR number then specified these features, and the top requests were incorporated into JDK 5. You can find out more about the Java Community Process, and have your own say in future enhancements, by visiting the JCP website at http://jcp.org/en/home/index.

We will provide a quick overview of the new features in this chapter, and then cover them in more detail in later chapters where they can be seen in the context of our assignment.

Generics

Generics (supporting generic types at runtime in a type-safe manner) allow us to specify at compile time what a generic object will contain at runtime. An example will probably make this easier to understand. The formatting rules used in the example will be summarized at the end of this section. Consider the following non-type-safe code:

```
public List getBreed(String breedName) {
    List dogs = new ArrayList();
    // do some work to find the correct dogs
    String dogName = "";
    Dog pooch = new Dog(dogName);
    dogs.add(pooch);
    return dogs;
}
```

```
public void listDogs() {
    Collection c = getBreed("labrador");
    for (Iterator i = c.iterator(); i.hasNext(); )
        String name = ((Dog) i.next()).getName();
        System.out.println(name);
    }
}
```

This does work; however, although we know that the returned List must contain a list of Dogs, there is nothing to stop someone else from compiling source code that assumes that the list contains Cats—it will compile without problems. However, if that happens, a ClassCast-Exception will be thrown at runtime.

To get around that, you would have to write explicit type checking into your code (using the instanceof operator) and/or catch ClassCastException.

It is much nicer when we can ensure that a generic class will be handled correctly at runtime. Consider the following replacement for the getBreed and listDogs methods:

```
public List<Dog> getBreed(String breedName) {
    List<Dog> dogs = new ArrayList<Dog>();
    // do some work to find the correct dogs
    String dogName = "Labrador";
    Dog pooch = new Dog(dogName);
    dogs.add(pooch);
    return dogs;
}
```

```
public void listDogs() {
    Collection<Dog> c = getBreed("labrador");
    for (Iterator<Dog> i = c.iterator(); i.hasNext(); ) {
        String name = i.next().getName();
        System.out.println(name);
    }
}
```

We have now specified that the return type of the getBreed method will be a List of Dogs. (It may help to read List<Dog> as List of Dog).

Note that the line String name = i.next().getName(); does not cast the class anymore—the line defining the Iterator specifies its type.

Attempting to cast an item in the collection to a nonrelated class produces the following error:

```
GenericExample.java:16: inconvertible types
found    : Dog
required: Cat
            String name = ((Cat) i.next()).getName();
                  ^
1 error
```

Note the formatting used in the above examples:

- There are no spaces within the angle brackets (< and >).

- There is no space between the collection name and the angle brackets.

- There is no space between the angle brackets and the curved brackets (when calling a constructor).

These are the coding conventions used in the JSRs and in several Sun documents describing the new features of JDK 5; however, currently there are no formal conventions.

Enhanced for Loop

In our example of generics, we used an `Iterator` to step through the items in the collection. To reiterate, our code example looked like this:

```
for (Iterator<Dog> i = c.iterator(); i.hasNext(); ) {
    String name = i.next().getName();
```

However, this is overly wordy: in most cases you will want to step through all the items in your iterator one by one. So why spell it out for the compiler in this way?

JDK 5 has made the use of iterators in for loops much easier. Consider the following construct, which does the same work:

```
for (Dog mutt : c) {
    String name = mutt.getName();
```

It may help to read the colon (:) as "in." Thus, the statement for (Dog mutt : c) would read "for each mutt in collection c."

■Note Many people are curious about why Sun chose to use the colon instead of using the words "in" or "foreach." Quite simply, Sun wanted to avoid introducing any new keywords, which might potentially break existing source code. All your existing code should compile and run without any problems under JDK 5.

The enhanced for loop can also work with standard arrays. The following code gives an example of iterating over an array of `Strings` without using the enhanced for loop:

```
public static void main(String[] args) {
    for (int i = 0; i < args.length; i++) {
        System.out.println(args[i]);
    }
}
```

The enhanced for loop allows this to be simplified, as shown here:

```
public static void main(String[] args) {
    for (String arg : args) {
        System.out.println(arg);
    }
}
```

Note that the new for loop can't be used in every scenario. In particular, it hides the iterator, so you can no longer call any methods on the iterator that might change the underlying collection.

The formatting rule for the new for loops is to have a space before and after the colon.

Autoboxing

JDK 5 allows for automatic type conversions between primitives and their wrapper classes. For example:

```
Integer myInteger = 5; // automatically converts 5 (int) into an Integer
```

No special coding convention is needed for handling this.

VarAgs

Variable argument lists (also commonly referred to as VarArgs) allow the coder to specify that the number of arguments in a constructor or method signature is variable. Using this facility can reduce the number of overloaded methods and constructors.

However, VarArgs come at a price: when you specify the exact number and type of parameters a given method requires, the Java compiler can perform type checking to ensure that your usage of the method is correct. When you use VarArgs, only minimal checking is possible.

To give an example, consider creating a class Dog, which has two optional attributes (fields): age and name. If you wanted to create constructors that can handle all potential ways that a user could create a Dog class, you would need the following constructors:

```
Dog();
Dog(int age);
Dog(String name);
Dog(int age, String name);
```

Unfortunately, it doesn't end there. The number of constructors you need is 2 to the power of the number of parameters. So if the Dog class has the following seven attributes—age, height, weight, name, owner, color, and pedigree—we would potentially need 128 constructors to allow for every combination!

We would then have additional problems, because Java would be unable to differentiate between constructors where the method signatures are effectively the same. For example:

```
Dog(int age, String name);
Dog(int age, String owner);
```

JDK 5 allows us to specify that there will be a variable number of arguments *of the same type* passed to the method or constructor. So you could specify that the exact number of Strings passed to the constructor is variable by specifying a constructor of

```
Dog(int age, String... args) {
    for (String parameter : args) {
        System.out.println("Received parameter " + parameter);
    }
}
```

As you can see in the previous code, the ellipsis (...) immediately follows the type it refers to. Once it's inside the body of your method, you can just treat the argument as an array of the named type.

■**Note** You can only have one variable argument list in a given method or constructor declaration, and it must be the last parameter in the method or constructor. For example, you cannot have Dog(int... ages, String name).

■**Caution** Be very careful when overloading constructors or methods with versions containing VarArgs. It is very easy to end up with overridden methods that cannot be differentiated by the compiler (e.g., Dog(String name, String... args) and Dog(String... args) are effectively the same), or end up with a generic method that matches more than you bargained for (e.g., Dog(Object... args) will match *all* constructors, due to autoboxing).

You may have realized that a similar effect was possible under earlier versions of the JDK: namely, you simply passed an array of the named type into your method. However, to use this, you effectively had to create a new array. For example:

```
public static void lookupDog(String... searchCriteria) {
    for (String criterion : searchCriteria) {
        // do work here
    }
}

public static void lookupCat(String[] searchCriteria) {
    for (String criterion : searchCriteria) {
        // do work here - no different than working with Dog method
    }
}

public static void main(String[] args) {
    // first the easy code: use the Dog method:
    lookupDog("Breed", "Terrier", "Color", "Brown");
```

```
    // now for the Cat method
    lookupCat(new String[] {"Breed", "Burmese", "Coat", "Silky"});

    // or
    String[] criteria = {" Breed", "Burmese", "Coat", "Silky"};
    lookupCat(criteria);
}
```

The code to use the lookupDog method is much easier to read, write, and maintain than the equivalent lookupCat method.

Static Imports

Prior to JDK 5 some programmers were defining constants in interfaces, as this allowed them to *implement* the interface, giving them a shorthand way of writing the constant name. This is shown in the following example:

```
public interface BadInterface {
    public static final int FIRST_NAME_POSITION = 1;
}

public class BadClass implements BadInterface {
    public static void main(String[] args) {
        System.out.println("First name = " + args[FIRST_NAME_POSITION]);
    }
}
```

There are a couple of problems with this:

- A class that implements an interface is said to "be" an instance of that interface. If you have a reasonable name for your interface, it probably doesn't make sense to say your class "is" an instance of it.

- If your class implements an interface, then any subclasses of your class will also implement the interface. Effectively, the constants will become part of the namespace of the subclass—even though the subclass may have no need of these constants.

To get around these problems, JDK 5 introduces the idea of *static imports*—the ability to import the static members from another class or interface.

For instance, if you were using the logging features (discussed in the section "Logging" later in this chapter), you would normally have to qualify the logging levels as this code snippet shows:

```
    myLogger.log(Level.FINE, "This message is at FINE level");
```

However, static imports allow us to refer to the static object FINE as though it had been defined within our own class:

```
import static java.util.logging.Level.*;
// ...
        myLogger.log(FINE, "This message is at FINE level");
```

It should be noted that this "feature" was introduced to work around a bad programming practice. You might want to use it when you would otherwise be tempted to declare local copies of the constants, or when you are tempted to abuse the inheritance as mentioned earlier. But, in general, we recommend that you avoid this where possible, and use qualified constants.

Javadoc

Javadoc is a very simple, yet powerful, tool that helps programmers provide API documentation for other programmers.

The default Javadoc tool is very simple. It parses your source code, looking for special comments. It then generates HTML documentation based on that. To make this easier to understand, let's start with some sample Javadoc comments, and describe them:

```
/**
 * The <b>main</b> starting point for this application.
 * Instantiates an instance of this class, and runs it.
 *
 * @param args an array containing the command line arguments.
 * @throws IOException if files cannot be created
 */
public static void main(String[] args) throws IOException {
    // ...
```

A Javadoc comment starts with the special comment start indicator of /**, and continues until the comment closing indicator of */. Tags are noted by the at symbol (@). All text from the comment start indicator through to the first tag is included directly in the generated output. Javadoc will ignore unknown tags and plain text after *any tag* has been found up until the next known tag, or the end of the doc comment—this bit of magic is how XDoclet can work.

The Javadoc code above produces the following HTML:

```
<A NAME="main(java.lang.String[])"><!-- --></A><H3>
main</H3>
<PRE>
public static void <B>main</B>(java.lang.String[] args)
                throws java.io.IOException</PRE>
<DL>
<DD>The <b>main</b> starting point for this application.
 Instantiates an instance of this class, and runs it.
<P>
<DD><DL>
<DT><B>Parameters:</B><DD><CODE>args</CODE> - an array containing the command
line arguments.
<DT><B>Throws:</B>
<DD><CODE>java.io.IOException</CODE> - if files cannot be created</DL>
</DD>
</DL>
```

When viewed in Microsoft Internet Explorer, this will appear similar to Figure 2-1.

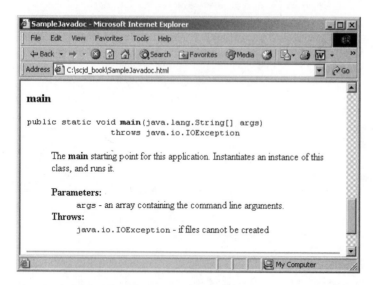

Figure 2-1. *Example Javadoc output*

■**Note** Javadoc is more powerful than many programmers realize. It was developed as an extensible tool, which can behave in different ways depending on which module is plugged in. By default, it will parse the Java source code, generating API documentation. But if you were to change the plug-in to XDoclet (http://xdoclet.sourceforge.net/), for instance, the Javadoc engine could generate additional source code based on comments in the code you wrote (very useful when building J2EE applications—you could have XDoclet create your interfaces and deployment descriptors for you). Or you could plug in DocCheck (http://java.sun.com/j2se/javadoc/doccheck), and you could get a report on how well you are adhering to Sun's Javadoc conventions.

Coding Conventions

Sun published an article titled "How to Write Doc Comments for the Javadoc Tool," which is available online at http://java.sun.com/j2se/javadoc/writingdoccomments/index.html. A quick overview of the topics covered in this article follows.

What to Write

The names of your classes and methods should be reasonably self-documenting, so there is no point in writing Javadoc comments that just restate the name of the class or method. Your Javadoc comments should provide information that will help the user of your class and/or provide information that would be needed by a third party if they wanted to reimplement your class from scratch (without looking at your source code).

For example, if you were creating a class to provide a network connection to your server, you might call the class `NetworkConnection`. There is no point in having a Javadoc comment that states that this class provides "a network connection"—the user already knows that. Instead, you might consider specifying that the class provides "a connection to the database server over the network through which remote access to the database functions can be used."

■**Caution** You should not write any implementation-specific details in your Javadoc comments.

Where to Put your Javadoc Comments

In theory, Javadoc comments can go anywhere in your source code. However, the Javadoc application will only include comments in specific locations:

- Class comments should appear immediately before the class declaration (Javadoc currently allows the comments to appear anywhere before the class declaration, even before the package declaration, but this behavior should not be relied on).

- Class and instance variable comments should appear immediately before the class or instance variable to which they belong.

- Method comments should appear immediately before the method signature.

The Javadoc tool will ignore Javadoc comments in any other locations entirely. If you want to put a comment inside a method, for example, there's no point in making it a Javadoc comment, as it won't appear in any generated API. Just use an implementation comment.

Formatting Codes and Special Tags

Javadoc comments can contain any HTML markup tags. Commonly used tags are shown in Table 2-4.

Table 2-4. *Commonly Used HTML Tags*

Tag	End Tag	Description
`<code>`	`</code>`	Text between these two tags will appear in monospaced font in the HTML output. This is usually designed for short words or phrases.
`<pre>`	`</pre>`	Text between these two tags will appear in monospaced font in the HTML output, maintaining your indentation. This is usually used for example code.
`<ul>`	`</ul>`	Denotes the start and end of an unordered list (not numbered).
`<ol>`	`</ol>`	Denotes the start and end of an ordered list (numbered).
`<li>`		Denotes the start of a list item within either an unordered or an ordered list.
`<p>`		Denotes the start of a new paragraph.

■**Note** Javadoc produces output conforming to HTML standard 3.2, which does not require closing tags for certain elements (e.g., there is no requirement for the `<li>` tag to be closed with a `</li>` tag, nor for the `<p>` tag to be closed with a `</p>` tag); however, you may use them if you wish. In addition, the HTML 3.2 standard does not specify whether tags should appear in upper- or lowercase. Throughout this book we will use HTML 3.2 tags, but we will format them according to the later HTML 4.0 and XHTML formats (we will use closing tags, and we will put the tags in lowercase). You may also use tags and HTML constructs that were only created in HTML version 4 or later if you wish (Javadoc will handle them without problems). However, if you do so, you may find that some older browsers may not be able to display your generated documentation.

There are many more HTML codes you may use in your Javadoc comments. You generally don't need many of them, though, as you are generating API documentation for other programmers to read.

■**Tip** You should use the `<code>` tag for Java keywords, package names, class and interface names, method names, field names, and argument names to make them appear in monospaced font when the browser supports it.

In addition to the HTML tags, Javadoc recognizes special *Javadoc tags*—and they will be handled in special ways. The Javadoc tags for classes and interfaces are shown in Table 2-5. The tags are listed in the order they should appear in your Javadoc comment.

Table 2-5. *Class and Interface Tags*

Tag	Description
@author	The name of the person who wrote the class or interface.
@version	The current version of the class or interface. You might choose to have your revision control software set this automatically as you check your code out of source control.
@see	Generates a link to the specified class or method—the link will appear in a special "See Also" section of the generated Javadoc. Refer to the comments below regarding the @see and @link tags for special instructions.
@since	Used to indicate the version number of your release in which this class first appeared.
@deprecated	Used to indicate that a class should no longer be used but still exists for compatibility reasons. The tag should be followed by text indicating what class the user should use instead of this class, or "No replacement" if there is no class with replacement functionality.

Tag	Description
@serial	Used to specify whether a class or field that would normally be serializable should be documented as being `Serializable`.
{@link *reference label*}	Generates an inline link to the specified class or method. Refer to the comments below regarding the @see and @link tags for special instructions. The label will appear in monospaced font.
{@linkplain *reference label*}	Same as the {@link} tag except that the label will appear in standard font.
{@docRoot}	Points to the base directory (where the `index.html` file resides) for your generated Javadoc. This will be correct no matter how many directories deep this tag is used.

The Javadoc tags for fields are shown in Table 2-6.

Table 2-6. *Field Tags*

Tag	Description
@see	Generates a link to the specified class or method—the link will appear in a special "See Also" section of the generated Javadoc.
@since	Used to indicate the version number of your package in which this field first appeared.
@serial	Used to specify whether a class or field that would normally be serializable should be documented as being `Serializable`.
@deprecated	Used to indicate that a field should no longer be used but still exists for compatibility reasons. The tag should be followed by text indicating what field or method the user should use instead of this field, or "No replacement" if there is no field with replacement functionality.
{@link *reference label*}	Generates an inline link to the specified class, method, or field. The label will appear in monospaced font.
{@linkplain *reference label*}	Same as the {@link} tag except that the label will appear in standard font.
{@docRoot}	Points to the base directory (where the `index.html` file resides) for your generated Javadoc. This will be correct no matter how many directories deep this tag is used.
{@value}	Displays the value of the constant being specified.

The Javadoc tags for constructors and methods are shown in Table 2-7.

Table 2-7. *Constructor and Method Tags*

Tag	Description
@param	Describes a parameter in the method signature. Each parameter should be described on its own line, with the list following the same order as the parameters in the method signature.
@return	Describes the value or object returned from the method.
@exception	Describes an exception that may be thrown from this method. (@throws is a synonym added in Javadoc 1.2.)
@see	Generates a link to the specified class, method, or field—the link will appear in a special "See Also" section of the generated Javadoc.
@since	Used to indicate the version number of your package in which this constructor or method first appeared.
@deprecated	Used to indicate that a constructor or method should no longer be used but still exists for compatibility reasons. The tag should be followed by text indicating what constructor or method the user should use instead of this constructor or method, or "No replacement" if there is no constructor or method with replacement functionality.
{@link *reference label*}	Generates an inline link to the specified class, method, or field. The label will appear in monospaced font.
{@linkplain *reference label*}	Same as the {@link} tag except that the label will appear in standard font.
{@docRoot}	Points to the base directory (where the index.html file resides) for your generated Javadoc. This will be correct no matter how many directories deep this tag is used.

The @see and @link tags will create hyperlinks to the first matching class, field, or method. The class name does not need to be specified when referring to a method or field within the current class; likewise, the package name does not need to be specified when referring to a class within the same package. Finally, unless you want to refer to a specific overloaded method, you do not need to specify the method parameters. Some examples are shown in Table 2-8.

Table 2-8. *Examples of @see Links*

Example	Comment
@see #field label	Creates a link to the specified field with the given label
@see #method label	Creates a link to the first matching method and gives the link the specified label
@see #method (parameters) label	Creates a link to the method with the matching signature and gives the link the specified label
@see class#method label	Creates a link to the first matching method in the named class and gives the link the specified label
@see package.class#method label	Creates a link to the first matching method in the named class in the named packages and gives the link the specified label

JDK 1.5 introduced two new tags that can be used anywhere within your document: {@code *text*} and {@literal *text*}. In both cases, the text will be displayed without interpretation. For example, if your text was <b>, normally this would be interpreted as the HTML tag to start bold text. However, using the tag {@code <b>} will result in the text <b> being displayed as desired. The {@code *text*} tag will display the text in monotype font and {@literal *text*} will display the text in normal font.

Package-Level Documentation

Javadoc can also incorporate package documentation into the generated output, and create a summary page for your overall submission. An example of the summary page is shown in Figure 2-2.

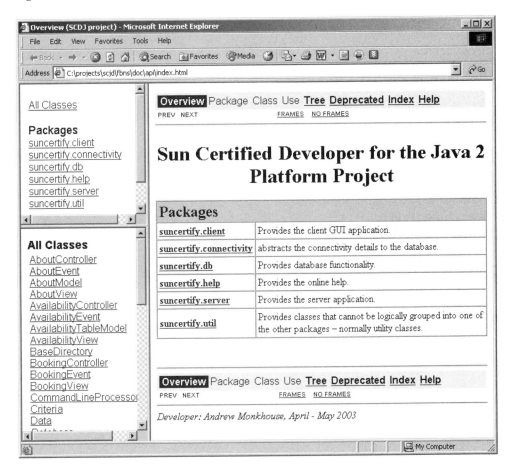

Figure 2-2. *Sample summary page*

To create package documentation, you will need to create a file named package.html in each package directory. A simple example might look like this:

```
<!doctype HTML PUBLIC "-//W3C//DTD HTML 3.2//EN">
<html>
<head>
<title>com.example.db</title>
</head>
<body>
Provides database functionality.
<h2>Package Specification</h2>
These classes are the base that provide the basic data creation, reading, updating,
and deleting functions required to process data in a database. Basic locking
functionality exists, but this is not an advanced package.

@author Unattributed person from example.com.
@author Andrew Monkhouse
@version 1.0
@since 1.0
</body>
</html>
```

JDK 5 Changes

The obvious changes to the Javadoc tool from earlier versions include support for the two new tags ({@code *text*} and {@literal *text*}) mentioned earlier, and the obvious support for the generics, enums, and VarArgs features.

When JDK 1.4 was released, Sun was planning to change the way Javadoc would determine how much of a comment should appear in the summary (where the break should be between the summary and the remainder of the comment). Sun incorporated the logic for the new break iterator in the Javadoc tool, which resulted in large numbers of warnings being generated when the proposed change would cause different summaries to appear in the future version. Sun has now reversed their plans, and removed the 1.4 logic.

Running Javadoc from the Command Line

The basic command format for Javadoc is

```
javadoc [options] [packagenames] [sourcefiles] [@files]
```

Following from this, you could generate the API documentation for all your source files that do not belong to any package by typing the following command in the same directory as the source files:

```
javadoc *java
```

If you have your source files organized in packages, you could list the package names on the command line instead:

```
javadoc com.example.mypackage com.example.more.packages
```

Both those command lines will generate the API documentation in the current working directory, which may not be desirable. You can specify the directory where API documentation should be stored by using the -d option:

```
javadoc -d doc/api com.example.mypackage com.example.more.packages
```

■**Tip** Javadoc will convert Unix-style pathnames into platform-specific pathnames. This is especially useful when you are developing scripts that may be run by unknown people on potentially any platform.

You can add many more options, turning features on or off as desired. For example:

```
 1  javadoc \
 2      -d doc/api \
 3      -version \
 4      -author \
 5      -use \
 6      -source 1.5 \
 7      -windowtitle "Denny's DVD application" \
 8      -doctitle "<h1>The SCJD Exam with J2SE 1.5 Project</h1>" \
 9      -bottom "<i>Developers: Andrew Monkhouse and Terry Camerlengo</i>" \
10      -sourcepath src \
11      -linkoffline http://java.sun.com/j2se/1.5.0/docs/api /jdk_1.5/api \
12      sampleproject.gui sampleproject.db sampleproject.remote
```

The meaning of the new tags is explained in Table 2-9.

Table 2-9. *Meaning of Common Javadoc Command-Line Options*

Line	Option	Meaning
2	-d	Used to specify the output directory for generated API.
3	-version	Specifies that the version information in your Javadoc comments will be incorporated into the generated API.
4	-author	Specifies that the author information in your Javadoc comments will be incorporated into the generated API.
5	-use	Tells Javadoc to include a "use" page for each class, detailing where it is used as either a parameter in a method or as a return value.
6	-source	Specifies which version of the JDK the Javadoc should maintain compatibility with.
7	-windowtitle	Specifies the title to appear at the top of your browser (where supported).
8	-doctitle	Specifies the title to appear on the package summary page.
9	-bottom	Specifies text that appears on the bottom of every generated page.
10	-sourcepath	Specifies the base directory containing your packages.
11	-linkoffline	Creates links to existing Javadoc entries. See the description in the paragraph that follows.

The -link and the -linkoffline options enable you to link to other preexisting APIs. For example, if you used the String class as a parameter in one of your methods, you might like to have your API documentation for your method include a hyperlink back to Sun's API documentation for the String method.

You would normally use the -link option whenever you do not have a copy of the preexisting API local to you, but you can access it over the Web.

The -linkoffline option is preferred when you have a local copy of the preexisting API documentation, or when you have a local copy of the package-list file from the preexisting API documentation, or when you cannot access the preexisting API over the Web.

■**Tip** Whenever possible you should refer to local documentation rather than looking at it over the Web, simply because it will be faster for you. Likewise, linking "offline" by using your local copy of the documentation will be faster than accessing the required file over the Web.

Obviously, you would not want to type such a complex command line every time you wanted to regenerate your API documentation. One way of working around this is to put all the options (one per line) into a plain text file, and then refer to that file on the command line. For example, if you had put all the options in a file named javadoc.options, you could use the following command line to generate your API documentation:

```
javadoc @javadoc.options sampleproject.gui sampleproject.db sampleproject.remote
```

Working with Packages

If you were to put all the files on your computer into one folder, this one folder would quickly become unmanageable, and finding any particular file would be a nightmare. To avoid this, you probably organize folders to store related files—one for accounting information, another for job hunting, another for music, and so on. Some of these folders may have subfolders to provide further subcategories.

Developing software has the same potential issue. Fortunately, Sun has provided us with a platform-independent equivalent of the folders: packages. You can locate classes belonging to a specific package by the fully qualified package and class name, even if the operating system has no concept of folders, directories, or a hierarchical file system.

When starting any project, consider what logical modules or functionalities your project might have, and place the classes related to that functionality into its own package. In the case of our project, we will have a set of classes that provide the graphical user interface, another set of classes that provide network functionality, and another set of classes that provide data access functions. We could therefore start with the following potential packages:

```
gui
network
database
```

After further investigation, we may decide to add more packages and/or refactor the existing packages—Chapter 3 will discuss how to analyze the sample project. For example, we might decide to subdivide the `network` package into two separate packages: one for RMI networking, and one for Sockets networking. We would therefore have the packages

```
network.rmi
network.sockets
```

Package names should be qualified to ensure that each class can be uniquely identified. That is, when you attempt to instantiate the `StartGui` class, you want to instantiate *your* class of that name, not mine. To do this, you create packages for your domain name, written in lowercase and in reverse. So if you worked for a company with the domain name `example.com`, then your package names should start with the same name in reverse (`com.example`). So our fully qualified package name would now become `com.example.network.sockets`.

On Microsoft Windows and Unix-based systems, each package should be in a separate directory. So for the `com.example.network.sockets` package mentioned earlier, we would have a directory for the first package `com`, which would contain a directory for the `example` package, which in turn would contain the directory for the `network` package, which finally would contain a directory for the `sockets` package. This final directory would contain all the Java class files that belong in that package.

Note Many operating systems differentiate between case for files and directories. So a file named `numberOfBoxes` will be different from a file named `NumberOfBoxes`. Since Java must request files from the underlying operating system, and cannot reasonably go through every permutation of upper- and lowercase, Sun has stipulated that the case of your files and directories must match the case of your classes and packages.

The Sun Java utilities are all designed to work with packages in the same way, so you can be sure that if the Java compiler can find and compile your classes, then the Java runtime and the Java documenter will also be able to work with your classes.

JAR files can also act as a package structure. After you change directory to the classpath root folder, running the command

```
C:\devProj\classes\> jar cf db.jar sampleproject.db
```

will result in a compressed file named `db.jar` containing the `sampleproject.db` package tree. Therefore, this file can now be added to a classpath the same way a directory is specified, and the compiler or Java Virtual Machine (JVM) will scan the file for referenced packages.

It is important to note the behavior of Java utilities when dealing with shared package definitions. For example, a situation could arise under which two directories containing different portions of a package definition exist on a computer's file system.

The classes for the first package are stored in `c:\devProj\classes`, and the second set of files is stored outside of the project's directory structure in `c:\tempClasses`. In the first directory, the package `sampleproject.db` is stored, while `sampleproject.testclient` is stored in the second directory (this means that the files will be stored in the directories `c:\dev\Proj\` `classes\sampleproject\db\` and `c:\dev\Proj\classes\sampleproject\testclient\`, respectively).

Next, both directories are compressed into separate JAR files using the JAR utility, as shown here:

```
C:\devProj\classes\> jar cf db.jar sampleproject.db
C:\devProj\classes\> jar cf testclient.jar sampleproject.testclient
```

Finally, both JAR files are specified in a classpath when compiling a Java application, as shown here:

```
C:\devProj\tmp\> javac -cp c:\devProj\classes\db.jar;c:\tempClasses\testclient.jar
 MyClass.java
```

The question at this point is, what happens to the classpaths? Does the first JAR file overwrite the package path of the second file? The answer is no. Packages with the same package tree can be stored in separate JAR files or separate directories, and in this case, the Java compiler will combine the contents of these two files at runtime.

■**Caution** If you have classes with the same name that are in the same package namespace in two JAR files, the first one found (based on classpath order) will be used—the second will be ignored.

The ability to store package definitions in different locations allows for a very modular structure. Thus, you should consider certain ideals when planning an application's package structure. First and foremost, packages should consist of all classes that are similar in function or are dependent on each other in design. This allows for the packages to function as complete units of functionality. Thus, a JAR file could conceivably contain an entire functional package that is "plugged" into a project.

■**Note** The sample project introduced later in this book uses package structure to isolate the different network implementations. This structure enables the entire networking layer of the sample application to be changed without impacting the application's other packages.

Classes in the base node of every package should be the building blocks of that tree's functionality, and therefore they should be the most stable portions of the tree. Lower-level packages designate the stable classes that all others are built upon, and package definitions should be planned using this principle.

If it is not possible to place only stable, nonchanging classes in the base nodes of a package, the classes should be replaced by interfaces, and the volatile implementations of these interfaces moved to a higher level of the package definition or into a whole different package altogether.

It is also very important to ensure that dependencies between classes are contained within a single package. Essentially, packages should be autonomous units that can be compiled separately. For the most part, if classes in a package have to be compiled in order for another package to compile, the package structure should be reworked so that all class dependencies fall within a single package. A proper package design will also ensure that an application is built on the most stable foundation possible.

In summary, packages act as a mechanism to compartmentalize portions of a project into functional blocks. Thus, an effective package design allows for portions of a project to be removed and swapped around without impacting other portions of your code.

Best Practices

In your programming career, you may have noticed practices that you (or others) follow that do not fit into the categories above, and yet they make the overall delivery of a final solution much easier. While these practices are not required, you should consider using them in your assignment.

Writing Documentation As You Go

It seems strange to have to mention this, but you really must write your documentation at the same time as you are working on your assignment, preferably before you write your code, or as you write it.

You must provide three major forms of documentation as part of this assignment:

- Design choices

- Javadoc

- User documentation

Design Choices

The design choices document will contain a quick overview of what *major* choices you made while developing your solution, and what alternatives you considered—possibly explaining why you discarded the alternative.

You do not need to write a book on your choices—the assessors are only interested in two things:

1. Did you consider alternatives?

2. Did you write the code you submitted?

If you go on to become a system architect, you will be expected to *know* multiple ways of achieving any software goal—often using multiple architectures and languages. As a developer, you should also be able to consider and reject alternative solutions within your area of expertise—J2SE. For example, in a case where you could use a radio button or a check box, you should be able to recognize that both alternatives are possible, and decide which is the correct choice (note that the choice between a radio button and check box is *probably* a minor decision, and possibly not something you would want to document).

■**Tip** Where possible, you should also put your design decisions in an implementation comment close to the code itself. For example, if you had chosen a radio button instead of a check box, having an implementation comment near the constructor for that button will save the person maintaining your code from spending time trying to decide whether this was the "right" choice or not.

Sun has a difficult task—how do they prove that *you* wrote the assignment that *you* submitted? One step in the process is to have multiple assignments (different business domains), each with multiple versions (different interfaces to be implemented), so it is unlikely that anyone you know will happen to have the same assignment as you. Another step is to check that the information you write in the written exam (where you must provide proof of ID) matches the design choices document, and that the design choices document describes the code. Combine these, and Sun can be reasonably certain that the person who sits for the exam is the person who wrote the code.

It is very important that you write down your design decisions as you make them. If you leave that task until the end of the project, you will have a hard time remembering what choices you made, let alone why you made them.

Javadoc

It has been shown time and time again that if the documentation is separate from the code, then it is often not updated at the same time as the code is updated, which renders it useless.

Javadoc, and similar code documenting tools, were designed to solve this problem. By putting the code documentation with the code itself, it is much easier to update the documentation at the same time the code is updated.

But this relies on one major premise—that you write and update the comments at the same time as you write and update the code.

If you wait until the end of a three-month assignment to do the source code commenting, you may find that you have another three-month job ahead of you just to finish the comments, simply because you have to reread all your code to work out what you were doing in order to document it.

User Documentation

In the section "Prototyping the GUI," we recommended drawing rough sketches of your user interface before starting the project. One of the benefits we mentioned is that you will then have a definite design to work toward, reducing the risk that you will end up with a less usable interface simply because it is easier to implement.

When you write the user documentation before coding, you get the same benefit: you have described up front what your user interface is going to do, so you have a definite target to achieve.

You also have a definite end point in mind—when your user interface meets your user documentation, you know that the user interface should be ready for testing.

User documentation is also where users go when they have a problem, or when they want to determine how they can do something more advanced. Incorrect or badly worded user documentation will cause frustration for the end user, and in your real employment will cause your support calls to be more aggravating than they need to be. Writing your documentation up front means that it is less likely to be rushed, and also means that you are more likely to go back to it several times during the course of your development and improve it.

Assertions

Assertions were added in JDK 1.4, and provide a useful confirmation and documentation of assumptions for you as the developer without affecting deployment of your application.

The syntax of assertions is as follows:

```
assert <expression with a boolean result>;
```

or

```
assert <expression with a boolean result> : <any statement>;
```

If `<expression with a boolean result>` returns false, and assertion checking is turned on at deploy time, an `AssertionError` is thrown.

Programmers sometimes make assumptions about how two parts of their program interact—for example, they might assume that the value of a parameter in a private method will never exceed a certain value. However, if the assumption is incorrect, the problems it causes might not become obvious for quite some time. In such a case, it can be worthwhile to include an assert statement at the start of the method that can be used while testing to confirm your assumptions but that will not have any effect on the deployed code.

■**Caution** You should never use assertions to validate the inputs on public methods—these are methods that other programmers may use, and they may not honor your requirements. You should validate these inputs regardless of whether or not assertions are turned on at runtime.

Here is some example code to show validating a value:

```
public class AssertionTest {
    public static void main(String[] args) {
        new AssertionTest(11);
    }

    public AssertionTest(int withdrawalAmount) {
        int balance = reduceBalance(withdrawalAmount);

        // reduceBalance should never return a number less than zero
        assert (balance < 0) : "Business rule: balance cannot be < 0";
    }
}
```

■**Note** In JDK 1.4 you had to specify the `-source 1.4` option to the Java compiler in order to enable the compilation of assertions. In JDK 5 this is no longer required.

By default, assertions are turned off at runtime. This has two major benefits:

- `AssertionError` is an `Error`, and as such you do not want it thrown in production.

- Evaluating the expression in the assertion could be time consuming—having it switched off by default ensures better performance.

■**Caution** You should never use assertions to perform actions required for the method to work—assertions should only validate that the values are correct. Since assertions are normally switched off at runtime, any actions you perform within the assertion will not normally be performed at runtime.

To enable assertions at runtime, you must specify either the `-ea` or the `-enableassertions` command-line option. For example:

```
java -ea AssertionTest
```

Without the `-ea` option, the `AssertionTest` program will run without errors. With the `-ea` option, it will throw an `AssertionError`.

Assertions can be enabled for individual classes or packages as well, by specifying the classes or packages on the command line:

```
java -ea:<packageName> -ea:<className>
```

Logging

When debugging, you will find it useful to know when you have reached a certain method, and what the values of some of your parameters and variables are.

In a debugger you might set breakpoints at certain locations and watches on some variables. But this can be tedious to do each time you want to debug a program.

The next logical step might be to add `System.out.println(...);` statements throughout your code. Watching the output in the command window will then give you an idea of what your program is doing. However, this is not a good idea for code that someone else (your client or assessor) is deploying: at best it is distracting for them; at worst they may assume that the "normal" debug messages are signs of an error. In addition, any application that may be deployed as a server application may not even have a window in which to watch the messages. And, if something does go wrong with your program, it can be difficult to get the user of the program to copy the correct messages and send them to you. Furthermore, some of the messages you want to appear while debugging the application make no sense at deploy time—you would want to be able to selectively turn off some of the messages.

Obviously this problem has cropped up many times, and there is a common solution: use a logging framework. Doing so ensures that we can

- Send logging messages to a desired location (file/screen/printer/nowhere)

- Log messages even if the application is running in "server" mode and does not have a window for messages to appear in

- Ensure that logging is done in a consistent manner throughout the entire application

- Turn logging on and off selectively throughout the application at deploy time

JDK 1.4 and later provide a standard API for logging. We recommend that you use this API throughout your application whenever you consider sending something to the standard or error output.

To use the logger, you must first get an instance of a logger you can use. Loggers are normally named (although there is an anonymous logger that everyone can use), allowing you to configure different loggers in different ways. To get a reference to the logger for the example.com.testApplication context, you would create code similar to this:

```
Logger myLogger = Logger.getLogger("example.com.testApplication");
```

All classes that "get" a logger using the same name will get the same instance of the logger. This ensures that the configuration applied to that logger will apply to all instances of that logger.

■**Note** The name of the logger is part of a hierarchical namespace, meaning that example.com. testApplication is a child of the namespace example.com. We will comment further on this later in this section.

You can define the level at which your messages will be logged. There are several predefined levels, and we recommend that you use them rather than define your own. The predefined levels are shown in Table 2-10 in order from the least amount of logging to the most amount of logging.

Table 2-10. *Predefined Logging Levels*

Logging Level	Recommended Usage
Severe	Serious failure
Warning	Potential problem
Info	Informational messages
Config	Configuration messages
Fine	Tracing (debugging) messages
Finer	Fairly detailed tracing messages
Finest	Highly detailed tracing messages

The logger class has several utility methods for logging information (`Logger.info(<msg>)`), warning (`Logger.warning(<msg>)`), and severe (`Logger.severe(<msg>)`) messages, allowing you to log simple messages, for example:

```
myLogger.severe("Sending message to standard error");
```

If you have been putting these commands into simple test applications, you may be wondering what the fuss is about—after all, so far we have not done anything that we cannot do with a `System.out.println(<msg>)` statement. But consider that you could turn off all logging to your *entire* application with one statement near the start of your application, such as

```
myLogger.setLevel(Level.OFF);
```

That is, all your classes could be logging messages, at different levels, and that one line could turn them all off—no need to go hunting for all those `System.out.println(<msg>)` statements.

You may want to execute a block of logging code only if you know that it is actually going to be logged. In such a case, you can make a call to the `isLoggable(<level>)` method first to determine whether you should call your (potentially performance-reducing) logging code.

One benefit we mentioned earlier was that we could log messages to a file—this is done through a `Handler` object. We can add a simple file handler to our logger with one simple command:

```
import java.util.logging.*;
import java.io.IOException;

public class TestLogging {
    public static void main(String[] args) throws IOException {
        Logger myLogger = Logger.getLogger("Test");
        myLogger.addHandler(new FileHandler("temp.log"));
        myLogger.severe("My program did something bad");
    }
}
```

■Note The `FileHandler` class can handle storing logs in common locations regardless of operating system, and can handle the usual issues such as rotating log files. Refer to the API for `FileHandler` to see how such options can be utilized.

Running this example produces the following log message:

```
C:\TEMP> java TestLogging
11/12/2004 19:22:40 TestLogging main
SEVERE: My program did something bad
```

■Note Your time and date will obviously differ.

There should also be a `temp.log` file in the current working directory, which contains the log message in XML format:

```
C:\Temp>dir temp.log
 Volume in drive C has no label.
 Volume Serial Number is EOF1-2766

 Directory of C:\Temp

11/12/2004  07:22p                    388 temp.log
               1 File(s)              388 bytes
               0 Dir(s)    2,066,956,288 bytes free

C:\Temp>type temp.log
<?xml version="1.0" encoding="windows-1252" standalone="no"?>
<!DOCTYPE log SYSTEM "logger.dtd">
<log>
<record>
  <date>2004-12-11T19:22:40</date>
  <millis>1102753360550</millis>
  <sequence>0</sequence>
  <logger>Test</logger>
  <level>SEVERE</level>
  <class>TestLogging</class>
  <method>main</method>
  <thread>10</thread>
  <message>My program did something bad</message>
</record>
</log>
```

When you have a program to analyze your log messages, you may find this useful. However, when you want to read the log messages yourself, you may find it more beneficial to have the output in plain text. You can do this by adding a `Formatter`.

Changing the code to read:

```java
import java.util.logging.*;
import java.io.IOException;

public class TestLogging {
    public static void main(String[] args) throws IOException {
        FileHandler myFileHandler = new FileHandler("temp.log");
        myFileHandler.setFormatter(new SimpleFormatter());
        Logger myLogger = Logger.getLogger("Test");
        myLogger.addHandler(myFileHandler);

        myLogger.severe("My program did something bad");
    }
}
```

will result in the following output on the screen:

```
11/12/2004 19:39:27 Test main
SEVERE: My program did something bad
```

and the following output in the `temp.log` file:

```
11/12/2004 19:39:27 Test main
SEVERE: My program did something bad
```

If you wanted to have some other form of output, consider making your own formatter. The source code to `SimpleFormatter` is available in the JDK sources, and is only 80 lines for the entire formatter—it would be easy to create your own formatter.

You will have noticed that logging has so far been going to the screen, even though we have not asked for this. This is because by default each logger will use its parent's log handlers in combination with its own. The default anonymous logger will, by default, send output to the screen. That is, if you get a logger for `example.com`, and another logger for `example.com.test`, the logger for `example.com.test` is a child of `example.com`. So any message logged to the `example.com.test` logger will also be sent to the handler for `example.com`. You can turn this behavior off by calling the `setUseParentHandlers(boolean useParentHandlers)` method on the child logger.

You should not remove logging code before deploying in production. Doing so runs the risk that you may remove something you didn't intend to remove, and if you later need the logging back again, you will have to add it all again manually. It is a much better idea to use the logger's rotating log scheme to ensure that log files never get too large, in combination with setting the log level so that you are not producing too many log messages—usually either the `Level.WARNING` or `Level.SEVERE` log level. You would normally also turn off any logging to the screen (if you have not already done so).

Summary

Spending a little bit of time up front in planning your project can pay big dividends in reducing total time spent on this assignment. Ensuring that your code is easy to read and maintain will win you better marks in this assignment, as well as more respect from your colleagues at work. And using the tools provided by Sun can make your submission far more professional.

We have introduced some of the features that will help you make a more professional submission, and assist you in your day-to-day life.

FAQs

Q Is it necessary to follow the methodologies and standards in this chapter?

A There are requirements in your instructions that you must follow, and using Javadoc is one such requirement. However, the use of methodologies and standards is not always fully stipulated—if you do not have a specific requirement, you can ignore the standard, but you do so at your own risk.

Q Should I include unit tests in my submission?

A Current assignments have a warning stating that you will not get extra credit for going beyond the specifications. That being the case, we recommend that you do not include the test cases in your submission: at best the assessor will ignore them, and at worst you may receive a lower score if the assessor finds a fault with additional code. Plus if you use JUnit, your test code won't compile without `junit.jar`—and that's external code you're not allowed to include for the assignment.

Q Should I leave logging code in my submission?

A As mentioned in the section on logging, we recommend that you leave the logging in your code—this saves you the effort of trying to remove it, and more importantly, saves you the effort of trying to re-add it if you later need it again. (Yes, we know this seems to contradict the answer about unit tests, but unit tests are separate from your major project code, and logging is integrated into your project code. Also, `java.util.logging` *is* part of the standard libraries, whereas JUnit is not. So that's another reason why it's okay to include logging code in your assignment, but not JUnit code.)

Q Can a custom directory structure be used instead of the one presented in the book?

A For your Sun assignment, check the instructions carefully—if they specify a directory structure, then you *must* follow it. Outside of any Sun restrictions, any directory structure may be used. If you intend to follow along with the sample project in this book but decide to change the directory structure, then the instructions and examples in the book may need alterations in order to run as explained. You should only use custom directory structures if you are already comfortable with Javadoc, classpaths, and package structures.

CHAPTER 3

■■■

Project Overview

In this chapter, we introduce the sample application, which will serve as a wellspring for the myriad of topics required for developer certification. The sample project, Denny's DVDs, has a structure and format similar to the one you will encounter during the Sun Certified Java Developer (SCJD) exam, and it will demonstrate each of the essential concepts necessary for successful completion of the certification project. Each chapter adds an integral component to the project and builds from the preceding chapter, so that by the end of the book you will have a complete and properly functioning version of Denny's DVDs version 2.0. As an added benefit, Denny's DVDs utilizes Java 2 Platform Standard Edition (J2SE) 5, and some of the "Tiger" features, such as autoboxing and generics, are elucidated in the following chapters.

■**Note** "Tiger" is the code name for J2SE 5, and the two terms will be referred to interchangeably throughout the book. Sometimes we will use the term "Tigerize," which means to add a J2SE 5 language feature to code originally composed as a J2SE 1.4 program. We do this quite a bit in the sample project, and even the DOSClient makes use of generics. For more information on J2SE 5 and the plethora of new features that have been added (some of which are discussed in this book), go to http://java.sun.com/developer/technicalArticles/releases/j2se15.

What Are the Essential Requirements for the Sun Certification Project?

To demonstrate "developer-level" competency for Sun certification, your project submission must successfully accomplish the following objectives:

- It must implement an application interface provided by Sun.

- It must use either RMI or serialized objects over sockets for networking.

- It must use Swing with a JTable for display.

- It must be entirely contained within one single executable JAR and, consequently, should not require any command-line options to run.

- Configuration settings must be persisted between application runs.

Your project submission must consist of these components:

- An executable JAR file, which will run both the stand-alone client and the network-connected client

- An executable server-specific JAR file, which will run the networked server

- A common JAR file, which will contain code common to both client and server applications:

  - An src directory containing the source files for the project

  - The original data file supplied with the instructions

- A docs directory that will contain

  - The API generated by Javadoc

  - The end-user documentation

- The file summarizing your design choices

The entire submission should be packaged in a JAR file, as described in Chapter 9.

■**Note** JARs were initially created to allow applets to be downloaded in a single HTTP request, rather than multiple round-trips (request-response pairings) to retrieve each applet component, such as class files, images, and so forth. Executable JAR files have file associations so that clicking on them will run javaw -jar on Windows and java -jar on Unix.

The Denny's DVDs sample will eventually be bundled into one JAR file. That JAR file will contain an executable JAR file named runme.jar, containing the database files, documentation, and source code. The runme.jar will handle both the server and the client depending on how it is invoked. Running the final application from the executable JAR file will be explained in Chapter 9.

■**Note** The previous edition of this book included a chapter on Java's New I/O, or NIO. At the time, NIO was a new 1.4 topic, and the extent that NIO could be used for the certification exam was unclear. Subsequently, after the publication of the first edition and the release of J2SE 1.4, Sun explicitly disallowed the use of NIO as a networking solution for the certification project, but permitted its use as a mechanism for file I/O. Admittedly, the main reason for including NIO in the previous edition was just to demonstrate this cool new technology. Our primary examples (downloadable from the Apress web site) did not use NIO in the networking layer. Unfortunately, there was some confusion since many believed that the inclusion of NIO indicated that our proposed solution required NIO. It did not. For this reason, we have decided to drop the discussion of NIO in the current edition of this book to avoid any further confusion, but would like to make it clear that sockets or RMI are required for the networking layer but that channels can safely be used for plain old file I/O.

Introducing the Sample Project

Denny's DVDs is a DVD rental store for a small community. The certification project requires that the application be built on a provided interface. Sun will include an interface as part of the assignment, and you will be responsible for implementing that interface and developing a fully featured application. Our sample project will take the same approach. We will imagine that the infamous Denny of Denny's DVDs will define an interface that he expects the developer (i.e., you the reader) to implement. That interface, DBClient.java, will be our starting point for development. Figure 3.1 shows a UML use case diagram for the primary operations the system must support.

■Note The acronym *UPC* will be bandied around quite a bit, so a little background information may come in handy. UPC, which stands for Universal Product Code, is an official designation for a product, whether it be a book, a CD, or a DVD. It is a unique number identifying that product worldwide. For more trivia-related information on UPC (and related concepts such as European Article Numbering [EAN] and checksums), refer to such sites as Wikipedia (http://en.wikipedia.org/wiki/Main_Page) and the various online UPC databases. Of course, such a topic is way outside the scope of this book. For our purposes, UPC is a nice surrogate for a system-wide identifier or primary key.

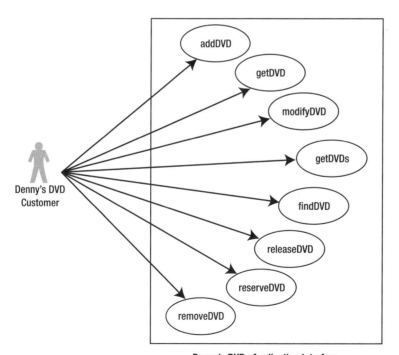

Denny's DVDs Application Interface

Figure 3-1. *Denny's DVDs use case diagram*

The operations in Figure 3.1 make up the public interface, DBClient.java, that the Denny's DVDs application must implement. Here are descriptions of the interface methods:

addDVD—Requires a DVD object as an input parameter. Will add the DVD to the system if the UPC is unique; otherwise, will throw an exception.

getDVD—Given a UPC value for a DVD, this method should return the corresponding DVD object. A null object is returned if the UPC is not found in the database.

modifyDVD—Requires a DVD object with a UPC that exists in the database. Will overwrite an existing DVD with new DVD values. If the database does not contain a DVD with the supplied UPC code, then false is returned and the database is not updated.

getDVDs—Should return a collection of all the DVDs in the database. If there are no DVDs in the database, then an empty collection should be returned.

■**Note** The Denny's DVDs system available for download comes with a starter database, which is referred to throughout the book's examples.

---

findDVD—This operation should use a regular expression query as the input parameter. The supplied input parameter should match on multiple attributes with a regular expression query. The input parameter is the regular expression query, so the application must translate the user's search criteria into a regular expression query prior to invoking this method. Transforming the user's search criteria into a regular expression can be done either in the GUI or via some intermediate class, but not in the findDVD method itself. Of course, you must not require or expect the user to enter the regular expression syntax as the search criteria. A collection of DVDs should be returned.

releaseDVD—Will increment the count of available DVDs. This operation is equivalent to a rental return. The operation should return true, which indicates whether the DVD identified by the UPC exists in the database and has copies out for rental. Otherwise, the operation returns false.

reserveDVD—Will decrement the DVD count indicating that someone has rented one of the available copies. Requires a UPC as an input parameter. If the UPC of the DVD to reserve does not exist, false is returned; false is also returned if no more copies of the DVD are available for rental.

removeDVD—Will remove the DVD with the matching UPC and return true. If the UPC is not found in the database, then no DVD is removed and the method returns false.

The interface must have a GUI to allow the execution of each of the required methods listed here. Also, the GUI must be capable of connecting to a server on a network, or work in stand-alone mode and connect to a server on the localhost. You must also consider design issues related to concurrent user access and record locking. Listing 3.1 contains the code for the DBClient.java interface.

■**Tip** Before inspecting the Denny's DVDs `DBClient.java` source code available for download, try writing the class yourself and see how close your interface is to the one used in the sample project. Since you will also be given the interface in the actual assignment, this exercise should be performed just for fun.

Listing 3-1. *The DBClient Interface*

```java
package sampleproject.db;

import java.io.*;
import java.util.regex.*;
import java.util.*;

/**
 * An interface implemented by classes that provide access to the DVD
 * data store, including DVDDatabase.
 *
 * @author Denny's DVDs
 * @version 2.0
 */

public interface DBClient {

    /**
     * Adds a DVD to the database or inventory.
     *
     *
     * @param dvd The DVD item to add to inventory.
     * @return Indicates the success/failure of the add operation.
     * @throws IOException Indicates there is a problem accessing the database.
     */
    public boolean addDVD(DVD dvd) throws IOException;

    /**
     * Locates a DVD using the UPC identification number.
     *
     * @param UPC The UPC of the DVD to locate.
     * @return The DVD object which matches the UPC.
     * @throws IOException if there is a problem accessing the data.
     */
    public DVD getDVD(String UPC)throws IOException;

    /**
     * Changes existing information of a DVD item.
     * Modifications can occur on any of the attributes of DVD except UPC.
     * The UPC is used to identify the DVD to be modified.
```

```
 *
 * @param dvd The DVD to modify.
 * @return Returns true if the DVD was found and modified.
 * @throws IOException Indicates there is a problem accessing the data.
 */
public  boolean modifyDVD(DVD dvd) throws IOException;

/**
 * Removes DVDs from inventory using the unique UPC.
 *
 * @param UPC The UPC or key of the DVD to be removed.
 * @return Returns true if the UPC was found and the DVD was removed.
 * @throws IOException Indicates there is a problem accessing the data.
 */
public  boolean removeDVD(String UPC) throws IOException;

/**
 * Gets the store's inventory.
 * All of the DVDs in the system.
 *
 * @return A List containing all found DVD's.
 * @throws IOException Indicates there is a problem accessing the data.
 */
public List<DVD> getDVDs() throws IOException;

  /**
   * A properly formatted <code>String</code> expressions returns all
   * matching DVD items. The <code>String</code> must be formatted as a
   * regular expression.
   *
   * @param query The formatted regular expression used as the search
   * criteria.
   * @return The list of DVDs that match the query. Can be an empty
   * Collection.
   * @throws IOException Indicates there is a problem accessing the data.
   * @throws PatternSyntaxException Indicates there is a syntax problem in
   * the regular expression.
   */
public Collection<DVD> findDVD(String query)
        throws IOException, PatternSyntaxException;

  /**
   * Lock the requested DVD. This method blocks until the lock succeeds,
   * or for a maximum of 5 seconds, whichever comes first.
   *
   * @param UPC The UPC of the DVD to reserve
```

```
 * @throws InterruptedException Indicates the thread is interrupted.
 * @throws IOException on any network problem
 */
boolean reserveDVD(String UPC) throws IOException, InterruptedException;

/**
 * Unlock the requested record. Ignored if the caller does not have
 * a current lock on the requested record.
 *
 * @param UPC The UPC of the DVD to release
 * @throws IOException on any network problem
 */
void releaseDVD(String UPC) throws IOException;

}
```

■**Note** The sample project is not a full-featured e-commerce system. Instead, think of it as a program that will demonstrate the concepts needed to successfully complete the project portion of the SCJD exam.

Application Overview

So, what's next? In this section, we present an overview of the new system and describe the steps necessary to successfully implement the sample project.

Architecturally, the application is a traditional client-server system composed of three key parts: the server-side database with network server functionality, the client-side GUI, and a client-side database interface that handles the networking on behalf of the user interface. Figure 3-2 shows a high-level overview of the new system.

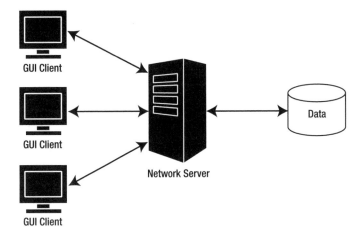

Figure 3-2. *Denny's DVDs system overview*

The users, Denny's employees, must be able to do the following:

- Perform the operations defined in the DbClient.java through a GUI interface.

- Enable multiuser networked access to a centralized DVD database.

- Allow network access via RMI or sockets.

- Make the database implementation thread-safe (implicitly required for multiuser networked access).

Tip Included in the source code available for download is a DOSClient.java class. This is a useful command-line program that was available in the download that accompanied the first edition of this book but, due to recent changes in the format of the certification project, is not necessary in the second-edition version of Denny's DVDs. Even though we do not discuss the DOSClient.java in this book, we include it anyway as a convenience to those downloading the code. Think of the DOSClient.java as a simplified command-line version of the GUI tool.

Creating the GUI

The GUI must allow an employee to view DVD information such as the UPC, title, rental status, director, actors, actresses, composer, and number of store copies. The GUI must also allow an employee to conduct a search on any of these DVD attributes. These attributes are listed in the class diagrams in Figure 3-3. The GUI should provide the user with the option of connecting to the database locally or through a network. It does not need to take into account any security features such as authentication and logon. Because the SCJD exam currently requires the use of Swing for the GUI, you will also use Swing for your project's GUI.

Note Swing is a Sun technology built on top of the Abstract Windowing Toolkit (AWT). AWT is part of the Java Foundation Classes (JFC). Knowledge of the AWT is no longer necessary for programmer-level certification, and a direct understanding of how Swing utilizes the AWT is not essential for developer certification.

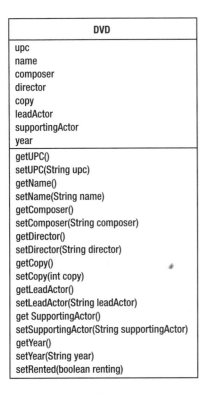

Figure 3-3. *Class diagrams*

Network Server Functionality for the Database System

Version 1.0 of Denny's rental-tracking system can be run either locally or across a network. In local mode, the GUI will connect to the database only if it is located on the same machine. In network mode, the GUI should connect to the data server from any machine accessible on the network. The network implementation can make use of either sockets or RMI (see Figure 3-4). We demonstrate both approaches in Chapters 5 and 6.

▓**Note** Even though there isn't a version 2.0 discussed in this book, we will still refer to the system we are describing as Denny's DVDs version 1.0. Perhaps version 2.0 will show up in a third edition.

Figure 3-4. *High-level client server functionality*

Because it is possible for multiple clients to connect over a network and attempt to modify the same records simultaneously, the application must be thread-safe. We discuss thread safety in more detail in Chapter 4. For now, it will suffice to know that thread-safe code protects an object's state in situations where multiple clients are accessing and modifying the same object. It is your responsibility to make sure that your certification submission is thread-safe, as you'll learn in Chapter 4 in the section, "Understanding Thread Safety."

There is no need to notify clients of *nonrepeatable reads*—that is, it is not a requirement that all clients viewing a record that has been modified be notified of the modification. However, if two employees attempt to rent the same DVD simultaneously, then only one customer will get the DVD. This is referred to as *record locking*. In Chapter 4, record locking will be explored in more detail (with an example given in Chapter 5).

The application should be able to work in a non-networked mode. In this mode, the database and user interface run in the same virtual machine (VM), no networking is performed, and no sockets should be created. Later, in Chapter 5 (which covers networking), separate implementations for both RMI and sockets are demonstrated.

Summary

In this chapter, we introduced the public interface of Denny's DVDs rental-tracking program. We discussed the project requirements and each method of the interface that you will be responsible for implementing. All of the code for the sample application can be obtained from the Source Code section of the Apress web site (http://www.apress.com).

The new system should be accessible by multiple clients either across a network or locally. The GUI should be intuitive and easy-to-use, and the application must be thread-safe. The remainder of this book examines the requirements covered in this chapter. Denny's DVDs rental-tracking program will evolve as each new concept is introduced.

FAQs

Q The Sun assignment instructions tell us that we must include the instructions and data file in our submission. Why is this needed?

A There are multiple assignments available from Sun, and multiple versions of these assignments. Some of the changes in the assignment versions include variations in the data file format, the provided interface, the required class names, or any combination of these variations. Providing both the instructions *you* implemented and *your* data file ensures that the assessor will be comparing your submission with your instructions, and not anyone else's. Likewise, this means that the assessor is guaranteed to receive the correct instructions at the same time he or she receives your submission.

Q The provided interface does not include an exception I would like to throw. Can I add it?

A No. As stated in the instructions, other applications are expecting to use this interface, so if you add exceptions, the other application will need to catch them. This could prevent the other application from working.

Q I think this application will work better if I add another method to the interface. Can I do this?

A You can; however, we advise against it for the Sun assignment. Adding new interface methods will break the contract between the data formats and user interface. Additionally, if you do this on the actual assignment you may end up failing. A better approach is to add methods to the implemented classes. We encourage you to add class methods (that is, not interface methods provided by Sun) or to modify implementations as a way to better understand the project and source code.

Q How similar is this chapter's example to the one Sun will provide?

A There is no guarantee what future exams will look like from Sun, but this sample demonstrates the concepts required to achieve the Java developer certification, and it also introduces new features in J2SE.

Q How should I use the provided code samples?

A The completed version of the Denny's DVDs system is available for download. Each chapter will describe the evolution of the project from the required DBClient interface developed in this chapter to the remainder of the application. As you read the book, refer to the relevant section of the code base in order to understand the full implementations. Chapter 9 explains in detail how to compile and execute the entire Denny's DVDs system in a manner similar to the way your actual Sun submission will need to be executed.

An alternative approach is to study the sample project source code first and then read the book to provide an explanation for the design choices made and how those choices relate to similar decisions you will encounter while developing the actual Sun certification project. We recommend reading the book first and then referring to the code, but the alternative approach of reading the code and referring to the book should also produce successful results. It really depends on which approach makes more sense for you and your natural learning methods.

Q Can I add features not discussed in this book?

A Of course you are free to modify the project and make it more sophisticated. In fact, inquisitiveness and a sense of experimentation are very important qualities for a software engineer. However, the project has been carefully designed with two goals in mind. The first and more important goal is to cover all of the concepts required for the SCJD exam. So if you do decide to ad-lib, keep in mind the purpose of the sample project. The second goal is to introduce the new features of J2SE 5, such as autoboxing and generics.

PART 2

Implementing a J2SE Project

CHAPTER 4

■■■

Threading

Welcome to threading. In this chapter we will demystify this topic by breaking it down into manageable sections and subsections using real-world examples and metaphors. The purpose of this chapter is to explain the conceptual and technical details you need to pass the SCJD exam, including the written part of the exam.

The first sections of this chapter introduce threading and the challenges of multithreading. Waiting is explained in detail, as is locking. Finally, there is a subsection on thread safety issues, including deadlocks, starvation, race conditions, and monitors.

The sections that follow discuss the various ways that Thread objects can be used directly, considerations of threading when working with Swing, and the dos and don'ts of threading. Finally, we'll conclude with a FAQ section that covers some common threading questions. Specifically the following topics are covered:

- An introduction to threads and multithreading

- Locking and synchronization

- The new locking capabilities of JDK 5

- Effective thread management through waiting, sleeping, and yielding

- The importance of thread safety

- Record-locking strategies

■**Note** This chapter is only designed to be an introduction to threading. If you want to gain an in-depth understanding of threading, we recommend Allen Holub's excellent book, *Taming Java Threads* (Apress, 2000).

Threading Fundamentals

Before you start this chapter, there are few things you should already know about threads. You should know that there are two ways to create a thread of execution in Java: the first by extending the Thread object, and the second by implementing the Runnable interface. You should know that to start a thread you must call the start method, and you should know that threads can appear to do their work in parallel with each other. This is the basic understanding required for the SCJP exam, and it should be material you have mastered if you are thinking about taking the SCJD exam.

A Brief Review of Threads

A *thread* is an independent stream of execution for a set of instructions. For example, imagine a word processor needs to accomplish two activities, as shown in Figure 4-1. It needs to print and save the document you are currently working on.

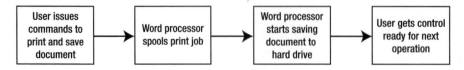

Figure 4-1. *Word processing program example*

If the word processor were single-threaded, it could not start saving the document until it was finished printing the document, as depicted in Figure 4-1. This approach would certainly work, but it would be overly inefficient, as those of us who remember the earliest word processors can attest. We can do better.

Now imagine that the program spawns two independent paths of execution, or threads. One is printing a document, and the other is quietly backing up the document in the background. This approach will yield potentially more efficient results, because there is no need for the two activities to wait on each other. For example, even as the network connection is being established with the printer, another thread could be saving the file. This concept of multithreading is illustrated in Figure 4-2 and described in detail in the next section.

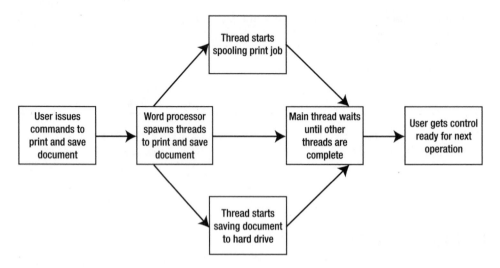

Figure 4-2. *Word processing program with threads*

Multithreading

Multithreading is the coordination of the various threads that run in a system. It is done for the purpose of improving overall system efficiency. This could mean taking turns with the resources or sharing them, decreasing overhead, or respecting the boundaries of other threads.

There are inherent challenges in managing multiple threads. These challenges arise as a result of the way in which central processing units (CPUs) handle threads. We will be discussing these challenges throughout this chapter, with explicit details in the section "Understanding Thread Safety."

A CPU will execute a number of instructions from a given thread, then switch over to executing a set of instructions from another thread, and so on. Because this switching happens quickly, an illusion of independent and parallel execution is created for all the threads. In addition, threads that are inactively waiting—say, for a network connection—will not act as bottlenecks for other threads. This is one of the greatest advantages of multithreading. However, this increased efficiency comes at a price: It is entirely possible for one thread to corrupt the data that another thread is using, unless precautions are taken. We will demonstrate these problems, and show you how to program defensively to counteract these problems in the section "Understanding Thread Safety."

■**Note** Throughout this chapter we will be discussing threading from the perspective of the JVM operating on a single CPU computer. On computers with multiple CPUs, it is quite possible for threads to be operating on different CPUs concurrently. Regardless, the issues that arise will be the same.

Returning to the word processing program example, suppose that another thread is justifying the text, and this thread makes no effort to coordinate with the thread that is printing the document. The result might be that some of the printed document is justified and some of it is not.

These are some of the challenges that come with the territory when you start to multithread. The SCJD exam requires that you have a strong understanding of multithreading and the dangers that lurk therein.

Java's Multithreading Concepts

Java is one of the few languages that has built-in support for multithreading. Two important behaviors arise from this support. First, every Java object can be locked down for exclusive use by a given thread. Synchronizing on an object achieves this. A locked object is inaccessible to any thread other than the one that explicitly claimed it as long as all the other threads honor the locking. Second, each Java object can keep track of all the threads that want exclusive access to it. Think of this as having a sign-up sheet for each object.

The basic challenge of multithreading is similar to one of the challenges of raising young children: How do you keep the threads (children) from fighting over a limited supply of resources (toys)?

The solution, at least in Java, is twofold. First, every method that potentially uses a global object must adhere to the convention of checking to see if it is currently in use by another thread. Second, every method that modifies the object needs to put a sign on it noting that the object is currently in use. (If only it were so easy with children...)

A real-world metaphor for the latter part of the solution is signing up to use the treadmill at the gym. If you (the thread) want to use the globally available object (the treadmill), then you have check to see whether other people (other threads) are using it. If somebody is using it, then you wait. If not, then you sign it out and use it.

The first activity is referred to as waiting. The next section explains waiting in detail.

Waiting

Waiting is the act of getting out of the way when you can't be productive. As the name implies, waiting is an inactive process. This means that a waiting thread does not waste CPU time it cannot use. If a thread is waiting, then other threads are free to use its allotted quota of CPU time. The waiting thread will certainly not need it.

Imagine a group of children trying to buy ice cream from an ice cream truck. If the boy who currently has the ice cream vendor's attention does not have enough money to pay for his ice cream, he won't force everyone else to wait while his father brings him the funds he needs. He will get out the way, probably weep quietly to himself, and wait. Then he'll step back into the fray and try to claim the ice cream vendor's attention. The other children won't wait for him, because he can't order anyway.

■**Note** The metaphor of children greedily trying to get ice cream is not an arbitrary one. Competing threads do not behave like polite adults in a grocery store line. There is no sense of order. All compete voraciously, and based on the underlying operating system, priorities, and other variables, one or another wins.

In general, there are two distinct families of pausing execution while waiting for something to happen. There is a version of pausing that maintains the lock(s) that your thread has, as well as a version that releases a lock. Typically the first type of pausing happens when you need some event to happen before continuing (for example, waiting for data to be sent over a network socket), and the second usually happens when you call some method that explicitly states that it will release the lock—for example, calling the `Object.wait` method will release the lock on the particular object it is invoked on.

■**Note** We will explore locking in the "Locks" section of this chapter. For now, think of locking as sticking an "in use" sign on an object.

If your thread goes into a wait state by calling `Thread.yield` or `Thread.sleep`, or needs something to occur before continuing, such as receiving I/O, then your thread will maintain all locks it holds. That means that other threads will not be able to use the locked objects. If they attempt to do so, they will block until those resources are released.

Calling myObject.wait for a given object myObject, however, does release that object's lock, assuming you have the lock on that object—if you do not have the lock on that object, attempting to call the wait method will result in an IllegalStateException being thrown. This is actually very useful, because it allows other threads to modify myObject. This is illustrated later in this chapter in the "Ice Cream Man" example.

To understand the wait method, think of the minister of a church passing around a collection plate. He expects people to modify the collection plate's state—as a matter of fact he's waiting for them to do so. If they don't, he'll probably continue to wait until they do. In code, this might look something like Listing 4-1. Don't be discouraged if the code samples aren't 100 percent clear to you right now. Read the entire chapter, and it will all fall into place.

Listing 4-1. *Waiting Example*

```
1  public class Minister {
2      private CollectionPlate collectionPlate = new CollectionPlate();
3
4      public static void main(String[] args) {
5          Minister minister = new Minister();
6
7          // create a Thread that checks the amount of
8          // money in the collection plate.
9          minister.new CollectionChecker().start();
10
11         //create several threads to accept contributions.
12         for (int i = 0; i < 6; i++) {
13             minister.new CollectionAcceptor(20).start();
14         }
15     }
16
17     /**
18      * the collection plate that get passed around
19      */
20     private class CollectionPlate {
21         int amount = 0;
22     }
23
24     /**
25      * Thread that accepts collections.
26      */
27     private class CollectionAcceptor extends Thread {
28         int contribution = 0;
29
30         public CollectionAcceptor(int contribution) {
31             this.contribution = contribution;
32         }
33
34         public void run() {
35             //Add the contributed amount to the collectionPlate.
```

```
36                synchronized (collectionPlate) {
37                    int amount = collectionPlate.amount + contribution;
38                    String msg = "Contributing: current amount: " + amount;
39                    System.out.println(msg);
40                    collectionPlate.amount = amount;
41                    collectionPlate.notify();
42                }
43            }
44        }
45
46        /**
47         * Thread that checks the collections made.
48         */
49        private class CollectionChecker extends Thread {
50            public void run() {
51                // check the amount of money in the collection plate. If it's
52                // less than 100, then release the collection plate, so other
53                // Threads can modify it.
54                synchronized (collectionPlate) {
55                    while (collectionPlate.amount < 100) {
56                        try  {
57                            System.out.println("Waiting ");
58                            collectionPlate.wait();
59                        } catch  (InterruptedException ie) {
60                            ie.printStackTrace();
61                        }
62                    }
63                    // getting past the while statement means that the
64                    // contribution goal has been met.
65                    System.out.println("Thank you");
66                }
67            }
68        }
69    }
```

In this case, there is one thread representing the minister waiting for the collection to exceed $100. There are a further six threads representing attendees adding $20 to the collection plate. Each of these threads synchronizes on the collectionPlate object. Since the threads adding to the collection plate need to obtain the lock on the collectionPlate object, the minister thread must temporarily release it from time to time, which it does by calling the wait method. As each thread adds to the collection plate, it wakes the minister by calling the notify method.

■**Note** In Listing 4-1, it does not really matter whether the collection threads call notify or notifyAll in line 41—either call will wake the minister thread. Since there is only one thread waiting on the condition (the amount in the collection plate) to change, we have chosen to call notify. If multiple threads were waiting on different conditions to change, then it would make more sense to call notifyAll.

Or imagine a producer/consumer relationship where one thread populates an object and another consumes that object when it is populated. In this case, the consumer thread wants the object to be modified; thus, the consumer wants to know when that modification occurs. `Object.wait`, `Object.notify`, and `Object.notifyAll` support the latter kind of waiting.

Calling the `wait` method is different than calling `sleep` or `yield`, or even pausing for I/O. The `wait` method actually allows other threads to acquire the lock on the object in question, while `sleep`, `yield`, and pausing for I/O do not.

Note The `wait` and `notify`/`notifyAll` methods almost always go together. If one thread `wait`s, there should be another thread that can call `notify` or `notifyAll`. The exception to this would be if you were doing something with timeouts and needed to release locks—but this would be a very rare situation. If there's no call to a `wait` method, then there's no reason at all to call `notify` or `notifyAll`.

Yielding

Yielding is the act of politely offering up your turn in the queue while maintaining your resources. For example, suppose you're trying to use a bank's automated teller machine (ATM). You know that this process will take a while because you're going to transfer funds, check your balance, make a deposit, and so forth. Yielding would be the act of offering the person behind you in line an opportunity to use the ATM before you. Of course, you wouldn't give that person your resources (money, ATM card, and so on). However, you would offer to give up your spot at the ATM (analogous to the CPU). The process of making this offer, even if there's no one to accept it, is yielding.

It is possible that, even though you yielded, you may still get first access. In our ATM scenario it is possible that the person behind you is too nice to accept your kindness. In computer terms, though, when you yield, all threads (including your own) then get to compete for the lock on the object—your thread does not get a lesser or greater chance of getting the lock on the object. But what decides which thread actually wins that competition and gets access to the lock on the object? The thread scheduler does.

The *thread scheduler* is like an office manager. It takes threads into consideration and decides which thread should be allowed to run based on the underlying operating system, thread priorities, and other factors.

There are two important points to note. First, you must be aware that your thread of execution is not guaranteed to be next in line when you yield, even though you originally volunteered to give up the CPU. Once a thread yields and the CPU is taken by another thread, the original yielding thread does not have any special status in being next in line. It must wait and hope, like every other thread.

Second, it's important to realize that your thread didn't give up resources that you have exclusive locks on. That is, even though you're letting someone else use the ATM, you didn't give him your ATM card. When a thread yields, it steps out of the CPU, but it retains control over any resources it had originally marked for exclusive use.

So why yield? Imagine that your thread entails six small bank operations: checking your balance, moving money from your checking account to your everyday account, checking your balance, moving money from your savings account to your everyday account, checking your balance, and finally withdrawing money. The thread you're yielding to might just put the money it owes you into your everyday account, making your financial footwork unnecessary and thus removing your need to continue. If your thread had not yielded, it might not have received the money until after it was done with all six bank operations. If your thread is performing a prolonged or expensive operation, it's a good idea to yield occasionally.

■**Caution** You should not rely on thread priorities, and by extension yielding, to resolve your threading issues. Implementation of thread scheduling, including yielding, is completely up to the JVM manufacturer. So it is possible that different operating systems, or even two different JVMs on one operating system, may deal with yielding differently. So go ahead and yield in your programs, but never count on the yielding to actually occur.

Blocking

Blocking is the act of pausing execution until a lock becomes available. If your thread is attempting to obtain a lock some other thread already owns, then it will block until the other thread releases its lock. This simply means that the thread goes into a state of hibernation until the event comes to pass. In this case, the lock becoming available is the event.

What does this mean for other threads? It means that they are free to use the CPU cycles that the blocking thread has a right to but is not using. However, the blocking thread keeps exclusive control over any other resources it had explicitly locked. Also, other threads should be prepared for the blocking thread to start again at any point, because the event that will trigger it could happen at any time.

■**Note** The JVM handles changing threads from the `Thread.State.BLOCKED` state to the `Thread.State.RUNNABLE` state for you. You do not have to do anything special in your code to tell any other threads that you are about to release a lock on an object.

Sleeping

Sleeping is the act of waiting for at least a specified amount of time. Imagine that you are using the ATM, but get a message on screen telling you that the system is congested. You might decide that you want to give up for 5 minutes and then wander over to try to use it again after that time has passed. This act frees up the ATM for at least the next 5 minutes. After that time period expires, you walk over to the ATM and join the line waiting for its use.

■**Note** A sleeping thread is guaranteed to wait at least as long as specified. However, it might wait longer, depending on the whims of the thread scheduler.

The difference between sleeping and yielding is that a yielding thread never knows how brief or long the wait will be. A sleeping thread, on the other hand, always knows that it will wait for at least the amount of time specified.

Child.java Example

This example is probably more complicated than anything you'll have to do on the SCJD exam, but it provides a good illustration of waiting. Study it carefully and you won't be overwhelmed by the threading demands of the SCJD exam.

The first 41 lines in this example are very straightforward. An IceCreamMan object is created in its own thread and goes into a loop, waiting for clients to hand him IceCreamDish objects. The IceCreamMan is a static object, which ensures that there will only ever be one IceCreamMan for all the children in our example.

In line 15 we set the IceCreamMan thread to be a daemon thread. The JVM will exit if the only threads still running are daemon threads. In this example, we have explicitly created several non-daemon threads: the three threads for each of the children. There is also one other non-daemon thread that was created for us: the main thread. When these four threads have completed, the only thread we *explicitly* created that is still running will be the IceCreamMan daemon thread, so the program will terminate.

Note You cannot change a thread's daemon status after the thread has started—if you want your thread to be a daemon, you must explicitly set it as such before starting the thread. A thread created from non-daemon threads defaults to being a non-daemon thread. Likewise, a thread created from daemon threads defaults to being a daemon thread. In either case, if you do not like the default type of thread, you can change it by calling the setDaemon method on the thread.

The IceCreamMan class extends the Thread class, so we can call the start method directly, as shown in line 16.

Line 25 shows an example of using the enhanced for loop to iterate over the items in an array. In this array we create several Child objects, each of which is an independent thread. Their role is to request a dish of ice cream from the IceCreamMan.

Lines 27 and 28 show how to create a thread based on a Runnable class. In line 27 we create a new thread from the Runnable class, and in line 28 we start the thread as we would any other thread object.

For this example we have decided that getting ice cream for our three children is the most important task—what happens after that is not important. So we have decided that we can end the application once all three children have eaten their ice cream. To do this, our main thread must pause until all three Child threads have completed running. We accomplish this in lines 32 through 38, where we call the join method on each of the child threads.

Tip If you are having trouble understanding the terminology of "joining a thread," it may make more sense if you refer back to Figure 4-2. In the diagram it *appears* as if each thread split from the main thread, then rejoined it after completion.

Once all the `Child` threads have completed, the main thread prints a status message, then exits. As mentioned earlier, at this point there will be no more non-daemon threads running, and the application itself will exit.

■Note If we did not have the join statements in lines 32 through 38, the application would still work in a very similar fashion. The major difference would be that the main method would complete before the `Child` threads complete. However, since the `Child` threads are not daemon threads, they would still continue to run. So all the children would still get their ice cream. Once all the children have their ice cream, the program would still exit.

```
1   /**
2    * a Child object, designed to consume ice cream
3    */
4   public class Child implements Runnable {
5       private static IceCreamMan iceCreamMan = new IceCreamMan();;
6       private IceCreamDish myDish = new IceCreamDish();
7       private String name;
8
9       public Child(String name) {
10          this.name = name;
11      }
12
13      public static void main(String args[]) {
14          // start the ice cream man's thread.
15          iceCreamMan.setDaemon(true);
16          iceCreamMan.start();
17
18          String[] names = {"Ricardo", "Sally", "Maria"};
19          Thread[] children = new Thread[names.length];
20
21          // create some child objects
22          // create a thread for each child
23          // get the Child threads started
24          int counter = -1;
25          for (String name : names) {
26              Child child = new Child(name);
27              children[++counter] = new Thread(child);
28              children[counter].start();
29          }
30
31          // wait until all children have eaten their ice cream
32          for (Thread child : children) {
33              try {
34                  child.join();
```

```
35                  } catch (InterruptedException ie) {
36                      ie.printStackTrace();
37                  }
38          }
39
40          System.out.println("All children received ice cream");
41      }
```

Child objects attempt to hand their personal IceCreamDish to the ice cream man, as shown in line 44. Then they eat the ice cream when it is returned to them—this is handled by the eatIceCream method.

■**Note** The Sun Code Conventions for the Java programming language recommend inserting a blank line between methods; however, there is no value in showing these blank lines when code listings have been split to allow room for comments within this book. Nevertheless, the blank lines do exist in the downloadable source, so to ensure the line numbers remain consistent between the book and the downloadable source, you may see cases where blank lines and Javadoc comments have been removed from the text. Therefore, while it appears that lines are missing, rest assured that all the relevant code is presented.

```
43          public void run() {
44              iceCreamMan.requestIceCream(myDish);
45              eatIceCream();
46          }
```

As we will see when we review the IceCreamMan code in the next section of this chapter, after receiving an IceCreamDish the IceCreamMan instance fills it and signals that he is done with that particular IceCreamDish. The Child instances wait until the IceCreamMan modifies their personal IceCreamDish objects and notifies them of the change. As soon as they receive that notification, they eat their IceCream.

Notice that in this example the Child instance actually releases its lock on the instance of the IceCreamDish by calling myDish.wait() in line 60. This then provides the opportunity for the IceCreamMan to gain the lock on the dish, after which he can fill it.

The next interesting part of the code happens between lines 48 and 69:

■**Note** You cannot call the wait method on an object unless you are in a block or a method that is synchronized on that object.

```
48      public void eatIceCream() {
49          String msg = name + " waiting for the IceCreamMan to fill dish";
50          /*
51           * The IceCreamMan will notify us when the dish is full, so we should
52           * wait until we have received that notification. Otherwise we could
```

```
53                * get a dish that is only half full (or even empty).
54                */
55            synchronized (myDish) {
56                while (myDish.readyToEat == false) {
57                    // wait for the ice cream man's attention
58                    try {
59                        System.out.println(name + msg);
60                        myDish.wait();
61                    } catch (InterruptedException ie) {
62                        ie.printStackTrace();
63                    }
64                }
65                myDish.readyToEat = false;
66            }
67            System.out.println(name +": yum");
68        }
69    }
70
71    class IceCreamDish {
72        public boolean readyToEat = false;
73    }
```

Line 55 synchronizes on the IceCreamDish reference, myDish. This means that the current Child thread will not move past line 55 until it has exclusive access to the IceCreamDish reference of this particular Child object.

Remember that each Child and the IceCreamMan share access to that particular child's IceCreamDish. The IceCreamMan could be modifying the IceCreamDish at any time; we don't want the Child object to use the IceCreamDish until the IceCreamMan is through.

Now assume that the Child has achieved access to the IceCreamDish. This could happen for two reasons. First, the IceCreamMan is not currently using that Dish (he does, after all, have other Child objects to attend to). Second, the IceCreamMan is finished with that Dish. Line 56 checks the value of dish.readyToEat. This value tells the Child whether the IceCream is ready to be eaten. A monitor is used between the Child objects and the IceCreamMan. Monitors will be defined shortly. For now, think of a monitor as a prearranged signaling device between the IceCreamMan and the Child objects.

If the dish.readyToEat value is false, then the IceCreamMan has not finished filling the bowl. The Child can release the lock on the Dish by calling wait on it, as in line 60.

Notice that the Child thread checks the condition of the dish.readyToEat variable in a while loop, not an if statement. The reason for this is due to a small problem with when the JVM will return control to the application after a call to the wait method. The Sun Javadoc comments for the wait method say, in part: "*A thread can also wake up without being notified, interrupted, or timing out, a so-called spurious wakeup. While this will rarely occur in practice, applications must guard against it by testing for the condition that should have caused the thread to be awakened, and continuing to wait if the condition is not satisfied. In other words, waits should always occur in loops.*"

IceCreamMan.java Example

The IceCreamMan object starts a loop inside his run method. The method checks to see if any IceCreamDish objects need to be serviced. This all happens in the run method between lines 15 and 32:

```java
1    import java.util.*;
2
3    public class IceCreamMan extends Thread {
4        /**
5         * a list to hold the IceCreamDish objects
6         */
7        private List<IceCreamDish> dishes = new ArrayList<IceCreamDish> ();
8
9        /**
10        * Start a thread that waits for ice cream bowls to be given to it.
11        */
12       String clientExists = "IceCreamMan: has a client";
13       String clientDoesntExist = "IceCreamMan: does not have a client";
14
15       public void run() {
16           while (true) {
17               if (!dishes.isEmpty()) {
18                   System.out.println(clientExists);
19                   serveIceCream();
20               } else {
21                   try {
22                       System.out.println(clientDoesntExist);
23                       // sleep, so that children have a chance to add their
24                       // dishes. see note in book about why this is not a
25                       // yield statement.
26                       sleep(1000);
27                   } catch(InterruptedException ie) {
28                       ie.printStackTrace();
29                   }
30               }
31           }
32       }
```

Line 16 starts an infinite loop for this thread. Remember that the thread for the IceCreamMan is a daemon thread, so even though this is an infinite loop it will not stop the application from exiting once all Child threads have eaten their ice cream.

Line 17 checks to see if any IceCreamDish objects have been queued up for processing. If not, the IceCreamMan thread sleeps for a second and then checks again, per lines 22 through 26. If the queue has an entry, then the IceCreamMan thread calls the serveIceCream method.

At line 26 we had a choice—we could have yielded to other threads, or we could sleep for some time. Either choice would have provided the Child threads a chance to run. However, sleeping provides a better chance for the Child threads to run, as the JVM knows that the IceCreamMan will not be running for at least a second—if we had yielded, any of the Child threads or the IceCreamMan thread could have started running immediately afterwards. In addition, yielding is something you would normally do before you start (or in the middle of) a lengthy or complex task—it is a way of being nice to other threads. However, this is not the case here. Finally, if there are no other threads that can run, the JVM will immediately pass control back to the while loop—this will result in the thread consuming as much CPU cycles as are available; it can even lead to your computer having the appearance of hanging.

The serveIceCream method is the most interesting part of our code. Assuming that there is currently a Dish in the queue, line 49 synchronizes on that IceCreamDish instance. This has the effect of forcing any Child objects that want to use the IceCreamDish instance to wait. Specifically, it causes line 55 in Child to pause until line 53 in IceCreamMan is reached or, if the Child thread had paused at line 60, it will not be able to resume until line 53 in IceCreamMan is reached.

Conversely, if a Child instance is executing a method that synchronizes on the IceCreamDish, then hitting line 49 in IceCreamMan will cause IceCreamMan to wait until lines 50 through 61 in Child finish executing, or until the Child instance releases the lock on the Ice-CreamDish by calling wait in line 55.

This is an example of the threads respecting each other's boundaries. By synchronizing on the same object, the two threads can be assured that they will not be simultaneously modifying or using the same object.

When the IceCreamMan owns the lock on the dish, he can fill it with ice cream, and then notify the Child that it is available. This happens in line 52. After line 52 is run, the Child thread that was waiting on that particular plate will no longer be waiting—the JVM scheduler will now be able to run it. However, until the IceCreamMan releases the lock on the dish at the completion of line 53, the Child will not be able to regain the lock on the dish, so it will remain blocked.

■**Note** You cannot call the notify method on an object unless you are in a block or a method that is synchronized on that object.

```
34      /**
35       * Serve Ice Cream to a Child object.
36       */
37      private void serveIceCream() {
38          // get an ice cream dish
39          IceCreamDish currentDish = dishes.get(0);
40
41          // wait sometimes, don't wait sometimes
42          if (Math.random() > .5) {
43              delay();
44          }
45
46          String msg = "notify client that the ice cream is ready";
47          System.out.println("IceCreamMan: " + msg);
48
```

```
49          synchronized (currentDish) {
50              currentDish.readyToEat = true;
51              //notify the dish's owner that the dish is ready
52              currentDish.notify();
53          }
54
55          //remove the dish from the queue of dishes that need service
56          dishes.remove(currentDish);
57      }
```

The synchronized blocks in lines 49–53 in the IceCreamMan's serveIceCream method here, and lines 55–66 of the Child's eatIceCream method, require both threads to synchronize on the same object. We have to assume that any programmers working on the Child class and the IceCreamMan class will continue to use the synchronized blocks. However, there is a risk that a Child may remove their synchronized code, which would mean that they could grab their dish back before it has been filled with ice cream. This actually gives us a safeguard against the program being changed—we can explain to other programmers that removing the synchronized code could result in the Child thread getting a dish that has not been completely filled (or could even be empty).

Tip Whenever code is written that depends on a particular way of implementing it, you should add an implementation comment to explain the details to other programmers. We have shown this in the comments in lines 50–54 of the Child class in the previous code listing.

While it is relatively easy to explain to a Child that they should not try to take the plate before they have been told it is full (because they won't want to miss out on more ice cream), it is harder to get them to agree not to try to hand their dishes over all at once—from their perspective the sooner they hand the dish over the sooner it will be filled. They don't particularly care about fairness to the other children, or how well the IceCreamMan can handle receiving multiple plates at once.

To guard against this, we have synchronized the IceCreamMan's requestIceCream method. By synchronizing the method, we can ensure that only one Child is ever handing a dish to the IceCreamMan at a time.

```
59      /**
60       * Allow client objects to add dishes
61       */
62      public synchronized void requestIceCream(IceCreamDish dish) {
63          dishes.add(dish);
64      }
65
```

```
66      /**
67       * build in a delay
68       */
69      private void delay() {
70          try {
71              System.out.println("IceCreamMan: delayed");
72              Thread.sleep((long) (Math.random()*1000) );
73          } catch (InterruptedException ie) {
74              ie.printStackTrace();
75          }
76      }
77  }
```

As Figure 4-3 shows, the IceCreamMan is waiting for clients in his own thread. Each Child object is also in its own thread. The Child objects interact with the IceCreamMan by giving him their IceCreamDish, and then they step out of the CPU and wait. The IceCreamMan prepares the IceCreamDish, which is the signal that the Child associated with that IceCreamDish needs to wake up and eat their IceCream.

Figure 4-3. *IceCreamMan waiting for clients*

Waiting Summary

A thread that needs a resource becomes paused without you specifically requesting that it pause. In contrast, a thread that pauses because of a call to yield, wait, or sleep is paused specifically at the request of the programmer. Regardless, all cases result in the thread pausing execution.

In the case of a thread paused until a resource becomes available and a thread that yielded to other threads, the programmer does not know when the thread will resume processing—for the former, it will be whenever the resource becomes available, and for the latter it will be at the discretion of the JVM thread scheduler. If you call wait without any parameters, you will not know when the thread will resume processing—it is dependent on another thread notifying it that it can continue operating. However, if you call wait with a time limit, you will know that the thread will resume processing when it has been notified, or soon after the time limit has expired. Remember that time limits cannot be strictly enforced; the JVM will pause the thread at least as long as you requested and make its best attempt to schedule the thread after the time limit has expired, but the exact time the thread resumes is not guaranteed. If you call sleep, you will know that the thread will resume processing soon after the time limit has expired—again, time limits cannot be strictly enforced. Returning to the ice cream example, imagine that little Sally has finally gotten the ice cream man's attention and given him some money, but she hasn't yet actually picked her flavor. If Sally yielded, then she would move out of the way voluntarily to let another child try, but she would be secure in the knowledge that the ice cream man won't sell the cone that she explicitly locked down. If no children were in fact interested, then she would jump back in and have her cone filled with ice cream.

If Sally decided to sleep, it might be as if she has put her money down for a cone but is delaying making her choice for up to 1 minute—say, for her younger brother to arrive. After the minute has elapsed, then she will try again (whether the younger brother has shown up or not). When she finally does get the ice cream man's attention, she will be confident that the ice cream cone she had locked down will still be there. But just because Sally has decided that the minute is up does not mean that she will be able to get her cone immediately—another child may be getting his or her cone filled at the end of Sally's minute. Sally is blocked whenever she cannot get the ice cream man's attention. Having slept for 1 minute in the previous example, she now finds that the ice cream man is serving another child. Although she still owns the lock on her cone, she does not own the lock on the ice cream man and is blocked until she can get that lock (and maybe her brother can turn up in the meantime).

However, if Sally had to wait for her father to bring her money, then she does not have any cone locked down, and by the time the money arrives, all the cones may be sold.

Locks

Locks are tokens of exclusive use. Each Java object has one. Think of locking as the ability to stick a note on any object and claim that object for your thread's exclusive use. By claiming an object's lock, your thread tells other methods (those that respect synchronization) not to modify that object in any way until your thread releases it. A method that respects synchronization is one that synchronizes on the object in question.

In Java, you can lock an object by synchronizing on it. Consider the following example:

```
public void addElement(Object item) {
    synchronized (myArrayList) {
      //do stuff
    }
}
```

This lets the JVM know that other threads should not modify the myArrayList object. Of course, this only applies to synchronized methods. For instance, in the following example the method elementExists might have no need to synchronize access, because it is a read-only operation:

```
public boolean elementExists(Object item) {

    return myArrayList.contains(item);
}
```

However, if it were required that elementExists be absolutely accurate (that is, if you could not afford to receive an incorrect answer while another thread was in the middle of inserting or removing elements into the ArrayList by another thread), then you would synchronize access here as well.

This section integrates some of the ideas already presented. The concept of locking is fundamental to understanding threading, and you will gain a lot by paying careful attention here.

Locking Objects

You lock objects all the time in everyday life. When you go the movies, you might "lock" your seat by leaving your coat on it. Even if you leave the seat to buy some popcorn, it is understood that no one should sit down in that seat. The act of leaving your coat on the seat effectively marks the seat for your exclusive use until you choose to release it.

Any Java object can be claimed for exclusive use. This is one of the explicit ways that Java supports multithreading. Java further supports multithreading by allowing objects to broadcast when they are freed and by forcing threads that want a locked resource to become inactive until those resources are freed.

If an object is not explicitly claimed, it is open for any thread's use. Similarly, a seat in a movie theater that is not explicitly claimed can be taken at any time. This means that if you leave your seat to buy some refreshments and don't lock the seat by leaving your coat on it, then you shouldn't be surprised if someone else has claimed your seat when you get back. Even if this strategy has worked in the past, it is not thread-safe for future use. The same is true in Java. Unless your classes are made explicitly thread-safe, the fact that they have been uncorrupted in the past is no guarantee that they will not be corrupted in the future.

There is a second level of depth to this metaphor. Someone might take your movie theater seat anyway, even though your coat is on it. The same is true in Java. A locked object can be violated if the thread that is modifying it does not respect synchronization.

For example, suppose you have a method that synchronizes on a member variable:

```
public void goodMethod() {
    synchronized (myObject) {
      //do stuff to myObject
    }
}
```

A second method could modify myObject if it chooses not to synchronize on myObject. Synchronizing on an object means "I'll respect other people's locks on this object, and I hope they respect mine." However, it is unenforced. Thus, the following example would refuse to respect the synchronization established in goodMethod, and would execute without complaint. This could cause problems if badMethod modifies myObject, as other threads that have synchronized on myObject would be expecting to have exclusive access to myObject.

```
public void badMethod() {
    //do stuff to myObject
}
```

Of course, these methods' names don't really imply that one way is "good" and another is "bad." For example, badMethod might just need to read myObject. If so, depending on context, it may be perfectly okay not to synchronize on myObject. As is often the case, "good" and "bad" are really just a matter of context.

Locking Class Instances

Java provides a mechanism for locking classes as well as objects. This can be a little confusing, but the concept is actually very straightforward. A class is just an object, used to create other objects, just as an axe is an object for creating firewood.

The JVM generates a `Class` object when your program initially loads for every class the program uses. Per JVM, there is a single `Class` object for all of the instance objects of a given class. You have limited access to the `Class` object. Because the `Class` object is itself an object, you can lock it just as you can lock any other object. What makes the `Class` object interesting is its capability to contain static variables and static methods.

Static variables are universal for every object of a class, which means that a single instance is shared by every object of that class. For example, for objects of the class `McBurgerPlace`, `chiefExecutiveOfficer` is a static member variable, because it is common to all. No matter which `McBurgerPlace` you are eating in, it shares the same `chiefExecutiveOfficer` with every other `McBurgerPlace`. If any `McBurgerPlace` restaurants were to change the `chiefExecutive➡ Officer`, every other `McBurgerPlace` would instantly be able to sense that change.

A static method is universal for every object of a class, which means that the single method is shared by every object of the class, per JVM. For example, objects of the class `McBurgerPlace` might have `createFranchise` as a static member method, assuming that creating a franchise happens at the corporate level. Any `McBurgerPlace` object can create a new franchise by calling corporate headquarters and asking to do so. No matter which `McBurgerPlace` store you are talking about, the exact same `createFranchise` method is called.

Using static methods is different from using instance methods in one very important way: The method exists on the class, not the objects. The proof of this lies in the fact that you can create a franchise, even if there is no `McBurgerPlace` store present, by getting in touch with corporate headquarters directly.

So what does all of this have to do with locking? Assume that you want to lock a given `McBurgerPlace` for exclusive use while executing a method. For example, if your `McBurgerPlace` (say the one on High Street) has a `waxFloor` method, then you don't want to be doing anything else while waxing the floor—after all, lawsuits abound.

How do you enforce this exclusivity? In the real world, you make sure that nothing else is happening in that particular store while waxing is in progress: no making burgers, no selling French fries, no preparing Joyful Meals. Almost every activity waits until you are done waxing the floor. To achieve the same exclusivity in Java, you synchronize the method in question by putting the keyword `synchronized` in the method declaration:

```
public synchronized void waxFloor()
```

This means that any other synchronized methods called on the `McBurgerPlace` on High Street will wait until the floor has been waxed.

■Note Unsynchronized methods do not respect synchronized methods. Thus, an unsynchronized method can be executed at any time. It is important to make sure that such methods can do no damage in your object's state. For example, `countMoney` is probably safe to leave unsynchronized because it cannot interfere with the waxing of the floor. The method `wipeDownTables` should probably be synchronized, however, because it does interfere with the floor waxing.

This exclusivity has nothing to do with other objects of the McBurgerPlace class. For example, the McBurgerPlace on Fifth Street is free to make burgers, sell French fries, and so forth, even if the McBurgerPlace on High Street is currently waxing the floor. Why shouldn't they?

What about dealing with an activity that does affect other objects? For example, what about receiving the chiefExecutiveOfficer? Obviously, you only want a single McBurgerPlace to receive the chiefExecutiveOfficer at a given time: She can't be in two places at once. How do you represent this exclusivity of access in Java? For that matter, how do you control access to her? You don't want one store to interrupt her while she is in the middle of talking to another store.

There are two steps in the solution to this dilemma. First, make sure that the chiefExecutiveOfficer variable is static—that is, it exists only at the class level. You can achieve this by using the keyword static when declaring the chiefExecutiveOfficer variable at the class level:

```
private static Object ceo = new Object();
```

The second step is to synchronize the static method that accesses the chiefExecutive▶ Officer, like this:

```
public static synchronized Object receiveCeo (){
    return ceo;
}
```

Because the method is static, this synchronization occurs at class level rather than at instance level.

Locking Objects Directly

There is a second way to lock objects (both instance objects and class objects). You can synchronize on the object you want to lock explicitly. For example, imagine that your McBurgerPlace class has a getSoda method that requires exclusive control of the sodaFountain member variable. You can lock the entire McBurgerPlace object, or you can lock just the sodaFountain member variable:

```
public void getSodaEfficiently() {
    synchronized (sodaFountain) {
        //do Stuff
    }
}
```

Locking a member variable object is like forcing only those people who want to use the sodaFountain to wait while you are using the sodaFountain, as opposed to forcing everyone in the entire store (including those who only want to purchase a burger) to wait.

Synchronizing a method is a form of locking an object—specifically, the this object. Synchronizing a method is really just shorthand for synchronizing on the this reference object. Thus, this code presented in Listing 4-2 is equivalent to the code presented in Listing 4-3.

Listing 4-2. *Synchronizing a Method*

```
public synchronized void myMethod() {
    //code
}
```

Listing 4-3. *Synchronizing on the this Reference Object*

```
public void myMethod() {
    synchronized (this) {
        //code
    }
}
```

Locking some object other than this can provide more concurrency than synchronizing a method because it allows other blocks of code that are synchronized on different objects to work concurrently. But efficiency, alas, is in the eye of the beholder. If an individual method needs to obtain multiple locks, then the steps of locking and unlocking the multiple locks can lead to more overhead than synchronizing the method.

In Listing 4-4, synchThisObjectExample is more efficient than synchAllLocksExample because it doesn't have the overhead of locking and unlocking three times. If your object is carefully constructed not to allow unsynchronized access to the resources you need to lock, then synchronizing methods is probably the simpler approach.

Listing 4-4. *Synchronization Example*

```
1   public class SynchExample {
2
3       private Resource resourceOne = new Resource();
4       private Resource resourceTwo = new Resource();
5       private Resource resourceThree= new Resource();
6
7       public synchronized void synchThisObjectExample() {
8           resourceOne.value = -3;
9           resourceTwo.value = -2;
10          resourceThree.value = -1;
11      }
12
13      public void synchAllLocksExample() {
14          synchronized (resourceOne) {
15              resourceOne.value = -3;
16          }
17
18          synchronized (resourceTwo) {
19              resourceTwo.value = -2;
20          }
21
```

```
22          synchronized (resourceThree) {
23              resourceThree.value = -1;
24          }
25      }
26
27      private static class Resource {
28          int value;
29      }
30  }
```

The notify and notifyAll Methods

Every Java object has the capability to broadcast a call, notifying threads that have called the
wait method on that object that some event that they might be interested in has occurred. If
you call the notify method, one of the threads waiting on that object is told to come out of the
waiting state and block until it can regain the lock on the object, after which it can continue
processing. If you call notifyAll, every thread waiting for the object is told to come out of the
waiting state and block until it can regain the lock on the object, after which it can continue
processing.

■Caution It is easy to become confused when talking about threads waiting. Thread.State.WAITING
has a specific meaning in Java, namely that the thread has called the wait or the join methods. When a
thread enters the Thread.State.WAITING state by calling the wait method, it consumes no CPU cycles
until some other thread calls either notify or notifyAll on the same object that wait was called on,
or until the thread is interrupted. When a thread enters the Thread.State.WAITING state by calling the
join method, it consumes no CPU cycles until the thread it is trying to join terminates, or until the thread is
interrupted. In contrast, if several threads attempt to obtain the same lock simultaneously, one will obtain it,
and the remainder will enter the Thread.State.Blocked state until the lock is released, at which time
another thread will obtain the lock—the JVM scheduler handles automatically selecting another thread from
those in the Thread.State.Blocked state.

Listing 4-5 demonstrates the difference between calling notify and notifyAll.

Listing 4-5. *NotifyVersusNotifyAll.java*

```
1   public class NotifyVersusNotifyAll extends Thread {
2       private static Object mutex = new Object();
3
4       public static void main(String[] args) throws InterruptedException {
5           for (int i = 0; i < 5; i++) {
6               new NotifyVersusNotifyAll().start();
7           }
8
9           Thread.sleep(2000);
```

```
10          synchronized(mutex) {
11              mutex.notifyAll();
12  //              mutex.notify();
13          }
14      }
15
16      public void run() {
17          try {
18              synchronized (mutex) {
19                  System.out.println(getName() + " waiting");
20                  mutex.wait();
21                  System.out.println(getName() + " woken up");
22                  mutex.wait(2000);
23                  System.out.println(getName() + " waking up another thread");
24                  mutex.notify();
25              }
26          } catch (InterruptedException ie) {
27              ie.printStackTrace();
28          }
29      }
30  }
```

Figure 4-4 shows the results of running NotifyVersusNotifyAll, first with line 12 and line 11 commented out (so that notify is called), then with line 11 and line 12 commented out (so that notifyAll is called).

Figure 4-4. *Notify returns one thread to the runnable state whereas notifyAll returns all threads to the runnable state.*

■Caution Although Figure 4-4 shows the threads being notified in the same order they called `wait`, this should never be relied on. The order in which threads are notified, and the order in which they regain owner-ship of the lock on the common object, is entirely at the discretion of the JVM's thread scheduler.

In general, you would use `notify` only when you are certain that the thread that will be notified will be able to use the notification. If you have multiple threads that you are certain will be able to use the notification but you want only one of them to transition to the runnable state, then you should use `notify`. However, in this case you must ensure that the remaining threads do not stay in limbo—some thread will have to notify them at an appropriate time that they can continue processing. This is complex and requires detailed analysis in order to get it right. If you have multiple threads waiting on one event but they have different condi-tions to meet, you are better off calling `notifyAll` so that all the threads will recheck their condition. As an example, consider the following code snippets:

Producer Thread:

```
synchronized (lock) {
    value = Math.random();
    lock.notifyAll();
}
```

Consumer Thread 1:

```
synchronized  (lock) {
    while (value < 0.5) {
        lock.wait();
    }
}
```

Consumer Thread 2:

```
synchronized (lock) {
    while (value >= 0.5) {
        lock.wait();
    }
}
```

This code shows one example where calling `notifyAll` is preferable to calling `notify`. By calling `notifyAll` after setting `value`, the producer can be sure that both consumers will check the current contents of the `value` variable, and one of them will be able to continue process-ing. If `notify` had been used instead of `notifyAll`, it is possible that after setting `value`, the wrong thread may have been notified, and upon finding that the `value` variable did not con-tain the desired number, would have gone back to the `Thread.State.WAITING` state, meaning that neither consumer thread would be working!

Dealing with Nonimplicit Locking

You should be aware of two important issues when you deal with locks. First, locking an object does not lock member variables of that object. This may seem counterintuitive at first, but it makes sense from the JVM's point of view. Specifically, it allows the thread to avoid locking objects that may be nested *n* layers deep. Imagine the overhead of locking an object, locking all of its member variables, locking all of their member variables, and so on. Listing 4-6 shows an example of locking objects but not their member variables. The output is shown in Figure 4-5.

Listing 4-6. *A Locking Objects Example*

```
1   import java.util.*;
2
3   public class LockObjectNotMemberVariables{
4       private List myList = new ArrayList();
5
6       public static void main(String args[]){
7           LockObjectNotMemberVariables lonmv =
8                   new LockObjectNotMemberVariables();
9           lonmv.lockTest();
10      }
11
12      public synchronized void lockTest(){
13          System.out.println("Is the THIS object locked? " +
14                              Thread.holdsLock(this));
15
16          System.out.println("Is the list object locked? " +
17                              Thread.holdsLock(myList));
18      }
19  }
```

Figure 4-5. *Locking an object does not lock member variables of that object.*

The second important point is that locking a class does not lock instance variables of that class. This is demonstrated in Listing 4-7. Notice that the method lockTest is both static and synchronized. This means that it achieves a lock on the Class object. Figure 4-6 shows that locking a class does not lock objects of that class.

Listing 4-7. *A Locking Example*

```
1   public class ClassLockNotObjectLock {
2       public static void main(String args[]) {
3           lockTest();
4       }
5
6       public static synchronized void lockTest() {
7           ClassLockNotObjectLock clnoc = new ClassLockNotObjectLock();
8           System.out.println("Is the class object locked? " +
9                               Thread. holdsLock(clnoc.getClass()));
10
11          System.out.println("Is the object instance locked? " +
12                              Thread. holdsLock(clnoc));
13      }
14  }
```

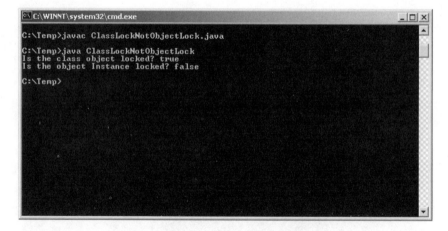

Figure 4-6. *Locking a class doesn't lock objects of that class.*

Locking in JDK 5

JDK 5 includes several packages that provide the ability to lock and wait on conditions separate from the synchronization and locking mechanisms described previously. These have several benefits, including the ability to specify whether locking should be granted fairly (remember that the methods described earlier make no guarantees about the order in which threads will be granted—a thread that has only just started waiting could be notified before a thread that has been waiting for a long time).

A new package, java.util.concurrent.locks, has been created in JDK 5, which provides some benefits to SCJD candidates, including the ability to have a ReadWriteLock (where multiple threads could all lock a record for reading, but only one thread could lock the record for writing—this will improve concurrency). We will examine ReadWriteLocks in the section discussing the DvdFileAccess class in Chapter 5.

In JDK 1.4, after returning from a call to wait(milliseconds), it was not possible to know *directly* whether the thread had been notified, or whether the timeout had elapsed. The Lock.tryLock(time, unit) method returns a boolean indicating whether it had gained the lock or whether the time expired. An example of using the similar Lock.await(time, unit) method is shown in the "Creating Our Logical Reserve Methods" section in Chapter 5. And while this technique is not required for the SCJD assignment, it is now possible to set multiple conditions upon which a thread might be notified.

Although the new lock code looks different from using synchronized blocks, it is not too difficult to convert code from one style to another. For example, the following code uses a synchronized block:

```
Object lock = new Object();
public void doSomething() {
    synchronized (lock) {
        while (true) {
            try {
                lock.wait();
                // something happens here
            } catch (InterruptedException ie) {
                // handle exception
            }
        }
    }
}
```

This code can be changed to the new format like this:

```
private static Lock lock = new ReentrantLock();
private static Condition lockReleased = lock.newCondition();
public void doSomething() {
    lock.lock();
    try {
        while (true) {
            lockReleased.await();
            // something happens here
        }
    } catch (InterruptedException ie) {
        // handle exception
    } finally {
        lock.unlock();
    }
}
```

An example of using the new locking classes is shown in the "Creating Our Logical Reserve Methods" section of Chapter 5, and further thoughts are presented in the same chapter, in the "Discussion Point: Multiple Notification Objects" section.

To ensure that a lock is released, we highly recommend that you place the call to unlock in a finally block as demonstrated earlier.

Regardless of whether you use synchronized blocks or the new concurrency classes, the same rules of thread safety apply.

Locking Summary

Object locks and locks on the member variable within the object do not interact in any way. That is, synchronizing an object does not lock member variables of that object. Nor does synchronizing a member variable lock the object that owns that variable. Threads that own locks on different objects can run concurrently as long as they do not also share a lock on a common object. In addition, locking a class does not lock instances of that class. Unsynchronized access to member variables can violate thread safety.

Understanding Thread Safety

Threading presents unique logical pitfalls, which can often be reached unexpectedly and seemingly randomly. In this section, we define some of the more common pitfalls and offer advice on ways to avoid them. The following subsections explain what thread safety is and the sorts of horrors it helps to prevent.

Deadlocks

Deadlocks occur when threads are blocked forever, waiting for a condition that cannot occur. Deadlock is like a cartoon where Daffy Duck and Bugs Bunny are stranded on an island. Daffy has a can of food, and Bugs has a can opener. Daffy won't give up the food until he gets the can opener, and Bugs won't give up the can opener until he gets some food. They are deadlocked.

In Listing 4-8, you can see that thread1 acquires a lock on lock1 but needs lock2. thread2 has acquired a lock on lock2 and needs to acquire lock1. Neither thread will allow the other thread to progress, nor will it progress itself. This is deadlock. Figure 4-7 shows the output.

Listing 4-8. *Deadlock Example*

```
1   public class DeadlockExample {
2       /**
3        * Entry point to the application. Creates 2 threads that will deadlock.
4        */
5       public static void main(String args[]) {
6           DeadlockExample dle = new DeadlockExample();
7
8           Object lock1 = "Lock 1";
9           Object lock2 = "Lock 2";
10
```

```
11          Runner thread1 = new Runner(lock1, lock2);
12          Runner thread2 = new Runner(lock2, lock1);
13
14          thread1.start();
15          thread2.start();
16      }
17
18      /**
19       * Lock two objects in the order they were specified in the constructor.
20       */
21      static class Runner extends Thread {
22          private Object lockA;
23          private Object lockB;
24
25          public Runner(Object firstLockToGet, Object secondLockToGet) {
26              this.lockA = firstLockToGet;
27              this.lockB = secondLockToGet;
28          }
29
30          public void run() {
31              String name = Thread.currentThread().getName();
32              synchronized (lock1) {
33                  System.out.println(name + ": locked " + lockA);
34                  delay(name);
35                  System.out.println(name + ": trying to get " + lockB);
36                  synchronized (lock2) {
37                      System.out.println(name + ": locked " + lockB);
38                  }
39              }
40          }
41      }
42
43      /**
44       * build in a delay to allow the other thread time to lock the object
45       * the delaying thread would like to get.
46       */
47      private static void delay(String name) {
48          try {
49              System.out.println(name + ": delaying 1 second");
50              Thread.sleep(1000L);
51          } catch (InterruptedException ie) {
52              ie.printStackTrace();
53          }
54      }
55  }
```

Figure 4-7. *Output from the deadlock example*

This is an example of bad design. There is almost always a better way to handle these sorts of situations than resorting to nested locks. If you find yourself unable to come up with a solution, reconsider the larger design of your project. Sun gives difficult problems on the SCJD exam, but most can be solved elegantly.

Race Conditions

Race conditions occur when two or more threads compete for the same resource, and the behavior of the program changes depending on who wins. For example, you and Johnson race to get be the first person to reach the test server in the morning. Depending on who wins, the server is tied up for a few minutes or for a few hours. Thus, based on somewhat random factors—say, who got stuck in traffic that morning—your program's behavior changes. This is rarely a good thing. Race conditions can be very difficult to track down because they happen sporadically and thus are difficult to reproduce.

Race conditions can also lead to deadlock because locks could be achieved in an order other than the one expected. Thus, your application, which had always achieved lock1 followed by lock2, could suddenly achieve lock2 first and attempt to release those locks in an unexpected order.

These sorts of problems are manifested when your application appears to "spontaneously" generate new behaviors, as shown in Listing 4-9. They are difficult to debug and often difficult to reproduce. That's why it's so important to make design decisions that will steer you clear of the general dangerous area of race conditions. Figure 4-8 shows the output of our example.

Listing 4-9. *Race Condition Example*

```
1  public class RaceConditionExample {
2      public static void main(String args[]) {
3          //create an instance of this object
4          RaceConditionExample rce = new RaceConditionExample();
5
```

```
 6          //create two runners
 7          Runner johnson = rce.new Runner("Johnson");
 8          Runner smith = rce.new Runner("smith");
 9
10          //point both runners to the same resource
11          smith.server =  "the common object";
12          johnson.server = smith.server;
13
14          //start the race, based on a random factor, one thread
15          //or the other gets to start first.
16          if (Math.random() > .5) {
17              johnson.start();
18              smith.start();
19          } else {
20              smith.start();
21              johnson.start();
22          }
23      }
24
25      /**
26       * Creates a thread, then races for the resource
27       */
28      class Runner extends Thread {
29          public Object server;
30
31          public Runner(String name) {
32              super(name);
33          }
34
35          public void run() {
36              System.out.println(getName() + ": trying for lock on " + server);
37              synchronized (server) {
38                  System.out.println(getName() + ": has lock on " + server);
39                  // wait 2 seconds: show the other thread really is blocked
40                  try {
41                      Thread.sleep(2000);
42                  } catch (InterruptedException ie) {
43                      ie.printStackTrace();
44                  }
45                  System.out.println(getName() + ": releasing lock ");
46              }
47          }
48      }
49 }
```

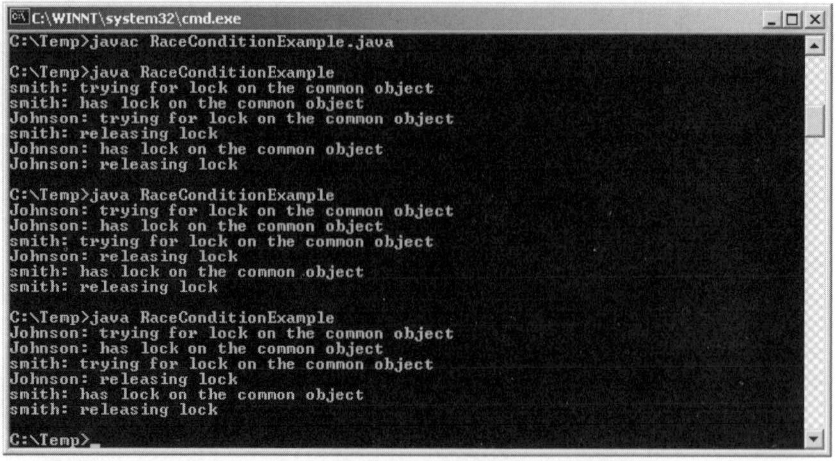

Figure 4-8. *Output from the race condition example*

It is clear here that there is no consistency in terms of who gets access to the server. This could be perfectly all right, or it could be catastrophic. It all depends on context. While it is not necessary to resolve every race condition in order to achieve thread safety, it is important to be aware of them.

Starvation

Starvation occurs when a thread never gets a chance to run. Its most common manifestation occurs when higher-priority threads keep getting preferential treatment over those with a lower priority. Imagine that your task requires that you speak to the CTO of your company. However, every time it seems as if she might be free, a senior executive steps in and takes the slice of time you were going to use. This could be for very legitimate reasons, but the end result is that you never get to speak with her (your thread never gets a chance to run).

The example in Listing 4-10 shows a contrived example of three high-priority threads and one low-priority thread all trying to use the same resource.

Listing 4-10. *Starvation Example*

```
1   /**
2    * Demonstrate the concept of a starving thread.
3    */
4   public class StarvationExample {
5       public static void main(String args[]) {
6           // Ensure the main thread competes with the other threads
7           Thread.currentThread().setPriority(Thread.MAX_PRIORITY);
8
```

```
9          // Create an instance of this object
10         // Create 4 threads, marking number 1 as a very low priority
11         for(int i = 0; I < 4; i++) {
12             //create a runner
13             Runner r = new Runner();
14             r.setPriority(Thread.MAX_PRIORITY);
15
16             //set the first thread to starve
17             if (i == 0) {
18                 r.setPriority(Thread.MIN_PRIORITY);
19                 r.setName("Starvation Thread");
20             }
21             //start the thread.
22             r.start();
23         }
24
25         // Exit as soon as we possibly can
26         System.exit(0);
27     }
28
29     /**
30      * Create a thread, then cycle through its command ten times.
31      */
32     static class Runner extends Thread {
33         public void run() {
34             for (int count = 10; count > 0; count--) {
35                 System.out.println(getName() + ": is working " + count);
36             }
37         }
38     }
39 }
```

The starving thread never ran, as you can see in Figure 4-9.

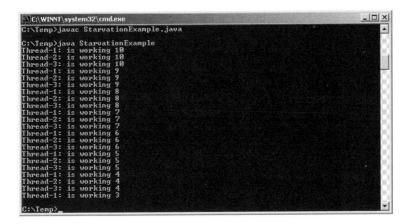

Figure 4-9. *Output from the starvation example*

■Note The exact output varies with each running of this application, as thread priorities and scheduling cannot be guaranteed. However, in the majority of executions of this application, you will note that the StarvationThread either does not run at all, or runs far fewer times than the other three threads. In the cases where the StarvationThread does run, it is almost always after the other three threads have completed.

Understanding Atomic Operations

Atomic operations are indivisible. A thread will not be swapped out while in the middle of an atomic operation. In practical terms, the only naturally occurring atomic operations in Java are assignments. For example,

```
x = 45;
```

is an atomic operation when x is an int. The only exceptions to this rule are assignments involving doubles and longs. Those are not atomic.

Operations involving longs and doubles are essentially two operations, because longs and doubles are so big. The first part of the operation sets the high 32 bits, and the next part sets the low 32 bits. This means that mid-assignment to a long or double variable, your thread could be sliced out.

Your thread consists of a number of programmatic statements. These in turn consist of atomic statements. Your thread of execution could be swapped out anywhere, except while Java is in the middle of an atomic statement. For example:

```
1          x = 7;
2          y = x++;
```

is really

```
1          x =7;
2a         int temp = x + 1;
2b         x = temp;
2c         y=x;
```

Assume x, y, and z are class member variables. A thread swap between lines 2a and 2b could lead to unexpected results, for example, if the thread that has swapped in changes the value of x to, say, 13. You could end up with the bizarre result of y being 13 (and a headache). Of course, this problem would not exist if x, y, and z were local method variables, because then no other method could have access to them.

By wrapping your method in a synchronized block, you are effectively treating the entire method as a single atomic operation, as far as other threads' clients of that object are concerned. Even if another thread swaps in before your method is done executing, as long as the thread calls methods on your object that are synchronized, you are guaranteed that corruptions such as the previous one will not occur, because those methods will not execute until your method returns.

The example in Listing 4-11 shows a contrived example of 10 threads yielding at an inopportune time, causing invalid results.

Listing 4-11. *Nonatomic Operation Example*

```
1  public class NonAtomic {
2      static int x;
3
4      public static void main(String[] args) {
5          for (int i = 0; i < 10; i++) {
6              new Runner().start();
7          }
8      }
9
10     static class Runner extends Thread {
11         private int validCounts = 0;
12         private int invalidCounts = 0;
13
14         public void run() {
15             for (int i = 0; i < 10; i++) {
16  //               synchronized (NonAtomic.class) {
17                     int reference = (int) (Math.random() * 100);
18                     x = reference;
19
20                     // either yielding or doing something intensive
21                     // should cause the problem to manifest.
22                     yield();
23  //                 for (int y = 0; y < 20000; y++) {
24  //                     Math.tan(200);
25  //                 }
26
27                     if (x == reference) {
28                         validCounts++;
29                     } else {
30                         invalidCounts++;
31                     }
32                 }
33  //           }
34
35             System.out.println(getName()
36                             + " valid: " + validCounts
37                             + " invalid: " + invalidCounts);
38         }
39     }
40 }
```

When you run this program, you will see that in the majority of cases, another thread has changed the value of x between when it is set (in line 18) and when it is checked (in line 28). An example of this is provided in Figure 4-10.

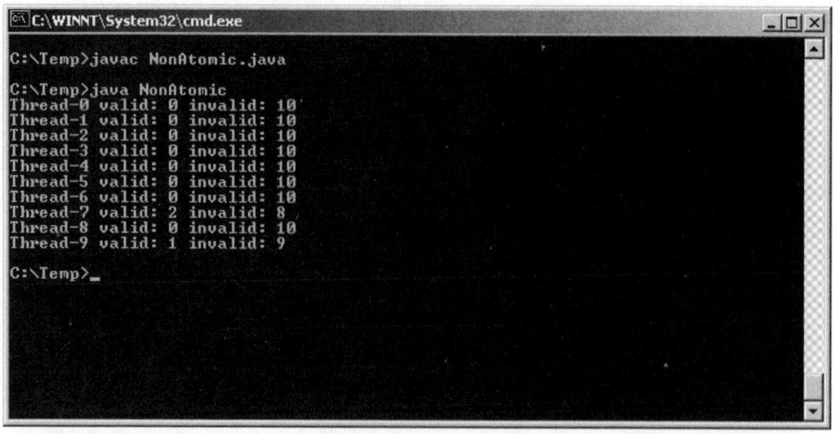

Figure 4-10. *Output from the nonatomic example*

In calling `yield` we caused this problem to be more obvious than would normally be the case; however, it is not the call to `yield` that is the problem—it is the coding itself. You can prove this by commenting out the call to `yield` in line 22, and uncommenting the for loop in lines 23–25. If you change the program in this way, and rerun the program, you will see that there are still often errors caused by the nonatomic nature of the code, even though there is no explicit yielding. You will also notice that changing the program in this way will cause it to take significantly longer to run, and if you watch your computer's CPU usage, you should find that these loops require a lot of computational effort.

If you put the code inside a synchronized block by uncommenting lines 16 and 33, you will find that the code now behaves in an atomic fashion regardless of whether you are using `yield` or the for loop.

Thread Safety Summary

You could code around any of the situations presented in this section as they occur, but that is the wrong approach. The best idea is to avoid the sorts of situations that lead to unsafe threading. There are exceptions to every rule, but in general don't nest locks, don't count on thread priorities, and watch for race conditions. The section titled "Threading Best Practices" later in this chapter helps you reduce the chances of creating situations where these sorts of problems can fester.

Using Thread Objects

This section contains some important general information you should keep in mind when working with thread objects directly.

Stopping, Suspending, Destroying, and Resuming

You should never use the `Thread.stop`, `Thread.suspend`, `Thread.resume`, or `Thread.destroy` methods, as they have been deprecated because they are inherently unsafe.

Instead of using these methods, you should have some variable that can be accessed by both the thread whose state you wish to change, and by the thread that wishes to change the state. The thread whose state is being changed should monitor this variable periodically, and safely change its state if the variable changes (by releasing any resources, closing files, etc.).

For more information, read the description of why these methods have been deprecated at `http://java.sun.com/j2se/1.5.0/docs/guide/misc/threadPrimitiveDeprecation.html`.

Thread States

Threads have six states: `Thread.State.NEW`, `Thread.State.RUNNABLE`, `Thread.State.WAITING`, `Thread.State.TIMED_WAITING`, `Thread.State.BLOCKED`, or `Thread.State.TERMINATED`. Java has specific rules about the transitions from state to state, and it's important to know them.

The most important rule is that a `Thread.State.TERMINATED` thread cannot go into any other state. Ever. The next most important rule is that a thread can only execute commands if it is `Thread.State.RUNNABLE`. When you first call the start method on a thread, the thread scheduler will transition it to `Thread.State.RUNNABLE`. At some point after that, depending on the whims of the thread scheduler, the thread will start to execute the statements in the run method body.

From the `Thread.State.RUNNABLE` state, a thread has four paths it can take, as illustrated in Figure 4-11:

- It can go on to completion, after which it enters the `Thread.State.TERMINATED` state.

- A thread can enter the `Thread.State.WAITING` state by calling wait or join.

- If the thread calls sleep or wait with a timeout value, it will enter the `Thread.State.TIMED_WAITING` state.

- If a thread cannot access a lock, it enters the `Thread.State.BLOCKED` state.

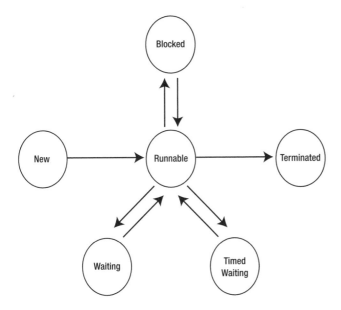

Figure 4-11. *Thread states*

More on Blocking

Blocking is an important phenomenon in threading and thus deserves a few more words of explanation. To quickly review, blocking threads do not use CPU cycles and are in a state of suspended animation. They do not wait for a time period to expire, but rather for an event to occur; specifically, a lock they were trying to acquire becomes available. Blocking threads deserve a healthy dose of respect because they do not release locked resources when they slice out of the CPU. A blocking thread that does not receive its lock can refuse to release resources that other threads might need, in addition to never coming out of hibernation, as shown in Listing 4-12. Figure 4-12 shows the output of this example.

Listing 4-12. *Blocking Example*

```
1   import java.net.*;
2
3   public class BlockingExample extends Thread {
4       private static Object mylock = new Object();
5
6       public static void main(String args[]) throws Exception {
7           LockOwner lo = new LockOwner();
8           lo.setName("Lock owner");
9           lo.start();
10
11          // Wait for a little while for the lock owner thread to start
12          Thread.sleep(200);
13
14          // Now start the thread that will be blocked
15          BlockingExample be = new BlockingExample();
16          be.setName("Blocked thread");
17          be.start();
18
19          // Wait for a little while for the blocked thread to start
20          Thread.sleep(200);
21
22          // Now print the two threads states
23          printState(lo);
24          printState(be);
25      }
26
27      // start a thread.
28      public void run() {
29          // wait for the mylock object to be freed,
30          // which will never happen
31          synchronized (mylock) {
32              System.out.println(getName() + " owns lock");
33              System.out.println("doing Stuff");
34          }
```

```
35              System.out.println(getName() + " released lock");
36          }
37
38      private static void printState(Thread t) {
39          System.out.println();
40          System.out.println("State of thread named: " + t.getName());
41          System.out.println("State: " + t.getState());
42          System.out.println("begin trace");
43          for (StackTraceElement ste : t.getStackTrace()) {
44              System.out.println("\t" + ste);
45          }
46          System.out.println("end trace");
47      }
48
49      static class LockOwner extends Thread {
50          public void run() {
51              synchronized (mylock) {
52                  System.out.println(getName() + " owns lock");
53                  try {
54                      ServerSocket ss = new ServerSocket(8080);
55                      ss.accept();
56                  } catch (Exception e) {
57                      e.printStackTrace();
58                  }
59              }
60              System.out.println(getName() + " released lock");
61          }
62      }
63  }
```

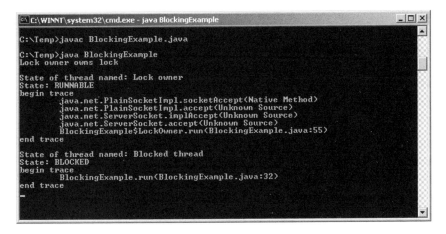

Figure 4-12. *Output from the blocking example*

■**Note** At line 54 we attempt to start listening on port 8080. There is no particular reason for picking this port, other than the fact that it is not a port that is officially assigned to any other application, and therefore there is a reasonable chance that this port will be available. However, if you are running another application that also uses port 8080 (for example, the Tomcat Web Application Server by default uses port 8080), then an exception (`java.net.BindException`) will be thrown. If you see that exception, just change the port number in line 54 from 8080 to some other number, for example 9090.

The `myLock` object is never released, because the `LockOwner` thread never finishes. Because the `myLock` object is never released, the thread that is waiting for `myLock` (in this case, the `BlockingExample` thread) is blocked and never gets a chance to execute.

The main thread would continue executing, however, if it were not dependent on the locked resource. Again, this is because blocking threads do not use CPU cycles.

■**Caution** When talking about an application or thread pausing until it can get some I/O, many publications use the standard terminology of saying that the thread or application is blocked for I/O. According to their terminology the `LockOwner` thread would be blocked until a client connects to the socket. However, as the previous example shows, the JVM state for a thread waiting for I/O may be `Thread.State.RUNNABLE`, or it may be some other state depending on how the code for the I/O class is implemented. When debugging your code, or when perusing other publications, you need to be aware that Java does not have a separate state for threads that are paused for I/O.

InterruptedException

`InterruptedExceptions` typically occur when a thread has been paused (sleeping, or waiting, or trying to join several threads) for too long, and another thread deliberately calls `interrupt` on the thread to be interrupted to bring it out of that state. Think of an `InterruptedException` as one thread violently shaking another thread back into consciousness. When a thread is shaken awake in this manner, the first thing it does is execute whatever code is inside its catch (`InterruptedException`) clause if it has one.

As an example, consider if you wrote a `Data` class that has a `lockRecord` method that must wait for a record to become available before locking it, but it does not have a timeout. After the `Data` class has been approved, you are asked to create a subclass of the `Data` class that does handle timeouts when locking. You could rewrite the entire locking code from scratch, or you could create a separate thread that interrupts the thread locking of the record if the lock is not acquired within the timeout period.

■**Note** It is possible for a thread to be interrupted at any time, even if it has not called `sleep`, `wait`, or `join`. In such a case the thread will continue to execute normally until it calls `sleep`, `wait`, or `join`, at which time an `InterruptedException` will immediately be thrown from the called method.

Synchronization

There are two natural divisions when you talk about synchronization: object synchronization and client synchronization. This section explains the differences between the two.

Internally Synchronized Classes

A Vector is a synchronized object and an ArrayList is not. What does this mean? It means all the methods that can access a Vector's internal data are synchronized. Any changes made to a Vector object by one thread are guaranteed to be immediately visible to any other thread, while changes made to an ArrayList are not so guaranteed. It does not mean that you are using the Vector object in a thread-safe way in your code. If you wanted that guaranteed, you would have to synchronize on the Vector object directly, just as you would have to synchronize directly on the ArrayList.

■**Note** Vector is an example of a thread-safe collection; however, it is rare that the thread safety offered by Vectors is required (see the next paragraph for information on what thread safety is guaranteed). If you do need this kind of thread safety, you may be better off using Collections.synchronizedCollection or similar methods to create a thread-safe collection with the characteristics of your preferred base collection.

A synchronized object only promises this: A method called on that object will behave atomically. For example, imagine that you are running two threads and that myVector and myArrayList are class member variables. Thread1 has started to run line 1, and Thread2 has yet to start line A.

Thread1:

```
1          myVector.add("Hello");
2          myArrayList.add("Hello");
```

Thread2:

```
A          myVector.add("Cruel");
B          myArrayList.add("Cruel");
```

Now, say that in the middle of line 1, Thread1 slices out. Thread2 will be unable to slice in because Vectors are synchronized,. You are therefore guaranteed that Thread2 line A will add "Cruel" after "Hello" for myVector.

This guarantee does not exist for myArrayList. That is, if Thread1 sliced out in the middle of line 2 and Thread2 sliced in, the order of adding the items to the ArrayList is indeterminate. Even worse, if one of the adds causes a resize of the internal array, all sorts of strange things can happen. We might see a NullPointerException or ArrayIndexOutOfBoundsException, or one of the adds might be "lost." All sorts of unpredictable nastiness can emerge from unsynchronized access by multiple threads.

■**Note** The reason that we've specified threads slicing out in the *middle* of line 1 or 2 is that the add method for both Vectors and ArrayLists are methods that perform several actions before actually adding the requested object to the underlying store.

Vectors are not superior to ArrayLists, nor are ArrayLists superior to Vectors. There are times when you do not need the overhead of synchronization on the Collection, and there are times when you absolutely must have it. For example, a local method variable might as well be an ArrayList, because it only exists in the context of that particular method; thus, there is no opportunity for any other threads to modify it.

However, where possible we recommend against using the Vector class. There is the possibility that a junior programmer may incorrectly believe that use of a Vector is providing thread safety other than what synchronized classes actually guarantee. Plus, there is the risk that a later programmer may change the Vector to some other class, not realizing that a synchronized class was required.

Synchronized objects have their purpose, as do unsynchronized ones. Part of earning your Java developer certification is knowing what those purposes are.

Client Synchronization

Client synchronization is the process of making sure that no other thread interrupts your method while it is mid-stride. For example, while myVector.add(Object) is a synchronized operation, the internal synchronization of the Vector object did not guarantee that another thread would not empty the myVector before the next step of your method executed. Consider the following example:

```
1    public boolean addDVD(DVD dvd ){
2        for (int i = 0; i < myVector.length(); i++) {
3            doSomethingWith(myVector.get(i));
4        }
5    }
```

While you are guaranteed that line 2 will not be hijacked mid-stride, you are not guaranteed that some other thread will not set empty the myVector object by the time you get to line 3. The current thread could slice out between lines 2 and 3, and the thread that picks up could just happen to be one that corrupts myVector. The chances are probably small, but the possibility for mischief does exist.

Be aware of such risks, even if you decide to accept them: Another thread could always slice in between two unsynchronized lines of code even if they're calls to synchronized methods.

To guarantee exclusivity, you could modify the method in one of two ways. The first way is to synchronize the method:

```
1    public synchronized boolean addDVD(DVD dvd ) {
2        for (int i = 0; i < myVector.length(); i++) {
3            doSomethingWith(myVector.get(i));
4        }
5    }
```

This denies any other threads the capability to call any synchronized methods on this particular object until addDVD returns. Depending on your class's structure, this may be sufficient.

The second way is to synchronize on the myVector member variable:

```
1    public boolean addDVD(DVD dvd ) {
2        synchronized (myVector) {
3            for (int i = 0; i < myVector.length(); i++) {
4                doSomethingWith(myVector.get(i));
5            }
6        }
7    }
```

This keeps any other method that calls from modifying the myVector object for the duration of lines 3, 4, 5, and 6. This holds even if your thread slices out during those lines.

As with all exclusivity, this only applies to methods that follow synchronization rules. If those methods do not internally synchronize on the myVector object, then they won't obey the protocol. Thus, the guarantee of thread safety would no longer hold.

Incidentally, this is a great justification for controlling access to your class's member variables through encapsulation. If all member variables are private, then you can control access to sensitive data by synchronizing all the relevant methods. This is exactly what the Vector object does. Synchronized objects such as Vectors do not synchronize on their internal data state; they synchronize the methods used to access that data. Sun recommends and encourages encapsulation. For example, it is explicitly evident in JavaBeans.

Multithreading with Swing

Swing components, by and large, are not thread-safe. Swing uses a single thread to deal with UI events from the underlying operating system. That is, in general Swing components don't *need* to be thread-safe as they're typically accessed from only one thread. This means that processing an event, such as a button click, will cause other events to be ignored until the first event is finished. Your UI could be very unresponsive if the event handler associated with the event is long.

The point here is that your Swing client could become slow if you are doing a big operation for a given event. This may be okay on the SCJD exam, but you need to be aware of it and document it. If your requirements state that UI responsiveness is very important, then you need to think about spawning threads to deal with more intensive operations, and that's when you have to worry about all the thread safety concerns, synchronizing as appropriate.

General Principles of Threading with Swing

Once a Swing component has called setVisible(true) or pack(), all updates should be done via the event dispatcher thread. This helps avoid race conditions that can occur as a result of the various requests from the RepaintManager.

In general, you only need to be concerned about threading in your Swing application when you are updating your components based on a thread other than the event dispatcher thread—specifically, in cases where you need a responsive GUI that cannot wait for RMI and/or socket calls across the network.

You should make sure that you can't afford to wait for these before you start down this path: It's a long and error-prone approach, and it will probably complicate your life unduly as far as the SCJD exam is concerned. If you do decide to take this route, execute your lengthier calls through a separate thread, or worker thread, and then feed your results back into the GUI using the event dispatcher. For an excellent example of this technique, please visit `http://java.sun.com/products/jfc/tsc/articles/threads/threads2.html`.

Caution You must not use the `SwingWorker` class directly in your assignment. The assignment specifies that you are only allowed to submit code you write yourself, so submitting the `SwingWorker` class could lead to disqualification. You can, however, use the `SwingWorker` class to learn the techniques needed, then make your own class(es).

Remember that calling the various setters on a component is not a thread-safe way to get that event into the event-dispatching queue. This process does generate events, but the event dispatcher thread does not always handle these.

Updating Components in the Event Dispatcher Thread

So how do you get your events into the event dispatcher thread? You use the `SwingUtilities.invokeAndWait` and `SwingUtilities.invokeLater` methods. The first method, `invokeAndWait`, blocks until the event fires. `invokeLater` does not block; it simply adds your code to the queue of events to be fired. The parameter to both of these methods is a `Runnable` interface. The `run` method of the parameter is then called by the event dispatcher.

Threading Best Practices

Here are some general practices that should help you avoid the dark side of threading:

- Don't nest locks. If you have two synchronized blocks on two different objects in your execution path, you're probably heading down the wrong road.

- Avoid multithreading with Swing, if possible. It can be argued that multithreading activities for distributed calls from a Swing front-end, for example, only offer illusionary responsiveness. That is, just because the GUI appears to respond quickly doesn't mean that it actually does so. Do you really want your client to think an operation is finished when in fact it isn't? Does the illusion actually serve a useful purpose in your application?

- For threads that are providing lengthy services, it's a good idea to yield occasionally. For example, if your thread is starting a lengthy process but the user wants to cancel, that canceling event might not get read until your thread stops executing. By yielding occasionally, you give other threads a chance to slice in at a time that is opportune for your thread's execution state. It's best to release any locks before yielding.

- There's no need to synchronize methods that don't use state information in the class. If your method doesn't use internal member variables, doesn't modify an external object, and doesn't modify an object that was passed in as a parameter, don't synchronize it.

- Don't oversynchronize. Make sure you know exactly why your method or data structure is synchronized. If you can't articulate the need for synchronization to your own satisfaction, you probably should reexamine the original need.

- Immutable objects, such as `Strings` and `Integers`, never need synchronization. This applies even to member variables, because immutable objects can't be modified. However, a member variable referring to an immutable object may still need synchronization if the member variable itself is mutable.

- Don't multithread needlessly. Unless your threads are doing a lot of blocking, single threading is often faster.

- When working with Swing, feel free to create and insert components into any container that hasn't been realized yet. To be realized, a component must be able to receive paint or validation events—this means before `show`, `setVisible(true)`, or `pack` has been called on the component.

- Don't get confused by internally synchronized classes such as `Vector`. All an internally synchronized class promises is to perform its actions atomically. This means that if one thread code executes `myVector.add("test")`, and another thread slices in, if that new thread executes `myVector.contains("test")` it will return true. This behavior is not guaranteed with, say, an `ArrayList`. You will usually need to use synchronized methods to interact with these variables.

- Try to minimize actions performed within your synchronized blocks, since no other thread will be able to obtain the lock your code is synchronized on for the duration, thus reducing concurrency.

- Avoid depending on thread priority as a mechanism of thread control. Different operating systems use distinct algorithms to deal with thread priority, and different JVMs use different algorithms still. This could lead to your program acting wildly different from one platform to the next. You best bet is to avoid the ambiguity of thread priorities, especially where the SCJD exam is concerned.

- Don't synchronize your thread's `run` method. Synchronizing your thread's run method can lead to a lot of complications, and it's a bad idea.

- If you are checking a condition in a synchronized block of code, use a while loop and not an if statement. If your thread slices out in the middle of executing your if statement, then the thread will resume exactly where it left off when it slices back in. Counterintuitively, this is not a good thing, because the condition that was true when your thread sliced out might no longer be true, because another thread could have changed it.

- While loops, on the other hand, are re-checked before your thread exits the block. Thus, relevant state changes will be detected. The following snippet shows an example of this technique:

```
synchronized (lockedRecords) {
    while (lockedRecords.contains(upc)) {
        lockedRecords.wait();
    }
    //do stuff
    lockedRecords.notifyAll();
}
```

- Use notifyAll instead of notify. notify only wakes a single waiting thread, while notifyAll wakes all waiting threads.

Summary

In this chapter, we discussed some of the possibilities available to you when using threads, and we pointed out some trouble spots to avoid. We discussed safe threading issues, threads and Swing, blocking, waiting, and a host of other topics.

The best way to understand threading is to design your threading scheme, make predictions about how it will function, and then test those predictions with the handy method in the Thread class, holdsLock(Object). Thread's getState() and getStackTrace() methods can be very handy for checking what another thread is doing. If your threads aren't behaving the way you expected them to, explicitly record your assumptions (we suggest writing them down) and then examine them one by one. Threading is a lot like grammar: There are a lot of rules, but eventually you develop a sense for what works and what doesn't. (Or so I'm told.)

As you read the next chapters, please don't hesitate to refer back to this chapter when needed.

FAQs

Q What happens when a synchronized block/method calls an unsynchronized one?

A The unsynchronized block/method is treated as if it was synchronized.

Q What happens when a synchronized block/method calls a synchronized one within the same object?

A If both methods are synchronizing on the same object, then nothing unusual happens as far as you're concerned—there's no double synchronization or risk of deadlock. The thread acquires an extra lock on the object, which in turn dissipates when the lock is released.

Q Does locking an object lock all of its internal variables?

A No, absolutely not. Doing so would place a tremendous burden on the JVM, because it would lock all their internal objects, and then the internal object of member variables in turn, and so on. Java assumes that you understand this, and that you are only locking what you mean to lock.

Q How much slower is a synchronized method than an unsynchronized one?

A It's difficult to say, but unscientific tests seem to indicate that a synchronized method is anywhere from 1.5 to 150 times slower than an unsynchronized method, depending on contention. Noncontended synchronization may have negligible impact on time.

Q Can you synchronize data?

A No, you can only synchronize access to data.

Q Aren't vectors synchronized data?

A No, vectors provide synchronized methods that access their data. It's an important difference.

Q What's the difference between synchronizing on a static member variable and a local one?

A There's no difference, really. You're still obtaining a lock on an object. But by synchronizing on a static member variable, the lock can be shared across multiple objects who share that static object as a class member variable.

Q What does it mean when people say that an object, such as a Vector, is synchronized?

A It means that all public methods of that object are synchronized when they access shared data. Generally, it means that calling a method on that object is an atomic action. Any other thread calling a method on that object will block until your thread completes its operation on that object.

Q What happens when one method synchronizes on a member variable, and another synchronizes on the this keyword, and the two have to interact?

A Then you are acquiring two locks on two distinct objects—namely this and the member variable—and it is very important to be careful. Otherwise, you are opening the door to deadlock. You should consider carefully whether you really need to do this, or whether you can synchronize on the one object.

Q How can I restart a thread after it has died?

A You can't. You will have to create a new thread.

Q Most of the examples provided show the main application implicitly waiting until all the created threads had finished before exiting. Is there a way of exiting the program without waiting for a thread to complete?

A Yes—you can explicitly call System.exit, or you can call Thread.setDaemon(true) on the thread you don't want to wait for *before* you start it running. See the creation of the IceCreamMan thread for an example of how to set a daemon thread.

CHAPTER 5

■■■

The DvdDatabase Class

In this chapter, we will start working on our assignment by developing a DvdDatabase class, which will implement the DBClient interface described in Chapter 3. Since both the client and the server need this class, starting the assignment with this class is quite logical.

As you work through this chapter, you will use several important concepts introduced in Chapters 2 and 3:

- Design patterns

- Generics

As mentioned earlier in this book, there are several areas in our sample project where we feel we *must* deviate from the project provided by Sun. Nowhere is this more important than with the classes presented in this chapter. Either the code used in this section of our sample assignment will quite often be more detailed than your assignment requirements, or we will use shortcuts that you cannot use in your assignment. In particular, we specify that java.io.IOException can be thrown in our interfaces and classes, greatly simplifying our development; we complicate our assignment by having timeouts on locks; and we use ReadWriteLocks to improve concurrency. Regardless, all the information you need to develop a good solution for *your* requirements is presented in this chapter.

We also discuss issues that you might want to consider for your assignment that are not required but that may make your submission more professional. This includes the topics of caching data, handling deadlocks, managing client crashes, and using multiple notification objects to reduce CPU usage by threads trying to obtain a logical record lock.

Creating the Classes Required for the DvdDatabase Class

The DvdDatabase class uses a few other classes as inputs, outputs, or exceptions. We need to build these before we can build the Data class itself.

The DVD Class: A Value Object

The DvdDatabase class uses a class named DVD to contain the data corresponding to a DVD that can be reserved. This type of object is referred to as a value object. The Value Object design pattern is also referred to as the Transfer Object pattern. The name *value object* represents the type of object it is; it contains all the values relating to a particular object (in our case, all the values we wish to track relating to a DVD). *Transfer object* is named for one of the more common uses of this design pattern: creating a single class to transfer data between two separate systems, usually between a client and a server.

The reason for such an object is fairly simple—it can make your code easier to read, and improve performance of your system as a whole. Your code will be referencing fields within a single object, which will make it clearer within your code that the fields are all related. And since you can send and retrieve the entire value object in one call to another method, your code will perform much better than if it had to retrieve each of the fields separately. This is especially useful when retrieving value objects over a network, as only a single network call is required, in contrast to the multiple network calls required if you were retrieving each field separately.

Sections of the DVD class are detailed next; however, since much of the code is repetitive, we won't display all the code here but only important sections of it. The entire code for this method can be downloaded from the Apress web site in the Source Code section; more details on what can be downloaded and how the code can be compiled and packaged are listed in Chapter 9. The line numbers shown here correspond to the real line numbers in the online source code—therefore, you'll note gaps in the numerical sequence because we skip comments and repetitive code.

```
1   package sampleproject.db;
2
3   import java.io.*;
4   import java.util.*;
5   import java.util.logging.*;
6
..
13  public class DVD implements Serializable {
..
19      private static final long serialVersionUID = 5165L;
```

We will be using this class to transfer the data that represents a DVD between the client and the server, potentially on different computers. Doing this, however, relies on the client and server both agreeing on what a DVD object is. If either system believes that the internal data structure is different (for instance, if the server believes that the issue date is a Java Date object, while the client believes that it is a String object), then the whole system of transferring data is called into question. If you are lucky, you will receive some form of class cast exception, or a similar problem. If you are unlucky, your client and server will be able to work with the data, even though it is potentially wrong, and your data will be corrupted.

Java provides a mechanism for classes that use a serialized object to confirm that the serialized object conforms to a known structure: the serialVersionUID. This is done for us by the JVM itself; if a class tries to deserialize an instance of a class where the serialVersionUID does not match the known value, an InvalidClassException will be thrown.

■**Note** Serialization is covered in detail in the first few sections of Chapter 6.

You can declare a `static final long serialVersionUID` in your code, as shown in line 19. Note that the `static final` and `long` modifiers are mandatory. Any access modifier may be used, including the `private` modifier we used in this code. This enables you to decide whether a change to your `Serializable` class requires recompilation of your client classes. For example, if we added an extra field to our DVD class to contain the number of Emmy nominations the DVD received, it would not affect those clients that were compiled prior to the addition of the field; they would still be able to access every field that they were previously able to access. The same would **not** be true if you deleted a field, even if it was one your clients were currently not using—*potentially* they would be unable to access the field, so the change to the class would require clients to recompile.

If you do not declare a `serialVersionUID` in your `Serializable` class, the Java compiler will generate one for you, based on various aspects of the class, such as the name of the class, the names of the methods, the names of the fields, and so on. If any of these change, then your `serialVersionUID` will change as well. So even for our example of adding an unimportant field earlier, an autogenerated `serialVersionUID` will change. For this reason, it is always recommended that you define your own `serialVersionUID`. (For those who are curious, the `serialVersionUID` we used is just the last four digits of the ISBN number for this book.)

■**Tip** To learn more about object serialization, refer to the Sun documentation available at `http://java.sun.com/j2se/1.5.0/docs/guide/serialization/`.

Our DVD class then specifies all the fields we want to associate with a DVD. Again, comments have been excluded, so the line numbers are not in numerical sequence:

```
89     private String upc = "" ; // The record UPC identifier
94     private String name = ""; // The movie title
100    private String composer = ""; // The music composer
106    private String director = ""; // The director's name
112    private String leadActor = ""; // The lead actor's name
118    private String supportingActor = ""; // The supporting actor's name
123    private String year = ""; // The movie's release date
129    private int copy = 1; // The number of DVDs in stock
```

■**Note** A UPC (Universal Product Code) number is a unique number assigned to retail items in U.S. and Canadian stores. The equivalent code in Japan is the JAN code, and the next standard will be the European EAN code, which has been designed to increase the number of potential codes to cater for the entire world. For the purposes of this book we have stuck with the original UPC code, which we use to ensure that each record in our data file has a unique index.

We then have three constructors: a default constructor (required for any serialized object), a constructor that assumes we have only one copy of the DVD in stock, and a constructor that allows us to specify how many copies of the DVD we have.

```
140     public DVD() {
141         log.finer("No argument constructor for DVD called");
142     }
...
157     public DVD(String upc, String name, String composer,
158                 String director, String lead, String supportActor,
159                 String year) {
160         this(upc, name, composer, director, lead, supportActor , year, 1);
161     }
162
163     /**
164      * Creates an instance of this object with a specified list of initial
165      * values.
166      *
167      * @param upc The UPC value of the DVD.
168      * @param name The title of the DVD.
169      * @param composer The name of the movie's composer.
170      * @param director The name of the movie's director.
171      * @param leadActor The name of the movie's leading actor.
172      * @param supportingActor The name of the movie's supporting actor.
173      * @param year The date the of the movie's release (yyyy-mm-dd).
174      * @param copies The number of copies in stock.
175      */
176     public DVD(String upc, String name, String composer, String director,
177                 String leadActor, String supportingActor, String year,
178                 int copies) {
179         log.entering ("DVD", "DVD",
180                     new Object[]{upc, name, composer, director, leadActor,
181                                 supportingActor, year, copies});
182         this.upc = upc;
183         this.name = name;
184         this.composer = composer;
185         this.director = director;
186         this.leadActor = leadActor;
187         this.supportingActor = supportingActor;
188         this.year = year;
189         this.copy = copies;
190         log.exiting ("DVD", "DVD");
191     }
```

The comments were left in the final constructor, to show how parameters are declared in Javadoc comments. As you can see, there is no requirement to specify the type of each parameter.

It might also be noted that there are no calls to the logger in the second instantiator. Since this instantiator immediately calls the third instantiator, we are relying on the logging available there.

For each variable listed in lines 89–129, we have a getter and a setter. For example, the composer variable specified in line 100 has a getComposer getter and a setComposer setter as follows:

```
199     public String getComposer() {
200         log.entering("DVD", "getComposer");
201         log.exiting("DVD", "getComposer", this.composer);
202         return this.composer;
203     }
...
211     public void setComposer(String composer) {
212         log.entering("DVD", "setComposer", composer);
213         this.composer = composer;
214         log.exiting("DVD", "setComposer", this.composer);
215     }
```

Using getters and setters (so named because the first verb of the method is either get or set) enables us to expose only the sections of the method we want to expose, and allow only certain operations on them. For example, we might decide that the number of copies of a DVD can never go below zero; if we allow clients to directly modify the field, then they can set it to any number they like, including negative numbers. But by having a setter for numbers of DVDs, we can include our business logic to ensure that the client cannot set a negative number.

Note In line 200 we call log.entering and then call log.exiting immediately afterwards in line 201. As always, there was a design decision to be made here: Do we create our own log message (probably calling log.finer), or do we use the two calls that really don't provide much useful information? Once again, there is no one "right" way to handle this. The disadvantage of our chosen method is that we are providing unnecessary logging, which does not produce much useful information. However, on the positive side we are still using the same standard logging format for **all** "entering" and "exiting" log messages—contrast this with the probability that if we were to write our own specialized log method for these getters and setters, it is likely that the log messages would vary from method to method. In addition, if we ever needed to do more work in this method, the work can be put directly between the two log messages; if we had created our own specialized log message, we would probably have to remove it and replace it with the standard log messages.

The logging provided for the getters and setters is possibly overkill; however, it does highlight one valuable debugging tool: It can be very useful to see what parameters are passed into a method, and what the end result of executing the method is. By logging the composer method parameter at line 212, we will have a record of what was passed into the method, and by logging the this.composer instance variable at line 214, we will have a record of what the end result of executing the setComposer method was. If at a later date this method is updated (for example, adding code to ensure the first letter of each part of the composer's name is capitalized), we will still get logging showing what the input and results are.

The remaining getters and setters have not been shown; however, they all follow the same form as the getComposer and setComposer methods shown earlier.

■**Tip** Most IDEs have the ability to automatically generate getters and setters for you, including generating rudimentary Javadoc comments. After using such facilities, you can go to each generated method, add any required business logic, and modify the Javadoc comments to suit.

One last point worth considering is whether we would ever want to compare two instances of a DVD to see if they are the same. In a stand-alone application, we might consider allowing only a single instance of each DVD object to be created, in which case we would be able to check that they were equal by using the == comparison. However, since we might be getting multiple copies of the same DVD record over a network, each copy will be deserialized into a separate instantiation of the DVD class, so we cannot use the == comparator. We should therefore look at overriding the equals method of the Object class.

```
416    public boolean equals(Object aDvd) {
417        if (! (aDvd instanceof DVD)) {
418            return false;
419        }
420
421        DVD otherDvd = (DVD) aDvd;
422
423        return (upc == null) ? (otherDvd.getUPC() == null)
424                             : upc.equals(otherDvd.getUPC());
425    }
```

At line 417, we ensure that we have been given an instance of DVD to compare against. Once we have confirmed this—and only when we have confirmed this—we can convert the supplied object into an object of type DVD, as shown in line 421. Finally, in lines 423 and 424 we utilize the fact that UPC numbers are unique for DVDs, and compare the UPC numbers.

■**Note** Lines 423 and 424 use a ternary operator to determine whether to return true or false. Everyone has their own opinion as to whether ternary operators increase or decrease readability. This is something you will have to decide for yourself, possibly on a case-by-case basis. In this particular case, we believe it improves readability, compared with the alternative:

```
if (upc == null) {
    return otherDVD.getUPC() == null;
} else {
    return upc.equals(otherDVD.getUPC());
}
```

In that last `return` statement, we can safely use the `String.equals` method to compare the contents of the two UPC fields. We could not use it earlier, as we did not know if the local UPC field contained `null` (in which case the last `return` statement would have generated a `NullPointerException`); likewise, we did not know if the other UPC value contained `null`, so we could not reverse the logic (`otherDVD.getUPC().equals(upc)`) as it may also have thrown a `NullPointerException`. It is only after we have validated that *at least* one of the two UPC values is not `null` that we can use the `equals` method.

If the UPC did not uniquely identify the DVD, we might consider having more complex logic; for example, we might compare the UPC, the title, and the main actor (it is unlikely that an actor would work in a film with the same title as one they had previously worked in, and that had the same UPC). However, we would probably not check the number of DVDs available, as they are not unique to the DVD.

It is **strongly** recommended that whenever you override the `equals` method, you should also override the `hashCode` method, as the two are often used together. Once again, we have used the fact that the UPC number uniquely identifies the DVD, and simply reused the UPC's hash code as the DVD's hash code:

```
462      public int hashCode() {
463          return upc.hashCode();
464      }
465  }
```

It is important to try to return different hash codes for instances of a class that are not considered equal where possible, while at the same time the same hash code value must be returned for instances of a class that are considered equal no matter how many times it is run on a single JVM (unless some of its internal field data is changed in such a way that it is no longer considered equal to the old instance). If we had added extra checking to our `equals` method (such as checking the actor's name), then we might want to consider modifying our hash code generator to take into account the extra uniqueness checking. For example, we might choose to add the hash codes for both the UPC and the actor's name, and return the sum as the new hash code.

Tip A unique hash code per unique instance of a class may not be possible. Furthermore, even if you spent considerable time developing an algorithm to generate a hash code that is highly likely to be unique, there would almost certainly be a loss of efficiency caused by the extra time required to execute the algorithm. If you need to generate your own `hashCode` methods, we recommend that you don't spend too much time in this method **unless** code profiling shows that a significant amount of time is being spent in methods that rely on the hash code (such as the `HashMap.get` method).

Discussion Point: Handling Exceptions Not Listed in the Supplied Interface

You may find that in order to create your Data class, you must call some methods that throw exceptions that are not listed in the interface supplied by Sun. You will then have to decide what to do with those exceptions, one by one. There is no single perfect solution for how to handle this (although there *are* some bad solutions).

You will have to decide for yourself which approach is right for you. Look at the instructions *you* downloaded from Sun (remember, each set of instructions can be different in small ways), and then decide how best to meet *your* requirements. Whatever you decide, be sure to document your decision in your design decisions document, as well as in the source code itself.

To help illustrate the various possibilities, let's use the following base code:

```
1   import java.util.logging.*;
2
3   public class InterruptedExceptionExample extends Thread {
4       static Logger log = Logger.getAnonymousLogger();
5
6       public static void main(String[] args) throws InterruptedException {
7           InterruptedExceptionExample iee = new InterruptedExceptionExample();
8           iee.start();
9
10          while (iee.isAlive()) {
11              log.info("main: waiting 5 seconds for other thread to finish");
12              iee.join(5000);
13
14              if (iee.isAlive()) {
15                  log.info("main: interrupting other thread.");
16                  iee.interrupt();
17              }
18          }
19          log.info("main: finished");
20      }
21
22      public void run() {
23          try {
24              getLock();
25          } catch (LockAttemptFailedException dle) {
26              log.log(Level.WARNING, "Lock attempt failed", dle);
27          }
28      }
29
30      public void getLock() throws LockAttemptFailedException {
31          // try to get some resource that we will presumably never get.
32          for (;;) {
33              try {
```

```
34                 synchronized (InterruptedExceptionExample.class) {
35                     log.info(getName() + ": waiting for some resource.");
36                     InterruptedExceptionExample.class.wait();
37                 }
38             } catch (InterruptedException ie) {
39                 // this is the bit we are interested in
40             }
41         }
42     }
43
44     public class LockAttemptFailedException extends Exception {
45         public LockAttemptFailedException(String msg, Throwable t) {
46             super(msg, t);
47         }
48     }
49 }
```

■**Note** When we call `join` in line 12 there is the risk that an `InterruptedException` may be thrown. Handling this exception is not relevant to our discussion point, so we have decided to allow the `main` method to throw the exception as specified in line 6.

As noted in the comment at line 31, the `getLock` method needs something to happen before it will complete—but for the purposes of this example we have not declared what that will be. If this were a section of code from a real-life application it might be waiting for a lock to be released, or it might be waiting for a resource to become free. All we care about for this example is that, regardless of what we were waiting for, it won't ever happen.

The important point of this example code is that we are calling the `wait` method in line 36, and the `wait` method can throw an `InterruptedException`; however, the signature for the `getLock` method states that only the `LockAttemptFailedException` (which does not extend `InterruptedException`) will be thrown. So we must do something with the `InterruptedException` that we are catching at line 38.

■**Tip** As shown in lines 34 and 36, every class can itself be used as the object to be synchronized on. You do not even need an instance of the class—you can just use the `class` literal. In most cases, you will find that there are specific objects you wish to synchronize on; however, if there are no apparent objects, do not automatically assume that you are going to have to create an object just so you can use it as a mutual exclusion lock (a lock that mutually excludes access to all other threads as long as one thread owns the lock; also known as a mutex). Conversely, don't use this feature where it doesn't apply—if you want to make explicit what a particular mutex is being used for, it might be worthwhile creating an `Object` with a suitably descriptive name just to make the code clear. Making these sorts of decisions is all a part of being a developer.

Swallowing the Exception

In the code shown in the previous section, lines 38 through 40 do absolutely nothing with the exception. This is commonly referred to as "swallowing the exception." Once those lines have completed, it is as though your code has swallowed the exception whole: there is no trace of it left for anyone to see.

While the Java language will allow you to get away with doing this, it is considered extremely poor programming, and will almost certainly cost you some marks in your assignment (and cause heated discussions between yourself and whoever has to maintain your code at work). An exception is, as its name states, something that should not have happened. But by swallowing the exception, we have not allowed for any handling of this event, nor have we provided any form of tracking down what went wrong later.

If we were to run this program now, we would find that the main method could never complete. This is shown in Figure 5-1.

Figure 5-1. *Swallowing the exception*

Logging the Exception

We might decide that for business reasons the exception should be ignored. For example, a business rule might state that for audit reasons transactions cannot be canceled—they must be processed fully, then a new transaction created to undo the first transaction (this is a common business requirement). In such a case, we might decide to ignore the fact that the client is trying to interrupt us, and just continue trying to gain the lock.

In such a case, though, we do not want to just swallow the exception—that would leave us with no evidence that the client is trying to interrupt the thread. So what we should do is some form of logging. Here are some examples:

```
38                } catch (InterruptedException ie) {
39                    log.info("Ignoring InterruptedException in transaction");
40                }
```

The output from this change is shown in Figure 5-2.

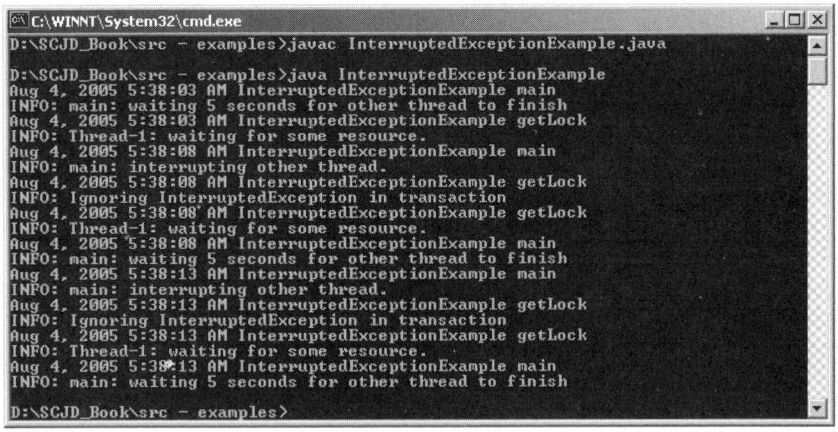

Figure 5-2. *Extremely simplistic logging*

However, this does not tell us much about what has happened but only that we have decided to ignore the exception. In this particular case, it is fairly easy to see which line caught that particular exception, and what it did with it. But what if we were running on a server, and the getLock method could have been called from any one of a number of different methods? In such a case, a stack trace might be useful to see why our getLock method was called. So we could use more sophisticated logging, as shown in the following code and in Figure 5-3:

```
38                } catch (InterruptedException ie) {
39a                   log.log(Level.WARNING,
39b                         "Ignoring InterruptedException in transaction",
39c                         ie);
40                }
```

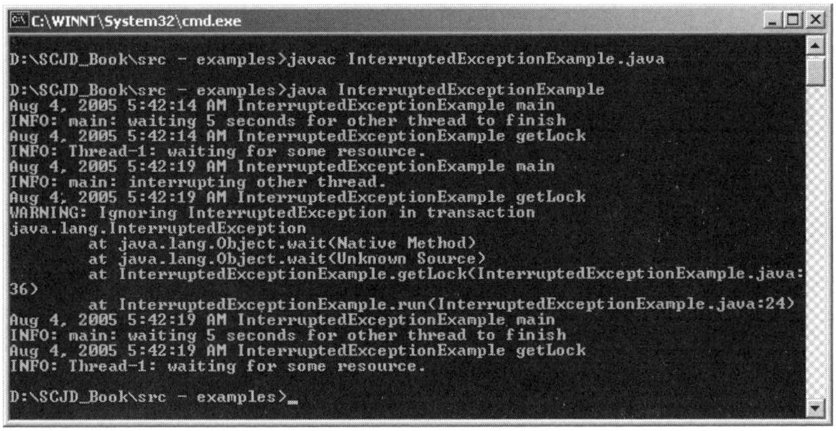

Figure 5-3. *More detailed logging*

If you decided that your method will ignore interruptions, then it would be wise to mention this in your Javadoc comments so that users are aware of this—and don't phone you in the middle of the night asking why they can't interrupt a thread they created.

Wrapping the Exception Within an Allowed Exception

In most cases exceptions cannot be as easily ignored as in the last example. If an IOException occurs while writing to file, you cannot just ignore it or you will end up with corrupted data. We created a fictitious business rule that allowed us to ignore the InterruptedException in the last example, but if that business rule did not exist, then clients may have a right to expect that they can interrupt their own threads.

One way to handle this is to wrap the caught exception within the exception we are allowed to throw, as shown in the next bit of code. The output from running this is shown in Figure 5-4.

```
38              } catch (InterruptedException ie) {
39a                 throw new LockAttemptFailedException(
39b                     "InterruptedException in getLock",
39c                     ie);
40              }
```

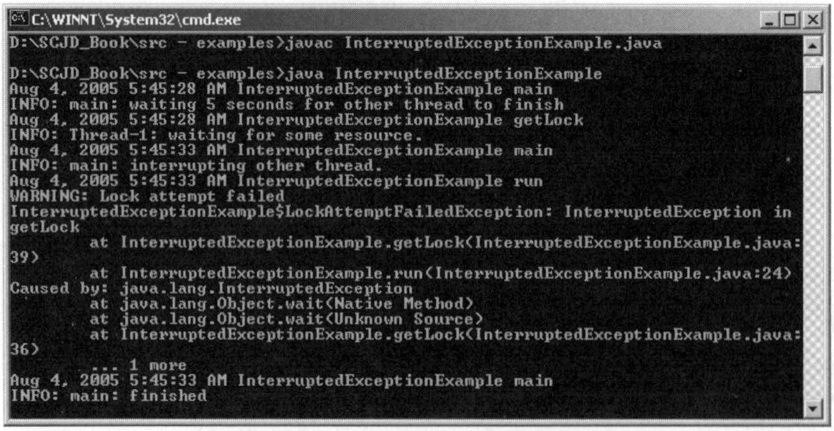

Figure 5-4. *Wrapping the exception within an allowed exception*

As can be seen in Figure 5-4, we received a warning message, telling us that we had a LockAttemptFailedException with the expected stack trace. This log message came from our LockAttemptFailedException handler at line 26. More importantly, though, the log also contains lines starting with Caused by:. If you look at these lines, you will see that they are the same lines that were output in Figure 5-3. By wrapping the InterruptedException inside the LockAttemptFailedException, we ensured that we still have the complete stack trace from the InterruptedException.

■**Caution** You need to consider carefully whether it will make sense to wrap an exception in this way. If the only exception you are allowed to throw is a RecordNotFoundException, you might consider that it is reasonable to wrap an EOFException within your RecordNotFoundException—if you got to the end of the file without finding the record, then it *might* be a reasonable assumption. However, it might also be an invalid assumption—if you received an EOFException halfway through reading a record, then your file may be corrupted, and implying that the record cannot be found might be misleading at best, or cause further problems and corruption. Similarly, it would probably not make sense to wrap an InterruptedException within a RecordNotFoundException—if you were waiting on a lock for the record, then presumably the record does exist.

Wrapping the Exception Within a RuntimeException

There are cases where wrapping the caught exception within a declared exception does not make sense, as discussed in the previous note. However, we may not be able to add a new checked exception to the method signature since this may stop other programs from working. This is especially true when writing a class that implements an interface—another programmer could write their program to use your class based on the published interface, and have their program fail in unexpected ways if you change the interface—or they may find that recompiling their code no longer works. Either way, you are probably going to become unpopular very quickly.

RuntimeException, and subclasses of RuntimeException, do not need to be declared in method signatures, nor do they need to be caught. So it is possible to wrap the caught exception within a RuntimeException as shown in the following code:

```
38              } catch (InterruptedException ie) {
39a                 throw new RuntimeException (
39b                     "InterruptedException in getLock",
39c                     ie);
40              }
```

Unfortunately, if you do this it becomes difficult for the user of your class to catch the exception and handle it properly. Consider the following code, which demonstrates a poor way to handle it:

```
22      public void run() {
23          try {
24              getLock();
25a         } catch (RuntimeException re) {
25b             log.log(Level.WARNING, "Caught the interrupt", re);
25c         } catch (LockAttemptFailedExceptiondle) {
26             log.log(Level.WARNING, "Lock attempt failed", dle);
27          }
28      }
```

If we try and catch RuntimeException, we risk catching a whole lot of subclasses of RuntimeException that we really probably don't want to handle in this exception block, where we're only trying to handle the "interrupted" exception. For example, let's assume that somewhere in the getLock method, something throws a NullPointerException. NullPointerException is a subclass of RuntimeException, so it will be caught in line 25a. However, we do not handle NullPointerException, so it will not be handled appropriately. To ensure that we only handle the one RuntimeException that we are really interested in, we have to look at the cause of the RuntimeException, and if it is not the RuntimeException we are interested in, we should rethrow the exception.

```
22      public void run() {
23          try {
24              getLock();
25a         } catch (RuntimeException re) {
25b             if (re.getCause() instanceof InterruptedException) {
25c                 log.log(Level.WARNING, "Caught the interrupt", re);
25d             } else {
25e                 throw re;
25f             }
25g         } catch (LockAttemptFailedException dle) {
26              log.log(Level.WARNING, "Lock attempt failed", dle);
27          }
28      }
```

If we make this change and run the program, we will see the now familiar output as shown in Figure 5-5.

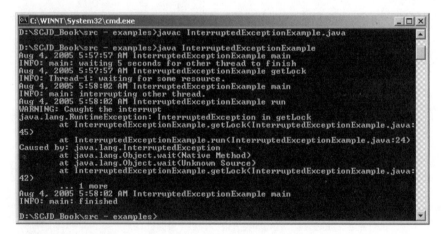

Figure 5-5. *Wrapping the exception within a RuntimeException*

Wrapping the Exception Within a Subclass of RuntimeException

We needed to add five lines of code to handle the RuntimeException, instead of the normal two lines we would have added for a checked exception, significantly adding to our code complexity.

However, as stated previously, subclasses of RuntimeException do not need to be declared or caught. So a better solution is to create a new exception that is a subclass of RuntimeException, similar to this:

```
public class UserInterruptionException extends RuntimeException {
    public UserInterruptionException(String msg, Throwable t) {
        super(msg, t);
    }
}
```

We can then use this in exactly the same way that we had used the RuntimeException in our previous example, namely

```
38                } catch (InterruptedException ie) {
39a                   throw new UserInterruptionException(
39b                       "InterruptedException in getLock",
39c                       ie);
40                }
```

However, our code for catching the exception returns to being nice and simple:

```
22      public void run() {
23          try {
24              getLock();
25a         } catch (UserInterruptionException uie) {
25b             log.log(Level.WARNING, "Caught the interrupt", uie);
25c         } catch (LockAttemptFailedException dle) {
26              log.log(Level.WARNING, "Lock attempt failed", dle);
27          }
28      }
```

Tip If you are creating a subclass of RuntimeException that you do not expect to be caught, then it is considered standard programming practice not to declare it in the method signature. However, if you are trying to work around a limitation of a provided interface, then you might want to declare it in your method signature and in your Javadoc documentation. Many common IDEs will show the exceptions a method will throw when it is entered, and some will even create standard catch blocks based on method signatures. In such cases, listing the subclass of RuntimeException will help your users.

If you do list the RuntimeException in the method signature and/or the Javadoc, it would be wise to add a code comment stating why you did this for the benefit of the person who is maintaining your code. In the specific case of the Sun assignment, you might also want to consider putting a comment in the Javadoc itself stating why you did it.

The big downside of using RuntimeExceptions and its subclasses is that they do not need to be caught. If a programmer left out the additions to lines 25a–c, the program will still run fine, but a RuntimeException will propagate up the stack to the top of the thread. This is shown in Figure 5-6.

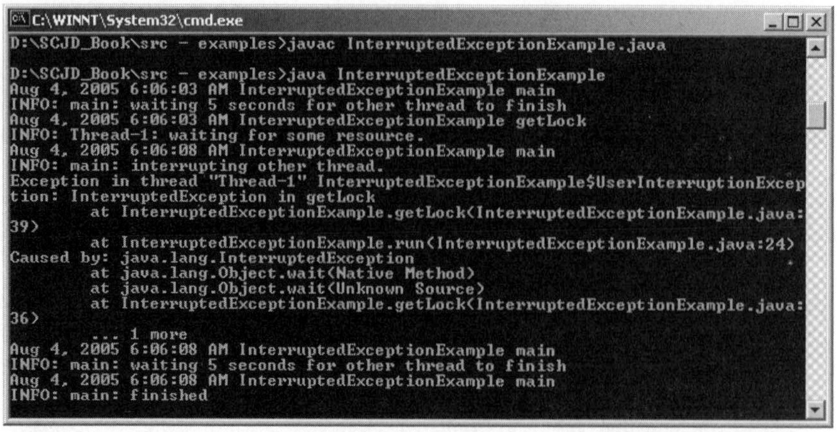

Figure 5-6. *RuntimeException propagating to the top of the thread stack*

■**Caution** It is important to realize that the `RuntimeException` propagates to the top of the stack *for the thread it is running in, not for the entire JVM.* As can be seen in Figure 5-6, even after the `RuntimeException` has been thrown, and Thread-1 has died, the main thread is still operational. This has important ramifications when developing your server code—if you throw a `RuntimeException` and don't catch it, it is possible that your server will still be running while being unable to process any requests.

The DvdDatabase Class: A Façade

Before building any class, it is worthwhile considering what it is that the class does. The same applies to methods—for each method, try to determine just what the method does. If you find yourself using the word "and" when describing a class or method, there is the *possibility* that the class or method is trying to be responsible for more than it should. You might then consider whether it makes sense to break a class or method into two or more classes or methods; it might make your code a bit more manageable and maintainable.

In the case of our `DvdDatabase` class, we have been told in our instructions that this is the public class that all other classes will use if they want to access the data file. However, when we look at what the `DvdDatabase` class provides, we find that there are two separate functions:

1. Physically accessing the data

2. Providing logical record locking

If we tried to describe what this class does in a short sentence, we would probably have to use the word "and": "This class provides physical access to the data **and** provides logical record locking."

We *could* provide both these functions in one class, but if we split them out, then the code will be more maintainable later. If you need to work on a method that physically accesses the database, you will be able to go to a class that only deals with accessing the database; you will not have to wade through all the logical locking code.

There is a design pattern that describes what we are trying to achieve here: the Façade pattern. The English meaning of the word "façade" is the front face of something, typically a building. So we might refer to the front of a shop or building as its façade: the view of the building that the average user gets to see. In the same way, we can think of the DvdDatabase as the front face, or façade, shown to external users, hiding the classes that external users may not need to know about.

■**Note** Although using a façade does not stop us from using the word "and" in our description of what the class does, it does change the class itself so that the faced class is not providing all the functionality; it is handing off to the other classes behind the scene.

Our DvdDatabase class is therefore very simple. We start by creating references to the classes that do the real work:

```
package sampleproject.db;

import java.io.FileNotFoundException;
import java.io.IOException;
import java.util.Collection;
import java.util.List;
import java.util.regex.PatternSyntaxException;

public class DvdDatabase implements DBClient {
    private static ReservationsManager reservationsManager
            = new ReservationsManager();

    private static DVDFileAccess database = null;

    public DvdDatabase() throws FileNotFoundException, IOException {
        this(System.getProperty("user.dir"));
    }

    public DvdDatabase(String dbPath) throws FileNotFoundException, IOException {
        database = new DvdFileAccess(dbPath);
    }
```

We now have to define our constructors for DvdDatabase. Since the instructions for our sample project do not specify how the DvdDatabase constructor should appear, we have some flexibility. This prompts two primary concerns:

1. What parameters should we use for the constructor?

2. What exceptions, if any, should be thrown from the constructors?

Regarding the parameters, we have to consider how this class will be used. We know that it might be used in a stand-alone application, and for that purpose it might be handy not to provide any parameters at all, and assume that the data file is in the current working directory. However, we also know that this class will be used in a server environment, and in such cases, it is common for the data file to reside in a different directory (and sometimes a different hard drive) than the application. In this case, we would need to be able to specify the directory where the data file can be found.

The first constructor is just a special case of the second constructor, and as such we might be tempted to leave it out. We should make a decision on whether it will be used often. If so, adding the constructor will make our users happy. If not, we can leave the constructor out, thereby simplifying our code, and in the rare cases where a user wants to use a database in the current working directory they can call the constructor that takes a directory as a parameter with the current working directory (System.getProperties("user.dir")) as the parameter.

We have decided to leave both constructors in the class, primarily to demonstrate the technique of having one constructor call the other constructor. This is a very common way of handling overloaded methods and constructors, as it ensures that the same business logic is executed no matter which version gets called.

Our constructors are going to open the data file, which means we could get a FileNotFoundException if the file is not in the specified directory, and we could get an IOException if there is a problem with opening the data file (for example, if we don't have adequate permissions). We're faced with the decision of handling them within our constructor, or passing them back to the calling class.

Another way of thinking about this issue is, what can we realistically do if we get either of those exceptions? About the only thing we can do within our DvdDatabase class is try the operation again, but if the file does not exist when we first look for it, is it likely to be there the second time we look for it? We cannot simply log these exceptions and ignore them; then the user will think that the DvdDatabase class was instantiated correctly and is ready for use when it isn't. So we have chosen to pass these exceptions back to the class that is constructing the DvdDatabase.

■**Tip** To keep this project simple, we have elected to rethrow the FileNotFoundException and IOException, but in doing this we have implicitly declared that we are dealing with a file-based data store. A future enhancement might be to convert this backing store to a SQL database, in which case these exceptions would no longer apply. A better solution might be to create our own DatabaseFailureException, and wrap FileNotFoundException and IOException in it where necessary. This way, if we later change to a SQL database, we could similarly wrap the SQL exceptions within the same DatabaseFailureException, and the client code should still continue to work. Doing this is left as an exercise for the reader.

For each method in our DBClient interface, we create a method that calls the appropriate method in our worker classes:

```java
    public boolean addDVD(DVD dvd) throws IOException {
        return database.addDVD(dvd);
    }

    public DVD getDVD(String upc) throws IOException {
        return database.getDVD(upc);
    }

    public boolean removeDVD(String upc) throws IOException {
        return database.removeDVD(upc);
    }

    public boolean modifyDVD(DVD dvd) throws IOException {
        return database.modifyDVD(dvd);
    }

    public List<DVD> getDVDs() throws IOException {
        return database.getDVDs();
    }

    public Collection<DVD> find(String query)
            throws IOException, PatternSyntaxException {
        return database.find(query);
    }

    public boolean reserveDVD(String upc) throws InterruptedException {
        return reservationsManager.reserveDVD(upc, this);
    }

    public void releaseDVD(String upc) {
        reservationsManager.releaseDVD(upc, this);
    }
}
```

Accessing the Data: The DvdFileAccess Class

We will present the DvdFileAccess class section by section, rather than trying to present all
the code at once. Once again, the code is available online at the Apress web site in the Source
Code section.

Since there is only one physical file on disk, it is tempting to consider making the
DvdFileAccess class a singleton—coding the class in such a way that only one instance
of DvdFileAccess can exist at any given time. However, a lot of work can be performed in

parallel if multiple clients are working on a multiple-CPU system, for example, converting between a DVD value object and the bytes on file, or searching through the data file. In addition, if we were to make the DvdFileAccess class a singleton, any class that uses the DvdFileAccess class would have to be coded differently than if it is a standard class—if we were to later decide that this same class can be used to process multiple data files (with some simple modifications), we would have to modify all the classes that use DvdFileAccess. Therefore, this class is not a singleton.

As mentioned earlier, DvdDatabase is the façade through which all other classes should access the data. Therefore, no other classes should call DvdFileAccess directly. To ensure this, default access is set on the class itself—only classes within the sampleproject.db package can access this class—as shown in line 31. As mentioned earlier, line numbers are not contiguous, as source code comments have been removed.

```
 1   package sampleproject.db;
 2
 3   import java.io.*;
 4   import java.util.*;
 5   import java.util.concurrent.locks.*;
 6   import java.util.logging.*;
 7   import java.util.regex.*;
..
31   class DvdFileAccess {
..
35       private static final String DATABASE_NAME = "dvd_db.dvd";
..
41       private Logger log = Logger.getLogger("sampleproject.db");
..
46       private static RandomAccessFile database = null;
..
51       private static Map<String, Long> recordNumbers
52               = new HashMap<String, Long>();
```

While most of the fields listed use the standard format from all previous versions of the JDK, the recordNumbers collection uses the new generics declarations so that the compiler can check that we are using the *generic* collection in a type-safe manner. This almost removes the risk of us getting a ClassCastException at runtime. We will discuss the use of this particular variable in the section following the class constructors.

```
58       private static ReadWriteLock recordNumbersLock
59               = new ReentrantReadWriteLock();
..
66       private static String emptyRecordString = null;
..
71       private static String dbPath = null;
..
77       static {
78           emptyRecordString = new String(new byte[DVD.RECORD_LENGTH]);
79       }
```

When writing a record to file, we could write each field separately, filling with spaces if required, or we could write the entire record in one operation.

Since a disk drive is constantly spinning when doing operations, writing field by field would be considerably slower than writing the entire record at once. This is because the disk would have continued spinning between each call to write the field, and there would be a small delay while the disk heads return to the correct location for writing (such an operation would be handled by the drive controller, but it would still slow down this operation). Although the delays caused by writing individual fields to a file would be small, they do exist, and they would be a bottleneck in a multiuser environment since only one user can ever be writing to the disk at any given time. We have, therefore, decided to write the entire record at once.

In the section describing the persistDvd method, we will show one method of building a record before writing it to disk. For speed and simplicity, we have decided to build a record by starting with a StringBuilder of known length, and replacing the bytes within it with the contents of the DVD fields. Since we want the StringBuilder to be a known length and contain all nulls before we start inserting our field data, we have created an emptyRecordString that can be used in the constructor of our StringBuilder to quickly create a known starting point. Since the emptyRecordString is a static field, it is constructed in the static initializer shown earlier.

```
90    public DvdFileAccess(String suppliedDbPath)
91            throws FileNotFoundException, IOException {
92        log.entering("DvdFileAccess", "getDvdFileAccess", suppliedDbPath);
93        if (dbPath == null) {
94            database = new RandomAccessFile(
95                    suppliedDbPath + File.separator + DATABASE_NAME, "rw");
96            getDvdList(true);
97            dbPath = suppliedDbPath;
98            log.fine("database opened and file location table populated");
99        } else if (dbPath != suppliedDbPath) {
100            log.warning("Only one database location can be specified. "
101                    + "Current location: " + dbPath + " "
102                    + "Ignoring specified path: " + suppliedDbPath);
103        }
104        log.exiting("DvdFileAccess", "DvdFileAccess");
105    }
```

Although the DvdFileAccess class is not a singleton, it does not make sense to rerun the constructor code each time the constructor is called. Setting the database field is one example of code we do not want run multiple times—the first time the constructor is called, the database field will be set to the RandomAccessFile for our data file, and after that there is no need or desire to reset it. As shown in line 93, we check whether the database path has already been configured, and if so, we do not perform initialization logic a second time. However, there is a risk that somebody may call this constructor multiple times with different paths; if they do this, a warning message will be logged stating that the newer path is being ignored.

We as developers must always be aware of how well our code performs. While it does not make sense to agonize over every line of code trying to make it perform better, we should attempt to spot common areas where code may perform badly.

■**Caution** If it has not already happened, then one day you may be asked to improve the performance of a class. While it can be useful to read through the code manually, looking for known problem areas, it is always recommended that you use a profiler—a program that will attach to your program while it is running, and tell you where your program is spending most of its time. When you know which methods take the most time to complete, you can look at improving their performance, rather than trying to fix random methods. The information provided here about improving the performance of our DvdDatabase class is designed to give us discussion points into several sections of the class and JDK 5. They are not necessarily the only (or even the best) places for us to concentrate on improving our programs.

Reading and writing from the disk is one of the slowest operations we have to deal with. We may also have multiple users all trying to access different records; with only one data file, they must queue up to access the file, effectively creating a bottleneck.

When reading or writing a record, we can speed up the operation if we can go straight to the location in the file where the record is stored. If our primary key was the record number, we would be able to calculate the file position on the fly based on the record number multiplied by the size of the record. However, our application is based on using the UPC string as the primary key, so we need a way to map UPCs to the location in the file. The only way to do this is to read the data file at least once, storing UPCs and file locations in the map as we go. We could create a method just to do this for us, but the interface we must implement already has a public method that we must implement that will read the entire file and return a List of the DVDs in that file, so we can piggyback that logic to populate our map.

However, there is a danger in doing this. Our constructor is relying on this method to populate a needed field. But it is possible for the getDVDs method to be overridden, which would result in our field not being populated. So we should either make this method final (which will stop any other class from overriding it), or call a private method that does the same function (private methods are similar to final methods, since they cannot be overridden, because no other class can even see them).

The getDVDs method is a business method. That is, we only created it because the business requirements stated that we must—we could easily write our client application without it. Likewise, although our implementation of it reads the entire database file from end to end, it would be possible to implement it differently, such that it does not access the file directly but rather calls other public methods (such as the getDVD method). Given this, it is possible that somebody might later decide to override our implementation, so it would not be appropriate for us to make this method final.

However, the getDVDs method is one of the methods that we must make public according to our provided interface.

Fortunately, we have a simple workaround for this dilemma: create a private method that does the work, and have the getDVDs method call it. That way, if somebody later overrides getDVDs, our private method will still exist in the background populating our required map.

This is still not quite a perfect solution, though. In using this method to populate our map, we will be creating the list for no purpose and discarding it immediately. Normally creating a collection and then destroying it without using it would be a bad thing, but in this case it is more than justified. It is only the constructor that wastes this List, and the alternative is to have a method that is almost identical but exists only to populate our map. Here is our method that reads all the records from file, and along the way populates our map of UPC numbers to file locations, along with the getDVDs method that calls it:

```
113    public List<DVD> getDvds() throws IOException {
114        return getDvdList(false);
115    }
```

Note The getDvds method in the DvdFileAccess class uses a different naming convention from the getDVDs method specified in the DBClient interface. We are able to do this because DvdFileAccess is the class behind the façade—it does not implement DBClient. We have made a design decision to use the Sun code conventions for the method names in our nonpublic classes, even though this means that they do not match perfectly with the method names in the public classes and interfaces. There is a trade-off here—a programmer working with the DvdFileAccess class may appreciate working with class and method names that conform to one convention, but changing the code convention between the public class and the nonpublic class could also be slightly confusing for a junior programmer.

```
130    private List<DVD> getDvdList(boolean buildRecordNumbers)
131            throws IOException {
132        log.entering("DvdFileAccess", "getDvdList", buildRecordNumbers);
133        List<DVD> returnValue = new ArrayList<DVD>();
134
135        if (buildRecordNumbers) {
136            recordNumbersLock.writeLock().lock();
137        }
138
139    try {
140        for (long locationInFile = 0;
141                locationInFile < database.length();
142                locationInFile += DVD.RECORD_LENGTH) {
143            DVD dvd = retrieveDvd(locationInFile);
144            log.fine("retrieving record at " + locationInFile);
145            if (dvd == null) {
146                log.fine("found deleted record ");
147            } else {
148                log.fine("found record " + dvd.getUPC());
149                if (buildRecordNumbers) {
150                    recordNumbers.put(dvd.getUPC(), locationInFile);
151                }
152                returnValue.add(dvd);
153            }
154        }
155    } finally {
156        if (buildRecordNumbers) {
157            recordNumbersLock.writeLock().unlock();
```

```
158                    }
159                }
160
161            log.exiting("DvdFileAccess", "getDvdList");
162            return returnValue;
163        }
```

As with the file itself, the map of UPC numbers to file locations is a single object used by many threads. However, in most cases, the threads will only be reading from the recordNumbers map—it will be much rarer for a method to update this map. Prior to JDK 5, we would have synchronized all access to the recordNumbers map, which would have meant that only one thread could ever access it at any given time. With JDK 5 we now have ReadWriteLocks that allow for greater concurrency. Instead of synchronizing code, we encapsulate the code inside calls to lock and unlock methods. Multiple threads can own a read lock on a single object at any given time, but only one thread can own a write lock at any given time.

If we are running this from the constructor, then we will be updating the recordNumbers map, so we will not want any other thread to be accessing the map in the meantime—a write lock will ensure this for us. This is set in line 136, and released in the finally block at line 157. It is important to ensure that the lock is released even if an exception is thrown; hence the call to unlock is in the finally block to ensure it is always run. This is recommended whenever you are using the new locking classes.

Line 150 adds our UPC string and the location in the file into the map. Using generics and autoboxing (introduced in Chapter 2) allows us to keep this code simple, while simultaneously ensuring that invalid data is not entered into our recordNumbers map. At the very start of the class we declared that the recordNumbers could only contain a String as the key and a Long as the value with the following code:

```
51        private static Map<String, Long> recordNumbers
52                = new HashMap<String, Long>();
```

The compiler will then use this to validate *at compile time* that we are storing Strings as the key and a Long as the value within this Map. Using autoboxing allows us to add a String and a *primitive* long to the Map, knowing that Java will automatically convert the *primitive* long to the wrapper Long class required for the Map.

Prior to JDK 5, there was no way for the compiler to validate that the type of data we were adding to a collection was the type of data we actually wanted to allow into the collection. You will now get an error message if you attempt to add the wrong type of data to our collection. If you would like to see an example of how this works, try changing line 150 as follows:

```
recordNumbers.put(dvd.getUPC(), (int) locationInFile);
```

The JDK 5 Java compiler will now produce an error message, because the type of data we are potentially adding to the Map no longer matches our declared allowable contents:

```
sampleproject\db\DvdFileAccess.java:150: put(java.lang.String,java.lang.Long)
in java.util.Map<java.lang.String,java.lang.Long> cannot be applied to
(java.lang.String,int)
                    recordNumbers.put(dvd.getUPC(), (int) locationInFile);
                                      ^
1 error
```

It is important to realize that this is a compile-time validation only—it is still possible to provide invalid data at runtime, resulting in a ClassCastException.

Line 143 calls a private method to read the DVD record based a location in a file. This method is also used by our public method that will read a DVD based on a UPC number. We will show the public getDVD method first:

```
172     public DVD getDvd(String upc) throws IOException {
173         log.entering("DvdFileAccess", "getDvd", upc);
174
175         recordNumbersLock.readLock().lock();
176         try {
177             // Determine where in the file this record should be.
178             // note: if this is null the record does not exist
179             Long locationInFile = recordNumbers.get(upc);
180             return (locationInFile != null) ? retrieveDvd(locationInFile)
181                                             : null;
182         } finally {
183             recordNumbersLock.readLock().unlock();
184             log.exiting("DvdFileAccess", "getDvd");
185         }
186     }
```

Line 175 requests a read lock on our mutex for the recordNumbers map. Remember that many threads can be operating simultaneously, so asking for a read lock allows the other threads to also gain read locks and work with the recordNumbers map.

If the UPC requested does not exist, null will be returned to the calling method, as shown in line 181. Otherwise, the retrieveDvd method will be called in line 180 and the results of that call will be returned to the calling method. If the retrieveDvd method throws an IOException or a RuntimeException, it is important to ensure that we do not leave the recordNumbersLock mutex locked, so we have put the call to unlock in the finally block at line 183. It is important to remember that the finally block is still executed, even though the return statement is at line 180.

```
196     private DVD retrieveDvd(long locationInFile) throws IOException {
197         log.entering("DvdFileAccess", "retrieveDvd", locationInFile);
198         final byte[] input = new byte[DVD.RECORD_LENGTH];
...
202         synchronized(database) {
203             database.seek(locationInFile);
204             database.readFully(input);
205         }
```

Multiple threads work with the recordNumbers map, but the majority of them will only be reading the map, and multiple reads can occur simultaneously without affecting the other threads. Therefore, access to the recordNumbers map is a perfect candidate for a ReadWriteLock.

However, in the case of reading from the data file, one thread could affect another thread if they were allowed to operate simultaneously. When reading from the data file, we need to perform two steps: move to the correct location in the file, then read the entire record. It is very important that these two operations behave as a single atomic operation; otherwise, if the position in the file was changed by another thread between lines 203 and 204 we would end up reading from the wrong location in the file. Using a ReadWriteLock would be counterproductive in this case, as all operations would need a WriteLock, and the extra overhead of confirming that there are no outstanding ReadLocks would result in poorer performance. A much better solution is to use a standard synchronized block, as shown in lines 202 through 205.

Since a synchronized block will block any other thread from accessing the data file, we want the block to be as small as possible to reduce the blocking time. Therefore, the synchronized block only lasts until the record is read fully. It is important to note that the read method does not guarantee that an entire record will be read but only that *at least* one byte will be read. It is therefore important to ensure that an entire record is read, which we achieved by calling readFully.

Having read an entire record into an array of bytes, we can extract the various strings for each field from that array.

```
211        class RecordFieldReader {
212            int offset = 0;
213            String read(int length) throws UnsupportedEncodingException {
214                String str = new String(input, offset, length, "UTF-8");
215                offset += length;
216                return str.trim();
217            }
218        }
219
220        RecordFieldReader readRecord = new RecordFieldReader();
221        String upc = readRecord.read(DVD.UPC_LENGTH);
222        String name = readRecord.read(DVD.NAME_LENGTH);
223        String composer = readRecord.read(DVD.COMPOSER_LENGTH);
224        String director = readRecord.read(DVD.DIRECTOR_LENGTH);
225        String leadActor = readRecord.read(DVD.LEAD_ACTOR_LENGTH);
226        String supportingActor = readRecord.read(DVD.SUPPORTING_ACTOR_LENGTH);
227        String year = readRecord.read(DVD.YEAR_LENGTH);
228        int copy = Integer.parseInt(readRecord.read(DVD.COPIES_LENGTH));
229
230        DVD returnValue = ("DELETED".equals(upc))
231                    ? null
232                    : new DVD(upc, name, composer, director, leadActor,
233                              supportingActor, year, copy);
234
235        log.exiting("DvdFileAccess", "retrieveDvd", returnValue);
236        return returnValue;
237    }
```

Finally, if the record is not marked as being deleted, we create a new DVD value object and return it. While creating the value object, we remove any trailing spaces or nulls from the field.

Once we have populated the recordNumbers map, it rarely needs to be changed. The only time we need to modify it is when a record is added or deleted. The addDVD method calls a private persistDVD method, which is also used when we modify a DVD record.

```
246    public boolean addDvd(DVD dvd) throws IOException {
247        return persistDvd(dvd, true);
248    }
```

We start the `persistDVD` method by seeing if the provided UPC is in our map of known UPCs, and verifying whether we are creating or modifying the DVD record. If we are creating a record the UPC must not be in our map. If we are modifying the DVD, then the UPC must be in our map. In any other case we cannot proceed, so we return false to indicate that the operation failed. Since we may be potentially adding the DVD's UPC to our map of known UPCs, we need to obtain a write lock on the `recordNumbersLock`.

▓Note Normally it is a bad idea to use return values to indicate success or failure of a call to a method— we should be able to throw an exception if we cannot continue. An exception would provide greater detail of what went wrong, and more importantly what the stack trace was at the time. However, the `DBClient` interface has specified that the `addDVD`, `modifyDVD`, and `removeDVD` methods must return a Boolean to indicate success or failure, so we must follow the dictates of the interface or we risk causing other programmer's code to fail. As with the assignment you get from Sun, we have simulated an interface where the reasons for the methods, parameters, return values, and exceptions have not been specified.

Leaving this method without releasing our write lock could be disastrous: no other thread would ever be able to gain a read or a write lock on `recordNumbersLock`, effectively rendering most of our methods inoperable. To guard against this, immediately after gaining the write lock we enter a try … finally block, and release the lock in the finally clause at line 357.

```
338    private boolean persistDvd(DVD dvd, boolean create) throws IOException {
339        log.entering("DvdFileAccess", "persistDvd", dvd);
340
341        // Perform as many operations as we can outside of the synchronized
342        // block to improve concurrent operations.
343        Long offset = 0L;
344        recordNumbersLock.writeLock().lock();
345        try {
346            offset = recordNumbers.get(dvd.getUPC());
347            if (create == true && offset == null) {
348                log.info("creating record " + dvd.getUPC());
349                offset = database.length();
350                recordNumbers.put(dvd.getUPC(), offset);
351            } else if (create == false && offset != null ) {
352                log.info("updating existing record " + dvd.getUPC());
353            } else {
354                return false;
355            }
356        } finally {
357            recordNumbersLock.writeLock().unlock();
358        }
```

The persistDVD method has a private StringBuilder variable that we will use to create a representation of a complete record. Prior to JDK 5, we might have used a StringBuffer to build this; however, the StringBuffer is internally synchronized to make it thread safe. Since the variable we will be using is a method variable, not a class variable, we do not need the synchronization. The StringBuilder class will therefore provide us with better performance.

Since each record is a fixed length, it is easy to start with a blank record of the correct length, then replace the blanks with the field data. We have a static empty field that was declared in line 66 and initialized in lines 77–79 as described earlier in the chapter. This makes it easy for us to create a StringBuilder of the correct length and contents in line 360:

```
360         final StringBuilder out = new StringBuilder(emptyRecordString);
```

Having created our variable, we will use StringBuilder's replace method to put the field data in the correct locations within the record field. By making a utility inner class we can save replicating the code:

```
362         class RecordFieldWriter {
363             int currentPosition = 0;
364             void write(String data, int length) {
365                 out.replace(currentPosition,
366                             currentPosition + data.length(),
367                             data);
368                 currentPosition += length;
369             }
370         }
371         RecordFieldWriter writeRecord = new RecordFieldWriter();
```

We can then use our utility inner class to convert the DVD record to the StringBuilder equivalent:

```
373         writeRecord.write(dvd.getUPC(), DVD.UPC_LENGTH);
374         writeRecord.write(dvd.getName(), DVD.NAME_LENGTH);
375         writeRecord.write(dvd.getComposer(), DVD.COMPOSER_LENGTH);
376         writeRecord.write(dvd.getDirector(), DVD.DIRECTOR_LENGTH);
377         writeRecord.write(dvd.getLeadActor(), DVD.LEAD_ACTOR_LENGTH);
378         writeRecord.write(dvd.getSupportingActor(),
379                           DVD.SUPPORTING_ACTOR_LENGTH);
380         writeRecord.write(dvd.getYear(), DVD.YEAR_LENGTH);
381         writeRecord.write("" + dvd.getCopy(), DVD.COPIES_LENGTH);
```

■**Caution** When working on your Sun assignment you must make the design decisions that make sense to you and that you are willing to defend when you go to do the exam portion of the certification. This can (and in some cases should) mean that you may make design decisions that contradict our design decisions— we are, after all, working on different assignments with different requirements. Do not be afraid to consider other options. A good place to discuss one of our design decisions or one of your design decisions is JavaRanch (http://www.javaranch.com).

Finally we write the record to file, and return true to show that the record was persisted to file.

```
384        // now that we have everything ready to go, we can go into our
385        // synchronized block & perform our operations as quickly as possible
386        // ensuring that we block other users for as little time as possible.
387
388        synchronized(database) {
389            database.seek(offset);
390            database.write(out.toString().getBytes());
391        }
392
393        log.exiting("DvdFileAccess", "persistDvd", persisted);
394        return true;
395    }
```

Most of the remaining methods do not need explaining. However, we will end with the find method, which shows the enhanced for loop, as well as using the regular expressions classes introduced in JDK 1.4.

```
311    public Collection<DVD> find(String query)
312            throws IOException, PatternSyntaxException {
313        log.entering("DvdFileAccess", "find", query);
314        Collection<DVD> returnValue = new ArrayList<DVD>();
315        Pattern p = Pattern.compile(query);
316
317        for (DVD dvd : getDvds()) {
318            Matcher m = p.matcher(dvd.toString());
319            if (m.find()) {
320                returnValue.add(dvd);
321            }
322        }
323
324        log.exiting("DvdFileAccess", "find", returnValue);
325        return returnValue;
326    }
```

In line 315 we take the string provided from our GUI application and compile it into a Java Pattern. We then need another class, the Matcher class, which can attempt to match the pattern against the provided string in various ways; we generate the Matcher for each DVD read in line 318. Finally, in line 319 we tell the Matcher to find the next occurrence of the pattern in the current DVD's string representation; if found we add the DVD to the collection of DVDs to be returned. While we are only interested in finding the pattern as a subset of the entire DVD, the Matcher can perform other types of matching as well; for instance, it can compare two strings in their entirety, or match starting with the beginning of the string.

Line 317 shows the enhanced for loop syntax in action. Using this form saved us the drudgery of manually creating our own iterator, and using generics saves us from casting objects. Contrast the simple use of line 308 with the code we would have had to use if the for loop had not been enhanced:

```
317a            List<DVD> dvds = getDVDs();
317b            for (Iterator i = dvds.iterator(); i.hasNext(); ) {
317c                DVD dvd =  i.next();
318                 Matcher m = p.matcher(dvd.toString());
319                 if (m.find()) {
320                     returnValue.add(dvd);
321                 }
322             }
```

Discussion Point: Caching Records

So far we have made minor concessions to speeding up the data access code, but we still have the situation where each DVD record is read from the physical file on disk—possibly the slowest operation of all. We have deliberately done this so that we have not overcomplicated this chapter; however, it is worthwhile considering whether or not we can cache the data.

The first question we should address is whether caching the data will save us any disk operations. If most operations on the data were writing to disk, then caching would not make much sense, since we would have to update the cache and update the file for the majority of operations. In fact, we might even end up with poorer performance than if we did not cache the data at all. However, the application we are developing is likely to have a large number of searches for matching records, and displaying of records, before one record is chosen for updating. Therefore, the majority of operations could benefit from having the records cached.

The next issue is whether the memory requirements would preclude caching. Each DVD record is relatively small, and it is likely that caching 1,000 DVD records would require far less than 10 MB of RAM. Because most new computers being sold have at least 128 MB of RAM, we should not have a problem caching our data.

Finally, we should take into account the impact this change will have on our code. If adding any feature makes the code significantly harder to read, then we should consider whether it is worth adding—certainly whoever maintains our code will not thank us if they have to maintain unreadable code. However, adding a cache to the existing code is reasonably simple; all we need is an extra map to hold the UPC keys and DVD records. Access to this cache can be handled in the same way as we use the recordNumbersLock mutex for the UPC-to-file-location map.

You should read the instructions you received from Sun carefully before deciding whether or not to implement a cache. Check whether there are any performance requirements, or any requirements for the simplest possible code. If there are no specific requirements, you can make your own decision as to whether to implement a cache—just remember to document your decision in your design choices document.

The ReservationsManager Class

The ReservationsManager class provides the ability to logically reserve a record so that a client can modify it, secure in the knowledge that no other client can modify it until the logical reservation is released.

To help explain the purpose of logical record locking, let's first consider a scenario where there is no logical record locking, and two clients try to rent the only copy of a particular DVD:

- Client A retrieves the DVD record for the movie *Office Space*.

- Client B retrieves the DVD record for *Office Space*.

- Client A verifies that there is one copy of the DVD still in stock.

- Client B verifies that there is one copy of the DVD still in stock.

- Client A rents the DVD.

- Client B rents the DVD.

We now have a problem; according to the electronic records, both clients A and B have rented the same DVD.

One way to solve this problem would be to make the retrieval-verification-rental operations atomic. However, this could only be done on the server side since two separate clients working in their own JVMs would be unaware of any synchronized blocks operating in other JVMs. Having this code operate on the server side makes building a thin client very simple, but we already know that we have to build a Swing client, so we know that the client computers can support thick clients. A bigger problem is that having this code within an atomic block will reduce concurrency.

THIN AND THICK CLIENTS

The term "thin client" is used to denote a client interface that can run on a computer with minimal processing power. A typical example is a web interface to an application—the computer accessing the web interface can be a very low-powered computer. It is even possible to set up a computer that has no hard drive or floppy disk drive that can access powerful software as long as there is a thin client interface for the software. It would be possible, for example, to set up a web browser on a personal computer with a 386 CPU running at 16 MHz with 4 MB of RAM. If you did this, you would still be able to access your e-mail, read news, and perform web searches, among other things.

For those who are not as old as the authors, before the current personal computers with Pentium 4 CPUs running in excess of 2 GHz with a minimum of 128 MB of RAM, there were personal computers with Pentium III CPUs. Going further back in the timeline were Pentium II CPUs, Pentium CPUs, 486 CPUs—and before that were 386 CPUs. Before the personal computers with 386 CPUs were 286, 8086, and 8088 CPUs, but the authors wouldn't want to set up a web browser on one of them (the first Unix-like system one of the authors worked on was a Coherent system on a 286).

A "thick client" (or a "fat client") is one where a large proportion of the processing is done on the client computer, and therefore a more powerful client computer is required. For example, Microsoft recommends running Microsoft Office on a PC with at least a Pentium III CPU, and 128 MB of RAM.

There is a trend toward using thin client software where possible within organizations for many reasons, such as the fact that thin clients can typically still run on older computers (the 386 was released in 1985, while the Pentium III was released in 1999; there are 14 years' worth of computers that would be obsolete if all software required a thick client running on a Pentium III), plus system administrators have an easier job if they only have to administer one or two servers running the applications, and all the client machines only run thin client software.

■**Caution** Before deciding whether to build a thin or a thick client for your submission, carefully read the instructions you downloaded from the Sun site to determine whether there are any requirements you must adhere to. There have been many discussions about this on JavaRanch (http://www.javaranch.com) regarding this topic (one, started by one of the authors, had 133 views put forward), and you are welcome to join in the discussions there.

But consider the same scenario with logical record locking:

- Client A logically locks the DVD record for *Office Space*.
- Client B attempts to logically lock the DVD record for *Office Space*; however, it cannot do so until client A releases the logical lock. Client B must now wait for client A to finish.
- Client A retrieves the DVD record for *Office Space*.
- Client A verifies that there is one copy of the DVD still in stock.
- Client A rents the DVD.
- Client A releases the logical lock for the DVD record for *Office Space*.
- Client B logically locks the DVD record for *Office Space*.
- Client B retrieves the DVD record for *Office Space*.
- Client B finds that there are no more copies of the DVD in stock.
- Client B releases the logical lock on *Office Space* and (hopefully) goes off to find some other DVD to rent.

One of the major advantages of logical record locking is that it allows a greater concurrency. It can also work across a network, so we can use the power of our thick clients.

Discussion Point: Identifying the Owner of the Lock

It is rarely good enough to simply have a way of logically reserving a record and releasing the reservation. You typically need some way of identifying which client has reserved the record, so that only they can release it.

An example from real life might help explain why we need this. Imagine if you rang the theater and reserved the last seat for a show. But then some other person turned up at the theater and claimed that they had reserved the seat. If the theater does not have some way of identifying who reserved the seat, you could lose your seat.

Likewise, if we don't identify the owner of a lock, an unscrupulous programmer could write a program in such a way that if they have not received a lock within a certain amount of time, they will just unlock the record anyway.

How you identify your lock owner depends on what your instructions state, and possibly on how you develop your network server. We will offer some suggestions in the following sections, but you will have to determine for yourself what will work for your specific instructions.

Using a Token to Identify the Lock Owner

If we can return a token from the lock method to the client requesting the logical lock, then we can mandate that the client must use that token when performing other operations, including when they release the logical lock.

The token itself (also referred to as a "cookie" or a "magic cookie") is something that our class would use to identify the owner of the logical lock. As such, it does not have to be a meaningful object, since the client does not need to do anything with this token other than store it for use when calling other methods. In fact, it is probably better that this token be random, since if the token has some meaning then the unscrupulous programmer might be able to guess it and still unlock our records.

However, our interface requires that our lock method return a Boolean and the releaseDVD method does not allow us to insert a token either, so this is unfortunately not an option for us.

Using the Thread to Identify the Lock Owner

If we opt to use sockets for our network interface, we will have total control over the threads used by each client. We will create a new thread when the client connects to the server, so we can use the thread identifier as a proxy for the client identifier.

When doing this, we would simply store the thread identification with the record identifier at the time we logically lock the record. Then, whenever the client attempts to do anything that needs the lock, we can compare the current thread identifier with the stored value; if they match, then we allow the operation.

This saves the client worrying about storing and reusing a token, but it will only work for our stand-alone client and for a network solution based on sockets. If our network solution uses Remote Method Invocation (RMI), this won't work.

Using a Class Instance to Identify the Lock Owner

The RMI specification states that there are no guarantees about which threads will be used for any given remote method. This means that the following scenario is possible according to the specification:

- Client A uses thread 1 to logically lock a record.

- Client B uses thread 1 to attempt to logically lock the same record; it waits for the logical lock to be released.

- Client A uses thread 2 to logically release the record.

- Client B uses thread 1 to logically release the record.

More complex scenarios are also possible. Listing 5-1 shows an example of this problem.

Listing 5-1. *An Example of Thread Reuse in RMI*

```java
import java.rmi.*;
import java.rmi.registry.*;
import java.rmi.server.*;

interface ServerReference extends Remote {
    public void serverThreadNumber(String id) throws RemoteException;
}

class Server extends UnicastRemoteObject implements ServerReference {
    public Server() throws RemoteException {
        // do nothing constructor
    }

    public void serverThreadNumber(String id) throws RemoteException {
        System.out.println(id + " running in thread "
                            + Thread.currentThread().hashCode());
        try {
            Thread.sleep(2000);
        } catch (InterruptedException ie) {
            ie.printStackTrace();
            System.exit(1);
        }
    }
}

public class RmiProblem extends Thread {
    public RmiProblem(String id) {
        super(id);
    }

    public static void main(String[] args) throws Exception {
        LocateRegistry.createRegistry(1099);
        Naming.rebind("rmi://localhost:1099/RmiProblem", new Server());

        Thread a = new RmiProblem("A");
        a.start();

        Thread.sleep(1000);

        Thread b = new RmiProblem("B");
        b.start();

        a.join();
        b.join();
```

```
        System.exit(0);
    }

    public void run() {
        try {
            ServerReference remoteCode =
                    (ServerReference) Naming.lookup("RmiProblem");

            for (int i = 0; i < 5; i++) {
                remoteCode.serverThreadNumber(getName());
                Thread.sleep(2000);
            }
        } catch (Exception e) {
            e.printStackTrace();
            System.exit(0);
        }
    }
}
```

Don't worry if you do not understand this code completely. Chapter 6 discusses RMI in depth, so it may be easier to come back to this code after reading that chapter.

Although the results of running this code will vary from computer to computer (and indeed from run to run), one example of running the code is shown in Figure 5-7.

Figure 5-7. *Example of thread reuse within RMI*

As can be seen in Figure 5-7, both client A and client B use threads 15655788 and 16112134.

With this in mind, if we cannot use tokens and we have chosen to use RMI, then we need to find some other way of uniquely identifying our clients.

One way of handling this is to build our server using the Factory design pattern, where our factory creates a unique object for each connected client. We can then use the unique instance of our DvdDatabase class to identify the client.

Using a factory works for both a sockets-based solution (although it is generally overkill) and for an RMI solution. Since we are presenting both solutions in this book, we have decided to use a factory, and we will describe it in Chapter 6.

Creating Our Logical Reserve Methods

To create the reserveDVD and releaseDVD methods needed for logical locking, we need some class variables. For a start, we need to track the owners of the locks; a Map containing the UPC number and the owner is ideal. We also need a common Lock object to ensure that different threads do not try to lock the record simultaneously. Finally, we need a condition that threads can monitor to determine when they can attempt to acquire a lock again. These three variables are as follows:

```
private static Map<String, DvdDatabase> reservations
        = new HashMap<String, DvdDatabase>();

private static Lock lock = new ReentrantLock();
private static Condition lockReleased  = lock.newCondition();
```

Listing 5-2 contains the reserveDVD method.

Listing 5-2. *The reserveDVD Method*

```
boolean reserveDVD(String upc, DvdDatabase renter)
        throws InterruptedException {
    log.entering("ReservationsManager", "reserveDvd",
            new Object[]{upc, renter});

    lock.lock();
    try {
        long endTimeMSec = System.currentTimeMillis() + 5000;
        while (reservations.containsKey(upc)) {
            long timeLeftMSec = endTimeMSec - System.currentTimeMillis();
            if (!lockReleased.await(timeLeftMSec, TimeUnit.MILLISECONDS)) {
                log.fine(renter + " giving up after 5 seconds: " + upc);
                return false;
            }
        }
        reservations.put(upc, renter);
        log.fine(renter + " got Lock for " + upc);
        log.fine("Locked record count = " + reservations.size());
        log.exiting("ReservationsManager", "reserveDvd", true);
        return true;
    } finally {
        // ensure lock is always released, even if an Exception is thrown
        lock.unlock();
    }
}
```

We have decided to allow any UPC to be reserved, even if no such record exists. This ensures that a DVD can also be reserved when we are first adding it to the system. The alternative would be to have the reserveDVD method start by verifying that the record does exist, throwing some exception if the record does not exist. If we had any delete methods, we would also have to verify that the record existed after we acquired the lock. However, if we did this, we would also have to change the logic of the addDVD method, and possibly the updateDVD method (remember, they both defer to the same private persistDVD method, which might also have to be updated).

Our reserveDVD method acquires a mutual exclusion lock, and then goes into a while loop, waiting until we either time out or acquire the lock.

Our DBClient interface specifies that we must return false if we were unable to lock the record within 5 seconds. Under JDK 1.4 there was no guaranteed way of determining whether a call to wait(timeout) had timed out or whether notification had been received. JDK 5 has a new Condition.await method, which will return a Boolean true if we were notified by the unlock method that we can continue processing, and false if we timed out.

If we have acquired the lock, we add a record to the map of lock owners, indicating that we own the lock.

Finally, we release the mutual exclusion lock.

The Logical Release Method

The releaseDVD method is the counterpoint to the reserveDVD method shown earlier, and the code is very similar.

```
void releaseDvd(String upc, DvdDatabase renter) {
    log.entering("ReservationsManager", "releaseDvd",
                    new Object[]{upc, renter});
    lock.lock();
    if (reservations.get(upc) == renter) {
        reservations.remove(upc);
        log.fine(renter + " released lock for " + upc);
        lockReleased.signal();
    } else {
        log.warning(renter + " cant release lock for " + upc + ": not owner");
    }
    lock.unlock();
    log.exiting("ReservationsManager", "releaseDvd");
}
```

First, we ensure we have a lock on the mutual exclusion Lock; then if it is the owner of the reservation who is releasing it, we remove our lock indication from the map. Then we signal any waiting threads that they can try to acquire locks. If the wrong renter instance is passed to this method, a warning message is logged. Finally, we release our mutual exclusion Lock.

Discussion Point: Deadlock Handling

Deadlocks occur when a thread is blocked forever, waiting for a condition that cannot occur. Chapter 4 discusses deadlock handling from a threading perspective, but the same issues apply at an application logic level as well. Consider what would happen if two clients were both trying to get logical locks on the same two records, but in different orders, as shown in the following example:

- Client A gets a logical lock on record 1.

- Client B gets a logical lock on record 2.

- Client A attempts to get a logical lock on record 2.

- Client B attempts to get a logical lock on record 1.

Our reserveDVD method times out after 5 seconds. But if both client A and client B immediately retried to get the lock, the result would be the same as if we didn't have a timeout: both threads would effectively be deadlocked.

There are many solutions to prevent deadlocks, among them:

- Don't allow a client to ever lock more than one record at a time. If they cannot lock multiple records, then you cannot get a logical deadlock.

- Only allow clients to lock records in numerical order. Under these rules, client B would not be allowed to attempt to lock record 1 in our previous example, and would have to give up the lock on record 2 at some point, which would allow client A to continue.

- Have a dedicated mechanism for tracking that locks are owned and which locks are in contention. Each time that a new lock goes into contention, this mechanism would be checked to see that a deadlock will not occur, and if it will, the lock is cancelled. This is the most complex of the possible solutions, but the code required is mostly recursive and can be written simply with a little thought.

- Ignore the problem. Seriously—is it a requirement of your assignment? Is there a possibility that attempting to handle this problem could result in you making a mistake that might cost you marks? Do you feel that this is out of scope for the assignment?

Once again, we are going to recommend that you read the instructions you received from Sun very carefully to determine what you need to do about deadlock handling (if anything). However, if your instructions do not mention this at all, you will have to decide for yourself whether you want to handle deadlocks. Some of the questions you might like to ask include the following: Is it more professional to have deadlock handling? Does deadlock handling add unnecessary complexity to the code? Can you handle deadlocks with the exceptions you are allowed to throw?

Whatever you decide, this is a design decision that you might like to document.

Discussion Point: Handling Client Crashes

Earlier in this chapter, we discussed the potential for having thick clients, where the client will be responsible for obtaining a logical record lock and later releasing it. But what happens if the client crashes (or is just shut down) sometime after requesting a logical record lock but before releasing the logical record lock? In such a case, the record will be locked for all time—no other client will ever be able to lock the record.

Once again there are many possible solutions, some of which include the following:

- Having a thinner client (where the client just calls a `rentDVD` method on the server, and the server calls both the `reserveDVD` and `releaseDVD` methods) will bypass the problem totally. The lock should never become totally unavailable. We recommend you refer back to the section on fat/thin clients earlier in this chapter to see the ramifications of this (and possibly join in the discussions on JavaRanch on this topic).

- If we have a socket network solution, then the server thread servicing the client will receive an exception when the client disconnects. If that thread keeps track of which locks have been granted, then it could release them if it receives this exception.

- If we have a server factory, with unique `DvdDatabase` objects as our client identifiers, we could store the reservation data in a `WeakHashMap` with the client identifier as the key. When the client disconnects, the `DvdDatabase` for that client will (eventually) be garbage collected and the lock will be automatically removed from the `WeakHashMap`. In this case, we would probably want a separate thread monitoring the `WeakHashMap` so that it can notify any waiting threads that a reservation has been cleared.

- If we have a server factory with unique workers per RMI client, we could have the worker implement `java.rmi.server.Unreferenced`. The `unreferenced` method from this interface will be called sometime after the RMI client disconnects. If the worker instance keeps track of which locks have been granted, then it could release them if `unreferenced` is called.

- Ignore the problem. Again, seriously—is it a requirement of your assignment? Is there a possibility that attempting to handle this problem could result in you making a mistake that might cost you marks? Do you feel that this is out of scope for the assignment?

Once again, we are going to recommend that you read the instructions you received from Sun very carefully to determine what you need to do about clients dying (if anything). However, if your instructions do not mention this at all, you will have to decide for yourself whether you want to handle the possibility of locks never being released. Some of the questions you might like to ask include the following: Is it more professional to handle disconnected clients? Does handling disconnected clients add unnecessary complexity to the code?

Whatever you decide, keep in mind that this is a design decision that you might like to document.

Discussion Point: Multiple Notification Objects

Consider what will happen if 100 threads are all waiting to reserve different records. When a thread releases its lock on any one record, it will call `lockReleased.signal`, and *all 100 threads* will be notified that a lock has been released, so all 100 threads will attempt to regain the `lock` mutex and check whether it is the record that they are interested in that was released—and potentially the released record was not of interest to any of them! So there would be a sudden burst of CPU activity each time a record is released, potentially lowering productivity on the server each time.

A better solution would be to have each thread get notified only when the record it is interested in becomes free.

Under JDK 1.4 this would have been difficult to achieve; you would have had to synchronize on different objects to be able to ensure that only a specific thread gets notified. Under JDK 5 you can have all your threads obtain a lock on the same object but use different Conditions upon which they should be notified.

JDK 1.5's reentrant locks, with their different syntax to synchronized blocks, provide the ability to create hand-over-hand locking, where a lock is requested, then a second lock is requested, then the first lock is released, and so on. No lock in the chain is released until the next lock is granted.

Conceptually the replacement for the reserveDVD method would look like the code in Listing 5-3. Note that the line numbers are specific to this discussion, and have no relationship to the line numbers for the original reserveDvd method.

Listing 5-3. *A Less CPU-Intensive reserveDvd Method*

```
1       private static Map<String, LockInformation> reservations
2               = new HashMap<String, LockInformation>();
3
4       private static Lock masterLock = new ReentrantLock();
5
6       public boolean reserveDvd(String upc, DvdDatabase renter)
7               throws InterruptedException {
8           LockInformation dvdLock = null;
9           masterLock.lock();
10          try {
11              dvdLock = reservations.get(upc);
12              if (dvdLock == null) {
13                  dvdLock = new LockInformation();
14                  reservations.put(upc, dvdLock);
15              }
16              dvdLock.lock();
17          } finally {
18              masterLock.unlock();
19          }
20
21          try {
22              long endTimeMSec = System.currentTimeMillis() + 5000;
23              Condition dvdCondition = dvdLock.getCondition();
24              while (dvdLock.isReserved()) {
25                  long timeLeftMSec = endTimeMSec - System.currentTimeMillis();
26                  if (!dvdCondition.await(timeLeftMSec, TimeUnit.MILLISECONDS)) {
27                      return false;
28                  }
29              }
30              dvdLock.setReserver(renter);
31          } finally {
```

```
32                  dvdLock.unlock();
33              }
34          return true;
35      }
```

We start by getting a lock on the masterLock, which allows us to retrieve the lock for our specific UPC at line 11 or create a new lock and add it to the map if necessary at lines 13 and 14. Without this master lock, another thread could be modifying the map while we are trying to get our lock.

In JDK 1.4 we would now have a problem—we no longer want to keep the lock on masterLock, but if we release the masterLock before we gain a lock on our particular dvdLock, there is the risk that some other thread could modify the dvdLock before we managed to lock it. However, because JDK 1.4 locking works in terms of synchronized blocks, it is not possible to lock dvdLock and then release masterLock.

Hand-over-hand locking solves this problem for us. Before releasing the lock on masterLock we lock dvdLock in line 16. At this point we own two locks, but we release the masterLock in line 18, bringing us back to a single lock. At no time did we own zero locks, and the time that we owned two locks was reduced to a minimum.

When we get to line 26, each client will be waiting for the condition specific to the lock they are after. They will no longer be woken up when *any* lock is released.

This relies on a LockInformation class, which is shown in Listing 5-4.

Listing 5-4. *The LockInformation Class*

```
1      class LockInformation extends ReentrantLock {
2          private DvdDatabase reserver = null;
3          private Condition notifier = newCondition();
4
5          void setReserver(DvdDatabase reserver) {
6              this.reserver = reserver;
7          }
8
9          void releaseReserver() {
10             this.reserver = null;
11         }
12
13         Condition getCondition() {
14             return notifier;
15         }
16
17         boolean isReserved() {
18             return reserver != null;
19         }
20     }
```

The releaseDVD method would use the Condition from the instance of the LockInformation class for the record being unlocked to only notify threads waiting on this particular record. If there are a large number of threads waiting for records, this could significantly reduce the CPU usage when a record is released.

Again, we recommend that you read the instructions you received from Sun very carefully to determine what you need to do about multiple threads receiving notification simultaneously (if anything).

■**Tip** We have presented this section on having multiple notification objects as it does appear to meet a requirement listed in at least some of the Sun instructions. However, at the time of this writing Sun does not appear to penalize those candidates who ignore this requirement.

Summary

In this chapter we showed how to build classes that can read the data file and provide locking. We discussed some of the common pitfalls that can occur, and explained how to avoid them. We also presented several examples of design patterns, and examined how they can be used.

We used many of the techniques that you need to use in your Sun SCJD assignment, including reading and writing from random locations in files, and locking and releasing records. We also used many of the new techniques introduced in JDK 1.5, and introduced some of the new APIs.

One word of caution: As we mentioned in Chapter 3, we have made some parts of our sample assignment more difficult than the real assignment. You may find far simpler solutions for your Sun assignment than those presented here (and we strongly recommend you look for them). Similarly, some portions of the Sun assignment may be more difficult than what we have presented here. You will also note that there are methods in your Data class you must implement that we have not even mentioned; we believe we have provided you with the basic information you need to create these methods on your own.

FAQs

Q Will I have to create my own data file in the Sun SCJD assignment?

A No; at the time of this writing, Sun provides a sample data file for you, along with the details of the file format necessary for you to read and write the file.

Q Should I provide my test classes and build scripts in my submission?

A We recommend against providing anything outside of the requirements. At the time of writing, the instructions from Sun include a statement that going beyond the requirements will not gain you extra marks. So providing the test classes and build scripts cannot gain you anything.

Q Should I build the Data class in stages?

A We strongly recommend you do build each of your classes in stages, ensuring that each part is correct before moving on to the next part.

Q Is it necessary/possible for my Data class to use a value object?

A You will have to check your instructions to see whether or not this is possible. All the instructions to date have been very explicit about the required method signatures for the Data class. However, even if you cannot use them in the Data class, your instructions might allow value objects to be used elsewhere in your solution.

Q Is it necessary for my Data class to use the Façade pattern?

A There are no specific patterns that must be used within your submission; you are free to use any that you feel fit your requirements. Similarly, there are no requirements for you to acknowledge which patterns you are using, but it is considered good programming practice to mention the patterns in your design decisions documentation and/or your Javadoc APIs as doing so will assist other programmers in understanding your code.

Q Should I use a cache in my Sun SCJD assignment?

A Usually the Sun instructions tell you that a clear design is preferred over a higher performance design. So you should decide for yourself whether the addition of a cache makes your code easier to read, and whether the gains are worth your while.

Q What happens if using a cache causes the JVM/computer to run out of memory?

A You could use lazy loading of records (only loading them when required) in conjunction with SoftReferences to ensure that the JVM can clear the records if it is running out of memory. If the JVM does clear the record from memory, using a lazy loading scheme will result in you reloading it next time you need it (and presumably some other low-usage object being cleared). That said, you might want to calculate just how many records it will take to use all the memory on your computer—and whether you could even access that many records with the provided APIs.

Q Am I allowed to use the java.nio (NIO) packages or the java.util.concurrent packages in my application?

A In the past Sun has displayed information on its web site indicating that use of the NIO packages was not allowed for the SCJD assignment. However, Sun has also stated that the instructions you download from its site are authoritative; if your official instructions state that you must not use a particular package, then you must not use it. However, if your instructions do not ban a particular package, then you are free to use it.

CHAPTER 6

■ ■ ■

Networking with RMI

In this chapter, you will develop the background needed to implement a complete networking solution using Remote Method Invocation (RMI). To that end, this chapter will cover RMI and, to a lesser extent, serialization. Figure 6-1 illustrates where the networking solution fits in the overall architecture of the system, which is nestled between the GUI and the data layer.

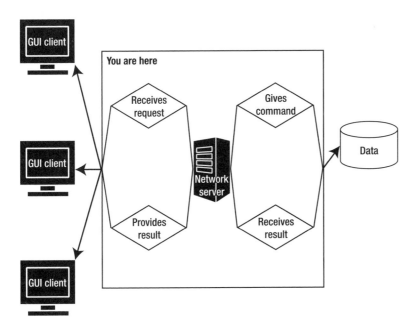

Figure 6-1. *The networking tier of Denny's DVDs version 2.0*

Before you can fully understand RMI, it is important to familiarize yourself with some of the ins and outs of serialization, since RMI relies on this feature. Serialization is a topic that you may already be familiar with from the Sun Certified Java Programmer (SCJP) exam, but we will still cover the topic briefly. These topics are some of the big-picture points developed in this chapter:

- Understanding object serialization in Denny's DVDs

- Evaluating the pros and cons of using RMI as a network protocol

- Implementing a remote object and defining a remote interface

- Examining the Factory pattern and learning why we are using it for our RMI implementation

- Marshaling and demarshaling in RMI

- Registering your remote objects

Caution The next chapter describes Java sockets, which is the other networking protocol the examinee may opt to use for the certification project. However, be advised that for the certification project, you must send serialized objects if opting for a sockets solution as a networking protocol. Java RMI requires serialization, but it is not absolutely necessary to use serialization in a Java socket implementation. You could, for instance, implement your own wire format in a socket implementation so that any client-side technology could submit requests to a Java socket server. In the next chapter, we explain the technique of using sockets with serialization objects. If you decide to implement your solution using sockets as the networking protocol, the next section, "What Is Serialization?", will still be useful.

What Is Serialization?

So what is serialization, and why would you need it in your program? Let's consider an example. Suppose there are two machines on the same network. Machine A sends a message to a Java program on machine B; how does machine B receive and understand the message? What's required is a transfer protocol. A *transfer protocol* will flatten the data that needs to be transferred by putting it into a format that can be sent across a network.

Part of the process of sending data across a network involves serialization. *Serialization* is the process of deconstructing an object into its components of type information and state, and then reconstructing a copy of the original object on the receiving end by reading in the type information and then the field values. The term often used to describe the process of transferring serialized objects across a network is *marshaling*. Sometimes the reverse process, restoring the serialized object on the other end, is referred to as *demarshaling*, or *unmarshaling*. Serialized objects can be persisted to a local file system, courtesy of Java file I/O, or sent across a network via a socket. This is accomplished by converting the object into a serial stream of bytes, transmitting that stream across a network or to a file system, and then reading the persisted byte stream back into memory in order to re-create the object graph (see Figure 6-2), which is Java vernacular for reconstructing the original object and its state as if nothing ever happened. When a byte stream is loaded into memory in the form of an object, it is said to be in an *active* state. When that same byte stream is located in a file, rather than in a Java Virtual Machine (JVM) memory bank, it is said to be in a *passive* state. Keep in mind the notion of an object being in an active or passive state, as it will come in handy when we introduce the `Activatable` interface later in this chapter. Let's discuss the process in a little more detail.

The first of three steps is converting the object to a serial stream of bytes. First, type information gets written as header information to the stream, and then state information is written. The state information consists of the values of the class members, except for the static and transient members (assuming the default serialization mechanism, which does not implement readObject and writeObject; this is discussed a bit later in more detail). On the deserialization end, the receiving remote object first reads the type information in from the header and creates an instance of the class. If the class cannot be located (either locally or remotely), then a ClassNotFoundException is raised. Once the class is instantiated, the field values are read in from the stream and the values set in the marshaled object.

■**Note** Serialized objects are a copy of the original, not a reference to them. Parameters and return values in RMI are passed by values or copies. An object can be referenced on another machine only if the object is a remote object—that is, the object is exported via the UnicastRemoteObject.export() method or UnicastRemoteObject is extended.

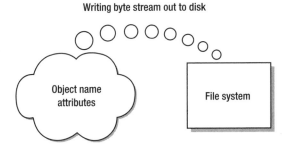

Writing byte stream out to disk

Object name attributes

File system

Figure 6-2. *Creating the byte stream from an object graph*

Using the serialver Tool

Serialization involves implementing the java.io.Serializable interface. This interface is of interest because it does not have any methods that require implementing. In fact, the main purpose of implementing Serializable is to inform the JVM that the object can be serialized. Serializable is often referred to as a marker interface. Formally a marker interface is an interface, which does not define any methods that a class or subclass would be required to implement but rather identifies the object as being of a certain type. To determine if a class is serializable, use the tool serialver. To start the serialver tool, from the project root enter the following at a command prompt:

```
serialver -classpath classes/. -show
```

Let's run the serialver tool on two of our classes, one that is serializable and one that is not serializable. We will use the DVD class as our serializable class and DvdFileAccess as the class that is not serializable. Figures 6-3 and 6-4 demonstrate the use of serialver on our DVD and DvdFileAccess classes, respectively.

Figure 6-3. *Running the serialver tool on the DVD class*

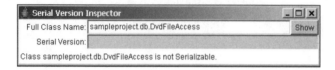

Figure 6-4. *Running the serialver tool on the DvdFileAccess class*

Since we started serialver from the DennyDVD classes directory, we can inspect our project's classes for the Serializable interface. If we had started from another directory, we would have had to make sure that our project was listed in our system classpath. *Inspecting* our classes for the Serializable interface is not very interesting since we have the source code and are well aware which classes are Serializable and which are not (i.e., we can simply inspect the file visually to see if Serializable is implemented). But using serialver on classes in which we do not have source code is much more useful—for instance, classes in a JAR file or classes that are part of the JDK.

For fun, try inspecting other classes in your classpath, such as those in the Java JDK (i.e., java.util.Date or java.lang.String).

If you inspect the source code for both the DVD and DVDFileAccess classes (downloadable from http://www.apress.com), you will note that DVD does indeed implement Serializable, while DVDFileAccess does not.

The Serialization Process

To actually persist an object's state, there are two classes in the java.io package that perform the bulk of work required for reading and writing serializable objects: ObjectOutputStream and ObjectInputStream. ObjectOutputStream has a method called writeObject, while ObjectInputStream has a method called readObject. In the Denny's DVDs project, serialization is used to send method parameters across the network between the GUI and the server using the default serialization mechanism (e.g., whether the server is an RMI or a socket server). We do not actually serialize our method parameters explicitly for RMI to work. In fact, our only concern is that the object sent across the network be serializable. Let's assume that we want to persist the state of our DVD objects explicitly to the file system. In that case, we could do so by implementing the persistDVD and retrieveDVD methods. When the client wants to save the state of a database record or DVD object, such as after a setRecordNumber call, the client invokes the DVDFileAccess method persistDVD. persistDVD serializes the DVD object using the ObjectOutputStream class and its writeObject method. The persistDVD method is shown in Listing 6-1. Keep in mind that the actual member we are serializing is a DVD. Our DVD class must be Serializable. The retrieveDVD method reads the serialized object and re-creates the object, as demonstrated in Listing 6-2.

Listing 6-1. *persistDVD Method Demonstrating FileOutputStream to Serialize a DVD Object*

```java
private boolean persistDVD(DVD dvd) throws IOException{
      boolean retVal=false;
      //open a FileIOutputStream associated with the data
      //notice that if the DVD does not already exist,
      //it will be created.
      String filePath = dbName+"/"+ dvd.getUPC() + fileExtension;
      FileOutputStream fos = new FileOutputStream(filePath);
      try {
              ObjectOutputStream oos = new ObjectOutputStream(fos);
              //Read in the data from the object
              oos.writeObject(dvd);
      }
       finally {
                  //close all references
                oos.close();
                      fos.close();
      }
}
```

Listing 6-2. *retrieveDVD Method Demonstrating FileInputStream to Deserialize a DVD Object*

```java
private DVD retrieveDVD(String upc, String fileExtension) throws IOException,
ClassNotFoundException {
              DVD retVal = null;
              //get the path to the object's serialized state.
              try {
                      String filePath = dbName+"/"+ upc + fileExtension;
                      FileInputStream fis = new FileInputStream(filePath);
                      //Read in the data from the object
                      ObjectInputStream ois = new ObjectInputStream(fis);
                      retVal = (DVD)ois.readObject();
              }
              finally {
                      ois.close();
                      fis.close();
              }
              return retVal;
}
```

■**Caution** The code shown in these listings is not contained in the actual project since Denny's DVDs relies on the JVM and the default serialization mechanism. The code is used as a pedagogical device to illustrate how to explicitly serialize an object.

As mentioned previously, information pertaining to the object's state is persisted to a file via a stream of bytes. But that is not all of the information that is saved. Information regarding the class type and its version number is also persisted. This is important because the class loader needs to properly deserialize the class from its persisted state. If the serialVersionUID is not declared, then the ObjectOutputStream will generate a unique version number for the class. Any subsequent changes to the class's members will generate a new version number at the next compilation. In the sampleproject.db.DVD class, the version ID is defined as a private member defined as follows:

```
private static final long serialVersionUID = 5165L;
```

■Note Often, serialization compatibility between versions needs to be maintained even though minor changes that will not break serialization compatibility have occurred. In these situations you need to declare the serialVersionID. You can use serialver to do this initially. This will allow you to define your own numbering schemes for the versionID for the class. Interestingly, even though this is a private field, the JVM knows it is there and uses it when defining a class.

Tweaking the Default Serialization Mechanism

There may be times when you want more control over how an object's state is serialized. For instance, perhaps you are only concerned with persisting part of the object's state, but not all of it. This is useful if the class contains a private member for holding a reference to a database connection, and you do not want to persist that information because the connections are only meaningful during a single session and are assigned on an as-needed basis. It wouldn't make sense to try to persist a database connection for the next time the application is run. The next time you load the object with the connection reference, you can simply assign that member a new connection. Another situation where you would not want to persist object information is when an object member is of a type that is not serializable. For instance, in our sample project the J2SE 1.5 Logger instance in the DVD class is not serializable.

But how do we indicate to the JVM that we don't want to persist a specific class member but would like to persist the other class members? Java provides for this functionality through the use of the keyword transient. The byte stream that gets persisted will not include any members that are declared using the keyword transient.

We use the keyword transient in our serialization implementation since the Logger instance cannot be serialized. (Hint: Try running serialver on the logger.) Conceptually this works out well since a logger member does not really add anything essential to the notion of a DVD. In general, a logger is the sort of thing that does not need to be persisted, and we can re-create a complete DVD record by reinitializing the logger. The following is an example of how you can use the keyword transient in the Logger instance in DVD.java:

```
private transient Logger log = Logger.getLogger("sampleproject.db");
```

There is another approach to serialization that we should mention. Rather than implement Serializable, an alternative approach is to implement a subinterface of Serializable:

the `Externalizable` interface. The big advantage of the `Externalizable` interface is performance. The algorithm for serialization uses reflection for marshaling and demarshaling. The serialization algorithm will systematically determine the nontransient and nonstatic class members through the use of reflection.

However, this can be quite expensive because the reflection algorithm costs in terms of CPU cycles and memory. The costs result from the JVM having to dynamically discover class properties during runtime. In situations where performance is more important than flexibility, consider using a reflectionless approach to serialization, such as `Externalizable`. For more information on reflection, refer to the following Sun tutorial: `http://java.sun.com/docs/books/tutorial/reflect/`.

Customizing Serialization with the Externalizable Interface

If performance is a must, then you can serialize using the `java.io.Externalizable` interface instead of the `Serializable` interface. So just how does `Externalizable` improve on the default serialization mechanism? `Externalizable` requires that you write the details of reading and writing the object's state to the byte stream. This is much more tedious than relying on reflection, but ultimately it provides more of a speed burst to your application. The `ObjectOutputStream` class no longer simplifies this process. You must use the methods `readExternal` and `writeExternal` and be aware of the member's type—whether it is a primitive type, a `String` (i.e., UTF), or some other type of object, other than `String`, that is serializable. Since you are involved in the low-level handling, you must read your object's members in the same order in which they were written to the stream.

Listing 6-3 presents an example of how our DVD class might look if it were `Externalizable`. For illustration purposes, the nuts and bolts of the class are not shown—just the code that relates to `writeExternal` and `readExternal`. Both methods can be private since the serialization mechanism can circumvent the normally applicable accessibility rules for classes (i.e., the JVM can invoke an object's private serialization methods).

Note If the `readObject` and `writeObject` methods are implemented in the `Serializable` object, the heavy reliance on reflection is not required and there is actually a performance edge over the default serialization mechanism (i.e., implementing `Serializable` without overriding the `readObject` and `writeObject` methods).

This approach is similar to externalization, with some minor differences with regard to inheritance and the handling of class metadata. The signatures of the methods to override appear in Listing 6-3. When you override these methods, it is crucial that the order in which the class attributes are written to the stream is the same as the order they are read back. As long as the serializable objects are not part of a class hierarchy, `readObject` and `writeObject` are implemented exactly as `readExternal` and `writeExternal`, as discussed later in this section. Here are the method signatures for `readObject` and `writeObject`:

```
private void writeObject(java.io.ObjectOutputStream out) throws IOException
private Object readObject(java.io.ObjectInputStream in) throws IOException, ➥
ClassNotFoundException
```

Listing 6-3. *An Externalizable Version of DVD.java: Implementing the readExternal and writeExternal Methods of DVD.java*

```
/**
 * Required method for Externalizable interface.
 * Specifies how the object graph gets converted to a byte stream.
 */
private void writeExternal(ObjectOutput out) throws IOException{
                out.writeUTF(upc);
        out.writeUTF(name);
        out.writeUTF(composer);
        out.writeUTF(director);
        out.writeUTF(leadActor);
        out.writeUTF(supportingActor);
        out.writeUTF(year);

        out.writeInt(copy);
}
/**
 * Required method for Externalizable interface.
 * Specifies how to recreate the object graph from
 * a byte stream. The order members are read must
 * match the order in which the object members were
 * written to the stream.
 */
private void readExternal(ObjectInput in) throws IOException{
                out.readUTF(upc);
                out.readUTF(name);
                out.readUTF(composer);
                out.readUTF(director);
                out.readUTF(leadActor);
                out.readUTF(supportingActor);
                out.readUTF(year);
                out.readInt(copy);
}
```

■**Caution** As was the case with `persistDVD` and `retrieveDVD`, the `readExternal` and `writeExternal` methods are not included in the actual project code base, but are used merely as a pedagogical device for demonstrating externalization.

Since `Externalizable` is considered a more advanced serialization approach, we will not cover `Externalizable` any further in this book. Rather, we have chosen to implement `Serializable` for simplicity, but `Externalizable` is mentioned so that you understand the alternative. `Serializable` is simpler to implement but sacrifices performance and flexibility.

Using Externalizable results in code that is more difficult to maintain. For instance, if we were to add a new class member to the DVD class—say, a serializable type such as boolean—our preceding read and write code would not change. However, if DVD implemented Externalizable instead of Serializable, then we would have to update the readExternal and writeExternal methods to incorporate the change. In addition, the externalization methods should include logic to check for specific versions of serial version IDs to determine if they were dealing with older versions of the class. In a production system, this can be an annoyance if you have a lot of classes that tend to change over time. Table 6-1 presents a comparison of serialization to externalization.

■**Tip** The use of transient in a class that implements Externalizable is not required. Since the Externalizable interface requires that the details of reading and writing the object's state be defined, the transient keyword is not necessary. In fact, it is completely ignored in an Externalizable object.

■**Note** Since application performance is not a consideration in our design; we have opted for plain serialization over externalization in our implementation of Denny's DVDs version 2.0.

Table 6-1. *Comparing Serialization and Externalization*

Serialization	Externalization	Advantage Goes To . . .
Easier to use. Just implement Serializable and use writeObject and readObject to persist state.	More complex. Must implement the Externalizable interface methods readExternal and writeExternal.	Serializable
Less efficient algorithm. Uses reflection to determine object's makeup.	Better performance. No need to use reflection since you write the code.	Externalizable
More data gets serialized due to larger class description and versioning information.	More control over what gets serialized.	Externalizable

Introducing RMI

An important objective of the SCJD exam is for the examinee to develop a solution that will allow machines on a network to exchange messages. Such communication, known as distributed computing, can be a challenging task, but RMI is one of the helpful tools at your disposal. However, RMI is not the only game in town. There are other technologies, such as RPC, Common Object Request Broker Architecture (CORBA), and Microsoft's .NET technology. In fact, RMI can be thought of as object-oriented RPC.

■**Note** .NET has a similar and competing technology called .NET remoting.

This is a good time to define some terms. When we use the term *server* in RMI programming scenarios, we are referring to a remote object that has methods that can be invoked from another JVM. A *client* is the object that invokes the remotely accessible methods of the server. An RMI *distributed object system* provides remote objects that can be invoked by clients. Communication between a client and a remote object is two-way. A client must be able to locate and communicate with remote objects, invoke their methods, and receive their return values.

RMI specifically enables Java objects on different machines to communicate with each other. One of the motivations behind RMI is for developers to interact with remote Java objects as if they were local objects. The actual location of the object is transparent to the developer. Network transparency is a very appealing feature, because it abstracts the complexities involved in distributed object systems so that they behave as if they were local object systems. So in an RMI system, the client runs locally, while the rest of the system runs on a different machine. These types of systems are often referred to as distributed object systems. Figure 6-5 illustrates this type of system.

■**Note** An alternative to sockets and RMI is Remote Procedure Call (RPC). RPC is language- and processor-independent, assumes that parameters are network representations of simple data types such as ints and chars, and can be run on almost any platform. RMI is only processor-independent, assumes an object-oriented framework, and requires the use of Java.

In addition to RPC, CORBA and Simple Object Access Protocol (SOAP) are other technologies that allow processor and language independence between different platforms. But because RMI assumes the use of Java, many of the tedious protocol-level tasks have been built into RMI, leaving the developer with more time to worry about application logic. Java's RMI is very good for Java systems, since it can assume that a JVM will be present on both sides of the network connection. For these reasons, RMI is preferable to RPC and CORBA in distributed object systems built entirely with Java. However, as a scandalous side note, CORBA systems tend to perform better than RMI systems, mainly because they can be written in C or C++. Closely related to RMI is RMI-IIOP, which stands for Java Remote Method Invocation Run Over Internet Inter-Orb Protocol. RMI-IIOP was coproduced by Sun and IBM in order to achieve interoperability between CORBA-compliant applications and Java. Using the Java development language, you can create the Interface Definition Language (IDL) that will work with CORBA applications written in languages such as C++. The rmic compiler supports the option -iiop, which will produce the IDL files.

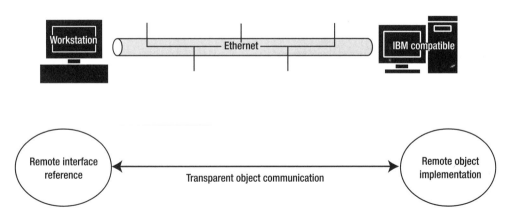

Figure 6-5. *Distributed object system*

The Delivery Stack

A transport protocol is a protocol built directly above the network layer; the two most common examples are TCP/IP and UDP. Above the transport layer is the transfer layer, which is responsible for the transparent transfer of data between hosts, flow control, and end-to-end error recovery and data transfer. The transport layer issues requests to the network layer. Figure 6-6 shows the technology stack complete with the network layer that RMI applications are built upon.

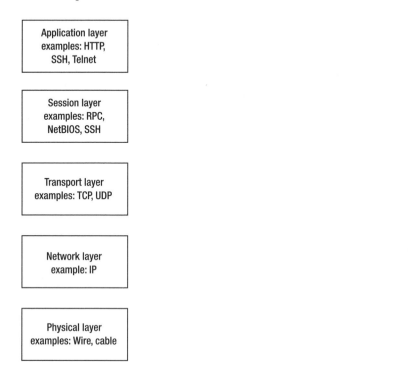

Figure 6-6. *The delivery stack*

A transfer protocol resides above a transport protocol and establishes how information is trasnferred between hosts. A very common example of a transfer protocol is Hypertext Transfer Protocol (HTTP). HTTP is the protocol for the World Wide Web. Java RMI does not use HTTP as a transfer protocol but instead uses the Java Remote Method Protocol (JRMP). One shortcoming to JRMP is that Java must be understood on both ends, the sending and receiving end, tying the solution to a Java RMI framework. To alleviate the dependency on Java, CORBA-related clients can be used by specifying -iiop for stub generation with the rmic tool. IIOP ensures the CORBA clients can be used with Java remote object implementations, thus reducing the dependency on a strictly Java solution.

Table 6-2 summarizes the three choices developers have for choosing a transfer protocol when using RMI.

Table 6-2. *RMI Transfer Protocols*

Protocol	Description
RMI-JRMP	The default transfer protocol for RMI. For client-server applications relying entirely on Java as the programming language. A Java-to-Java solution.
Java-IDL	For CORBA developers wanting to use Java in conjunction with interfaces defined in CORBA-compliant applications. Essentially this is a CORBA-to-Java solution.
Java RMI-IIOP	For Java developers needing to maintain compatibility with legacy applications. A Java-to-non-Java solution.

Return values and parameters are copies. Objects that are exported, or that implement a remote interface, are referenced via their stub, or client-side proxy. To export an object, extend UnicastRemoteObject or explicitly call UnicastRemoteObject.export(<remote object>).

The Pros and Cons of Using RMI as a Networking Protocol

For the developer exam, the examinee can choose between RMI or serialized objects over sockets for the networking protocol. Here are some of the reasons for selecting RMI over sockets:

Object-based semantics—Remote objects look and feel just like local objects. The complexities of network-aware objects can be hidden from the programs using RMI remote objects.

No protocol burden—Unlike sockets, when working with RMI there is no need to worry about designing a protocol between the client and server, a process that is error-prone.

Method calls are type-safe in RMI—RMI is more strongly typed than sockets. Errors can be caught at compile time.

It's easy to add new objects with RMI or extend the protocol—You can more easily add new remote object interfaces or add methods to an existing remote object.

IIOP can be used for non-Java end points—You are not explicitly tied to a Java-to-Java solution.

Generating stubs just got easier with J2SE 5.0—If JRMP is used, there is no need to generate stubs explicitly with rmic any longer. But we will still be required to do so for our project.

■**Caution** Even though Java 5.0 has added dynamic stub generation to alleviate RMI developers from explicitly invoking `rmic` on their remote classes prior to runtime, you must still do so for the certification project. This is important: **The use of `rmic` is still required** as of this writing for the Java developer certification project.

However, the relatively intuitive object semantics of RMI come at the expense of the network. There is communication overhead involved when using RMI, and that is due to lookups in the RMI registry and client stubs or proxies that make remote invocations transparent. For each RMI remote object, there is a need for a proxy, which slows the performance down.

Also it is important to be aware that thread management can sometimes cause issues if working with classes that are not designed around thread safety. Control and management of threads in RMI is delegated to the JVM and not the program.

The Classes and Interfaces of RMI

Figure 6-7 presents an overview of the classes and interfaces of RMI.

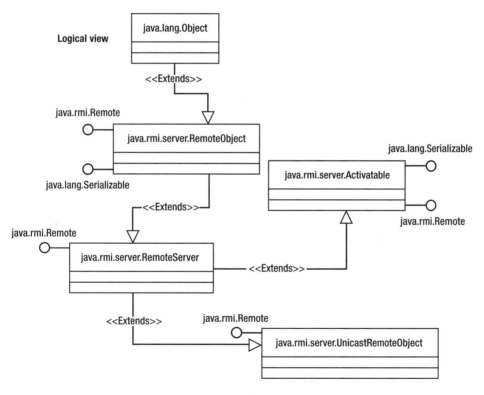

Figure 6-7. *The RMI classes and interfaces*

The Interfaces

The Remote interface is another marker interface, similar to the Serializable interface discussed earlier. The term *remote* indicates that the methods defined may be accessed from a different virtual machine than the one containing the remote object. For an object to be considered a remote object, the Remote interface must be implemented. Implementing this interface is accomplished by extending java.rmi.Remote.

Any public method defined in the Remote interface must throw a java.rmi.RemoteException or a super interface of java.rmi.RemoteException such as an IOException, Throwable, or Exception. This is the super class for all communication exceptions that occur during the invocation of a remote method. RemoteException is a checked exception and must therefore be enclosed in the try/catch block or specified in the method signature of any object that uses a remote object. A RemoteException may occur for either of the following reasons:

- The server is down, unreachable, or has terminated communication with the client.

- Errors were encountered during marshaling of params and return values.

One more interface is needed to create a remote object. The abstract class java.rmi. RemoteObject, which is displayed in Figure 6-7, must also be extended. You can think of RemoteObject as a remote object analog to java.lang.Object. RemoteObject provides the network implementations for the java.lang.Object methods toString(), hashCode(), and equals() that are appropriate for remote objects. Figure 6-8 shows the RMI layers.

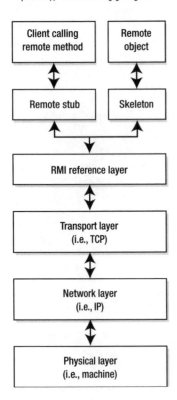

Figure 6-8. *RMI layers*

Another abstract class required for writing RMI programs is java.rmi.RemoteServer. The RemoteServer class is the common super class for server implementations and provides the framework to support a wide range of remote reference semantics. Specifically, the functions needed to create and export remote objects (i.e., to make them remotely available) are provided abstractly by RemoteServer and concretely by its subclasses. RemoteServer has two important subclasses: java.rmi.server.UnicastRemoteObject and java.rmi.Activatable.

Exporting remote objects is the responsibility of Activatable or UnicastRemoteObject. An Activatable object executes when requested and can turn itself off when necessary, whereas UnicastRemoteObject runs only when the server is up and running. An active object is one that has been instantiated and exported to a JVM. A passive object is one that has not been instantiated. Activation is the process of transforming a passive object into an active one. Lazy activation is the process of deferring activation until its first use. The Activatable interface provides RMI with the option of delaying access to persistent objects until needed. It is undesirable to permit an RMI server to use extensive system resources by loading a lot of remote objects that are infrequently used or not needed. Ideally, distributed systems should have access to thousands of persistent objects over very long, even indefinite, periods of time.

An RMI server that makes use of UnicastRemoteObject requires that remote objects be instantiated prior to a remote client invoking one of the remote methods. But in the case where we have many remote objects and the cost of instantiating all of them is prohibitive, an Activatable RMI server is an excellent alternative. With the Activatable interface used in conjunction with rmid, the RMI daemon, the server will instantiate the remote object when it is needed.

Luckily, we do not need to worry about this facet of resource management when implementing our RMI server, since we have only one remote object, BookDatabaseImpl, that acts as our RMI server and gateway to the database. We do not demonstrate an Activatable implementation in this book. Instead, we extend the UnicastRemoteObject class.

What Is an RMI Factory?

An RMI factory is just what the name would imply: an RMI version of the software design pattern aptly named the Factory pattern. As explained in Chapter 5 (which discussed data locking), we make use of an RMI factory to have a proper identifier mechanism for lock ownership. By ensuring that each RMI client has its own version of the DvdDatabase class, we avoid the issue of thread reuse, which is common in RMI and cannot be controlled explicitly through a JVM or RMI property. Since we cannot be sure how threads are being used and we are not allowed to use cookies or tokens to identify the requester, we exploit the Factory pattern to produce discrete instances of the DvdDatabase. The sequence-like diagram in Figure 6-9 depicts the typical actions and actors in a Factory pattern.

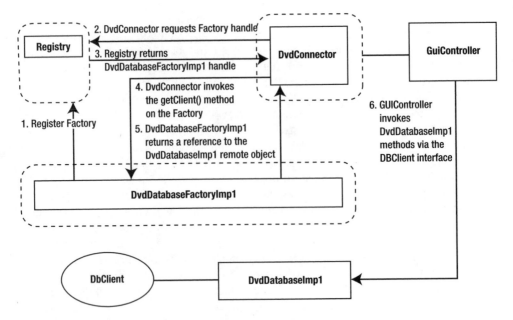

Figure 6-9. *The RMI Factory pattern applied to Denny's DVDs*

The Factory Pattern—What Is a Factory?

A *factory* is a software entity that creates other types of software entities. The client makes a request to a factory for a certain type of object, and out that object comes. Request a different type, and the factory will create and return the type requested. Of course, the factory needs to know how to create the requested object; otherwise the factory will complain that it doesn't understand the request. For instance, you wouldn't request a personal computer from a factory specializing in producing cars. Likewise, our factory will understand how to create remote objects. In particular, our factory will make a special type of remote object, a DvdDatabase.

Our factory is not a very robust factory in the sense that we only mass-produce one object type, a DvdDatabase. One of the most common motivations for implementing an RMI factory is to reduce the number of remote objects that need to be registered. This allows us to register the factory only once and gradually evolve and add new remote classes without having to register the new classes or even restart the registry. This is a nice by-product of an RMI factory even though it doesn't apply in our situation.

The RMI factory we implement in Denny's DVDs is an example of a parameterized Factory pattern, which is a type of creational pattern (i.e., patterns that involve the creation of objects and/or types; a singleton is another common example of a creational pattern). It is a variant of the parameterized pattern because we do not actually supply a name or parameter to the getClient method. It could be written getClient(String class_name_to_create). However, since our application only has one remote interface, DvdDatabaseRemote, the type of class is implied. We do not need to specify. But we could easily modify this method or the factory to return multiple remote objects.

The RMI Implementation

To create a version of our server that acts as a factory, we first define the factory and its only method, getClient(), which allows us to obtain a unique instance of the DvdDatabase class (see Listing 6-4).

■**Note** In this section we are talking about using the Factory pattern with our RMI solution, but it would work equally well with a sockets solution. However, the socket server already works essentially as a factory, creating a unique thread for each connected client, so we don't really need to explicitly create a unique object for each connected client. The very nature of a multithreaded socket server addresses the issue of thread reuse in an RMI thread pool.

Listing 6-4. *DvdDatabaseFactory.java*

```
interface DvdDatabaseFactory extends Remote  {
    public DvdDatabaseRemote getClient() throws RemoteException;
}

class DvdDatabaseFactoryImpl extends UnicastRemoteObject
    implements DvdDatabaseFactory {
    /**
     * A version number for this class so that serialization can occur
     * without worrying about the underlying class changing between
     * serialization and deserialization.
     */
    private static final long serialVersionUID = 5165L;

    public DvdDatabaseFactoryImpl() throws RemoteException {
                //do nothing constructor
    }

    public DvdDatabaseRemote getClient() throws RemoteException {
                return new DvdDatabaseImpl();
    }
}
```

Now we define the DvdDatabase remote class, which like any other Remote object, extends java.rmi.Remote in the interface and extends UnicastRemoteObject in the Implementation class:

```
public interface DvdDatabaseRemote extends Remote, DBClient {
}
public class DvdDatabaseImpl extends UnicastRemoteObject implements
DvdDatabaseRemote {
 ... refer to code base for the rest of implementation...
}
```

Finally, we can export the factory instance to the RMI registry found in the register() method in the RegDvdDatabase class. The createRegistry() method starts the Java RMI registry programmatically:

```
public static void register(int port) throws java.rmi.RemoteException, ➥
                        java.net.MalformedURLException{

        //the default rmi port is 1099.
        java.rmi.registry.LocateRegistry.createRegistry(port);

        DvdDatabaseFactoryImpl dvdFactoryImplementation
                = new DvdDatabaseFactoryImpl();

        //register
        Naming.rebind("DvdMediator", dvdFactoryImplementation);
    }
```

■**Note** Starting the registry programmatically is a new project requirement. Sun no longer allows starting the RMI Registry in a separate step.

Our RegDvdDatabase class binds the name DvdMediator to our remote object instance. When the client (soon to be a Swing GUI in the next chapter) requests a remote reference to our database application, it will require the services of the DVDConnector class. The DVDConnector either returns a remote object or a DvdDatabase, which is the database wrapper for the DvdFileAccess class; both are DBClients.

It is important to realize that we are only exporting the factory—we do not ever need to export the DvdDatabase remote object. In the DvdDatabaseFactory class we return the remote object DvdDatabase:

```
        public DvdDatabaseRemote getClient() throws RemoteException {
                return new DvdDatabaseImpl();
            }
```

And the reason for the factory in the first place is the new instance of the database itself, which can be found in the constructor of our DvdDatabase remote implementation:

```
public DvdDatabaseImpl() throws RemoteException {
        try {
            db = new DvdDatabase();
        } catch (FileNotFoundException e) {
            throw new RemoteException(e.getMessage());
        } catch (IOException e) {
            throw new RemoteException(e.getMessage());
        }
    }
}
```

We now have a unique instance of the DvdDatabaseImpl class for each connected client. If each DvdDatabaseImpl has its own instance of DvdDatabase, then the instance of DvdDatabase can be used to identify the client to the ReservationManager.

Since using a factory will work for both a socket solution and an RMI solution, and since we are building **both** socket connectivity and RMI connectivity in this book, we will present the ReservationManager code as though a factory solution is being used.

Let's demonstrate the use of a factory and compare it to a nonfactory scenario. Included in the downloaded code are two classes, RmiFactoryExample.java and RmiNoFactoryExample.java. As you can probably surmise from the names, one class serves as a factory implementation test case, while the other serves as a test case for a nonfactory implementation. The RmiFactoryExample class demonstrates how multiple instances of the DvdDatabase is instantiated, and the RmiNoFactoryExample class demonstrates how multiple requests result in reuse of our DvdDatabase instance.

Both sample programs extend Thread and implement the run method. The main in each sample test program also spawns two threads to simulate a multiuser environment. The only difference between the two test programs involves which remote object gets registered. The RmiNoFactoryExample registers a DvdDatabase remote object, while the RmiFactoryExample registers the DvdDatabaseFactory remote object. Correspondingly, the run methods must cast the appropriate remote interface returned from the lookup method. Refer to Listings 6-5 and 6-6.

Listing 6-5. *The Main Method in the RmiNoFactoryExample Class*

```java
public static void main(String[] args) throws Exception {
    LocateRegistry.createRegistry(1099);
    Naming.rebind("RmiNoFactoryExample", new DvdDatabaseImpl());
    Thread a = new RmiNoFactoryExample("A");
    a.start();
    Thread.sleep(1000);
    Thread b = new RmiNoFactoryExample("B");
    b.start();
    a.join();
    b.join();
    System.exit(0);
}

public void run() {
    try {
        System.out.println("getting a remote handle to a DvdDatabase."
            + this.hashCode());
        DvdDatabaseRemote remote
            = (DvdDatabaseRemote)Naming.lookup("RmiNoFactoryExample");
    }
    catch (Exception e) {
        System.err.println(e);
        e.printStackTrace();
    }
}
```

The code for RmiFactoryExample is very similar, with the following differences in the main method:

```
Naming.rebind("RmiFactoryExample", new DvdDatabaseFactoryImpl());
```

Listing 6-6 shows the run method for RmiFactoryExample.

Listing 6-6. *The Main Method in the RmiNoFactoryExample Class*

```
public void run() {
    try {
        System.out.println("Getting a remote handle to a factory. " ➥
            + this.hashCode());
        DvdDatabaseFactory factory
            = (DvdDatabaseFactory)Naming.lookup("RmiFactoryExample");
        DvdDatabaseRemote worker = factory.getClient();
    }
    catch (Exception e) {
        System.err.println(e);
        e.printStackTrace();
    }
}
```

To run the RmiNoFactoryExample test program, type the following command in the classes directory of the sampleproject:

```
java sampleproject.remote.RmiNoFactoryExample
```

And to run the RmiFactoryExample, type:

```
java sampleproject.remote.RmiFactoryExample
```

Figure 6-10 shows the output of running the two test programs.

In the DvdDatabase class, an output line was added to indicate that the constructor was called. The following println statement has been inserted into the DvdDatabase constructor:

```
System.out.println(" constructing a DvdDatabase object " + this.hashCode());
```

Examining the output of the two test programs indicates a critical difference: the number of DvdDatabase objects constructed. The RmiFactoryExample constructs two separate instances of the object. The RmiNoFactoryExample constructs only one. This demonstrates how RMI reuses threads. Each thread has a separate DvdDatabase object, but since the RmiNoFactoryExample reuses one of the threads, the DvdDatabase instance is shared between the two remote invocations. Thus we cannot ensure thread safety and our locking strategy fails. (Refer to the section in Chapter 5 on locking to review why the locking strategy requires a unique DvdDatabase object.)

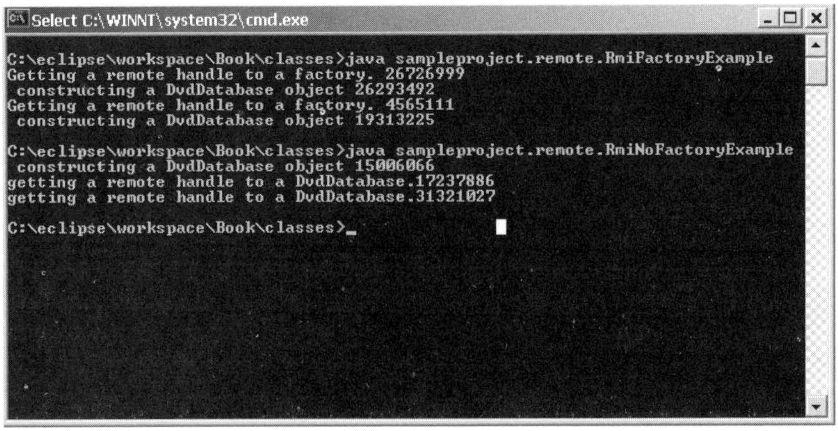

Select C:\WINNT\system32\cmd.exe
C:\eclipse\workspace\Book\classes>java sampleproject.remote.RmiFactoryExample
Getting a remote handle to a factory. 26726999
constructing a DvdDatabase object 26293492
Getting a remote handle to a factory. 4565111
constructing a DvdDatabase object 19313225
C:\eclipse\workspace\Book\classes>java sampleproject.remote.RmiNoFactoryExample
constructing a DvdDatabase object 15006066
getting a remote handle to a DvdDatabase.17237886
getting a remote handle to a DvdDatabase.31321027
C:\eclipse\workspace\Book\classes>_

Figure 6-10. *RMI factory examples*

However, the `RmiFactoryExample` creates two separate instances of the `DvdDatabase` object, as evidenced by the two constructor output messages, for each remote invocation.

We would like to expose the public methods as remote methods so our Swing GUI can invoke them. Figure 6-11 shows a class diagram of our remote class.

java.rmi
Remote
sampleproject.db
DBClient
sampleproject.remote
DVDDatabaseRemote
sampleproject.remote
DVDDatabaseImp1

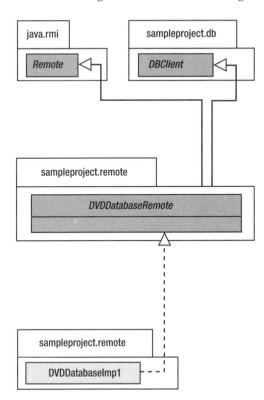

Figure 6-11. *DvdDatabaseRemote class diagram*

■**Note** Since the advantages that `Activatable` bestows are beyond the requirements of our project, we have opted to extend the simpler, more straightforward `UnicastRemoteObject` class.

The code for the remote interface is rather concise, as shown in Listing 6-7.

Listing 6-7. *The DvdDatabaseRemote.java*

```
package sampleproject.remote;

import java.rmi.Remote;
import sampleproject.db.*;

/**
 * The remote interface for the GUI-Client.
 * Exactly matches the DBClient interface in the db package.
 *
 * @author Denny DVD
 * @version 2.0
 */
public interface DvdDatabaseRemote extends Remote, DBClient {
}
```

To understand what behavior this interface is actually defining, it's useful to examine the DBClient class. That class diagram is shown in Figure 6-12, and the code file is shown in Listing 6-8.

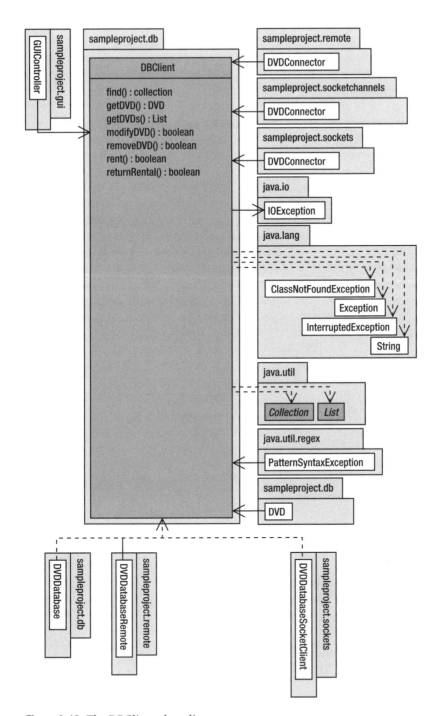

Figure 6-12. *The DBClient class diagram*

Listing 6-8. *DBClient.java*

```java
public interface DBClient {
    /**
     * Adds a DVD to the database or inventory.
     *
     * @param dvd The DVD item to add to inventory.
     * @return Indicates the success/failure of the add operation.
     * @throws IOException Indicates there is a problem accessing the database.
     */
    public boolean addDVD(DVD dvd) throws IOException;

    /**
     * Locates a DVD using the UPC identification number.
     *
     * @param UPC The UPC of the DVD to locate.
     * @return The DVD object which matches the UPC.
     * @throws IOException if there is a problem accessing the data.
     */
    public DVD getDVD(String UPC)throws IOException;

    /**
     * Changes existing information of a DVD item.
     * Modifications can occur on any of the attributes of DVD except UPC.
     * The UPC is used to identify the DVD to be modified.
     *
     * @param dvd The Dvd to modify.
     * @return Returns true if the DVD was found and modified.
     * @throws IOException Indicates there is a problem accessing the data.
     */
    public  boolean modifyDVD(DVD dvd) throws IOException;

    /**
     * Removes DVDs from inventory using the unique UPC.
     *
     * @param UPC The UPC or key of the DVD to be removed.
     * @return Returns true if the UPC was found and the DVD was removed.
     * @throws IOException Indicates there is a problem accessing the data.
     */
    public  boolean removeDVD(String UPC) throws IOException;

    /**
     * Gets the store's inventory.
     * All of the DVDs in the system.
     *
     * @return A List containing all found DVDs.
```

```
 * @throws IOException Indicates there is a problem accessing the data.
 */
public List<DVD> getDVDs() throws IOException;

 /**
  * A properly formatted <code>String</code> expressions returns all
  * matching DVD items. The <code>String</code> must be formatted as a
  * regular expression.
  *
  * @param query The formatted regular expression used as the search
  * criteria.
  * @return The list of DVDs that match the query. Can be an empty
  * Collection.
  * @throws IOException Indicates there is a problem accessing the data.
  * @throws PatternSyntaxException Indicates there is a syntax problem in
  * the regular expression.
  */
public Collection<DVD> findDVD(String query)
        throws IOException, PatternSyntaxException;

/**
 * Lock the requested DVD. This method blocks until the lock succeeds,
 * or for a maximum of 5 seconds, whichever comes first.
 *
 * @param UPC The UPC of the DVD to reserve
 * @throws InterruptedException Indicates the thread is interrupted.
 * @throws IOException on any network problem
 */
boolean reserveDVD(String UPC) throws IOException, InterruptedException;

/**
 * Unlock the requested record. Ignored if the caller does not have
 * a current lock on the requested record.
 *
 * @param UPC The UPC of the DVD to release
 * @throws IOException on any network problem
 */
void releaseDVD(String UPC) throws IOException;
}
```

To complete an RMI implementation we need one more class. The class that actually implements the remote interface is displayed in Listing 6-9. Most of the code has been omitted for brevity, but the unexpurgated version can be viewed in the project download from the Source Code section of the Apress website. One of the important things to note is that we extend UnicastRemoteObject rather than Activatable. We also implement DVDDatabaseRemote. This will ensure that the proper methods are implemented.

Listing 6-9. *DvdDatabaseImpl.java*

```java
public class DvdDatabaseImpl extends UnicastRemoteObject
        implements DvdDatabaseRemote {
    /**
     * A version number for this class so that serialization can occur
     * without worrying about the underlying class changing between
     * serialization and deserialization.
     */
    private static final long serialVersionUID = 5165L;

    /**
     * The Logger instance. All log messages from this class are routed through
     * this member. The Logger namespace is <code>sampleproject.remote</code>.
     */
    private static Logger log = Logger.getLogger("sampleproject.remote");

    /**
     * The database handle.
     */
    private DBClient db = null;

    /**
     * DvdDatabaseImpl default constructor
     * @throws RemoteException Thrown if a <code>DvdDatabaseImpl</code>
     * instance cannot be created.
     */
    public DvdDatabaseImpl() throws RemoteException {
        try {
            db = new DvdDatabase();
        } catch (FileNotFoundException e) {
            throw new RemoteException(e.getMessage());
        } catch (IOException e) {
            throw new RemoteException(e.getMessage());
        }
    }

    /**
     * Returns the sampleproject.db.Dvd object matching the UPC.
     *
     * @param upc The upc code of the DVD to retrieve.
     * @return The matching DVD object.
     * @throws RemoteException  Thrown if an exception occurs in the
     * <code>DvdDatabaseImpl</code> class.
     * @throws IOException Thrown if an <code>IOException</code> is
     * encountered in the <code>db</code> class.
     * <br>
     * For more information, see {@link DvdDatabase}.
```

```
 * @throws ClassNotFoundException Thrown if a
 * <code>ClassNotFoundException</code> is
 * encountered in the <code>db</code> class.
 * <br>
 * For more information, see {@link DvdDatabase}.
 */
public DVD getDVD(String upc) throws RemoteException, IOException {
    return db.getDVD(upc);
}

/**
 * Gets the store's inventory.
 * All of the DVDs in the system.
 *
 * @return A collection of all found DVDs.
 * @throws IOException Indicates there is a problem accessing the data.
 * @throws ClassNotFoundException Indicates the Dvd class definition cannot
 * be found.
 */
public List<DVD> getDVDs() throws IOException {
    return db.getDVDs();
}

/**
 * A properly formatted <code>String</code> expressions returns all matching
 * DVD items. The <code>String</code> must be formatted as a regular
 * expression.
 *
 * @param query A regular expression search string.
 * @return A Collection of DVD objects that match
 * the search criteria.
 * @throws IOException Thrown if an IOException is
 * encountered in the db class.
 * @throws ClassNotFoundException Thrown if an
 * ClassNotFoundException is encountered in the
 * db class.
 * @throws PatternSyntaxException Thrown if a
 * PatternSyntaxException is encountered in the
 * db class.
 */
public  Collection<DVD> findDVD(String query)
        throws IOException, PatternSyntaxException {
    return db.findDVD(query);
}

/**
 * Modifies a DVD database entry specified by a DVD object.
```

```
 *
 * @param item The DVD to modify.
 * @return A boolean indicating the success or failure of the modify
 * operation.
 * @throws RemoteException  Thrown if an exception occurs in the
 * <code>DvdDatabaseImpl</code> class.
 * @throws IOException Thrown if an <code>IOException</code> is
 * encountered in the <code>db</code> class.
 * <br>
 * For more information, see {@link DvdDatabase}.
 */
public boolean modifyDVD(DVD item) throws
                                        RemoteException,
                                        IOException {
    return db.modifyDVD(item);
}


/**
 * Removes a DVD database entry specified by a UPC.
 *
 * @param upc The UPC number of the DVD to remove.
 * @return A boolean indicating the success or failure of the removal
 * operation.
 * @throws RemoteException  Thrown if an exception occurs in the
 * DvdDatabaseImpl class.
 * @throws IOException Thrown if an IOException is
 * encountered in the db class.
 * <br>
 * For more information, see {@link DvdDatabase}.
 */
public boolean removeDVD(String upc) throws
                                        RemoteException,
                                        IOException {
    return db.removeDVD(upc);
}


/**
 * Lock the requested DVD. This method blocks until the lock succeeds,
 * or for a maximum of 5 seconds, whichever comes first.
 *
 * @param upc The UPC of the DVD to reserve
 * @throws InterruptedException Indicates the thread is interrupted.
 */
public boolean reserveDVD(String upc)
        throws InterruptedException, IOException {
    return db.reserveDVD(upc);
}
```

```
/**
 * Unlock the requested record. Ignored if the caller does not have
 * a current lock on the requested record.
 *
 * @param upc The UPC of the DVD to release
 */
public void releaseDVD(String upc) throws IOException {
    db.releaseDVD(upc);
}

/**
 * Adds a DVD to the database or inventory.
 *
 * @param dvd The DVD item to add to inventory.
 * @return Indicates the success/failure of the add operation.
 * @throws IOException Indicates there is a problem accessing the database.
 */
public boolean addDVD(DVD dvd) throws IOException, RemoteException {
    return db.addDVD(dvd);
}
}
```

This DVDDatabaseImpl source code is interesting since it accesses the database via a wrapper, or an adapter, called the DvdDatabase. We could have easily placed the actual database method implementations, found in the class DvdFileAccess, directly in the remote object DvdDatabaseImpl. Or we could have extended UnicastRemoteObject on DVDFileAccess and made that object the remote object. We chose to do it this way for the following reasons:

- Adding a level of abstraction between the RMI implementation and the actual database-level code makes it a clearer object-oriented design and helps to separate the RMI details from the application logic details. We wanted to create a level of separation from the application logic and the two networking approaches: RMI and sockets. With the preceding design, we will be able to easily use either the socket or the RMI code depending on our preferences. We have eliminated any dependencies between the networking packages and the database packages. This will be clarified in the project wrap-up in Chapter 8.

- In order for our locking strategy to work properly, it is important that all database modification requests first achieve a lock prior to the modification identified with a unique DvdDatabase object. We require a unique instance of DvdDatabase in order to have a unique identifier for the lock method; otherwise we cannot ensure that the client who locked a record is the same one who is modifying, deleting, or even unlocking that same record. Once the lock is granted, the modification may safely occur. Finally we unlock the record. Because these operations must not occur in a synchronized method (see the "Locks" section in Chapter 4), and all of the modification methods in the database must be synchronized, we must access the database by way of our adapter.

All RMI implementations must be thread-safe because invocations on a particular object could occur concurrently if the RMI runtime spawns multiple threads. There is no guarantee regarding RMI thread management. Thus, it is your responsibility to make sure that remote object implementations are thread-safe. In our case, using an RMI factory pattern in collaboration with the reserveDVD and releaseDVD methods in the DvdDatabase class ensures that our implementation is thread-safe.

If you choose not to extend UnicastRemoteObject but rather call the class method UnicastRemoteObject.export in the constructor, then the object methods such as hashcode, toString, and equals must be implemented. Listing 6-10 shows how the class constructor and declaration would accommodate that approach (the rest of the code has been omitted for conciseness).

Listing 6-10. *Exporting UnicastRemoteObject*

```
public class DvdDatabaseImpl implements DvdDatabaseRemote
{
        public DvdDatabaseImpl() throws RemoteException {
                UnicastRemoteObject.exportObject(this);
            this.dvdDatabase = new DvdDatabase();
        }
}
```

Stubs and Skeletons

Only clients actually invoke methods on a *stub*, which is a local representation, or proxy, of the remote object. While it appears that the client is calling the remote object directly, unbeknownst to the client it is actually calling a proxy method in the stub that initiates communication with the destination VM. The stub is responsible for packaging the parameters of the remote method call prior to sending them across the network. The process of packaging the parameters prior to shipping them across a network is called *marshaling*.

On the other side of the wire, or server side of the network, the incoming invocation is eventually received by the remote reference layer, which demarshals the arguments and dispatches the call to the actual server object. The server then marshals the return value back to the caller on the client side.

J2SE 1.5 introduces a new feature that alleviates the need to separately generate stub classes for the client using the tool rmic. Now stub classes can be dynamically generated at runtime by the JVM. (However, we are still required to use rmic for stub generation in our submission.) To unconditionally generate stubs dynamically, set the JVM parameter java.rmi.server.ignoreStubClasses to true. This can be done using the -D option (i.e., java -Djava.rmi.server.ignoreStubClasses=true).

■**Note** You must still generate stub classes with rmic for backward compatibility with pre-J2SE 1.5 clients.

The tool `rmic` can be used in a number of ways depending on context. `rmic` allows for compatibility with previous versions of Java such as Java 1.1 (stubs and skeletons) and Java 1.2 (stubs only). J2SE 1.5 does not require the use of skeletons, but as we mentioned earlier, you must still use `rmic` with your project submission.

■Note The skeleton interface has been deprecated in the Java 2 platform (i.e., JDK version 1.2 and greater). To create stubs for version 1.2 only in our RMI implementation, we use the following syntax with `rmic`:

```
rmic -v1.2 sampleproject.remote.DVDDatabaseImpl
```

■Note RMI makes use of the Proxy design pattern. The Proxy pattern designates a surrogate object that controls access to the real object. There are three key players in this design pattern: a `Subject`, a `Proxy`, and a `Real-Subject`. The Proxy object has a reference to the `Real-Subject` and is responsible for communication to and from the `Real-Subject`. The `Subject` displays the same interface for both the `Proxy` and the `Real-Subject`. The `Real-Subject` is the actual implementation of the object the `Proxy` represents and that the `Subject` has defined. In RMI, the `Subject` corresponds to the remote implementation. The stub is the `Proxy` and the remote object implementation is the `Real-Subject`. Figure 6-13 illustrates the various elements in the Proxy design pattern.

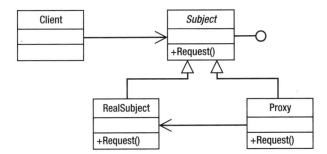

Figure 6-13. *The Proxy design pattern*

For backward stub//skeleton compatibility with previous versions of Java, you can read more about `rmic` at `http://java.sun.com/j2se/1.5.0/docs/tooldocs/windows/rmic.html` for Windows. For Unix, visit `http://java.sun.com/j2se/1.5.0/docs/tooldocs/solaris/rmic.html`.

Parameter Passing

RMI method invocations require communication between objects on different machines and in different JVMs, even though the call behaves as if it is a local call within the same JVM. This section describes how RMI transfers parameters and return values between different

JVMs. There are three classes of parameters and return values to consider: primitive types, Serializable objects, and remote objects.

■Note Arrays of primitives and arrays of Serializable objects can also be safely passed as a remote method parameter.

Primitive Types

RMI makes a copy of the primitive type for both method arguments and return values. When a copy of the primitive is sent across the wire, we say that the parameter or return value is *pass-by-value*.

Serializable Objects

When an object is marshaled across the wire as a method parameter or a return value, RMI makes a copy of the object and all of the objects it references as one large object graph. Object parameters are sent across the wire as pass-by-value, just like primitive types.

The object being passed must be Serializable or a NotSerializableException will be thrown. In addition, all of the class members of the object being marshaled must also be Serializable, unless the member is declared as a transient member or the Externalizable interface is implemented instead of Serializable.

Remote Objects

This is the most complex scenario of the three. When the item being returned is a remote object (i.e., one that implements java.rmi.Remote), the proxy for that object, or the stub, is returned in place of the Real-Object. In this way, remote objects are pass-by-reference and the stub is marshaled back and forth.

Remote objects, by default, implement Serializable. Table 6-3 summarizes how RMI handles various parameters and return values. RMI uses one of two mechanisms to obtain remote object references. The RMI registry is one way, and another is simply passing the proxy or stub, which was discussed previously. The RMI registry uses java.lang.Naming to store references to remote objects. java.rmi.Naming provides URL-based methods to associate name-object pairs located on a particular host and port. RMI can also load bytecodes with a valid URL naming protocol such as FTP or HTTP. When a client interacts with a remote object, it also interacts with the remote object interface, not with the actual remote implementation.

Table 6-3. *RMI Parameter Passing*

Object/Type	Parameter/Return Value
Remote objects	Pass-by-reference: A stub is passed instead of a copy.
Nonremote/serialized objects	Pass-by-value: An actual copy of an object is passed as a serialized object.
Primitive types	Pass-by-value: A copy is made.

Security and Dynamic Loading

Running an RMI application over a network requires that certain files be accessible to the server and client class loaders. Table 6-4 summarizes which files are required.

Table 6-4. *Class Loader Requirements*

Client Class Loader Requires	Server Class Loader Requires
Remote interfaces	Remote interfaces, remote implementations
Stubs for remote objects	Stubs for remote objects
Server classes used as return values	Skeletons for remote objects (JDK version 1.1 only)
Miscellaneous client classes	Miscellaneous server classes

When a client has the remote object stubs and class files locally, the task is much simpler and there are no special runtime considerations. However, if a client only has the remote interface, Java provides the capability to load the classes and stubs dynamically. Dynamic loading is the feature in RMI that allows for an object not available locally to be retrieved. Two important classes make dynamic loading possible: RMIClassLoader and SecurityManager. Besides these two important classes, you need to know the location of the classes to be loaded.

This is referred to as a code base. Think of a code base as similar to a classpath, except on a different machine accessible with a URL. A classpath would be analogous to a local code base. The codebase property is java.rmi.server.codebase. It would be specified on the command line as follows:

```
java -Djava.rmi.server.codebase <URL>
```

The java.rmi.server.RMIClasssLoader class is required for dynamic class loading when using RMI.

The RMIClassLoader class makes use of the codebase property. The RMIClassLoader class can load classes from either an applet or an RMI application. For our purposes, and the purposes of the certification exam, our discussion on security will be brief. We do not need to worry about security or policy files in our implementation, since our application does not use a security manager. Java 2 makes use of a security manager option due to compatibility with pre–Java 2 applications. However, in a professional RMI application, a security manager is a given. In addition, if your network application uses dynamic class loading, a security manager is required.

Firewall Issues

When the client and server are separated by a firewall, the RMI transport layer is forbidden from creating socket connections. In situations where a socket connection is prohibited, RMI makes use of a technique called HTTP tunneling. Tunneling is the process of wrapping RMI calls in an HTTP POST request, which firewalls typically allow.

Tunneling is done automatically. When a socket connection is denied by the transport layer, a last-ditch effort is made to service the request via HTTP tunneling.

■**Note** Java programs have permissions that are governed by policy files. The Java 2 security model requires that programs and the RMI registry have permission to create sockets. After all, RMI is based on sockets. The client also needs to specify a policy file on start-up. Here is how we would start the RMI registry to load a policy file other than the default: `rmiregistry -J-Djava.security.policy=ourSecurityFile.policy`.

Port 80 is used as the default port unless one is specified in the server property `http.proxyHost`. However, HTTP tunneling comes with a number of costs. Performance is sacrificed and security can be compromised. Tunneling can be disabled by setting the server property `java.rmi.server.disableHttp` to true.

Summary

This chapter covered a great deal of information. First, we reviewed serialization.

Any object that can potentially be sent across a network must be serialized prior to its trip across the wire. Both sockets (which will be discussed in the next chapter) and RMI require serialization. In RMI, both the return values and the method parameters must be serializable for the application to work.

Finally, we explored RMI in depth and implemented an RMI solution for Denny's DVDs. Considering the amount of effort that went into building the socket implementation, we were able to appreciate the amount of work RMI does under the hood. We did not have to worry about writing a multithreaded server, since RMI handles that aspect for us. We also did not have to worry about creating command and result objects in order to implement an application protocol.

However, RMI did require us to define a remote interface and make sure that all of our method parameters were serializable. Additionally, we had to concern ourselves with registering our remote object with the RMI naming service and starting the RMI registry so that our object is accessible to a remote client. We hope you have learned enough about serialization, sockets, and RMI so that you can design and implement a complete networking solution for the SCJD exam. Using this project networking package as a guide, along with the chapter, you should be adequately prepared.

FAQ

Q Is RMI thread-safe?

A No. The J2SE 1.4 RMI specification makes no guarantee regarding the number of threads that will have access to your remote object. For this reason, your design has to take into account issues of thread safety. See Chapter 4 for details on locking and thread safety. The approach we used in this chapter was to create an RMI factory ensuring a distinct instance of the `DvdDatabase` wrapper class and using that as our unique identifier for record locking.

Q Which method is better, RMI or sockets?

A Each approach has its strengths. Sockets are useful for sending large amounts of data (with or without a protocol) without a lot of overhead. With RMI it is much easier to implement a multithreaded server, since RMI handles the threading aspect for you. The remote object also behaves as if it is a local object complete with a protocol or set of public methods, whereas sockets require that you implement a protocol. It is really up to you, but both approaches should work fine as long as you understand the key technical issues pertaining to the protocol.

Q Is a security manager, or some sort of authentication, required?

A This depends largely on the details of your exam. Read the instructions very carefully! Each test is different. In this chapter, we briefly discussed a number of security issues such as policy files, dynamic class loading, HTTP tunneling, firewalls, and security managers. However, in our implementation, we do include a security manager and do not make use of policy files.

Q Do I need to include the skeletons in my J2SE 5.0 implementation of RMI?

A Yes. Skeletons are only required for those Java versions prior to 1.2 (i.e., version 1.1). By default, skeletons are generated when `rmic` is run on your remote object implementations, but you can control this feature by using the `-keep v1.2` option of `rmic`. However, at the time of this writing, the certification project still requires that stubs be included with your submission and that you do not rely on the dynamic stub generation technique in the Tiger version (i.e., J2SE 5.0).

Q Am I required to start the RMI registry manually?

A No. The registry must be started programmatically. Again, read the instructions on your exam. But most likely, you will be required to start the registry as we did in the `RegDVDDatabase` class. The class has a `register` method that binds the remote object implementation class in the RMI naming service and uses the `LocateRegistry.register` method. When running this across a network, as we will in Chapter 8, you should call the `getRemote` method in `Connector` from a `main` method.

CHAPTER 7

■■■

Networking with Sockets

This chapter describes how to build the Denny's DVDs networking layer by using sockets. Sockets are a software abstraction that allows applications to communicate with each other across a network. Any connection between two machines over IP (Internet Protocol) requires the use of sockets. Java provides programmers with the ability to connect application sockets, but as we will see in this chapter, much work needs to be done to ensure that clients and servers can communicate effectively using standard sockets. To alleviate some of that effort, Java also provides the Remote Method Invocation (RMI) framework, which is built on top of sockets. As you learned in the previous chapter, however, using RMI introduces its own problems. Either networking solution has its pros and cons, and it is up to you as a developer to determine which one you feel is better for a given situation. In this chapter, we will detail a simple sockets solution for our sample project, providing you with what you need to make an informed decision regarding which solution to use in your Sun assignment.

Our major areas to cover include

- An overview of sockets

- Why you would want to use sockets

- The basic information required for connecting sockets

- How to build a TCP socket client

- How to build a TCP socket server

- Serialized objects with sockets

- Socket lifecycles

Socket Overview

A *socket* is one of the endpoints in a communication link between two programs and is always bound to a port. A socket connection is useful for connecting to remote machines, and sending and receiving data. To create a socket connection, you will need the host address to which you want to connect and the port number. Sockets are not specific to Java. However, all versions of Java since JDK 1.0 have provided facilities for creating sockets. As with RMI, the discussion is demarcated by client and server considerations.

The server is a listening service that receives connection requests from socket clients. When a request is granted, the server establishes a socket-to-socket connection. The client will use the server's hostname (or IP address) and port to request a connection. On the server side of the network, `java.net.ServerSocket` is the class that listens for connection requests from socket clients. The class `java.net.Socket` is one of the endpoints of a socket connection. Both the server and the client will have an instance of `java.net.Socket` per socket connection.

Why Use Sockets

Choosing between sockets and RMI is one of the biggest decisions you will have to make for the certification project. But each choice comes with its own advantages and trade-offs. If the JavaRanch web forum on the certification exam is any indication, it seems that most developers opt for the RMI solution. In fact, in the first edition of this book we recommended using RMI instead of sockets just because we believed at the time that the approach seemed more intuitive from a Java programmer's perspective. However, since then we have backed off from this assertion. Either RMI or sockets will work fine and both are reasonably straightforward to implement. But for the adventurous at heart, let's discuss some of the reasons you might opt for a socket solution.

Socket servers are more scalable and faster than RMI servers. Acquiring a remote object handle requires a network call in the form of a Registry lookup. In addition, each remote object has a client-side proxy, or stubs, which effectively adds an object layer between the client and the actual remote object implementation class. This communication overhead is paid for in terms of performance.

Typically one of the reasons mentioned for *not* using sockets is the implicit contract, or application protocol, that needs to be in place between the socket clients and the socket server. We discuss this in more detail later in this chapter in the section "The Application Protocol." However, what if the protocol is very simple? In cases where the socket interface is simple, sockets are an excellent choice.

One final reason worth considering a socket implementation involves threading. Each socket client request in our socket solution spawns a new thread, which we can use to maintain a lock on the `DvdDatabase`. This means we do not have to worry about implementing a factory as we did with RMI. The very nature of our socket solution avoids this potentially complicating issue. Of course, you now have to deal with the problem of developing a multithreaded socket server, but help is on the way! Denny's DVDs is a multithreaded socket server, and we describe our server implementation later in this chapter.

Socket Basics

In this section, we will explore the types of sockets available to the Java programmer as well as some of the fundamental concepts related to socket development.

Addresses

An address is a unique number used to identify a device connected to a network, much like a postal address identifies the location of a building in a city. An IP address is a unique number, usually consisting of 12 digits or more, that is technically a 32-bit or 128-bit unsigned number used by the Internet protocol (i.e., IP) and for sending messages between socket addresses on TCP- or UDP-based networks. The `java.net.InetAddress` class is the Java class that encapsulates an IP address for use with Java sockets.

■**Note** The 32-bit addressing scheme used by TCP/IP has been around since the 1970s. With more and more devices requiring Internet addresses, it is estimated that all currently available addresses will be used somewhere between 2016 and 2023 (however, previous estimates on Internet growth have been far below reality, so this figure is not to be relied on). To alleviate this problem, a new addressing scheme has been recommended and is slowly being implemented. The 32-bit addressing scheme is known as IPv4, and the new addressing scheme is known as IPv6. Java supports both schemes with the `Inet4Address` class and `Inet6Address` classes, respectively. In this chapter we will be using IPv4 as this is the most common addressing scheme currently in use.

TCP and UDP Sockets Overview

Over the years programming has evolved from manually setting binary instructions (1GL or first-generation languages), through assembly language (2GL), human-readable languages (Java, C++), and specification languages like SQL (4GL). The later languages do not eliminate the need for the lower-level languages—they just do the hard work of translating the programmer's code into lower-level code. For example, when programming in Java your code will be translated into bytecode by the Java compiler (corresponding roughly to the output from an assembly language program), which is later translated into the binary instructions for the computer by the JVM. While you can still find work as a machine language programmer, many programmers find that such work is slow and error prone—working in a higher-level language such as Java can greatly improve productivity and quality of work.

Similarly, network protocols have evolved over the years, so that we no longer need to worry ourselves with the lowest-level network details. When you are programming your Java program, you typically do not care how to physically send signals over a piece of wire (or other medium), nor do you care whether your computers are communicating over an Ethernet or a Token Ring network; all you care about is how to make the connection. Finally, in order to use sockets, we will be using IP rather than one of the other network layers (X.25, ICMP, IPX). But even having chosen to use sockets, leaving all the low-level communication to the IP layer and layers beneath it, we still have a choice between TCP and UDP sockets.

UDP Sockets

User Datagram Protocol (UDP) enables machines on a network to send datagram packets to each other. UDP sockets work in much the same way as the U.S. postal system. Messages, or letters, are sent to a particular address and an immediate response by the server, or addressee, endpoint is not necessary. UDP sockets do not require a two-way connection. Similarly, the postal system does not require that the recipient be present when a letter is delivered.

Let's consider the mail analogy a little more. A letter is dropped off at a mailbox and delivered to the stated address. The mail carrier then places the letter in the destination mailbox. The mail system does not require that someone be there to accept the letter (of course, I realize that sometimes packages require signatures, but for the sake of convenience let's ignore those kinds of packages for now). Once the individual to whom the letter is addressed returns home, he or she can then collect the mail.

UDP discards corrupted messages (datagrams) so there is no guarantee that messages sent via UDP will make it to their final destination, just as there is no guarantee that a letter sent through the postal system will make it to the intended recipient. The main classes used are DatagramSocket and DatagramPacket in the Java API. A *packet* is information in the form of byte sequences that are sent across a network. Since messages are not guaranteed to be delivered and can be received out of order, UDP socket applications have to deal with reordering and data loss.

Efficiency and flexibility are the main reasons you would choose a UDP socket approach. We do not use UDP for a few reasons. First, efficiency is not something that is an overriding concern. Second, and most important, the exam does not permit a UDP approach. So that sort of makes our decision rather clear-cut. But if we were to use a UDP approach, then both the client and the server would use a DataGramSocket class for sending and receiving DataGramPacket objects. The remainder of this chapter and the sample project use TCP sockets instead of UDP sockets, so our discussion of UDP will end here.

■**Caution** The exam requirements tend to be vague regarding this point. Most likely the instructions read "You must use either serialized objects over a simple socket connection, or RMI." It is not precisely clear as to what a simple socket is and whether this precludes a UDP solution. We take it to mean that you should use the java.net.Socket class and not the java.net.DatagramSocket class. While it would be technically feasible to create a UDP solution for this assignment, doing so would require a lot of work in developing packet-handling code, and would go against the standard expected usage of UDP (simple, short [often less than 100 bytes] messages). We therefore recommend that, if you're using sockets as the networking protocol, you use the simpler TCP approach. However, that being said, you should always refer to your specific exam for instructions.

UDP is designed for minimal messaging applications—the very small messages that you might use if you were trying to monitor network applications, such as SNMP (Simple Network Management Protocol)—or for very simple query/responses, such as DNS (Domain Name System) queries. It is better to use TCP for larger messages, such as the large messages that are possible in response to a database query in our sample application. The next section describes how to develop a socket solution using TCP.

TCP Sockets

TCP stands for Transmission Control Protocol—a protocol that controls the transmission of packets so that messages are guaranteed to be received and that packets are received in the same order as they were sent. To meet these guarantees, the TCP protocol uses slightly more network traffic than UDP (and since RMI provides more features and guarantees than a plain TCP socket, it uses even more network traffic than TCP). However, since the protocol provides these features for us, we do not have to verify the order in which packets are received in our application. This makes it a much better choice for Denny's DVDs.

A TCP socket is a socket connection that utilizes a TCP/IP connection as its underlying transfer protocol. Each end of the connection is identified with an IP address and a port number. TCP socket clients send requests, and TCP socket servers listen for requests.

The following are the basic steps involved in TCP socket communication:

1. Create an instance of a socket class.

2. Send serialized messages using the socket I/O streams.

3. Close the socket connection.

■**Note** For the initial connection there are two requirements: a socket client that sends the initial connection request and a socket server that is listening for incoming connection requests. But once the connection has been set up, you have a connection between two sockets, and either one can send or receive data. It is up to the communication protocol to determine which socket is sending data and which socket is receiving data at any given time. We will cover application protocols in the section "The Application Protocol" later in this chapter. As you might imagine, if either client or server does not follow the application protocol, the point-to-point communication will break down.

TCP Socket Clients

The class `java.net.Socket` is responsible for implementing a socket-to-socket connection.

The constructor for this class, which actually attempts to connect to the destination machine, requires both the hostname as a URL (as a string) and the port of the destination machine. Table 7-1 lists the various public constructors for `java.net.Socket`.

Table 7-1. *Public Constructors for java.net.Socket*

Socket Class	Socket Class Constructors
`public Socket()`	Creates an unconnected socket.
`public Socket(InetAddress address, int port)`	The most commonly used. Creates a connected socket to the supplied address and port.
`public Socket(InetAddress address, int port, InetAddress localAddr, int localPort)`	Creates a socket that connects to the remote address and port and also binds to the local address and port.
`public Socket(String host, int port)`	Creates a stream socket and connects it to the specified host and port.
`public Socket(String host, int port, InetAddress localAddr, int localPort)`	Connects to a remote host and port and binds to the local address and port.

Once a socket connection is made, you can obtain information about the connection through a variety of getter methods. The client-side socket is not bound to the port number the server is residing on. Rather, the client-side socket is assigned a local port it uses to communicate with the server.

A number of constants are defined in the interface SocketOptions. These constants are used as settings to customize a client socket. We do not implement the SocketOptions interface directly, but we have access to its constants through getter and setter methods in the Socket class. In the sections that follow, we discuss a few of the more useful options.

Using SO_TIMEOUT

When reading data from a socket through the use of the input stream's read method, the call blocks other requests as determined by this setting. The SO_TIMEOUT option determines the amount of time in milliseconds that blocking operations can block until they time out. If the operation does not complete in the allotted time, then a java.net.SocketTimeoutException is thrown, as shown in Figure 7-1. If this option has not been set or is set to 0, then the call blocks requests until complete and will not time out.

Figure 7-1. *A SocketTimeoutException*

The Socket methods used for setting and getting this option are as follows:

```
public void setSoTimeout(int timeout) throws SocketException
public int getSoTimeout() throws SocketException
```

We use this option in DVDSocketServer.java, although we could just as easily have used this option in our socket client, DVDSocketClient.java. The following line will shut down the socket server after 1 minute, or 60,0000 milliseconds, of inactivity:

```
serverSocket.setSoTimeout(60000);
```

After the specified time elapses, a java.net.SocketTimeoutException is thrown. Figure 7.1 illustrates the DVDSocketServer console when the exception occurs.

Using SO_SNDBUF

This option sets the buffer size for data transmissions from this socket. When setting this option, it is merely a suggestion, or a hint, to the platform about the size of buffer the application requires for output operations over the socket. The getter indicates the actual size of the output buffer. These two methods can be used together to determine whether the platform was able to make use of the hint in the set method by a call to the get method after the output operation. The Socket methods used for setting and getting this option are as follows:

```
public int getSendBufferSize() throws SocketException
public void setSendBufferSize(int size) throws SocketException
```

The send buffer size value determines how many packets will be sent before waiting for an acknowledgment that the packets have been received at the other application. On a reliable network, you can set this to a high value to get the best throughput of data. In a worst-case scenario, you could set the send buffer to the same size as the packet size. In this case, for every packet sent, an acknowledgment would have to be received—if you needed to send 100 packets, you would need to receive 100 packets. Contrast this with a send buffer that is 100 times larger than the packet size—when sending the 100 packets you would have to receive only one packet; it would complete in nearly half the time.

Using SO_RCVBUF

This option is similar to SO_SNDBUF, which is used for setting the send buffers. The difference here is that this option deals with the receive buffers. As with the send buffer option, setting the receive buffer size value is actually a hint to the platform. To verify the size the buffer was set to, use the getReceiveBufferSize method. To improve the performance of a high-volume socket connection, increase the size of the receive buffer. Decreasing this value can reduce incoming backlog.

```
public void setReceiveBufferSize(int size) throws SocketException
public int getReceiveBufferSize() throws SocketException
```

Using SO_BINDADDR

This option indicates the local address that a socket is bound to. This option is read-only. A socket address cannot be changed after it is created and must be specified in the constructor. The method signature is as follows:

```
public InetAddress getLocalAddress()
```

One of the possible uses for this method is determining what IP address you are bound to when running on a computer with multiple IP addresses (e.g., a server with multiple network cards, a PC with both a local IP address and a networked address, or a computer with both a network address and a virtual private network address).

The DvdSocketClient

There are a few important points to note about the DVDSocketClient. The socket implementation in our sample project uses port 3000 by default. Also by default, we use localhost as the hostname. This is useful when we want to run our application in networking mode on one machine (i.e., when we do not have access to a network). If we run our application on different machines, we will have to specify the IP address of the machine that is running the socket server.

Another key point regarding the socket client is that it implements DBClient. This ensures that our rent and return methods are available to any client using DVDSocketServer. The DvdSocketClient.java is displayed in Listing 7-1. The entire source code for the sockets package can be downloaded from the Apress web site (http://www.apress.com) in the Source Code section—more details on what can be downloaded and how the code can be compiled and packaged are listed in Chapter 9.

■**Tip** On Linux and most Unix computers, you can also specify localhost.localdomain as the hostname. You can also use the loopback addresses (127.0.0.0–127.0.0.254) instead of the hostname. Accepted practice is to use 127.0.0.1 as the standard loopback address, leaving the other potential loopback addresses for specialist purposes (e.g., for testing multiple identical applications on different addresses simultaneously).

Listing 7-1. *DVDSocketClient.java*

```java
public class DvdSocketClient implements DBClient {
    /**
     * The socket client that gets instaniated for the socket connection.
     */
    private Socket socket = null;
    /**
     * The outputstream used to write a serialized object to a socket server.
     */
    private ObjectOutputStream oos = null;
    /**
     * The inputstream used to read a serialized object (a response)
     * from the socket server.
     */
    private ObjectInputStream ois = null;
    /**
     * The IP address of the machine the client is going to attempt a
     * connection.
     */
    private String ip = null;
    /**
     * The port number we will be connecting on.
     */
    private int port = 3000;
    /**
     * Default constructor.
     */
    public DvdSocketClient () throws UnknownHostException, IOException {
        this("localhost", "3000");
    }
```

```java
/**
 * Constructor takes in a hostname of the server to connect.
 *
 * @param hostname The hostname to connect to.
 * @throws NumberFormatException if portNumber is not valid.
 */
public DvdSocketClient(String hostname, String portNumber)
        throws UnknownHostException, IOException {
    ip = hostname;
    this.port = Integer.parseInt(portNumber);
    this.initialize();
}

/**
 * Adds a DVD to the database or inventory.
 *
 * @param dvd The DVD item to add to inventory.
 * @return A boolean value that indicates the success/failure of the
 * add operation.
 * @throws IOException Indicates there is a problem accessing the data.
 */
public boolean addDVD(DVD dvd) throws IOException {
    DvdCommand cmdObj = new DvdCommand(SocketCommand.ADD, dvd);
    return getResultFor(cmdObj).getBoolean();
}

/**
 * Gets a <code>DVD</code> from the system using a UPC.
 *
 * @param upc The UPC of the DVD you want to view.
 * @return A DVD that matches the supplied UPC.
 *
 * @throws IOException Indicates there is a problem accessing the data.
 */
public DVD getDVD(String upc) throws IOException {
    DVD dvd = new DVD();
    dvd.setUPC(upc);

    DvdCommand cmdObj = new DvdCommand(SocketCommand.GET_DVD, dvd);
    return getResultFor(cmdObj).getDVD();
}

/**
 * Attempts to rent the DVD matching the provided UPC.
 *
 * @param upc is the UPC of the DVD you want to rent.
 * @return true if the DVD was rented. false if it cannot be rented.
```

```
     *
     * @throws IOException Thrown if an <code>IOException</code> is
     * encountered in the <code>db</code> class.
     * <br>
     * For more information, see {@link DVDDatabase}.
     * @throws InterruptedIOException Thrown if an
     * <code>interrupted Threading exception</code> is
     * encountered in the <code>db</code> class.
     * <br>
     * For more information, see {@link DVDDatabase}.
     */
    public boolean rent(String upc) throws IOException {
        DVD dvd = new DVD();
        dvd.setUPC(upc);

        DvdCommand cmdObj = new DvdCommand(SocketCommand.RENT, dvd);
        return getResultFor(cmdObj).getBoolean();
    }

    /**
     * Attempts to return the DVD matching the provided UPC.
     *
     * @param upc The UPC of the DVD you want to rent.
     * @return true if the DVD was rented. false if it cannot be rented.
     *
     * @throws IOException Thrown if an <code>IOException</code> is
     * encountered in the <code>db</code> class.
     * <br>
     * For more information, see {@link DVDDatabase}.
     * <br>
     * For more information, see {@link DVDDatabase}.
     */
    public boolean returnRental(String upc) throws IOException {
        DVD      dvd    = new DVD();
        dvd.setUPC(upc);

        DvdCommand cmdObj = new DvdCommand(SocketCommand.RETURN, dvd);
        return getResultFor(cmdObj).getBoolean();
    }

    /**
     * Gets the store's inventory.
     * All of the DVDs in the system.
     *
     * @return A collection of all found DVD's.
     * @throws IOException Indicates there is a problem accessing the data.
     */
```

```java
public List<DVD> getDVDs() throws IOException {
    DvdCommand cmdObj = new DvdCommand(SocketCommand.GET_DVDS);
    return getResultFor(cmdObj).getList();
}


/**
 * A properly formatted <code>String</code> expressions returns all matching
 * DVD items. The <code>String</code> must be formatted as a regular
 * expression.
 *
 * @param query A regular expression search string.
 * @return A <code>Collection</code> of <code>DVD</code> objects that match
 * the search criteria.
 * @throws IOException Thrown if an <code>IOException</code> is
 * encountered in the <code>db</code> class.
 */
public Collection<DVD> findDVD(String query)
        throws IOException, PatternSyntaxException {
    DvdCommand cmdObj = new DvdCommand(SocketCommand.FIND);
    cmdObj.setRegex(query);

    DvdResult serialReturn = getResultFor(cmdObj);

    if (serialReturn.isException()
            && serialReturn.getException() instanceof PatternSyntaxException) {
        throw (PatternSyntaxException) serialReturn.getException();
    } else {
        return serialReturn.getCollection();
    }
}


/**
 * Removes a <code>DVD</code> from the system using a UPC.
 *
 * @param upc The UPC of the DVD you want to remove from the database.
 * @return true if the item was removed, false if it was not removed.
 * @throws IOException Indicates there is a problem accessing the data.
 */
public boolean removeDVD(String upc) throws IOException {
    DVD     dvd    = new DVD();
    dvd.setUPC(upc);

    DvdCommand cmdObj = new DvdCommand(SocketCommand.REMOVE, dvd);
    return getResultFor(cmdObj).getBoolean();
}
```

```java
/**
 * Modifies a DVD database entry specified by a DVD object.
 *
 * @param dvd The DVD to modify.
 * @return A boolean indicating the success or failure of the modify
 * operation.
 * @throws IOException Thrown if an <code>IOException</code> is
 * encountered in the <code>db</code> class.
 * <br>
 * For more information, see {@link DVDDatabase}.
 */
public boolean modifyDVD(DVD dvd) throws IOException {
    DvdCommand cmdObj = new DvdCommand(SocketCommand.MODIFY, dvd);
    return getResultFor(cmdObj).getBoolean();
}


/**
 * Lock the requested DVD. This method blocks until the lock succeeds,
 * or for a maximum of 5 seconds, whichever comes first.
 *
 * @param UPC The UPC of the DVD to reserve
 * @throws InterruptedException Indicates the thread is interrupted.
 * @throws IOException on any network problem
 */
public boolean reserveDVD(String upc) throws IOException,
InterruptedException {
    DVD dvd = new DVD();
    dvd.setUPC(upc);
    DvdCommand cmdObj = new DvdCommand(SocketCommand.RESERVE, dvd);
    return getResultFor(cmdObj).getBoolean();
}


/**
 * Unlock the requested record. Ignored if the caller does not have
 * a current lock on the requested record.
 *
 * @param UPC The UPC of the DVD to release
 * @throws IOException on any network problem
 */
public void releaseDVD(String upc) throws IOException {
    DVD dvd = new DVD();
    dvd.setUPC(upc);
    DvdCommand cmdObj = new DvdCommand(SocketCommand.RELEASE, dvd);
    getResultFor(cmdObj).getBoolean();
}
```

```java
    private DvdResult getResultFor(DvdCommand command) throws IOException {
//        this.initialize();
        try {
            oos.writeObject(command);
            DvdResult result = (DvdResult) ois.readObject();
            Exception e = result.getException();

            if (! result.isException()) {
                return result;
            } else if (e instanceof ClassNotFoundException ) {
                IOException ioe = new IOException(
                    "problem with demarshaling DvdCommand)");
                ioe.setStackTrace(e.getStackTrace());
                throw ioe;
            } else if (e instanceof IOException) {
                throw (IOException) e;
            } else {
                // well, we still have an exception, but it is up to the
                // calling method to handle it
                return result;
            }
        } catch (ClassNotFoundException cnfe) {
            IOException ioe = new IOException(
                "problem with demarshaling DvdResult)");
            ioe.setStackTrace(cnfe.getStackTrace());
            throw ioe;
//        } finally {
//            closeConnections();
        }
    }

    public void finalize() throws java.io.IOException {
        closeConnections();
    }

    /**
     * A helper method which initializes a socket connection on specified port
     *
     * @throws UnknownHostException if the IP address of the host could not be
     *         determined.
     * @throws IOException Thrown if the socket channel cannot be opened.
     */
    private void initialize() throws UnknownHostException, IOException {
        socket = new Socket(ip, port);
```

```
        oos = new ObjectOutputStream(socket.getOutputStream());
        ois = new ObjectInputStream(socket.getInputStream());
    }

    /**
     * A helper method which closes the socket connection.
     * Needs to be called from within a try-catch
     *
     * @throws IOException Thrown if the close operation fails.
     */
    private void closeConnections() throws IOException {
        oos.close();
        ois.close();
        socket.close();
    }
}
```

Socket Servers

In this section, we discuss the various types of socket servers and the techniques often used to build them. We also introduce the concept of an application protocol and how we implemented the protocol in the Denny's DVDs socket server.

Multicast and Unicast Servers

A unicast server involves one-to-one communication between a client and a server. The sockets developed in Denny's DVDs are unicast. However, in addition to unicast sockets, there are multicast sockets.

Multicast sockets are connections between groups of machines. Multicasting, or broadcasting, is used when data is sent from one host to multiple clients. The class java.net.MulticastSocket is used when writing applications that broadcast messages to many clients. We will not discuss multicast sockets any further, but you should at least be familiar with the concept. Figure 7-2 highlights the differences between multicast and unicast sockets.

Multitasking

An iterative, or single-threaded, server is one that handles client requests sequentially. As one request comes in, the server responds and begins listening again once the request is completed. Client requests that come in while the server is processing a prior request are placed on a queue and serviced as prior requests are completed. In addition, as long as one client maintains the port connection to a single-threaded server, no other client can connect—if the connection is held for too long, some of the waiting clients may time out. (Refer to the SO_TIMEOUT setting earlier.) Figure 7-2 shows the lifecycle of an iterative, or sequential, socket server.

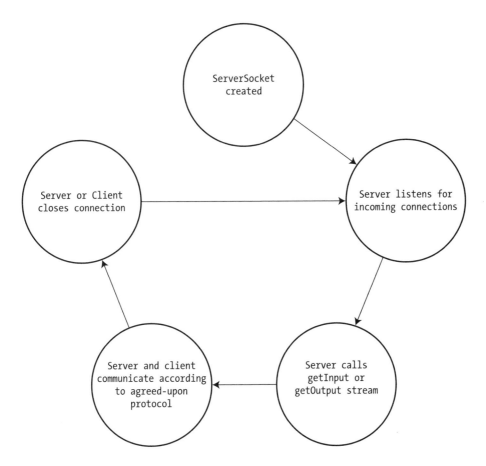

Figure 7-2. *Iterative socket server lifecycle*

Socket servers that can multitask can process multiple client requests simultaneously. This is accomplished with a multithreaded socket server. If you are anticipating a lot of requests, or requests take a long time to process, then multitasking is a very useful feature for a socket server to have. The Denny's DVDs socket version is a multithreaded socket server.

Each client gets serviced with its own thread, which makes the socket solution operate much like our RMI factory solution. We can thus be assured that each client has its own DvdDatabase object. (See our discussion on the RMI factory in Chapter 6.) The next section describes the details of our multitasking socket solution.

The Server Socket Class

The class java.net.ServerSocket allows you to create servers that listen to incoming connections on a specified port. A ServerSocket can send and receive data as well as act upon that data. Figure 7-3 illustrates the lifecycle of a multithreaded server. The public constructors for ServerSocket let you specify the port, queue length, and binding address. The server is responsible for implementing the protocol, or the rules that both the client and server must conform to in order to communicate. If the port you try to open is being used when you try to instantiate your ServerSocket, then an IOException is thrown. If the socket is successfully created, the server listens on that port for incoming connections by using the accept method. The ServerSocket.accept method returns the client socket that is connected to the client.

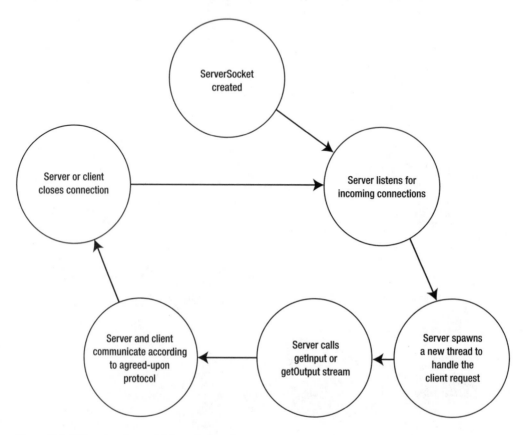

Figure 7-3. *Lifecycle of a multithreaded socket server*

■Note More accurately, if the port you try to open is already being used when you try to instantiate your ServerSocket connection, a BindException will be thrown. However, the constructor for ServerSocket only specifies the superclass of BindException (IOException) will be thrown, as other exceptions may also be thrown during construction.

Next, the server opens readers and writers on the socket and communicates with the client by writing and reading to the socket. The ServerSocket.accept method blocks the port until a client connects, and then it returns a Socket object. The socket connection is then used to execute the client request, and the connection can be closed for that client.

SocketServer has many of the same socket options available as the Socket class. One important option that they share is the SO_TIMEOUT option. With the ServerSocket class, the SO_TIMEOUT option specifies how long the server should wait for an incoming socket connection with the accept method.

When the accept method times out, a java.net.SocketTimeoutException is raised. Let's look at a sample socket implementation in Listing 7-2 for our networking version of Denny's DVDs. Figure 7-4 shows a high-level view of how we must implement our socket solution.

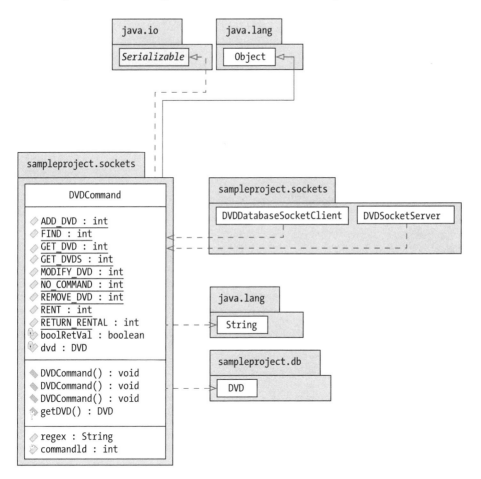

Figure 7-4. *Socket classes*

Listing 7-2. *DVDSocketServer.java*

```java
package sampleproject.sockets;
import java.io.*;
import java.net.*;
import java.util.*;
import java.util.logging.*;
import sampleproject.db.*;
```

```java
/**
 * DVDSocketServer is the class that handles socket client requests and
 * passes the request to the database. The class recieves parameters in
 * <code>DVDCommand</code> objects and returns results in
 * <code>DVDResult</code> objects.
 * @version 2.0
 */
public class DvdSocketServer extends Thread {
    private String dbLocation = null;
    private int port = 3000;

    /**
     * Starts the socket server
     *
     * @param argv Command line arguments.
     * @throws IOException Thrown if the socket server fails to start.
     */
    public static void main(String argv[]) {
        register(".", 3000);
    }

    public static void register(String dbLocation, int port) {
        new DvdSocketServer(dbLocation, port).start();
    }

    public DvdSocketServer(String dbLocation, int port) {
        this.dbLocation = dbLocation;
        this.port = port;
    }

    public void run() {
        try {
            listenForConnections();
        } catch (IOException ioe) {
            ioe.printStackTrace();
            System.exit(-1);
        }
    }

    public void listenForConnections() throws IOException {
        ServerSocket aServerSocket = new ServerSocket(port);
        //block for 60,000 msecs or 1 minute
        aServerSocket.setSoTimeout(60000);

        (Logger.getLogger("sampleproject.sockets")).log(Level.INFO,
                "a server socket created on port " +
                aServerSocket.getLocalPort());
```

```
        while (true) {
            Socket aSocket = aServerSocket.accept();
            DbSocketRequest request = new DbSocketRequest(dbLocation, aSocket);
            request.start();
        }
    }
}
```

The main method creates a ServerSocket object on port 3000. There is a loop that listens for requests from any Java or non-Java clients on port 3000. Once a request is received, the connection is accepted, meaning that the accept method stops blocking and the Socket object is returned. The resulting socket is passed in as a parameter to the DBSocketRequest. The server socket then spawns a new thread for the client request. This design enables multiple clients to connect to the socket server since each request is serviced in a separate thread.

The DBSocketRequest class extends Thread. You will recall that one of the requirements is that multiple clients need to be able to use the DVDDatabase services.

Now our socket server can create multiple threads as needed. Once an object is accepted on the port (port 3000 in our case), which happens in the run method, the execCmdObject method is called. This method is a big switch statement. It inspects the command object for the action to be performed and then calls the matching method in DVDDatabase. Refer to the project download for the entire DBSocketRequest class. For brevity, Listing 7-3 only shows the run method.

Listing 7-3. *DBSocketRequest.java*

```
/**
* Required for a class that extends thread, this is the main path
* of execution for this thread.
public void run() {
    try {
        ObjectOutputStream out =
        new ObjectOutputStream(client.getOutputStream());
        ObjectInputStream in =
            new ObjectInputStream(client.getInputStream());
        DVDCommand cmdObj = (DVDCommand) in.readObject();
        out.writeObject(execCmdObject(cmdObj));
        if (client != null) {
            client.close();
        }
        out.flush();
    }
    catch (SocketException e) {
        logger.log(Level.SEVERE,
          "SocketException in Socket Server: " + e.getMessage());
    }
    catch (Exception e) {
        logger.log(Level.SEVERE,
            "General Exception in Socket Server: "
            + e.getMessage()
    );
}
```

A final point about DBSocketRequest is that DBSocketRequest is where we implemented our application protocol. We have separated the protocol from the actual socket, DVDSocketServer.

The Application Protocol

The socket client transmits a serialized object to the socket server. But how does the server know how to respond to the object? A serialized object is technically just data in the form of a byte stream; on the surface it does not communicate action. This is where we need a *protocol*, or set of rules, that defines how our client is to interact with our server.

At a high level, here is how our protocol will work:

1. The client will make a request, such as rent or return rental, of the server.

2. The server will execute the request.

3. The result status or return value will be sent to the client.

Deliberating on the preceding list should lead to the following two questions: "How will the server interpret the request?" and "How will the result be sent back to the client?"

The Denny's DVDs application adopts an approach of encapsulation. The request is encapsulated in a command object and the result is encapsulated in a result object. Let's take a closer look at the command and result objects.

The Command Enum

The DvdCommand class encapsulates the client request by storing it as a SocketCommand member, commandId. When a GUI client calls one of the DBClient methods on DVDSocketClient, the socket client sets the commandId property and sends it off to the socket server, DVDSocketServer. Since DVDCommand is sent, or marshaled, across the wire, it must be serializable. When the server receives the DVDCommand object, it uses the commandId to call the corresponding method on the DVDDatabase, which is a local call to our server. Any parameters (for instance, the UPC value) that are required for the request are passed in the DVD class member. The regex attribute is used exclusively for the find method.

Listing 7-4 shows the constructors that take a SocketCommand enum ID (see the sidebar "Using Enum Constants") and a dvd object as a parameter. The dvd object is useful for storing the UPC for rent and return. For the modify method, a dvd parameter can be used to set the other dvd attributes for a particular DVD. We do not actually use the modify method publicly in our implementation, but the class has been designed with this enhancement in mind.

■**Note** The DVDCommand object is an example of the Command pattern. A command object encapsulates a request as an object. You can find more information about the Command pattern in the book *Design Patterns: Elements of Reusable Object-Oriented Software*, by Erich Gamma, Richard Helm, Ralph Johnson, and John M. Vlissides (Addison-Wesley, 1995). The Proxy and Adapter patterns are also described in this literary software masterpiece.

Listing 7-4. *The Public Methods of DVDCommand.java*

```
/**
 * Default constructor
 */
public DvdCommand() {
    this(SocketCommand.UNSPECIFIED);
}

/**
 * Constructor that requires the type of command to execute as a parameter.
 *
 * @param command The id of the command the server is to perform.
 */
public DvdCommand(SocketCommand command) {
    this (command, new DVD());
}

/**
 * Constructor that requires the type of command and the DVD object.
 *
 * @param command The id of the command the server is to perform.
 * @param aDvd
 */
public DvdCommand(SocketCommand command, DVD dvd) {
    setCommandId(command);
    this.dvd = dvd;
}

/**
 * Gets the query that was used for searching.
 *
 * @return The string representing the regualr expression to use in find().
 */
public String getRegex() {
    return regex;
}

/**
 * Sets the regular expression
 *
 * @param re The regular expression to use in find().
 */
public void setRegex(String re) {
    regex = re;
}
```

DVDSocketClient makes use of the DVDCommand object in each of its DBClient methods. For example, in the find method, the command object is constructed with the FIND enum value of SocketCommand. Next, the regex attribute is set using the query parameter of the find method. These two steps are shown again here:

```
DvdCommand cmdObj = new DvdCommand(SocketCommand.FIND);
cmdObj.setRegex(query);
```

The Result Object

The DVDResult object is used to encapsulate the result of the request. When the DVDDatabase has completed a request, the result is sent back to DVDSocketServer, which in turn wraps the result in a DVDResult object and sends it back to the socket client. As in the case of the command object, DVDResult must be serializable since it is sent across the network. Even exceptions are wrapped in DVDResult and sent back to the client.

The result object is similar to the DVDCommand object in its operation. There are a number of constructors that take the varying types of return values from the DBClient methods. You can find the code in the project download, but the following is an example of its usage in the find method of DVDSocketClient:

```
DVDResult serialReturn = (DVDResult)ois.readObject();
if (!serialReturn.isException()) {
retVal = serialReturn.getCollection();
}
```

The DVDResult is received from the socket server. The result object is checked for exceptions, and if no exceptions are detected, the Collection is extracted from DVDResult. We know it must be a Collection since our protocol ensures that for DBClient's find method, a Collection is always returned.

■**Note** Our application protocol was separated from our socket server, based on good design principles. Thus, changes in our protocol, or even additional protocols, can now be handled without affecting the socket server directly.

USING ENUM CONSTANTS

The Application protocol is implemented by specifying the command type. This was performed with the following code taken from the constructor of the DvdCommand class:

```
public DvdCommand(SocketCommand command, DVD dvd) {
    setCommandId(command);
    this.dvd = dvd;
}
```

Prior to JDK 5, the `commandId` variable in the `DvdCommand` class would probably have been constants, of the form:

```
public final static int FIND = 0;
public final static int RENT = 1;
public final static int RETURN = 2;
```

There are many problems with doing this, though, including the possibility that someone might directly set the `commandId` variable to an integer value that is not supported, or they might do something illogical with the constants (such as try to add them). Furthermore, we cannot enumerate over the number of modes, and if we tried to print the value of the `commandId` variable, a number would be returned—we would have to look up this number in the documentation or in the source code to determine what the number really means.

JDK 5 provides us with a simpler way of defining these constants: using an enum. The `SocketCommand` enum is defined as

```
package sampleproject.gui;

public enum SocketCommand {
    UNSPECIFIED, /* indicate that the command object has not been set */
    FIND,         /* request will be performing a Find action */
    RENT,        /* renting a DVD */
    RETURN,       /* returning a DVD */
    MODIFY,       /* updating status of a DVD */
    ADD,        /* creating a new DVD record */
    REMOVE,       /* delete a DVD record */
    GET_DVD,    /* retrieve a single DVD from database */
    GET_DVDS,    /* retrieve multiple DVDs from database */
    RESERVE,
    RELEASE

}
```

Now any variable of type `SocketCommand` can *only* contain one of these listed options—no other options are possible.

We also have the benefit that anytime we print (or log) the contents of the `commandSocket` variable, the string UNSPECIFIED, FIND, RENT, RETURN, MODIFY, ADD, REMOVE, GET_DVD, GET_DVDS, RESERVE, or RELEASE will be printed (or logged)—it will be instantly clear from looking at the output what the variable was set to.

There are many more benefits of using enums. We recommend you read the release notes related to enums available at `http://java.sun.com/j2se/1.5.0/docs/guide/language/enums.html` for more information.

Summary

In this chapter, we discussed the Denny's DVDs socket implementation. We also provided a brief overview of the different types of sockets, and the various types of TCP socket development strategies. We laid out the application protocol for our socket implementation and demonstrated the Command pattern with the help of Java enums. The choice of sockets as the network protocol in your exam solution should not be perceived as something esoteric and frightening that is to be avoided at all costs. Even though most students opt to not develop a socket solution, we believe that the choice isn't any more challenging than an RMI solution and should be fairly straightforward, given the sample code base that accompanies this text. Sockets are a technology that underlies most networking protocols. Most of the cool new technologies, such as web services and EJBs, ultimately rely on sockets. As we have discussed, even RMI is built on top of sockets. So you would be well served to become acquainted with sockets, if only to help deepen your understanding of these other networking technologies. The next chapter covers the graphical user interface (GUI) for the Denny's DVDs application.

FAQs

Q Do I need to implement a multithreaded socket server?

A Yes. The certification exam requires that the server allow multiuser access. If you use a single-threaded solution, then there will never be a way to demonstrate concurrent access. Your application will block serially until each request is resolved one at a time. This may be an interesting solution and will circumvent the need to figure out a locking strategy, but one that Sun will not permit.

Q Should I utilize a thread pool for the socket server implementation?

A This is completely up to you. You could do so and it would be a good practice. Every time a new connection is accepted, our server spawns a new thread to handle the request. However, creating and destroying threads is not a free lunch. On a really busy, highly trafficked server, it might be better to control the creation of threads. A thread pool will instantiate a set number of threads, a number that can be calibrated based on your application performance requirements, upon startup. When the server receives a new request, it is serviced with one of the threads from the pool. When the request is completed, the thread is returned to the pool for later use. A thread pool will eliminate the overhead associated with creating and destroying new threads. We do not make use of a thread pool in Denny's DVDs and you will not have to implement a thread pool for your certification project since the exam does not require that your server perform well under a heavy load.

Q What is meant by TCP sockets being a connection-oriented protocol?

A Sometimes in the literature, the term "connection-oriented" will be used when referring to TCP sockets. What this means is that before communication can occur between the endpoints, a connection must exist. Contrast this with UDP sockets, a connection-less protocol.

Q Was it necessary to use the `SocketCommand` object to indicate which command to perform on the database?

A No. We chose this implementation for clarity: it was a nice way to enumerate over the possible commands and demonstrate the command pattern. The drawback is that if new commands were added to the database, the client would have to receive an updated `SocketCommand` class in order to submit future requests since we would no longer be able to deserialize older command objects on the server. (Of course, we could check the `serialversionID` so that we could be backward compatible, but you get the idea.) A different approach would be to embed the command as a string in the `DvdCommand`. This way, as new commands are added, there would be no need to add them to the `SocketCommand` class, but the server would be able to recognize the new command.

Q Should I allow the user to change the port to be used in this application?

A While not strictly necessary, doing so is generally considered a good idea. Otherwise, if another server application is using your desired port, your server application will be unable to start.

Q When choosing a port number to use in my application (whether hard-coded or a default value), are there any numbers I should avoid?

A The Internet Assigned Numbers Authority (IANA) specifies a list of well-known ports (from port number 0 through 1023), registered ports (from 1024 through 49151), and dynamic and/or private ports (from 49152 through 65535). It is recommended that you choose a port number from the private port range to avoid conflict with any other service. You should avoid using a well-known port since, depending on your operating system, you may also find that you cannot run your server using a well-known port without administrator privileges.

Q How can I perform system cleanup when a client disconnects?

A If the thread that is dedicated to that client is listening for a new command from the client, then it will receive an exception when the client disconnects. Alternatively, if the client disconnects before your server has an opportunity to respond to a previous request, then the thread dedicated to that client will receive an exception when you attempt to send the response to the client. In either of these cases, you can add cleanup code to your catch block.

Alternatively, if you are only interested in cleaning up any outstanding locks, you can use the thread dedicated to the client as a key within a `WeakHashMap` containing the locks. When the client disconnects (and the thread dies), then eventually the lock will be automatically removed from the `WeakHashMap`. Refer to Chapter 5 for more information.

Q How can I automatically update all clients whenever a booking is made by any other client on the server?

A This is not required for the Sun assignment; however, you would have to open an additional socket between the server and the client so that the server can send messages to the client. You could combine this with the Observer design pattern (described in Chapter 8) so that clients can register their desire to be notified of bookings.

CHAPTER 8

∎∎∎

The Graphical User Interfaces

In the preceding chapters, the implementation of the data and network tiers for the Denny's DVD application were discussed in detail. Now it is time to deal with the final development tier: the graphical user interface (GUI).

In this chapter we will cover the following topics:

- Designing simple yet usable GUIs

- Reviewing Swing components and the event model

- Implementing a `JTable`

- Implementing the Model-View-Controller (MVC) design pattern

- Implementing the Observer design pattern

It is not necessary to have read the networking chapters prior to reading this chapter. The majority of this chapter details how to design your GUI, and as such, the networking sections are not required. The sections of this chapter that deal with connecting to the database use the Factory design pattern, which will provide an instance of a class that implements our connection interface. Naturally, though, you will not be able to connect the GUI to the database using the networking options described in this chapter until after you have completed the networking chapters.

∎**Tip** The way we are using the connection interfaces shows one of the benefits of using an interface: the interface provides a contract that we can assume will be implemented—we don't need the actual implementation to develop our factory and use it.

While developing the Sun assignment, you might choose to start development of the GUI prior to developing the networking classes. This is also a reasonable approach, and might even be the preferred approach in real life—developing the GUI before the networking code means that the customer could start working with the stand-alone application before the final code is written.

For the purposes of this book, it made sense for us to develop the networking code first, as we will be connecting to the database via direct connection and via the various networking options from within our GUI.

■**Caution** A common misconception made by end users is that when they have seen the user interface, then the entire project is close to completion. It can save a lot of confusion if you spend extra time with the client to make sure that they understand how much additional work is required at the time you show them the user interface. One attempt to get around this misconception is the Napkin Look & Feel for Swing applications. See `http://napkinlaf.sourceforge.net` for further details.

Of all components in an application, none affects the user quite as much as the GUI. This is true by an interface's nature: It is the method by which an end user interacts with a system. Unfortunately, the GUI is often the most de-emphasized part of the application development process. This is truly a fallacy, since a user interface can sometimes make or break an entire system. If a GUI is convoluted and difficult to navigate, users will quickly become frustrated and the result will be a poor overall user experience. In the end, a system is only successful if people can successfully use it.

This chapter aims to introduce concepts of GUI layout, design, and implementation to those who may not have given it much thought in the past. An interface is a required portion of the SCJD exam, and this chapter provides novices with all the information they need to get one up and running.

GUI Concepts

The SCJD exam requires that one individual complete all development work. This includes development of all three tiers of the application: the server tier, the middle tier, and the presentation tier. This is different from the more common working environment, where developers often specialize in a certain tier. It is common practice in the workforce to have a group of back-end developers and a separate group of front-end developers working on a three-tiered project. In the case of the SCJD exam, one developer must create all three tiers.

■**Tip** The fact that you are doing the work that might normally be split into three teams can cause confusion when reading Sun's instructions. Often candidates feel that requirements in the GUI section of the instructions contradict instructions in the Data section. But when considered from the perspective of individual teams, you should find that the instructions do not contradict each other; the team building the Data class has clear instructions to carry out. The team building the GUI has been told what the Data class will provide, and can then add their own restrictions to meet the requirements of the GUI.

Creating the front-end can be a daunting task, especially for those who are primarily not front-end developers. There are many Java developers who never write a line of interface code but who are still extremely fluent programmers in general. This is further exacerbated by the fact that only a limited textual description of the interface is provided; we have not been given any examples of what the end user would like to see. The crux of the next two sections is to ease the burden of developing the GUI.

Layout concepts are discussed at a high level, in addition to some basic human interface concepts that can be incorporated into the interface for the SCJD exam.

■**Note** Layout concepts and human interface concepts are courses of study unto themselves. The next two sections only introduce ideas of relevance to the SCJD exam.

Layout Concepts

It is a common misconception that GUI layout is more an art than a science. This is a slight misrepresentation of the process of layout design and information architecture. In the early days of computing, computer programming was considered more of an art than a science. This fact seems almost ludicrous by today's standards. It was only after an engineering process was applied to the art of programming that it quickly became more of a science or an engineering practice. The same can be said for interface design concepts.

Layout design revolves around the presentation of information in a clear and concise manner. The user should be able to process the information a user interface presents with little or no effort. This last statement is vague, but for a reason. No matter how standards oriented a process may become, there is always a level of intuition in decision making. Not all roads can be anticipated and laid out in a standard process. Intuition is where the art of layout design comes into play, in deciding how to deal with those gray areas of development where no one has treaded before.

Fortunately for us, many have treaded into the design considerations presented in the SCJD exam. In fact, the layout of data has become so standardized that Sun actually includes a Swing component, the JTable, to deal specifically with this "database"-style data. Sun even goes so far as to require the use of the JTable component for the SCJD exam. The JTable component, which is discussed in detail later in this chapter, is the main method of data presentation in this book's example application.

On a high level, let's take a look at how the JTable efficiently displays data. The JTable uses the spreadsheet paradigm of presenting items divided into rows and columns. This spreadsheet-style layout is illustrated in Figure 8-1. Notice that when users need to locate data under this paradigm, they only need to cross-reference a column value with a row value. Where the two values intersect is the location of the data. The paradigm also is the ultimate reconciliation of data versus display space. If another row of data is added to the table, the size will increase by approximately the height of the font used. Adding an additional column impacts the size of more than a row, but the layout is extremely flexible, so updates to the underlying system data are easily represented in the presentation. In addition to all of these features, the table schema presents a great quantity of data in a very small area.

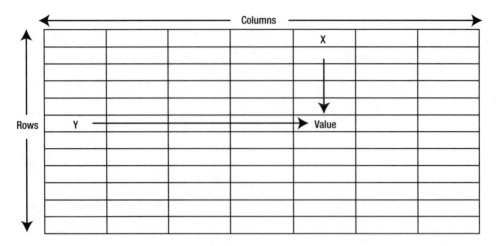

Figure 8-1. *A high-level table schema*

While the preceding analysis may appear to be stating the obvious, it does emphasize the layout principles the table schema does very well. The analysis performed on the JTable can and should be done for the overall layout of any GUI interface. You should look for these criteria in a user interface:

- All data is presented in the minimum amount of space, without being cluttered or disorganized.

- The user should be able to locate necessary information quickly.

- In most cases, the interface must scale to fit more or less data.

Human Interface Concepts

Human interface concepts go beyond simple data layout organizational techniques. Human interface design schemas organize the user's flow of events when attempting to complete a task. For instance, deciding how to lay out data in order to maximize its readability is a *layout* decision. Deciding how to lay out the entire act of selecting a data item and modifying it is a *human interface* decision. In short, human interface decisions determine how users interact with the system.

The point of a GUI is to create an easy method of interaction between a user and a system. The GUI, in a certain sense, acts as a layer of shielding, abstracting the actual functions of the system away from the user. When the user clicks a button to save a document, the system may have to go through a number of steps to save the file:

1. The application validates the file integrity.

2. The system calculates the physical size of the file.

3. The system checks the hard disk to see if there is enough available space to save the file.

4. The application writes the file to the file system.

These are steps almost every application takes in order to save a file. But most applications require only one item of input from the user to initiate these actions: selecting the Save option from the File menu.

Imagine if an application required the user to select a Validate File menu item, followed by a Calculate File Size option, followed by a Check Hard Drive Space option; to then enter the calculated file size obtained from the previous step; and finally, after confirming that there is enough hard drive space, to select a Write File to File System option. This application would make saving a document more trouble than it is worth.

The previous example is extreme, but it still demonstrates the notion of abstracting the operations of the system away from the user as much as possible. The system should be able to complete many of the tasks listed previously without any input from the user. The only time the user needs to be notified of the system's activities is if an error should occur. For instance, if there is not enough space on the file system to save the file, the user should be prompted and notified that the system can no longer complete this step on its own. Beyond these circumstances, the user should be allowed to simply select Save and have the system abstract away all necessary substeps.

This is one of the primary focuses of interface design: reconciling system instructions with the actions a user must take to actually interface with the system. This may seem like an obvious and simple task, but quite frankly, it is not simple. It requires an individual to view a system from the standpoint of the average person who has never used the application. Being objective is challenging for many application designers and developers. Their intimate knowledge of the entire system may make it difficult to judge what actions are necessary for the user versus what actions are necessary for the system.

This is where the time taken to get a fresh reading of the requirements can be extremely valuable. To detach yourself from the system design and approach the application from the point of view of the user, step back and reread the requirements for the application and look for certain interaction information:

- Who are the primary users of the system?

- What do users employ the system for? What tasks must it allow them to complete?

- What actions are required by the system in order to complete these tasks?

Write down the answers to these questions. To give an example, if you were considering creating software that allows the user to add footnotes to a document, you should get a list that looks something like Table 8-1.

Table 8-1. *Sample Use Case Skeleton*

User	Interactions with Footnote Facilities
Writer	Add a Footnote
Writer	View a footnote
Writer	Edit a footnote
Writer	Delete a footnote

Those who are experienced in project requirements by now have noticed that what we are doing is creating a set of simple use cases. *Use cases* spell out items such as how all of the actors interact with the system and what tasks the system will allow them to complete. A set of use cases will usually go into further detail and spell out the additional steps required for the completion of a task. A simple use-case diagram for Table 8-1 would look similar to that shown in Figure 8-2.

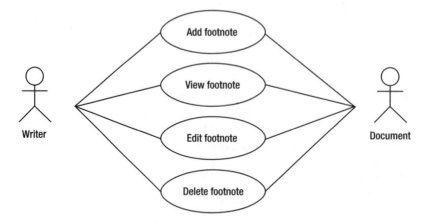

Figure 8-2. *Use case diagram for user interactions with footnote facilities*

■**Note** User interfaces should attempt to bridge the gap between the use cases and the functionality of the system. The system should, by design, allow for all the actions detailed in the use cases. The interface's job is to make these tasks as easy as possible for the user. If the system architecture does not allow for all of the actions detailed in the use cases, it indicates a serious flaw in the application's design.

Next, fill in the details of each action, like this: "The user may add a footnote to text by first selecting the text to attach a footnote to. Next, the user may optionally specify a name for the footnote, and then add some body text for the footnote. The user then saves the footnote."

Now there should be enough detail to begin the interface design. First and foremost, consider how to reconcile the actions the system requires versus the actions required by the user. Plan an interface that requires the minimum number of steps from the user in order to complete a task. This should be the guiding principle in your interface design.

■**Tip** Usually, user interfaces allow for multiple ways to complete a task. For example, an application may allow a user to save a document via a menu item, or a designated keystroke, or an onscreen button. This is considered good interface design, and users will memorize and use the method that works best for them. While not explicitly listed as a requirement for the SCJD assignment, developers are expected to follow standard practices, and you would do well to consider adding common features such as keystroke shortcuts to button operations and menu operations.

Another simple principle to consider is how users actually traverse and interpret the user interface. In most Western societies, users generally begin analyzing an interface at the upper-left corner. The tendency from that point is to continue down and to the right. This is due to the nature of the written word in Western nations: Words on a page flow from left to right, so most Western users tend to perceive the left portion of the screen as a beginning point and the right portion as the end. Anything in between these two points represents the necessary steps to travel from the beginning to the end. This concept is illustrated in Figure 8-3.

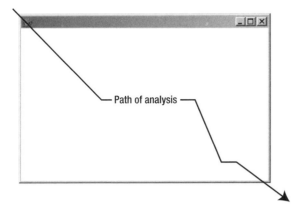

Figure 8-3. *Path of a Western user's eye when interpreting a GUI*

■**Tip** Even if you're an Asian developer working in Asia, for the purpose of the Sun assignment you should probably assume that the assignment is being evaluated with Western expectations.

When you plan the workflow of an interface, it is advantageous to the user to arrange items in order of importance along this path. The elements we want the user to be aware of first should, of course, be closest to the upper-left corner. The order in which the interface items are placed descending from the starting corner also suggests an order to the actions. For example, consider Figure 8-4.

The path illustrated in Figure 8-4 suggests that users should perform operations on the table and then click the Enter button when they have completed the operations. If the Enter button was placed before the table, the user would likely still figure out and interpret the order of operations, but the interface would seem nonintuitive and clearly not as well organized.

Grouping items also suggests similar functionality. This is why document-storage buttons, such as Open, Save, and New Document, are located in close proximity to each other in most word processing programs.

■**Tip** If you have a question about how to design an action that is intuitive for the end user, the answer is sometimes very easy to find: Look for another popular program with similar functionality. Designing an interface that is similar to other application interfaces to which the user may be accustomed is a helpful way to ensure your application is intuitive as well.

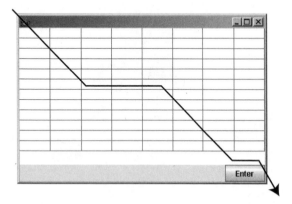

Figure 8-4. *An applied path*

Also, placing a button next to a text field suggests that the button performs some type of action associated with the text field. This principle dictates a significant design error you should be cautious of committing. Because the user interprets grouped items as grouped functionally, placing a Quit button directly next to a Save button is a very bad idea. The Quit item is considered a destructive action because it terminates program execution, whereas the Save button is a nondestructive and frequently used action. This particular interface design error could result in users quitting the program when they really intended to save their work.

It is important to always remember that the average user is accident-prone. Developers must assume that users will make mistakes and click a wrong button every now and then. A good interface design with proper button groupings and placements will minimize this possibility. In many real-world applications, the user interface might even go a step further and implement an "undo" mechanism using the facilities available in the javax.swing.undo package. This enhanced functionality allows the user to revert the application state to a preceding point in time and erase the ramification of an action that may have been a mistake. Although this functionality is useful, it is far beyond what is required for the SCJD exam.

Another consideration to keep in mind when designing a user interface is that you as the developer may have assumptions about an application's operating environment, but these assumptions can never be considered fact. For example, just because your development computer has a mouse attached to it does not mean you can assume that every computer your application runs on will have a mouse. This is especially true for Java applications because they aim to target almost every platform in existence. To ensure the functionality of your user interface, each functional widget on the screen should have a keystroke mnemonic mapping, an equivalent function key, or even a hotkey. That way, if your application is run on a platform that does not have a mouse, the end user will still be able to navigate the application via the keyboard.

An excellent final interface principle is to place items in stationary, predictable locations. Following this principle helps the user develop what is known as muscle memory. The phenomenon occurs when the user becomes so accustomed to the location of an item on the screen that his or her mind subconsciously knows where it is located. Thus, working with the interface becomes less thought-intensive and more like second nature to the user. For example, think about the web browser you have used for the past three years. Even if you have switched browsers numerous times, the Back and Forward buttons are almost always located in the same place. Therefore, locating these buttons with the eye and targeting them with the mouse has become quicker for you, basically because you always know where they are. It is like riding a bicycle: You may stop riding for a few years, but you never forget how to keep your balance.

■**Note** Users adapt to new UI standards, and therefore what is intuitive is always in flux. Over the years, popular new UI concepts have been introduced. For example, when the tabbed panel metaphor was introduced, it became an instant hit with developers since it offers a highly efficient method to display multiple panels of data in a single window. Due to its efficient nature, the tabbed panel was, and still is, used quite liberally by developers. Because the metaphor has been used so often, users have become accustomed to using it. Some other examples of new UI paradigms that have entered the average user's interface vocabulary include the icon button bar and the web browser-style "back and forward" navigational interface.

As you design and develop an interface for your application, it's always a good idea to test it. Testing an interface isn't as cut and dried as testing application code, however. The best way to test the GUI is to have someone who has never seen or used the application sit down and use it.

First, create an interface prototype. The prototype can be a simple, nonfunctional version of the proposed interface. At this stage, even an interface mock-up sketched out on paper is sufficient. The point is, don't put too much work into a prototype before you're certain of its usability value.

Next, present the test subject with a written list of tasks and ask the user to complete those tasks. Observe the user while they attempt to complete the list using your interface prototype. While you observe the tester, do not instruct them on how to get past areas they may misinterpret or get hung up on. During this process, expect the user to get hung up on your interface prototype and fail at some tasks. This is very common, so be careful not to become aggravated with the testing process. When hang-ups occur, simply ask the test user what they are trying to accomplish and the location where the user expects their next action. Take note of these comments—they are actually suggestions on how to adjust the interface for the next user. Continue this process as many times as you see fit or until the supreme moment when all your testers can use the interface with few or no problems. For more extensive information on usability testing and usability design issues in general, please refer to the FAQs section of this chapter for some valuable URLs.

Model-View-Controller Pattern

The previous section demonstrated the necessity of reconciling system functionality with a user's interaction with the application through the GUI layout. The Model-View-Controller (MVC) pattern limits the dependencies between a system's interface and implementation, and buffers the data and middle tiers from design decisions that may affect the presentation tier.

Why Use the MVC Pattern?

The main purpose of the MVC pattern is the separation of responsibility for the various tasks involved in the user interface (UI). A typical UI can be split into the following areas of responsibility:

1. The interface to the system

2. The displaying of the data to the end user

3. Accepting input from the user, then parsing and processing it

These three areas of responsibility correspond to the Model, the View, and the Controller, respectively.

It is possible, using the MVC design pattern, to keep these three areas of responsibility logically separate. On large teams it might be possible to assign these areas of responsibility to teams who have the best skills to perform the work—for example, those who have good layout skills might be assigned to work on the View, while those who are better at parsing inputs from various sources might work on the Controller.

Using the MVC design pattern allows us to change the UI rapidly. For this book's sample assignment and for the Sun SCJD assignment we will be creating a GUI that will run as a stand-alone application. However, by changing the View and the Controller, we can easily create a web-based application. Another View and Controller can be used to provide a web services interface to the application.

■**Tip** It is often recommended that when learning any new subject you should try to put the concepts into practice. If you are planning to study for the Sun Certified Web Component Developer certification, you could try creating a web interface to your assignment. This can be easier than trying to implement a brand-new project as part of your studies, as you will have already created the business logic and will therefore only be concentrating on the information pertinent to your new certification studies.

MVC in Detail

As its name suggests, the MVC pattern consists of three primary players, as shown in Table 8-2.

The MVC pattern may seem complex, but it's actually an incredibly simple concept. The concept is very easy to follow when it's boiled down to a real-world example. Let's consider it from the perspective of ordering from your local fast-food restaurant.

Table 8-2. *Components of an MVC Architecture*

Component	Role
Model	The Model is the interface to the remainder of the application. It provides a consistent way for the Controller(s) to access and/or modify data, and returns data in a specified format. It is not uncommon for the Model to incorporate other design patterns—for example, the Façade pattern to hide low-level application details; the observable side of the Observer pattern to provide automatic updates to view(s); the Singleton pattern to ensure that only one instance of the model can exist; and so on.
View	The View is the actual visual representation of the data. The underlying system may store data in a number of ways, but it is the function of the View to interpret and transform the system data into an appropriate format. Some appropriate presentation formats may include an HTML page, a PostScript document, or the GUI of a Java application. No matter what type of data display is chosen, the fact remains that the View is solely responsible for transforming the system's internal data format into the presentation format. The View must also allow for human interaction. The user may click a button in the GUI interface, and the View must handle and dispatch that action. This translates into a call to the Controller. It is important to realize that a View does not necessarily have to correspond to a screen layout—it is also possible in a business-to-business (B2B) scenario that the View may be an XML document that is being sent to a remote application.
Controller	The Controller is the mediator between the data and presentation portions of an application. The View calls the Controller and instructs it to execute a certain action. The action may require data passed from the View, or it may pass data back to the View. In any case, one thing is certain: All interaction between the data tiers and the presentation tiers must occur through the Controller. To preserve the high level of abstraction the MVC allows, the View must never bypass the Controller and communicate directly with components below it. For instance, the View should never call the database directly and tell it to execute a query. Instead, the View should call the Controller and instruct it to call the database component.

When you get to the restaurant you look at the menu and decide the salad looks really nice. So you ask the counter person for a salad and a milk shake. That individual goes to the kitchen, collects your food, and returns it to you.

This is a pretty common scenario, but it is a perfect representation of the MVC pattern. Let's break down the main actors in this scenario and map them to their equivalents in the MVC pattern.

The View in this example is the menu being presented to you. The type of View may vary—you may be inside the restaurant looking at a menu in your hands, or you may be in the drive-through looking at a menu on the wall. The same information is presented in either View, but it might be presented in different formats—a paper menu for patrons inside the restaurant or a painted menu for those in the drive-through.

The Controller in this scenario is the counter person who takes your order. That person acts as the buffer between you and the actual operations of the fast-food restaurant. The counter person takes note of the meal you request, and arranges for it to be provided to you.

■**Note** It is possible to consider the counter person as part of the View, since they are asking the customer questions and possibly requesting payment for the meal. However, for the purposes of simplicity, we are ignoring the multiple roles the counter person may play.

It is the Controller's job to handle the actual details of getting the meal for you, and you do not need to see or understand how they get your meal. The Controller may go to the kitchen and ask the chef to prepare your salad and milk shake, or the Controller may have to ask two separate people to do these two tasks. The fact is, when you order your food, you never go in and tell the individual employees to go off and make your meal, and you certainly do not prepare the meal yourself. Organizing the supply of food is the job of the Controller, and all you care about is getting the next View (the meal itself).

The next component of the MVC is the Model. In the fast-food example, the Model is the kitchen. The kitchen will provide the various Views—the standard menu, any "specials of the day" menus (which might be listed on a separate page on the menus used inside the restaurant, or on a blackboard for the drive-through customers)—then take the order and present the data (the food) for the next View.

Benefits of MVC

The main benefit of the MVC pattern is the abstraction of the data presentation from the system operations. The implications of this fact are many. For example, if a system must display data to many different output methods, this pattern is the ideal solution. Under the MVC pattern, the data model remains the same, but the method of display can very easily change. Thus, the same system could have a GUI front-end and a web-based HTML front-end, all without any changes to the rest of the system.

The MVC pattern also helps limit the scope of changes to a system. The majority of the time, a client will get preoccupied with the functionality of the presentation tier. This is quite understandable, considering that this is the portion of the application the end user will actually use. Many times, clients will request numerous changes to the front-end design. The MVC pattern limits the scope of these changes and often precludes them from impacting other portions of the system. This is not to say that the MVC pattern makes system updates a snap, but it certainly does make the front-end of the system much more flexible.

Drawbacks of MVC

Everything has a good side and a bad side, and the MVC pattern is no exception. MVC is not the best option for every system. For instance, a system that does not need the capability to display data through multiple sources may not be a good candidate for this pattern. MVC does employ a large amount of data abstraction, and sometimes the associated overhead is not worth the cost, both in development time and performance.

The MVC pattern is generally a good idea, and it is one of the more lightweight design patterns. It is also widely used, and is supported by most development platforms. Its usefulness almost directly correlates with the size of a project. If the development task requires several programmers and substantial expandability, the MVC pattern is a sure win. If the project is very small in scope and will probably never be updated, the MVC pattern is probably unnecessary.

Alternatives to MVC

The most obvious alternative to the MVC pattern is not to use it at all. A system can be designed and implemented that tightly integrates the actual system functions with the user interface. This will, of course, limit the flexibly of the GUI. All changes will directly impact all areas of the system, since the system is basically one unit.

On some programming platforms, tight integration of the presentation and data tiers is possible. Due to the event-driven nature of the Java platform, some aspects of the MVC pattern are inherent in any user interface. All interface components produce actions, and there are always classes that are created to deal with these actions. In this sense, the MVC pattern is built in, but the programmer can choose to limit its effect and not use the full MVC architecture.

Swing and the Abstract Windows Toolkit

The previous sections emphasized some high-level methodologies of interface design. Most of the ideas, such as the MVC pattern, are platform agnostic and apply to the architecture of development projects, which can then be developed in almost any language. The next sections shift to a platform-specific approach using the Abstract Window Toolkit (AWT) and Swing to explain methods of interface implementation on the Java platform.

Entire books have been written on how to program with AWT and Swing. This section offers only an overview of some of the basic concepts. For more complete coverage of these topics, we recommend you read the tutorials available online at `http://java.sun.com/docs/books/tutorial/uiswing`.

Layout Manager Overview

`Components` (buttons, text areas, graphics, etc.) are added to `Containers` such as a `JFrame`, `JPanel`, or a `JWindow`. Containers use layout managers to specify how components should be laid out within the container. `Window` and `Frame` containers use `BorderLayout` as their default layout manager. This particular layout schema has some peculiar functionality you may want to review.

First, the `BorderLayout` divides the container into five areas, as shown in Figure 8-5.

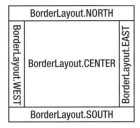

Figure 8-5. *The areas of BorderLayout*

A Component can be placed into a specified region of the BorderLayout by calling the Container's add method, with the first parameter being the object to add, and the second parameter being the constraint, which for BorderLayout will be one of the five regions of the BorderLayout, as represented by the following String constants:

- BorderLayout.NORTH

- BorderLayout.SOUTH

- BorderLayout.EAST

- BorderLayout.WEST

- BorderLayout.CENTER

When a component is placed into one of these five regions, it will immediately expand to fill that area, observing any constraints for that area. For instance, in Listing 8-1 a button is added to each of the regions. Figure 8-6 shows the result.

Listing 8-1. *BorderLayoutExample*

```
import java.awt.*;
import javax.swing.*;

public class BorderLayoutExample extends JFrame {
    public static void main(String[] args) {
        new BorderLayoutExample().setVisible(true);
    }

    public BorderLayoutExample() {
        setDefaultCloseOperation(EXIT_ON_CLOSE);
        add(new JButton("North"), BorderLayout.NORTH);
        add(new JButton("South"), BorderLayout.SOUTH);
        add(new JButton("East"), BorderLayout.EAST);
        add(new JButton("West"), BorderLayout.WEST);
        add(new JButton("Center"), BorderLayout.CENTER);
        pack();
    }
}
```

■**Note** Prior to JDK 1.5, it was necessary to get the content pane for a JFrame, and then add components to the content pane. JDK 1.5 provides overridden add methods for JFrame that allow the code shown earlier to make it appear that we are adding components directly to the JFrame—in fact we are not; the components are being added to the component pane in the overridden add method.

Figure 8-6. *An example of the BorderLayout in action*

As can be seen, the buttons that were added to the "North" and "South" regions have expanded to fill the region from the far left to the far right of the JFrame; however, they have not expanded to fill space above or below the button. The buttons added to the "East" and "West" have expanded to fill the space above and below the button, but they have not expanded to fill to the left or right. The button added to the "Center" can expand in all directions.

Caution If more than one component is added to a region, the newest component placed inside the region is drawn on top of all other previously added components. This often causes confusion when programmers are first adding components, as it appears that some of their components have been lost. There is probably no reason why you would ever want to intentionally add two components in the same region.

There are multiple strategies you can use to lay out components in a container and prevent the preceding anomalies. The best, and perhaps easiest, way to control component flow is to first place all components into a JPanel container and then place the JPanel container into one of the five BorderLayout areas. Unlike the BorderLayout, the JPanel's default layout manager is the FlowLayout. The properties of this particular type of layout are much easier to deal with than that of the GridBagLayout or even the GridLayout. Every component placed in the FlowLayout will maintain its suggested size and will flow from left to right.

The FlowLayout also accepts some justification parameters. The constructor FlowLayout (int index) may be used with one of the following constants in the FlowLayout class:

- FlowLayout.CENTER

- FlowLayout.RIGHT

- FlowLayout.LEFT

Listing 8-2 uses a JPanel combined with a JFrame container to display three buttons. You should also try resizing the JFrame to see the effect this has on FlowLayout. Some examples are shown in Figures 8-7, 8-8, and 8-9.

Listing 8-2. *A FlowLayout with Three Centered Buttons*

```java
import java.awt.*;
import javax.swing.*;

public class ExampleFlowLayout extends JFrame {
    public static void main(String[] args) {
        new ExampleFlowLayout().setVisible(true);
    }

    public ExampleFlowLayout () {
        setDefaultCloseOperation(EXIT_ON_CLOSE);
        JPanel thePanel = new JPanel();
        thePanel.add(new JButton("One"));
        thePanel.add(new JButton("Two"));
        thePanel.add(new JButton("Three"));
        add(thePanel, BorderLayout.CENTER);
        pack();
    }
}
```

Figure 8-7. *FlowLayout showing the default operation—all components laid out at their preferred size next to each other*

Figure 8-8. *An example of FlowLayout when the container has been expanded*

Figure 8-9. *An example of FlowLayout when the container has been reduced in size*

Notice that the button sizes are calculated by the FlowLayout and displayed at just the right size to show their text labels. Also note that the default justification for the FlowLayout is CENTER. Listing 8-3 demonstrates an alteration to the code segment in Listing 8-2 that changes the justification of the buttons. An example of how this might appear is shown in Figure 8-10.

Listing 8-3. *A FlowLayout with Three Buttons Aligned to the Right*

```java
import java.awt.*;
import javax.swing.*;

public class MyFrame extends JFrame {
    public static void main(String[] args) {
        new MyFrame().setVisible(true);
    }

    public MyFrame() {
        setDefaultCloseOperation(EXIT_ON_CLOSE);
        JPanel thePanel = new JPanel(new FlowLayout(FlowLayout.RIGHT));
        thePanel.add(new JButton("One"));
        thePanel.add(new JButton("Two"));
        thePanel.add(new JButton("Three"));
        add(thePanel, BorderLayout.CENTER);
        pack();
        setSize(300, 70);
    }
}
```

Figure 8-10. *An example of FlowLayout with components aligned to the right*

Tip The combination of the `JFrame` and `JPanel` containers is a powerful yet simple way to lay out graphical components. There are certainly more complex ways to handle interface layout, but the combination of these two containers will probably be more than enough to lay out the client interface for the SCJD exam.

Look and Feel

Swing supports a pluggable look and feel. This feature is a welcome side effect of Swing's lightweight components that can be overwritten with programmer-defined design and functionality. A prime example of this feature is the Ocean look and feel. This interface style can be used on any platform that supports Java and graphical user interfaces, and it can be used as a standard interface across all platforms. If an interface absolutely must look and behave the same on every platform, then the Ocean look and feel is the right choice.

The look and feel of any Swing-based GUI can be changed on the fly programmatically within the application.

Here are some common LookAndFeel subclasses:

- javax.swing.plaf.metal.MetalLookAndFeel

- com.sun.java.swing.plaf.windows.WindowsLookAndFeel

- com.sun.java.swing.plaf.motif.MotifLookAndFeel

- com.sun.java.swing.plaf.gtk.GTKLookAndFeel

- com.apple.mrj.swing.MacLookAndFeel

■**Caution** The only look and feel that is guaranteed to exist on all platforms is the one that is in the standard Java packages: javax.swing.plaf.metal.MetalLookAndFeel. All other look-and-feel packages are in nonstandard packages—the com.sun or com.apple (or other vendor) packages. The vendor packages probably won't exist in JVMs produced by other vendors, and may not even exist in all JVMs produced by a particular vendor. For example, the WindowsLookAndFeel is only available on Microsoft Windows platforms, and the GTKLookAndFeel is only available on platforms supporting GTK (typically Unix and Unix-like systems).

Since we have been using the Ocean theme from the Metal look and feel for the previous examples, Listing 8-4 will show an example of setting the look and feel to the Microsoft Windows look and feel, or to a look and feel specified on the command line. An example of how this will look is shown in Figure 8-11. Other look-and-feel examples are shown in Figures 8-12 through 8-15.

Listing 8-4. *Setting the Microsoft Windows Look and Feel*

```java
import java.awt.*;
import javax.swing.*;

public class MyFrame extends JFrame {
    public static void main(String[] args) throws Exception {
        new MyFrame(args).setVisible(true);
    }

    public MyFrame(String[] args) throws Exception {
        String lookAndFeelName = (args.length > 0)
                ? args[0]
                : "com.sun.java.swing.plaf.windows.WindowsLookAndFeel";

        UIManager.setLookAndFeel(lookAndFeelName);

        setDefaultCloseOperation(EXIT_ON_CLOSE);
        Panel topPanel = new Panel(new FlowLayout(FlowLayout.LEFT));
        topPanel.add(new JTextField(15));
        add(topPanel, BorderLayout.NORTH);
```

```
        Panel centerPanel = new Panel(new FlowLayout(FlowLayout.RIGHT));
        centerPanel.add(new JButton("One"));
        centerPanel.add(new JButton("Two"));
        centerPanel.add(new JButton("Three"));
        add(centerPanel, BorderLayout.CENTER);
        pack();
        setSize(210, 100);
    }
}
```

Figure 8-11. *An example of using the Microsoft Windows look and feel*

Figure 8-12. *An example of using the Motif look and feel*

Figure 8-13. *An example of using the Metal look and feel with the Ocean theme*

Figure 8-14. *An example of using the Metal look and feel with the Steel theme*

Figure 8-15. *An example of using the GTK look and feel (Unix platforms)*

You may have noticed that Figures 8-13 and 8-14 both use the Metal look and feel but different themes. Prior to JDK 1.5, the Metal look and feel looked like Figure 8-14; however, with JDK 1.5 Sun has improved the standard look and feel, making the Ocean theme shown in Figure 8-13. To revert to the old theme, the following command line was used:

```
java -Dswing.metalTheme=steel MyFrame javax.swing.plaf.metal.MetalLookAndFeel
```

Caution The layout managers have been designed to perform the hard work of determining where components should be placed relative to one another, as well as determining the size of containers. It is possible to explicitly place components with the setLocation method, and set their size with the setSize method (which we used in Listing 8-4); however, as shown in Figures 8-11 through 8-15, the size of components varies depending on the look and feel used, so deliberately setting the size or location of a component or a container can result in strange-looking GUIs. We strongly recommend that you leave the work of component placement and container sizing to the layout managers.

When a different look-and-feel package is used, the interface adopts not only the look of that particular platform but also the functionality of its interface widgets. For example, a drop-down menu in the Motif look and feel is vastly different from the menu functionality under the Windows or Metal look and feel. This is because Motif represents the interface look and also the functionality of an X Window system.

The JLabel Component

Standard user interfaces have labels near any component that accepts input, providing the user with a brief explanation of what the user input is for. An example of this might be having the label "Surname" next to the text field that accepts the surname data—the label serves to remind the user what sort of data is to be entered in the text field.

The Swing component that holds a label is the JLabel. A simple constructor for this could be

```
JLabel zipCodeLabel = new JLabel("Zip code");
```

While this on its own is not very exciting, you can also specify which character will be displayed as the mnemonic (which character will be underlined). Since it does not make sense for a label to have focus, you normally set the displayed mnemonic, and at the same time set which field will get focus if the mnemonic is pressed. This could look similar to

```
zipCodeLabel.setDisplayedMnemonic('Z');
zipCodeLabel.setLabelFor(zipCode);
```

In this case, if a user presses the mnemonic key (by pressing the Alt and Z keys simultaneously), then focus will be transferred to the zipCode field.

This technique will be demonstrated in Listing 8-5 in the next section, with a sample GUI displayed in Figure 8-16.

The JTextField Component

The JTextField is the basic data entry field. It allows the user to enter plain text up to a specified length. Here's a simple constructor for the JTextField with a size of 15 columns:

```
JTextField zipCode = new JTextField(15);
```

Other constructors for the JTextField allow you to specify a default value to be displayed in the text field, and a Document to validate data entry (data validation will be covered in the next subsection).

A very simple application to demonstrate the use of JLabels and JTextFields is shown in Listing 8-5, and the GUI that this creates is shown in Figure 8-16. A JButton has been included in the GUI to allow you to experiment with transferring focus away from the JTextField and then use the mnemonic to transfer focus back again.

Listing 8-5. *Demonstration of JLabel and JtextField Components*

```java
import java.awt.*;
import javax.swing.*;
import javax.swing.text.*;

public class MyFrame extends JFrame {
    public static void main(String[] args) throws Exception {
        new MyFrame().setVisible(true);
    }

    public MyFrame() throws Exception {
        setDefaultCloseOperation(EXIT_ON_CLOSE);
        setLayout(new FlowLayout());

        JLabel zipCodeLabel = new JLabel("Zip code");
        JTextField zipCode = new JTextField(15);

        zipCodeLabel.setDisplayedMnemonic('Z');
        zipCodeLabel.setLabelFor(zipCode);

        this.add(zipCodeLabel);
        this.add(zipCode);
        this.add(new JButton("A button for focus"));
        pack();
    }
}
```

Figure 8-16. *Demonstration of JLabel and JtextField components*

Validating the Contents of a JTextField

In a perfect world, users would only ever enter valid data into our applications. However, in the real world, people make mistakes, and unfortunately, if not caught in time, major problems can occur if invalid data is entered. So we should make a reasonable effort to prevent invalid data from being entered, and possibly validate data once it has been entered.

Listing 8-5 contained a field named zipCode. In the United States, zip codes are five digits long, and are used to identify the area where a letter or parcel is to be delivered. Unfortunately, our sample program will allow any data to be entered, regardless of length or content.

If we want to limit the zip code field to accept only five-digit zip codes, we can use a subclass of the JTextField: the JFormattedTextField in combination with a MaskFormatter. A JFormattedTextField will only allow characters to be entered that match a specified mask. The MaskFormatter provides a simple method of specifying a text formatter based on a mask—any characters that do not match the mask will be discarded. The mask for a number is the # character. So we could change our definition of the zipCode variable from Listing 8-5 as follows:

```
MaskFormatter fiveDigits = new MaskFormatter("#####");
JTextField zipCode = new JFormattedTextField(fiveDigits);
zipCode.setColumns(5);
```

If you make these changes, you will find that you can no longer enter any character other than a number, and you cannot add more than five digits.

Taking validation a step further, let's consider the case where users want to enter the zip+4 code, where the original five-digit code is followed by a dash and an additional four digits to further narrow down the delivery address—for example, the first five digits specify the delivery office (post office), the next two digits identify a set of blocks on a major street, and the final two digits identify the particular block on the street.

However, zip+4 is not used everywhere, nor is it mandatory to use this format even where it's available (for that matter, it does not appear to be mandatory to use zip codes for anything going through the US Postal Service, but it is probably advisable if you want your letter to arrive in a timely fashion).

One method of handling this is by creating our own text field, with its own document model, in which we override the insertString method. So once again, our definition of the zipCode variable is changing:

```
JTextField zipCode = new ZipTextField(9);
```

The ZipTextField extends JTextField, but all it overrides are the constructors and the createDefaultModel method:

```
private class ZipTextField extends JTextField {
    ZipTextField() {
        super();
    }

    ZipTextField(int columns) {
        super(columns);
    }
```

```
        protected Document createDefaultModel() {
            return new ZipDocument();
        }
    }
}
```

You could override more constructors if you wish, or you could even leave out the constructors (just use default constructors, and call the inherited setColumns method).

The hard work is all done in the model for our ZipTextField. For JTextField (which we are subclassing), the default model is a PlainDocument. We will subclass that to form our ZipDocument, in which we will validate text entered.

Note JTextField, like many Swing components, uses the Model-View-Controller design pattern internally. This gives us two potential areas where we can control data entry—in the Model that contains the data entered, and in the Controller before data is passed to the Model.

```
    private class ZipDocument extends PlainDocument {
        public void insertString(int offs, String str, AttributeSet a)
                throws BadLocationException {
            if (str == null) {
                return;
            }


            for (char c : str.toCharArray()) {
                if (! ((Character.isDigit(c) && offs < 10 && offs != 5)
                        || (b == '-' && offs == 5))) {
                    return;
                }
            }

            super.insertString(offs, str, a);
        }
    }
```

To keep this example simple, we have only overriden the insertString method, and only checked that the character being entered is valid in the location it is being entered. If it is valid, we call the insertString method of the super class to perform the work of actually inserting the string.

Because we have chosen to keep this simple, we have not shown code for validating the deletion of entered data for which we would have to override the remove method. A more complete example is provided in the downloadable source code for this book in the port number validation.

■**Caution** Nothing shown so far prevents the user from entering something like 12345-67 and then moving to the next field or clicking elsewhere in the document. Therefore, some additional validation is in order somewhere, an example of which is shown in the full code.

The JButton Component

The JButton is a "click to do something" type of button. What it does when the user clicks it is up to you. An example of a constructor for this is

```
JButton exitButton = new JButton("Exit");
```

Other constructors allow for an icon to be used instead of or as well as the text, and setting an Action for the button.

The constructor on its own is not very useful—we have not specified what should happen when the button is clicked. For that, we need to add an ActionListener:

```
exitButton.addActionListener(anActionListener);
```

The ActionListener interface allows you to listen for actions: button clicked on, button clicked on while a modifier (the Ctrl, Alt, Shift, or Meta key) was pressed, and so on. When such an action occurs, your actionPerformed method will be called by the event dispatcher thread.

The ActionListener can be an anonymous inner class, a private class, or an external class, or (since ActionListener is an interface) your View can implement the ActionListener.

Here is an example of creating an anonymous inner class for your ActionListener:

```
JButton exitButton = new JButton("Exit");
exitButton.addActionListener(new ActionListener() {
    public void actionPerformed(ActionEvent ae) {
        System.out.println("Somebody clicked the Exit button");
        System.exit(1);
    }
});
```

■**Note** The last line of the code snippet above may look confusing, but if you count backwards, you will find that the closing brace (}) matches the opening brace for the new ActionListener() {, and the closing bracket ()) matches the opening bracket for the addActionListener(.

As with all choices, there are good points and bad points for using an anonymous inner class. Some of the good points are as follows:

- There is no need to create a separate class to handle user events.

- There is no need to check which component triggered the action event.

- The code to handle the event is right with the component that triggered the event.

The first point can be worth consideration, but if you are using the MVC pattern, you might prefer to have the Controller handle the user events. Alternatively, a simple anonymous class can call a method in the Controller class, making the Controller class less dependent on the GUI architecture.

The last point can be both good and bad as well—you might not want the code *handling* the event with the code that is *configuring* the View. It might make more sense to keep event-handling code separate.

If you do decide to have a separate class or method handling events, you might want to consider using the setActionCommand method to set a string by which your component can be easily identified. The string you set can then be retrieved from the ActionEvent handed to the actionPerformed method. This is demonstrated in Listing 8-6 in the next section.

The JRadioButton Component

Radio buttons are small buttons that are logically grouped together, but only one of the group can be active at any given time. This is similar to the way a radio with buttons for several pre-set stations should only have one button pressed at any given time—you can only listen to one station at a time.

A simple constructor for a JRadioButton could be

```
JRadioButton serverButton = new JRadioButton("Server");
```

Other constructors allow for an icon to be used instead of or as well as the text, setting the initial state of the radio button, and setting an Action for the radio button.

As with the JButton, an ActionListener can be added to each JRadioButton. You might use this if you needed to enable or disable fields dependent on which button a user clicked. However, it is not always necessary to have an ActionListener—if you don't care about which button is clicked until after the user performs some other action, then you can use the isSelected method to check the user's choice.

For JRadioButtons to be effective, several of them should be logically grouped together, so that only one of the logical group can be selected at any given time. You do this by creating a ButtonGroup, and adding the radio buttons to it:

```
ButtonGroup applicationMode = new ButtonGroup();
applicationMode.add(serverButton);
```

A complete example of JButtons and JRadioButtons is demonstrated in Listing 8-6, and the window it would create is shown in Figure 8-17.

Listing 8-6. *Demonstration of JButton and JRadioButton Components*

```java
import java.awt.*;
import java.awt.event.*;
import javax.swing.*;

public class MyFrame extends JFrame {
    private static final String EXIT_COMMAND = "EXIT";
    private static final String CLIENT_COMMAND = "CLIENT";
    private static final String SERVER_COMMAND = "SERVER";
```

```java
    public static void main(String[] args) throws Exception {
        new MyFrame().setVisible(true);
    }

    public MyFrame() throws Exception {
        setDefaultCloseOperation(EXIT_ON_CLOSE);

        ActionListener buttonHandler = new MyFrameActionListener();

        JButton exitButton = new JButton("Exit");
        exitButton.setActionCommand(EXIT_COMMAND);
        exitButton.addActionListener(buttonHandler);

        JRadioButton serverButton = new JRadioButton("Server");
        serverButton.setActionCommand(SERVER_COMMAND);
        serverButton.addActionListener(buttonHandler);
        JRadioButton clientButton = new JRadioButton("Client");
        clientButton.setActionCommand(CLIENT_COMMAND);
        clientButton.addActionListener(buttonHandler);

        ButtonGroup clientServerGroup = new ButtonGroup();
        clientServerGroup.add(serverButton);
        clientServerGroup.add(clientButton);

        JPanel clientServerPanel = new JPanel();
        clientServerPanel.add(serverButton, BorderLayout.NORTH);
        clientServerPanel.add(clientButton, BorderLayout.SOUTH);

        this.add(clientServerPanel, BorderLayout.CENTER);
        this.add(exitButton, BorderLayout.SOUTH);

        pack();
    }

    private class MyFrameActionListener implements ActionListener {
        public void actionPerformed(ActionEvent ae) {
            if (EXIT_COMMAND.equals(ae.getActionCommand())) {
                System.exit(0);
            } else if (SERVER_COMMAND.equals(ae.getActionCommand())) {
                System.out.println("Server selected");
            } else if (CLIENT_COMMAND.equals(ae.getActionCommand())) {
                System.out.println("Client selected");
            }
        }
    }
}
```

Figure 8-17 shows the result from Listing 8-6.

Figure 8-17. *Demonstration of JButton and JRadioButton components*

The JComboBox Component

Sometimes it makes sense to give users a clear choice of options, rather than requiring them to type in a choice (which is an error-prone approach). The JComboBox provides us with a simple box that, when clicked, pops down a list of options from which the user can choose.

If you know the items that are to be used in the list, then there are constructors that allow you to specify the initial items. Alternatively, you can dynamically add or remove items from the list using the addItems and removeItems methods, respectively.

As with the JButton and JRadioButton, an ActionListener can be added to each JComboBox. You might use this if you needed to take action immediately after the user selects an option. However, it is not always necessary to have an ActionListener—if you don't care about which button is clicked until after the user performs some other action, then you can use the getSelectedIndex method to determine the index of the item chosen, or the getSelectedItem method to find out the object selected.

JComboBox usage is demonstrated in Listing 8-7 shown in the next section, with the window created displayed in Figure 8-18.

The BorderFactory

So far all the components demonstrated have appeared to the end user to be in the same JFrame—there is nothing to logically separate one component (or set of components) from another.

However, there are times when it makes sense to logically group components together by drawing a border around them. One of the most common uses of borders is to create a perceived link around several radio buttons or check boxes. We did not put a border around our radio buttons in the previous section because we want to emphasize that the border only creates a **user perception** that the buttons are logically linked—it is possible to have a border drawn around buttons that are not logically linked, and just creating a border around buttons does not logically link them.

Unlike with most Swing components, we do not create a border directly. Instead we call one of the static methods of the BorderFactory class to create a border for us, which we can then use in a JPanel or JFrame.

■**Note** The Factory design pattern, used by the BorderFactory, is often used when many similar objects need to be created, but the user of the objects does not need to know the implementation details—all the user of the object needs to know about is how to use it. Each of the BorderFactory's create methods will create a Border, where Border is an interface. Since we have an interface for all potential borders, we can use the created border in any JFrame or JPanel without concerning ourselves with what type of border was created. Furthermore, we don't have to worry about how a particular border will be created on different operating systems—the factory handles all that for us.

Which particular border to create and use is up to you. Frequently status bars use a lowered bevel border (which you can create using the createLoweredBevelBorder method), groupings of radio buttons use a titled border (createTitledBorder), and groupings of buttons might be enclosed in a beveled border without a title (createBevelBorder).

An example of creating a titled border around a JComboBox is shown in Listing 8-7, with the window created shown in Figure 8-18. For this example we included some spacing labels to make the border more obvious.

Listing 8-7. *Demonstration of the JComboBox Component and the BorderFactory*

```java
import java.awt.*;

import javax.swing.*;


public class MyFrame extends JFrame {
    private final static String TITLE = "Title goes here";

    public static void main(String[] args) throws Exception {
        new MyFrame().setVisible(true);
    }

    public MyFrame() throws Exception {
        setDefaultCloseOperation(EXIT_ON_CLOSE);

        String[] items = {"One", "Two", "Three", "Four", "Five"};
        JComboBox choosableItems = new JComboBox(items);

        JPanel clientServerPanel = new JPanel();

        clientServerPanel.setBorder(BorderFactory.createTitledBorder(TITLE));
        clientServerPanel.add(new JLabel("Pick a number:"), BorderLayout.EAST);
        clientServerPanel.add(choosableItems, BorderLayout.CENTER);

        this.add(new JLabel("    "), BorderLayout.NORTH);
        this.add(new JLabel("    "), BorderLayout.SOUTH);
        this.add(new JLabel("    "), BorderLayout.EAST);
```

```
        this.add(new JLabel("    "), BorderLayout.WEST);
        this.add(clientServerPanel, BorderLayout.CENTER);

        pack();
    }
}
```

Figure 8-18. *Demonstration of the JComboBox component and the BorderFactory*

Listing 8-7 was designed to show how to make a simple border without introducing too many new features at once. To that end, we put empty labels around the border just to make it stand out—normally you would not do this in practice. Instead, you might consider using a compound border, as shown in Listing 8-8. This will produce an almost identical result to that shown in Figure 8-18.

Listing 8-8. *Demonstration of a Compound Border*

```java
import java.awt.*;
import javax.swing.*;

public class MyFrame extends JFrame {
    private final static String TITLE = "Title goes here";

    public static void main(String[] args) throws Exception {
        new MyFrame().setVisible(true);
    }

    public MyFrame() throws Exception {
        setDefaultCloseOperation(EXIT_ON_CLOSE);

        String[] items = {"One", "Two", "Three", "Four", "Five"};
        JComboBox choosableItems = new JComboBox(items);

        JPanel clientServerPanel = new JPanel();
        clientServerPanel.setBorder(
                BorderFactory.createCompoundBorder(
                        BorderFactory.createEmptyBorder(10, 10, 10, 10),
                        BorderFactory.createTitledBorder(TITLE)));
```

```
            clientServerPanel.add(new JLabel("Pick a number:"), BorderLayout.EAST);
            clientServerPanel.add(choosableItems, BorderLayout.CENTER);
            this.add(clientServerPanel, BorderLayout.CENTER);

            pack();
        }
}
```

The JTable Component

As discussed earlier in this chapter, the table paradigm has developed into a de facto data display mechanism. As you may recall, the table schema is a great way to display data because it offers ease of interpretation for the user and efficiently displays large amounts of data in a small area.

The JTable renders data in the familiar "data table" style. For the developer, it is the perfect combination of ease of use and extensibility. You can create a JTable for casual use by simply calling the JTable constructor method JTable (Object rowData [][], Object columnNames[]) and defining two arrays containing header names and the data rows, as demonstrated in Listing 8-9.

Listing 8-9. *A Simple JTable Constructor*

```
Object [ ][ ] rows = {{"Data 1", "Data 2"}, {"Data 3", "Data 4"},
                       {"Data 6", "Data 6"} };
Object [ ] colNames =  {"Header 1", "Header 2"};

JTable table = new JTable (rows, colNames);
```

Listing 8-9 creates a table composed of three rows. This table is shown in Figure 8-19.

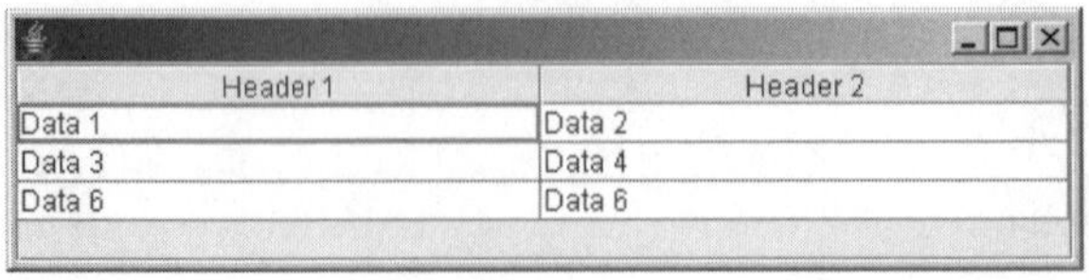

Figure 8-19. *A sample table*

Note that each row is labeled with a header. If an array of table headers is not specified, the table will only display the rows and columns without any headers. Also notice that the table columns are automatically sized, but they may be resized and even rearranged. The following methods can be called on a JTable instance to enable and disable these capabilities:

- setSelectionMode(ListSelectionModel.SINGLE_SELECTION)

- setAutoResizeMode(JTable.AUTO_RESIZE_ALL_COLUMNS)

The preceding table example is perfect if the data in the table only needs to be displayed once, but the example is not a very malleable method with which to display data. To become a more flexible data display, a good table class would need additional methods and constructors to fit within the paradigm of the MVC pattern. It so happens that the JTable fits incredibly well into this pattern—so much so that the JTable actually defines its own model: the TableModel interface.

Note Many Swing components, such as the JTable and the JTree, implement their own MVC architecture.

The TableModel

The TableModel is one of the easiest and most flexible ways to display a data set in a JTable. Earlier in this chapter, the interaction between the Model and the View in the MVC pattern was discussed in detail. As you may recall, the View is solely responsible for taking the data contained in a Model object and converting it into a visual representation. The JTable actually incorporates this part of the MVC pattern into its standard API. An implemented TableModel interface acts as the Model in this case, and the JTable instance acts as the View. The TableModel is essentially handed off to a JTable instance, and the table widget renders the data model into the visual representation. The Model may be specified in the JTable constructor:

```
JTable table = new JTable (TableModel model);
```

or set via the void setTableModel (TableModel model) instance method. Once the TableModel is passed to the table instance, the JTable class literally takes care of the rest.

At this point, the JTable may seem like a snap to use. While the JTable is quite easy to use, the bulk of the work for the developer comes in the task of implementing the TableModel interface.

As with event listener interfaces, not all of the methods specified in the TableModel interface are always necessary for a given data set. For instance, if a developer wanted to implement a simple TableModel, it would be inefficient to have to provide implementations for all the interface methods, such as removeTableModelListener(TableModelListener modListener). Thus, an adapter class is provided that functions in a manner similar to event adapter classes. The AbstractTableModel class implements the TableModel interface such that each method already has a default implementation. Therefore, extending the AbstractTableModel class is usually the best starting point when creating a custom TableModel.

In version 2.0 of the Denny's DVDs application, the DVDTableModel class is an extension of the AbstractTableModel class. The DVDTableModel does not need to implement the getColumnClass, removeTableModelListener, and addTableModelListener methods, so their default implementations provided by the abstract implementation will suffice. All other methods in the TableModel interface will be implemented.

First, notice the addition of the two member variables in the DVDTableModel class in Listing 8-10.

Listing 8-10. *The DVDTableModel's Internal Members That Hold the Table Rows*

```
private String [] headerNames = {"UPC", "Movie Title", "Director",
                                 "Lead Actor", "Supporting Actor", "Composer",
                                 "Copies in Stock"};

private List<String[]> dvdRecords = new ArrayList<String[]>(5);
```

Remember that Model objects act as data containers. The View object that transforms a Model into a display format does not require knowledge of how they internally represent data. On a very abstract level, tables encapsulate two things:

- The names of the columns

- The data contained in each row

These two items require a TableModel to internally represent two types of collections: one that contains a list of header names and one that contains a list of row values. The only decision that remains is what type of collection is appropriate to represent these two types of data.

In the case of the JTable contained in our client application, the header names will remain the same throughout the life of the application. Therefore, an array of String objects will be the perfect data structure to hold the column names. Next, the row column values for each row are immutable in the sense that once a row is created, the number of values in a row does not need to change. Thus, an array of String values can also represent a row of DVD data.

The actual collection that holds the rows is entirely different from the table headers and column data in that the number of rows changes—and changes quite often. If a user searches for a list of DVD records, there is no way to ensure how many rows will result, and therefore it will be impossible to anticipate the size of the data structure required to hold the values. The best option to hold rows of data is a dynamic collection that can have values easily appended, removed, and iterated through. The order of the results also matters, so a set collection is obviously a poor choice. The best choice is some type of dynamic list. The list can now be narrowed to a Vector, a LinkedList, or an ArrayList. As mentioned in the "Internally Synchronized Classes" section of Chapter 4, Vectors provide little benefit in most cases, but can provide a false sense of thread safety—we therefore generally recommend against their use. In this particular case, the values in our TableModel do not have to be thread-safe because only one thread is manipulating their values in a single instance. Thus, a Vector provides unneeded overhead in this application without providing any benefits. A LinkedList provides us with some additional methods over an ArrayList—specifically the ability to add and remove the first and last objects in the collection; however, we do not need this additional functionality. The best choice for the representation of DVD data rows in our TableModel is clearly an ArrayList.

Next, our TableModel must implement some of the required methods that the JTable uses to render the Model into a View. For instance, the TableModel must have a way to inform the JTable of how many columns it encapsulates. The method getColumnCount shown in Listing 8-11 provides this functionality.

Listing 8-11. *Our TableModel's getColumnCount Method*

```
public int getColumnCount() {
    return this.headerNames.length;
}
```

In this case, the number of columns is always equal to the number of header titles, so this method can simply return the length of the headerNames member. Our TableModel must also return the name of each column. Listing 8-12 returns the String value from the headerNames member at a specified index.

Listing 8-12. *The TableModel's getColumnName Method*

```
public String getColumnName (int column) {
    return headerNames[column];
}
```

Next, the TableModel returns and sets a cell value at a given row and column index. The methods shown in Listing 8-13 allow the assignment and retrieval of values at specific row and column indexes.

Listing 8-13. *The TableModel's set and get valueAt Methods*

```
public Object getValueAt(int row, int column) {
    String[] rowValues = this.dvdRecords.get(row);
    return rowValues[column];
}

public void setValueAt(Object obj, int row, int column) {
    Object[] rowValues = this.dvdRecords.get(row);
    rowValues[column] = obj;
}
```

Note, it would have been possible for the getValueAt method to have been written as

```
public Object getValueAt(int row, int column) {
    return this.dvdRecords.get(row)[column];
}
```

Whenever you are tempted to take a shortcut like this, though, you should consider what benefit it gives you. Is the creation or destruction of the rowValues **reference** to the array so expensive that this will gain much efficiency? Alternatively, will this code be harder to read and therefore harder to maintain?

Next, the method getRowCount shown in Listing 8-14 returns the number of data rows encapsulated in the TableModel. In our TableModel, the number of rows is the size of the DVD ArrayList.

Listing 8-14. *The DVDTableModel's getRowCount Method*

```
public int getRowCount() {
    return this.dvdRecords.size();
}
```

The isCellEditable method in our TableModel class (see Listing 8-15) indicates whether or not a cell is editable. No cells in our particular TableModel implementation are editable, so the method returns false by default. If particular cells in the TableModel were editable, this method would take the column and row indexes into account and evaluate whether or not a cell was editable.

Listing 8-15. *The TableModel's isCellEditable Method*

```
public boolean isCellEditable (int row, int column) {
     return false;
}
```

■**Note** Unlike the other methods shown so far, isCellEditable is already implemented in AbstractTableModel. As it happens, the AbstractTableModel implementation provides the same functionality as our overridden method. We therefore did not need to override this method; however, doing so makes it easier for you to experiment with this method.

Finally, our DVDTableModel class contains two methods beyond those required by the TableModel interface. These extra methods are included as a matter of convenience. As mentioned earlier in this chapter, the DVD object, which is used by the rest of the system, is not the same Model that is used by the View. In this case, the View object is a JTable and the Model object is the DVDTableModel. The GUIController class must go through the process of converting a DVD object (or a collection of DVD objects) to a DVDTableModel object. To make this task easier, the DVDTableModel implements the two methods in Listing 8-16.

Listing 8-16. *Convenience Methods Within the DVDTableModel Class*

```
public void addDVDRecord (String upc, String name, String director,
                          String leadActor, String supportingActor,
                          String composer, int numberOfCopies) {
    String [] temp = {upc, name, director, leadActor, supportingActor,
                      composer, Integer.toString(numberOfCopies)};
    this.dvdRecords.add(temp);
}

public void addDVDRecord (DVD dvd) {
        addDVDRecord(dvd.getUPC(), dvd.getName(), dvd.getDirector(),
                 dvd.getLeadActor(), dvd.getSupportingActor(),
                 dvd.getComposer(), dvd.getCopy());
}
```

The methods in Listing 8-16 take in a DVD object (or the equivalent data) and append the new row to the data set encapsulated within the DVDTableModel. The first method receives the data contained in a DVD object as parts, whereas the second method simply requires a DVD object. In order to add a DVD to the DVDTableModel, the GUIController will simply call one of these two methods, thus avoiding a conversion process from within the GUIController each time an alteration to the data view occurs.

■**Tip** The preceding `DVDTableModel` has the capability to convert DVD model objects one at a time, but sometimes it is more convenient to provide a method that will convert entire collections of model objects. That way, a search method could use a single call to convert its entire set of search results.

Using the TableModel with a JTable

Once a `TableModel` has been implemented, using it with a `JTable` is a simple task. A `TableModel` may be specified in the constructor of a `JTable` object. For example, the following snippet will create a new `JTable` using the `DVDTableModel` that was described in the previous section:

```
JTable table = new JTable (new DVDTableModel ());
```

The preceding statement will create a `JTable` using a `DVDTableModel`, but the table display will be empty, since no data is contained in the specified `DVDTableModel` instance.

■**Note** A `JTable` instance can have its internal table model modified after it is instantiated. The `setModel` method updates a `JTable`'s internal `TableModel` member and therefore updates the data the `JTable` displays. Data can also be added to a `JTable`'s `TableModel` reference by calling the method `getModel` method on a `JTable` instance. In our case, this method can be called to get a reference to the `JTable`'s internal `DVDTableModel` reference. Then the method `addRecord` can be called to add a row to a `JTable`.

Because alterations to a `JTable`'s `TableModel` translates into an updated View, the client must be set up to take advantage of this schema. The `MainWindow` class contains the private member

```
private DVDTableModel tableData;
```

This data member will always hold the main `JTable`'s `TableModel`. Because all data transfer between the View and the Controller is done via a `DVDTableModel` object, this member is always updated to reflect changes to the database's state.

Once the database has been updated or queried, the resulting table model is placed into the `tableData` member. After calling the Controller, the `MainWindow` class calls its internal private method `setupTable`. This method contains the statements in Listing 8-17.

Listing 8-17. *The setupTable Method*

```
private void setupTable() {
        // Preserve the previous selection
        int index = mainTable.getSelectedRow();
        String prevSelected = (index >= 0)
                            ? (String) mainTable.getValueAt(index, 0)
                            : "";
```

```
        // Reset the table data
        this.mainTable.setModel(this.tableData);

        // Reselect the previous item if it still exists
        for (int i = 0; i < this.mainTable.getRowCount(); i++) {
            String selectedUpc = (String) mainTable.getValueAt(i, 0);
            if (selectedUpc.equals(prevSelected) ) {
                this.mainTable.setRowSelectionInterval(i,i);
                break;
            }
        }
    }
}
```

Notice that the setupTable method refreshes the MainWindow's JTable instance by calling the setTableModel method. As soon as the table's internal TableModel is replaced, the View will refresh and display the updated data set. If the JTable does not update its contents, the updateUI method can be called, effectively forcing the table to redisplay its contents.

Also notice that the setupTable method stores the last selected row before refreshing the table model. After the table model is reset, the method loops through the new data set and locates the previously selected row by the UPC number. After that, the table's setRowSelectionInterval method is called to reselect the previous row.

The JScrollPane

Occasionally we get a situation where we need to display more on the screen than will fit. For the Denny's DVDs application, it is possible that there could be so many DVDs in the database that displaying them all on screen simultaneously is impossible.

In these cases, we can add the component that is too large for the screen to a JScrollPane, which will put scrollbars around the component, *where necessary*, to allow scrolling to a different region and viewing the contents there. Note that, by default, the scrollbars are only shown when needed—if they are not needed, they will not appear.

Listing 8-18 shows an example of an application where there is too much data to appear in the desired text area, and the way this would appear on screen is shown in Figure 8-20.

Listing 8-18. *An Application That Has Too Much Data to Appear in the Window*

```
import javax.swing.*;


public class MyFrame {
    public static void main(String[] args) throws Exception {

        JFrame theFrame = new JFrame();
        theFrame.setDefaultCloseOperation(JFrame.EXIT_ON_CLOSE);
```

```
        String outputString = "";
        for (int i = 0; i < 100; i++) {
            outputString += "The quick brown fox jumped over the lazy dog. ";
        }

        JTextArea textDisplay = new JTextArea(20, 60);
        textDisplay.setLineWrap(true);
        theFrame.add(textDisplay);
        theFrame.pack();
        textDisplay.setText(outputString);
        theFrame.setVisible(true);
    }
}
```

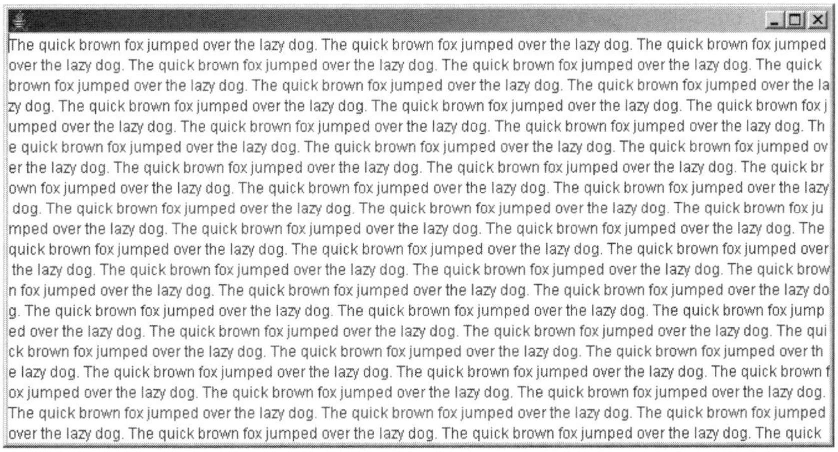

Figure 8-20. *Display when attempting to show too much text*

In most cases, the simplest solution to this problem is changing the line

```
        theFrame.add(textDisplay);
```

to read

```
        theFrame.add(new JScrollPane(textDisplay));
```

The results of this change are shown in Figure 8-21.

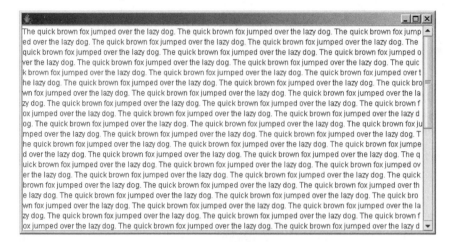

Figure 8-21. *Making a GUI object scrollable using a JScrollPane*

Bringing Denny's DVDs Together

Now it is time to bring the Denny's DVDs application together. The best way to launch the Denny's DVDs client is through the use of a shell class. The entire responsibility of this class is to initiate the launch of the application. Usually, an application shell will initialize some global settings, such as the application's look and feel, and resolve any preconditions that must exist for the application.

For the DVD client application, the main precondition is setting up the look and feel. In order to provide users with a look and feel they are familiar with, we have chosen to set the look and feel based on the system look and feel.

We also check the command-line options provided, as the command-line options set the mode for the application.

Application Startup Class

The ApplicationRunner class is essentially an application loader. The only thing the main method creates is an object of type ApplicationRunner. The ApplicationRunner class's constructor sets up the application's look and feel and instantiates either the MainWindow or the ServerWindow class, as shown in Listing 8-19.

Listing 8-19. *Denny's DVDs Main Application Loader*

```
public ApplicationRunner(String[] args) {

    if (args.length == 0 || "alone".equalsIgnoreCase(args[0])) {
        // Create an instance of the main application window
        new MainWindow(args);
    } else if ("server".equalsIgnoreCase(args[0])) {
        new ServerWindow();
    } else {
```

```
            log.info("Invalid parameter passed in startup: " + args[0]);
            // Logging may be turned off, or may be going to a file, so
            // send usage information to the error output (usually the screen).
            System.err.println("Command line options may be one of:");
            System.err.println("\"server\" - the server application will start");
            System.err.println("\"alone\"  - client start in non networked mode");
            System.err.println("\"\"       - (no command line option): " +
                            "networked client will start");
        }
    }
```

The ApplicationRunner class also contains the static method handleException. The method takes in a String argument and prompts the user with an error message box containing the string message. This method exists for the sole purpose of presenting application error feedback to the user. All exceptions that occur in the MainWindow class will be caught, and during the try/catch process a call to the handleException method will be made that will display error information for the user.

The Client GUI

The bulk of the GUI logic is contained within the MainWindow class, which we will present here.

GUI Design and Layout

As mentioned in Chapter 2 and at the start of this chapter, we recommend you start by hand-sketching your GUI. To give an example of what we mean, consider the sketch of the GUI we will be developing for our client application that is shown in Figure 8-22.

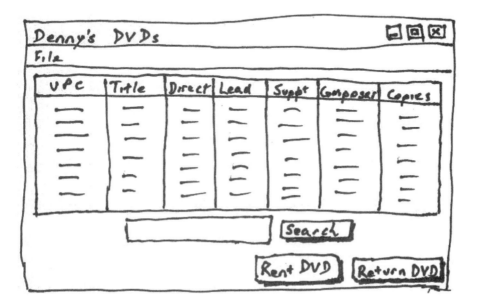

Figure 8-22. *A hand-drawn sketch of the client GUI interface*

Sketching a prototype in this way gives us the following advantages over coding the GUI directly:

- We can sketch a sample GUI quicker than we can write code to create a mock-up of the application.

- Following that point, if the end user would like a change made to the interface, you won't have to throw out code.

- The sketch can be shown to your sample audience/testers anywhere—you do not need a computer handy.

- When you show it to potential users, they will *know* that it is a sketch, and not a complete application, whereas if you show potential users a mocked-up GUI, there is the tendency for the users to believe that a large proportion of the work is complete.

- Having made an up-front decision about what looks good, we are more likely to stick to it. When coding without the up-front sketch, there is the temptation to change parts of the design whenever it appears to difficult to do.

- Having made an up-front decision about what will appear in the GUI, there is less temptation to add more as we go along.

Just like assembling a puzzle, there are many ways to solve a single problem. The preceding layout structure is, of course, merely the way we have chosen to lay out Denny's DVD application—you might choose a totally different layout for your application. The Denny's DVDs application interface takes a simple approach that incorporates very few additional bells and whistles. A basic Swing implementation is all that Sun requires for the SCJD exam, but you can choose to go above and beyond what is required and add more features than required. A JToolBar, for example, could be provided for additional ease of use, even though it is not specifically required to pass the exam. Whether to add such features is up to you. On the one hand, there are many features that you can add that will make your GUI more user friendly, and hence improve your score. On the other hand, your instructions may warn against going beyond specifications. Where to draw the line is up to you.

When we look at the sketch in Figure 8-22, we can see that there are three major areas (excluding the title bar and menu bar), as shown in Figure 8-23.

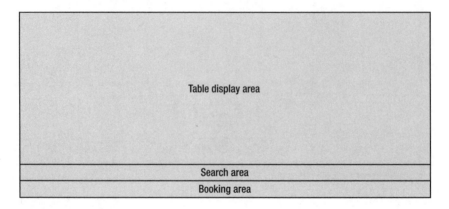

Figure 8-23. *The three main areas of the client GUI application*

We might be tempted to try to add our components directly into a `BorderLayout`; however, if the user should resize the screen, the object to the north and south will only stretch horizontally—it is the object in the center that will stretch vertically. This could lead to an awkward-looking screen, as demonstrated in Figure 8-24.

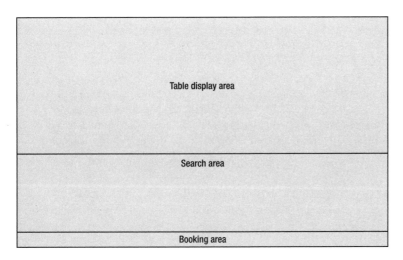

Figure 8-24. *Resizing the GUI application if the table is in the north, the search panel is in the center, and the booking panel is in the south*

■Note This is an example of where creating a sketch of our application before coding helps ensure we end up with a GUI that the users want, not what is easiest for us. Without that sketch, we might be tempted to change the user-approved design just to make our life easier.

So what we need to do is to change how we break up the GUI. The major amount of information is going to be displayed in the table, so that is the component we want in the center. This means that we are going to need to create another panel that will contain both search options and booking options to go in the south of the main panel, as shown in Figure 8-25.

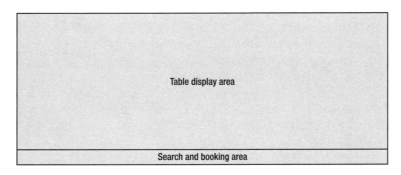

Figure 8-25. *The new panels for the main window*

We will create a JPanel that contains the search panel and the booking panel. Since these two panels do not need to change size when the user resizes the window, we will place the search panel in the north, and the booking panel in the south, as shown in Figure 8-26.

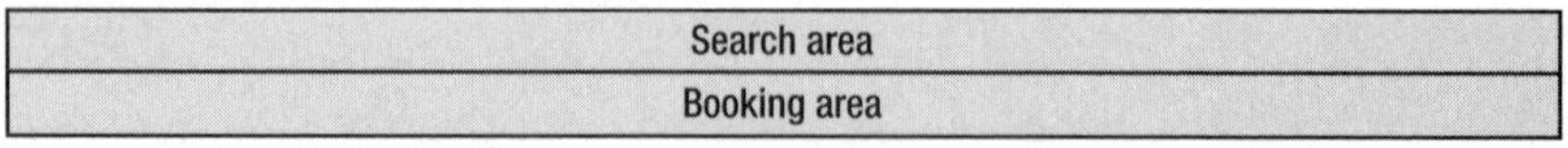

| Search area |
| Booking area |

Figure 8-26. *The new panel for searching and for booking*

We can then take the panel shown in Figure 8-26 and add it to the south of the panel shown in Figure 8-25, which results in a GUI that will resize the table pane where needed, while leaving the search and booking panes the desired size. The code shown in Listing 8-20 demonstrates this techinique. Note, however, that labels are used in place of the real components—this is done so that the code may be easier to understand.

Listing 8-20. *Combining Several Panels to Form One Overall GUI*

```java
import java.awt.*;
import javax.swing.*;
import javax.swing.border.*;

public class MyFrame {
    public static void main(String[] args) throws Exception {
        Border border = BorderFactory.createLineBorder(Color.BLACK);
        JFrame theFrame = new JFrame();
        theFrame.setDefaultCloseOperation(JFrame.EXIT_ON_CLOSE);

        // This is the panel for the table - that is all it contains
        JPanel tablePanel = new JPanel();
        tablePanel.setBorder(border);
        JLabel table = new JLabel("Table display area",SwingConstants.CENTER);
        table.setPreferredSize(new Dimension(650,225));
        tablePanel.add(table);

        // The search options panel
        JPanel searchPanel = new JPanel();
        searchPanel.setBorder(border);
        JLabel search = new JLabel("Search area",SwingConstants.CENTER);
        search.setPreferredSize(new Dimension(650,15));
        searchPanel.add(search);

        // the booking options panel
        JPanel bookPanel = new JPanel();
        bookPanel.setBorder(border);
        JLabel book = new JLabel("Booking area",SwingConstants.CENTER);
        book.setPreferredSize(new Dimension(650,15));
        bookPanel.add(book);
```

```
        // The search & booking options panels are both added to an extra panel
        JPanel optionsPanel = new JPanel(new BorderLayout());
        optionsPanel.add(searchPanel, BorderLayout.NORTH);
        optionsPanel.add(bookPanel, BorderLayout.SOUTH);

        // The the tablePanel and optionsPanel are added to the JFrame
        theFrame.add(tablePanel, BorderLayout.CENTER);
        theFrame.add(optionsPanel, BorderLayout.SOUTH);

        theFrame.pack();
        theFrame.setVisible(true);
    }
}
```

Listing 8-20 shows roughly how we will be laying out the MainWindow for our client application. We will be providing the complete code for the MainWindow class next; however, it is worthwhile reading through the code presented in Listing 8-20 to ensure that you are comfortable with the layout concepts before continuing.

The contents of the screen generated by Listing 8-20 are shown in Figure 8-27.

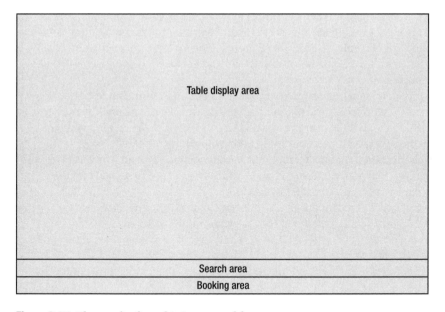

Figure 8-27. *The result of combining several frames*

The search area and the booking area each contain multiple items laid out in a row. We can use the FlowLayout for these two panes, as will be shown in Listing 8-21 in the next section.

■**Tip** This technique of developing small sections of code to show a concept is very useful in developing and debugging code. It is often the case when attempting to incorporate some feature that does not appear to work correctly, or trying to debug some existing code, that a large portion of the code is not relevant to your problem. When you create a simple application just for testing the issue, you do not have irrelevant code to distract you. It also means that you have a small bit of code with which to ask a friend or colleague for help if necessary—asking a friend or colleague to help debug a thousand-line application is really pushing friendship.

The MainWindow

The MainWindow class extends JFrame and is the actual implementation of the Denny's DVDs main window. The constructor of the MainWindow goes through the process of setting up the application menu bar, the main data table, adding the DVDScreen (described after Listing 8-22), and setting the main window in the center of the operating system screen.

First, the DVDMainWindow constructor creates an instance of its super class, JFrame, setting the title of the application. Following this, a dialog box is created where the user can enter the location of the database (described in the upcoming section, "Specifying the Database Location"). The initialization procedure then continues to create the menu bar and all menu items.

As shown in Listing 8-21, there is one JMenuBar for the frame. The menu bar may have several JMenus attached (for example, one for the File menu, one for the Help menu, and so on). Each menu may have several JMenuItems attached—one for each action your user is likely to perform via a menu.

Each menu and menu item may have an optional mnemonic key and an optional icon attached. We have shown attaching the mnemonic key F to the File menu, and the mnemonic key Q to the Quit menu item. If the user presses the Alt and F keys, the File menu will pop down, and if they then press the Q key, the application will quit.

Normally each menu item has an actionListener attached to respond to events. We have shown attaching an instance of the QuitApplication class to the quitMenuItem (the QuitApplication class will be shown in Listing 8-22).

After the menus have been configured, and the data loaded from the database, an instance of the DVDScreen class is added to the MainWindow frame. DVDScreen is a JPanel that contains the elements described in the "GUI Design and Layout" section earlier. It will be shown in Listing 8-23.

Finally, an initial size for the application window is set, and the application window is centered on the screen.

Listing 8-21. *The MainWindow Constructor: Setting Up the Menu*

```
public MainWindow(String[] args) {
    super("Denny's DVDs");
    this.setDefaultCloseOperation(this.EXIT_ON_CLOSE);

    ApplicationMode connectionType = (args.length == 0)
                            ? ApplicationMode.NETWORK_CLIENT
                            : ApplicationMode.STANDALONE_CLIENT;
```

```
        // find out where our database is
        DatabaseLocationDialog dbLocation =
            new DatabaseLocationDialog(this, connectionType);

        try {
            controller = new GuiController(dbLocation.getNetworkType(),
                                    dbLocation.getLocation(),
                                    dbLocation.getPort());
        } catch (GUIControllerException gce) {
            ApplicationRunner.handleException(
                    "Failed to connect to the database");
        }


        // Add the menu bar
        JMenuBar menuBar = new JMenuBar ();
        JMenu fileMenu = new JMenu ("File");
        JMenuItem quitMenuItem = new JMenuItem ("Quit");
        quitMenuItem.addActionListener(new QuitApplication ());
        quitMenuItem.setMnemonic(KeyEvent.VK_Q);
        fileMenu.add(quitMenuItem);
        fileMenu.setMnemonic(KeyEvent.VK_F);
        menuBar.add(fileMenu);

        this.setJMenuBar(menuBar);

        // A full data set is returned from an empty search
        try {
            tableData = controller.getDVDs();
            setupTable();
        } catch (GUIControllerException gce) {
            ApplicationRunner.handleException(
                    "Failed to acquire an initial DVD list." +
                    "\nPlease check the DB connection.");
        }

        this.add(new DvdScreen());

        this.pack();
        this.setSize(650, 300);

        // Center on screen
        Dimension d = Toolkit.getDefaultToolkit().getScreenSize();
        int x = (int) ((d.getWidth() - this.getWidth())/ 2);
        int y = (int) ((d.getHeight() - this.getHeight())/ 2);
        this.setLocation(x, y);
        this.setVisible(true);
    }
```

If the user chooses to quit the application using the Quit menu item, the event handler will call the QuitApplication class. This is one of the simplest event handlers we could write—all it does is call System.exit(0). It is shown in Listing 8-22.

Listing 8-22. *The QuitApplication ActionListener*

```
private class QuitApplication implements ActionListener {
    public void actionPerformed (ActionEvent ae) {
        System.exit(0);
    }
}
```

Listing 8-23 contains the DVDScreen constructor. The major components of this have all been introduced in the earlier sections.

DVDScreen starts by adding a scroll pane for the table holding the DVDs—this is added to the center of the JPanel.

Following this, the panel for the search options is created, along the way creating the text field for entering the search parameters, and the button to begin a search. An action listener is added to the search button, and will be described after Listing 8-23 since it is a little more involved than our application listener for the Quit menu item.

Then the buttons and panel for the Rent and Return options are created, along with their action listeners.

A bottom panel is created to hold both the search options and the hiring options, with the search options panel added to the north, and the hiring options panel added to the south. The bottom panel is then added to the south of the master JPanel.

Finally the table is configured and some tooltips are added.

Listing 8-23. *The DVDScreen*

```
public DvdScreen() {
    this.setLayout(new BorderLayout());
    JScrollPane tableScroll = new JScrollPane (mainTable);
    tableScroll.setSize(500, 250);

    this.add(tableScroll, BorderLayout.CENTER);

    // Set up the search pane
    JButton searchButton = new JButton ("Search");
    searchButton.addActionListener(new SearchDVD ());
    searchButton.setMnemonic(KeyEvent.VK_S);
    // Search panel
    JPanel searchPanel = new JPanel(new FlowLayout(FlowLayout.CENTER));
    searchPanel.add(searchField);
    searchPanel.add(searchButton);
```

```java
            // Setup rent and return buttons
            JButton rentButton = new JButton ("Rent DVD");
            JButton returnButton = new JButton ("Return DVD");

            // Add the action listenters to rent and return buttons
            rentButton.addActionListener(new RentDVD ());
            returnButton.addActionListener(new ReturnDVD ());
            // Set the rent and return buttons to refuse focus
            rentButton.setRequestFocusEnabled(false);
            returnButton.setRequestFocusEnabled(false);
            // Add the keystroke mnemonics
            rentButton.setMnemonic(KeyEvent.VK_R);
            returnButton.setMnemonic(KeyEvent.VK_U);
            // Create a panel to add the rental a remove buttons
            JPanel hiringPanel = new JPanel(new FlowLayout(FlowLayout.RIGHT));
            hiringPanel.add(rentButton);
            hiringPanel.add(returnButton);

            // bottom panel
            JPanel bottomPanel = new JPanel (new BorderLayout ());
            bottomPanel.add(searchPanel, BorderLayout.NORTH);
            bottomPanel.add(hiringPanel, BorderLayout.SOUTH);

            // Add the bottom panel to the main window
            this.add(bottomPanel, BorderLayout.SOUTH);

            // Set table properties
            mainTable.setSelectionMode(ListSelectionModel.SINGLE_SELECTION);
            mainTable.setAutoResizeMode(JTable.AUTO_RESIZE_ALL_COLUMNS);
            mainTable.setToolTipText("Select a DVD record to rent or return.");

            // Add Tool Tips
            returnButton.setToolTipText(
                    "Return the DVD item selected in the above table.");
            rentButton.setToolTipText(
                    "Rent the DVD item selected in the above table.");
            searchField.setToolTipText(
                    "Enter infromation about a DVD you want to locate.");
            searchButton.setToolTipText("Submit the DVD search.");

        }
    }
```

The GUI created by the MainWindow class and the DVDScreen class can be seen in Figure 8-28.

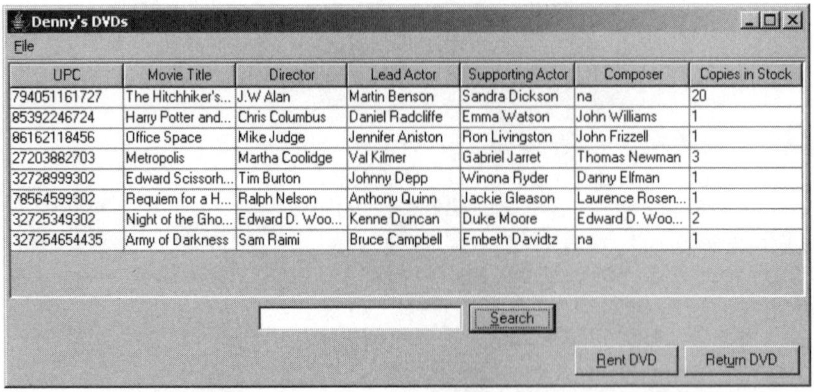

UPC	Movie Title	Director	Lead Actor	Supporting Actor	Composer	Copies in Stock
794051161727	The Hitchhiker's...	J.W Alan	Martin Benson	Sandra Dickson	na	20
85392246724	Harry Potter and...	Chris Columbus	Daniel Radcliffe	Emma Watson	John Williams	1
86162118456	Office Space	Mike Judge	Jennifer Aniston	Ron Livingston	John Frizzell	1
27203882703	Metropolis	Martha Coolidge	Val Kilmer	Gabriel Jarret	Thomas Newman	3
32728999302	Edward Scissorh...	Tim Burton	Johnny Depp	Winona Ryder	Danny Elfman	1
78564599302	Requiem for a H...	Ralph Nelson	Anthony Quinn	Jackie Gleason	Laurence Rosen...	1
32725349302	Night of the Gho...	Edward D. Woo...	Kenne Duncan	Duke Moore	Edward D. Woo...	2
327254654435	Army of Darkness	Sam Raimi	Bruce Campbell	Embeth Davidtz	na	1

Figure 8-28. *The GUI created by the MainWindow class and the DVDScreen class*

Just like all other action handlers in the Denny's DVDs application that communicate with the GUIController, the search action shown in Listing 8-24 must be ready to receive a GUIControllerException from the GUIController. This particular method, however, handles the exception a little differently. The GUIControllerException that is thrown from the find (String query) method may contain a PatternSyntaxException as its cause. This particular exception is thrown if the user enters a search string that is not a properly formatted regular expression. In this case, the exception message may contain important information for the user pertaining to the incorrect syntax of the search. In order to present this information to the user, J2SE's exception chaining facility is put to use. When the actionPerformed() method in Listing 8-24 catches an exception, it checks the exception's cause to see if it is of type PatternSyntaxException. If it is this type, the exception message is added to the message that is passed to the handleException method. The end result is a very useful error dialog box that looks like the one shown in Figure 8-29.

Listing 8-24. *The SearchDVD Event Handler*

```java
private class SearchDVD implements ActionListener {
    public void actionPerformed (ActionEvent ae) {
        previousSearchString = searchField.getText();
        try {
            tableData = controller.find(previousSearchString);
            setupTable();
        } catch (GUIControllerException gce) {
            // Inspect the exception chain
            Throwable rootException = gce.getCause();
            String msg = "Search operation failed.";
            // If a syntax error occurred, get the message
            if (rootException instanceof PatternSyntaxException) {
                msg += ("\n" + rootException.getMessage());
            }
            ApplicationRunner.handleException(msg);
```

```
            previousSearchString = "";
        }
        searchField.setText("");
    }
}
```

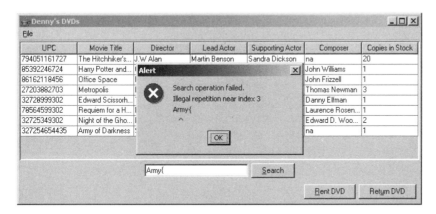

Figure 8-29. *The error message from a regular expression compilation failure*

Specifying the Database Location

When users start the client or server applications, they need to be able to specify where the database is located.

For the Denny's DVDs application, we have determined that this entails the following:

- In stand-alone client mode, the user must specify where the physical file is located.

- In networked client mode, the user must be able to specify the URL or IP address of the server computer, the type of server running (RMI or sockets), and the port number the server is using.

- In server mode, the user must be able to specify where the physical file is located, the type of server (RMI or sockets), and the port number the server will use.

▪Note You should not need anything so complex for your solution. Some of the options we are allowing for are specifically to allow for all the options of this book.

To allow these options to be entered in client mode, we are going to develop a dialog box, as shown in Figure 8-30. The major part of this dialog box is the reusable panel shown in Figure 8-31.

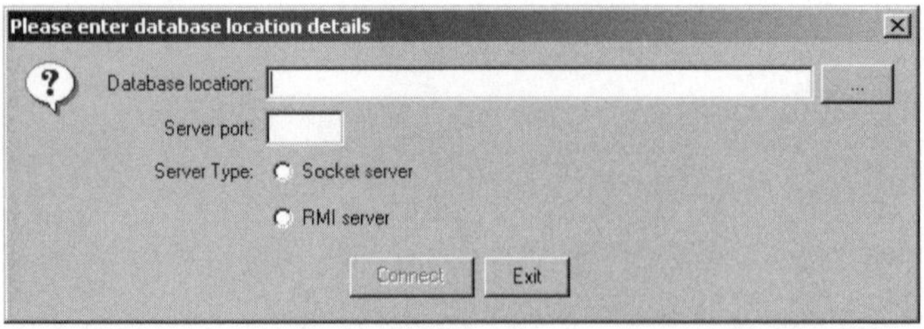

Figure 8-30. *The client application's dialog box for entering the database location*

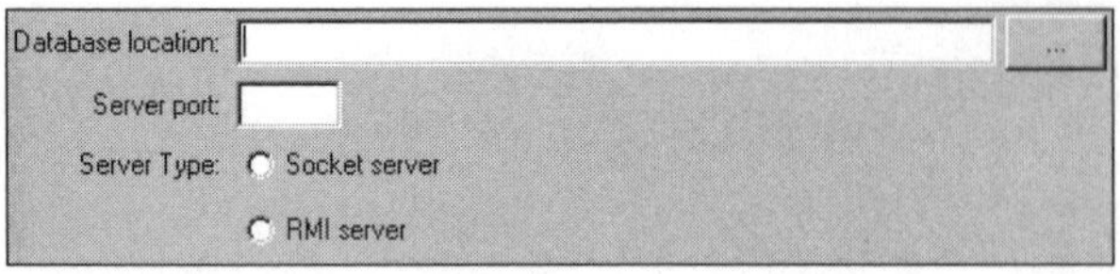

Figure 8-31. *The JPanel for getting common parameters in both the client and the server application*

In Listing 8-28 we will see that the constructor for the common frame will change which options are displayed, and what tooltip text is displayed, depending on a parameter in the constructor. This allows us to use the same frame for stand-alone client, networked client, and server applications.

For the main client GUI, we used the simple graphical layout managers: BorderLayout and FlowLayout. These layout managers will serve in most cases. However, in some circumstances you may find that you want to lay out a panel in some form that cannot be readily achieved using these simple layout managers. The common frame is one such case—we want to have up to four rows of components, but each component has a label that we want to align vertically on its right edge.

In this section we introduce one of the most powerful layout managers—the GridBagLayout. We deliberately delayed introducing this layout manager until now, as it is more complicated to use than the other layout managers.

■**Tip** Although this layout manager is very powerful, and works well in the Denny's DVD example application, you may find that you do not need to use this layout manager in your application. We recommend that you use the simplest solution that works for you—you will not get extra marks for proving that you can use all the layout managers.

The GridBagLayout

Java has two grid-based layout managers: the GridLayout and the GridBagLayout manager.

The GridLayout is the simpler of the two; however, it forces all cells in the grid to be the same size, as shown in Figure 8-32. The program that produced this is shown in Listing 8-25.

Listing 8-25. *A Simple GridLayout Application*

```java
import java.awt.*;
import javax.swing.*;

public class MyFrame {
    public static void main(String[] args) throws Exception {
        JFrame theFrame = new JFrame();
        theFrame.setLayout(new GridLayout(2,2));
        theFrame.setDefaultCloseOperation(JFrame.EXIT_ON_CLOSE);
        theFrame.add(new JButton("One"));
        theFrame.add(new JLabel("A very long component"));
        theFrame.add(new JTextField("Three"));
        theFrame.add(new JTextArea("Four\nFive\nSix"));

        theFrame.pack();
        theFrame.setVisible(true);
    }
}
```

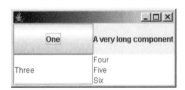

Figure 8-32. *Example of GridLayout demonstrating consistent cell sizes*

As you can see in Figure 8-32, the width of all components is the same as the width of the longest component—the JLabel with the contents "A very long component"—and the height of all components is the same as the height of the tallest component—the JTextArea that contains multiple lines of text.

While this layout can be very useful if most of the components are the same size, it is not very useful when you have considerable differences in component sizes, as we do in our common frame. If we were to use the GridLayout, then the space allocated to the labels would be the same as the space allocated to the largest component—the Database location field.

The GridBagLayout also works on a grid of cells; however, components are allowed to occupy more than one cell, the width of a column is calculated based on the width of the widest column that does not span multiple columns, and the height of a row is calculated based on the height of the tallest component in that row that does not span multiple rows.

We will start off with a simple example that contains the same components as used in Figure 8-32, but this time we will use the GridBagLayout. Listing 8-26 shows the program that creates the GUI shown in Figure 8-33.

Listing 8-26. *A Simple GridBagLayout Application Similar to Listing 8-25*

```java
import java.awt.*;
import javax.swing.*;

public class MyFrame {
    static GridBagLayout grid = new GridBagLayout();
    static GridBagConstraints constraints = new GridBagConstraints();

    public static void main(String[] args) throws Exception {
        JFrame theFrame = new JFrame();
        theFrame.setDefaultCloseOperation(JFrame.EXIT_ON_CLOSE);
        theFrame.setLayout(grid);

        constraints.anchor = GridBagConstraints.WEST;

        JButton one = new JButton("One");
        grid.setConstraints(one, constraints);
        theFrame.add(one);

        constraints.gridwidth = GridBagConstraints.REMAINDER;
        theFrame.add(constrain(new JLabel("A very long component")));

        constraints.weightx = 0.0;
        constraints.gridwidth = 1;
        theFrame.add(constrain(new JTextField("Three")));
        theFrame.add(constrain(new JTextArea("Four\nFive\nSix")));

        theFrame.pack();
        theFrame.setVisible(true);
    }

    private static Component constrain(Component c) {
        grid.setConstraints(c, constraints);
        return c;
    }
}
```

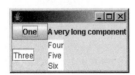

Figure 8-33. *Example of GridBagLayout demonstrating inconsistent cell sizes*

As can be seen in Figure 8-33, the components are no longer forced to the same height and width as the highest and widest components. The first row's height has no relationship to the second row's height, and the first column's width has no relationship to the second column's width.

The basic concept when using GridBagLayout is to configure the constraints to be used for the component, notify the GridBagLayout manager of these constraints, and then add the component to the pane. This is best exemplified in the following code snippet from Listing 8-26:

```
constraints.anchor = GridBagConstraints.WEST;

JButton one = new JButton("One");
grid.setConstraints(one, constraints);
theFrame.add(one);
```

Prior to this code snippet, the constraints were set to default values (starting in row 1, column 1, centered in the grid, occupying one grid position, etc.). The first line changes the location of each component so that they will now be left-justified. We then created our component and notified the GridBagLayout that the specified constraints were to be used with that particular component. Finally, we added the component to the panel.

Note Only one set of constraints is used throughout the application—when the setConstraints method is called, the layout manager clones the constraints provided. This makes it easier for developing, as you can set common constraint configuration at the start of your layout code and use those constraints throughout the program.

Since components can span multiple rows and multiple columns, the GridBagLayout cannot determine whether or not a component is the last component. Therefore, before adding the last item to row 1, we must specify via the constraints that this will be the last component in the row. The following line does this:

```
constraints.gridwidth = GridBagConstraints.REMAINDER;
```

As noted, we use the same set of constraints for all components. We set the constraints to specify that the component will be the last component in the row, and then used that constraint when adding the component to the container. However, if we do not reset the constraint, all future components will also appear as the last component in the row. The following line does this:

```
constraints.gridwidth = 1;
```

To close this section, we will demonstrate how to specify that components span multiple rows or columns. The program to do this is shown in Listing 8-27, and the output is shown in Figure 8-34.

Listing 8-27. *A GridBagLayout Application Demonstrating Components Spanning Multiple Cells*

```java
import java.awt.*;
import javax.swing.*;

public class MyFrame {
    static GridBagLayout grid = new GridBagLayout();
    static GridBagConstraints constraints = new GridBagConstraints();

    public static void main(String[] args) throws Exception {
        JFrame theFrame = new JFrame();
        theFrame.setDefaultCloseOperation(JFrame.EXIT_ON_CLOSE);
        theFrame.setLayout(grid);

        constraints.fill = GridBagConstraints.BOTH;

        constraints.gridheight = 2;
        theFrame.add(constrain(new JButton("Deep")));

        constraints.gridheight = 1;
        constraints.gridwidth = GridBagConstraints.REMAINDER;
        theFrame.add(constrain(new JButton("Wide")));

        constraints.gridwidth = 1;
        theFrame.add(constrain(new JButton("One")));
        theFrame.add(constrain(new JButton("Two")));

        theFrame.pack();
        theFrame.setVisible(true);
    }

    private static Component constrain(Component c) {
        grid.setConstraints(c, constraints);
        return c;
    }
}
```

Figure 8-34. *Example of GridBagLayout demonstrating components spanning multiple cells*

■Note GridBagLayout is one of the most useful layout managers available, and it is capable of far more than we can show in one section of one chapter. Unfortunately, going into all its capabilities is beyond the scope of this book.

The Common Database Location Frame

Now that the basics of the GridBagLayout have been explained, we can show the code that creates the common frame for displaying the database location.

The ConfigOptions constructor stores a local variable to show what mode it was configured with, and then constructs a GridBagLayout with a gap between components of 2 pixels in every direction.

Regardless of which mode we are in, we will be displaying the label for the Database location field, so we add that next.

The remaining options are configured depending on the mode we are in. If a component or option does not make sense in the mode we are in, then it is not added to the panel. If it does make sense to add it, then it is added, and the tooltip text is set relevant to the mode. Listing 8-28 demonstrates how the components used within a particular mode are laid out using the GridBagLayout.

Listing 8-28. *The ConfigOptions Constructor*

```
public ConfigOptions(ApplicationMode applicationMode) {
    super();
    this.applicationMode = applicationMode;

    GridBagLayout gridbag = new GridBagLayout();
    GridBagConstraints constraints = new GridBagConstraints();
    this.setLayout(gridbag);

    // Standard options
    // ensure there is always a gap between components
    constraints.insets = new Insets(2,2,2,2);

    // Build the Data file location row
    JLabel dbLocationLabel = new JLabel(DB_LOCATION_LABEL);
    gridbag.setConstraints(dbLocationLabel, constraints);
    this.add(dbLocationLabel);

    if (applicationMode == ApplicationMode.NETWORK_CLIENT) {
        locationField.setToolTipText(DB_IP_LOCATION_TOOL_TIP);
        constraints.gridwidth = GridBagConstraints.REMAINDER; //end row
    } else {
        locationField.setToolTipText(DB_HD_LOCATION_TOOL_TIP);
        // next-to-last location in row
        constraints.gridwidth = GridBagConstraints.RELATIVE;
    }
```

```
locationField.addFocusListener(new ActionHandler());
locationField.setName(DB_LOCATION_LABEL);
gridbag.setConstraints(locationField, constraints);
this.add(locationField);

if ((applicationMode == ApplicationMode.SERVER)
        || (applicationMode == ApplicationMode.STANDALONE_CLIENT)) {
    browseButton.addActionListener(new BrowseForDatabase());
    constraints.gridwidth = GridBagConstraints.REMAINDER; //end row
    gridbag.setConstraints(browseButton, constraints);
    this.add(browseButton);
}

if ((applicationMode == ApplicationMode.SERVER)
        || (applicationMode == ApplicationMode.STANDALONE_CLIENT)) {
    // Build the Server port row if applicable
    constraints.weightx = 0.0;

    JLabel serverPortLabel = new JLabel(SERVER_PORT_LABEL);
    constraints.gridwidth = 1;
    constraints.anchor = GridBagConstraints.EAST;
    gridbag.setConstraints(serverPortLabel, constraints);
    this.add(serverPortLabel);

    portNumber.addFocusListener(new ActionHandler());
    portNumber.setToolTipText(SERVER_PORT_TOOL_TIP);
    portNumber.setName(SERVER_PORT_LABEL);
    constraints.gridwidth = GridBagConstraints.REMAINDER; //end row
    constraints.anchor = GridBagConstraints.WEST;
    gridbag.setConstraints(portNumber, constraints);
    this.add(portNumber);

    // Build the Server type option row 1 if applicable
    constraints.weightx = 0.0;

    JLabel serverTypeLabel = new JLabel("Server Type: ");
    constraints.gridwidth = 1;
    constraints.anchor = GridBagConstraints.EAST;
    gridbag.setConstraints(serverTypeLabel, constraints);
    this.add(serverTypeLabel);

    constraints.gridwidth = GridBagConstraints.REMAINDER; //end row
    constraints.anchor = GridBagConstraints.WEST;
    gridbag.setConstraints(socketOption, constraints);
    socketOption.setActionCommand(SOCKET_SERVER_TEXT);
    socketOption.addActionListener(new ActionHandler());
    this.add(socketOption);
```

```
        // Build the Server type option row 2 if applicable
        constraints.weightx = 0.0;

        constraints.gridwidth = GridBagConstraints.REMAINDER; //end row
        constraints.anchor = GridBagConstraints.WEST;
        constraints.gridx = 1;
        gridbag.setConstraints(rmiOption, constraints);
        rmiOption.addActionListener(new ActionHandler());
        rmiOption.setActionCommand(RMI_SERVER_TEXT);
        this.add(rmiOption);

        ButtonGroup serverTypesGroup = new ButtonGroup();
        serverTypesGroup.add(socketOption);
        serverTypesGroup.add(rmiOption);
    }
}
```

If the choice between RMI and sockets is displayed, we want to display two radio buttons under each other, with only one label on the left.

There are several ways we could have approached this. We could have set the label to be two columns deep, or we could have created another frame to hold the radio buttons. However, both these techniques have been shown before, so we opted instead to set the absolute grid position for the rmiOption radio button, with the instruction:

```
        constraints.gridx = 1;
```

This tells the GridBagLayout to add the specified component in position 1, where cells start at column 0.

If you would like to see how this common frame would look in the server application, you can skip forward to Figure 8-35. We recommend that you return to this section to find out how we have handled passing information from the common frame to the enclosing frame or dialog box.

The Observer Design Pattern

There are many options to be configured, but the client and server applications cannot start unless all the correct options are configured. However, in the client application, our common frame will be used in a dialog box, while in the server application it will form part of the server GUI. So we need some common way for either of these applications to create an instance of the common frame and receive notifications whenever a field changes. In effect, we want the dialog box and the server application to observe any changes in the common frame.

This is one occasion where we can use the Observer design pattern. In this pattern, you set up one class as the Observable class, and any classes that want to be notified of changes implement the Observer interface. The Observer classes then register themselves to the Observable class, and the Observable class notifies registered Observer classes of any changes.

■**Note** The Observer design pattern is not normally used for one part of a GUI to receive notifications of changes to another part of the GUI. It is more common to have an `Observable` model in an MVC pattern with one or more `Observer` views. Or you might have an `Observable` server that notifies all the `Observer` clients whenever something changes on the server.

Normally you would have the class you wish to observe extend the `Observable` class, but our `ConfigOptions` panel already extends `JPanel`, so we cannot do this. Instead, we have created an inner class that extends `Observable`, and provided a convenient `getObservable` method that the client and server applications can use in order to register themselves as observers.

When using Java's inbuilt implementations of the observer pattern, you can specify an object that should be passed to the observers. We have created a value object class that can be used to pass the field that was changed along with the field contents. This class is presented in Listing 8-29. For more information on the Value Object design pattern, refer to Chapter 5.

Listing 8-29. *The OptionUpdate Value Object*

```java
package sampleproject.gui;

public class OptionUpdate {
    public enum Updates {
        NETWORK_CHOICE_MADE,
        DB_LOCATION_CHANGED,
        PORT_CHANGED;
    }

    private Updates updateType = null;
    private Object payload = null;

    public OptionUpdate(Updates updateType, Object payload) {
        this.updateType = updateType;
        this.payload = payload;
    }

    public Updates getUpdateType() {
        return this.updateType;
    }

    public Object getPayload() {
        return payload;
    }
}
```

When the user changes something in the common dialog box (which is the class that might have some `Observers`), one of the event handlers will be called. If this is an event we want to notify our Observer classes of, an OptionUpdate value update is constructed and sent to all the observers.

For example, when the user leaves the locationField or the portNumber field, then the following code is executed:

```
public void focusLost(FocusEvent e) {
    if (DB_LOCATION_LABEL.equals(e.getComponent().getName())
            && ( ! locationField.getText().equals(location))) {
        location = locationField.getText();
        updateObservers(OptionUpdate.Updates.DB_LOCATION_CHANGED,
                        location.trim());
    }

    if (SERVER_PORT_LABEL.equals(e.getComponent().getName())
            && ( ! portNumber.getText().equals(port))) {
        port = portNumber.getText();
        updateObservers(OptionUpdate.Updates.PORT_CHANGED, port.trim());
    }
}
```

Assuming that the user has changed one of these fields, the following method is called:

```
private void updateObservers(OptionUpdate.Updates updateType, Object payLoad) {
    OptionUpdate update = new OptionUpdate(updateType, payLoad);
    observerConfigOptions.setChanged();
    observerConfigOptions.notifyObservers(update);
}
```

■**Note** We called the setChanged method on the Observable object before calling the notifyObservers method. If you call notifyObservers without first calling setChanged, no Observers will be notified.

That is all we need to do to notify however many observers we may have. While it may appear that we have gone to a lot of work to pass some information back to either the Client Database Location dialog box or to the server GUI, the advantage is that we have decoupled the panel from the users of the panel—any class can use this panel, and simply by registering themselves as an Observer of the panel they can get notification whenever anything changes on the panel.

The next two sections—"The Client Database Location Dialog Box" and "The Server GUI"—show the other half of the Observer-Observable pair. Both will be Observers of the panel described here.

The Client Database Location Dialog Box

Having created a common frame for the various modes, we can add it to a dialog box, as shown in Listing 8-30.

Our dialog box will not allow users to start the client application until they have entered the required details; however, the required details change depending on the client application mode—in stand-alone mode, we only need to know the URI of the data file. But in networked mode we need to know the URL of the server, its port number, and the type of server we are connecting to. The constructor starts by assuming that if we are building a dialog box for stand-alone mode, then we don't need a port number or connection type. It then goes on to create an instance of the ConfigOptions pane and add itself as an observer of the pane.

A simple OK/Cancel question JOptionPane is then created, with the common pane as its main object. We then override the buttons that will be displayed so that we can enable the connect button when the user has entered the required data.

If the user closes the dialog box rather than clicking the Connect or Exit button, we want to treat it as though they had clicked the Exit button. So we set the dialog box to do nothing on close, and then we add a window listener to the dialog box.

Listing 8-30. *The DatabaseLocationDialog*

```
public DatabaseLocationDialog (Frame parent, int connectionMode) {
    // the port and connection type are irrelevant in standalone mode
    if (connectionMode == ApplicationMode.STANDALONE_CLIENT)
        validPort = true;
        validCnx = true;
    }

    configOptions = (new ConfigOptions(connectionMode));
    configOptions.getObservable().addObserver(this);

    options = new JOptionPane(configOptions,
                              JOptionPane.QUESTION_MESSAGE,
                              JOptionPane.OK_CANCEL_OPTION);

    connectButton.setActionCommand(CONNECT);
    connectButton.addActionListener(this);
    connectButton.setEnabled(false);

    exitButton.setActionCommand(EXIT);
    exitButton.addActionListener(this);

    options.setOptions(new Object[] {connectButton, exitButton});

    dialog = options.createDialog(parent, TITLE);
    dialog.setDefaultCloseOperation(JDialog.DO_NOTHING_ON_CLOSE);
    dialog.addWindowListener(this);
    dialog.setVisible(true);
}
```

When the user makes a change in the common frame, all the observers are notified. The notification is sent to the method with the signature public void update(Observable o, Object arg). In that method, we first confirm that we did receive an instance of the OptionUpdate value object, and if not we ignore the entire message. If it is an OptionUpdate, then we recast it so that we can easily get access to information about what has changed, as shown in the following code snippet:

```
if (! (arg instanceof OptionUpdate)) {
    log.log(Level.WARNING,
            "DatabaseLocationDialog received update type: " + arg,
            new IllegalArgumentException());
    return;
}

OptionUpdate optionUpdate = (OptionUpdate) arg;
```

▨Caution You should always check for nulls or for the type of an object before recasting it. However, if you check the type of the object, you may not need to explicitly check for null since instanceof will return false if passed a null reference. You should also check for nulls being passed into any API you have made public. Even though we know that the class we are currently observing should only send us instances of the OptionUpdate class, we cannot guarantee that this will never change in the future. Should this change, we will get a warning log message giving as much information on what has been received and where it came from as possible.

▨Tip Even though we created an IllegalArgumentException for the purposes of creating a stack trace in the log message, we never threw it, so the application will continue to run. Creating an exception simply for the information available from the exception can be a useful tool if you ever need to debug your code.

▨Note It may not be desirable to log all updates received that your particular code is not interested in. When AWT was first released, **all** events would be sent to any class that was interested in any event. This could mean that a class that was only interested in learning when the mouse moved over a particular field might get millions of updates as the mouse moved over other areas of the screen—in such a case you would not want to log all the unwanted events. However, in this particular case where we know all the events that can be generated at this time, it makes sense to log a warning if we receive an event we were not expecting.

We then perform validation on the field the user has entered, setting the Boolean flag if the user has entered valid data, as shown in the following code snippet for validating a field name:

```
location = (String) optionUpdate.getPayload();
if (configOptions.getApplicationMode()
        == ApplicationMode.STANDALONE_CLIENT) {
    File f = new File(location);
    if (f.exists() && f.canRead() && f.canWrite()) {
        validDb = true;
        log.info("File chosen " + location);
    } else {
        log.warning("Invalid file " + location);
    }
}
```

Finally we check whether we have all the required fields, and if so, we enable the Connect button as shown in the following code snippet:

```
boolean allValid = validDb && validPort && validCnx;
connectButton.setEnabled(allValid);
```

The Server GUI

The server GUI is shown in Figure 8-35. As can be seen, the majority of this GUI is the common panel developed earlier.

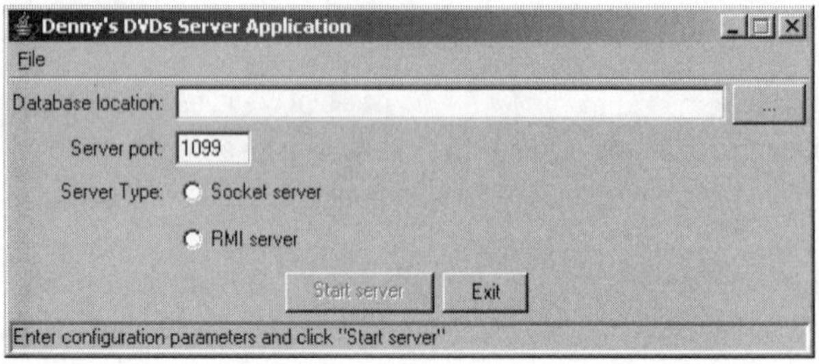

Figure 8-35. *The server GUI*

The constructor used to create the server GUI is shown in Listing 8-31. We start by setting the title of the GUI, configuring the application to exit if the close button is clicked, and ensuring the GUI cannot be resized.

We then create our menu bar the same way we did for the client application, and add our ConfigOptions panel to the main window. We then add the buttons to start the server (disabled until configuration options are set), and load any stored configuration options. Finally, we center the server window on the screen, and set it to be visible.

Listing 8-31. *The ServerWindow Constructor*

```java
public ServerWindow() {
    super("Denny's DVDs Server Application");
    this.setDefaultCloseOperation(this.EXIT_ON_CLOSE);
    this.setResizable(false);
    Runtime.getRuntime().addShutdownHook(new CleanExit());

    // Add the menu bar
    JMenuBar menuBar = new JMenuBar ();
    JMenu fileMenu = new JMenu ("File");
    JMenuItem quitMenuItem = new JMenuItem ("Quit");
    quitMenuItem.addActionListener(new ActionListener() {
        public void actionPerformed (ActionEvent ae) {
            System.exit(0);
        }
    });
    quitMenuItem.setMnemonic(KeyEvent.VK_Q);
    fileMenu.add(quitMenuItem);

    fileMenu.setMnemonic(KeyEvent.VK_F);
    menuBar.add(fileMenu);

    this.setJMenuBar(menuBar);

    configOptionsPanel.getObservable().addObserver(this);
    this.add(configOptionsPanel, BorderLayout.NORTH);
    this.add(commandOptionsPanel(), BorderLayout.CENTER);

    status.setBorder(BorderFactory.createBevelBorder(BevelBorder.LOWERED));
    JPanel statusPanel = new JPanel(new BorderLayout());
    statusPanel.add(status, BorderLayout.CENTER);
    this.add(statusPanel, BorderLayout.SOUTH);

    // load saved configuration
    SavedConfiguration config = SavedConfiguration.getSavedConfiguration();

    // there may not be a default database location, so we had better
    // validate before using the returned value.
    String databaseLocation =
            config.getParameter(SavedConfiguration.DATABASE_LOCATION);
    configOptionsPanel.setLocationFieldText(
            (databaseLocation == null) ? "" : databaseLocation);

    // there is always at least a default port number, so we don't have to
    // validate this.
    configOptionsPanel.setPortNumberText(
            config.getParameter(SavedConfiguration.SERVER_PORT));
```

```
                status.setText(INITIAL_STATUS);

                this.pack();
                // Center on screen
                Dimension d = Toolkit.getDefaultToolkit().getScreenSize();
                int x = (int) ((d.getWidth() - this.getWidth())/ 2);
                int y = (int) ((d.getHeight() - this.getHeight())/ 2);
                this.setLocation(x, y);          this.setVisible(true);
            }
```

When the user has entered all the valid information and clicked the Start Server button, all the user fields and buttons with the exception of the Exit button are disabled, as shown in Figure 8-36.

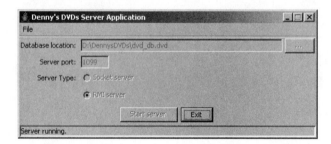

Figure 8-36. *The running server GUI*

This is achieved with the following code in the action listener for the Start Server button:

```
                configOptionsPanel.setLocationFieldEnabled(false);
                configOptionsPanel.setPortNumberEnabled(false);
                configOptionsPanel.setBrowseButtonEnabled(false);
                configOptionsPanel.setSocketOptionEnabled(false);
                configOptionsPanel.setRmiOptionEnabled(false);

                startServerButton.setEnabled(false);
```

We then add a shutdown hook to handle any exit events:

```
        Runtime.getRuntime().addShutdownHook(new CleanExit());
```

Finally we start the appropriate server depending on what type of server the user has chosen.

The shutdown hook code is very simple—it is simply an initialized thread that gets called when the application is shutting down. It locks the database so that no other thread can attempt to write to the file while we are shutting down, and then exits. The complete code for the shutdown hook is shown in Listing 8-32.

■**Tip** Adding a shutdown hook is a good way of handling shutdowns within an application that will be running on a server. No matter whether your code calls System.exit, or the user clicks the close button, or the application is told by the operating system that it must shut down, the same hook will be run. Handling the cases where the operating system tells the application to shut down is especially valuable—consider the case where the server is running on an uninterruptible power supply (UPS) and the power goes out. Normally the UPS runs for a while on battery power, but that can only last so long. So before the battery is likely to run out, the UPS sends a message to the operating system telling it to shut down. The operating system then sends a message to all running applications telling them to shut down. The shutdown hook allows your application to receive this message and perform a clean shutdown.

Listing 8-32. *The Shutdown Hook Code*

```
package sampleproject.gui;

import java.io.IOException;
import java.util.logging.*;
import sampleproject.db.*;

public class CleanExit extends Thread {
    private Logger log = Logger.getLogger("sampleproject.gui");

    public void run() {
        log.info("Ensuring a clean shutdown");
        try {
            DVDDatabase database = new DVDDatabase();
            database.setDatabaseLocked(true);
        } catch (IOException fne) {
            log.log(Level.SEVERE, "Failed to lock database before exiting", fne);
        }
    }
}
```

Swing Changes in J2SE 5

Sun has introduced several changes to Swing for the latest release of J2SE. Several of these improvements can be used to provide a more polished submission. We will briefly discuss them in this section.

Improve Default Look and Feel of Swing

Prior to JDK 5, if you wanted to provide a common look and feel for your application on multiple platforms, you had to use the Metal look and feel, which by default used to look like Figure 8-37.

Figure 8-37. *An example of using the Metal look and feel with the Steel theme*

With JDK 5, Sun has modified this look and feel, as shown in Figure 8-38.

Figure 8-38. *An example of using the Metal look and feel with the Ocean theme*

To help reduce confusion, Sun has named these two versions of the same look and feel "Steel" and "Ocean," respectively.

If you wish to use the old theme, you can set the following system property:

```
-Dswing.metalTheme=steel
```

Skins Look and Feel

A "skin" (also called a "theme") is a way of changing the look and feel of an application or website, without changing any code. This is usually achieved by modifying a configuration file.

Sun has created `javax.swing.plaf.synth.SynthLookAndFeel` as a skinnable look and feel, allowing the look and feel to be specified in a file. This means that your users could modify this file to make your application meet their preferred look and feel without needing any coding changes.

Adding Components to Swing Containers Has Been Simplified

Prior to JDK 5, it was not possible to directly add components to any class that implemented `RootPaneContainer`, namely `JApplet`, `JDialog`, `JFrame`, `JInternalFrame`, and `JWindow`. Instead, you had to get the content pane, then add the components to it. This resulted in code that looks like this:

```
JFrame theFrame = new JFrame();
theFrame.setDefaultCloseOperation(JFrame.EXIT_ON_CLOSE);

Container thePane = theFrame.getContentPane();

thePane.add(new JButton("Exit"));
theFrame.pack();
theFrame.setVisible(true);
```

A large number of users of classes that implement `JRootPane` do not need to use the various panes that exist—they only need to add content to the content pane. So in JDK 5 Sun has rewritten the `add` methods of these classes so that they perform in the way most users would expect. This allows us to rewrite the previous code as shown here:

```
JFrame theFrame = new JFrame();
theFrame.setDefaultCloseOperation(JFrame.EXIT_ON_CLOSE);

theFrame.add(new JButton("Exit"));
theFrame.pack();
theFrame.setVisible(true);
```

This reduces confusion as to when we should be dealing with the frame itself or the panel, and makes the code a little more readable.

Summary

A sound interface design will bridge the gap between the user and the system. By using solid design patterns, such as the Model-View-Controller (MVC) architectural paradigm, you can ensure that changes to the data display have minimal impact on the rest of the system. On a superficial level, the end user will most likely judge the quality of an application based on the functionally of its interface, so it is important to plan and design a quality front-end to a system.

In this chapter we introduced GUI design, and provided some examples of how you can combine various layout managers and components to achieve your desired design. It is important to realize that there is no "one right way" to develop a GUI, so you can use the techniques introduced here to develop GUIs that you believe will be usable for your instructions.

FAQs

Q The instructions state that I may only use Swing components, but none of the layout managers are part of the `javax.swing` package—will this cause me to fail?

A You will be fine using any of the layout managers. However, you must not use an AWT component where there is a Swing replacement. For example you should not use a `Button` since there is a Swing replacement: the `JButton`.

Q Does Swing replace AWT?

A Swing is not a replacement for AWT. Swing is built on the patterns and groundwork set forth in AWT. Both Swing and AWT components can be mixed and matched in any interface, to an extent (however, only Swing components may be used in the Sun assignment).

Swing does offer some large improvements over AWT both in performance and functionality. Therefore, Sun now emphasizes Swing over AWT. As a result, Swing is a required part of the SCJD exam.

Q How do I center a window on screen?

A To center a window on screen, get the window dimensions from the
`java.awt.Toolkit.getDefaultToolkit().getScreenSize()` method. Use the returned
`Dimension` to calculate the vertical and horizontal center of the screen while taking into
account the dimensions of the window you want to center. Finally, place the window at
that location, as in the following code snippet used for centering our `connectionDialog`
object:

```
// Center on screen
Dimension d = Toolkit.getDefaultToolkit().getScreenSize();
int x = (int) ((d.getWidth() - connectionDialog.getWidth())/ 2);
int y = (int) ((d.getHeight() - connectionDialog.getHeight())/ 2);
dialog.setLocation(x, y);
```

Q How do I create keystroke mnemonics for my GUI components?

A You can add keystroke mnemonics to virtually any component via the `setMnemonic(int keyValue)` method. Lists of predefined key values are located in the `KeyEvent` class.

Q Can I use the Macintosh look and feel on a Windows operating system, or vice versa?

A Sun provides several cross-platform interface look and feel packages. Metal and Motif
were the only guaranteed look-and-feel libraries prior to JDK 1.5. With the release of
JDK 1.5 Sun has included Ocean (a custom Metal theme), and Synth (a skinnable look
and feel). Most other libraries are operating system–specific. Although it might be
technically possible to use the Windows look and feel on a Mac, or vice versa, it is usually not legal to distribute an application that uses one operating system's look and feel
on another platform.

Part of the power of Swing is its capability to be extended and make custom look-and-
feel libraries. Some custom libraries are available that are cross-platform, but they are
not part of the standard Java distributions and are difficult to rely on for interface
design.

Q I found a look and feel on the Web that I prefer to any of Sun's look and feels. Can I use
it instead?

A Check your instructions carefully—most instructions state that **all** code submitted
must be your own. If you use a look and feel that you did not write and that is not part
of the JDK, then you will be violating this rule.

Q Where can I find out more about Java look-and-feel guidelines?

A You can find extensive information pertaining to Java interface design and standard
practices at `http://java.sun.com/products/jlf/`.

Q Where can I find out more information on interface design and usability testing?

A The following URLs are great places to begin research into usability engineering and
testing:

```
http://www.useit.com
http://www.asktog.com
```

PART 3

Wrap-Up

CHAPTER 9

■■■

Project Wrap-Up

Congratulations! You've made it through a myriad of complex topics and intricate details. We've covered a lot of information that will help you pass the Sun Certified Java Developer (SCJD) exam, and we've exposed you to some of the new features of JDK 5. This chapter summarizes some of the architectural decisions we confronted during the completion of our sample project, and it wraps up some of the loose ends regarding packaging and running the application. In this chapter we will cover

- Understanding the design decisions

- Finding out where to get the code samples

- Compiling and packaging the application

- Creating a manifest file

- Running the application in local mode

- Running the application in network mode

- Running a multithreaded test client

- Packaging the submission

Figure 9-1 presents an overview of the Denny's DVDs 2.0 application.

■Note Normally you would expect to see an overall diagram of an application drawn from left to right, or top-down—in other words, the client would normally be in the far left of the diagram or in the top location. There is a reason we have drawn the diagram bottom-up, though: it matches the way we have developed the project through this book. We started with the DvdDatabase class in Chapter 5, proceeded with the RMI and sockets classes in Chapters 6 and 7, and built the GUI classes in Chapter 8.

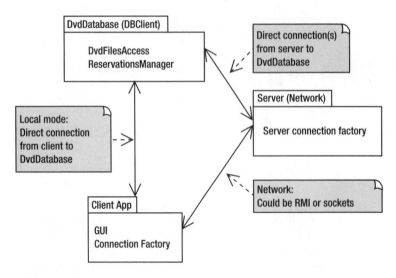

Figure 9-1. *Denny's DVDs 2.0 overview*

The design decisions we made centered around the three tiers of the application, which are central to the SCJD exam. The areas of interest are locking in the db package, choosing between RMI and sockets for the network layer, and using the MVC pattern in the GUI package.

We also need to cover how to package, install, run, and test the application.

You can find all of the sample code in the Source Code section of the Apress web site (http://www.apress.com). This chapter explains how to compile and package the final version, Denny's DVDs 2.0.

Let's get started!

Thread Safety and Locking

Thread safety was covered in depth in Chapter 4. The main thrust of Chapter 4 was to explain threading and related topics such as synchronization, locking, and concurrency and the new concurrent package of JDK 5. Waiting was also explained in detail, as were other issues relating to sharing a single resource across multiple client threads.

Chapter 5 also implemented a locking strategy that demonstrated these concepts. For example, the networking code base creates separate instances of the DvdDatabase class for each client so that we can identify the owner of the lock as described in the discussion points.

The Choice Between RMI and Sockets

It can be difficult to choose whether to develop an RMI solution or a serialized object over sockets solution to the Sun SCJD assignment. Sun will accept either solution, with no extra marks awarded or deducted for the choice alone. Many candidates simply choose the technology they are least familiar with as that gives them greatest scope for learning. But if you do not know either technology, or if you are equally comfortable with both technologies, it is beneficial to be able to look at the benefits of each.

> **■Note** When reading these benefits you should be aware that the benefit might be a disadvantage of the other choice. Also, many of the perceived benefits can be easily countered in an argument—where possible we provide counterarguments in our discussions in the same place we discuss the benefit.

Benefits of Using a Serialized Objects Over Sockets Solution

In real-world applications, the choice between RMI and sockets often comes down to the scalability and performance requirements of your application.

Sockets are ideal if performance is a must since you can limit the degree of overhead and sockets are well suited for sending data, often in compressed form that does not require a heavy protocol. As you may recall, the larger and more complex your protocol becomes, the more you may want to use RMI. A well-designed, simple socket interface can outperform an RMI-based server. If you must handle a large number of requests efficiently, sockets may be for you.

This does not mean that you cannot compress or encrypt your data using RMI—if you want to, you can use custom socket factories with RMI to provide specialist functionality (for more information, refer to `http://java.sun.com/j2se/1.5.0/docs/guide/rmi/socketfactory/`). However, when you implement a straightforward sockets solution, you can easily incorporate only the functionality you need, and leave out the functionality you do not need. For example, you might decide to drop the "heartbeat" functionality that is incorporated into every RMI solution. The heartbeat functionality simply ensures that at regular intervals the server sends a signal—a heartbeat—to the RMI registry to let the registry know that the server is still alive; similarly the RMI clients send a signal—a heartbeat—to the server to let it know that they are still alive.

Another advantage to sockets is that most system administrators are already familiar with what needs to be done to implement a server that listens on a particular socket, even if they need to go through a firewall. Few are familiar with setting up an RMI registry, and even fewer know how to configure RMI to work through a firewall. RMI can work through a firewall, but it is not quite as simple as setting up a simple sockets solution through the firewall.

> **■Note** Sockets have been a standard method of performing network connectivity for many years, whereas RMI is a relatively new standard. However, this alone does not justify using sockets over RMI; using serialized objects over the sockets connection almost ensures that only another Java class can connect to your server (only "almost" because the Java specifications make it explicitly clear how a serialized class will appear, which means it is *possible* for somebody to develop a client in a different language—just very difficult). Conversely, using RMI over IIOP (the Internet Inter-Orb Protocol used by CORBA) would allow any CORBA-compliant client to connect to your server (although using RMI over IIOP is not allowed in the current assignments). For more information on IIOP and CORBA, refer to the Wikipedia pages `http://en.wikipedia.org/wiki/IIOP` and `http://en.wikipedia.org/wiki/CORBA`, respectively.

It may be easier to propagate changes to remotely accessible methods over a sockets solution than an RMI solution. Unless you do something major like remove a method that is being used, or change the port it is running on, you can usually change a sockets-based server without the clients even being aware of it—they just won't get the new functionality. In comparison, an RMI solution that has pre-JDK 5 clients or that doesn't allow stubs to be dynamically generated will require recompilation of the client stubs, and redistribution to clients if you do not use dynamic downloading. If you do use dynamic downloading, you may also have associated issues with security and setting the codebase option.

A sockets solution should also require less sockets and network traffic between client and server. A sockets solution for this assignment might need only one socket per client, and the network traffic can be minimal depending on how minimal you make your solution. An RMI solution, on the other hand, will always open a listening port for your RMI registry, a listening port for your RMI server, a connected port between the server and the registry, and one socket per client between the clients and the server. The RMI solution will also require more network traffic while connecting (doing the lookup on the registry) and also while idling (performing distributed garbage collection and sending heartbeat messages).

This brings up another point: with RMI you always have an extra process running (the RMI server). While most computers are not going to be taxed by this extra process, if you were using most of the CPU and memory resources of your server, this could become an issue.

A *well-written* sockets solution *can* be easier for a junior programmer to understand and maintain than an RMI solution. This contradicts the commonly accepted view that RMI is simpler. But there are several items to consider here. If you write your sockets code well, the networking code will be hidden from the client and server applications—they will just be calling your sockets API, in the same way that in an RMI solution the clients and servers are just calling the RMI API. But in this case, the junior programmer does not need to learn about registries, or how to use rmic, or how to deal with the RMI stubs. So there is less of a learning curve for them. However, there is little doubt that once that learning curve has been passed, an RMI solution is easier to develop, understand, and maintain. And most likely, the only way a sockets solution can be clearer than an RMI solution is if the sockets solution is really well written (and possibly also if the RMI solution is not well written).

General client identification is easier in a sockets solution—you can use the connection's thread to identify the client. However, if your assignment requires you to use cookies for locking, unlocking, and modification calls, then you can use the cookie as the client identification. Likewise, if you decide to use thread pooling for scaling reasons, then you will no longer be able to use the thread identifier. Regardless, for either RMI or sockets, using a connection factory will provide a simple client identifier.

There is less chance that somebody will accidentally disable your server. With RMI, if another server happened to do use the Registry class's rebind method with the same remote reference name, they will replace your code. With sockets, once you have bound to a particular port, no other server can bind to that port. However, this can also work to your disadvantage— if somebody deployed another server that happened to use the port number, then restarted the computer, it may not be possible to predict which server will bind to the port first, so you may not know which server will be accepting connections. This is called a race condition; a race condition in relation to threads is discussed in Chapter 4.

Benefits of Using an RMI Solution

However, let's be blunt. **For the SCJD exam, scalability and performance are not design considerations**, and as shown in the "Benefits of Using a Serialized Objects Over Sockets Solution" section earlier, neither solution provides a method of allowing non-Java clients to connect.

We mentioned that a *well-written* sockets solution *might* be easier for a junior programmer to understand and maintain. However, as a developer you would be expected to know both of these technologies anyway so that you can make a valid choice between them (and to help you, we have devoted Chapter 6 to RMI and Chapter 7 to sockets). Once you know the two technologies, you may find that your job could actually be a lot less tedious using RMI. And the assessor is expected to understand RMI, so there is no problem with submitting an RMI solution. Let's quickly list a few of the advantages of RMI.

Implementing socket servers and socket clients involves creating a custom protocol. A sockets implementation must send serialized objects across the network that the receiving socket point must know how to handle at runtime. Thus, a sockets-based application can be a little more tedious and awkward to write than an RMI program. This can be negated slightly if you write well-factored code, such that each class has only one responsibility, and the methods are likewise well factored. However, using the Command pattern for the client-server communication protocol trivializes building the new protocol.

The details of object serialization and network communication are hidden by RMI, whereas using sockets you have to implement it all yourself. In other words you will be reinventing a basic technology that already exists.

No matter how well you write your code, there is no doubt that you will write more code for a socket-based solution than an RMI one. And the more code you write, the more chance of making mistakes—it can be safer to leverage off the code written by the RMI developers, which has been tried and tested for many years; much of the RMI code base has been around since JDK 1.1, which was released in September 1997.

RMI provides network transparency, which means that to the client a remote object seems to behave as if it is a local object. Thus there is no need to implement a handshake protocol or worry about low-level details such as opening and closing socket connections.

Due to the use of interfaces and remote methods behaving as though they were local, developing code to call a remote method is usually type safe. The same can apply to a sockets solution, but unlike RMI there is no requirement to use interfaces. Consequently, it is easy to end up with a solution that does not provide any form of compile-time (or even runtime) type safety.

RMI also relieves you of the responsibility of having to write multithreaded servers, which can be tricky. You are still required to write thread-safe code in either protocol, but the actual server does not have to spawn threads or manage thread pools.

Thread pooling can provide a significant performance improvement when systems are scaled to large numbers of simultaneous users, and RMI provides it for free. Yet this comes at a cost: client identification is slightly more complex if you cannot use cookies.

RMI is also extensively used in Enterprise JavaBean (EJB) technology, so learning and using RMI for the SCJD assignment will assist you in EJB projects.

The RMI registry helps you deploy your server side code dynamically—using the `Registry` class's `rebind` method allows you to load the new server functionality with a minimum of downtime. With a sockets solution you would either have to stop the old server and then start the new server (with a longer downtime than RMI's `rebind`), or use a different socket port (which would require reconfiguring or replacing clients).

Using RMI frees you from the requirements of specifying which port a particular service will be available on. With a sockets solution you must specify which port your server will be listening on, and the clients must make a connection to that port. If you do not make this configurable and some other application is developed in such a way that it uses the same port (and is also not configurable), then one or the other will have to be recompiled. Even if the port number is reconfigurable you would have to reconfigure all the clients to use the new port number, which may not be easy or practical. RMI solutions, by default, use random port numbers for the servers, where the port number is specified by the RMI registry. The clients need only know the port number of the registry, which they then query to determine how to contact the server they are interested in.

Although not permitted within the SCJD assignment, RMI allows you to download executable classes. You could use it, for instance, to download some security algorithm that will encrypt all the data between clients and server—since the code is downloaded dynamically, the programmer for the client side never gets to see how you implemented it (indeed, you could even hide the fact that it is being used at all), thus reducing the chances of someone trying to hack your encryption algorithms if they never get to see them.

Choosing Between the Two Solutions

Probably by now you have seen that there are good arguments for both solutions, and no absolute differentiator between either. We believe that Sun has deliberately done this to see your decision-making logic.

You must decide which of the arguments we've listed (or others that you determine for yourself) make the most sense to you, and which of them you are willing to defend if you are asked to explain your decision.

The MVC Pattern in the GUI

Chapter 8 covered GUI-related design decisions ranging from general information on interface layout principles all the way to the discussion of specific Swing components, such as the `JTable`. Unlike the choice between an RMI and a sockets-based network implementation (discussed in Chapters 6 and 7 as well as earlier in this chapter), Sun literally requires the use of the `JTable` in order to pass the SCJD exam, so the decision to use it is a no-brainer if you want to pass the exam.

The design decision therefore shifts from what GUI widget is appropriate for use in the Denny's DVDs application to how to properly incorporate the `JTable` into a Swing user interface. The solution we suggest in Chapter 8 is the application-level use of the MVC design pattern. As you learned in Chapter 8, Swing components, such as the `JTree` and the `JTable`, implement the MVC pattern internally, but the choice to use the MVC pattern beyond these components is entirely up to the developer. The main benefit gained through the use of an application-wide MVC architecture is increased abstraction between the data display and the actual data implementation. The `JTable` and its own MVC implementation in turn becomes a smaller player in the overall application display layer and works in cooperation with the application's MVC implementation.

Locating the Code Samples

You can find the code samples for this book in the Source Code section of the Apress web site (`http://www.apress.com`). There you will a zip file with the final code base (i.e., Denny's DVDs version 2.0). In this chapter you will be concerned with the version 2.0 zip file.

Unzip the final code base in the location of your choice on your machine. There should be one directory, `sampleproject`, which contains four directories: `db`, `remote`, `sockets`, and `gui`. These directories correspond to four packages:

- `sampleproject.db`

- `sampleproject.remote`

- `sampleproject.sockets`

- `sampleproject.gui`

Unless you've skipped around quite a bit and started out with Chapter 9, you should be very familiar with each of these packages. Once you've unzipped all of the Java source files into something resembling the preceding directory structure, you're ready to compile the application.

Compiling and Packaging the Application

Bring up a command prompt and type `java -version`. Make sure that you are using J2SE 5 or later (see Figure 9-2). If you aren't, please download it and install it from the Sun J2SE download site (`http://java.sun.com/j2se/1.5.0/download.jsp`).

■**Note** The "b05" shown in the version number in Figure 9-2 indicates that this is build number 05; it does not imply a beta version of the software.

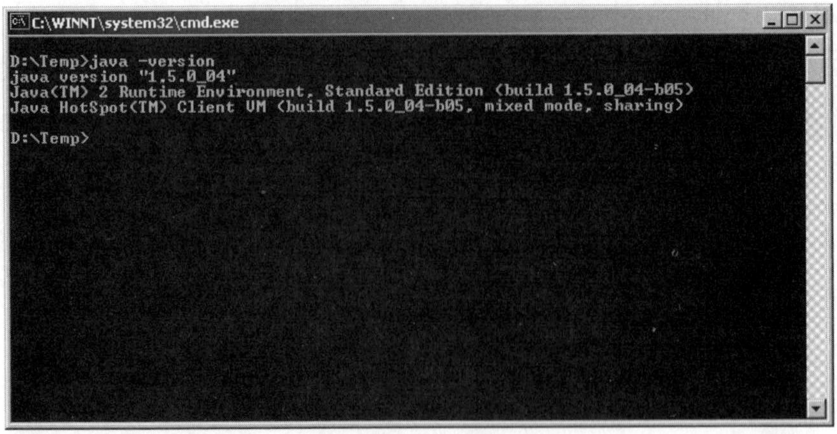

Figure 9-2. *Verify that J2SE 5 is properly installed.*

Navigate to the root directory of Denny's DVDs. This is the directory where you unzipped the project's .java files. For demonstration purposes, we created a directory called dennysDVDs2.0 and chose that as the root directory.

■**Tip** Zip files can usually be decompressed with the jar executable, as shown in Figure 9-3. Both zip files and JAR files use the same compression algorithms.

Next, you'll want to compile the .java files into a destination directory. By default, Java will place the .class files in the same directory as the source files. Using the Java compiler's -d option allows you to separate the source and compiled files. Separating the source and compiled files helps you organize your project.

You need to decide where to direct your .class files. For simplicity, we decided to place the compiled files in a directory below the root called classes. Using the command mkdir classes from the command prompt will create the necessary directory. Or you can add the directory using Windows Explorer.

Next, compile each package separately using javac with the -d option set to your destination directory. Figure 9-3 illustrates the battery of commands needed to successfully compile the sample project. Make sure that you compile the packages in this order: db, remote, sockets, and finally gui. This order highlights the project dependencies. Recall from Chapter 5 that we only had the db package. We added the other packages as topics were introduced in Chapters 6, 7, and 8, respectively.

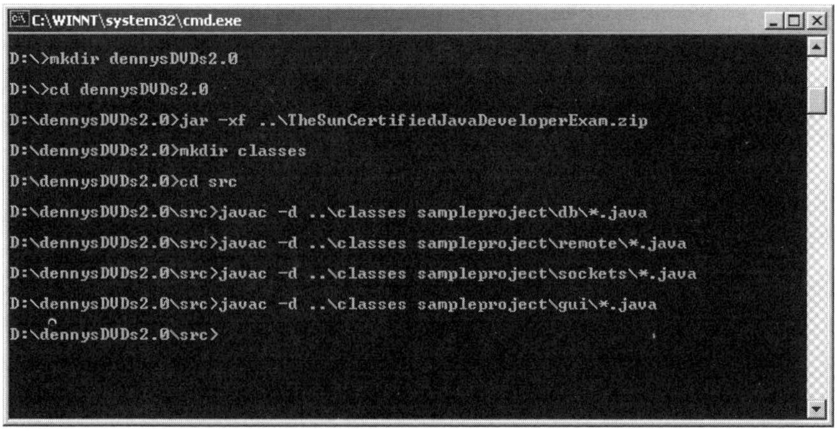

Figure 9-3. *Compiling the source into the classes directory*

Creating a Manifest File

Now you'll want to create a manifest file. This file will be packaged in your project's JAR file and used by the JVM to load the correct class and run the application. The key entry in the manifest file is the class name of the main method you want to execute when running the application. In our case, this is the `ApplicationRunner` class in the `gui` package.

The contents of the manifest file are minimal. Insert the following two lines of code and save them in a new file called `Manifest.mf`. We have placed the manifest file in the root directory, `dennysDVDs2.0`.

```
Manifest-Version: 1.0
Main-Class: sampleproject.gui.ApplicationRunner
```

■**Note** The name of the manifest file can be anything you like if you are using Sun's `jar` tool to create the JAR file. We will go into this in more detail when we describe using the `jar` tool in the section "Packaging the Application" later in this chapter. If you are not using Sun's `jar` tool (there is really no reason not to use it, though), then the final manifest file **must** be named `MANIFEST.MF` and must be placed in the `META.INF` directory, which must be in the root directory of the JAR file.

The location of the manifest file comes into play when we actually create a JAR file containing our project's class files. All JAR files contain manifests, and the manifest can be used to specify many attributes for the JAR file. Some of the more common attributes are shown in Table 9-1.

Table 9-1. *Manifest Attributes*

Attribute	Use
Manifest-Version	Specifies which version of the Manifest.mf definition you are conforming to. At present only version 1.0 has been defined.
Created-By	Specifies the jar tool's creator and version number. This is automatically added by the jar tool itself, so you should not set it.
Class-Path	You may optionally use this to specify libraries needed at runtime. These must be specified relative to the current JAR file (so you can specify lib/another.jar but you cannot specify an absolute path like d:\libs\another.jar). If you have multiple JAR files, separate them by spaces.
Main-Class	Tells the JVM which class to execute if the JVM is started with the -jar parameter.

There are many other attributes that can be set as well, but delving into them is beyond the scope of this book. If you are interested in reviewing these options, we recommend you look at the Sun documentation for JAR files available online at http://java.sun.com/j2se/1.5.0/docs/guide/jar/jar.html#JAR Manifest.

The jar tool needs to know where to load the manifest file so that it can be included in the JAR file. Otherwise, the jar tool will create one by default. The manifest file that is created by default when you do not specify one will not include a main class label.

Running rmic on the Remote Package

One of the benefits of using JDK 5 is that using rmic to create stubs is not strictly necessary; the stubs can be generated dynamically. However, as explained in Chapter 6, stubs are still required if you have pre-JDK 5 clients or if you are not allowed to dynamically generate stubs. This section has been provided for the benefit of those who may require stubs.

■**Caution** At the time of this writing, all current assignments have a prohibition against *requiring* the dynamic downloading of stubs—you must provide all stubs precompiled in your executable JAR file. Since dynamically generating stubs would result in the stubs being dynamically downloaded, you cannot use the JDK 5 dynamic stub generation feature. However, you should still check the assignment instructions **you** downloaded from Sun; future assignments may remove this prohibition.

Using RMI involves creating stubs with the Java tool rmic. The stubs need to be packaged up with the JAR file in order to run the program using RMI via the remote package.

The rmic command only needs to be run on the remote object implementation class file. In our case, that class is DvdDatabaseImpl of the remote package. Make sure you run the rmic command from the destination directory because the class files are required by rmic. Figure 9-4 shows rmic being run against the DvdDatabaseImpl class. In addition, rmic also needs to be run against the DvdDatabaseFactoryImpl class.

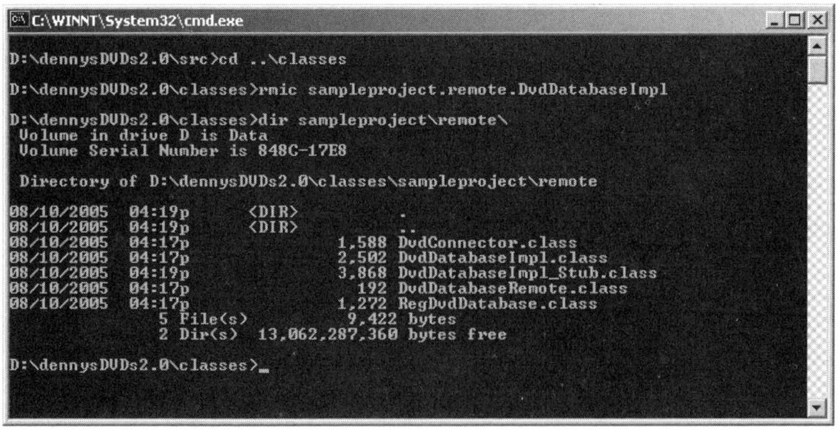

Figure 9-4. *Running rmic on the remote object DvdDatabaseImpl*

If you would like more detailed information than what is shown in Figure 9-4, run `rmic` with the `-verbose` flag. The `-help` option will display all of the other options that are available. The file displayed in the remote directory, `DvdDatabaseImpl_Stub.class`, is the result of the `rmic` command.

Packaging the Application

You are ready to create your JAR file. The `jar` command allows you to create archives of files of various types into a single compressed file based on the zip format. To run the `jar` command, make sure you comply with the following syntax:

`jar [options] [manifest] destination input-file [input-files]`

To create your JAR file, use the c, v, f, and m options, which are described in Table 9-2. You will also need to specify the location of your manifest file, which is in the `dennysDVDs2.0` root directory.

Table 9-2. *jar Tool Options Used to Create sampleproject.jar*

Option	Description
c	**C**reates a new archive; unless the f parameter is provided, the archive will be created on standard output.
v	Generates **v**erbose output.
f	Indicates that the name of the JAR **f**ile to be created (not on stdout) will be specified as the next argument in order.
m	Includes a **m**anifest file that will be specified as the next argument in order. The `jar` tool will read the contents of the file you specified and store them in the file named `MANIFEST.MF` in the `META.INF` directory.

■**Note** When more than one `jar` command-line option requires a parameter, the parameters must appear in the same order as the command-line options. That is, if the command-line options are `-cvfm`, then the output filename must appear before the manifest file name (since the `f` appeared before the `m`). However, if the command-line options provided were `-cvmf`, then the manifest file name must appear before the output filename (since the `m` appeared before the `f`).

There are other options you can use with the `jar` tool. Running `jar -help` will give a brief synopsis of the various arguments and usage options. Figure 9-5 captures the `sampleproject.jar` file creation in the root directory using the command:

```
jar -cfm sampleproject.jar Manifest.mf -C classes .
```

■**Caution** There is one period in the command line following the directory named classes. It is easy to miss that period in a book, particularly when it occurs at the end of a sentence. If you are unsure of the command line we used, compare it with Figure 9-5.

Using the `-v` option will display verbose output detailing which files are being added to the JAR and information related to file compression. To display verbose information, replace `-cfm` with `-cvfm` in the `jar` command.

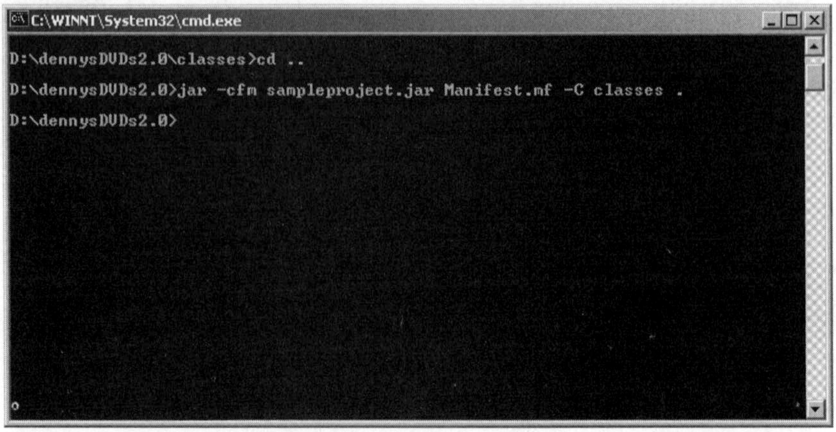

Figure 9-5. *Creating the sampleproject.jar file*

Running the Denny's DVDs Application

The Denny's DVDs application runs in multiple modes, depending on the command-line options provided. These modes are presented in the following sections.

Running the Client Application in Stand-alone Mode

Running in local mode is easy. Navigate to the directory where the `sampleproject.jar` file is located.

The `java` and `javaw` executables allow you to specify a JAR that you want to execute using the `-jar` option. At the command prompt, type the following:

```
javaw -jar sampleproject.jar alone
```

The `sampleproject.jar` file can be anywhere on your machine since the entire project classes are packaged in the JAR. This should bring up the database location dialog box shown in Figure 9-6. Select the location of the database (it should be in the root directory) and click `Connect`. The main window will then load as shown in Figure 9-7.

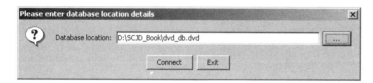

Figure 9-6. *Starting the application in local mode*

UPC	Movie Title	Director	Lead Actor	Supporting Actor	Composer	Copies in Stock
794051161727	The Hitchhiker's...	J.W Alan	Martin Benson	Sandra Dickson	na	20
85392246724	Harry Potter an...	Chris Columbus	Daniel Radcliffe	Emma Watson	John Williams	1
86162118456	Office Space	Mike Judge	Jennifer Aniston	Ron Livingston	John Frizzell	1
27203882703	Metropolis	Martha Coolidge	Val Kilmer	Gabriel Jarret	Thomas Newman	1
32728999302	Edward Scissor...	Tim Burton	Johnny Depp	Winona R	Laurence Rosen...	1
78564599302	Requiem for a ...	Ralph Nelson	Anthony Quinn	Jackie Gleason	Laurence Rosen...	1
32725349302	Night of the Gh...	Edward D. Woo...	Kenne Duncan	Duke Moore	Edward D. Woo...	1
327254654435	Army of Darkness	Sam Raimi	Bruce Campbell	Embeth Davidtz	na	1

Figure 9-7. *The application running in local mode*

Running Denny's DVDs Server

Running Denny's DVD server requires you to specify the location of the database file, which port you want to use, and the type of server (RMI or sockets). To start the server, at the command prompt, type the following:

```
javaw -jar sampleproject.jar server
```

This should bring up the server configuration window shown in Figure 9-8. Select the location of the database (it should be in the root directory), change the port number if desired, select the network type, and click the Start Server button. The server window will then display information that it is running and will disable most controls, as shown in Figure 9-9.

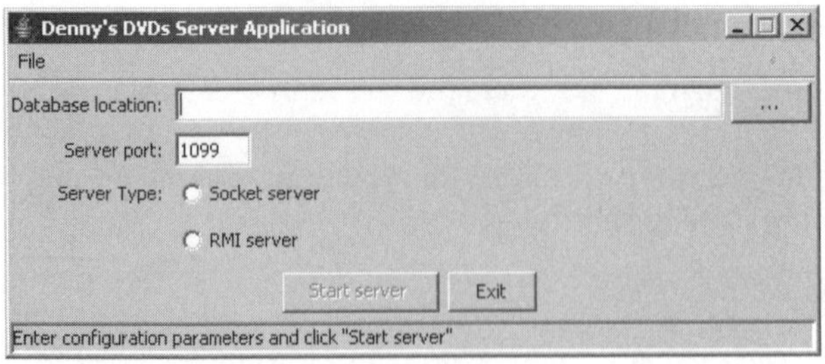

Figure 9-8. *Configuring the network server*

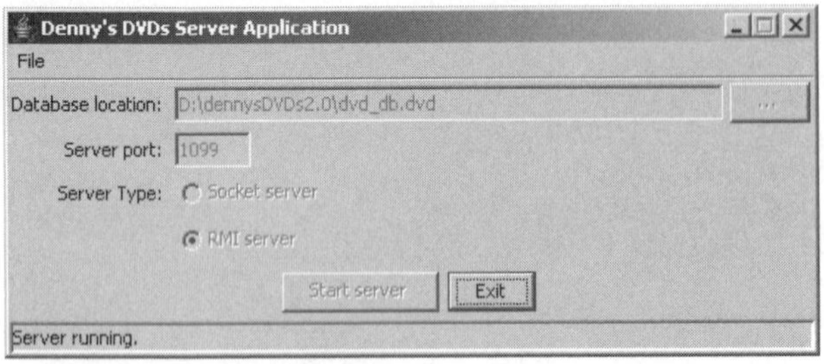

Figure 9-9. *Running the network server*

We specified that the server should use port 1099 in Figure 9-8. With our RMI solution, this means that the RMI registry will be listening on port 1099 (if we had chosen the socket server, it would have meant that our server itself would have been listening on port 1099). We can confirm this by running the netstat -a command to show all connected or listening ports, as shown in Figure 9-10.

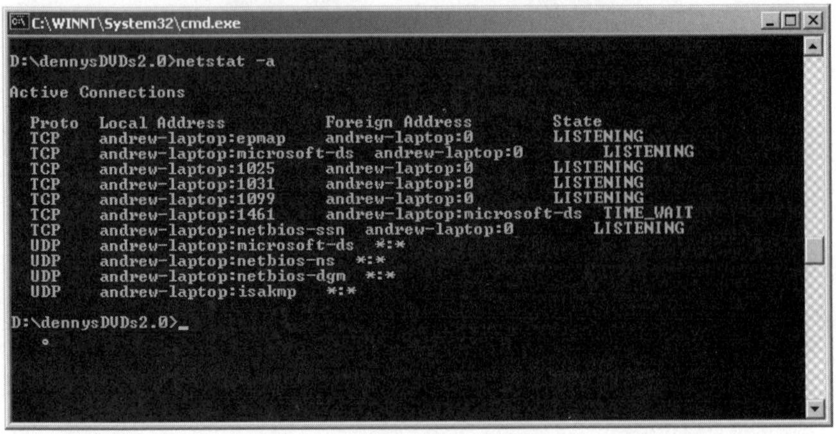

Figure 9-10. *Checking which ports are in use*

In Figure 9-10 we can see that the fifth `Local Address` is listening on port 1099. The port that the server itself is running on is unknown—it will be dynamically configured by the RMI registry.

Running the Client Application in Networked Mode

Running the application in network mode requires specifying the IP address or host name of the machine that the server and database files are located on, the port number the RMI registry or the server is listening on, and the server type. To start the networked client, at the command prompt type the following:

```
javaw -jar sampleproject.jar server
```

This should bring up the connection configuration dialog box shown in Figure 9-11.

Figure 9-11. *Starting the networked client*

Enter the location of the database (either by the name of the computer hosting the database, e.g., `localhost`, or by the IP address of the computer host, e.g., `127.0.0.1`), change the port number if necessary to match the port number specified when starting the server, and select the same network type as specified when starting the server. Then click `Connect`, and the main window will load as shown in Figure 9-7 earlier.

Testing

In version 2.0 of Denny's DVDs is a package called `test`, which is in a different directory structure than the standard source. The standard source is in the directory named `src`, while the test package is in a subdirectory called `test`. The different directory structures will assist us to ensure that we do not submit any classes we do not want to submit—this will be explained in the "Packaging Your Submission" section later in this chapter.

This may be a little confusing, so we recommend you look at the directory tree structure displayed in Figure 9-12. If you have been following along with this chapter, you will have a root directory similar to `D:\dennysDVDs2.0` (the actual drive and directory can be different). In that root directory so far are the directories `classes` (where `javac` has been storing our compiled classes), `src` (which is the root directory for our sample assignment source), and `test` (which is the root directory for our test source). Our package structure appears within each of those directories, starting with the top-level package named `sampleproject`.

> **■Note** There should also be a bonus directory in the root directory named `src - examples`. This has not previously been described anywhere in the book, but it contains sample code for many of the topics discussed in the book that are not part of the project itself.

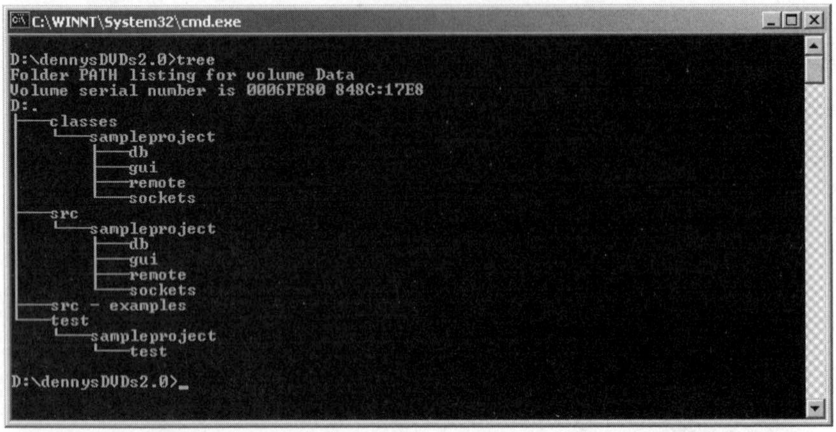

```
C:\WINNT\System32\cmd.exe                                          _ □ X

D:\dennysDVDs2.0>tree
Folder PATH listing for volume Data
Volume serial number is 0006FE80 848C:17E8
D:.
├───classes
│   └───sampleproject
│       ├───db
│       ├───gui
│       ├───remote
│       └───sockets
├───src
│   └───sampleproject
│       ├───db
│       ├───gui
│       ├───remote
│       └───sockets
├───src - examples
└───test
    └───sampleproject
        └───test

D:\dennysDVDs2.0>_
```

Figure 9-12. *Tree structure for the development project so far*

The test package contains our multithreaded test harness. Testing your application with multiple clients is a must. We will use our test harness to simulate a group of users all vying voraciously for database access.

In the test package are two classes. One called DBTester, which extends Thread and simulates the client that attempts to rent and return DVDs. The other, called DBTestRunner, it spawns multiple DBTester test threads, waits for them to finish running, and then reports on their success (or failure).

Since the test package is in a different directory structure from our standard source, we must compile it separately. To do this, we can change into the test directory and run the following command:

```
javac -cp ..\classes -d ..\classes sampleproject\test\*.java
```

Listing 9-1 shows the test client code. Unlike the real application, we have chosen to directly connect to the RMI DvdConnector or the sockets DvdConnector just to show how this could be done. To simplify the connection code, we have commented out one of the two network connector import statements.

Listing 9-1. *DBTester.java*

```java
package sampleproject.test;

import sampleproject.db.*;
import java.util.Date;
```

```java
// rather than going through a factory, we are directly calling the connector
// Uncomment the DVDConnector of the protocol you want to use.
import sampleproject.remote.DvdConnector;
//import sampleproject.sockets.DvdConnector;

/**
 * A DBTester is the test equivalent of a client who is trying to book one or
 * more DVDs. However we know exactly how the DBTester is going to behave,
 * therefore we can predict the results of this testing.
 */
public class DBTester extends Thread {
    // various status for what can happen when we try to book over the network
    public enum Status {
        SUCCESS, OUT_OF_STOCK, TIMEOUT
    }

    private String dvdUpc; // the DVD we are supposed to rent
    private int numberOfRentals; // number of times to rent it
    private DBClient db; // connection to the remote database

    private int successfulRentals = 0;  // number of times we rented the DVD
    private int outOfStock = 0; // number of times we failed due to no copies left
    private int timeouts = 0; // number of times timed out trying to reserve DVD

    // To make the screen output easier to read, we are using a pretend logger
    // If we chose to convert to the real JDK logger, we could just change this
    private PretendLogger log = new PretendLogger();

    public DBTester(String title, int numberOfRentals, String dvdUpc)
            throws Exception {
        super (title);
        this.numberOfRentals = numberOfRentals;
        this.dvdUpc = dvdUpc;

        db = DvdConnector.getRemote();
    }
```

Most of the work is performed in the run method—the client goes into a loop based on the number of times they are supposed to rent the DVD. Within that loop, they try to rent the DVD. If they are successful, they watch it for two seconds, then return it. If they are not successful because the store is out of stock, they complain to management for a second. If they are not successful because trying to obtain the lock took longer than five seconds, they just take note of the fact. No matter which of those events happened, they will then wait for another two seconds before trying to obtain another lock.

Note We have used specific times for each of these events, providing us with some degree of certainty that we can duplicate our tests. We cannot be absolutely guaranteed that we can get exactly the same result every time since minor changes in how long network traffic takes over multiple bookings could have an effect. But for a small number of bookings on a local area network with low traffic (or on a single machine), we should be able to predict with confidence what the outcome will be.

```java
public void run() {
    int secondsForWatchingDvd = 2;
    int secondsForComplaining = 1;
    int secondsForBrowsingStore = 2;

    try {
        for (int i = 0; i < this.numberOfRentals; i++) {
            switch (rentDvd(dvdUpc)) {
                case RENTAL_SUCCESS:
                    successfulRentals++;
                    // watch the DVD
                    Thread.sleep(secondsForWatchingDvd * 1000);
                    // then return it so somebody else can rent it
                    returnDvd(dvdUpc);
                    break;
                case RENTAL_OUT_OF_STOCK:
                    outOfStock++;
                    // complain that it is not in stock
                    Thread.sleep(secondsForComplaining * 1000);
                    break;
                case RENTAL_TIMEOUT:
                    // just track that we had the problem, and continue
                    timeouts++;
                    break;
            }
            // wander around the DVD store looking at DVDs.
            Thread.sleep(secondsForBrowsingStore * 1000);
        }
    } catch (Exception e) {
        // This should never ever go into production code, but for testing
        // we are simply catching *every* exception and displaying it
        System.err.println("Exception thrown by " + getName());
        e.printStackTrace(System.err);
        System.err.println();
    }
}
```

The rentDvd method duplicates the business logic required by our application. It reserves the DVD so that no other client can modify it (assuming, of course, that the other client also follows the protocol of reserving a DVD before modifying it), retrieves the DVD (to ensure we have the latest copy), checks that there are enough DVDs available (and if so it removes one), and saves the modified DVD back to the database.

```
private int rentDvd(String upc) throws Exception {
    if (db.reserveDVD(upc)) {
        try {
            DVD dvd = db.getDVD(upc);
            int copiesInStock = dvd.getCopy();
            if (copiesInStock > 0) {
                copiesInStock--;
                log.info(getName() +
                            "        -> (Rent)       " +
                        "Copies in stock = " + copiesInStock );
                dvd.setCopy(copiesInStock);
                db.modifyDVD(dvd);
                return RENTAL_SUCCESS;
            } else {
                log.info(getName() + "    00     (No stock)");
                return RENTAL_OUT_OF_STOCK;
            }
        } finally {
            db.releaseDVD(upc);
        }
    } else {
        log.info(getName() + "    XX     (Timeout)");
        return RENTAL_TIMEOUT;
    }
}
```

Similarly the `returnDvd` method reserves the DVD so no other client can modify it, retrieves the DVD (to ensure we have the latest copy), increases the number of copies, and then saves the modified DVD.

```
private void returnDvd(String upc) throws Exception {
    if (db.reserveDVD(upc)) {
        try {
            DVD dvd = db.getDVD(upc);
            int copiesInStock = dvd.getCopy() + 1;
            dvd.setCopy(copiesInStock);
            log.info(getName() +
                        " <-        (Return)   Copies in stock = " +
                    copiesInStock );
            db.modifyDVD(dvd);
        } finally {
            db.releaseDVD(upc);
        }
    }
}
```

When the client has finished running, the test harness will want to know how many successful and unsuccessful bookings were made. So we have a number of getters to provide that information.

```
public int getSuccessfulRentals() {
    return successfulRentals;
}

public int getOutOfStock() {
    return outOfStock;
}

public int getTimeouts() {
    return timeouts;
}
```

Finally, we want to display information on what is happening while the test is running; however, we do not want to use the standard logger as it can make the resultant screen output hard to decipher. In a larger test environment we would probably consider creating our own log Formatter, but this is overkill for this chapter, so we have opted to create a pretend logger instead. This provides a very simple logging facility, and if we later decided to change to using the JDK's logger, we would only need to change the definition of our log variable.

```
private class PretendLogger {
    void info(String logInformation) {
        System.out.format("%tT %s%n", new Date(), logInformation);
    }
}
}
```

The test harness code is very simple—all it needs to do is to create multiple clients, run them, wait until they have finished, and then display some statistics. The code for this is displayed in Listing 9-2.

Listing 9-2. *DBTestRunner*

```
package sampleproject.test;

import java.util.Calendar;

public class DBTestRunner {
    private int numberOfClients = 4; // how many test clients we will start
    private int rentalsPerClient = 2; // number of rentals each client will make
    private String dvdUpc = "32725349302"; // the DVD they will rent

    private DBTester[] clients = null; // an array of the test clients
```

```
public static void main(String[] args) throws Exception {
    new DBTestRunner();
}

DBTestRunner() throws Exception {
    clients = new DBTester[numberOfClients];

    startClients();
    waitForClientsToDie();
    displayStatistics();
}

private void startClients() throws Exception {
    for (int i = 0; i < numberOfClients; i++) {
        String clientName = "Client " + i;
        clients[i] =  new DBTester(clientName, rentalsPerClient, dvdUpc);
        clients[i].start();
    }
}

private void waitForClientsToDie() throws Exception {
    // wait for them all to finish
    for (DBTester client : clients) {
        client.join();
    }
}
```

It is important to realize that even though the client threads are all in TERMINATED state by the time the statistics are being generated, the DBTester objects still exist, and we can still call the public methods on that object to get the information needed for our statistics.

```
private void displayStatistics() {
    // display some statistics
    System.out.println();
    formatLine("========", "========", "========", "========", "========");
    formatLine("Client #", "Rented", "No stock", "Timeout", "Total");
    formatLine("--------", "--------", "--------", "--------", "--------");
    for (DBTester client : clients) {
        formatLine(client.getName(),
                client.getSuccessfulRentals(),
                client.getOutOfStock(),
                client.getTimeouts());
    }
    formatLine("========", "========", "========", "========", "========");
}
```

```
    private void formatLine(String name, int rentals, int noStock, int timeout) {
        formatLine(name,
                    "" + rentals,
                    "" + noStock,
                    "" + timeout,
                    "" + (rentals + noStock + timeout));
    }

    private void formatLine(String name, String rentals, String noStock,
                            String timeout, String total) {
        System.out.format("%tT %8s %8s %8s %8s %8s%n",
                    Calendar.getInstance(),
                    name,
                    rentals,
                    noStock,
                    timeout,
                    total);
    }
}
```

When printing statistics (and in our PretendLogger), we use the PrintStream.format method that was introduced in JDK 5. Remember that the System out static variable is an instance of PrintStream, so we get to use this new method in defining our output.

The format method takes a String argument that describes the formatting of the output, and then takes a variable number of arguments (VarArgs in action). This means that no matter how many arguments you provide, one definition of the format method can handle them all.

The String argument that describes the formatting of the output has many options—far too many to mention here. Table 9-3 describes the options we have used in our test harness. For more information, we recommend you look at the documentation for PrintStream's format method, and the Format class available online at http://java.sun.com/j2se/1.5.0/ docs/api/index.html.

Table 9-3. *String Format Options Used in the Test Harness*

Option	What It Does
%tT	Declares that the corresponding argument after the format string should be displayed as time (the lowercase t), and that the time format should be 24-hour format (the uppercase T)
%8s	Declares that the corresponding argument after the format string should be displayed right justified in a minimum of 8 characters, and it should be a String (the lowercase s)
%n	Outputs the correct characters to start a new line for your operating system

As shown in Figure 9-13, the DVD database as supplied contains three copies of the movie *Night of the Ghouls*. In our test harness, we have specified that there should be four clients trying to rent this movie—therefore we know that at least one will miss out. Furthermore, we have declared that each client should try to rent this movie twice, and because of our explicit timings, we know that the client who missed out first time should get the movie the second time, and one of the other clients should miss out.

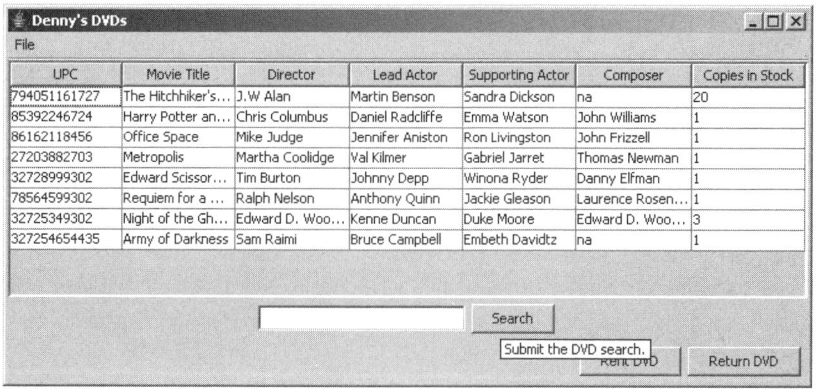

Figure 9-13. *The database contents prior to, and after, running our test*

Figure 9-14 shows a sample run of the test harness. As expected, one of the clients (client 2 in this particular run) missed out on their first attempt to rent the movie, and a different client (client 3) missed out on their second attempt to rent the movie.

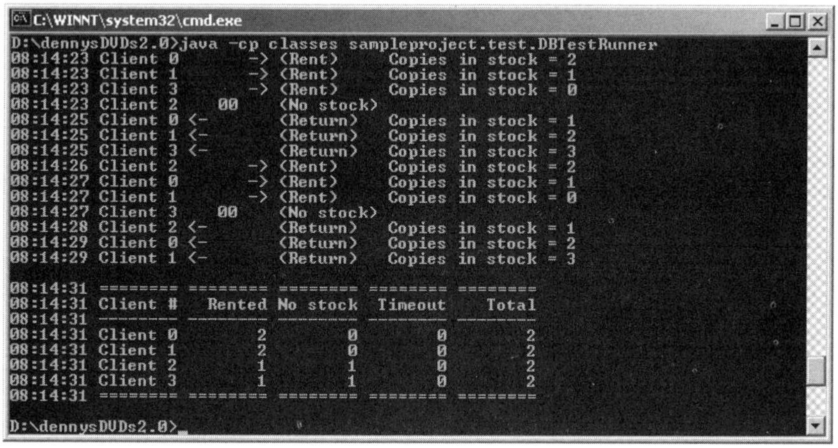

Figure 9-14. *Test harness output*

■**Caution** Although we have made a reasonable attempt to make a multithreaded networked test harness that will produce repeatable results, you should be aware that the JVM thread scheduler and network latency may result in slightly different results.

Packaging Your Submission

We now have to check our instructions to determine what needs to be packaged up and sent to the assessor. Since we don't have any instructions in our assignment, we are going to follow something that will be *similar* to your instructions—namely we are going to create a JAR file that contains the executable runtime, the database, the source code in a directory called src, and the API documentation for our project in a subdirectory of the docs directory. What we will end up with is a JAR file *containing* a JAR file, several directories, and our database file, as shown in Figure 9-15.

■**Caution** The Sun assignment instructions are likely to have a few other requirements as well (such as requiring a design decisions document), and may require slightly different directory structures. You *must* read the instructions you received from Sun carefully, and follow them to the letter. If you get one part of the packaging incorrect, the assessor could fail you on the spot.

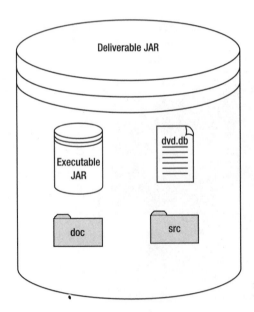

Figure 9-15. *Submission contents*

We have already created our executable JAR file, and since we created it prior to compiling the test classes, we know it does not contain anything we do not want to submit. If we were unsure, or if there's a chance we might go through this sequence more than once, we could just delete the contents of the classes directory, then recompile the source in the src directory, and we could be certain we have a clean code base. This is where having separate directories for the main project source and the test programs source comes in handy.

Naturally we have all the source code sitting in the src directory, so that can easily be incorporated into our submission. Likewise we already have the database file sitting in the root directory, so the only thing remaining is the Javadoc API documentation.

First up we need to create a directory to hold the documentation. We can do that with the following command:

```
mkdir doc\api
```

The command to build the Javadoc API would be

```
javadoc -quiet  -link http://java.sun.com/j2se/1.5.0/docs/api/
  -d doc\api -sourcepath src -public
  sampleproject.db sampleproject.gui sampleproject.remote sampleproject.sockets
```

■**Note** Note That Javadoc command line is all one line—we have just spread it over three lines in this book to make it easier to read.

An example of running that command line is shown in Figure 9-16.

Figure 9-16. *Building the Javadoc API on the command line*

A full explanation of the options we used in our command line, plus many more options we have not used (but you may want to), are listed in the "Running Javadoc from the Command Line" section of Chapter 2.

A simpler option, especially if you are likely to be re-creating the API documentation on a regular basis, is to store all the options in one or more option files. These can be any plain-text file, and each option can be space delimited or newline delimited. An example of using such a file is shown in Figure 9-17.

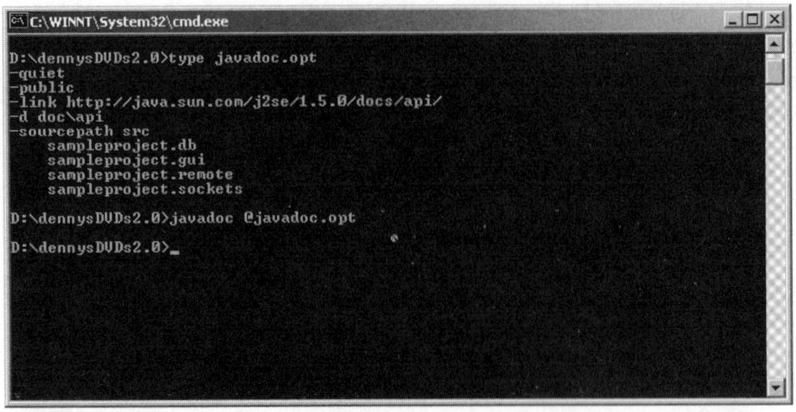

Figure 9-17. *Building the Javadoc API using a file to contain the Javadoc options*

Once we have done this, we can create a single JAR file, holding all the necessary parts. The following command line will perform this for us:

```
jar -cf submission.jar sampleproject.jar dvd_db.dvd src doc
```

■**Note** We did not specify a manifest for this JAR file, as this JAR is only meant to be a container to get your submission to the assessors—it is not meant to be an executable JAR file. So the default manifest file that the `jar` tool creates for us will suit us perfectly.

An example of building the submission JAR file is shown in Figure 9-18.

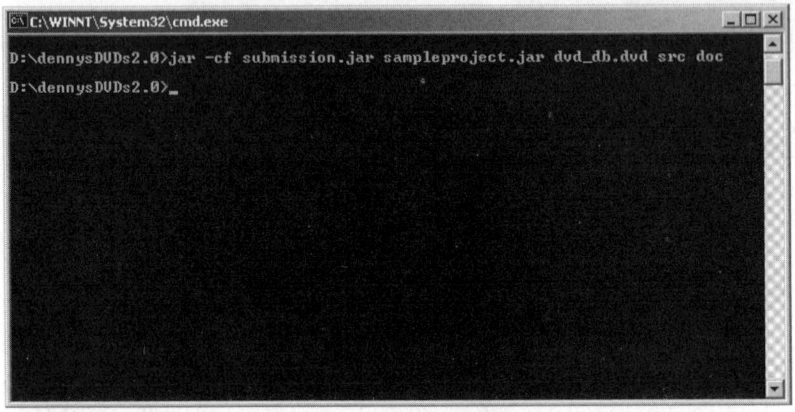

Figure 9-18. *Building the Javadoc API using a file to contain the Javadoc options*

We are now ready to submit. Remember to refer to the information you received from Sun for *your* specific submission instructions. If your instructions differ from the ones in this chapter, then you *must* follow *your* instructions.

At the time of this writing, you upload your Sun submission JAR file to the same site that you downloaded the initial JAR file that contained your Sun instructions and database. When you go to upload the JAR file, you will be given explicit instructions on the naming convention for the submission JAR file (the one that *contains* everything, including the executable JAR file).

Tip Currently you have to request upload permission before you can upload your submission. Unfortunately, we cannot guarantee that this will always hold true, though, and the only way to find out is to try to submit the assignment—which might not be a good idea if your assignment is not complete (although you could always close your browser window at the point where it asks you to select your submission JAR file). Since you are supposed to submit your assignment before you sit for the exam, you should allow a couple of working days between when you plan to submit the assignment and when you sit the exam, just in case you find you must ask permission first.

Summary

We hope that you have enjoyed this book. More important, we hope that you are now prepared to complete the SCJD exam. You have been exposed to a lot of material, and putting everything that you have learned into context is a large task. Undoubtedly, you have some lingering questions, such as "Have I tested my application properly?" and "How will my application behave in this scenario?"

There always seems to be some change or enhancement that can make your application better, and at some point you need to feel confident that your project will pass Sun's scrutiny. After all, your goal is to pass the exam, not develop a commercial project. Sun estimates that about 100 hours of development time is needed to develop a working solution.

To ensure that you pass your exam, here is a list of to-dos:

- Read the SCJD exam instructions very carefully. Even though many of the tests have the same name, their details differ.

- Read this book. At the very least, look at the sample project to see how we solved some of the basic problems such as locking, networking, and the GUI implementation, especially the JTable. We believe that if you understand the code, you should have all of the tools you need to pass your exam.

- Refer to this book throughout your development process.

- Join the JavaRanch SCJD forum (see the FAQs section).

- Test your application. Write a test harness similar to the one we discussed in this chapter. If possible, test it across an actual network. Test all of the use cases. Test your application in a multithreaded environment with a test class such as DBTestRunner.

- Package up all of your ReadMe and design documents along with your application and submit the project to Sun as your exam directions stipulate.

Good luck!

FAQs

Q Where do I get the database files to run the sample project?

A It is included in the zip file you can download from the Apress web site (http://www.apress.com).

Q Do I have to package my application as a JAR file?

A The answer to this question depends on the specifics of your exam. However, our experience has been that most exams require that the examinees use JAR files for their submission. It is recommended that separate JAR files be included in a master JAR file for submission.

Q What do I need to include with my exam submission?

A The basic elements are typically as follows:

- Source files
- An executable JAR file
- Database file(s)
- A design document explaining some of the key design decisions
- A file that explains the development environment you used
- Javadocs
- User documentation

However, you **must** carefully read the instructions provided to you by Sun to ensure that you meet the submission requirements. If there is a discrepancy between what we have described and what is in the Sun instructions, you must follow the Sun instructions.

Q What platform should I test my submission on?

A Since Java is platform independent, your submission should run on either Unix or Windows. We strongly recommend that you test your exam on Windows, Unix, Linux, and Mac OS X (i.e., Macintosh), since there can be subtle platform differences that could cause problems with your submission. For consistency and simplicity, the examples in this book have been demonstrated on Windows 2000. Even though there is no guarantee what platform your application will be tested on once it is submitted, make sure you document the platform you worked on in your ReadMe.

Q What should I do after I have passed the exam?

A Celebrate. Then send us an e-mail at scjd@apress.com.

Q If I have comments or questions regarding this book, whom should I contact?

A You can contact the authors at scjd@apress.com.

Q Are there any online resources useful for passing the SCJD exam?

A There are many excellent online resources. Here are just a few that we found particularly helpful:

- The JavaRanch web site at `http://www.javaranch.com`
- The SCJD discussion groups on Yahoo! (`http://groups.yahoo.com`)
- Java 2 Development Kit, Standard Edition Documentation page (`http://java.sun.com/j2se/1.5.0/docs/`)
- The Java Tutorial: RMI (`http://java.sun.com/docs/books/tutorial/rmi/`)
- The JFC Swing Tutorial (`http://java.sun.com/docs/books/tutorial/books/swing/`)
- JavaWorld article: "Sockets programming in Java: A tutorial" at (`http://www.javaworld.com/javaworld/jw-12-1996/jw-12-sockets.html`)
- Portland Pattern Repository (`http://c2.com/ppr/`)
- Java Coding Conventions (`http://java.sun.com/docs/codeconv/html/CodeConvTOC.doc.html`)
- Sun's Javadoc Style Guidelines (`http://java.sun.com/j2se/javadoc/writingdoccomments/index.html`)
- Java Look and Feel Guidelines (`http://java.sun.com/products/jlf/`)
- User interface design and testing information (`http://www.useit.com` and `http://www.asktog.com`)

Index

REVOLUTIONS
IN EASTERN EUROPE

REVOLUTIONS
IN EASTERN EUROPE

The Religious Roots

Niels C. Nielsen

ORBIS BOOKS

Maryknoll, New York 10545

The Catholic Foreign Mission Society of America (Maryknoll) recruits and trains people for overseas missionary service. Through Orbis Books, Maryknoll aims to foster the international dialogue that is essential to mission. The books published, however, reflect the opinions of their authors and are not meant to represent the official position of the society.

Copyright © 1991 by Orbis Books
Published by Orbis Books, Maryknoll, New York 10545
Manufactured in the United States of America
All rights reserved

Library of Congress Cataloging-in-Publication Data

Nielsen, Niels Christian, 1921-
    Revolutions in Eastern Europe : the religious roots / Niels C.
Nielsen.
        p. cm.
    Includes bibliographical references and index.
    ISBN 0-88344-764-9
    1. Europe, Eastern — Church history — 20th century. 2. Communism
and Christianity — Europe, Eastern. 3. Church and state — Europe,
Eastern — History — 20th century. 4. Europe, Eastern — Politics and
government — 1945 5. Revolutions — Europe, Eastern — History — 20th
century. 6. Revolutions — Religious aspects — Christianity.
    I. Title
BR738.6.N54   1991
274.7'0828 — dc20   91-23592
                                                                CIP

CONTENTS

PREFACE

What was religion's role in the "peoples' revolutions" in Eastern Europe during the second half of 1989? This book has been written in response to this paradoxically simple but complex question. It does not argue that faith in God was the only factor or that it always had positive consequences — only that it often was crucial in opening the way to freedom without violence.

Evident to a visitor to the former Russian satellite countries was not only the deep and intense anticommunist feeling, which could have been anticipated, but the isolation that had prevailed. Citizens in the different nations were engaged primarily with their own national traditions and problems. This book seeks to develop a general overview while at the same time recognizing the distinctiveness of events in each of the countries discussed.

The dramatic changes which have taken place with great suddenness in Eastern Europe — cessation of the persecution of religion, the reunification of Germany, and the end of the cold war — have only begun to be evaluated in long-term historical outlook. The order of presentation in this book is not simply chronological.

Considerable research has been available on the Communist persecution of religion in Eastern Europe, which now belongs largely to the past. Information about the revolutions and the pattern of events since the change of governments still comes in major part from magazines and newspapers. Often reporting of the news had more contemporaneity than perspective! The information provided by French and German as well as English sources has been combined with data gathered during personal visits to the first four countries considered (Germany, Hungary, Poland, and Czechoslovakia as well as the USSR) in the late spring and summer of 1990.

1

THE VARIED FACES
OF REVOLUTION

GAINING PERSPECTIVE ON THE EVENTS

Suddenly the Iron Curtain was torn down — just a decade before the end of the twentieth century! Revolution came quickly and decisively to the Russian satellite countries of Eastern Europe: Poland, Hungary, East Germany, Czechoslovakia, and Romania. No one had expected communism to be displaced from power so suddenly. Historians would long study and debate the causes and meaning of what happened. This much was evident: the continent would never be the same again. It was the end of an era.

Clear and immediate gains could be seen. The threat of nuclear warfare was being diminished, although massive armaments remained. The Berlin wall was dismantled; soon West and East Germany would be united in a single democratic nation. No one was quite sure about future developments in Russia, although it was clear that *perestroika* in that country had been a major dynamic of change. International power structures were being reconstituted in a pattern that could determine the future of generations to come.

At the outset of 1989, citizens were living under atheist rule in the so-called Russian satellite countries of Eastern Europe. Personal faith was repressed through a wide range of strategies that varied from nation to nation. Economies were centrally controlled; free elections were not allowed. At year's end, the totalitarian regimes in all of these nations had collapsed in the face of popular democratic protest. Dissidents, only recently persecuted, found themselves called upon to give new leadership in society.

What did the anticommunist revolutions really mean, viewed in long-term historical perspective? The second half of 1989 was a watershed comparable in consequences with the French Revolution of 1789, two hundred years earlier. A major period of human history was coming to an end — that of the Cold War between East and West. A new era was beginning, with

1

all its risks and dangers. Still there was a difference as compared with the French and Russian revolutions. The 1989 revolutions in Eastern Europe were nonviolent, with the exception of that in Romania.

Jewish philosopher-historian of culture Hannah Arendt finds the positive side of revolution in the human capacity for beginning new things.[1] This much was evident: civil society and its humane values would have a chance to prosper again, no longer inhibited by Communist intolerance of dissent. Democratic pluralism, a market economy, and religious freedom were again the order of the day. Both the French and Russian revolutions had been anticlerical and antireligious. In 1989, religion most often was on the side of revolution.

Some commentators attempted to explain what happened simply in political, economic, or social terms, without reference to belief in God; their analysis, however, was incomplete. The fact remained that religion had played an important role in the peoples' revolutions of 1989. Religious leaders saw dangers as capitalism and the cross at times appeared together in popular imagination, confusedly symbolizing the revolt against communism.

This much was clear: historians will record that a deliberate and prolonged persecution of faith in God came to an end. Citizens in East Germany and Hungary, Czechoslovakia and Poland—where the churches had been persecuted for nearly half a century—suddenly found that all restrictions had been lifted. The change reached even to the USSR, where the abandonment of atheism was still incomplete. The Communist attack on religion—carefully orchestrated and often intense—in all probability ranks as the most powerful since the end of persecution in the late Roman Empire. Millions of Christians suffered imprisonment and death under Stalinist and neo-Stalinist regimes.

To be sure, state policy differed from country to country. Attempts were made to play off one party of believers against another; generally minority religious communities were given more privileges than majority ones. Even in these circumstances, religion sustained trust and community among citizens who otherwise lived in isolation, often shuddering under opportunistic and ruthless rulers. In fact, one reason that the revolutions of 1989 were nonviolent and that "the Chinese solution" was not invoked (with the possible exception of Romania) was that religious influence was present even in the midst of repression.

The Yugoslav dissident and former Communist Milovan Djilas wrote after the recent wave of revolutions:

Coming back to religion ... why, freedom of religion is important. Because with freedom of religion, or religions, it might be better to say, one is opening the way to the political freedoms. When there is freedom of religion, there is freedom of thought, there is freedom of belief and this opens up the possibility of other freedoms, for political theories and political beliefs. This is the essential reason why communists are against the freedom of the Church and religions.[2]

Djilas's point was that freedom of belief and the right to worship according to the dictates of one's conscience did not stand alone. Demands for civil rights, disarmament, respect for the environment, freedom of communication and travel, as well as liberty of religion, literally were carried through the streets by protesters. Oppressive regimes suddenly found themselves confronted with unprecedented mass uprisings. Living in a country not immediately affected by revolution, Djilas expressed surprise not only at the speed of communism's dissolution, but the absence of any internal resistance in its defense.

Revolution would not have taken place without courageous leaders—not all of whom were Christians—who were ready to speak out. What they achieved was not just the rebirth of personal liberty and the right to worship God without state interference. This was accompanied by a parallel and reawakened concern for civil society free from totalitarian repression and for normal political life. Václav Havel, elected president of Czechoslovakia following the 1989 revolution in his country, was a leader among the hundreds of dissidents who signed Charter 77, a careful and outspoken protest issued ten years after the repression of the 1968 Prague Spring. An internationally acclaimed playwright whose plays were performed abroad even while he was imprisoned, Havel borrowed words from the Communist manifesto ("a spectre is haunting"), using them in his own ethical analysis. A charismatic leader, he summed up well the ethos of despair and the imperative for change long before he came to power:

A spectre is haunting eastern Europe. . . . This spectre has not appeared out of thin air. . . . It was born at a time when this [communist] system, for a thousand reasons, can no longer base itself on the unadulterated, brutal and arbitrary application of power, eliminating all expressions of nonconformity.[3]

Havel was sure that

life in the system is so thoroughly permeated with hypocrisy and lies. . . . the complete degradation of the individual is presented as his or her ultimate liberation. . . . banning individual thought becomes the most scientific of world views. . . . the regime is captive to its own lies, it must falsify everything.[4]

Havel's concern, like that of his fellow dissidents, was for the kind of autonomous civil society that churches, in their subcultures, had protected and nurtured even under Communist rule. Protestors' interests were necessarily economic and political as well as religious. It was clear to them that the ethical bases of civilization had been eroded. One reason was that institutional religion, viewed cynically by party cadres, had become a plaything of state bureaucracies. In the Eastern European revolutions of 1989, it was liberated and given freedom to lead its own life. Even "in captivity," the Christian churches had played an important and often indispensable role in keeping hope alive and structuring change.

Havel, in a 1978 essay entitled "The Power of the Powerless," pointed out that two diverse patterns and life-styles were in fact existent: the lie versus the truth. Public discourse was dominated by so-called real socialism and its lies that virtually no one any longer believed. Havel described this state of affairs as one of "living in the lie." Rulers in power sought to crush all opposition, forbidding any alternative culture to that of the ruling party. But this was not fully possible. Citizens knew better, even when they remained silent out of fear. Because their consciences called them to "live in the truth," there was hope in spite of all oppression, Havel believed.

Havel illustrated the widespread general attitude by the figure of a manager of a fruit-and-vegetable shop. The manager was given a sign to be placed in his shop window with the long-standing Communist slogan: "Workers of the world, unite!" By the simple act of displaying it, Havel remarked, he signaled his conformity. "If the greengrocer had been instructed to display the slogan, 'I am afraid and therefore unquestioningly obedient' . . . the statement would reflect the truth." Havel proposed the following:

> Let us now imagine that one day something in our greengrocer snaps and he stops putting up slogans merely to ingratiate himself. . . . He begins to say what he really thinks at political meetings. And he even finds the strength in himself to express solidarity with those whom his conscience commands him to support. In this revolt the greengrocer steps out of living within the lie. . . . He discovers once more his suppressed identity and dignity. . . . His revolt is an attempt to live within the truth.[5]

Revolution was indigenous; it did not come primarily from outside the countries or from anticommunists in the West. For participants, there was an unambiguous cause and clear-cut options. Communism had proved itself inhumane; its dream of utopia had been fully dissipated. In the streets protesters chanted: "If not now, when?" Under communism, a totalitarian system alone had prescribed truth and falsehood, and nothing was to be done outside of its sphere of influence and control. All of life was to be bent to its utopian promise that it would create a new type of human being. This dream had become fully bankrupt.

The Polish philosopher Leszek Kolakowski, first a Marxist and then later an anticommunist, argues that the church did not oppose communism primarily because it was atheistic but because it was totalitarian.[6] It was noteworthy that under Communist regimes, the role of institutional religion was changed from that of oppressor (so it often had been viewed in the past) to that of the oppressed. Patrick Michel points out that respect for institutional religion was in reverse proportion to its so-called normalization. Clergy who conformed to state wishes — in effect serving Caesar rather than the church — were not effective or trusted. In measure as they spoke for God and not Caesar, at times at great price, they had leadership in both personal life and society.

Westerners might not understand fully the reasons for the spiraling anticommunism. Eastern Europeans knew why! Notoriously, for more than four decades, Communist rulers had attempted to prohibit any free assembly in Eastern Europe. Religion was to be limited to worship and the sanctuary. In such a setting, Christianity was regarded as a foreign body that governments must seek to subvert and in the end destroy. But it was not destroyed. Instead churches (especially in Poland and East Germany) became shelters for dissidents who in the end could not be silenced and led the population to overthrow the system. Religion was not, as the Marxists had claimed, an expression of alienation but of the freedom of the spirit.

No doubt it was change in Russia, perestroika, which made possible the overthrow of discredited and defunct regimes. An economic crisis, accompanied by the demise of belief in Communist ideology, threatened to collapse the Russian empire. The supply-and-demand systems of all Eastern European nations were in crisis. The lethargy and repression of Stalinism and neo-Stalinism had taken their toll. The stagnation brought by these forms of totalitarianism would have remained longer, had it not been for leaders such as Havel who took the risk of open dissent and protest. Of course, they did not know in advance whether they would succeed or fail in bringing about change.

Havel used the imagery of the fairy tale to illumine the situation: suddenly it had become clear that the ruling emperor (the Communist party and its ideology) had no clothes. As in the case of the imaginary king who paraded naked before his subjects, citizens had been forced to cheer for a nonexistent reality. Even though they knew better, no one had dared to say that the emperor's clothes (like Communist claims) were a myth. Now faltering communist regimes were no longer supported by citizens who not only distrusted but hated their self-important leaders and the corruption they had imposed. Unlike the Russian Revolution of 1917, the 1989 revolutions renewed continuity with the past, even as they looked to a new beginning. The watershed for captive populations was not only a fresh opportunity for economic, social, political, and religious freedom but for a more normal life in a democratic civil society.

Stalin's statue had been everywhere in Eastern Europe for more than forty years. Often larger than life, his visage gazed down on towns and their citizens. Strangely, even in his lifetime, the dictator had been both hated and loved; he took on what appears to be a semireligious mythical significance. Even citizens who knew how much he had done to destroy their land wept when he died. His legacy lived on during the Khrushchev and Brezhnev eras. In 1989, Stalin's statue disappeared from public squares. Whole groups of them could be seen thrown together on the ground, waiting to be destroyed after they had been taken down. Perestroika had tried to moderate his legacy, to break with the past he had dominated. But it was not enough. The revolt was against Stalin and his influence. Needless to say, citizens' feelings ran high. It was a revolution!

Patrick Michel, in a discerning study, *La société retrouvée, politique et religion dans l'Europe sovietisée*, argues that the church provided what he calls a triple vector against Communist totalitarianism: against the alienation of individuals, against the totalization of society, and against the sovietization of the nation. This in his judgment was the reason it inspired resistance in a diversity of settings in Eastern Europe.[7] The Soviet project had been the homogenization of a vast empire, the maximum of uniformity in a minimum of space. This meant the destruction of both personal freedom and national traditions. Religious conviction, in opposition, supported both—often together. Communism had its own counter symbols, and in the peoples' revolutions of 1989, these—along with Stalin's statues—were attacked.

In summary, it was said popularly that the change required ten years of struggle in Poland, ten weeks in Germany, ten days in Czechoslovakia, and ten hours in Romania. With the peoples' revolutions of 1989 there was a positive pattern of change, of restoration and revival in public life. Citizens who long had lived in isolation under communism finally learned what was going on beyond the borders of their own countries, and the revolutions cross-fertilized.

For forty years—to employ a simple but often-used figure—life had been put in a deep freeze. The conflict that surfaced as it was taken out—for example, a renewed and often intense nationalism—was to be expected. What was amazing was that civilization had endured so well. Surprisingly few persons in the populace wanted anything further to do with Marxism as it had existed in Eastern Europe; its earlier appeal had been destroyed by the attempt to embody it in Communist societies. Of course, there were pressing economic problems in Eastern Europe. Now they could be faced openly.

A useful category for understanding what has taken place is to be found in the concept of *kairos*.[8] A biblical idea that has been applied beyond the scope of scripture, it means the right moment, "the fullness of time." Thus the New Testament recounts that Jesus was born when the prophecies about him had been fulfilled; a series of events in history had prepared the way for his coming. In the contemporary setting, kairos, the convergence of a variety of circumstances, prepared the way for the revolutionary events of late 1989; it was the right time.

If the protests had come earlier, they would have been repressed by the

Russian army, as they were in Berlin in 1953, Budapest in 1956, and Prague in 1968. On the other hand, if they had come later, other strategies—perhaps more violent—might have taken over. A favorable setting had been developing internally within the satellite countries in reform communism as perestroika was taking shape in the Soviet Union. It had not been the moment of kairos when the Solidarity movement grew up in Poland in 1980–1981, for example. The year 1989 was the right time for change.

All revolutionaries were not saints, nor all government officials incompetent. In fact, there were reform Communists in all countries, with the possible exception of Romania. The "return to politics" following the revolutions revealed a wide range of grays, in addition to black and white. Eastern Europe was never the single whole that Communist propaganda and Western ignorance had made it out to be, but there was a common "Yalta experience." Citizens in all of the satellite countries felt deeply that they had been betrayed to Stalin by Roosevelt and Churchill. The cost in human suffering had been very high. At the end of 1989, events moved farther and faster than Russian leadership had expected.

What was in the minds of the students ready to risk more than their elders as they took to the streets in Leipzig, Prague, and Budapest? Often the police were waiting. Not a few were beaten and arrested before citizens in general joined in the protest. The changes which took place during the second half of 1989 can be understood from two different points of view. Externally, in terms of the law, they represented the restoration of basic human rights: freedom of personal expression (conscience, belief, and worship) in civil society. The 1975 Helsinki accords were a widespread inspiration. Protesters called on governments to observe the treaty guarantees to which they had been signatory.

Internally, from the point of view of the motives of citizens who made and participated in the revolutions in different settings, the revolutions were a victory of nonviolence over violence, of spirituality over the debasement of human beings. Statements and public letters by the churches in particular had made clear the crisis. In East Germany and Poland, the churches stood for peace, convincing their constituencies that Europe's problems could not be solved by a third world war.

No one understood the situation better than Adam Michnik, a Polish dissident of Jewish descent. He identified the role of religion very clearly in his writings. Michnik was held for two and one-half years and then rearrested six months later. Following his second arrest, he was given an additional three-year sentence. In his *Letters from Prison*, he wrote of his captors at the Bialoleka Internment Camp:

> To these people, with their lifeless but shifting eyes, with their minds that are dull but skilled in torture, with their defiled souls that yearn for social approval, you are only raw material to work with. They have their own particular psychology: they believe that anyone can be

talked into anything (in other words, everyone can be either bought or intimidated). . . .

And so you find yourself engaged in a philosophical debate with them about the meaning of your life. . . . you score a victory not when you win power but when you remain faithful to yourself.[9]

Michnik's life-style long had alternated between activism and imprisonment. While he was in confinement, he reflected and wrote influentially on what he called the regime's war against the Polish people. Finally released from his second term and resuming his activism, he helped to guide the Solidarity movement to its stunning electoral victory of June 4, 1989. Michnik describes the experience of large numbers of his fellow countrymen who helped to bring about change:

> You know that you are no hero and that you never wanted to be one. You never wanted to die for your nation, or for freedom, or for anything else, for that matter. . . . Nevertheless, they did declare this war on you and over thirty million other people, and so you are forced to recognize that amid the street roundups, the ignoble court sentences, the despicable radio programs, and the distribution of leaflets by underground Solidarity you will not regain the normalcy that was based on respect for yourself. . . . And you will not for the sake of life's enjoyments, give in to the tempting offers of freedom made by the policeman, who seeks to delude you with promises of happiness but really brings suffering and inner hell instead.[10]

The state police tried to force Michnik to sign a declaration of loyalty to the regime on the promise that it would bring him immediate release. "The steel gates of Bialoleka will open up before you, and instead of the prison yards you will see the streets of your hometown, filled with strolling army patrols and rolling tanks," he wrote.[11] Friends and relatives were asking, "So what's stopping you from making these few inconsequential gestures?" Michnik gave his answer:

> Impotence in the face of armed evil is probably the worst of human humiliations. When six hulks pin you to the ground, you are helpless. . . . When they take you from your house, beat you with all their might, burn your eyes with tear gas, break open your front door with a crowbar and wreck your furniture right in front of your family, when in the middle of the night they drive you to the police station in handcuffs and order you to sign statements, then your ordinary instinct for self-preservation and your basic sense of human dignity will make you say NO.

Because even if these people were doing it all in the name of the best and noblest cause they would be destroying that cause with their misdeeds.[12]

Michnik's two jail terms followed, but a new political savoir faire also emerged. Michnik wrote of the situation:

Solidarity knew how to strike but not how to be patient; it knew how to attack head-on but not how to retreat; it had overall ideas but not a program for short-term actions. It was a colossus with legs of steel and hands of clay; it was powerful among factory crews but powerless at the negotiating table. . . . The Polish communist system was a colossus with legs of clay and hands of steel.[13]

In the end, Marxist communism lost, both intellectually and practically. Materialism simply proved an inadequate philosophy of life, unable to account for either moral value or human freedom. Michnik observed: "Alexander Wat wrote somewhere that there is only one answer to the question of how intellectuals who lived in countries ruled by Stalin should behave. It is the Shakespearean answer: they should die."[14]

The central issue was clear, and it had profound overtones: it was one of freedom. Michnik replied to the alleged Shakespearean answer he had cited: "Perhaps it is the true answer. But I believe that this is an answer that one can give only to oneself, a measure that one can apply only to oneself, a sacrifice that one can ask only of oneself. Anyone who demands an answer to this question from others is arbitrarily giving himself the right to decide others' lives. And this usually ends badly."[15]

Michnik understood that the Roman Catholic church, frequently represented in the past as identified with a conservative status quo, suddenly was thrust into a prophetic role. In his book, *L'église et la gauche, le dialogue polonais (The Church and the Left, The Polish Dialogue)*, translated into French but not into English, he was sure that the old antithesis between anti-church laicist and clericalist movements was no more.[16] Persecution helped to accomplish what would not otherwise have been possible.

In Communist propaganda in Eastern Europe, the Roman Catholic church long had been identified with reactionary forces, including fascism. On December 11, 1989, the president of the USSR, Michail Gorbachev, visited Pope John Paul II in the Vatican. What did the two Eastern Europeans say to each other as they spoke together for a brief period without any other observers present? The Russian's interests were no doubt political as well as cultural; he wished peace and stability within his remaining empire.

The practical and symbolic meaning of the meeting for Eastern Europe is not to be underestimated. In a variety of ways, sometimes subtle, sometimes more overt, believers had been persecuted ever since the end of the Second World War—for more than forty years. Job and educational discrimination belonged to the pattern of oppression. In the USSR, the Uniate Greek Catholic Church, loyal to Rome, had been outlawed by Stalin at the end of the Second World War. It was to be allowed to worship openly again under perestroika.

Cardinal König of Vienna envisages the Soviet citizen "now standing baffled before the ruins of the edifice he had thought indestructible, because he had held communist dogma to be infallible."[17] The citizen asks what the fundamental error could have been that led to such chaos? König cites Djilas's claim that communism of necessity had to fail because of its radical contradiction of human nature. A second reason is that it is a system—political, economic, and social—that "excludes in principle any possibility of reform."[18]

What, if any, are the analogies of the situation in Eastern Europe? What can it be compared to? Visibly there was the end of the Russian empire in the satellite countries. Was the situation comparable to the end of French, Dutch, and British colonialism? To the extent that the comparison holds—and it does so only in part—one may consider religious parallels with the role of Hinduism in preserving Indian identity against the British. Islam has had a similar role against the Dutch and French as well as the British. Religious institutions became the place where longer cultural traditions could be asserted and religious identity preserved.

What was most remarkable was how very little violence attended the demise of the Marxist regimes of the so-called satellite countries. Romania was the exception, but even there—as elsewhere throughout Eastern Europe—the army finally refused to attack civilians. In an era of atomic and hydrogen weapons, the case for nonviolence had become far more convincing than before. When free elections finally took place, results only confirmed what everybody seemed to know: neo-Stalinist party leaders had lost touch with reality. Havel's distinction between "living in a lie" and "living in the truth" identified the moral issue. From the theological point of view, "living in a lie" can be called the blindness of sin.

At the same time it must be said that the stereotype of a group of steadfast true believers giving unqualified prophetic witness against a brutal state is all too easily invoked. Such situations existed, and there were faithful martyrs, but the larger problem was the conflict between religion and culture, church and state in the Communist setting. Religion is a social phenomenon, not simply a matter of individual belief. It exists in community. Even religious communities that were compromised under communism stood apart from totalitarianism, challenging it. The continued life of the churches in spite of state control indicated that Marxist atheism had not won fully.

Historians recognize that Christianity has had a variety of different models in its relation to society and civilization. It cannot simply endorse the status quo, as its founder proclaimed the kingdom of God. The kingdom of God poses an eschatological (last things) horizon with respect to both history and personal life. At the outset, Christian faith was set radically against the imperialism of the Roman Empire, as it has been against all earthly empires that claim ultimate authority. Throughout its history, Christianity has existed in tension as both a stabilizing and destabilizing force. A rich diversity of religious patterns continued under communism, expressed in different forms of polity. Some types of churches have been more sanctuary centered than others. Consider, for example, the differences between the Russian Orthodox and Baptist practices in the Soviet Union. The latter's prayer services require no special sanctuary. What has become clear in the persecution of a variety of confessions is that religion is not about to disappear. Its practice has deep roots in personal psychology as well as social tradition.

FIVE COURAGEOUS EXEMPLARS

"Tearing down the curtain" was not just the work of movements and ideas; it happened because courageous men and women resisted apathy and fear. What has happened can be illustrated through the careers of five churchmen.

JAN KOREC, S. J., AND CZECHOSLOVAKIA

Following the people's revolution the Jesuit Jan Korec was appointed the Roman Catholic bishop of the diocese of Nitra in Slovakia. Everything has changed very rapidly for him! Even late in 1989 he still was being harassed by the state police; they had questioned him some thirty times throughout the year. At the beginning of the Communist terror against religion in Czechoslovakia, Father Korec was secretly ordained a priest in 1950 and ten months later, a bishop. Only twenty-seven, he was encouraged by his fellow Jesuits to accept the office of bishop. Most of his life has been spent in the so-called underground church. There were long years in prison. Following his release from imprisonment, he lived with a family in Bratislava, the capital of Slovakia, suffering from tuberculosis. In the apartment, they never spoke above a whisper, as there were informers living in the same house on the floor above.

During the day, Bishop Korec was a worker, lifting heavy gasoline and asphalt drums. Nights he was active as a priest and author. No religious publication was allowed in the country, so the bishop wrote books that circulated in typed *samizdat* form. A few of them were printed in Canada and smuggled into the country. The bishop carefully chose and secretly ordained new priests. Generally, they came from the forbidden monastic orders.

Bishop Korec was finally able to visit Rome in 1969, where Pope Paul VI honored him with the gift of the pectoral cross and bishop's ring that he himself had worn as Bishop of Milan. (Korec had trouble getting them through customs at the Czechoslovakian border.) As the persecution continued, Bishop Korec worked in the underground church for two more decades. Early in 1990, an estimated crowd of sixty thousand people attended Bishop Korec's installation ceremony as Bishop of Nitra. Many of his priests did not live in the underground church, uncompromised with the state. There was no simple answer about whether to do so or not. At Nitra Bishop Korec has had the task of reactivating a large community, reopening a seminary, and training teachers for religious education in state schools—all with a minimum of financial resources. In May 1991 Korec was made a cardinal by Pope John Paul II.

PIORT DUDZINSKI AND POLAND

A very different responsibility belongs to Piort Dudzinski, secretary of the Polish Bishops' Conference in Warsaw and himself a bishop. For more than four decades the Roman Catholic hierarchy had a leading role in the struggle against communism in his country. Now the Communist regime has collapsed, but what Jerzy Holzer has called "Solidarity's [the trade union's] adventures in wonderland" were not at an end. "Poland's revolution did not end in blood but in a state of hopelessness and topor," Holzer wrote.[19] There were new and awesome difficulties as a Roman Catholic-led government tried to rectify past mistakes. Dudzinski, spokesman for the bishops' conference, drove hurriedly from place to place as he worked to mediate divisions in the Solidarity movement, trying to keep the Catholic adversaries of communism together in a time of very great economic hardship. It was very different from the situation Christians had found themselves in before the revolution. Asked about the future prospects for religion in Poland, Dudzinski replied bluntly that he was too busy with the present to speculate about the future.

LÁSZLÓ TÖKÉS AND ROMANIA

Following the revolution in Romania, László Tökés, a Hungarian, was elected bishop of the Reformed Church in Romania. A sophisticated intellectual, he was long in conflict with the totalitarian government of the land. It was the defense of Pastor Tökés by his fellow citizens and parishioners—when he was about to be deported from the city of Timisoara by order of the government ministry of cults—that sparked the first bloodshed in Romania. Unhappily, even after the revolution, Tökés was attacked by the Orthodox bishop in his area. An advisor to the new government early in 1990 (he has since resigned), Tökés has the stature to have become a major national leader, were he not a Hungarian. (The Hungarian minority to which he belongs numbers 1.75 million in the country.)

GÁBOR ROSZIK AND HUNGARY

Gábor Roszik, pastor of the small Lutheran congregation in Godollo, Hungary just outside Budapest, was the first noncommunist in his country to be elected to parliament. It was his election that gave "the slap in the face," as he calls it, to the government, warning it that it had long since lost public confidence. The Lutheran minister never had intended to enter political life. His election occurred after he publicly criticized the incumbent Communist member of parliament for her corruption in a newspaper letter, forcing her to resign. Having effected her removal from office, he was told that he was obligated to run for the open seat. When he did so, he won overwhelmingly.

In time Roszik was joined by two other noncommunist MPs who had won in by-elections, together with four others who had bolted and become part of the opposition. Roszik's own Lutheran bishop, an appointed member of parliament, did not welcome his presence, but the young minister retained his seat after the first open national election, and the bishop did not. The pastor's standard of living in Godollo was not a luxurious one. He worked long hours, day and night, for his constituency. Parliament no longer met sporadically, as under the Communists; it became a full-time legislative body. Roszik has remained uncorrupted and represents a new kind of dedicated public servant. He harbors no illusions about the problems that lay ahead for his country in the post-Communist era.

WOLF KRÖTKE AND GERMANY

By the spring of 1990, former students of Professor Wolf Krötke, who taught at the Protestant Church Academy in East Berlin, were serving worldwide in the government of the GDR. They included ambassadors as well as members of parliament. The building where Krötke taught and lived is not impressive. A former language school, it was taken over by the Protestant church to train future pastors. Most of the students refused to become informers for the Stasi (the state security police), and instead became leaders of protest in East Berlin. Many of the persons who came to study at the academy could not attain admission to the university department of theology, often for political reasons.

At the academy, they studied not just theology but the contemporary social program and pronouncements of their church. Faculty members such as Krötke knew that they were working with activistic students, restless and courageous. The professors had as their goal not indoctrination—only that their students should learn to uphold the truth: Christians cannot compromise the Word of God! Students at a similar academy founded at a mission school in Leipzig were also leaders of the resistance. They faced a largely secular society, acquiescent in the face of totalitarian oppression. Teachers such as Krötke helped bring about change—drastic change.

If one looks for a biblical analogy for totalitarianism, it is to be found in the vast pre-Christian empires of the type described in the Book of Daniel: Babylon, Greece, and Rome. Even when they were oppressed by them, the Hebrews saw hope in God's judgment and redemption in history. Biblical religion had earlier rejected idolatry in a critique that is still relevant against modern totalitarianism. With the demise of dictatorship, it is important to guard against a return to an earlier kind of establishment linked to the status quo.

Mere adherence to the past—simple restorationism—clearly will not answer contemporary needs. The churchmen we have described were effective because they refused to bow down to the Communist's idolatrous "golden image."

Cardinal König cited Dostoyevski as his own appraisal of what went on: "Why use so many words? One cannot be a man without bowing down to something. Such a man who cannot bow down to himself cannot bear his own company, and there is indeed no such man. He who denies God bows down to an ideal, whether it is of wood, of gold, or just in his mind."

König concludes: "And I would add: he who does not bow down before God does so before one of the many idols that a dechristianized society has created as a substitute for God: one bows to the power of the State, to the masses, to capital or the State itself.[20]

REVOLUTIONS WITH UNCERTAIN PROSPECTS

"All this seems to indicate that totalitarianism will one day simply disappear, leaving no other trace in the history of mankind than exhausted peoples, economic and social chaos, political vacuum and a spiritual tabula rasa." Thus Hannah Arendt described what might take place in her study, *The Origins of Totalitarianism*, written shortly after the end of the Second World War.[21] Did this finally come to pass in 1989?

This much was clear: the overthrow of reigning regimes did not necessarily bring lasting economic or even political solutions—only the possibility of such solutions. As the euphoria inevitably faded following the peoples' revolutions of 1989, everyone could see that utopia was not in sight (any more than it had been for the Marxists). A vacuum existed! "The road to serfdom has been mapped by many, the road to freedom leads through largely uncharted territory." This was the warning of Sir Ralf Gustav Dahrendorf, the longtime director of the London School of Economics and now warden of St. Anthony's College at Oxford University.[22]

In the period after revolution, the former satellite countries were often in turmoil. Timothy Garton Ash, who had chronicled the Polish revolution, now wrote of the apprehension of the "Angry New Eastern Europe."[23] Ash quoted a joke current in the Soviet Union: "We know that you can turn an aquarium into fish soup; the question is, 'Can you turn fish soup into an aquarium?' " He commented: "In East Central Europe things are not quite

so hopeless. Here one has something more like a goulash than a fish soup.
. . . There are large lumps of civil society swimming around like meat in
the goulash: private farmers, Churches, universities, small-scale entrepreneurs."[24]

Ash saw hope in two considerations. Writing for the *New York Review
of Books*, he cited Czeslaw Milosz's remark when he was asked what citizens
in his country, Poland, might have learned from the postwar experience:
"Resistance to stupidities." Ash quoted another Pole as saying, "I may not
know what freedom is, but I know what unfreedom is."[25]

President Havel, speaking at the opening of the Salzburg festival in
Austria at the end of July 1990, emphasized that for him the central question was one of truth. It was not just political and economic policy but
beliefs about the meaning of history and personal destiny that had been
debated in the life-and-death struggle between communism and its opponents. What was needed was not another grand scheme, a this-worldly plan
of salvation. It was instead common decency and truthfulness in a free civil
society.

Havel remarked that the revolutionary events in his own country often
seemed to him unreal and like a dream. More than this, fear returned to
him from time to time, even in the new situation of freedom. Long he had
lived with fear as he worked for goals that he knew might never be realized
in his lifetime; suddenly there was success. Now there were new goals, and
these were yet to be realized. Understanding that there were difficulties
ahead, he was plagued by a new kind of apprehension and even fear — that
the goals of the revolution might not be vindicated in his land.

What did the future hold? Helga Königdorm, writing in the German
magazine *Das Argument*, describes a series of stages in revolutionary movements: stage one — the beautiful stage, as she calls it — is a period in which
change is greeted with happiness.[26] It is followed shortly by a similarly
hopeful stage which she identifies as one of enthusiasm; new plans are
made. In a third stage, elections are held; in a fourth one, economies begin
to be rebuilt; and finally consolidation develops. Was this the sequence to
be followed in Eastern Europe? Assuredly, it was a very optimistic if not
utopian one, not a pattern that citizens in Poland, Hungary, Czechoslovakia,
or even East Germany would accept glibly. To identify the stages is easy
enough; to live through them (or bring them about) is far more difficult.

Dahrendorf pointed out that there are few, if any, known models of
change from a Communist to a more open market economy. He warned
especially against "the democratic deception."[27] Democracy is what citizens
hoped for and sought after in Gdansk, Leipzig, and Timisoara. *Democracy*
was a glamorous word, but it was not always clear what it meant. It meant
at least a plurality of political groupings, free elections, and parliaments.
"Self-appointed leaders must be removed, the monopoly of one party broken." There are questions of human rights. At the same time, Dahrendorf
agrees with Winston Churchill that democracy is a pretty bad system of

government—although all others are worse. Its messiness is too often overlooked in revolutionary euphoria. Democracy does make sure that those who govern have the support of the people, at least when they start. But it does not necessarily guarantee firm policies or success.

Dahrendorf continues that it is imperative that the illusion be dispelled that "removal of tyranny will by itself release the energies of freedom. . . . it does not guarantee a constructive process of economic—or for that matter—political reform." "An open society is not a system, but a mechanism for exploring alternatives."[28] "The economic valley of tears must be passed through." Dahrendorf calls "the road to freedom . . . a race against the clock." The task before Eastern European leaders is a daunting one. Democratic communities take time to grow; they cannot be built simply on command. More important still is a growing concept of civil society—an idea rediscovered with the demise of Marxism. To be sure, political change came first and suddenly. Economic revolution would require much more time.

Required are recognition of personal and social rights and the absence of privilege. In Dahrendorf's judgment, this consideration must not be allowed to be overshadowed by security and monetary problems. Our argument will be that the churches have nurtured civil society in a totalitarian era when others could not or would not. Their continued role in giving society moral value and integrity—even in the new pluralistic era that Dahrendorf expects—remains.

Arendt points out that dictators such as Hitler and Stalin established a fictitious world that could be sustained in its rootlessness only by continued and systematic lying. (It led to crimes so horrendous as to be unpunishable.) Were the peoples' revolutions the watershed—the final dismantling of Stalin's legacy that had lingered on longer than that of Hitler? Roy Medvedev, the Russian historian and dissident, author of *Let History Judge*, argues, "From the standpoint of iron will and cruelty, Stalin was unique. As an executioner of his own people and a tyrant, he had hardly any equals in history."[29]

V. Calikova wrote in the magazine *Neva* in 1988:

Stalinism is our misfortune and our weakness. It is inseparable from badly baked bread, from sticky-dirty trays in dining halls, from drunken vomit, from stinking public toilets, from the production of statistics instead of real goods, from clever slimy speeches and slavish silences, from the gaping void between word and deed.[30]

Were the revolutions in Eastern Europe a case of tyrannicide, the execution of a reigning tyrant? Stalin's paranoia, glasnost now has made clear, led to the death of millions of innocent persons; the number is not an exaggeration. The peoples' revolutions of 1989 did bring about the (political) death of Stalin's heirs and finally of his legacy. Paradoxically, Stalinism lingered on most of all in Romania, the only country in which the ruling head of state was put to death. A number of theologians have acknowledged that the killing of a tyrant can be morally justified in the case of an over-whelmingly wicked ruler. Some of them have added a qualification, how-ever: tyrannicide is morally acceptable only if a better ruler follows, in short, if there is not anarchy.

Alec Nove points out that until 1988 the Russian Institute of History was in the hands of dogmatists.[31] Questions which could be discussed only in samizdat (underground illegal) literature or abroad are now being researched. Earlier it was literary figures, writers like Solzhenitsyn, who had led the way. The novelist Anatoli Rybakov, in his novel *Deti Arbata (Children of the Arbat')*, imagines Stalin reflecting:

> To convert in the shortest possible period a peasant country into an industrial power requires countless material and human sacrifices. The people must accept them. But this cannot be achieved by enthu-siasm alone. The people must be compelled to make sacrifices. For this there must be a mighty state-power, inspiring fear in the people. This fear must be maintained by all and any means, and the theory of the unextinguished class struggle provides great help in this. If as a result a few million people perish, history will forgive comrade Stalin for this. If he leaves the state defenseless, causes it to perish, history will never forgive him.[32]

While Stalin was still living, at the end of the Second World War, Com-munist persecution was directed against the established religious order in the occupied countries. Totalitarian regimes came to power in Poland, East Germany, Czechoslovakia, Hungary, and Romania after the end of the Second World War and remained in control until 1989. To be sure, there was modification of Stalin's legacy following Khrushchev's famous "secret speech," as millions of political prisoners were released from the gulag. But it was Khrushchev who gave the command to invade Hungary. In spite of all the moderation of the later Communist rule in that country (whose leadership understood that Stalinism could not be reimposed), citizens would never regard Russian troops as anything but invaders on their soil. Nationalists were only waiting their time to expel the foreigners and their alien utopian ideology!

Stalinism was economic nonsense. Arendt cites one of the dictator's most sympathetic biographers, Isaac Deutscher, who characterized Stalinism as "a piece of prodigious insanity, in which all rules of logic and principles of economics were turned upside down."[33] Private property was abolished; today the mayor of Moscow calls openly for its return as a way of insuring responsible order.

As part of the same pattern of nihilism, Stalin expected to close all religious institutions and end the worship of God in the country. He had nearly realized his first goal just before the beginning of the Second World War. Only a handful of bishops remained active in office. Then the coming of war brought a respite for institutional religion. When the occupying Germans reopened church buildings, services were attended en masse. Stalin, in response, appealed to patriotism and allowed the Orthodox hierarchy to be reconstituted. As part of the war effort, religious institutions were given a recognized place in society. However, Roman Catholic Uniate churches were turned over to the Orthodox at the end of the war. The same pattern was followed in Romania.

It was Stalin's successor, Khrushchev, who renewed religious persecution in the USSR. Approximately half of the remaining Orthodox churches were closed on his initiative, and their priests "faded away into the woodwork." The repression of religion continued under Brezhnev, even though he showed moderation in negotiating limited disarmament with the West. It was he who sent troops into Czechoslovakia, ending the Prague Spring, and later into Afghanistan. Czechoslovakian friendship and admiration for the Russians, which dated from the time of the Munich accord and Hitler's conquest, came to an end in a new occupation. Amid apathy, citizens felt they were only biding their time. Neo-Stalinism and the persecution of religion continued in the USSR with few modifications. A major change of direction came only in 1988, with the celebration of a millennium of Christianity in Russia.

The Communist strategy had been to attempt to isolate Christians and to confine them to a kind of ghetto existence. Nonetheless, church leaders were in the forefront of the movement for change: clergy such as Rainer Epplemann, the Lutheran pastor in East Berlin; Václav Malý, the priest whose license was long revoked in Czechoslovakia; and Zoltán Dóka, the courageous Hungarian pastor who called for the replacement of collaborating clergy even while the Communists were in power in his country. The question of how institutional religion will adjust to new political developments is still an open one—still being decided. Now that civil society has been reestablished, the issue is how much the new opportunities will be utilized. What leadership will churchmen undertake in the new Europe of the twenty-first century?

In January 1989, the Russian atheist monthly *Nauka i religiya* (*Science and Religion*) published an article entitled "Reevaluation."[34] Its author was V. I. Garadzha, director of the Communist party's Institute of Scientific Atheism. He wrote: "In my opinion, the very fact that religion continues to exist in a socialist society demands a new theoretical approach. Up until now we have had a simplified, 'one track' attitude towards the evolution of religion under conditions of socialism. . . . setting up 'good atheists' against 'bad believers' has in practice undermined social unity."[35]

Garadzha concluded that it is "both senseless and ludicrous" to view religion as the greatest hindrance to the development of a socialist society. Perestroika and glasnost have made it clear that stagnation was not due to outmoded attitudes of believers or to religious prejudices, but to far deeper causes. Garadzha speaks of the personality cult's distortion of the basic mechanisms of society. Citizens were uprooted and alienated from creative activity. In this way, an immeasurable blow was dealt to morality and spirituality. Drunkenness, social apathy, and drug addiction have followed. The article protests that continuing stereotypes in atheist reflection still correspond to the spirit of the times when quick results were promised.

> The biologist Lysenko promised a total revolution, an abundance of agricultural foods. Likewise atheist education had its own Lysenkos, who somehow believed that with the wave of a metaphorical magic wand believers would become atheists. They considered religion to be ... a remnant of the "accursed past." ... A new society, they believed ... would not need the assistance of religion.[36]

Garadzha found that religion was blamed falsely for drunkenness, absenteeism from work, an anti-scientific worldview clouding and even poisoning the consciousness of the Soviet people. It was identified with bourgeois ideology, but religion itself long antedated the birth of capitalism. In his article he urges that the political aims advocated by churches have not been the same in all periods of history. There has been not only clerical anticommunism but "also the participation of clerics in the anti-imperialist struggle for the social and national liberation of peoples of Latin America and of many oriental countries."[37] Church leaders have been active in the campaign for nuclear disarmament and in promoting "green" policies. "Ministers of the church as well as atheists are engaged in the struggle against drunkenness and drug addiction, crime and alcoholism, against the dislocation of moral values."[38]

Such an attitude, to say the least, signals the end of persecution. The rebuttal was sharp. One letter replying to Garadzha's opinions suggested that he turn his magazine over to priests. It pointed out rightly that the article would not have been written or published in Brezhnev's time. In fact, it makes clear some of the reasons why atheism became unattractive at the time of the peoples' revolutions toward the end of the century.

A typology of a variety of outlooks needs to be identified in order to evaluate what has gone on. Different models can be distinguished: naturalistic, humanistic, or theistic. Marx identified his philosophy as dialectical materialism. *Dialectic* was a term borrowed from the early nineteenth century German philosopher Hegel. Marx's dialectical materialism can be described as a form of naturalism. His premise was that nature is all-inclusive. There is nothing "outside" or "above" it—in particular, no supernature.

Marx had studied the early Greek materialist philosophers during his university career and sought to revive their views in dynamic contemporary form. Fundamental is his understanding of the foundation and base of all philosophical construction. One may speak of it in terms of the relation of the lower to the higher, matter to consciousness and spirit, as it has often been described. The "lower"—Marx believed Darwin's discovery of evolution proved—not only precedes the more developed but determines what it is. The reverse is not the case, as religionists have traditionally believed. Matter is not based on spirit, but the reverse. Refusing all religious truth on principle, Marx rejected Hegel's idealism for materialism that he judged more accurately describes the course of events and history. In his view, history is not the working out of Idea in the metaphysical sense, but is constituted by concrete forces, economic and material.

In this setting, there are no absolute values such as freedom and justice, only the morality of class struggle. Communism found concrete expression in the Russian Revolution of 1917, and we may ask about its relation to other revolutions. The French Revolution was directed against feudalism and the old regime and signalized their demise. Older aristocratic traditions were replaced by those of a more democratic bourgeois society, which in turn was attacked and overthrown in the Russian Revolution of 1917. Bourgeois democracy was suppressed later in other Eastern European countries as Communists came to power. Attention was directed to the destruction of its ethics and its outlook on religion.

A whole variety of premises were insisted upon dogmatically in the Russian Revolution: materialism, determinism, class struggle, and a reductionistic view of morality. Any life after death was denied. Practically, it was the incompetence of centrally controlled economics which forced a crisis late in the twentieth century. The revolutions—in both their political and economic aspects—did not arise out of abstract ideas alone but from concrete circumstances: lack of food, lack of consumer goods, political repression, and the prolonged attempt to destroy religion. Still, ideologically (to use the Marxist term), leaders such as Poland's Michnik and Czechoslovakia's Havel represented humanism as against a reductionistic naturalism.

In opposing communism, humanists and Christians joined in a new alliance. John Anderson, of Keston College, explains: "In the same way that believers began to reveal more sympathy for secular dissidents, the latter began to show a greater understanding of religious values." There was what the German writer Heinrich Böll called "courtesy toward God."[39] As distinguished from philosophical naturalism, humanism may be said to give a larger place to human beings' uniqueness in transcending nature through freedom and reason. In terms of Hegel's philosophy, which Marx studied but rejected in part, there is spirit as well as matter. How the two are related had long been debated in the philosophical tradition. Still, from the nonreductionistic, humanistic point of view, the lower does not control the higher; matter does not determine consciousness. The charge is that dialectical materialism—Marx's naturalism—is unable to account for non-negotiable and absolute moral values. For communism, moral values have no intrinsic status in reality, apart from matter.

In the peoples' revolutions, absolutes were reaffirmed in terms of human dignity and freedom. Dissidents have affirmed that these simply are not negotiable or to be given up in the face of the totalitarian state. Christians have insisted that morality is not to be determined by the state or the regime or the party. Morality's ultimate source is deity, the giver of the Ten Commandments, for example. Philosophers have long identified what they call a naturalistic fallacy: one cannot derive what ought to be from what is (might does not make right). To do so is not possible logically; these are two different orders of understanding and reality.

Arendt clearly states that communism has broken with the moral as well as the religious traditions of Western European civilization.[40] As we have already suggested, humanism more than naturalism is related to the third position that we have mentioned, namely, that of theism. Theism affirms belief in a personal God who is both immanent in the world and transcendent over it. This is the view of both the Old and New Testaments, Judaism, and Christianity. Neither matter nor spirit explain life or human existence in their fullness. "Beyond" and "above" them (these are spatial metaphors) is the fullness of Reality.

The Communist position has been to deny any such Reality. An attempt was made to exile religion from culture. In this step, however, regimes were disavowing the traditions of their own people. Not surprisingly, national and religious loyalties remained together in social memory and personal motivation, resurfacing in 1989. The call for freedom was significantly a call for reinstatement of earlier cultural meanings and traditions. "Without solidarity, there is no freedom" echoed in the streets of Poland. It applied not only to the trade union movement but to the destruction of national identity and past loyalties that communism had attempted. What was called for in terms of freedom in Eastern Europe was something other than secularization in the pattern of Western Europe. Freedom was linked to both morality and religion.

The fact is that most Communists did not argue or seek communication; instead, they persecuted religion and those who made an open profession of belief in God. Their antireligious campaigns have been long and determined. The question has often been asked as to whether their ideology is not really a pseudo-religion. Does it not in itself have religious roots—negatively, at least—in the revolt against God? Actually, it is a revolt against a pseudo-deity, an idol which few if any Christians would recognize as the living God.

Whatever dialogue existed earlier in Western Europe between Christians and Marxists largely came to an end with the 1968 Prague Spring and the imposition of external military force. It is not an accident that artists and churchmen joined in protest in Prague's Velvet Revolution. It is the dimension of symbolism which communism's reductionistic materialism is unable to account for. In Czechoslovakia, as indeed elsewhere throughout the Soviet empire, the works of a whole generation of writers were refused publication. Symbolism (the term is not necessarily vague) has expression in art and literature as well as in religion. It is a dimension that materialism simply cannot handle in any positive way. Communists regarded religious symbolism as especially nonsensical and meaningless.

What are the immediate religious issues and needs in Eastern Europe today, following the peoples' revolutions against neo-Stalinism? Renewal, as against mere restorationism, requires that believers find new cultural relevance in their expression. First and outstanding is the problem of dechristianization, which came from decades of atheist rule. Much ground has been lost institutionally by the churches. Religious leaders sometimes designate East Germany, Czechoslovakia, and Hungary as "missionlands." Of course there is similar overwhelming secularization in West Germany, France, and Great Britain, as well. Part of the explanation for the dechristianization is very simple—practical, not abstract or intellectual. Communist regimes built large apartment housing blocks for tens and even hundreds of thousands of citizens without any new churches. Churchgoing habits dissolved! In East Germany, where a few churches were built, they were paid for with funds from the West. In the same pattern, governments worked very hard to keep young people away from the churches. Two generations have received little religious education.

Secondly, there is the question of what religious institutions' relations should be with governments, now that Communist repression has passed. The oppressive ministries of cults, through which Communist regimes attempted to control the churches, have been abolished. However, in the present situation of reconstruction, it is not possible to immediately disengage totally in relations with the government; new church-state policies are being formulated. The more fundamental consideration is whether Christians have a continuing responsibility for society and culture. Their religion makes ethical demands on public life, and church leaders and theologians were conscious that these remain even when the regime is no longer overtly hostile.

Very high on the list of problems and needs is the question of credibility. A large number of clergy were compromised by working with the Communist state. To be sure, this was less the case in East Germany and Poland, where the ecclesiastical community had more *Lebensraum*. But many of the collaborators with the regime still remain active as priests and/or pastors. The churches' position, in general, has been that their loyalties to the old regimes are to be condemned, but not their persons.

Thirdly, there is the problem of tension between nationalities (a problem that overlaps that of interconfessional relations). Communism in effect covered up the nationalities problem. Century-old hostilities among Orthodox, Roman Catholic, and Protestant continue, especially in Romania and Russia today. One religious group was pitted against the other whenever possible by the Communists. Romanians are Orthodox or Uniate. Hungarians are Roman Catholic or Protestant. Long-standing confessional tensions have presented enough difficulties in themselves. When they are joined with nationalism, they become explosive. As the Pope recognized when he visited Czechoslovakia, they still remain to be overcome in a variety of situations.

With the collapse of Communist ideology, nationalism has taken on immense and renewed power throughout Eastern Europe. Simply put, Marxist initiative has failed. A renewed nationalism is in effect pulling the Russian empire apart even as it earlier destroyed the Austrian-Hungarian empire.

Géza Németh is a Hungarian Reformed church pastor who was suspended from office for his opposition to the regime. His son was recently elected to parliament on an anticommunist platform, and the pastor has been outspoken against what he calls "KGB Bishops." These should be replaced by freely elected ones in the new postrevolutionary situation, he insists. Németh works with Hungarian refugees from Romania. The article that he wrote for *The Hungarian Observer* after the change of regime in his country, "Christianity's Answer to Nationalism," came not out of theory but practice.[41] What is needed is a combination of the ideas of Reinhold Niebuhr and Martin Luther King, Németh said. He wrote: "For 2,000 years this leaven of Jesus has been a yardstick, sometimes winning and often losing, even within the church itself, but still to this day the sole transcendent mentality able to cure a world driven by nationalism and the urge to conquer."[42]

Throughout history, Christianity has not always succeeded in its desire to foster brotherhood and justice, Németh observed. Often it has stood on the side of rulers against the ruled. This was the case in both Hungary and Romania, where many church officials often became instruments of Communist regimes. So reform in the churches is needed, drastic reform, along with renewed civic consciousness.

For more than four decades, Moscow directed church policy in Eastern Europe. Németh's most important (and in some respects disconcerting) conclusion is that this was the case more because of national than ideological motives. There was little more than expediency—power politics rather than a sincere belief in atheism—in much of the attack against religion. One had to deny God to be a Communist. Atheism had political (often cynical) roots as Russian Messianism was transferred from Orthodoxy to communism. Németh argued in his article:

The one aim of internationalism and atheism was Russification. Paradoxically, the oppressive power achieved its purpose only with its own people, which it robbed of its own Russian values and the thousand-year heritage of Russian Christianity. All other nations' national and religious identities seem to have strengthened, as the national movements currently flaring up show.[43]

Earlier affiliated with the state, the Russian Orthodox church championed Russian Messianism. Under communism, this emphasis was joined to belief in a new totalitarian world order. Refusal of faith in God became the new state religion, and any national church inside or outside of Russia that seriously held to Christian belief was to be destroyed. Specifically, the goal was that churches in the satellite areas should be phased out.[44] Churchmen who cooperated with authorities were given hierarchical powers, even as they were manipulated by the KGB.

As Eastern Europe lacks traditions of democracy comparable to those in the West, Németh observed, impatient nationalism and bigotry continue to be present. The outstanding question is not whether religion will continue to live on, but only how. Will it be joined to a reactionary nationalism? Németh concluded: "The churches, with their responsibility for peace in Eastern Europe, must underline that Christianity is a common heritage of all Eastern European peoples; the essence of the Christian message is to bind, not to part, and it cannot, under any circumstances, be an ideology of antagonism."[45] The challenge to religious institutions was immense: not to return to old parochialisms or to sectarian conflict. Unfortunately as Communist power in the state declined, ecumenical (interchurch) cooperation more often declined rather than increased throughout Eastern Europe.

2

GERMANY

Springtime in Autumn

The East German revolution of 1989 was called "the Revolution of Light." Thousands of candles lit the way as worshipers filed out of church buildings after Monday evening prayers for peace. In one hand the worshipers clutched a lighted candle; their other hand shielded its flame and indicated that the bearer held no weapon.

Such a peaceful revolution was without precedent in German history. Its leaders did not seek military victory as in earlier revolutions in their country or in the French, American, or Russian revolutions. A radical change of government took place without any major bloodshed. Of course, the motivation was not simply religious. It was, however, a determined minority of Christians that led the way out of both apathy and hate.

OVERCOMING THE MOST EFFICIENT POLICE STATE IN EUROPE

The East German government long had suppressed the free dissemination of ideas. Reflecting "German efficiency," state security police supervision was in many respects more severe in East Germany than in any Eastern European satellite country except Romania. Telephones were bugged. One could never be quite sure which colleague or alleged friend was an informer. A bishop remarked that he would utter in conversation only what could be said before God and the security police, the Stasi!

As identification of their allegiance, East German Communist party members were required to wear badges on their lapels. Citizens were not allowed to assemble or organize for free expression of opinion on any topic; hence the churches' unique role as a place of meeting. Dissident writers, censored and silenced, were not a major threat to the status quo. Many of the most creative of them had moved to West Germany, where they could continue their work in the same language. Others remained and were persecuted. University professors were carefully screened for party loyalty before being appointed, and their classes were infiltrated with informers. It is estimated that more than 90 percent of the faculty were Communist party members in Leipzig, for example.

In Berlin, the Stasi, the state security police, had long been successful in suppressing street demonstrations. Leipzig, not Berlin, became the first center of protest. World renowned for its trade fair and long a publishing center, it was only a shadow of its earlier glorious past. Pathetically run-down under Communist rule, more dwellings had been abandoned than were lost to bombing in the Second World War, it was rumored.

As the Revolution of Light grew in Leipzig, multitudes of dissatisfied citizens could be seen streaming out into its streets in the early evening following Monday night prayers for peace at Nikolai Church and other sanctuaries in the city. First there were thousands, and then tens of thousands. Finally, the Stasi headquarters itself was stormed by activists.

Of course, there was fear in the populace: fear of personal arrest and torture, fear of death on the street. Nonetheless, on Monday, September 25, an estimated six to eight thousand persons demonstrated on the major boulevard encircling the city. Next week, on October 2, the crowd had grown to over ten thousand. On October 9—the crucial watershed evening—more than seventy thousand were demonstrating. Many of the protesters were young people who had grown up in the GDR. The Communist government they had always lived under was all that they had ever known. At the end of the eighth year in school, young citizens swore eternal allegiance to the East German fatherland. They promised to be true patriots who, in firm friendship with the Soviet Union, would deepen and strengthen the brotherly ties between the socialist states.[1] Now they were calling for radical change.

During the early fall months the Stasi had beaten demonstrators and made hundreds of arrests. Students in particular were abused. Stasi informers were everywhere. In fact, the government had asked citizens in general for reports on their fellows, and information came in so fast that its computers could not sort out the charges. In Dresden, on October 4, ten thousand citizens assembled before the central railroad station. Trains were moving through the city loaded with East Germans who had been granted permission to pass from Czechoslovakia (where they had fled) on to the West. Dresden citizens, many of whom also wanted to leave, were dispersed with water cannons and tear gas. On October 7, the demonstrators, thirty thousand in Dresden, ten thousand in Plauen, and thousands in Berlin, were attacked by the police in force.

Pressure had mounted as thousands of citizens fled to West Germany during the summer months. It was not lost to Communist leaders that "the Great Escape" was a life-and-death threat to their regime. The majority of the population no longer believed in communism—if it ever had. Everyone knew that a totalitarian structure had been imposed from without at the end of the Second World War. Suddenly the country lost all its ideological moorings and spun out of control.

Would the protest remain nonviolent? At the time, no one could be sure, least of all the pastors who had allowed dissenters to meet in their churches. In Leipzig, police with full riot gear and live ammunition were waiting outside, and worshipers were forced to walk out one by one, single file, before they could move further on to Karl Marx Allee. Granted that the Stasi had informers everywhere; they might also have provocateurs to incite violence.

Inside churches, protesters often joined together with raised hands and sang the American folk song, "We Shall Overcome." No one could be sure that they would. Even while religious leaders insisted on nonresistance—the renunciation of force—the situation had become fully revolutionary. Unrest had been developing over the years. There was especially strong resentment that election results had been manipulated by the government in the spring. Although it probably had won only 80 percent of the votes (under duress), it claimed 95 percent. In the late summer and early fall of 1989, the outcry reached no longer controllable proportions. In Leipzig, the first few thousand Monday night worshipers had been joined by tens and then hundreds of thousands. Soon millions of citizens protested throughout East Germany.

In the face of the mounting crisis, the head of the East German government, Erich Honecker, stonewalled; he was at loggerheads with both the West and the East. Reform communism was not to be allowed in the GDR, he insisted. Egon Krenz, his successor, reports having argued with the chief. Remaining adamant against reform, even in the face of the exodus of his population, Honecker denigrated Gorbachev's policy of perestroika. "If your neighbour wallpapered his flat, would you feel the need to decorate yours?" asked the party's chief ideologist, Kurt Hager.[2]

Gorbachev visited East Berlin on October 7 to join the celebration of the fortieth anniversary of the Communist state. His arrival at the airport was not shown on East German television. Speaking publicly, the Russian leader admonished patience. "Don't panic, don't be depressed," he told East Berliners. His remarks were meant for the entire nation: "I think that dangers exist only for those who don't grasp the situation, who don't react to life." Privately, he is reported to have told Honecker, "Those who delay are punished by life itself."[3]

Two days later, the evening of October 9 in Leipzig, the decisive Communist retreat from the use of force took place; it became clear that the people's revolution would not be further suppressed by police violence. Asked about the sources of the revolution, President Weiszäcker of West Germany replied, "Gorbachev and the churches."

East Germany is mainly a Protestant country. It is the heartland of the Reformation, the homeland of Luther. The churches had been the only possible peaceful gathering point. In a hard-fought battle over the years, they had won the right to schedule religious meetings without state interference. As it developed, the leadership of the Monday night prayer services had been turned over to the small so-called base groups made up largely of activists who wanted change. On principle the churches claimed the right to allow men and women to pray, unhindered by the regime.

The sole alternative to imprisonment for most individuals seeking freedom of expression lay in flight to West Germany. It was only the concessions that the churches had won from the state that left a small loophole. Theology became the one major field that a young person could study without a Communist party membership card. But teaching communism was required even in theological faculties. In the course work, Communist atheism was not to be called into question, as it was established as the only acceptable truth by the government.

By 1989, an urgent question in the minds of the Monday evening worshipers was whether to stay in the GDR or to leave the country. Many of the protesters were awaiting permission to emigrate. The churches urged them to remain in East Germany and attempt to change the situation. Was that at all possible? At the outset, the 1989 street demonstrations echoed with the cry, *Wir wollen raus* — we want out. But then, under church influence, it changed to *Wir wollen bleiben*, we want to stay; *Wir sind das Volk*, we are the people. It was largely a Protestant movement but included many (secular) persons who had long since lost interest in religion.

Until the building of the wall in August 1961, Berlin had been the point of exit. Millions had left since the end of the Second World War. When East Germans met West Germans traveling on vacation, the vast economic discrepancies of the nation became evident. In the summer of 1989, alleged vacationers renewed the large-scale flight of East Germans — this time not through Berlin but Czechoslovakia and Hungary. From Hungary they pressed over the newly opened border between that country and Austria, when necessary leaving their small Trabant and Wartburg cars behind.[4] When the governments of these countries decided to allow the immigrants free passage, the impact was especially depressing in the home areas from which they had come. Suddenly there was a dearth of doctors, nurses, craftsmen, skilled laborers, and professional people. To be sure, their departure mitigated only in a small way the housing shortage. There was not that much space to spare.

Despite closed borders, East Germany did not live in total separation from the outside world. In much of the country, including Berlin and Leipzig, citizens could see West German television. In cities such as Dresden, where reception was not so easy, there was always radio. A Dresden pastor reports listening to the West Berlin radio reading of dissident Walter Jankas's book, *Difficulties With the Truth* — under the bedcovers.[5]

A vast network of informers and provocateurs infiltrated even church ranks, as recovered police records now make clear. But there was also a network of information among dissenters. Names of recently arrested protesters still in prison were given out in evening prayer services. As for the official press, citizens long since had learned to read between the lines; in conversation, there was double-talk, and language was corrupted. Even church newspapers were censored. Listening to preaching in the church was one of the few occasions that one could hear the truth without such corruption.

As elsewhere in Eastern Europe, the demand to know the truth—an end to deception and lying—led to a new espousal of human rights and democracy by the churches, particularly after the signing of the 1975 Helsinki accords on human rights. Citizens knew that the revolution would not have happened as it did without the churches' influence. Church leaders had prepared the way in a long conciliar process—year after year offering an alternative worldview and way of life. Peace, human rights, and concern for the environment were the chief themes—all defined on Christian rather than Marxist premises. These themes became the program for revolution.

To continue to supply its clergy under Communist rule, the Protestant church found it necessary to establish a number of training centers outside the usual university faculties of theology. In other countries they might have been called seminaries; the German name was *Kirchliche Hochschule*. One such institution was located in the building of the Sprach Convent (a language school) in East Berlin. A second was established at a former missions school in Leipzig. A third such school, smaller and concerned especially with religious education, was in Naumburg. In such circumstances, supervision was less strict by the Communist state bureaucracy. In order to avoid friction with the government, teachers in these institutions were registered with the state and paid as pastors. The curriculum was not limited just to classical theological interests, although these were included. Questions of immediate political relevance could not be avoided.

Students studying under the state-supported theological faculties at universities—in Leipzig, for example—were less activistic, although both groups participated in the demonstrations. One reason was that the Hochschule student bodies included many persons who had been barred from other educational opportunities. Some were sons and daughters of pastors, who were ineligible because of their family background. Others were in trouble with state authorities because of their known opposition to communism. In the church academies, they had an opportunity to study intensely their church's conciliar pronouncements on social issues. Not surprisingly, these students actively supported the Monday evening prayer services for peace that had been going on since 1982. Persons of such conviction, informed and convinced, were crucial to the success of the revolution.

Indeed, they were at the forefront of protest when the regime faltered and drew back in Leipzig. Why was the order for police intervention never given from above on the crucial evening of October 9? Why were the waiting security forces not instructed to shoot? True, in Leipzig that afternoon there had been a public appeal for nonviolence by the so-called Leipzig Six: Dr. Kurt Masur, the respected director of the Leipzig Symphony; Bernd-Lutz Lange, a popular entertainer; and Dr. Peter Zimmerman, a theologian, along with some of the regional socialist party leaders. When it became clear that there would be no "Chinese solution," no repetition of the massacre of Tiananmen Square on German soil, the number of Leipzig protesters grew to 120,000 on October 16 and 300,000 on October 30. At the same time, the way was now open for peaceful change and dialogue. The first dialogue between demonstrators and the representatives of the government took place in Dresden on October 9. Then a spiraling cycle of demonstration and discussion continued until a new noncommunist regime was in power.

A number of explanations have been given for the course of events. Police monitoring reports (volumes of them are now available for public reading) were required to be filtered through party officials before the final orders were given. Dissidents saw to it that there was a wealth of confusing and conflicting data coming in through police informers. In short, they overloaded police communication channels with a variety of possible scenarios. Egon Krenz, who ruled briefly as the head of the East German government after Honecker, claimed that he himself intervened. Krenz's statement is not fully credible, as he remained passive until late in the evening. Where were his sympathies? He had only recently returned from China, where he had been loud and vocal in his praise of "the Chinese solution," namely, suppression by violence. Clearly the Brezhnev doctrine was dead and the Russian army would not be used in support of such a strategy.

When Erich Honecker resigned on October 18, Krenz, as his long-intended successor, knew the situation was out of hand. Still he hoped to control it and keep the Communist regime in power. Lacking the public's confidence, he resigned in less than two months. In his autobiography, Krenz indicates that the government was well aware that its representatives had signed the 1975 Helsinki treaties on human rights. Did he know as well that when his government opened the Berlin wall on the night of November 8–9 (which had closed off East Germany from the West since August 16, 1961), the end of the GDR was being signaled? Reporters observed:

> On the stroke of twelve, both sides of Berlin erupted. Laughing, crying, shouting and singing, the crowds poured through the crossings and, where they were packed tight, climbed up and over the wall. As morning dawned, the Ku'damm, West Berlin's glitzy main street, was transformed by tens of thousands of poor relations from the East, wide-eyed as little children.[6]

CHURCHES AS ZONES OF FREE SPEECH

The remarks of Dr. Christa Grengel, ecumenical staff representative for the Reformed churches in East Berlin, provide an informed commentary and background on the pattern of events in her country. She had lived her entire lifetime under totalitarian regimes, first in the Nazi period and then amid communism. As a church leader and official, she has been especially sensitive to the nuances of the changing situation and has had access to more than the usual sources of information. Dr. Grengel was born in 1939, just before the Second World War began. To escape the bombings in Berlin, her family fled to Schleswig-Holstein, but then came back to live in a small city near Berlin after the war's end. Dr. Grengel's father, a pastor, never returned home from the war; the family believes that he was killed in the battle for Stalingrad. Her mother had studied theology in the 1930s and after the war undertook further training. She was ordained a Protestant pastor and was assigned to work in seven small villages with five preaching places.

The pastor's daughter was not allowed to be a member of the Communist youth organization, the Young Pioneers. What was she to do when her third-year school class was required to write an essay about why one should join it? Scholar Grengel recalls writing about "Why I am not a young pioneer." The legacy of the war was evident in the Soviet occupation in the Berlin area. Russian troops had their headquarters near the house where the family lived, and its members could not venture safely into the woods nearby alone. There was more official terror: the KGB prison was located on the street where the family lived, and Dr. Grengel's biology teacher disappeared into it. The presumption was that she was taken to Siberia. Two members of the church youth group also suffered a similar fate.

Large numbers of Christian young people left for the West when Russian tanks rolled into East Berlin to repress the June 17, 1953, workers' revolution. In Grengel's high-school class, Christians still numbered about 10 percent, thirty out of three hundred. They were told that they were the last of the bourgeoisie; twenty years into the future there would be no more Christians. Christians were identified with fascists. How could they be so unprogressive? Still, Grengel reports, she had no sense of being a martyr. When many school friends left the GDR for the West, her family stayed, out of a sense of religious responsibility. (The option to leave was an open one until the wall was erected.)

Her ambition was to study mathematics and theoretical physics, but this was not possible for a pastor's daughter. Later, she researched the boundaries between these disciplines and theology. The option open to her was to enroll in theology, and subsequently she became a pastor of a congregation that was divided (geographically) when the wall was erected. Recently, since the revolution, its two separated parts have been able to worship together again. After her work in the pastorate, she accepted a position in the central church office. She speaks fluent Russian, and her international contacts have been many. Now she has friends in the USSR to whom she sends CARE food packages.

How does Grengel evaluate the East German revolution of 1989? First of all, she points out that it was not planned. The churches' stance moved from a position of watchman to critical distance, critical solidarity, and then the church for others—ready to intervene wherever humans suffered or were threatened by power and force. What was achieved when revolution came? she asks herself. Very much, is her answer. A new and positive self-consciousness is expressed in the phrase, "We are the people." Personal life—the soul—has been liberated.

Dr. Grengel lists the following accomplishments: a set of individual rights—freedom of speech, information, and travel. The precarious economic situation of East Germany was made public, armed groups disarmed, and party pluralism achieved. There were also threatening potentialities, some overtly criminal, such as the growth of the black market and the illegal use of drugs. There were weapons in private possession amid calls for lynch justice. Among the population at large there was a growing number of suicides. Social differences were sharper than before as unemployment and homelessness increased. Dr. Grengel regretted most of all the loss of the positive social idealism that socialism had generated at its best and the rising rightist extremism.

Grengel is sure that the revolution would not have been peaceful without the churches. It is a gift of God that their representatives and stance were widely trusted by the public, she comments. Out of their experience, Christians have been compelled to formulate their beliefs more clearly. They have come to understand that the freedom of the Christian person does not depend simply on the political situation. Realization that "We are the people" was the most beautiful experience. But questions linger on about the people's real nature and guilt from the past. It was not difficult to say, in its absence, what freedom meant under communism. What freedom means positively today, as more than the absence of compulsion, is more difficult to identify, Dr. Grengel believes. Will the churches keep the trust of the populace and continue to be critics of society in the new Germany?

Theologically, for German Protestants in particular, Bonhoeffer's thought and ideas had a strong influence. Dietrich Bonhoeffer was hanged by the Nazis in the closing days of the Second World War. A young theologian who came from a secularized family, he had been hailed as an especially promising and creative thinker by Karl Barth, the older major Protestant theologian. Barth, although a leader of the anti-Nazi German Confessing Church, had Swiss citizenship and taught and wrote safely in Basel during the war. Bonhoeffer had studied at Union Seminary in New York City and because of a sense of mission, returned to Nazi Germany rather than remain in the United States. He participated in the resistance movement out of religious motivation and was involved in the unsuccessful plot on Hitler's life. Imprisoned and finally executed, before his death Bonhoeffer reflected on and wrote about what he called "religionless Christianity."

God had been pushed to the edge of the world, as it were. Older super-naturalisms, with their doctrines of divine causation, no longer seemed relevant in the modern, highly secularized setting. But even in this situation, Christianity was not destroyed but had become more rather than less relevant, according to Bonhoeffer. God is most of all present not as ruler but in terms of the cross. What Bonhoeffer—like his friend and mentor Barth—proposed was not a new establishment Christendom but, paradoxically, strength in weakness. Religionless Christianity gave up old supports—philosophical, cultural, even theological—but found new relevance in the cross amid the crisis. This was the antithesis of restorationism. Bonhoeffer's outlook, expressed in particular in his letters from prison, seemed especially illuminating to many reflective Christians living in East Germany.

By comparison with this stance, there were concerned Christians—Protestant and Roman Catholic—who defended Christian integralism.

> Minister, you are a Marxist. I am a Catholic Christian. Our philosophies of life have nothing in common. There is no bridge over the chasm that separates us. . . . We Catholics, however, live in a house whose foundations we have not built. These foundations we believe to be based on falsehood. If we are going to live together in this house, the only subject for us to discuss is —please forgive the trite saying—whose job it is to clear the staircase.[7]

This statement, made by Dr. Otto Spuelbeck, who was Apostolic Administrator at Meissen in 1956, is cited by Arvan Gordon of Keston College in a 1990 article on "The Church and Change in the GDR." Its citation reflects a specialist's view of the long-term stance of the Roman Catholic church in East Germany. Of course, Roman Catholics did support efforts for change in the GDR. They were specifically instructed to do so by Pope John Paul II. But they were not the majority. Their response to Communist rule—as a minority group—commonly was a conservative, defensive one.

Neither the Protestant nor the Roman Catholic church hierarchies were appointed in cooperation with the state, as in Hungary, Czechoslovakia, or Romania. Organized in regional synods, the Protestant churches encouraged their members, as a matter of principle, to work loyally within socialism and not to defect to the West. "The churches, indeed, have far more influence than they had forty years ago," Broun observed in 1988.[8] "Neither past repression nor present privilege has caused them to compromise." Actually, the kind of *Lebensraum* achieved and used effectively by East German Protestant officials has been compared to that afforded Roman Catholics by the papacy in other situations, such as Poland. Although organizational ties with the West German Protestant churches had been broken off in 1961 at the state's insistence, major funding continued to come in from West Germany. There was also East German participation in World

Council of Churches programs. The following is a fair description of the Protestants' situation:

> The social base of the [Protestant] church lies in the former bour-
> geoisie—many of whom had to become manual workers because of
> their Christian allegiance—and some farmers. The church has had
> little impact among the working class in industrial cities, which pro-
> vided the basis for the Communist Party, in the vast new housing
> developments, or until recently, among the young generation.[9]

The Protestants saw their role as a positive one, living in tension between the church and the world. Such an outlook did not call for withdrawal but for political involvement. A working relationship (in tension) between church and state was evident even in late 1989. When Krenz replaced Honecker, Protestant church leaders met with the new head of government. Gordon cites a Roman Catholic lay response:

> The Protestants have their slogan "the church in socialism," and imag-
> ine that they can achieve something by cooperating with the state.
> How naive they are! I know that communists seem on the face of it
> to be more humane and civilized than the Nazis. The truth is that
> they are more cunning and sophisticated. Their aim is to get total
> control of society—and of the individual—just as surely as the Nazis
> did.[10]

Since Christians and Communists had both struggled against fascism, socialism had a sympathetic hearing among some Protestants after the war. Still, Protestant leadership was politically sophisticated, especially following its experience under Nazi rule. When Bishop Moritz Mitzenheim, chairman of the Lutheran bishops, proposed greater cooperation with the regime in 1961, his fellow bishops drew back. Mitzenheim had been a staunch oppo-nent of Nazism.[11] At the same time, it must be said that Protestant spokes-men were effective in the crises of 1989, because in East Germany, Protestants—more than in other countries of Eastern Europe—had con-ducted a dialogue with socialism. Socialist ideals of peace and security were honored; the problem was that they had not begun to be realized.

The church and state together celebrated the quincentenary of Martin Luther's birth. But the Protestant churches did not remain silent in the face of a growing militarism. Military preparedness was introduced as a separate subject in East German state schools. Among the population, it was commonly called "education in hatred." In response, churches openly asked for education in peace rather than war. In 1982, a Lutheran synod even suggested the unilateral disarmament of the GDR. As plans were being made for the stationing of rockets with nuclear warheads on East German soil, the Protestant churches expressed strong opposition.

Communist propaganda long had cited the century-old union of throne and altar that continued until the end of the Second World War. But its claims were at best only partially justified. The fact is that Prussia (with its state-supported Protestant church) was one of the first countries to begin to practice religious tolerance in the eighteenth century. Following World War I (as elsewhere in Europe), a church which had long functioned under monarchy had problems of reorganization. It had hardly come to terms with the democratic pluralism of the Weimar Republic and accepted the new separation of church and state, when the Nazis appeared on the scene. It was the Confessing Church, a minority of Protestants, who opposed the so-called German Christianity and the anti-Semitism of the Nazi dictatorship.

Under communism, the churches faced a new range of issues and problems. The East German government could boast that under its state planning the standard of living was higher than that in any other satellite country. (Czechoslovakia also did relatively well.) Everyone had a place in which to live and work. (The quality did vary; there was a long waiting time for new but cheap apartments or the purchase of an automobile.) For each citizen, all of life was "scientifically" programmed from the cradle to the grave. Food was cheap and subsidized. State medicine cared for all, even though facilities often were primitive, so much so that doctors and nurses left in large numbers for the West (where they could also earn more).

Social security itself did not prevent the bleeding of the country, the flight of hundreds of thousands of dissatisfied citizens to West Germany, seeking freedom from the Stasi as well as new prosperity. The East had not kept up with technological change. Manufacturing plants were outmoded; the environment was polluted. By contrast, West Germany was unique. To persons who wished to leave, there was nothing to compare with West Germany in any other Eastern European country. Émigrés were immediately guaranteed citizenship as soon as they crossed the border, as was required by the West German constitution. They were given funds to live on during their transition period, and jobs were readily available for most of them.

Among Germans, the religious community was not strongly identified with nationalism, as in Poland. Indeed, nationalism was often played down in West Germany because of memories of past wars. In the East, by contrast, the regime tried to resurrect both nationalism and militarism. The churches, in reply, developed a multisided program for peaceful change. Pastor Friedrich Schorlemmer, who now preaches in the very *Schlosskirche* on whose door Luther nailed his ninety-five theses, received nationwide attention in 1983 when he attempted to mold a sword into a plowshare. Soon it became widely known that a Russian sculpture on the same theme, depicting the prophecies of Micah and Isaiah, had been donated to the United Nations in 1961. Citizens began to wear copies of it as an emblem, and GDR state authorities, enraged, forbade it.[12] Schorlemmer continued to have the support of his church.

Environmental issues also were an important part of the church program, with the Christian position based on the biblical doctrine of creation. Of course, the defense of human rights and personal freedom had the sanction of the Helsinki accords. Most of the items on the churches' agenda of causes were ones that the East German regime could tolerate, it even having espoused them at times on its own Marxist premises. Peace and disarmament had long been proclaimed Communist goals in propaganda, even as local elites were obliged to defend Russian power politics. In terms of its own interests, the East German regime appears to have been not too happy about the stationing of new Russian rockets on its soil; hence, the Christians could speak somewhat more freely. But they went further, asking fundamental questions about the meaning of peace as well as freedom.

Traditionally, church confirmation had initiated young citizens into civil society. Now the society was no longer Christian, even in a nominal sense, and the state developed its own *Jugendweihe* ceremony that included both nationalism and militarism. Confirmants promised unconditional loyalty to the state. In the early period of Communist rule, many pastors resisted the replacement of the church ceremony, insisting on a choice between the rite and Christian initiation. State pressure was very heavy, and the churches lost constituency in major numbers. Still, as the situation developed over the years, the churches had much more freedom in the GDR than in most other Communist-dominated lands. They were allowed to do social work, evangelism, and some religious education. Church hierarchies were not compromised or controlled, in the pattern of Hungary, Czechoslovakia, Romania, or the USSR. Of course, there was a contest for the loyalties of citizens.

Gordon concludes:

Perhaps the greatest tribute to the vitality of Christians in the GDR has been the attitude of the Socialist Unity Party. For 40 years the party tried unsuccessfully to infiltrate and subvert the churches. In the last days of the regime there were (as has been pointed out) plans to arrest considerable numbers of churchgoers. Such schemes would never have been necessary had the party leaders been dealing with a handful of protesting bishops, unsupported by masses of faithful lay people.[13]

BASE GROUPS AS CENTERS OF RESISTANCE

Protestant church headquarters in Berlin were not just a center of action. Long-term reflection and research also were undertaken. In the headquarters building after the revolution, one might visit sociologist Dr. Ehrhart Neubert, an early activist who later withdrew from politics. Neubert dresses informally and is obviously an intellectual; his theories are searching and discerning, to say the least. Even before change took place, he was describing its roots very accurately in detailed sociological research. The monographs he wrote as early as 1986 remain unusually rich source material.[14]

For example, Neubert's description of the roots of protest in small base groups sponsored by the Protestant churches is illuminating, retrospectively. He understood what could happen—how revolutionary the situation was, as well as the churches' role in it. Neubert's sociological thesis is that even under communism, the churches were socializing parts of the population which otherwise would have lived in isolation and bitterness. Members of the small base groups, refusing Marxist indoctrination, asked searching personal, existential questions. These were questions that were supposed to have been answered "scientifically" in a Marxist society but had not been. Failing to go to the root of problems and the curiosity which attended them, Marxist determinism made persons into objects rather than subjects. It minimized, indeed derogated, both individualism and introspection. Neubert marshals the evidence to show that the base groups had influence far beyond their numbers. Religion showed itself to have revolutionary power against totalitarian oppression and the fear it evoked, encouraging intellectual and cultural life.

All kinds of persons were attracted—not just the pious and devout—to a wide range of church-sponsored special-interest groups. Unlike what went on in the country at large, these groups encouraged interpersonal communication, reflection, and the growth of ideas. Small church-related subcommunities, they attracted a variety of participants, only some of whom were primarily interested in religion: peace activists, the environmentally concerned, human rights advocates, even persons not fitting into the mainstream, such as homosexuals. The churches' "umbrella" enabled them to voice their hopes and, over a period of time, to carry on dialogue about the issues, concern for which set them apart from more complacent citizens. Generally the groups were not very highly structured. Nor were they dogmatic, authoritarian, or even necessarily theological in orientation.

Neubert finds it especially significant that discussions on questions of contingency versus determinism were not welcomed under communism. This lack of interest, of course, does not preclude the fact that a large element of contingency, indeterminacy, and chance still remains in human existence. Neubert cites as an example the very highly personal concern about death, the end of one's own existence: it is certain that each individual person will eventually die. When this will take place is not known to us; it is contingent. Communism was not able to come to terms with the phenomenon of contingency, much less reflect critically on it.

The dialogue in the churches centered on ethical issues such as human rights, feminism, the environment, and disarmament. This was deepened and enriched by introspective reflection about the meaning of life, which encouraged dissidence. The net result often was protest and even public demonstrations. These in turn led to a host of problems for church officials in their relations with the state. The East German state had recognized the churches as a stabilizing force and given them more opportunities and responsibilities—for example, in social service activities—than in other Communist countries. In practice, the strategy of the church administration had been carefully balanced between support and criticism of the system until the late 1980s. Then, under pressure of the type engendered by discussion in the base groups, as well as the conviction of its own membership reflected in the so-called conciliar process, the balance began to collapse.

There were practical results as the churches' Lebensraum and the degree of freedom it afforded became public knowledge. Neubert reports that more than a few professed atheists who had the courage to oppose the system marched in church processions with their candles in hand. A religious symbol such as a lit candle assumed new meaning and power against the threat of a brutal totalitarian police force and its armaments. Labor leaders who had never darkened a church door asked that their constituencies be allowed to meet in sanctuaries when they could not assemble elsewhere. Churchmen were called on to become public spokesmen at mass rallies on the streets. Bishops and pastors understood the overwhelming motivation of young people and helped to constructively structure their protest. They did not see their own role as being one of political revolution. They did, however, claim responsibility for the truth and the Christian message of nonviolence.

These church leaders were too wise to allow the enemy to be defined simply in black-and-white terms. At the same time, both Marxists and Christians knew that their respective outlooks did not converge. Neubert observes that only a small percentage of the population, probably not more than 5 percent, were deeply committed to Christianity or Marxism. It was the Christians who turned out to be "the creative minority" in a crisis situation. In the end, they helped to humanize "the death of communism" in East Germany, even though in early 1990 they no longer held the loyalty of the majority of the population, which was first of all hungry for economic improvement.

Even a minority expression of a long-suppressed Christian conviction (initially, activists were estimated to number at most twenty thousand) was able to trigger a revolution. Under totalitarian repression, convinced Christians had taken seriously their faith's message (and institutional relation) to the world, and had not sought to escape into other-worldliness or mysticism. As a living subcommunity, a second force even in the Communist-ordered society, they had kept morality and culture more alive than their opponents had recognized.

REFLECTIONS ON REVOLUTION

Berlin

No place in all of Europe symbolizes the peoples' revolutions more dramatically than Berlin. It was there that the wall was torn down. Poland,

Hungary, Czechoslovakia, or Romania had no comparable divided city. To be sure, the protest in the streets of Leipzig took place earlier and was at first larger than in East Berlin. The Stasi thought it important to keep the capital of the GDR under control, and they succeeded in doing so for a period. When the regime in desperation finally opened the wall, all that Berlin symbolized and stood for was celebrated for days and weeks.

"Tearing down the Iron Curtain" is a metaphor. Tearing down the wall was an unexpected physical experience, a visible event in space and time. The wall's demise signaled the end of the cold war. Following the Second World War, Vienna, the Austrian capital city, like Berlin, had been divided among the occupying powers of Great Britain, France, the United States, and Russia. Each of the victors had its own zone, but the division of Vienna lasted for only a decade. Berlin was held captive four times as long. It was not that attempts at liberation were lacking. As early as 1953, a workers' revolution had been suppressed by the Russians. The city was so strategic that it could not be given up.

Politically, Berlin's heritage has been an authoritarian one. Located in Prussia, it had been the city of King Friedrich the Great, Bismarck, and Hitler. German power had been extended from it in two world wars, and it was ruthlessly bombed during the second one. Everyone recognized that the occupied city could be the place where a third world war would explode, as East and West met there in conflict. President Truman had saved the city through an airlift when the Communists attempted to isolate it fully and starve it out. Eventually, a compromise was worked out with the Russians about its status. West Germany became a show window for capitalism, well stocked with consumer goods. The East Germans, possessing the more spacious part of the city, rebuilt it in grand style but were not able to supply their stores as well.

Even religion took on a different pattern in the postwar era because of the Berlin show window. Capitalism and religious freedom (including the freedom not to believe either in communism or Christianity) belonged to the West, not the East. Poles could not in any large numbers escape from their country and its ideology or personal restrictions, any more than Czechoslovakians or even Hungarians. In Germany there were common radio and television links; most of all, there was a common language. Overshadowing religious concerns, although often linked with them, was the desire for freedom and democracy. As the pattern developed in time, freedom and interest in a more prosperous and consumer-oriented capitalist society—symbolized by the West Berlin show window—engaged the populace.

The symbol of Berlin bore very heavily on how and why Germans acted as they did after the people's revolution. Secularization had become widespread, beginning in the last century. Philosopher Friedrich Nietzsche, sure of its reality, had argued that "God is dead." No one wanted to cry out in the marketplace that this was true, like the mad man Nietzsche described. Still, there are no major signs of religious revival in the united nation.

Nonetheless, Neubert is sure that what took place was "Protestant revolution." More than sociological analysis is intended by this description. Assuredly, the majority of demonstrators were Protestants, many of them with only weak ties to the institutional church. Still, in principle, Neubert believes that the strength and the weaknesses of their revolution reflected their Protestant heritage as it was linked to capitalism. This thesis must now be examined.

Street demonstrations, like mass exodus to the West, were symptoms of the demise of the legitimacy of "real socialism," Neubert believes. Of course they reflected the economic and political situation, but much more than this needs to be said about them, quite apart from any value judgments. Neubert begins (somewhat indirectly) by probing why theologians led the resistance, more than artists and writers. The latter were active, but their influence did not compare with that of the Protestant churchmen. Neubert has no intent of derogating the contribution of artists, but he notes that they were highly individualistic and divided among themselves. This made it much easier for the Communist regime to disperse their occasional protests. After the revolution, they all too easily fell under the control of the capitalist market economy. Religious leaders, by contrast, felt more keenly a living relation to a longer past and tradition. The essence of Neubert's argument is that they could not avoid working against "real existent socialism." Why?

Neubert turns to the classic German sociologist Max Weber for an explanation. Weber would never have accepted a reductionistic economic interpretation of the events of the revolution, Neubert insists. For this classic sociologist, economic factors were perennial, but they were not the primary root of change. Even the Stasi knew this much, Neubert argues: economics is not the all-determining factor that Marx claimed it to be. Economics has a political base—and it was change in the political milieu that the regime was trying to suppress. To support his claim, Neubert cites police reports that recognized clearly the distinct threat posed by the church activists. The officials who wrote them, unlike Marx, were not economic determinists; they recognized the dynamic character of the opposition—how dangerous church activism really was.

At this point, Neubert begins to expound his larger case. Communism in East Germany rejected without reservation the entire pattern in which capitalism organizes both society and the economy. This rejection in fact rendered the East German regime helpless and hopeless. The churches had agreed in good faith not to attempt to overthrow the state, but even unintentionally they were supporting the spirit of capitalism. Paradoxically, institutional religion was playing a double role, agreeing with the regime in part in critique of capitalist exploitation (as in the third world) and at the same time propagating the spirit of capitalism. The churches' stance was not hypocritical, Neubert is sure. Communism's recourse against such opposition was only threats and irrationality.

Neubert provides an answer to the very common question: why is it that less than fifty years after their loss of the Second World War, the Germans and Japanese lead the world economically? Neubert points to a joining of religion and economics (even in a secularized situation when individuals think very little about the holy). He also raises the all-important question of the relation of Protestantism and capitalism and with it Protestantism and secularism. Neubert relates his theory to his earlier-cited discussion of small base groups. He notes that their members, organized under the umbrella of the churches, worked not only for human rights (the Enlightenment had taken root, he says) but for economic reform.

Neubert recognizes, of course, that Lutheranism, not Calvinism, has been the dominant form of Christianity in East Germany. Weber's thesis linking Protestantism and capitalism was developed in relation to Calvinism in particular. Nevertheless Neubert is sure that Protestantism, by its doctrine of calling, encouraged a sense of vocation and duty in the world. This is the essence of Neubert's case. In this pattern, there was a strict rational organization of life and use of time. For verification, Neubert argues that Protestant churches in his country have had as members significant numbers of people intent on planning and directing their own careers, their own bibliographies, as he says. The churches had long since ceased to be related to the workers and provided no sacred canopy, as in Poland. For Protestants in particular, the world had been significantly demythologized. Still their outlook had relevance. The weakness of the socialist ideology of work was that it was premised simply on claims about the physical needs of persons. By contrast, the Protestant work ethic had deeper roots as it advocated thrift and discipline, what Weber identified as a this-worldly asceticism.

Neubert understands religion—especially Protestantism—as perennially related to and developing in concrete situations. Often led by recognized dissidents, members of the base groups spoke out vigorously for freedom—peace, righteousness, and the protection of the environment. Their protest became part of the official church program. Even when the churches seemed neutral, they actually were engaged. Their place in society hardly allowed them to be otherwise. Indeed, their political engagement for peace and justice was intrinsic to their preaching.

But it was the members of the base communities, not primarily the larger constituency of the churches, which came to make up a subculture of resistance. Political opposition became especially intense as church prayer services served as a place of information, a voice for the voiceless. Bishops and theologians were not only leaders but symbolic figures. Religion played a larger place in reform and renewal than it would otherwise, because reform communism was lacking in the regime. When even "liberal Marxists" were bridled, there was nowhere else to turn.

According to Neubert, a leader of one of the new political parties that grew with the revolution in East Germany, Edelbert Richter of *Demokratischer Aufbruch* ("Democratic Awakening"), understood clearly what was going on. Mass protest was directed against the socialist way of constructing society, in particular against the central organization of the state. Citizens were asking for a distancing, a differentiation between the state and the Communist party. This was denied. Whether they knew it or not, Neubert claims, such political liberalization was in measure a restoration and reconstruction of capitalism. Capitalism had been symbolized and shown in the West Berlin show window. What Protestant religious leaders in East Germany had tried to advocate earlier, in their slogan "the Church in Socialism," had lost its power and appeal amid the growing social and economic crisis.

Honecker was not alone in rejecting calls for the revision of socialist ideology. Old party members were intent to keep a long-developed social identity that had grown up over two generations. Protest might have been accommodated if the regime had been less intransigent. Even the most vocal, outspoken opposition groups were calling only for democratic socialism. The later dominant interest in capitalism and a consumer-oriented economy had not yet surfaced.

Neubert believes the larger problem, seen in historical perspective, is that German liberalism had no base in collective consciousness comparable with that in England, France, and America. Liberalism in Germany could claim no key historic event other than resistance against Prussian centralism, for example. Neubert claims that religion was the force which gave liberal revolution legitimacy and goals. This is part of the reason that Protestantism was so powerful in East Germany. Individual Protestants, more than other citizens, identified with revolutionary events.

Neubert's argument leads him back to his claim that we examined initially, that in their subculture the churches had their own distinctive pattern of socialization, their own way of introducing members into their realm through baptism and confirmation, pastoral care and preaching. By their very nature as public institutions, they had influence on the national community. This influence grew and was legitimatized, even under a Communist government, because the state wanted something from the churches, namely, not only their stabilizing moral influence but recognition of its own legitimacy, as well. In this circumstance, a monistically intentioned society allowed factual plurality, and the church was respected among the populace in spite of widespread secularization.

The mistake of the GDR leaders—seen from this perspective—was that they ignored the rationality of capitalism and Protestantism and relied instead on irrational principles and dogmatic doctrines. The course of events made clear how much communism is in fact an enemy of the spirit; for example, it destroys art. Communist party leaders ignored facts and refused to recognize social and ethical conflicts. Protestantism was given a great opportunity for what in German is called *Entzauberung*, destruction of such "false magic." Neubert does not find it hard to understand why the church had an appealing rationality in the time of revolution. It stood for liberalism and human rights against positivism and reductionism. It was communism that appeared fuzzy, vague, and irrational; indeed, it was the antithesis of science, which it invoked rhetorically in justification.

Not to be ignored, however, is the fact that Christianity carries within itself a critique of a growing and ruthless capitalism, especially as it impacts on third world and ecology problems. Weber's claim was that capitalism became emancipated from its religious roots. It did not control its own hubris. Neubert finds that the socialism proposed as a remedy tried to kill the patient. Now pluralistic democracy, a market economy, and respect for the legal structures are in style again. These, too, require Christian criticism. Much more is at stake than the popularity of the church as an institution. Church leaders did not protest as they did under communism to attract a mass following or to fill churches. They did it because they believed and knew that it was right.

The case of Pastor Rainer Eppelman is an illustration:

A brick-layer by training, he was sentenced in the mid-1970s to eight months' imprisonment for refusing to take the military oath after having been conscripted. He then served as a "construction soldier," and went on to study theology. In 1975 he became pastor of the *Samariterkirche* in East Berlin where he organized the already-mentioned "blues masses." In 1981 he wrote a letter to Erich Honecker, requesting him—among other things—to work for the withdrawal of all troops from central Europe and gradual total disarmament. His letter began with a phrase that has later become famous, "It is five minutes to 12."[15]

Gordon notes that the church protected its pastor against the state, although it did suggest that citizens not sign the appeal he circulated, as he disagreed with some aspects of church policy. After the revolution, large numbers of pastors became involved in politics for at least two reasons: they had already been identified as leaders in the struggle against totalitarianism, and they were also one of the few groups in the society that had not been corrupted by collaboration with the Stasi. These considerations explain why Eppleman, a pacifist, became the defense minister and minister for disarmament in the noncommunist East German government. Paradoxically, he even defended the continued existence of NATO. That government has ceased to be. The Protestant pastor's role in it was a short-lived one.

LEIPZIG

Leipzig, a center of the revolution, was a city in transition six months after the overthrow of communism. What had happened to the people's revolution in East Germany? Like all the nation, Leipzig was awaiting monetary union with West Germany early in July. Soon the Western mark would be the currency of both Germanies. In anticipation of the change, there were long lines of citizens in front of banks and other savings institutions. New accounts were being arranged so that citizens could exchange the maximum number of Eastern marks for Western ones as soon as possible. Already Western goods and food supplies were appearing. Soon they would replace the shoddier East German merchandise which was being disposed of at greatly reduced prices.

One-fourth of the city's buildings were destroyed during the Second World War, and its center has been rebuilt unevenly. Modern structures, many of them ugly, stand side by side with older ones and their more gracious style of architecture. The city was the target of a terror attack by the Royal Air Force toward the end of the war; thousands of persons were killed in a single night. But this was not the end of the destruction. Walter Ulbrich, while head of Communist East Germany, evoked widespread opposition when he ordered that one of the city's oldest and most beautiful churches be blown up in order that a new skyscraper university could be erected on the site. The skyscraper's basement became a headquarters of the Stasi from which the police came out in large numbers to attack demonstrators.

St. Thomas Church, in the middle of the city, remains standing. Although it is not too far from city hall, it was not destroyed in the war. It is the church where Johann Sebastian Bach worked and wrote in the eighteenth century. Many of his most distinguished compositions were first performed as part of its worship. Its world-renowned boys' choir still sings from the balcony. Twenty-five years ago, the pastor, with his large Northern European-style pleated collar, preached vigorously to a very small congregation in a largely empty church.

In the summer of 1990, much had changed and little had changed! St. Thomas Church had about the same number of East German worshipers as it had a quarter of a century earlier. However, many tourists also were present. In his sermons, the pastor was now urging East Germans to welcome West Germans as fellow citizens in a soon-to-be-unified country. Christ, after all, had accepted fellow men, he emphasized. It was a theme that no one would have believed he would be preaching about only a year earlier!

Events moved faster and farther than the initiators of change inside and outside the country, the dissidents or Gorbachev, had expected. If Protestant church leaders, holding a strategic place, contributed powerfully to the revolution in East Germany, most of them did not intend the outcome. Indeed, they had looked for evolution, not revolution. Not a few Protestant theologians regretted that the GDR came to an end, rather than being improved and rectified. In the course of merger with West Germany, their influence was bound to wane. Economics, not religious concerns, were in the forefront.

The continuing question was whether the idealists who lead revolutions are anything more than froth or foam on the sea of history. The question is not necessarily asked cynically! American Protestant theologian and ethicist Reinhold Niebuhr directed attention to it when he wrote *Children of Light and Children of Darkness*.[16] His primary concern in this book was the United States, but he also intended a wider application. The children of darkness—the nonidealistic "realists" and cynics—more "worldly wise," often seem more effective and successful than the children of light, Niebuhr argued.

Events occurred as they did in East Germany because the country was going broke. The majority of the émigrés who left for West Germany were not idealists. They wanted freedom from personal harassment, but they also wanted a very much higher standard of living. In East Germany, by contrast with the West, the establishment simply did not know how to manage a modern economy—to protect the environment or to give young people creative or satisfying work. Revolution came because it was bankrupt, in terms of ideas as well as economically.

Geography no doubt remains an important consideration in power politics. At the simply geographical level, one may argue that the two Germanys could not remain forever divided. The land areas are too small, their populations too dynamic. The events of late 1989 bear on the larger question of the integration of Europe and the promise of the European Common Market. Peoples trade with each other not just for altruistic reasons. Commerce can help to destroy old animosities. To be sure, with the revolutions in Eastern Europe came enormous economic problems. But there was at least the possibility of attacking and solving them with combined resources. Threats to the environment could be faced up to, along with the need for a market economy.

Before the Revolution of Light, there had been a deliberate effort on the part of church leadership to overcome the isolation and parochialism enforced by the Communist regime. Church leaders took their cue from the World Council of Churches program for peace, justice, and protection of the environment. This triple emphasis had strong appeal in third world countries. Of the three foci, Eastern European concern was most of all for peace. In the GDR there was intense anxiety and fear that a third world war might begin in Germany. Both great powers had atomic weapons on German soil. Roman Catholic participation in the conciliar process came late, but eventually it became ecumenical as representatives of all major churches joined in. But it was not the World Council of Churches' idealism but Russian perestroika that offered hope of avoiding a third world war.

Church leaders had taken on a relatively secular program, and brilliantly revolution had been made with it. (They had no symbolism available comparable with that of the black Madonna in Poland.) Conservative religionists suspected that the threefold World Council of Churches program stood on the edge of secularism. It was a program that believers and nonbelievers could both subscribe to. Theological issues were being skirted. From the point of view of the World Council of Churches, theology, at least in part, could be worked out later in relation to praxis. The persecution of religion, always a part of the Communist program in one way or another, was over. What had been feared in East Germany was not so much sin and damnation in Luther's sense, but the terror of hydrogen warfare. That atomic energy could go out of control was clear from Chernobyl; it could destroy humanity even without war.

On October 2–3, 1990, at midnight, East and West Germany were reunited into a single country. Kurt Nowak, professor of church history at the University of Leipzig, sees a very different role for both church and state in the new situation. The latter, no longer totalitarian, will function as "an organ of political civility."[17] To their great credit, in a time of persecution, churches have defended the rights of citizens against the regime, Nowak acknowledges. Issues are very different in the reunited country: will the state function simply as a party machine or as a living democracy? What will be the role of citizens; how will they participate in the democratic process? Nowak suspects that politics is more pragmatic and more significantly regional than has been recognized. More than demonstration in the streets is called for. Encouraged by a new national pride, old structures can linger on, but the wave of the future, Nowak believes, is pluralistic democracy, and religious institutions must adjust to it.

On the night of unification, the Nikolai Church, from whose sanctuary demonstrators had come a year earlier, was closed. There was no service in St. Thomas Church, where Bach had worked and written. But it was open and the organ played Bach's chorale prelude "Now Thank We All Our God." Pastor Christian Fuehrer explained:

> There are some people for whom we could hold a service of thanksgiving to celebrate the fact that the borders are open and the state security is gone.
>
> There are others for whom we could better hold a service of intercession—the people who have lost their jobs already or are about to and don't have any idea what's to come. There are still others, triumphant nationalists, for whom we could hold a service of penitence. So instead we will simply keep quiet, and let the silence move people to think.[18]

CONCLUSIONS

The series of events that had Leipzig as a center were equally as dramatic as those in Prague and Budapest. Compared with the Czechoslovakian and Romanian revolutions, the East German revolution was played out on a larger stage—that of many cities throughout the nation. The time span was longer, although short when compared with that in Poland.

If the Polish revolution was a Catholic one, as we will argue, the East German was Protestant led. But one took place in a country where the sacred canopy was still intact; this was the case in Poland. The East German revolution was set in a highly secularized country. The problem facing German religious leadership in both sections of the country has been identified by Jürgen Moltmann, who teaches at Tübingen in West Germany.[19] The churches could remain in their own precincts, as it were, nurturing piety for a very limited number of persons. This stance led to irrelevance. Or they could plunge into the middle of events and the public struggle. In this case, they risked losing their identity and becoming just one force among others. Actually, leaders avoided both pitfalls most of the time.

In Poland (and even in Hungary, Romania, and Russia), nationalism was an asset on the side of the church. The East German Communists had not been able to capture the national identity, and when the Berlin wall finally was opened, their experiment in communism had come to an end. Reunification was a uniquely German problem. It was not the goal of the religious activists, as many of them said very openly. In 1990 German nationalism turned out to be an important motivating factor in reunification, but it did not seem as important as elsewhere because it lacked a religious basis.

West Germany was always over the border, luring citizens away simply by its own prosperity and offering asylum to refugees. No one could overlook its presence. In the end, that presence became overpowering and took over the East German revolution in a pattern different from that in any other country. There were lingering resentments between East and West Germans. But most of all there were West German financial resources and know-how, and this made a great difference. When freedom from Communist rule had been achieved, the people of the land chose economic prosperity and unification rather than perestroika and glasnost. Yet the latter could not be avoided. This was clear in the lasting controversy about persons who had worked for the Stasi; millions had!

Questions of reconstruction engaged all of the satellite countries after revolution. Moral dilemmas from the Second World War would continue for years and could not be papered over. Communism had made for mass corruption. Nearly the only persons about whose character one could be sure in East Germany were churchmen, and even among these there had been informers. Still the verdict had to be that in its own way, the East German revolution was an outstanding success and religionists were at the center, using the very limited options available to them very carefully and wisely.

In East Germany, the churches did have greater freedom than elsewhere. Still they were not in power, and it was in terms of justice and faith that Christianity seemed to be most relevant. A kind of action was developed that fit the situation. The stance was not sectarian or traditional. Nor was it highly dogmatic or confessional, and it allowed ecumenical outreach. To the degree that it carried over into the new situation after the revolution, it is still struggling against secularism—no longer Marxist socialist but capitalist.

Larger church attendance is not a prospect. Religious institutions will persist in an era of nominal culture Christianity. After the revolution, it very soon became clear that the Eastern part of the Protestant church would merge with the Western one. The religious situations were diverse in the two different sections of the country. East German Protestantism had ceased to be a majority folk church under communism. In West Germany, religion still continued in this mode in the part of the population it counted as constituency.

West Germans were divided nearly evenly between Protestants and Roman Catholics. The East German polity had become one of voluntary financial support, but this was not the case in West Germany. All West German citizens who did not declare themselves atheists or not to be church members automatically continued to be billed for church tax. In return, they could be baptized, confirmed, married, and buried, even if they were not otherwise religiously practicing. Church tax also became state policy in the Eastern part of the country

The situation was not as simple as critics, declared unbelievers, or free churchmen often supposed. If only active Christians contributed to financial support in the reunited Germany, there would be a vast lack of funds for international as well as national religious activities. Social services would suffer greatly. Much of what had been done to keep religion alive under communism in East Germany had been paid for from West German church taxes. But if the churches turned to active voluntary support in West Germany, among Protestants at least, their character would be changed drastically—possibly renewed. This was the dilemma of leadership.

Germans had been "inside" the Nazi experience, occupying rather than occupied. They lost in World War II. Now they are on top again. There was a larger German issue. Following the Second World War, a spiritual vacuum was evident with the demise of Nazism. The churches had an opportunity to fill it; for the majority of the population, it can be argued, they failed to do so. Of course, the problems were not simple—either the theoretical or the practical ones. Will this failure be repeated again? There are religious impulses and interests in the society, but many come from outside the churches, moving into them, and not the reverse.

3

HUNGARY

Revolution Delayed, Not Denied

A SINGULAR PEOPLE, A CHECKERED HISTORY

A quarter of a million people filed solemnly through Heroes Square [in Budapest] on 16 June, [1989] in front of six coffins containing the exhumed remains of Imre Nagy, his Defense Minister Paul Maleter, and three of their colleagues in the revolution. . . . The sixth coffin was empty, a symbolic gesture for the Historical Justice Committee who organized the events of the day, to represent all the others who died in the course of the revolution. The coffins lay on the steps of the main Exhibition Hall. . . . Black flags flew in the streets, and at noon church bells rang out all over the country.[1]

The ceremony was carried internationally by television, as well as throughout Hungary. All the world had been shocked at the Stalinist repression of the 1956 revolt in Budapest. Now it was being relived in memory in 1989. Representing the government at the ceremony were Miklos Nemeth and Imre Pozsgay. The latter, a reform Communist and general secretary of the Patriotic People's Front, had urged that the state abandon the evidently negative strategy of restricting church activities.

What took place could be called a delayed revolution—the conclusion of the tragic and failed 1956 revolt. Paul Lendvai, in his study entitled *Hungary, The Art of Survival*, cites the long-imprisoned writer, Tibor Dery:

Hungary always was the weakest, always came off second-best in conflicts with other peoples, in historic struggles, in its revolutions. . . . That experience has imbued the Hungarian character with what is possibly its most beneficent and appealing quality—that of sober

49

realism. The vanquished is always more soberly realistic than the victor. . . .[2]

When the new Hungarian minister for culture and education minister, Bertalan Andrásfalvy, came to Vienna for a conference on the future of Eastern Europe in June of 1990, he cited a haunting memory which continued to nourish fear and remorse. It was one of young people, too young to be executed when the 1956 revolution was put down. Subsequently, they were put to death secretly by the state some years later.[3] Andrásfalvy added: "Democracy does not yet function in Eastern Europe, because the human mentality—forty years long oppressed by the totalitarian system of fear, lying and repression, does not change so quickly."

More than three decades after the Russian invasion in 1956, the memory of the terror which had followed still lingered on vividly. To be sure, there had been sporadic street demonstrations over two decades. The traditional but unofficial independence day is March 15. Citizens wear the red, white, and green emblem of the nation. Even under the Communists, an official celebration was held each year with the usual schoolchildren, students, and patriotic adults. Following the ceremony, unofficial groups took over. In 1973 and 1986, the police used truncheons to disperse the several thousand young people who sang patriotic songs and marched to national memorials.[4]

In their national anthem, Hungarians sing of past sorrows:

> Land so long by shame dismayed,
> Lord, grant it joy long vanished!
> Price enough our nation's paid
> For all guilt to be banished.

Situated in central Europe, Hungary was overrun by the Mongols and then the Turks, dominated by the Austrians and then the Russians. To be sure, there have been great heroism and moments of respite. Perhaps the present is one of the latter. Today Hungary seems to typify a situation in which religion changes more slowly than secular politics. There has been no major religiously inspired renewal. Certainly, government interference and control of church life has been removed, but religious institutions are still dependent on the state for funding.

Question to a Hungarian theologian: "How much did the cardinal, bishops, and other leading church officials contribute to change in 1989?"

Answer: "Nothing!"

Question: "Did their ties with the state prepare the way for the new situation of religious freedom?"

Answer: "Not in any way!"

Question: "But was there not a mutual exchange of ideas and some Christian influence?"

Answer: "Influence and control came to the churches from the state and not the reverse."

Janos Kádár ruled the country for the Russians during more than thirty years with his "goulash communism." Repression had been sharp after the defeat of the Hungarian revolution in 1956. There were hundreds of executions, tens of thousands of imprisonments. Shortly into the new decade, however, the introverted typewriter mechanic whom the Russians had placed in charge initiated a more moderate and compromising line. Kádár himself had spent years in jail and had been tortured by Communist jailers. He was determined as head of state that conditions should not again arise to provoke revolution. Lendvai, who interviewed Kádár personally, praises him as "a technician of power gifted with uncanny political intuition."[5] As a pragmatist, he wished to keep the nation intact. Lendvai characterizes Kádár as a conservative reformer and comments:

Hungary's development testifies to the enormous importance of leadership style and the personality of the Party chief. Would Hungary's fate have been the same if the Soviets had not chosen Kádár in 1956 as Party leader and Hungary's Number One? Certainly not. As the Swiss historian Herbert Luthy has rightly observed, "History is not anonymous. . . . Facts and dates really mean nothing unless we can think our way into the minds of the persons involved."[6]

It was Kádár's policy to give individual citizens a measured degree of freedom in work and personal expression, as long as they left politics to the Communist party. The policy carried over into religion. Religion was not driven underground, Czechoslovakian style, following the suppression of the 1956 revolution by Russian troops. On the contrary, in better Communist fashion it was to be controlled by the state, and this was accomplished so well that public Christian witness was by and large emasculated. There was no experience comparable with that of the Lutheran and Calvinist Confessing Church in Germany in the period of the Second World War. The German Protestant church had been significantly a middle-class-citizens' church. Protestantism in Hungary, by contrast, was more rural than urban in spirit. A major element among others was a highly individualistic Pietist conviction—largely apolitical.

Within a decade, the Kádár regime was successful in dramatically raising the national standard of living. Citizens had automobiles and were allowed to travel a limited number of times to the West. It has been suggested with some justification that Communist bureaucracy in Hungary was the most sophisticated and least dogmatic in any Eastern European satellite country. Its middle ranks included persons who were prepared to challenge Communist dogma, the so-called reform Communists. Many of them were "technocrats" and not ideologues. They were a significant part of the power structure as an alarming economic crisis forced the change of government and ideology in the period of the peoples' revolutions.

> The Hungarian nation has drifted into one of the serious crises of its history. Its national strength is broken, its self-confidence and bearing are shaken, the bonds of cohesion are tragically loosened, its self-knowledge is startlingly inadequate. It anticipates a possible economic collapse. . . . Our nation does not possess a commonly accepted vision of the future.[7]

This statement was issued by 160 writers, economists, and scientists who met in the village of Lakitelek in the fall of 1987. Many of them had been associated with the government. Hard-core dissidents and political activists were not among them. Two years later, a new Hungarian Republic was declared on October 23, 1989. The nation was indeed altering course with a change of symbols as well as of political power. Suddenly, quite unexpectedly, the restrictive working relation of so-called normalization between the Communist state and the churches came to an end. Unlimited freedom of conscience took its place.

Events need to be seen against the background of a unique national consciousness based on language. The Hungarian speech stands alone in Central Europe, unrelated to the Germanic or Latin languages or even to the Slavic. It belongs to the same family as Finnish and Estonian. The Hungarian people came from their original home west of the Urals and settled in the Carpathian Basin in 896. Christianity in the Latin tradition was opted for by King Stephen, who was enthroned on Christmas Day in the year 1000. His crown, donated by Pope Silvester II, remains a national symbol. Half a millennium after Christianization, the Hungarians experienced one of the most brilliant epochs in their history in the second half of the fifteenth century. Then, in 1526, their army was defeated by the Turks at the battle of Mohacs. National independence was possible again only after the Ottoman army was driven back from the gates of Vienna by a Catholic army in 1683. Buda was liberated three years later.

THE CHURCH AND NATIONAL IDENTITY

The struggle for national identity has been a long one and has continued to the present in the confrontation with communism, an ideology never accepted by the majority of Hungarians. Hungary belonged to the once much larger Hapsburg Empire, and Hungarian rule extended into parts of what are now Czechoslovakia, Yugoslavia, and Romania. Today there are 1.75 million Hungarians living in Romania—a constant source of tension and bitterness. In the era between the two world wars, much of the nation's concern focused on attempts to recover lost areas, with their Hungarian-speaking peoples. This was achieved in part by cooperation with the Nazis during the Second World War. But when the Germans at last were defeated, Stalin saw to it that the Hungarians, whom he is reported to have disliked, had no more territory than before. Religiously, the country is divided into approximately two-thirds Roman Catholic and one-third Protestant (Calvinists, the larger denomination, and Lutherans), and Communist officials exploited the distrust between the churches to the full.

Hungary was liberated from the Turks by the Austrian Hapsburg monarchy, which at the same time imposed the Counter-Reformation on a largely Protestant population. Roman Catholicism never was identified with the national consciousness as much as in Poland. Some Calvinists still regard themselves as the "true Hungarians." Essentially, the Hapsburg Counter-Reformation policy bred subservience of the church to the political regime. The words of a dissident, written before the recent change of government, are still echoed in criticism: " 'He who is lame learns to live with his lameness.' . . . Our . . . Church . . . burdened by a long and often dubious history, seems to accept the surrender to Caesar, the identification with the interest of the rulers of the day."[8] Once it was the Hapsburgs, then the Communists, and there is now a new regime, often restorationist in spirit and polity.

Patrick Michel argues that the more church-state relations were "normalized," — the more religious institutions accepted and spread official government values — the less effective and believable were the churches' claims. This assuredly was the case in Hungary. Dissidents argued that the malaise of the regime reached to institutional religion. Indeed, so-called normalization was one of its chief causes.

The options available to church officials were extremely limited. Cardinal Mindszenty had fled to the American embassy in 1956. The Vatican, encouraged by the regime's apparent willingness to compromise, accepted a strategy of rapprochement. Externally, it appeared attractive; within the country, it did not check the decline of church attendance and religious education. A dissident who did not "want to be followed, spied upon, exposed to harassment, limited even more in my freedom of movement" wrote for self-protection under a pen name:

Those in power . . . would like to achieve the alienation of religion . . . This is not a very difficult task: all they have to do is to ensure that leading posts in the Church are filled by men who (willingly or not, it is all the same) are prepared to serve the interests of the secular power. Having settled this, they can even proclaim the independence of the Church — at least as far as appearances go. Once this has been achieved, they have to interfere only infrequently in ecclesiastical matters — church leaders will follow the rules of the game.[9]

With the change of government in 1989 and 1990 came a new restructuring of religious life. A statute adopted by parliament insured genuine freedom of religion. More than this, the newly elected head of state, Minister President József Antall, and a number of his ministers were openly Christian.[10] The change in religious polity was drastic and sudden, and events seemed to be moving too fast for religious leaders whose appointment had been controlled by the government. Ever since the repression of the revolution in 1956, clergy had been forced to submit and conform to state policy. Those who did not had been dispossessed. The Lutheran bishop, Lajor Ordass, was sent to prison even before the 1956 revolution on a fake charge. Liberated by the uprising, he was forced out of office again in 1958. His successors had better relations with the regime under Kádár. State-appointed bishops sat in parliament while ministry of cults officials participated in personnel and financial decisions of the church.

Swiss Protestant theologian Karl Barth wrote to the bishop president of the Reformed church as early as 1951:

> You are at the point of making an article of faith of your agreement with Communism, of making it part of the Christian message. . . . You are at the point of wandering into an ideological Christian wonderland. . . . How is it that you put socialism on your banner as if it were the perfect thing? How can you dare to put it on the banner of Jesus Christ? How can you claim in your propaganda that socialism is heaven on earth?[11]

The theology of diakonia of Bishop Zoltán Káldy, who was the head of the Lutheran church in Hungary from 1967 to 1985, was notorious. He had been elected bishop soon after the failure of the Hungarian Revolution. A year before Káldy's death, the Lutheran World Federation met in Budapest, sponsoring a dramatic mass assembly to symbolize, among other things, religion's place in Eastern Europe. Thousands of Hungarians attended its sessions, along with representatives of the Lutheran communion throughout the world from Europe and the Americas as well as Africa, Asia, and Australia. International leaders of the church processed in their robes at the opening worship service, which was televised to other European countries. Eucharist was received en masse at altars throughout the stadium. Later on the opening day, the Roman Catholic cardinal, along with bishops from the Reformed church in Hungary and high government officials, welcomed the delegates. Christianity in its worldwide outreach finally had come behind the Iron Curtain! But not in a rebirth of freedom.

Bishop Káldy's theology of diakonia—if indeed it can be called a theology—had put his church at the service of the state, promising to support government policies without exception. Káldy came to prominence when he replaced Bishop Ordass in office in 1958. The new bishop, unlike his predecessor, argued: "There is no 'third way' for travellers between socialism and capitalism. Our Protestant churches are not neutral; we stand unambiguously on the side of socialism."[12] A number of German Lutherans opposed his election as president of the Lutheran World Federation, a courtesy generally given to the leader of the church in the host country. Some joked that they did not know whether Káldy was a Christian or a Communist; in their own country, the East Germans had fought hard for a less-committed stance. Káldy lived only a brief period after his election as head of the Lutheran World Federation.

Vocal and informed opposition came from Zoltán Dóka, a parish minister who received an honorary doctor's degree from the University of Zurich in the spring of 1990. Under the Communist regime, church officials tried to drive him out of the ministry after he sent an open letter to leaders of the Lutheran World Federation on the eve of the Budapest assembly:

> In the HLC [Hungarian Lutheran Church] there is no religious freedom. . . . Theological terror reigns. . . . The church leadership maintains this terror by telling the civil authorities that those who dare criticize Diakonia Theology are enemies of the state. In this way they skillfully make theological debate impossible. This is a real and perilous slander."[13]

Dóka was persistently outspoken, but he was also a competent theologian who had studied abroad and understood clearly the teaching of his church. Attacking Diakonia Theology, he invoked the traditional Lutheran doctrine of two kingdoms. Christians live in two worlds, the kingdom of this world and the kingdom of God, Luther taught. The reformer insisted that the church is not primarily a political entity; it has the religious mission of bringing salvation. With this role, it lives of necessity in tension with evil and the powers of this world. This was the truth that seemed to have been forgotten by church leadership in Hungary.

By its nature, the church is not of the world. On principle, it does not seek to control the state. But even in living with it as a second kingdom, it must obey God and not men. Dóka understood that religious institutions in Hungary were being controlled by the state, which centralized authority and appointed church officials, disregarding the opinions and needs of members of the congregations. After his open letter to the Lutheran World Federation, Hungarian denominational authorities sought to remove Dóka from his congregation, but its people were loyal to him and fellow clergy would not vote to sanction the bishop's decree of expulsion.

Personally, Dóka had strong pastoral ability. Intellectually, he was clear that a critical theology with historical bases was not being developed in the country. Instead, preaching was corrupted by a compromising emphasis on social ethics. Diakonia Theology followed a pattern of conformity to the will of the secular power. Natural theology, the wisdom of the world, philosophy of religion, and social ethics took the place of the Gospel. Christianity could not be itself. Dóka demanded, and continues to demand, the resignation of church officials who compromised. He clearly identified the basic issue on Protestant religious grounds.

Central in the history of post-World War II Roman Catholicism is the figure of Cardinal József Mindszenty. His stance was a very traditional one, hierarchical and intransigent, and he was openly at war with the government, which tortured him and arranged a show trial. The cardinal had a brief respite of freedom during the 1956 revolution before he took refuge in the American embassy in Budapest. He left the country in 1971 and was removed from office by the Pope in 1974. Assuredly, the Hungarian cardinal's very aristocratic authoritarian view of the role of bishops and clergy was hardly that of the Second Vatican Council. Still, his strategy and character are being reassessed in Hungary today. Patrick Michel compares the Hungarian cardinal's inflexible stand unfavorably with that of Cardinal Stefan Wyszyński in Poland.[14] Both saw themselves as regents in the absence of a ruling monarch. But Hungary was a secular, confessionally mixed country; Poland was almost unanimously Roman Catholic.

Eventually Kádár, as head of state, did visit Rome, and the empty bishops' seats were filled with compromise candidates approved by the regime. Some of the new bishops were "Peace Priests" who had cooperated with the regime. Still, Khrushchev's war on religion, which closed half of the churches in the USSR, had only faint echoes in Hungary. Religion in Hungary reflected Kádár's tolerance as compared with the attitude of officials in charge in other satellite states. Religion was not to be crushed entirely, although atheism remained the state ideology. It was to be forced out of community and public life. So far as the individual citizen was concerned, religion was privatized. For more than three decades, the Communist regime lived under a trade-off with the populace. Kádár's slogan was, "he who is not against us is for us."[15] A ministry of cults was set up, and a department of state police empowered to deal with the churches. Under the velvet glove was an iron hand—the state church office.

The anonymous dissident quoted earlier observed:

What is the use of a flood of marvelously courageous articles, when it can happen—as it recently has—that a bishop reports a priest of another diocese because he holds catechism classes at his presbytery? When policemen surround the pupils and take their names, in order to intimidate them and their parents? When the State Church Office holds dozens of snapshots taken at religious gatherings as material exhibits against the participants?

Another ... aspect of the opting-out process is that of becoming an informer. Some people may be kept on a string, as a result of some moral peccadillo; they are forced to "grass" for the files of the State Church Office.[16]

Under Communist rule, there was the characteristic Communist attempt to limit religion to the sanctuary. Religious education, church publication, and social services were restricted when not dismantled entirely. (Some publication was allowed, but church books were more expensive than others.) Major church leaders were subservient to the government minister of religion, Imre Miklós, who was for all practical purposes the ruling hierarch in the country. (He left office in the spring of 1989.) In fact, Marxist rule was successful in achieving major dechristianization. Church attendance dropped drastically during the 1960s and 1970s and has by no means recovered.

The dissident Piarist Father Gyorgy Bulányi has summarized the situation discerningly: the majority of the populace has been baptized, but only a minority is seriously religious and practicing. Perhaps half of this number are traditionalists; some of the remainder are open to change and renewal. It is Bulányi's claim that an older folk piety—prayer for rain, for example— has been given up by the populace. It cannot be brought to life again in the face of modern science. The church has no choice but to confront the contemporary world, if it is to continue its ministry effectively.

The Roman Catholic community to which Bulányi still belongs claims approximately two-thirds of Hungarian Christians. Of its some 6 million baptized members, it is estimated that, at most, not more than 1.5 million remained actively church related during the more than four decades of Communist rule amid growing secularization and dechristianization. Probably only one-third (half of them over fifty-four years of age) of the still-church-related group attend services regularly. No doubt with the end of communism in the country, these figures will now improve somewhat, but not drastically. Most serious is the lack of young priests, and even those available are not used efficiently, according to Roman Catholic church sociologists. Participation is high, percentage wise, in the 440 Baptist congregations spread throughout the country. Still, these are mostly very small communities, and Baptist increase has not been outstanding. Religious instruction among Reformed young people shrank to only 5 percent under Communist pressure.

Asked about the causes of the 1989 revolutionary change of power in Hungary, even theologians reply in terms of economics. It was evident that Kádár was successful in the first part of his reign in stimulating economic life. The standard of living doubled, even tripled as he managed to distance himself from Russian economic stagnation while still supporting the Kremlin's foreign policy unqualifiedly. After the 1968 Warsaw Pact invasion of Czechoslovakia, in which Hungarian troops participated, Kádár was cautioned by Brezhnev during a visit to Moscow against too much economic innovation. The Hungarians drew back for a few years and then continued to work for change. Critics claim that Kádár did not accept it soon enough or side drastically enough with the reformers. In the end, this failure of strategy brought down his reign.

In the summer of 1987, Karoly Grosz, an authoritarian but pragmatic Politburo member, was appointed Prime Minister with the task of tackling the economic crisis. What shocked him most on taking up the post was the extent of Party control over Government decisions, and the mess the economy was in. The money borrowed from the West had not been spent on modernizing industry, which was having difficulty producing goods of high enough quality for Western markets, while the burden of servicing the debt had become ever more crippling.[17]

Grosz in time maneuvered to replace Kádár. He was eloquent and commanded wide attention and following through skillful use of the media. After he achieved power, however, he was not able to hold the situation together. Outmaneuvered by reformers as well as non-Communists at round-table talks in 1989, Grosz consented on June 21 to "fully free and democratic elections."[18] When they were held on March 25, 1990, it became clear that again "the emperor had no clothes." The major vote went to the Democratic Forum, a relatively conservative coalition with Christian sympathies.

It needs to be emphasized that religious life continued even under atheism, most of all because of the faith of individually committed Christians. In 1985, the underground journal, *Beszélö*, published an article written by a young teacher under a pseudonym:

You see, the main problem with the atheistic answers is that they ring hollow. In today's schools there are probably fewer convinced materialists than believing Christians. ... And what is meant by poverty, what is meant by violence, what is meant by omnipresent selfishness? The rousing Marxist-Leninist answers to these questions are hopelessly contrary to the child's experience.

Only some people should become teachers: those who have determination and flair for it, who can come to terms with never making a career of it, who have enough strength to bear an excess burden, and who are well aware that their employment could come to a sudden end.[19]

Simply keeping religious communities alive was not easy. Cardinal Lékai, Catholic primate from 1977 to 1986, was anything but an aristocrat on the Mindszenty model. In fact, he chose a very different life-style. After being appointed to his office, he commented: "It would be an anachronism for me to present myself as 'first baron' or 'prince primate' of Hungary. The Church must not look backward but must accept reality as it exists. ... Although the world view and ideology of Christians and Marxists are different, we must nevertheless look for ways to work out a common future."[20]

Neither Cardinal Lékai nor his successor as primate, Archbishop László Paskai of Kalocsa, have been major figures in change. They have not had a leadership role comparable to that of the primate in Czechoslovakia or

Poland. The Pope is supposed to have said, with respect to Cardinal Lékai, that he would visit Hungary only "When the cardinal has learned to bang his fist on the table."[21] No doubt Paskai was a compromise candidate between the wishes of the Vatican and the state. He had taken a leading role in rallying priests behind state foreign policy and had been head of a collaborationist organization, Opus Pacis.

Even when Cardinal Mindszenty was still living at the American embassy, a small delegation of clergy was allowed to attend the Second Vatican Council in 1962. The council's ideas remain relevant as against entrenched traditionalism in the country. The subordination of religion to the state did not begin with communism! Under the Hapsburgs, the church and its hierarchy were identified with the nobility. There was mutual support between the church and state under the Horthy regime between the two world wars, although Rear Admiral Horthy himself was Calvinist in background. However, this did not preclude his cooperation with the Nazis. Lendvai observes: "Hungary was on Hitler's side until the end, as was all too graphically confirmed for victors and vanquished alike by the flight — probably without parallel in modern history — of the entire Hungarian military and civil administration, complete with St. Stephen's crown."[22]

Hungary never had the unity among Christians, either within or without the Roman Catholic church, that existed in Poland. Protestants have not forgotten that Calvinist pastors were sent as slaves to the galleys in the late sixteenth century. A whole legacy of religious hostilities and hatreds remained and were exploited by both the Nazis and the Communists. Even though the Nazis and the Hungarian police massacred most of Hungary's Jewish population in the last period of the war, some anti-Semitic feeling has surfaced in recent elections. After the Second World War, the Protestant churches began to collaborate with the Communist regime as early as 1948. In explanation, it can be said that there were economic as well as political reasons. The lands from which church income had earlier been derived were seized by the state and a subvention given for a term of years in their stead. This was true of Roman Catholic as well as Protestant establishments.

As we have already suggested, the contrast with Catholic Poland is doubly evident. Hungary is a confessionally mixed society with major dechristianization. Yet, as in Poland, there is a distinct language community with a common history. Most recently, the discrimination against Hungarians in Romania has been renewed, and it looms large in the Hungarian national consciousness. At the same time, Hungary is not the same country that it was before Communist rule. There has been significant economic change and industrial development, in spite of all the inefficiency. Farms have been collectivized. In terms of the sociology of religion, it is noteworthy that, as in other Eastern European countries, large housing satellite cities with no new churches were built for tens of thousands of citizens by the Communist regime. Apart from all arguments about atheism, this made for dechristianization. Church-going habits were broken off by a large part of the population.

Moreover, difficulties are internal and not just external to religious vocation. A dissident's comments may be biased, but they are perceptive and identify a widespread Roman Catholic traditionalism:

> The majority of those who want to enter a seminary do not really have, strictly speaking, a priestly vocation; rather it is that of a "prophet" or perhaps "prophet priest."
>
> [The novice's] superiors are also talking in terms of the priestly vocation, but they mean, on their part, an identification with priestly institutions, a formal loyalty to the Church, nothing more. The novice slowly completes his five years' course and hardly notices at the end that the "priestly vocation" he had been taught is far from his original "call." Everything is in aid of this formalism: from the daily routine, through lifeless ideologies, to the virtual automation of spiritual life.[23]

The organizational problem for religious leadership is that the state has paid clergy and directed ecclesiastical activities, overtly and covertly. Now when its direction is gone, other organizational patterns and authority must be established. Even before the Communist demise, church officials felt strong enough to make demands for change. Bishop József Szendi of Veszpram met with Prime Minister Károly Grosz in March of 1988 and asked for:

> freedom for the church to operate off church premises, a free hand with young people, an end to bureaucratic interference in religious instruction, the rehabilitation of religious orders, expansion of the eight church schools to meet the demand for places, access to radio and television and the right to reply to false anti-church allegations, the right of priests to visit hospitals, prisons, and schools, and the right to establish youth groups.[24]

Politically, the Hungarian national scene lacks any commanding public figure, as in Czechoslovakia or Poland. At the beginning of the 1990s, its ethos is one of restorationism, nationalism, and refusal of dogmatic atheism. In short, there are echoes of an earlier romantic view of church-state relations in the past. Monarchy is not desired by the majority of citizens, yet Otto of Hapsburg, a link to the once-ruling house as the heir to the throne, is honored when he visits the country. He has been active in organizations for European unity. As a symbol, small farms are being given back to their former owners. The minister of education advocates compulsory religious instruction in all state-supported schools. Perhaps all of this was to be expected in reaction to more than forty years of Communist oppression.

When the Communist party accepted free elections, the populace rejected its ideology and rule en masse as soon as it had the opportunity to do so. Yet all problems were not solved by this decision. Political leadership has been changed in the top ranks. In the middle ranks, much of the same continues. Part of the population is not even quite sure that change has come to stay! The economic situation will be difficult for some years to come, but in all probability the crisis will not be decades long.

A major problem is that Hungary has had what is known as a double economy. The system is two-tiered: socialist and free market. A remaining government command base with state monopoly continues. At the same time, many workers have been obliged to take a second or even a third job in order to have an adequate living standard. The second job belongs to the growing free-market system. There is, as well, a growing underclass, a kind of new class struggle that raises serious ethical problems for Christians.

The most powerful and in many respects most important religious phenomenon in Hungary, sociologists point out, is that of the so-called base groups. With the decline of church attendance in the face of state repression during the 1960s and 1970s, the base groups became a primary resource for still practicing Christians. A refugee to the West wrote in 1985:

> It is astonishing how deeply many church groups live their faith today, even though they must live completely or at least half underground. They pray a lot. Christian solidarity leaves its mark on daily life. Nevertheless, man living under Communism is in danger right down to the very roots of his personality, because he lives under the constant pressure of atheistic propaganda. Communism destroys the human values on which religious values are built. Confronted by an all-powerful state, man becomes insecure, loses hope, and finally gives up thinking for himself.[25]

There was a significant brutalization of Hungarian society under communism. Even the Marxist sociologist, Miklós Tomka has acknowledged that without such Christ-centered associations as the base groups, the nation as a society could soon disintegrate. The base groups commonly are classified into four to six different types, and their membership is estimated at from 60,000 to 100,000 persons. Some are Protestant, others ecumenical. In the majority, the groups are Roman Catholic. They are significantly a reaction to the church's subordination to the state. When the religious orders were closed down by the Communists as they came to power, the phenomenon of such intense, dedicated groups appeared in another guise. A number of them originated as unofficial Bible study groups; others came to center around a particular priest. By the early 1970s, the groups were so strong that in 1976 the Roman Catholic hierarchy was called on by the state to control them. Church officials came to terms with the charismatics and so-called independents with some difficulty, while another group, the

Regnumists ("Regnum Marianum") were easier to deal with, as they adhere strictly to church rules.

It was "the Bush," led by Piarist Father Gyorgy Bulányi, that made the assigned task of control a complicated one, especially as the Vatican refused to excommunicate their priest-leader. He has continued to present difficulty for the Roman Catholic Hungarian bishops. Today, approximately thirty priests remain affiliated with Bulányi and his movement. His goal has never been mass conversion; instead, he has sought to convince a small minority "in depth" of the truth of Jesus' Sermon on the Mount as a way of life. Today, "the Bush" still has some two hundred small groups of eight to fifteen members each and remains strongly missionary minded. Broun explains:

> Many of those who became spiritual leaders of the base groups had been imprisoned during the early 1950s. Father Bulányi, then a student chaplain involved in organizing small underground religious groups, received a life sentence in 1952, was freed in 1956, was sentenced again, and was released in the general amnesty in 1960.
>
> Now in his seventies, Bulányi is a vigorous man, a powerful, charismatic leader, and a superb organizer. It is a tragedy that a person of such uncompromising integrity, a rarity in Hungary today, should have become a focus of a debilitating conflict in the church.[26]

Bulányi and his followers attempt to live out the Gospel strictly, and are pacifists. He is of the opinion that the hierarchy of his own church is so compromised that it no longer expresses the Christian Gospel. He cites as example the bishops' support of military conscription when the government was insisting on army service, irrespective of conscientious objection. Christian pacifism was ruled out as an option. Now that the government has made a place for alternative service, the bishops claim that this is the will of God.

The potentially schismatic character of the Bush arises from its emphasis on individual conscience and advocacy of a New Testament life-style. At the same time, Bulányi is very clear that he is theologically Roman Catholic and not Protestant. He is a conservative, not a liberal. Broun points out that Communist authorities saw in the movement he organized "the quintessential Catholic resistance to atheism. The Bush members' insistence that the spiritual values of Christianity transcend political and temporal expediencies marks them as the true heirs of Mindszenty."[27]

The Russian invasion and occupation had destroyed Hungarian civil society more completely than it did in Poland or East Germany. Police repression continued until 1989, even though church attendance had grown and was becoming more acceptable in the society. A new law enacted by Parliament on January 24, 1990 guaranteed full freedom of religion to all citizens and insured separation of church and state. State control of religion, which dated from the Hapsburg monarchy and was continued under different form under Communist rule finally came to an end. In the new situation, with a large pastoral and evangelistic task ahead for the churches, it is understandable that the base groups often provide centers for renewal, as their members are among the most active practicing Christians.

It is not clear that József Antall, who became head of the new government that took office after the March elections, will remain the leading political figure in the future. Nonetheless, it is significant that he, along with three other ministers of the regime, graduated from the Piarist order's preparatory school in Budapest. Two other ministers graduated from similar Catholic schools. The Democratic Forum, his party, initially included four Reformed pastors. Antall, with a strong Christian background, describes himself as "patriotic, liberal and Christian democratic."

Antall's statement of Christian conviction was very clear when he attended the ninetieth German *Katholikentag* in Berlin:

Where the revolution was peaceful, for example in Hungary, a question arises about the motivation of the old guard [when its members gave up office]: was it insight or admission of error or simply clever foresight about the irreversibility of the reform process? Was it fear of a repetition of the events of 1956 in Hungary, now without Soviet intervention? Or was it solidarity with one's own people? We have no answer to these questions and perhaps never will have.

Antall continued: "The Christian is conscious, that the history of salvation itself is a history of sorrow. He is conscious that human life has a higher meaning above the material. . . . Christian inspired values had lived in the shadow of dictatorship."[28]

CONCLUSIONS

The Hungarian Revolution was "the longest walk to Europe"—from 1956 to 1989. In the short-term perspective, religion had little to do with changing the situation. If one accepts the judgment that Christians were successful in Germany, Poland, and Czechoslovakia, in Hungary this was not the case. Hungary is a confessionally mixed country and had major secularism even before the Second World War; religion did not play an all-important part in public life and thought, as in Poland. Bishops were taking an oath of loyalty to the regime soon after Cardinal Jozséf Mindszenty was imprisoned. The Roman Catholic hierarchy was not as united as in Poland. Mindszenty was more inflexible than his counterpart in Poland, Cardinal Stefan Wyszyński, and less successful. But the historical situation was very different.

The revolutionary changes of 1989 were most of all the work of reform Communists, and religion benefited from them. Freedom and tolerance came with the revolution, but collaboration with the Communist regime had reached inside the church in a way that it had not in Poland and East Germany. The differences between the Hungarian and Polish models, and even with the German model, stand out clearly. There was a Communist-ordered hierarchy of control. Protestant bishops, directly or indirectly (often with pretexts for their legitimacy), were state appointed. Persons designated to rule over different religious groups by the state were held responsible for what went on in their respective communities. In turn, they stood at the head of a pyramid of power, little dependent on or responsible to their constituencies. They were expected to control their underlings. The negative consequences for the internal life of the churches can hardly be overstated.

What emerged was a polity in which most of the faithful understood that their religious leaders were compromised and corrupted. Church attendance dropped drastically in the 1960s and 1970s. Although at times it seemed that Christians were persecuted less harshly than in Czechoslovakia, there was often job and educational discrimination. The net result was major dechristianization, which continues to the present. The situation was one in which the state ministry of cults was trying to destroy religion and, when it could not accomplish this task, to corrupt and compromise it largely for reasons of expediency.

The greatest tragedy of all, perhaps, is that church leadership did not support the small base groups with any enthusiasm. The best that can be said is that the Roman Catholic hierarchy sought to control their pattern. Its rejection of a number of the most courageous and prophetic dissidents will continue to weaken Christianity in the land for a generation. A considerable number of younger Protestants, not trusting church leaders, are becoming increasingly secular. When one asks about Christian intellectuals, they are hard to locate. Persons of this type could not publish or advance in academia. Ecumenical concern has been weak even when existent and is being organized by laymen who have German and French contacts more than by church hierarchies. To be sure, there will be help from the Vatican with new appointments. International contacts will be unrestricted and wider. With Communist pressure against it removed, religious interest will grow and be accepted. It is increasing in a pattern of recovery which can scarcely be called revival, much less renewal. The struggle for a higher living standard in a more open market-economy society, often with more than one job, seems to leave no time for piety.

4

POLAND

To Live with Dignity

"We don't care about life, the pig also lives. We want a life of dignity."[1]

"We don't want vodka or sausage. The times are past when they closed our mouths with sausage."

"The Christ child says, I've had enough of those asses. . . . Let's get rid of them!"[2]

Such folk sayings tell what the populace really believed: the Polish nation had been occupied and raped by Communist Russia ever since Stalin's conquest.

There was no single climactic moment with tens of thousands in the streets. On the contrary, leaders of the Solidarity movement, outlawed at the end of 1981, were imprisoned to prevent such demonstrations. Still, they had the trust of the vast multitude of the Polish people.

The people's revolution has been summed up as follows:

Poland's struggle for freedom was a heroic test of endurance, which encompassed the whole of the 1980's. The final year of the decade was an extraordinary one, in which Poland produced the first non-Communist government in the Soviet bloc and led the way for the other people's revolutions that followed, but this historic event was the culmination of a long struggle against increasingly effete Communist rulers who in the end surrendered power not with a bang but with a whimper.[3]

A university student explained: "The end of the Second World War came here in 1989."

65

The round-table accord that restored freedom was signed on April 5, 1989, between the Solidarity leadership and the Marxist government.

Ending seven years of martial law, it made possible a revolutionary change of ethos. When the first free elections were held in early June, Communist candidates met unanimous rejection.

THE ROOTS OF THE STRUGGLE

"Since 1917, there has been darkness, great darkness throughout Eastern Europe. Now the light is breaking." So Bishop Dabrowski summed up the matter. To the majority of Poles, communism had been seen as a national enemy ever since the outset of its rule in the USSR. "When did change begin?" the bishop was asked. His answer was that "the coming death of communism was evident even in 1917, as soon as it came to political power in the Soviet Union."[4] The bishop agreed with the Marxists on this much: the course of history was inevitable. But it did not turn out as they expected.

The Polish Revolution's strength lay in a unique and massive popular piety which reached to every part of the population. To be a Pole generally meant being a Roman Catholic. Polish culture and civilization had been Christian ever since King Mieszko I was baptized in 966. The millennium of this event was celebrated in 1966, even under Communist rule. Rome, not Constantinople, received the Poles' allegiance when they were Christianized. Polity was different than in the Byzantine Orthodox tradition; the church did not become subordinate to or part of the state.

In the sixteenth century, the Poles were the ruling party in what was then a vast empire that stretched out into the Ukraine. The Reformation never took really deep roots. To their credit, however, the Poles practiced religious tolerance early on; it was guaranteed to Catholics and Protestants by a 1573 law. In 1683, a Catholic army led by a Polish king rescued the city of Vienna from siege. The Turkish threat against all of Europe was turned back decisively. It was the Roman Catholic church and its hierarchy that remained the guardian of the nation's identity when it was partitioned among Russia, Germany, and Austria, first in 1772 and finally in 1795. Nationalist insurrections against foreign occupation in 1794, 1830–31, 1863–64, and again in 1905 were not successful. Poland's freedom and independence were re-established only after the end of the First World War, and even as late as 1920, Poles were forced to fight against the Russians to maintain their borders.

Nationality has not been easily preserved in the face of Nazi and Stalinist attempts to destroy its spirit. Citizens are deeply conscious that Poland's recent history has been one of suffering. Pictures of Father Maximilian Kolbe are for sale with other religious objects outside of churches. He was put to death by the Nazis, giving his life in exchange for that of a family father whom the occupying army had scheduled for execution. Some 1,996 priests, 4 bishops, 238 nuns, 170 monks, and 113 seminarians are known to have died in concentration camps. The presiding Lutheran bishop, Julius Bursche, was also among the victims.[5] Then, after the war, came the new and overwhelming Communist persecution of religion. Bishops and priests continued to be imprisoned. The Russians empowered some 1.5 million *nomenklatura*, Communist party officials who became notorious for their inefficiency and corruption. In this setting, attendance at Sunday Mass was not only an affirmation of Polish identity, but virtually the only available act of protest.

Warsaw, the capital city of the nation, suffered massive destruction from the Nazis, and its Jews were massacred during the Second World War. It is charged that the Russian army had orders to hold back before taking the city, allowing the Nazi carnage to continue and its Polish defenders to be destroyed. (The Communists carried on their own anti-Semitic campaign after they came to power, under Stalinist sponsorship.) It is not forgotten by patriots that the last Polish king to rule from Warsaw died in prison in St. Petersburg.

Earlier monarchs had lived in Kraków, whose buildings still stand today. During the Second World War, the Nazis left the city untouched. Instead, they ruled from its castle and assembled Polish art, which they looted from throughout the country. Today Kraków and its glorious churches—the place from which Cardinal Karol Wojtyla presided before being elected Pope John Paul II—is threatened by destruction from the polluted air from the smokestacks of nearby Nowa Huta. This postwar center of steel manufacturing erected by the Communist regime has virtually no clean-air controls.

The Yalta treaty, which surrendered Eastern Europe to the Russians and communism, carved out a nation almost entirely Catholic. The new Poland was to be a buffer against any renewed German might to the West. The parts of prewar Poland populated by members of the Orthodox church were given to the USSR. Not all, but most, Protestants were Lutherans, and the majority fled the country. The new regime attacked the Roman Catholic church in particular because the Vatican was slow to recognize the new postwar borders of the nation. Still, time after time the party made promises to the Catholic primate and the bishops as it sought to avail itself of their influence to assure public order. More often than not, the promises were not kept. In the new setting, secularization was much less evident than in Western Europe, and as the antireligious campaign grew, nationalism remained on the side of the church. The following is a fair appraisal of potentialities:

The country's geographical position, sandwiched between the Germans and the Russians, must rate as one of the least enviable in the world. But with over 35 million inhabitants, a strong sense of nationhood, a large industrial base, agriculture in private hands, and rich mineral resources, it should not have been impossible for Poland to have become a successful nation with secure borders, given skilled leadership.[6]

The most skilled leadership was in the church, not the Communist party. Moreover, the proletariat, which Communist theory had envisaged as a main base of support, in fact turned out to be Christian, not Marxist. Nothing could make more clear that communism has remained an alien force in Poland, opposed by the family as well as the intelligentsia. Roman Catholic intellectuals from Kluby Inteligencji Katolickiej, supported by the church, have now come to power. The change was sudden and unexpected. The mass of the population had long since seen through what Havel called "life in the lie." But even the leaders who had worked for change in the face of years of martial law were surprised at the extent of their victory.

There had been a long and protracted struggle. On August 14, 1980, a Solidarity-led strike began at the Gdansk shipyards. It was not church sponsored. In fact, Cardinal Wyszyński's first response to it was one of caution, suggesting that the strikers return to their work. Nonetheless, they were overwhelmingly Roman Catholic, and from August 17, Mass was held each day at 5:00 P.M. Striking workers gathered in front of and behind the gate at the shipyards. Visible were pictures of the Pope and a huge cross.

One day, suddenly, the dramatic figure of Lech Walesa appeared, appealing to the crowd: a monument should be erected to workers who had been killed in an earlier strike. If the state would not supply the materials, a year hence, then the people themselves should bring the stones, he argued.

> Solidarity was lucky to have found Walesa. For in modern times Poland had produced nothing but a long series of disastrous leaders.
> Though it was his boast that he never read books ... Walesa's brilliant off-the-cuff oratory was peppered with references to Polish classical literature. But he also had a cool head, and his shrewd sense of timing was to be a crucial factor over the following decade as Poland stumbled hesitantly towards democracy.[7]

The government was forced to come to terms with the workers' demands. For fifteen months Solidarity functioned as a free trade union, with as many as ten million members before it was outlawed shortly before Christmas 1981. This fifteen-month period was also a time of freer religious expression. Nevertheless, the great concern was: "What would the Russians do?" The consensus is that they would have invaded the country, had Solidarity come to power in the early 1980s. Later, under Gorbachev, the Brezhnev Doctrine was abandoned. Solidarity was a worker-led, not a clerical-led movement, although there were priests who participated. Actually, the church hierarchy's commitment for the farmers' wing of Solidarity was the most explicit and strong. The Polish situation was a unique one, with workers' support for the church. The end was a nonviolent people's revolution that became a model for other countries. The yearning for liberation through truth (as against all lies and propaganda) was a clearly recognized theme of the shipyard workers' struggle. Religion joined the intellectuals and the workers in Solidarity. (Intellectuals even slept with workers under their benches in factories.) A common Christian conviction gave a sense of meaning to suffering.

Polish workers again and again refused violence. The symbol of the cross meant that the struggle for liberation must be free of hatred. Solidarity leaders persistently spoke out against force and sought to restrain their followers. Not a single person was killed in the sixteen months that the union was legalized. If not a peace movement, it was nonetheless peaceful; hate had been harnessed. Walesa remarked: "If I did not believe in God I would become a very dangerous man."[8]

True, there was no full counterpart to the Hungarian Revolution of 1956 and its repression by the Russian army, but there had been "incidents." When the workers in Poznan revolted on June 28, 1956, 53 persons were killed, and it took two days to restore order. Most tragically, it was not invading Russians who carried out the repression; Pole was killing Pole. (This was the difference with Hungary.) For a moment in 1956, the government under Wladyslaw Gomulka, the new head of state, seemed to represent nationalism and the workers' cause. But this hope was short-lived. Oppression of workers, low wages, and poor working conditions continued. Time after time the workers were given pay raises, but the price of living was set even higher by comparison. This cycle, which antedates Solidarity by more than two decades, was a major factor in bringing it into being.

In 1970, the state chose the Christmas season as the time to raise prices, and on December 15, revolt flared again. It was so strong, in fact, that a change of government followed. On January 24, 1971, the new prime minister, Edward Gierek, came to the factory gates to ask for worker support. As he borrowed billions of dollars from the West, the standard of living did improve during the first part of his term in office. In the later 1970s, decline set in. After renewed arrests and violence against workers, the KOR, the Workers' Defense Committee, was organized in 1976. This was a watershed event, as it joined workers with intellectuals. Five years later Solidarity continued the interrelation of these two groups. The intellectuals who had joined the workers were imprisoned with them when the union was outlawed.

No rhetorical eulogy is needed for the workers (who soon lost their political naïveté), the intellectuals, the church hierarchy, or the Pope. The long-term explanation of the Solidarity victory is not hard to come by. It roots in the separation of the Communist regime from the lives and beliefs of the Polish people. The church supported civil society and eventually the subculture it protected (as a kind of umbrella) became very much larger, especially after suppression of the workers' revolt in 1976. The church was the one place where there could be freedom of ideas and discussion. It gave order to the situation, working against chaos even as some activist priests were murdered. Over ten thousand members of Solidarity were arrested when it was outlawed and martial law declared by the Communist government on December 13, 1981. The overwhelming majority of them were Roman Catholic Christians. But they were not arrested because of their church membership but because of their opposition to the regime. Politics and religion could not be sorted out simply in watertight compartments.

Atheism never had been chosen by the whole Polish people; Communist rule had been imposed from without. The Roman Catholic church suddenly was thrust into a new prophetic role. To be sure, secularization had never been large among the peasant population, and as we noted, the Polish working class had not been lost to religion. Of course, Poland has had its atheistic movements claiming the death of God and protesting against clericalism. On the other hand, between the two world wars, church sanction and influence supported a highly authoritarian regime. Now, later in the century, force was employed on the other side, in support of atheism. In the changed setting, the dominant religious institution was given a unique opportunity.

The intellectual defeat of Marxist materialism in Poland has been narrated by philosopher Leszek Kolakowski, who himself helped to bring it about. He now teaches in the United States at the University of Chicago and in England.[9] Even as the Workers' Defense Committee coordinated the raising of funds to aid the workers in 1976, the samizdat press expanded. So-called flying universities, often with lessons in private houses, came into being. They became even more important after Solidarity was outlawed in 1981. It is important to understand that Polish government officials were ineffective in maintaining control of culture, whether the theater or education. They lost immense ground ideologically. Together with the growing failure of Communist economics, the developing noncommunist subculture in the drama and the schools made the situation inevitably revolutionary.

The situation began to change with the selection of a non-Italian, Polish Pope in October of 1978. John Paul II understood firsthand the meaning of terror in Eastern Europe. During the first of three visits to his homeland (June 1979), millions of Poles assembled to hear his message and found themselves no longer intimidated. It was an emotional occasion. The multitude cried out together, "We want God, we want God—in the family, in books, in schools, in government orders."

Christianity both stabilized and destabilized the situation. Politically, the Communists had power and controlled the state but not the country. Civil society was sustained by the church, which had already become a shelter for cultural pluralism and dissent. When, for example, in 1968 the regime had forbidden public discussion of Orwell's *1984*, it was Karol Wojtyla, who as it were "ordered it to be read and discussed in the churches." The family, religion, and human rights all were under siege, and the 1975 Helsinki declaration was appealed to by church leadership.

In his book *The Polish Revolution: Solidarity,* Timothy Garton Ash points out that the strategy of dissent was to act as if Poland were a free country.[10] No doubt religion was joined to nationalism, but something more than a return to traditional authority was taking place. There was forced dialogue between Christians and the state. Solidarity leaders were careful that all of their activities were carried out in the open. Names and addresses of signatories to statements were given with them. Obviously, the church had a unique role. It was the one last autonomous place of freedom in the midst of a totalitarian setting. Without it, the revolution of 1989 would not have been possible. In crucial moments the Roman Catholic hierarchy did support change, but in principle it was a conservative, stabilizing force. Without its influence, violence could have been nationwide.

Today between 80 and 90 percent of all Poles are practicing Roman Catholics. What this means and how much this strong popular base will remain under the new circumstances is debated among sociologists, Roman Catholic and non-Roman Catholic. After all, this is not just a religious issue but a question for historians and social scientists. Unfortunately, political freedom does not necessarily bring economic prosperity.

"DEALIENATING" THE INDIVIDUAL, "DETOTALIZING" SOCIETY

Patrick Michel gives the rationale for what developed in the church struggle in Eastern Europe. He first identifies a succession of images and models by which the church in Eastern Europe has been understood in the West: the church of silence, of martyrs, of resistance, and finally, in Poland at least, the church triumphant. Writing before the events of 1989, he was sure that communism had been defeated in Poland. We noted earlier what he calls religion's triple vector in Eastern Europe as it worked for the "dealienation" of the individual, the "detotalization" of society, and the "desovietization" of the nation. Michel accepts Kolakowski's judgment that Solidarity represented the first true workers' revolution in history.[11]

Michel points out that the survival of different peoples and national groups in Eastern Europe had always seemed uncertain and menaced. During the war period, the clergy had suffered with the people. Michel cites René Rémond to this effect.[12] In the face of Nazi persecution, they had their own confrontation with death. The longer result was that religion was not just identified with morality and civic order—it remained that—but at the same time increased as a living existential faith.

Michel emphasizes that the struggle against totalitarianism was church oriented. Institutional religion, not just isolated individuals, provided a moral base for the preservation and renewal of human freedom and civil society. Old antitheses, clerical and anticlerical, were no longer relevant in the face of Communist totalitarianism. The situation in Poland took on uniquely new dimensions. Against communist "homogenization"—sometimes called internationalism—the church, although itself an international body, affirmed patriotism and ethnicity and supported the national consciousness.

Marx had claimed the proletariat for his atheism. Now there was a new kind of struggle against the denial of God—practical and not just theoretical: liberation from atheism was sought. It was not just among workers (although in Poland their position was crucial) that religion became a formidable instrument as freedom was defended against the totalitarian state. Communists had attempted to push religion into the sphere of private life and in this way to combat it in practice. The continuing vitality of institutional religion was for them a problem and a barrier.

Michel emphasizes that in Poland, the stereotype of an uncompromisingly conservative church did not fit. The church was flexible. Church leaders such as Cardinal Wyszyński were much more in touch with the people and their needs than were the Communist party cadre. As ideology confronted reality in everyday life, Michel argues, erosion set in. Communists, controlling the government, insisted on the subordination of the spiritual and moral to the political; Christians refused. This forced a uniquely new dimension: the overwhelming majority of the population was Catholic, and this large community was now seeking to protect a plurality of worldviews.

Communists frequently charged Christians with introversion, exaggerated individualization, and empty theological speculation. On the Marxist premise of sociological determinism, Polish society was supposed to be undergoing a process of secularization. The persistence of religion was taken to be a sign of alienation. Actually, it often was desecularization that took place under the Communists' rule. They mistakenly believed that when and if traditional worldviews and values were given up, the next step would necessarily be socialism. This turned out not to be the case. Michel shows that it was the Catholic church which offered alternative possibilities and became the symbol of the new humanity, safeguarding the world.

The corruption and incompetence of Communist leaders was clear. Their illusions had brought the country to poverty and economic ruin. For Communists seeking to cooperate with the dialectic of history—for their part envisaged economically—change finally came, but not as they had expected. New leadership appeared in Lech Walesa and the new intellectual prime minister, Tadeusz Mazowiecki. In the round-table negotiations with the Communist regime, Solidarity leaders demanded and received government funds for capitalization of a new independent free newspaper, *The Gazete*, which now has more than a million readers daily throughout the nation.

The Communists really gave no alternative to Christianity; in the course of the struggle against them, Christian faith was purified, and the church grew. Even secular intellectuals no longer saw it as the defender of an old status quo. Christianity stood for justice and integrity, the antithesis of oppressive power. Indeed, the practice of religion by virtually all parts of the citizenry has been compared in size to that of the high Middle Ages in Europe: thanks to Communism, it took on a dominant role in culture.

In a sudden change of circumstances, Russian troops are being withdrawn and the struggle against Marxism wanes. Roman Catholicism's closed situation has brought community and discipline. What will happen now as an old enemy suddenly has been defeated and the siege is over? Responsible leaders call for the implementation of the outlook of the Second Vatican Council in a situation of new religious openness. Now that borders are no longer closed, isolation will be mitigated by contact with a wider world of international relations and ecumenicity. The Jewish question is especially sensitive and remains important. Jews were expelled from Poland by the Communist regime as late as 1968. Christian ecumenical and even world interfaith religious issues cannot be avoided. But other concerns are more immediate and pressing. Economic conditions have worsened. The state campaigned against the widespread drunkenness. When he took office, the first non-Communist prime minister expressed the hope that conditions will improve so that young people will no longer continue to want to leave the country.

The Polish situation can be summed up by a visit to four cities. Polish piety looks to *Rome*. Polish priests live very close to St. Peter's Church, just off the main square in Vatican City. When one visits them, the conversation is not about theology or even politics but about poverty in the home country. Poles who have come to Rome, most of them young people, constantly pass in and out of their doors, seeking aid. Poor, desperately poor, they come to the city and are helped with church funds — simply to stay alive. In Poland today, some 20 percent of the population lives below the poverty line; another 20 percent is on the edge of it. Communism has been defeated in the nation but its economy has not yet been reconstructed. In fact, there has been a 30 percent decline in the standard of living since the new government came to power.

The press as well as intellectuals and the leaders of the Austrian government hailed Lech Walesa as a charismatic and courageous leader when he visited *Vienna* and lectured in midsummer of 1990. Of course, the price for his leadership of the Solidarity movement had been years in prison when Solidarity was made illegal by the Communist regime. In his lecture, he recounted how he struggled against Communist rule. All this seemed secondary to his concern that Poland be admitted to the European Common Market as soon as possible and receive massive funds from the West for reconstruction.

In *Warsaw*, there is a new Sheraton Hotel that is too expensive for any but the most prosperous tourists and businessmen to visit. It is filled with scientists, foreign government representatives, and entrepreneurs, all part of the change that is slowly coming to the country. Citizens ask whether the aid will come in time.

Kraków, the ancient capital of Poland, is one of Europe's jewels, with its historic churches and palaces which remained undestroyed during the Second World War. Sometimes called a second Rome, it was from this city that the present Pope once ruled as cardinal. A very Catholic city, it had too many seminarians according to the complaints of the Communists. At the cathedral overlooking the city, on a Sunday morning, young boys in scout uniforms sold portraits of Field Marshall Józef Pilsudski, who ruled the country until his death in 1935. Having led a victorious Polish army against the Russians, he first ruled democratically as head of the country. In time he gave up office. Then when chaos set in, he returned to power and ruled autocratically, in near-fascist fashion. Adam Michnik has warned against the repetition of such a sequence.

The Jesuits in Kraków have a century-long tradition; today, they are owners of a small religious publishing house. Some of their members managed to travel in the West, even worldwide, while the Communists were still in power. One of them, a student chaplain, took a group of his university students to Budapest for an ecumenical conference. There they encountered for the first time Orthodox and Protestant Christian students and returned very confused. In short, the question of interfaith relations was raised for them as they were able to travel to Western Europe and throughout the world. Although they have little money, Poles are now at liberty to travel as they wish.

THE POLISH MODEL

The course of events in Poland provides a pattern against which the people's revolutions can be measured. The revolt there was the longest: from the end of 1981 to the spring of 1989. In fact, Polish Roman Catholics had resisted Communism for more than forty years before it was finally defeated. Their country was isolated, largely cut off from the Western world. In this setting there was a life-and-death struggle against Marxism. Final victory against it was won because of a unique workers' revolution (including strikes led by the Solidarity movement—but strikes do not enhance production). Politically, the country looked eastward to Moscow, religiously its people looked to the West and to Rome.

In Warsaw a young Polish intellectual writes for KIK (the Polish Catholic Intellectuals' Clubs) and ZNAK (Catholic parliamentarians), Zbigniew Nosowski. He describes the circumstances in which he has spent most of his life:

I was born in the year when the Berlin wall was built. Then it seemed that it would stand eternally. .... I was born in the state of the dictatorship of the proletariat, which was trying—strictly according to the rules of scientific socialism—to come through a developed socialist society to an unantagonistic classless communist society. .... I was born in the system when the alleged cause of every evil—a private ownership of the means of production—was eliminated by nationalization and suddenly everybody became an owner of everything. But everybody had nothing, especially no influence on the decisions. . . . I will try to be kind enough not to mention the wasted "human resources," i.e. millions of people murdered in camps, prisons and nobody knows where; thousands of people that were oppressed and persecuted. These are now things of the past. There is no wall, no dictatorship of the proletariat, no communist party (here and there) no leading role, no persecutions, economic reforms are being introduced.[13]

The young Pole studied sociology at Warsaw University during the Communist regime. Even in his student days, he reports, his professors had abandoned Marxist analysis. Following the end of the Communist regime in his country, he has traveled to Western Europe and the United States. His reaction to this experience in many ways may be said to be very characteristically Polish Roman Catholic. For example, he has expressed shock at the prestige still assigned to Marxism by many intellectuals, including Christians, especially those espousing Liberation Theology: "I beg of you not to build a new society on this theory of quasi-'scientific' socialism. It is better to learn . . . [from] the faults of others. Do not go through this lesson from the beginning. Do not believe the Marxist theologians."

The journalist identifies three Polish thinkers as having been theologically important in the Polish struggle: Fathers Józef Tischner, who teaches philosophy at Kraków, Franciszek Blachniki, the founder of the Light-Life renewal movement, and Jerzy Popieluszko, an outspoken priest who was murdered by the secret police. It was the killing of Popieluszko by members of the police that roused the country and made doubly clear the moral issues.

BLACHNIKI

Father Blachniki can be considered briefly; Professor Tischner will be discussed later. The founder of the Light-Life movement, Father Franciszek Blachniki, spoke of this-worldly as well as other-worldly salvation. He emphasized in particular that the end of slavery requires more than simply shaking off a yoke. Just a change in power or a change of roles does not bring true freedom. Indeed, there can be tragedy when the slave becomes master! His mentality may remain slavish. The Light-Life movement was an important resource for the church. It grew rapidly beginning in the early 1970s, and the estimate was that some 300,000 young people were formed by it in fifteen years. Forty percent of religious vocations came from its work.[14]

POPIELUSZKO

The Solidarity ideal was exemplified in the life and death of the outspoken priest Father Jerzy Popieluszko, who enthusiastically espoused it in his preaching. Often he cited Romans 12:21, "Do not let evil defeat you; instead, conquer evil with good." Still, from the Communist point of view, the priest was inciting resistance: "In preaching I speak about what people think and what they speak, often only personally because sometimes they have no courage or no possibility to say it loudly."[15] He has been compared to Oscar Romero, the Central American bishop who was killed while saying Mass. Romero insisted: "We commit the heaviest sin when we do not say the truth to people, for we betray the truth and the nation." Father Popieluszko became a symbol, and his murder was crucial in arousing the population.

Father Popieluszko's parish church, St. Stanizlaw Kostka, was a white twin-spired building in the Zoliborz area of Warsaw. It could accommodate some three thousand worshipers, and as many as ten or twelve thousand often stood outside when special masses were said for the fatherland on the last Sunday of the month. Popieluszko had been reprimanded repeatedly by Cardinal Glemp for his outspokenness, and cried bitterly after one such occasion. Nonetheless, he continued to withstand church pressure to "keep out of politics." Michael T. Kaufman of the *New York Times* recorded parts of what turned out to be one of Father Popieluszko's last sermons:

> The solidarity of the nation had its roots in earlier appeals for law and justice in the years 1956, 1968, 1970, and 1976. It had its roots in the tears, injuries, and blood of workers. It had its roots in the humiliation of university youth. That is why it grew so quickly into an imposing tree whose branches spread over the entire land.
>
> That which is in the heart, that which is deeply tied to man, cannot be liquidated with this or that regulation or statute. We have to fight our way out of the fear that paralyzes and enslaves reason and the human heart. . . . Our only fear should be the fear that we might ever betray Christ for a few pieces of silver. We have a duty to bear witness to the truth of what happened in August of 1980. We have a duty to demand that the hopes of the nation begin, at last, to be realized. . . . Of course, we have to act with care. We have to realize the geopolitical situation in which we find ourselves, but at the same time that situation should never be a convenient excuse to justify the waiver of national rights.[16]

On the morning of Saturday, October 20, 1984, Popieluszko did not return to his home church to conduct the early morning service as scheduled. His driver, a former paratrooper, recounted how he and the priest had been kidnapped by three men; it turned out that one of them wore the uniform of a traffic policeman. Father Popieluszko was beaten and thrown into the trunk of a car.

Since Popieluszko was missing, masses for him began to be said in virtually every parish throughout the land. Having more knowledge than the populace, the regime in a matter of days secretly arrested four members of the national police's Department Four, the part of the security apparatus charged with monitoring outspoken priests. The youngest of the four policemen involved broke under questioning and revealed the details of the killing. Popieluszko's body was recovered from a deep lake behind a dam, where it had been thrown into the water, weighted with rocks. The subsequent trial of the murderers was to engage the attention of the nation. The entire police apparatus was exposed in all its ruthlessness and bungling.

The funeral was held at the priest's parish at his mother's request, and nearly half a million people came to honor his life and martyrdom. It was an emotionally charged occasion, which illustrated the ingredients of the Polish ethos. One of the mill hands who had worked closely with him, Karol Szadurski, spoke directly to the slain priest:

> My friend, I believe all of Warsaw is here. Do you hear how the bells of freedom are tolling? Do you hear how our hearts are praying? Your ship carrying the hearts of Solidarity sails on with more and more of us. Let the Lord accept you among Polish martyrs. For the fatherland you have suffered the most. You are already victorious with Christ. It is that you wanted the most, Jerzy, our priest, farewell.[17]

Cardinal Glemp said: "Let the strangely latent instinct for self-preservation be awakened and let Poles of different social groups meet not crying over the coffin of a martyred priest, but at the table of dialogue to strive toward peace." The dialogue was delayed for nearly five years!

Indeed, Solidarity had not only popular martyrs, but intellectual depth as well. The journalist commentator whom we have cited, Zbigniew Nosowski, is sure that the Solidarity movement, the workers' revolt, had an implicit theology hidden within it. This seems a good way to put the matter, revealing both strength and weakness. The journalist describes the hidden theology which he believes to be implicit in the Solidarity movement with two key Polish words: *niepodległość* and *podmiotowość*. Their exact translation, he notes, is difficult. One he translates as "independence," although it means something more, and the other "subjectivity." Subjectivity is intended in the sense of "one's situation of being subject of one's destiny or the right of human person/society to decide about its life, its public life, the right to be the subject of this life and not to be the object of decisions taken by anybody else." Both words are seen to express the fundamental essence of the word *freedom*—freedom as related to human dignity.[18] This is what the Poles had in mind when they changed the words of a song sung

in church from "God bless free Poland" to "God give us free Poland back."
Nationalism is joined to religion with a new call for human freedom.

TISCHNER

The intellectual vitality of Solidarity was kept alive by persons like Father
Tischner, who was in many respects its leading theologian. Basically, he is
an ethicist more than an exegete or metaphysician. Tischner understood
the limitations of the situation in which he was working. His theological
insights as a social ethicist have become explicit in practical application.
Tischner preached in Kraków's cathedral to assembled worker delegates
when Solidarity was still legal, and he has written an excellent history of
the decline of Marxist philosophy in Poland.[19] Teaching in both Kraków
and Vienna, he has been an international interpreter of Solidarity's conviction, participating very actively in its life.

After the movement had been outlawed and driven underground, Tischner, attempting to explain what had gone on, remarked at a congress of
Polish theologians that they had yet to create an inclusive intellectual
expression of their faith in his country.[20] As compared with Latin American
Liberation Theology (which in general is not understood or favored in
Poland), it does not have a full-blown theoretical basis. In short, Solidarity
was not primarily an intellectual movement. Poles were too busy just sur-
viving! The Communist state imprisoned more than ten thousand members
of the opposition when it outlawed the union.

In his writings, Tischner recognizes the Marxist promise to build a society
free from the exploitation of one human being by another, but he emphasizes that the dialogue in his country was not between equals. One side did
not have full freedom. He compares the situation of Christianity in Poland
to that of Socrates in prison. In his judgment, the meeting between Christianity and Marxism in his own country was one between "two contradictory
concepts of bringing happiness to humankind." In Poland, "a great process
of historical verification of Marxism was going on," he writes. It failed.
Even simpleminded people in Poland knew that it had done so.

While Solidarity was still legal, Tischner asked publicly, "for what and
for whom is Marxism still needed?" His answer was "almost nobody." This
view was shared by the Catholic workers who defeated it. Tischner wrote:
"The essential defeat of Marxism happened at the level of labor. Marxism
did not lead to the liberation of labor that it had promised. . . . The crisis
of labor became a consequence of doctrinal mistakes of socialization."
Wastefulness emerged as a socialist form of exploitation.[21] If in Poland
practice was the ultimate, as Marxists claimed, judged by this standard, it
clearly failed. Tischner argued:

> A truly deep revision of Marxism could have occurred in the name of
> Marxism itself. To accomplish this, it would be sufficient to look more

incisively at social life, to sympathize more deeply with the working man. But such a revision did not take place. Why? Was this because the party did not permit it? One who goes to ask [the] party's secretary permission in matters like this is not a philosopher. I think that the lack of revision proves something else. Marxism as a method of comprehending the world exhausted its theoretical possibilities. Instead of sharpening the Marxists' view toward reality, it directed it toward something entirely different—toward an illusion or appearance of reality.[22]

This was indeed the issue raised by reform communism; it was not taken seriously enough. Communism had failed to provide adequate motivation for work. But in spite of all the emphasis on practice, issues of principle could not be avoided in critical reflection. "The problem of the Polish economy," Tischner argued, "was not so much one of poverty as of distress." In his judgment, the Solidarity movement faced a phenomenon unparalleled in history in terms of wastefulness of labor. "The pain of poverty was not as deep as the pain of wasting resource—energy, talents and people's good will. A reform of the system of labor became a basic goal for Solidarity Movement." Tischner finds that the word *poor*, (the Gospel's preference for the poor) spoken about so widely in Latin American Liberation Theology, "does not touch the essence of the Polish situation." He was speaking as a Pole from the Polish experience—about the Polish model!

As Ash has emphasized, Central Europe is not just a geographical designation. It has its own particular ethos. This became doubly clear as communism attempted to assimilate national traditions in the region. To its disadvantage, this effort took place in the face of a growing renewal of religion tied significantly to nationality. Michel identifies a sequence: religion first took on a strong moral expression and then became political.

CARDINAL WYSZYŃSKI AS PARADIGM OF THE POLISH CHURCH

The struggle had not been just about ideas or theology; it involved personalities. Today a life-sized statue of Poland's postwar primate, Cardinal Stefan Wyszyński, stands in front of a church, not far from Copernicus Square in Warsaw, where scientist Nicolaus Copernicus is also depicted with a larger-than-life statue. Wyszyński was a commanding figure in Eastern Europe, a leader who exemplified the strengths and weaknesses of the Polish experience. The cardinal is reported to have regarded himself as the interregnum sovereign of Poland, a role played earlier in history by the primate of the church when there was no king. He believed the struggle against communism called for authority, not popular democracy in the church. Often he functioned independently and with more outspokenness and courage than the Vatican; at times he challenged its judgment. His form of leadership was possible because Polish faith was deeply anticommunist, conservative in orientation, and supported by home and family traditions.

Born in 1901, Wyszyński became bishop in Warsaw after the Second World War, in 1948, and was made cardinal in 1952. Eastern Europe was significantly shaped by what he stood for and did. He led the opposition to Marxism in his country and set the tempo until his death in 1981.[23]

To guard against eulogizing Wyszyński uncritically, one needs to take note of those who disagreed with his leadership. An example: a Polish priest in a Jesuit monastery near Paris had just been sent to France via air by the cardinal and was very angry. What had the priest done? He had become too active in ministry to students and had become highly controversial in the eyes of the government, and it was seeking to silence and destroy him. Rather than carrying the dispute further, Wyszyński had sent him out of the country. The cardinal's response can be judged only in view of the situation.

Doctrinally the Polish primate was conservative and firm. Second Vatican Council reforms were to be implemented only slowly in his jurisdiction. They were only one alternative among others, in his view; priests serving under him had to understand this. Most important was a united church under the hierarchy in the land. As a matter of both principle and expediency, the Communist goal was the destruction of religion. The state used every device it could command against the church, seeking to divide it and to separate believers from the hierarchy.

In his day-by-day existence, the Polish leader lived between Rome and his Communist opponents in the state regime. Cut off by the Iron Curtain, the Vatican did not always understand all of the nuances of the local situation. Cardinal Wyszyński understood very well that no outside support could be effective in deterring persecution. His situation and strategies were different from those of Cardinal Mindszenty in Hungary. It was Wyszyński's conviction—criticized by those who thought that they knew better—that it was necessary to reach a *modus vivendi* with the state. On this premise, he agreed to a nineteen-point accord that included concessions on both sides. It was the cardinal who was deciding policy, not the curia in Rome. In return for state concessions, the Polish Roman Catholic church acknowledged the new social order in a way that the Vatican had not done to date.

Actually, it was all part of a struggle that continued for more than four decades; neither side was strong enough to fully defeat the other. In 1953, the Communist state set up an office for religious affairs, claiming the right to appoint and dismiss priests and bishops. The Catholic bishops met in Kraków under the cardinal's leadership and replied with a non-possumus, "We cannot." They would rather leave church positions open than place the spiritual rule of souls in unworthy hands. State authorities labeled the reply high treason, and Cardinal Wyszyński was arrested on September 23, 1953, and confined to a convent. Before the end of the year, eight other bishops and nine hundred priests had been imprisoned.

But, as happened again and again, the government could not control the situation. A pattern emerged which was repeated a number of times, almost regularly, in 1970, 1976, and 1980. Following a 1956 workers' riot in Pozan, a new party secretary, Wladyslaw Gomulka, came to power. Gomulka requested the cardinal to return to Warsaw and help calm the populace. He agreed to the release of the imprisoned bishops and priests and the continuance of monastic orders, along with church hospital care. Five Catholic intellectual clubs were authorized, along with Catholic parliamentary representation in a group called ZNAK.

Michel's sociological analysis of religious symbolism adds a fresh dimension to the interpretation of the struggle led by the cardinal.[24] He identifies the terrain of interrelation of church and state in Poland as social, aesthetic, and symbolic. Michel is sure that questions of secularization are not just, as Communists have often supposed, primarily political. Assuredly, Cardinal Wyszyński understood this. Michel's claim is that acceptance of religious symbols in community sociologically constitutes a break in the monism of the Communist-imposed setting. Religious symbolism, he points out, has the power both to stabilize and to destabilize. What sociologist Peter Berger calls the sacred canopy was shattered in Poland during two world wars, but did not remain so. Still, the sense of the holy persisted, thanks to the Roman Catholic church. When Christians continued to affirm their religious symbols in the face of totalitarian power, they were at the same time asserting autonomy: the state was delegitimatized and the church legitimatized.

The Communist state understood itself as intrinsically antireligious, and the struggle against it lasted throughout Wyszyński's lifetime. When the regime ordered religious instruction abolished in the public schools, the church set up its own catechetical centers, and in the end these functioned more effectively. But the cardinal did not stop at this point. Recognizing the importance of devotion as well as education, his appeal was to both Polish history and piety. He issued a call for a year-long round of Marian devotions, a "Great Novena." It was to culminate in 1966 with the celebration of the millennium of Christianity in Poland. All Catholics personally were to take the vows of loyalty to God and the Virgin Mary made by Polish noblemen after they had successfully defended the monastery of Czestochowa against the Swedes in 1656. The icon of our Lady of Czestochowa, the Black Madonna, was to be sent to visit all churches throughout the country. Communist officials made a maximum effort to hinder the visitation, and the icon was at times "arrested." Many churches were visited only by its empty frame![25]

The importance of symbolism was again publicly evident when Pope John Paul II visited his homeland in June 1979.[26] Civil society, the church, and power were the foci of the Pope's speeches. Michel observes that they were more patriotic than anticommunist, as they called for an independent nation. Humanization and peace were together in the teachings of the church. For General Jaruzelski, the Polish president, the state was final, and Michel judges that at times he was given to cynicism. For the Pope, governments are only a normalization of the political order. Civil liberty has bases in respect for the dignity of the individual. The state's sovereignty is an expression of the autodetermination of the people and the nation; it is to be evaluated from its achievement in promoting liberty and justice. Religion is not to be confused with culture, but the two intersect, John Paul II argued.

The Polish sociologist Jadwiga Staniszkis has called the struggle in his country a self-limiting revolution: Solidarity wanted radical change but did not use radical means. Its goal was to change the organization of public life; the state was blocking change by its ownership of all property. The strategy fit the situation. Ash spoke of the Polish "refo-lution" as combining evolutionary reform with revolutionary effect.[27]

Solidarity leaders had emphasized nonviolence. "It was a common-sense agreement that Communists had shed too much of Polish blood and therefore no more Polish blood should appear on the streets."[28] In reality, a violent revolution was excluded because of the Russian presence; judged on Communist premises, of course, the Polish situation was postrevolutionary. In such a setting it was both ethical and pragmatic to be nonviolent and evolutionary. The journalist we cited earlier paradoxically identifies a consensus that if the Soviet army had invaded, Poles would have fought, even though defeat seemed certain.

As we have already suggested, Eastern Europeans share the common convictions that their countries were unnecessarily given over to the Russians at the Yalta Conference. Had they been able to participate in the Marshall Plan and adopt capitalism, they believe their economies would be flourishing like those in Western Europe. Some supporters of the revolution were not yet fully conscious of the abuses which an unrestrained capitalism can bring.

Political freedom is being bought at a price. Stabilization of the currency as a measure against inflation has brought a sharply reduced standard of living, with even more citizens than before living below the poverty line. Solidarity leaders are dividing and competing against one another. The issue, of course, is how to speed the slow recovery of a drastically ailing economy. Initiative and capital are lacking. The "surgery" of the economic revolution is radical. As a member of the new government explained: to change anything it is necessary to change everything.

CONCLUSIONS

The Polish model has been a distinctive one, indeed a unique and seminal one, as revolution took place in a country where religion has had large public acceptance and played a highly visible role in change. Yet it cannot be said that the Roman Catholic church has been simply revolutionary. The cardinals in charge when the Solidarity Union strike began and when the union was outlawed by the government—cardinals Wyszyński and Glemp respectively—urged calm.[29] The larger setting was that of a long seesaw battle between the church and the Communist party, not of sudden mass demonstrations in the streets. In the struggle, neither side had been able to destroy the other. The contest came to an end when one of the contestants collapsed in the face of a workers' revolution.

The Communists' pretext for remaining in power was that they were preventing a Russian invasion. To do so, they even shed Polish blood as workers' revolts were put down—Pole killing Pole. When the Communists finally exited, they left the country bankrupt. Unlike in the rest of Eastern Europe, Polish agricultural land was privately owned. But most farms were outdated, and it was estimated that at least 80 percent of them would not be profitable in the new economy. Experts from the West estimated that most factories and their machinery needed to be replaced in entirety. Part of the difficulty was the squandering of earlier loans from the West in the early 1970s, from which there still remained large indebtedness. In spite of talk about the matter, there was no 1990 Marshall Plan to rescue the country; the major powers were engaged elsewhere. Catholic political leaders came to power at a difficult time, economically. It might have been easier if others had remained to take the well-deserved blame for conditions.

There was a limited amount of dechristianization and secularization in the early 1950s and 1960s; communism had a certain appeal as modern and progressive. Still, remarkably the church had not lost the confidence of the farm boys who moved to the cities to work in industry following the Second World War. There was not the pattern of secularization evident in East Germany, Hungary, and Czechoslovakia. In the contest for the lives of the people and their beliefs, the Communists were neither convincing nor effective. There was growing popular participation in worship and church life. The Roman Catholic church's continued vitality had international ramifications. A Polish Pope probably would not have been elected (to be sure, more than a decade before the change of regime) had it been in decline.

Eastern European theology is notably conservative. There has not been as much exposure to new post-World War II systems and philosophies as in Western Europe. Religious vocations remained high in the Communist period, and traditional interpretation was not overtly challenged. Liberation Theology has not been an issue; the situation has been very different than in Latin America. Our journalist commentator asks:

> Has there been in Poland any equivalent of the key-questions raised by Latin American theologians? No, the questions about God's stance within the system have never been asked, because it was clear and obvious on whose side God stood. This question has not been asked, because from the very beginning of the imposed system, its ruling powers have fully identified themselves with atheistic ideology in its

militant edition. Just here I see the main reason why serious and wide Polish theology of liberation (or of prophetic witness of the Church) has not been developed. We did not have to ask about God's place, because it was obvious. And without such a question, any theology of social reality and social struggle could not appear. It was widely accepted that "God is with us," but very few people tried to ask what it really meant in theological terms. It was the key-question, but it did not really exist as such, because there was only one possible answer to it.[30]

Now there was the possibility of more than one answer. The old enemy — atheism — seemed to be defeated. It was no longer there to fight against. Whose side was God on? Questions remained about the Christian ethos internally! Self-criticism became more open and necessary, following the revolution. Clearly religion was closely tied to nationality in Poland. Mass was said only in Polish, younger priests complained. Fundamental questions about God's place needed to be asked afresh.

In the central state government, change took place at the top echelons of society, as the result of a general election — more than at the lower levels. This is a problem throughout much of Eastern Europe; a large body of apparatchiks remained in the state bureaucracy. At the middle and lower ranks and even at some of the top ones (in a number of ministries), for a while control remained in the hands of Communists or those who had compromised with them. Still, Poland was distinctive and different, with real autonomy and a common Christian culture. There is every indication that the latter will continue into the twenty-first century. The inherent weakness is that its orientation is national more than international or ecumenical.

5

CZECHOSLOVAKIA

Fruits of Persevering Resistance

The Communist Party bears full responsibility for all that happened in our country in ... forty years. Our house received a new owner who dispossessed the former owners and promised an earthly paradise to the tenants.

This paradise was ushered in by the elimination of the most able occupants of the house. The most active people were executed or forced to spend long years in the concentration camps and prisons, hundreds of thousands of skilled people went into exile. The power had one single ideal: uniformity. The thinking artists and scientists were replaced by the advocates of a doctrine that pretended to be able to explain everything only to prove its lack of understanding of almost everything. The worker, officially flattered, became in reality a recklessly manipulated production instrument.[1]

A REVOLT LONG IN THE MAKING

This statement was issued by Civic Forum, the group organized by Václav Havel and his friends that led the peaceful revolution in Czechoslovakia. The people of the nation were complacent and apathetic, it had been alleged. Suddenly revolution erupted and swiftly took its course. Prague seemed an ideal city for public demonstrations. Citizens live very close together and could assemble quickly in Wenceslas Square. Encouraging the 200,000 people who marched on November 20, 1989, Cardinal Frantisek Tomášek sent the following message:

In this fateful hour of our history, no one of you dare stand aside. Raise anew your voice, this time together with ordinary citizens, with

Czechs, Slovaks and members of other folk, together with believers and unbelievers. The right to believe cannot be separated from other democratic rights. Freedom is indivisible. ... With God's help our fate now lies in our hands.[2]

Public protest began on November 17, 1989, the fiftieth anniversary of the death of Jan Opletal, a Czech student killed by the Nazi occupiers. Half a century earlier, in 1939, Czechoslovakian students had demonstrated against fascist rule. Suppressing the unrest, the Nazis not only closed all universities and institutions of higher learning, hundreds of their members were sent to concentration camps; many were executed. On the fiftieth anniversary of Opletal's funeral, not the day of his death, students again marched. The Socialist Youth Movement, the SSM, gave official sponsorship to the assembly at the medical university; students then moved on to the national cemetery at Vysehrad.[3] Clearly the demonstration was not directed just against the Nazi past. An initial crowd of 20,000 grew to 50,000. Banners called for the release of political prisoners, "Justice for all," and "Freedom."

After the observance at the cemetery, most of the crowd dispersed. Some three thousand students did not, however. They remained, and cries rang out, "To Wenceslas Square." The students moved in that direction. On Narodni Street, en route to the square, riot police were waiting. Confronted by them, the students sat down and began to sing: old Beatles' hits, hymns, and the national anthem. "We have no weapons," they chanted, and with loudspeakers the police instructed them to go home. Actually, they could not leave, as the government forces blocked the way. Eventually, riot police began attacking and clubbing students.[4]

"Police were called in to preserve public order in the city centre. They checked the identity of the demonstrators, and approximately 100 people were detained at the police station. By 10 P.M. peace was restored to the city centre."[5] This was the way the Communist newspaper, *Rude Pravo*, reported the matter the next morning. But most citizens knew better than to trust the official media. The rumor grew and spread that a mathematics student, Martin Smid, had been killed by the riot police. The news came initially from his girlfriend, Drahomira Drascka, who was herself beaten and told by the police that Smid had been "finished off" in a dark street. She gave this information to Petr Uhl, a human rights activist. Eventually, Smid turned up alive, but the pattern of events had been set in motion. The tale that he had been murdered activated the populace.

The sequence that led to the end of communism in the country can be chronicled as follows. Beginning on Saturday, citizens gathered in Wenceslas Square to protest. On November 20, 200,000 of them demonstrated. The entire Politburo resigned on November 24, but human rights advocates were not deceived. The old guard was still in power, and a general strike was called on November 27. Still the Communists persisted, announcing a new government in which they remained the majority. The next day 300,000 citizens protested in the streets, and the regime collapsed three days later. Finally, on December 10, a new government, made up of a majority of noncommunists, was sworn into office. In spite of the first "Bloody Friday," no one had been killed in the revolution.

The revolution was brought about by students, writers, artists, actors, intellectuals, and churchmen. In the end, the public at large joined in. The mass demonstrations were the greatest in the history of Prague. The protesters called initially for the end of police repression and open dialogue among all groups of society. The revolution succeeded very quickly because it was not simply amorphous or without program. Civic Forum was founded on November 19 by Václav Havel and his associates. Elected president of the republic on the last day of the year, he and his friends had been in and out of jail numerous times. For years, they were the object of a relentless campaign of oppression.

The group of leaders that assembled in Prague's Cinoherni Theater during the demonstrations came primarily from the Charter 77 human rights movement. They included not only Havel, but the foreign minister of the Dubcek era, Jiří Hajek, a disenfranchised young priest, Václav Malý, and the leader of the Socialist party, Jăn Skoda.[6] Ideologically diverse, they included Christians and non-Christians. It was Civic Forum that led in the negotiations which brought about the resignation of the government and its leaders. The failure of an attempt by Premier Ladislav Ademec to limit the general strike of November 27 to only a token few minutes underscored the impotence of the established Communist leadership.

When asked about the causes of the peaceful revolution, Dr. Jan Carnogursky, deputy prime minister in the new Czechoslovakian government and a leading Roman Catholic Slovak layman, listed "first of all society's total conviction that these changes were necessary. . . . The second most important factor was our historical experience in Czechoslovakia: . . . violent coups d'etat and violent changes in the past usually led to further deformations. . . . In the third place, I would put the moral influence of religion and the church."[7]

In Czechoslovakia, the repression of religion was especially overt and severe, with clergy arbitrarily prohibited from exercising their office at the will of the state. It was almost inevitable that priests and pastors would be among the opposition. Initially, Cardinal Tomášek did not trust the human rights activists, and it is reported that it was conversations with a young priest who had been banned by the state from functioning publicly, Father Václav Malý, (probably along with urging from Rome) that helped to change his mind.

The outlook of Civic Forum was set forth during the political campaign for the election of a new government as follows:

Our main aim is to return to Europe. . . . The Democratic Political System is considered by us as an essential condition. . . . Foreign Policy must be aimed mainly at our return to Europe. .... Economic Policy should be aimed at a speedy creation of market economy conditions. ... Our Social Policy will be mainly oriented to assist the social groups who are disadvantaged through no fault of their own. ... Ecological Policies will focus primarily on preventing the destruction of our environment. ... Our Cultural Policy will be based on the principle of freedom of the arts, cultural and religious freedom, and freedom of information.[8]

Exiled Czech theologian Jan Milic Lochman has underscored the radical change of ethos brought about by the hopes expressed in this program. Fear and terror dissolved. A sense of happiness and hope has reappeared in his native country. Fortunately—unlike Hungary and East Germany— Czechoslovakia has had a charismatic leader in Havel, who was born in 1936, two years before the Nazis occupied Czechoslovakia and twelve years before the beginning of Communist rule. Havel's class and family precluded his admission to the university. He has described himself as a privileged bourgeois child—"a well fed piglet."[9] Havel went to work as a stagehand at the Theater on the Balustrade in 1960. There he met the philosopher Jan Patočka, who like Havel became a leading intellectual spokesman for Charter 77.

Havel's importance can hardly be overstated. In the end he may have a place in Czechoslovakian history parallel with Tomáš G. Masaryk, the country's first president, as a democratic leader. As early as 1975, Havel wrote in an open letter to then President Husak:

Life must needs sink to a biological, vegetable level amidst a demoralization "in depth," stemming from the loss of hope and the loss of the belief that life has a meaning. It can but confront us once more with that tragic aspect of man's status in modern technological civilization marked by a declining awareness of the absolute, which I propose to call a crisis of human identity.

A world where "truth" flourishes not in a dialectic climate of genuine knowledge, but in a climate of power motives, is a world of mental sterility, petrified dogmas, rigid and unchangeable creeds leading inevitably to a creedless despotism.[10]

Charter 77, issued in 1977, ten years after the repression of the Prague Spring, was signed by citizens with a wide spectrum of beliefs. Its signatories were drastically persecuted out of fear by the regime—much more than their numbers seemed to call for. Dr. Václav Benda, a signer of Charter 77 and a member of VONS, the Committee for the Unjustly Persecuted, commented before his arrest:

After I had signed Charter 77—we several times rejected offers of an assisted passage to Austria. .... If a man is so eccentric as to allow himself to be thrown to the lions, it would be very silly of him to complain that their teeth were not clean enough. . . .

The conflict with the state into which I have entered will be long, exhausting, and, by all human standards, hopeless, and in this country means that my whole family down to the third generation will also be brought into the conflict, together with all my friends who were not quick enough to disown me publicly. . . .

Your rights no longer count, your claims will not be considered, your qualifications and contracts will be annulled; you will be dismissed from your job or thrown out of college without a chance of being accepted elsewhere, you will be denied medical care.[11]

The general populace on the surface remained docile. In his first New Year's speech as president, Havel proclaimed:

My dear fellow citizens,

For forty years you heard from my predecessors on this day the same thing in different variations: how our country flourishes, how many millions of [tons] of steel we produced, how happy we all are, how we trust our government and what right perspectives were unfolding in front of us. I assume you did not nominate me to this office so that I, too, would lie to you.

Our country is not flourishing. The enormous creative and spiritual potential of our nation is not used meaningfully. . . . A state which calls itself a workers' state humiliates and exploits workers. Our obsolete economy is wasting the little energy we have available. . . . We have polluted our soil, our rivers and forests, bequeathed to us by our ancestors. . . .

All this is still not the main problem. The worst thing is that we live in a contaminated moral environment. We fell morally ill because we became used to saying something different from what we think. We learned not to believe in anything, to ignore each other, to care only about ourselves. Concepts such as love, friendship, compassion, humility or forgiveness lost their depth and dimensions and for many of us they represent only psychological peculiarities, or they resemble greetings which wandered in from ancient times, a little ridiculous in the era of computers and spaceships. Only few [of] us were able to cry out loud that the powers-to-be should not be all-powerful.[12]

Even before the revolution, Havel knew that public opinion had changed more than the rulers of Communist regimes had imagined. In his essay on the power of the powerless, a year after the issuance of the Charter 77 protest, he spoke bluntly of

the continuing and cruel tension between the complex demands of that [Communist] system and the aims of life, that is, the elementary need of human beings to live, to a certain extent at least, in harmony with themselves, that is, to live in a bearable way, not to be humiliated by their superiors and officials, not to be continually watched by the police, to be able to express themselves freely, to find an outlet for their creativity, to enjoy legal security, and so on.[13]

Havel's concerns, like those of his fellow dissidents, were culturally inclusive—for civilization itself. In short, their interests were necessarily political, social, and economic, as well as philosophical and religious. When Havel took office as president of the republic following the revolution of 1989, the traditional relation between the presidential and bishop's palaces, which stand together on a hill above Prague, was resumed in a new setting. Neither side envisaged a uniting of church and state. Nonetheless, it was symbolic of the new situation that Havel, not a practicing Catholic, requested that a Mass be held to mark the occasion in St. Vitus Cathedral. In spite of all confessional division and controversy, the Christian heritage of the land was acknowledged.

Havel signaled a new era of religious freedom to which the Helsinki accords of 1975 had shown the way. They had often been invoked by Havel and his fellow Chartists as they set up the Committee for the Defense of the Unjustly Persecuted. With the revolution, religion would no longer be suppressed in the common life—a drastic, sudden, and surprising change. Welcoming Pope John Paul II to Czechoslovakia on April 22, 1990, Havel the playwright was at his rhetorical best:

> Your Holiness, dear citizens. I do not know whether I know what a miracle is. None the less, I dare to say that in this moment I am experiencing a miracle. A man who less than six months ago would have been arrested as an enemy of the state, today, as President greets the first Pope in the history of the Catholic Church to step on the ground of this state. . . .
>
> I do not know whether I know what a miracle is. None the less I dare to say that in this moment I am experiencing a miracle. In our land destroyed by the ideology of hate comes a message of love; . . . in a land until recently destroyed by the idea of confrontation and division of the world, comes a message of peace, of dialogue, of reciprocal tolerance, respect . . . the preaching of brotherly unity.[14]

There was an acknowledged religious dimension in Havel's letters to his wife, Olga, written earlier from prison. He did not know what his destiny would be when he sent them to her, and they were not intended to be published. Much of their content concerns details of everyday life. On October 3, 1981, he wrote:

> Today I understand, perhaps better than I ever did before, that one can become embittered. The temptation of Nothingness is enormous

and omnipresent, and it has more and more to rest its case on, more to appeal to. Against it, man stands alone, weak and poorly armed, his position worse than ever before in history. And yet I am convinced that there is nothing in this vale of tears that, of itself, can rob man of hope, faith and the meaning of life. He loses these things only when he himself falters, when he yields to the temptations of Nothingness.[15]

Havel's attitude toward religion was designated "courtesy toward God" by his German writer friend, Heinrich Böll.[16] Havel is himself very sympathetic to Christianity, both morally and intellectually. However, in his letters to his wife from prison, he is explicit that he is not a professing Christian believer. But he did understand the religious problematic.

On September 4, 1982, Havel composed the following reflection in a letter to his wife from prison:

I think that religious archetypes accurately mirror the dimensions of this ambiguous essence of humanity—from the idea of paradise, that "recollection" of a lost participation in the integrity of Being, the idea of a fall into the world as an act of "separation" . . . the idea of last judgment as our confrontation with the absolute horizon of our relating, right down to the idea of salvation as supreme transcendence, that "quasi-identification" with the fullness of Being, to which humanity is constantly aspiring.[17]

Imprisonment clarified issues for many.

Havel recalls how he was tutored at Ruzyne prison by philosopher Jan Patočka. Together they were awaiting officials. "At any moment," Havel writes, "they could have come for us, but that didn't bother Professor Patočka: in an impromptu seminar on the history of the idea of human immortality and human responsibility, he weighed his words as carefully as if we had all the time in the world ahead of us."[18] Patočka died two months later of a stroke after extended police interrogation.

An underground of students, artists, and churchmen had in fact believed in Charter 77 and had been working for change, even while both men were in prison. Philosophical and religious concerns—the depths of selfhood, the meaning of life, society, history and suffering—surfaced in revolt against a reductionistic materialism. After the revolution, religion was to play an open role again as part of the normal life of culture, in terms of pluralism not intolerance.

CZECHOSLOVAK RELIGIOUS TRADITIONS AND RELIGIOUS DISSENT

It must be remembered that the Counter-Reformation was imposed on Bohemia and Moravia after the defeat of the Protestants at the Battle of

White Mountain in 1620. Tolerance came only at the end of the eighteenth century in Hapsburg-ruled lands. Divisions between Roman Catholics and Protestants have been centuries long. It was not without reason that Pope John Paul II invited the rehabilitation of pre-Reformation martyr Jan Hus when he visited Czechoslovakia in spring 1990. Trevor Beeson, an English church historian who has specialized in Eastern Europe, observes: "In the course of over three hundred years the talented Central European peoples who now constitute the population of the State of Czechoslovakia have experienced no more than twenty years of real independence. Their history constitutes a major example of the struggle between freedom and oppression in human experience."[19]

Christians were driven together by persecution. In Czechoslovakia, during more than forty years of Communist rule, the repression of religion was in many respects the most overt and oppressive outside the USSR. It continued, in fact, until the overthrow of the ruling Communist regime in November 1989 (even after policy in Russia had begun to moderate). For a very brief period, the Prague Spring of 1968 had brought respite to the churches. But this did not continue long. The presence of Warsaw Pact armies, along with direct Russian intervention in police supervision, reinforced a hard-line policy. More than half a million former Communist party members who had joined in the Prague Spring were disenfranchised. An intellectual dialogue had been developing between Marxists and Christians. With the imposition of force, it came to an end.

A Charter 77 document issued in 1984 explained:

> Membership in a religious order automatically involves the loss of the fundamental rights that are guaranteed to all citizens, and the continual threat of penal sanctions. . . .
>
> The internment camps for religious were not part of the regular penal system, so its regulations did not apply. Conditions of life there were even worse than in the prisons, and in fact the political leadership was quite prepared to tolerate this since it killed them off more quickly. The internment had no time limits—it was for life, and some served twenty years. . . .Though they worked eight to ten hours a day they were not given enough food.[20]

To say the least, the neo-Stalinist strategies used in the repression of faith in God were commonly dogmatic and blatant. After a six-hour interrogation by state officials, Cardinal Štefan Trochta, age sixty-nine, collapsed and died in 1974. A slogan used in a Slovak high school ran, "There will never be prosperity until the last remaining priest is struck down by the last remaining stone from the last remaining church."[21] Church publications were restricted, and religious education forcibly discouraged. The overall strategy was to confine religion to the sanctuary, separating clergy from their people. Priests and ministers who became too active or outspoken were disenfranchised.

Roman Catholicism has not been a symbol of national unity, as in Poland. Still, Slovakia, in the predominantly Catholic eastern part of the country, in Communist eyes suffered from "the Polish disease." During the "Velvet Revolution," crowds of believers, Protestant and Roman Catholic together, joined in organized street demonstrations. The November 25 mass meeting calling for the release of religious prisoners in the capital of Slovakia, Bratislava, the second-largest city in the country, received less worldwide attention than the protests in Prague.[22]

Crucial under Communist rule was the state's direct exercise of authority to license or refuse to license clergy. This was not the pattern in Poland or East Germany, for example. As we have already noted, suspected clergy — those too active or potential dissenters — were not allowed to function in their office. Those who were tolerated were stipended by the state — given a pittance (less than a menial laborer). In fact, hundreds of clergy were forced into nonreligious work when they were so restricted. Czechoslovakia is more than 80 percent Roman Catholic, and the larger church suffered more than the smaller Protestant bodies. The regime favored the so-called peace priests, clergy in tension with the hierarchy, using them to infiltrate virtually every branch of church life.

Relations with the Vatican were cut off, and when the government ministry of cults could not control the appointment of bishops at its wish, de facto rule was exercised by lesser clergy whom it favored. Of course, Christians were not eligible for professions such as teaching and state civil service. All of this belonged to the regime's Communist-inspired attempt to control and suppress all religion.

Like their Roman Catholic counterparts, Protestant ministers who dared to speak out were disenfranchised and imprisoned. A number of them signed Charter 77. Those who were deprived by the state of their license to preach experienced personal hardship, together with their families. Beeson describes the Czech Protestant ethos as follows:

> The pattern has five elements. There is in Czech Protestantism a marked emphasis on personal discipleship, based on a concept of the Kingdom of God which demands that the Christian believer shall express his faith in a recognizably Christian life-style. . . . There is also the recognition that suffering is an integral part of Christian experience, involving for some actual martyrdom and for all acceptance of a servant role in the world. The Hussite movement was basically a movement of the oppressed, and, in contrast with other parts of Europe, the Czech Protestant communities consisted mainly of the underprivileged. Another element is the historical concern for ecumenism. . . . Last but not least, there is a strong concern for reconciliation and peace.[23]

The synod of the Czech Brethren was meeting on the same November 1989 day that the police began to attack students. When the report of their attack was brought into it, the synod immediately broke off the discussion of its business and sent a protest to the government.[24] This denomination has a Calvinist-oriented heritage, and students for its ministry are educated at the Comenius Theological Faculty in Prague. The Czechoslovak National church, also known as the Czechoslovak Hussite church, developed out of a schism with Rome in the post-World War I era. It was compromised heavily during the Communist era under state pressure, and its influence seems to have declined.

Even in Slovakia, the most thoroughly Roman Catholic part of the country, church attendance was reduced through persecution. Still, as in other Eastern European countries, the state's campaign against religion was in many respects counterproductive. Thousands of persons, many of them from atheistic backgrounds, continued to join the churches annually, even in the years before the revolution. Of course, statistics were hard to confirm. State reports estimated Christians as 30 percent in Czech areas and 51 percent in Slovakia.[25] The continuing vitality of religion became evident as pilgrimages turned into mass assemblies of Roman Catholics. The eleven hundredth anniversary of the death of Saint Methodius, who brought Christianity to the region, was celebrated at the Moravian shrine of Velehrad. In July of 1985, between 150,000 and 250,000 believers came together for prayer and worship in a highly impressive demonstration.

William Echikson, who worked for the *Christian Science Monitor* for five years in Eastern Europe, says that of all the stories he reported, that of Moravian dissident Augustin Navrátil was the most moving. Identifying Navrátil as a peasant, he describes him as "A short, stocky figure with big, calloused hands . . . [whose] intense gaze, mighty handshake and rapid-fire passionate speech suggested an iron will."[26] Navrátil and his family of nine lived five hours east of Prague in the village of Lutopečny. In addition to his work as a signalman at a one-room railroad station, he farmed two acres of land and kept two cows. Navrátil explained: "People in Prague told me that the petition wouldn't work, that it wasn't the proper time, that people wouldn't listen. I replied, No, we can't just talk, we must act."[27]

Echikson recounts how after Navrátil began petitioning for religious freedom in 1977, he was sent to a mental hospital with a diagnosis of paranoia. After his first release following seven months confinement at the Kroměřóiž Psychiatric hospital, he read all the mental-health books he could find and afford. He also read the laws which bore on his case and then wrote out an argument against his incarceration—charging that it was illegal—and sent off copies to the president, the prime minister, and the police, along with several ministries. Then he continued to write open letters. One of them protested the murder of the monk and secretly ordained priest Poemysl Coufal.

In 1987, Navrátil, in and out of confinement, was still circulating his petitions. Cardinal Frantisek Tomášek had replied to one of his letters: "I remind you with all strength that cowardice and fear are not worthy of a real Christian." Navrátil made over a thousand copies of the cardinal's reply and mailed them throughout the country, along with petitions ready for signing. Josef Zvěřina, a Roman Catholic leader, noted: "If it had just come from us intellectuals, it could have been ignored." Some priests spoke at Mass in support of the petition.

Before the petitions were presented to the cardinal, over 500,000 persons, including Protestants, Jews, and agnostics, had given their signatures. Navrátil's 1987 petition listed thirty-one demands.[28] He asked that the appointment of new bishops be made an internal matter of church affairs, without state interference. Religious instruction of children should no longer be forbidden on church premises. Copying and dissemination of religious texts ought not to be considered an illicit business activity or a legally punishable act. Priests and people were to be allowed to proclaim Christian ideas in public. The construction of new churches should be sanctioned by the state where necessary. All unlawfully sentenced priests and laypeople were to be speedily and consistently rehabilitated. The regulations that make a considerable part of the activity of priests and laypeople illegal were to be rescinded. The list of demands not only made clear the abuse of religion in the country; it also revealed a widespread knowledge of what was going on.

Echikson tells how, in one of his imprisonments, Navrátil was confined in a cell that measured only fifteen feet. It had only a bucket for a toilet, no running water, no soap, no towels. Other prisoners threatened to kill him. When Echikson met Navrátil, he had some missing upper front teeth and a nasty scar above his right cheekbone that gave him headaches. In 1988, following a Mass at St. Vitus Cathedral in Prague, some of the worshipers had demonstrated and shouted: "We want bishops. Bring us the Pope!" The police attempted to dampen public feeling by making an example of Navrátil and again sent him to a psychiatric hospital in reprisal.[29]

As Echikson points out, Navrátil initiated the most significant protest in Czechoslovakia since the Prague Spring. František Jelinek, Director of Religious Affairs, remarked: "This Navrátil, he thinks he is the spokesman of the Catholic Church. The petition means nothing. We will negotiate only with the official representatives of the Church."[30] But the state did not hold to this position. In a very different way than Havel, the peasant galvanized the opposition. Even before the people's revolution in 1989, the Communist regime had begun to liberalize its religious policy.

The history of the underground church that developed among Roman Catholics is one of the most fascinating chapters of the resistance. Mass was said in secret. Unlicensed priests and nuns had their own respective communities in which they lived together in defiance of the state ban. Strict secrecy was necessary, and many of the arrangements were known only to immediate superiors.

The 1984 Charter 77 document about religious orders cited earlier ended with a comment about the dreary period of persecution which "has been more damaging to society as a whole than to the orders themselves": "In the long history of religious orders in our country, the last thirty-five years represent a heroic era. This period will come to an end only when the doors of the convents open again."[31] In 1990, they were reopening, slowly and painfully, with the possibility of a new beginning. The Charter 77 document included the following observation:

> Religious orders have shown themselves able to adapt creatively to new conditions. They have divided themselves into smaller groups and trained for all sorts of professions; they live in apartments like other citizens, and yet in these outwardly anonymous conditions they continue the tradition of their rules, at the same time adapting themselves to fresh forms of spirituality and new possibilities for working in very different social conditions.[32]

The "underground church" developed in Czechoslovakia more than other satellite countries as a result of the intense persecution of religious orders. An information network emerged, and there was an underground monthly newspaper, *Informace o Církvi (Church Information)*, which reported what was going on. Because it had no central headquarters, the movement was difficult for the police to control. It included many young people who had become interested in religion and the priests to whom they had turned. The latter generally were not state-authorized clergy, and more often than not they were those who had distanced themselves from the regime. Forbidden to pursue a normal religious vocation, hundreds of priests, monks, and nuns still continued a Christian witness in the world.

The police used informers, telephone tapping, and house searches to suppress the underground church, but they were not successful in stamping it out. Bishop Korec reports that after one of his more recent arrests toward the end of the Communist period, the Voice of America broadcast news of what had happened to him the same evening for its clandestine listeners in the country. The civil rights movement that had developed, in addition to the religion information network, had conveyed the information. The civil rights movement operated more in the open, making complaints through official channels, especially following the Helsinki accords.

In the initial period of persecution, when Bishop Korec was apprehended and sentenced to twelve years imprisonment, his fellow prisoners included six bishops and two hundred priests, many of whom had been in prison for more than a decade. Following his 1960 arrest, Korec was kept underground in solitary confinement, without light. Most of the period, however, he was able to say Mass daily with the help of friends in and outside the prison. His Jesuit training strengthened his belief, and his pastoral role continued, irrespective of the setting.

With great inner strength, Korec found the energy to work as a laborer during the day and write and carry on a pastoral ministry the rest of the time. He used his authority very carefully, building up the underground church. Virtually all his ordinations were of persons who had belonged to suppressed religious orders. The polity of the orders provided a religious discipline and life rules by which their lives had been regularized. Any overt expression of piety outside the sanctuary was forbidden. The underground church was harassed. When even a few Christians met together with their priest in the woods for Mass, the police were soon upon them. Where was their authorization to meet? they were asked.

If a professional person ever ventured to attend Mass, it was permanently on his record, and he could be blackballed. If one was a Christian, word was telephoned from employer to employer, and he could not find work. Cardinal Korec has reflected retrospectively about the reasons for such drastic persecution: Christianity was the one force that the Communists feared, because they could not root it out with totalitarian means. It persisted in the inner lives of persons (and thus in society), an area which Communism simply could not access.

The constituency with which the secret bishop-priest worked most closely was a select one. It was made up of intellectuals, persons who are now doctors, lawyers, government officials—in short, "the creative minority." They were either practicing Christians or persons searching for religious meaning. Even after the revolution, the bishop still found fear among the populace. Citizens remembered the repression of the Prague Spring and asked if there would be a repetition. "Will the Russians come back?" they asked. Indeed, Russian troops were still in the country. The church had a major role to play in activating public life and overcoming suspicion.

Of course the events of November 1989 and the new freedom they brought seemed miraculous in themselves. Bishop Korec attributed them in part to Providence, God's care for the moral order. In his diocese in Nitra, hundreds of laywomen are willing to be trained for the religious teaching that is now possible in the public schools. But building facilities are lacking. Citizens are willing to work without wages in their reconstruction, but materials must be paid for, and there is a lack of funds. In Bratislava, the capital city of Slovakia, the priests' seminary—long small because of government restrictions—is now overflowing with candidates for the priesthood.

INTELLECTUAL HERITAGE OF RECONSTRUCTION EFFORTS

Leaders realize that time will be required for reconstruction. Prague theologian Professor Josef Zvěřina (imprisoned for many years) was interviewed about future prospects when he attended the 1990 German *Katholikentag* in Berlin.[33] His commentary was balanced and sober. At the outset, he warned against any expectation of miracles. Monastic orders can only be reconstituted slowly, with new recruits. Was there increased church attendance? Zvěřina's answer was yes, more in the cities than in the towns. The Pope's visit drew large crowds.

With respect to society in general, it is not so much the older or even the middle generation that needs to be considered most, Zvěřina believes. Factually, there has been significant dechristianization. It is important that the church become relevant for young people, a significant number of whom are interested in religion. Mere affirmation of past traditions will not draw their attention, and there is the ever-present looming threat of secularization in a consumer-oriented economy. The standard of living is already better than in most other Eastern European countries. In a few years, however, Czechoslovakia will have begun to substantially recover.

It is important not to idealize what has taken place religiously or politically. There remains a large group of priests, mainly older ones, who cooperated with the Communist regime. The church's policy is not to reject them personally but to reject what they stood for. The resources of both the church and state are limited. After much debate, parliament decided that only 10 percent of former church-related buildings were initially to be given back for ecclesiastical use.

Professor Zvěřina grounds his hope in terms of the longer history of the area. When the Czech royal house had no heirs at the beginning of the fourteenth century, he notes, there was trouble for a period comparable with that of Communist rule. The land was ravaged during the Thirty Years War, but cultural life re-emerged in richness. Now national and religious life are together recovering again after the crushing of the Prague Spring in 1968 and the Russian occupation. The situation in Slovakia is recognized to be different than in the western part of the country. Slovakia was under Hungarian rule during the Austro-Hungarian Empire. It was granted independence during the Second World War by the Nazis; the head of state was, in fact, a priest who was hanged for treason at the war's end. There are still calls for Slovakian independence, and the question is a sensitive one. The government hoped that the Pope's visit would help improve matters.

Havel stands in a distinctive national tradition with such concerns. From the beginning of the Czechoslovakian Republic, there had been significant interaction between philosophy and statecraft. This is evident not only in Havel, but in the writings and work of Tomáš G. Masaryk, the first president of the newly founded nation after the First World War. Masaryk had had a career in philosophy as well as politics and was sixty-five when he took office as head of state. Earlier he had been a member of parliament in Vienna and advocated Czechoslovakian independence only after he lost belief in federalism in the Austro-Hungarian Empire. (Masaryk's critique of Marxism was a careful one and is in part still relevant today.)

Both Masaryk and Havel have approached religion from a philosophical perspective more than that of churchmanship. Both were Roman Catholic in background. Masaryk converted to Protestantism, he said, to find a more vital, living faith. His *Conversations with Karel Čapek, Masaryk on Thought and Life*, seems to express the convictions of a modernist liberal.[34]

The differences in life philosophy between the two presidents reflect what happened between the two world wars as well as after the Second World War. Masaryk, relying on philosophical common sense, was a liberal Christian. Havel was more strongly influenced by existentialism. Havel stood outside the sanctuary, as it were, and was not a practicing Christian. On the other hand, it may be that he understood religious meaning in greater depth. His opponent was not Austro-Hungarian imperialism but a more inclusive totalitarianism. He believed the ethical bases of civilization were being destroyed. Nazism and communism were destructive of humanism as well as faith in transcendence. Common sense was not enough, as religious questions had been radicalized immeasurably.

Havel, not a professional philosopher like Masaryk, claims as his tutor Professor Jan Patočka. Part of the common lines between Masaryk and Havel, interestingly run through Patočka. Patočka, an unusually creative philosopher, taught at Charles University in Prague, and was respected beyond the borders of his own land. It is not an exaggeration to say that his writings will be read well into the next century. That he was hounded by the police until he died tells much about the Czechoslovakian scene. Havel and Patočka both were signatories and leading spokesmen for Charter 77. Erazim Kohák, in his study of Patočka's philosophy published prior to the 1989 revolution, emphasizes that Charter 77 was not a really radical document, judged in terms of perestroika and glasnost.[35] Nonetheless, the political situation before the revolution in Czechoslovakia was such that it brought an overpowering police reaction.

Description of Masaryk's career and ideas is necessary for an understanding of Patočka's outlook. To his credit, the first president, unlike less-active philosophers, marshaled troops and worked to bring about Czechoslovakian independence at the end of the First World War. More than many others in public life, he recognized the intellectual and religious crisis which was the background of the First World War. In his essays, *Modern Man and Religion*, he singled out what he regarded as modern humanity's titan-like tendency to kill either oneself or others as part of the crisis. Suicide — which he found to be widespread — seemed an expression of the disintegration. Masaryk wrote:

> Psychologically, the opposite of suicide and suicidism is murder and murderousness; suicide is violence of a soul turned inward . . . ; murder is violence of a soul outward, an abnormal objectivation. Subjectivist individualism rising into solipsism and titanic godlikeness is unbearable for man — in the end he violates either himself or his fellow man: suicide and murder are the extremes of violence.[36]

In Masaryk's view, the major destabilizing factor was the loss of religious faith. Modern science had produced a crisis but provided no answer, he argued.[37] Patočka discussed this claim in his first substantial article. The first president of the republic had been confident about a morally ordered world, and on this premise wrote his detailed and respected critique of Marxism. This was the position that Patočka no longer accepted. Masaryk was a believer in common sense and Christianity. Patočka was a seeker, not a believer. His father, the classical philologist Josef Patočka, had been a militant atheist. The son became caught up in the crisis of modernity from a very different perspective.

The intellectual history of the young Patočka is a revealing one. He once came close to joining the Czech Brethren Protestant church, but J. B. Soucek, a leading Protestant theologian, dissuaded him. Patočka's reason for not accepting Christianity was that for him the natural world did not seem to include prereflective experience of God. But what Masaryk had called titanism—the radical self-destructiveness of persons—confronted him. Because he did not share Masaryk's faith in the community of technical and human rationality, Patočka was more concerned than ever to find an existential ground for human rationality.[38]

Rejection of Masaryk's position radicalized the matter. Masaryk had identified titanism as the product of a religious consciousness that feels betrayed by God. Patočka put the matter differently: without a clear word from deity, it is a gigantic task to heed the call of the ideal in the face of evil. This is what Patočka set out to do. His philosophy embodies the full problematic of classical philosophy, often expressed, as in the case of Havel, in existential form.

Patočka's theme of "seeking" continues in Havel (and is very different from Masaryk's common sense). The letter that Havel sent to his wife, Olga, dated October 10, 1981, makes this clear:

> Only the deeply held belief that "nothing that is done can be undone," that "everything is, somehow," that "everything is known somewhere, somehow," and that everything, therefore, is completely evaluated and assigned a meaning "somewhere"—only this conviction enables one to live with the awareness of death and to overcome it. . . .
>
> Without this central assumption (though it remain unthought and be denied a hundred times) none of those human actions is either explicable, thinkable or even possible.[39]

Havel's statement exemplifies the experience that led his nation to reject Marxism.

Of course with such a view, the way is opened up for religious reflection and even practice. Especially interesting is Patočka's volume (written under Communist rule) entitled *Heretical Essays*, material which was first circulated in samizdat form. Embittered by the Soviet occupation, he seemed to many of his readers to have entirely turned away from the outlook of Masaryk. Kohák does not agree that this is the case. He writes:

Where Patočka differs from Masaryk is in his conviction, quite possibly reflecting his times as much as his philosophy, that moral maturity, the freedom and responsibility of the citizen, cannot simply grow organically as the extension of our mundane concerns. By themselves, those lead only to consumerism, and ultimately war. It takes a shock to let man break free of the lockstep of everydayness.[40]

This stance, more radically existential (less common sense) than that of Masaryk, tells much about what had transpired in Czechoslovakia. Profoundly more had been put at risk than in Masaryk's time. Havel knew it as well as Patočka. Together their perspectives would lead to a revolution without utopian expectations. Neither religion nor philosophy could be taken for granted as giving explicit answers, as they had seemed to do in the time of Masaryk. There was instead the necessity for intellectual quest, which Patočka undertook with full earnestness. It was not dogma but openness to religion that concerned them. From prison, Havel wrote to his wife on September 4, 1982:

An unqualified orientation to the "here" and "now," however bearable that may be, hopelessly transforms that "here" and "now" into desolation and waste and ultimately colors it with blood.

Yes: man is in fact nailed down—like Christ on the cross—to a grid of paradoxes: stretched between the horizontal of the world and the vertical of Being; dragged down by the hopelessness of existing-in-the-world on the one hand, and the unattainability of the absolute on the other, he balances between the torment of not knowing his mission and the joy of carrying it out, between nothingness and meaningfulness.[41]

CONCLUSIONS

The Czechoslovakian experience opens up perspectives "in depth" on the revolutions of 1989 which were not as immediately evident in other countries. It helps to define some of the issues more clearly. This is particularly the case with respect to the meeting of humanism and Christian faith—what the German writer Heinrich Böll (describing Havel's orientation) called "courtesy toward God." Comparatively, it can be said that from the beginning of the republic in 1918, there was a very different attitude toward religion than in the French and Russian revolutions. Separation of church and state, but not the destruction of religion, was envisaged. In the revolution of 1989, the churches were not as prominent as in Poland and East Germany, although they were very much present and active.

The events of that year in Prague need to be seen against the particular background of Czechoslovakian history. The nation came into existence after the First World War and had a prosperous and democratic life until the Munich crisis before the Second World War. Its republican cause—the best in Central or Eastern Europe—was surrendered to Hitler by Great Britain and France, and with the outbreak of hostilities, the Germans moved in. War casualties were not large, although the occupation was brutal. After liberation from the Nazis, communism became fully dominant by 1948, and Stalin's imperialism in Czechoslovakia soon evoked the organization of the North Atlantic Treaty Organization. The nation was separated from the Western European community of nations. When reform Communist leaders attempted to re-enter it in the Prague Spring of 1968, an overwhelming barrier was put in the way by the Warsaw Pact invasion under Russian direction. Moscow's troops continued to occupy the country, and communism's impact on intellectual and religious life was more devastating than ever.

The victory of the so-called Velvet Revolution in Prague was an artists' and writers' as well as churchmens' one. In fact, its victory showed how little the country and its faith had changed in the long run under communism. The Czechoslovakian revolution came very suddenly, late in the year. Rumors were wrong that the Czechoslovaks were apathetic, continuing long traditions of submissiveness they had learned under earlier empires, especially under Hapsburg rule. A whole generation of writers had been unable to publish. The 1989 Czechoslovakian revolution not only undid the ruling tyranny but before long evoked a promise of the withdrawal of Russian troops.

Noteworthy was the fact that there was a very charismatic popular leader, Václav Havel, who came from a very different segment of society than Lech Walesa of Poland. An intellectual who writes brilliantly, he proved not only courageous but politically astute. For example, he had contact with the Russian embassy through an intermediary (a popular singer) during the revolution, even as vast crowds of people were in the streets. (In this way he protected his flank!) Elected president, Havel appointed an ex-Communist as prime minister because of his ability—another act of political realism. Of course, Havel's political career is not yet finished, although he speaks of wishing to return to writing. He has been stubbornly ethical in his judgment. Immensely popular, he has helped to hold the nation together in a time of crisis and transition.

Ecumenical cooperation among Christians increased appreciably in the period of persecution, and Cardinal Tomášek was looked to as a common leader. How much cooperation will endure is a question. There is also the long-term issue of secularism as the nation integrates with Western Europe. Still, the nation has its own subculture and democratic models. Marxism had a chance to win a popular following in reform communism in 1968. When the Prague Spring was put down by the Russian army, all faith in "real socialism" was lost.

6

ROMANIA

Where Only Force Could Succeed

The Romanian revolution was different. In Poland and East Germany, citizens had not answered force with force; the churches held the populace back from a futile display of violence. In Hungary and Czechoslovakia as well, the change was peaceful. Not so in Romania. Blood was shed first on the evening of December 16, 1989, in the West Romanian provincial city of Timisoara. Rumors swept the country that thousands had been killed in the bloodbath; women and children were said to have been among the victims. In the end, the count ran only into the hundreds. Assuredly, that was terrible enough. When citizens returned the day after the first massacre, crying, "Give us our dead," troops fired again, and more innocent civilians were killed.

The crisis had begun quite unexpectedly in Timisoara when friends and parishioners of the pastor of the Reformed church, László Tökés, came to protest his departure. On orders from his bishop, the pastor was to be transferred to another area of the country. Everyone knew that the bishop was only conforming to the wishes of the Communist ministry of cults, to which he was fully subservient. He could not have been appointed without state permission and was paid by the government.

Pastor Tökés' father had long taught at the Protestant seminary in Western Romania. The son, a well-trained and capable preacher, had not limited his sermons to theology but spoke out against the mistreatment of the nation's 1,700,000 ethnic Hungarians. It was a provocative issue that the dictatorial regime had long suppressed. There could be no nationality conflicts under Communist rule — that was the official line. Istvan Tolnay, one of Tökés' supporters, explained: "They shut down our schools, our universities, our cultural institute. Pastor Tökés was the only one who stood up and said 'no' and spoke the truth."[1]

As the crowd in front of Tökés' home grew, the authorities hesitated, not sure what to do. Soon the Romanian army was ordered to intervene, and it killed hundreds, if not thousands, of civilians. "TI-MI-SHA-RAAA" became a rallying cry for what has been called Romania's half-finished revolution.

Events in Bucharest five days later were the watershed: the public defiance of dictator Nicolai Ceausescu—face-to-face by the multitude on the square in front of Communist party headquarters. Naively, he had supposed that the majority would cheer on his hardline rejection of perestroika. Instead, the echoing cries of "killer" and "Timisoara" called him to account for what he had labeled as only an incident set up by "foreign agents, hooligans, fascists and traitors."[2] Four days later, on Christmas Day, Ceausescu and his wife were executed in an act of tyrannicide.

ROMANIAN CHRISTIANITY AND CEAUSESCU'S COMMUNISM

Some 80 percent of Romanians belong to the Orthodox church. Their language is of Latin origin, but their religious heritage came from Byzantium. Certainly, even in Communist bondage, the Romanian Orthodox church was not as suppressed as the Russian church. It had its own national hierarchy and nearly as many sanctuaries as the Russian Orthodox church in the Soviet Union. Still, the fact was that in Romania, the Orthodox church was by no stretch of the imagination an agent of protest. Indeed, even as the revolution was taking place, its patriarch wrote a letter to the president, wishing him many more long years of happy rule. Ceausescu had long been eulogized uncritically, in Stalinist style. When the nation's tragedy became evident with the revolution, the patriarch resigned, but he was returned to office by the Holy Synod on the grounds that it had never accepted his resignation.

Nicolai Ceausescu was not above using religion to enhance his own image. The lie was that there had been freedom—at least some religious freedom—throughout the land. But there never was, under Communist rule. A church long subservient to secular rulers became the agent of the Communist regime. Ceausescu convinced the United States government to give his nation most-favored-nation status in foreign trade until he had to give up the farce. Ceausescu ruled Romania, carrying on his charade for nearly a quarter of a century. Stalinism, with its cult of personality, lived on, even when it was dead and dying throughout most of the rest of the world. The tragedy of Romanian life since the revolution is significantly and overwhelmingly his legacy. Neither an intellectual nor an imaginative person, he resisted perestroika to the end. His wife, Elena, who claimed to be a scientist, was deputy prime minister, while his relatives were interspersed everywhere throughout his dynasty. The land had become his fiefdom.

In Romania, religion has a popular following comparable only with that in Poland, in Eastern Europe. Folk piety lives on in power. Under the

Communists, institutional Christianity was fully encompassed by state tyranny and allowed no prophetic role. When the Communists came to power, the Romanian Orthodox church hierarchy, led by Patriarch Justinian, accepted and supported their rule. An enigmatic although somewhat charismatic leader, Justinian is said to have gone about his duties with a New Testament in one pocket and a copy of Marx's writings in the other. Many of his fellow countrymen could not have read either book! Still significantly a peasant land, the country was 27 percent illiterate when the Communists came to power at the end of the Second World War.

Support of the regime seemed a small price to pay for keeping religious observance alive in a Balkan ecclesiastical setting. After all, the country had been liberated from Turkish occupation hardly a century earlier. The hierarchy would save as much as could be saved; there would not be "an Albanian solution" in which all sanctuaries were closed and the practice of religion forbidden. The long-term problem was that patriarchs and bishops repeatedly went farther than was necessary to keep religion alive in the atheist state. As a village priest, Patriarch Justinian had been a friend of the Communist head of state, Gheorghiu-Dej. In fact, he had sheltered the young political radical when he was on the run from the secret police in fascist times. Justinian, at the politician's behest, was made first metropolitan and when Patriarch Nicodemus died early the next year, he became head of his church.

The Orthodox hierarchy under Justinian actually facilitated the Communist takeover and benefited from it. Uniates, Roman Catholics who observed the Eastern rite, had existed in the country since the end of the sixteenth century. Uniate Roman Catholic bishops and priests who were not prepared to be assimilated and become members of the Romanian Orthodox church were imprisoned. The Uniate church has been given freedom and reconstituted since the 1989 revolution. Thousands of Christians who opposed communism, not just the Uniates, were imprisoned and/or executed in the post-World War II terror. Most of those who remained alive were amnestied in 1964, when the regime looked for wider support in the population, seeking to reawaken nationalism against Russian influence.

The Orthodox church funeral ceremony was televised when Gheorghiu-Dej died and was buried in March 1965. To be sure, he was Ceausescu's predecessor as first secretary of the Communist party. Why a church burial? Romanian policy often eclectically combined a variety of motives and outlooks. Some party members did attend church from time to time, and many had their children baptized.

The lot of the nation could have been better if Ceausescu had not come to power. Communism had been imposed by the Russians in their conquest of Eastern Europe, and Ceausescu gained popularity at home and abroad by defying them. In particular, he refused to allow Romanian troops to participate in the 1968 invasion of Czechoslovakia and denounced it vehemently. During the cold war, many in the West nurtured the illusion that Ceausescu was promoting democratic freedom against the Soviet Union, in spite of all the evidence to the contrary. In fact, he ruled in the worst Stalinist fashion, allowing no ecclesiastical shelter for dissenting parties under the umbrella of the churches, as in Poland and East Germany.

After Ceausescu and his wife were executed by a firing squad on Christmas Day 1989, the political and ideological vacuum was all too clear. A small group of intellectuals called for the resignation of the patriarch after he was reinstated in office by the synod. The case against him was strong. He had long praised the dictator in extravagant terms that scandalized the religious conscience. No one in either church or state seemed to speak for the populace in general, which was preoccupied with day-to-day survival.

With respect to the churches, Orthodox and others, at least for the moment the problem was no longer one of state repression, although in the absence of private property and capital they still were dependent on government subsidies. Reform was the issue; all social criticism had been crushed in church ranks. Now the question was what leadership the churches could give, if any, to a new democratic order. The World Council of Churches had often been petitioned by dissenters asking it to speak out in protest against Romanian violations of human rights. The leadership of the Romanian Orthodox church threatened, virtually up to the revolution, to withdraw from the World Council if the Christian conscience was expressed in this way.

ROOTS OF RESISTANCE

All this does not mean that Romanians were entirely silent. In 1977, writer Paul Goma issued a human rights document comparable to the Czechoslovak Charter 77, but he found no support in Bucharest comparable to that in Prague. In fact, there were courageous martyrs tortured, exiled, and killed. Still the Orthodox hierarchy was so subservient that most of the time it did not even defend its own priests. Bishop Gherasim Cocosel, who was bold enough to speak out, had long since been "retired" to a monastery.[3] It is not debated that police oppression in Romania was among the worst in any satellite country. Typewriters were required to be registered with the police, along with a copy of their typeface; any underground press was thus preempted.

Romanian jails were brutal in their torture and inhumane procedures, and like the land itself under Ceausescu, they were places of terror. At least four thousand clergy passed through prisons and camps as the Communists consolidated power. An Orthodox monitoring group is reported to have a list of seventeen metropolitans and bishops and sixty-four priests who died in prison, the majority in the early period of the regime. Pitesti, used for Soviet dehumanizing experiments after the Second World War, was notorious.

It is important to understand what was distinctive about the revolution in Romania. The historical background must be considered, both short-term and long-term. Following the Second World War, the king attempted to change sides, joining the Allies rather than the Germans. He was not successful, and a Communist regime was installed by Stalin as he annexed eastern sections of the country to Russia. There were only a minimum of Communists in the nation. Some of them had been in Russia during hostilities; others had been in Romania. These two groups struggled against each other, and the locals won; their opponents were either jailed or executed.

By the early 1960s, the locals felt strong enough to begin to break ties with the USSR. No Russian troops were stationed on Romanian soil, even though the nation belonged to the Warsaw Pact. There was strong but suppressed resentment about the USSR's annexation of a large section of Moldavia. Russian names and signs disappeared from streets. The government was fostering nationalism, attempting to restore a distinctively Romanian consciousness. Romanian nationalism worked against russification. Indeed, it even reached to religion. Only when the Romanian government learned that Russian delegates or observers would not be present at the Second Vatican Council was a small Romanian delegation dispatched to Rome.

In Romania there was no Russian military intervention or military occupation against which to revolt, as in East Germany, Hungary, and Czechoslovakia (1953, 1956, and 1968). What was the Romanian revolution directed against? Not against outsiders or a regime that continued to be propped up from without. It was against a Romanian dictator, and this made the situation more difficult. No subculture, supported by religion or otherwise, had preserved national identity before Ceausescu's onslaught. Police suppression of opposition had been thorough and relentless.

At year's end in 1989, the revolution developed quite spontaneously, beginning at a Timisoara Protestant church and with university student protest, first in the provincial city and then in Bucharest. Its power and extent became clear as the head of state addressed a mass rally in the capital. Timisoara, the provincial center where the revolution began, has been described by an English reporter who was in Romania in late December 1989:

Timisoara is an unlikely town to have changed history. Like everywhere else in Romania, it is numbingly poor. Its medieval center is crumbling and its anonymous new apartment blocks, hurriedly built to house the villagers that the old regime had forced out of their homes, were in need of repair before they were even completed. Once a centre of learning, when it was part of Hungary, it is a kind of bleak town you want to forget as soon as you have passed through it.[4]

The scene of the massacre in Timisoara was renamed "Red Square," not in honor of communism but because of the blood that flowed there. "Romania was like a great glass with water full to the brim," one dissenter explained.[5] In Timisoara, it overflowed. Only recently, before his last trip to Iran, a major party congress had applauded Ceausescu with scores of standing ovations as he had attacked perestroika.

In Bucharest, workers were bussed in by the thousands, in usual fashion, for the mass rally that Ceausescu had called after his return from abroad. As they arrived on the morning of Thursday, December 21, they were told to be ready to cheer as he spoke from his balcony at midday. But as the students yelled out their jeers, the workers joined in, too, trampling on their banners. On television screens throughout the nation, viewers saw Ceausescu look bewildered and touched with terror as he left the balcony escorted by two bodyguards. So influential was the media coverage that what transpired subsequently was called a "tele-revolution."

Violence and hatred were the order of the day. Crowds continued to mill in the square throughout the afternoon and into the evening. Securitate forces observed them for hours, and then in the evening took their revenge on students in particular. Firing began at about 10:30 P.M. and continued for more than an hour. Then bodies were stacked up, identification removed, and they were taken away in trucks. Street-cleaning equipment was brought in, and the square cleared of bloodstains. But the revolution would not go away that easily.

The next day, part of the army seems to have changed sides. It became known that Defense Minister Vasile Milea had refused to order troops into battle. For this he was murdered and a false report given out that he had committed suicide. The army had an ambiguous role throughout the revolutionary period. It is significant that Ion Iliescu, the new head of state, used miners, not troops, to suppress demonstrations in the middle of 1990. Even some persons who wish him to stay in power, as there is no alternative, charge that he lies.[6]

Food supplies retained by the government were opened to the public after the revolution. Very soon they were exhausted, and many citizens were left hungry again. The economy was in shambles, and officials from the old regime, especially in the police and industry, remained in power in many places. Reporters from the English newspaper *The Observer* comment:

> In most traditional revolutions—the French and Russian revolutions, for example—one political class is replaced by another. The Romanian revolution has been more of a liberation than a revolution.
>
> The country's provisional Government [was organized] along lines that were all too familiar to the Romanian public—Communist Party lines. There was a Government, with ministers, but the real power lay in an Executive Council, a Politburo by another name. ... Many of the leaders of the Front were former Communists, who had held high

office under Ceausescu before falling from grace. At the provincial level, it includes many Army generals and bureaucrats who simply switched sides when it became clear that the dictatorship was crumbling.[7]

There is good evidence that the first student demonstrations in December were spontaneous and unplanned; later ones against the new regime were planned, and the government strategy was also reflected on in advance. In the initial days of the revolution, words like liberty, freedom, and democracy were shouted through the air. Feelings on both sides—the oppressor and the oppressed—were out of control. Everyone knew that the killing had been brutal in Bucharest the night after Ceausescu had been yelled down publicly. Securitate attacks on innocent civilians became promiscuous and random, intended to produce confusion, panic, and terror. It was only after a film clip of the dictator's death was shown on television that his supporters knew the end of his rule had finally come.

A LEGACY OF PROBLEMS IN BOTH STATE AND CHURCHES

Not surprisingly, Romania has been described as an enigma in which ambiguities and contradictions abound. Of course political and religious sentiments cannot be fully separated from each other. A strong Orthodox folk piety continues among a population that is still significantly peasant in orientation. Exiled Romanian historian of religion Mircea Eliade described its traditions and spirit at length. The intellectuals, to whom he belonged, remain only a small group, largely oriented toward the French culture. Romania was still under Turkish domination as the Enlightenment developed in Western Europe, and it did not reach Romania.

Both Orthodox and Protestant churches are filled with worshipers. Hungarians in Transylvania are Roman Catholic and Protestant (not Orthodox), and they attend services in larger numbers than citizens of the nearby motherland. In short, there is not the degree of secularization that there is in Western Europe, a situation that both Orthodoxy and communism are in part responsible for. Atheistic propaganda was often counterproductive. University students are sometimes reported to have come to church, especially after their required examinations in Marxism.

The end of the Communist regime left an enormous vacuum. A student remarked: "We don't know what freedom means. We don't know how to use freedom. We don't know to walk, to talk and to think free. We have only seen darkness and silence."[8]

Visitors interested in religion who came from abroad during the Ceausescu years were well advised to visit the minister of cults in Bucharest before proceeding elsewhere. Citizens living in the country knew that it was dangerous to speak with foreigners without state permission, and even then there could be harassment. At the ministry of cults, visitors would often receive an hour-long lecture eulogizing the status quo as one of freedom. However the facts were warped by what officials said, visitors still needed their permission to visit churchmen. State polity reflected the paradoxes of the Romanian situation, with its combination of Communist rule and widespread, deep piety. The Ceausescus, with all their idolatrous self-adulation, did not follow the pattern of Stalin or even of Khrushchev or Brezhnev. They were known to have attended baptismal services (with many bishops present) for their grandchildren.

In a country where private ownership of property was outlawed, the state gave subsidies to all officially recognized religious groups. These did not include the Uniate Greek rite Roman Catholic church, which was outlawed along with the Lord's Army, an Orthodox evangelical renewal group that still has a major following in the country. The latter grew up after the First World War around Orthodox priest Iosif Trifa and began to function openly again in 1990.[9] Most priests and pastors received a salary from the government comparable to that of a high school teacher; high-ranking clergy were paid more. Of course this meant control. Historic church buildings have been maintained by the state, but numbers of them were destroyed on Ceausescu's orders in an attempt to rebuild his capital city on a grand scale.

The fact is that, nurtured by the Orthodox church, Romanian popular piety remains alive; it has not died out under persecution as in Hungary or Germany. Of course the historical background is a very different one. Romania is a Balkan country that was long occupied by the Turks. From time to time, heroic Romanian leaders defeated the enemy, but the Turks just kept coming (as one Romanian put it), so close was their empire and so large their numbers. Christianity was tolerated as another "religion of the book" by the Muslim conquerors, and the Orthodox church and its hierarchy kept it alive under Turkish rule.

Citizens became accustomed to being passive under foreign sovereignty. The same outlook has continued in part under communism. To put the matter somewhat simply, Romanians have been more easygoing than the East Germans or Poles. Orthodoxy as a folk church from time to time evokes contempt from secular intellectuals. Still, one of the leading contemporary Romanian poets, Ion Alexandrn, a person of outstanding religious insight and fine literary ability, is significantly motivated by it, and his writings reflect its profundity.

The nationalities question exists primarily in western Romania. Transylvania, which became part of the country after the First World War, has a more religiously mixed population than the eastern part of the country. Germans have lived in Transylvania since the Middle Ages. They even had their own Protestant Reformation under the leadership of Honterus. Now, under economic and nationalist pressure, virtually all of them are leaving for Germany. The Germans in the Banat, in the majority Roman Catholic, were sent to the region by Empress Maria Theresa of Austria in the eighteenth century. Hungarians, Calvinist Reformed or Roman Catholic and not

Orthodox, constitute a larger community. Pressure on them to assimilate (to speak Romanian in the schools, for example) evokes tension and hatred on both sides. Nationalism was not acknowledged publicly in the Communist period, and now it has become inflammatory on both the Romanian and the Hungarian sides. Pastor Tökés, now Bishop Tökés, toured Hungary as a hero but lost in his attempt to win a seat in parliament in his own home in Romania. Non-Hungarians refused to vote for him.

The Orthodox form of Christianity came to the area under the influence of Byzantium especially in the ninth to eleventh centuries. Romanian nationalists have claimed a much earlier date for the beginning of Christianity in their country, even as early as the period of the Council of Nicea. When the Latins came into the area, they intermarried with the native people. Today Romanian, a Romance language, is interspersed with many Slavic borrowings. When Austrian Hapsburg armies recovered Transylvania from the Turks, the German and Hungarian parts of the population became dominant economically, politically, and even culturally. Now power relations have been reversed and the Romanians are in charge, insisting that citizens of all backgrounds speak their language in the schools. Religion is looked to for the defense of linguistic and ethnic heritages. In view of this background, Timisoara was not the unlikely place for violence that it first appears to have been.

Romania became a fully independent state in 1877. The two principalities of Wallachia and Moldavia had joined together earlier, in 1859. The Romanian Orthodox church was made autocephalous and given its own jurisdictional powers in 1885.[10] Baptist and other low-church Protestant movements entered only early in the present century. Their doctrine of the separation of church and state, as well as their emphasis on adult baptism, has not conformed to the Romanian Orthodox tradition. Partly for this reason, they have had significant growth. They have survived through persecution because of the conviction and sacrifice of believers. In the Communist period, even large church buildings erected by the free churches without state permission were bulldozed.

Following a decade of tolerance under their rule, the Communists began persecution of the Orthodox church itself. Monasticism was an excellent target from the state's point of view. At the beginning of the Communist takeover, there were some 10,000 religious. Their number dropped to 7,000 and then to 2,000 as functioning monasteries were reduced from 200 to 100. Recently the count has risen to nearly 125, and it is reported that monastic life is vital and alive. After the revolution, the head of one of the monasteries was proposed as replacement for the patriarch following the revolution, but he declined to be considered.

To care for its 80 percent of the population, the Orthodox church has over 8,000 parishes. Educational standards at the Orthodox academies in Sibiu and Bucharest are very high, and students are more numerous than in the USSR. Two of the most outstanding scholars, Constantin Galeriu and Dumitru Staniloaie (a systematic theologian whose writings are published in translation in the West), belong to the Group for Reflection and Renewal in the Orthodox church. This group is taking the lead in seeking a way out of the present dilemmas and weakness of the establishment.

One reason that Patriarch Justinian, who ruled from 1948 to 1977, was successful in preserving his church from more harm was that he had the help and support of Petru Groza, a leading Communist who was also a lay member of the Orthodox synod. It has been observed by a careful critic: "Justinian was the epitome of the enigmatic and complex Romanian character, with its astonishing—and to outsiders, infuriating—capacity to ignore, even to transcend, contradictions, a characteristic typical of the church today."[11] Caesaro-Papism, submission to and support from the state, dates from the time of Emperor Constantine. What was new was Communist supervision and control.

Justinian died in 1977 and was succeeded by Patriarch Justin, who was followed in 1986 by the present patriarch, who resigned and was reinstated after the revolution. Actually, all of the leading bishops had been compromised as collaborators with the old regime. At the same time, plans were made for a successor who was less tainted. Daniel Ciobetea was appointed the new Metropolitan of Moldavia and is unofficially in the line of succession to be the new patriarch. How large the change will be is not clear, and much depends on subsequent political developments. Religion changes more slowly than politics, a leading Romanian priest-émigré who lives abroad has observed.

Orthodox commentators in the West seem confident that there will not be regression or a return to subservience to the state on the pattern of the Ceausescu era. A law enacted in 1947 allowed the regime to dismiss a bishop for other than religious reasons.[12] How much of a change in policy will come about depends significantly on the courage of church leaders. The pattern of state repression so visible before the revolution is no longer in evidence.

In 1978 a religious-rights group called ALRC, initially organized by a number of Baptists, soon became a focus for grievances from all the churches.[13] Pavel Nicolescu was its chief spokesmen. "Our ideal is a free church in a free state that would allow dialogue and cooperation between the two," the founders observed. In spite of the fact that the first organizers were Baptists, Orthodox priests were attracted to it. Those who cooperated with it soon were disciplined by their bishops. A terror campaign was initiated against the organization in 1979. Some of its members were beaten and imprisoned, given truth drugs, and threatened with death.

The case of Orthodox priest Father Gheorghe Calciu-Dumitreasa, who now lives in exile in the United States, was an important one.[14] A medical student imprisoned for fourteen years, he vowed to become a priest, should God bring about his release. After he was ordained to the priesthood in 1973, he was appointed professor of New Testament theology at the

Bucharest Orthodox seminary. Calciu preached courageously against atheism as a "philosophy of despair" from the pulpit of the patriarchal cathedral. He drew crowds of young people including students and non-Christians, and copies of his sermons were distributed secretly throughout the country. Communism's ethical relativism, he argued, repudiates the value of the individual.

Calciu, as a member of the Lord's Army, sought to renew the Orthodox church. At the same time, he was concerned about the persecution of Christians of all nationalities and denominations. When he denounced the deliberate destruction of historic churches that had been personally ordered by Elena Ceausescu he was transferred from his seminary post and then arrested in March 1979. The Orthodox hierarchy did not come to his defense. Tortured, he was sentenced to ten years imprisonment by a closed court. When he was finally released, he was allowed to emigrate.

Baptists stand at the opposite pole from the Orthodox, as they insist on the complete separation of church and state. In this tradition, a group of Baptists even refused to work with the ALRC. Distancing themselves from all political action, they wished to devote their full efforts to evangelism instead. To their credit, they did articulate the clear separation of church and state as set forth in their own tradition. On the other hand, they proved impotent politically and failed to support others of their own number who protested against state abuse. Actually, political and religious issues were not fully separable. As far back as 1954, the president of the Baptist Union was given restrictive regulations by state officials and told to sign them in approval. When he refused to do so, a new president was forced on the union in his place. Three hundred is the figure commonly cited for the number of Baptist churches closed by the state in the 1960s.

By becoming apolitical, some ministers did escape arrest for a period. Among those not persecuted at first was Iosif Ton, a Baptist who had been sent to study at Oxford University in England. It is speculated that authorities had hoped that his faith would be weakened there by modernist theology. In all events, this was not the case. On his return, Ton championed the historic Baptist position on the separation of church and state, protesting against the submission to government control by his own denomination's leadership. He has been praised as the first Romanian to articulate the case for internal freedom in church life in the Communist era.

Ton went further, however. He preached that the "communist new man," unselfish and incorrupt, was best realized by becoming a committed Christian. Today the congregation where he once preached is still the fastest growing one among Baptists in the country, but he was long since dealt with by the regime. Attempting to be apolitical, Ton did not support his politically active fellow Baptists of the ALRC when they were expelled from the Baptist Union for their activism. The charge was that they were damaging its prestige by participating in an illegal political group. The union must enjoy the trust of the state, it was argued.[15] Ton was arrested following the March 1977 earthquake, held a month, and then released subject to the discipline of the Baptist Union's Central Council. Both his preaching and writing had a wide influence.

Baptists, with their doctrine of the complete separation of church and state, have a polity radically different from that of the Orthodox and their tradition of cooperation with the government. How the postrevolutionary situation will develop ecumenically remains to be seen. A third party is now represented officially. The Uniate Church, which practices the Eastern rite but is nonetheless Roman Catholic, has now been legalized, and diplomatic ties have been taken up with the Vatican. Orthodox members living in the West complain of the aloofness and very exalted view their hierarchy has of itself. How much the situation will improve ecumenically, if at all, remains to be seen. Christians of different traditions have lived together in the land for eight hundred years with little ecumenical progress. Yet there were positive developments in Romania's unfinished revolution. When President Iliescu met with leaders of the Orthodox church on July 10, 1990, they are reported to have asked for the release of student dissident leader Marian Munteanu. He had been beaten by a group of vigilante "miners" in the middle of June. Munteanu was released; for what reasons is not fully evident. The Orthodox church request was not a public one. Representatives of the four major churches belonging to the World Council of Churches came together in Cluj in the latter part of June to set up a national ecumenical platform. They expressed hope that other churches would join them and issued a statement saying that "the churches, whose identity is often linked with national identity, have a special responsibility to help reduce tension and create positive models of a multi-racial, multi-cultural society."[16]

CONCLUSIONS

The Romanian revolution was the most discouraging for a variety of reasons. Socially, religion was impotent. Ethnicity was an often determining factor in confessional differences. True, there was less dechristianization than in Hungary, Germany, or even Western Czechoslovakia. Folk piety remained; the sacred canopy had not been broken, as in Western Europe, in the period of two world wars. The Orthodox hierarchy showed little interest in any fundamental change and was unable to exercise influence for reform at all comparable with that of their Roman Catholic or Protestant counterparts in other Eastern European countries. Violent nationalist sentiment was rampant, and a large part of the population was not convinced of the value or necessity of popular democracy.

Anneli Ute Gabanyi, a longtime informed observer, argues that the Romanian revolution was in fact a stolen revolution.[17] Her thesis is that what took place was not a change of polity — the ethos and structure of government remained the same — but only of the ruling elite. Of course, there was revolt in the streets; the population was enraged against an incredibly self-eulogizing dictatorial regime that had lost touch with reality. The new regime understood that frenzied anti-Ceausescu sentiment was loose throughout the country. Early in 1990, some of the most notorious figures of the Ceausescu era were put on trial and given prison sentences, but most of the state functionaries continued as before. Almost immediately after the revolution, the Communist party in Romania was abolished. But the kind of government that was organized was one made up of a central committee and an accompanying body of officials on the Stalinist model.

Ideologically, Brezhnev's ideas, not those of Gorbachev, were in the forefront. Gabanyi cites the dossiers of the new minister president, Peter Roman, the leader of the Front's Council, Dumitrud Mazilu, and the oldest of the group, Silvan Brucan, to show that all were convinced Marxists. Much turns, of course, on how one views the ambiguous role and person of the new head of state, Ion Iliescu. Gabanyi describes him and his associates as internationalists who were opposed to self-contained isolationism practiced by the former dictator. But they were not, like Havel and Walesa, from an anticommunist background.

Gabanyi describes what took place in Romania as a "tele-revolution." The television station in Bucharest was the nerve center of the revolution, and its programs were telecast internationally to Budapest, Sophia, and Moscow. The individual in charge of the station, Stelian Pintilie, had been a high securitate functionary, and it was he who arranged for international programming. Iliescu showed up very early on national television, four days before the Ceausescus were executed, and was presented to viewers as the son of a revolutionary and a patriot.

Amid all the fury against the dictator and his personality cult, no non-Marxist ethical basis was provided in its stead. Incumbent officials by and large were left in place, and this was true religiously as well as politically. Drastic reform was not to be the course. Gabanyi charges that the populace was not politically mature in its election decisions. Students and other dissidents remained unsatisfied. They occupied streets of the inner capital city for weeks, and finally Iliescu called in the miners, who attacked and drove them away with violence. Western European governments, put off by what was a clear violation of human rights, slowed down their aid.

Romania had no democratic tradition comparable with that of Czechoslovakia or Western European countries. What was lacking most of all was an active citizens' movement that could attract widespread support, as in Poland. The new government, the Revolutionary Salvation Front, was no longer Communist in name, but opponents charged that it remained so in spirit and practice. What the future would hold was not clear. There was hunger in a potentially very rich agricultural country that stood on the edge of economic chaos. Many young people left for the West. The popular revolutionary cause which had done so much for freedom in other places had not succeeded in Romania. We have argued that part of the explanation was in the person of its dictator, Ceausescu. Religion did not have either the stabilizing or prophetic influence that it had elsewhere.

7

BULGARIA

An Ambivalent Revolt

As late as 1988 one of the best informed observers of religion in Eastern Europe wrote: "The situation of Bulgarian Christians in unlikely to change in any major way."[1] This evaluation proved mistaken because of the people's revolutions.

Actually, many Westerners paid little attention to Bulgaria until the attempted assassination of Pope John Paul II by a Turk who was apparently in the employ of the Bulgarian secret police. Sophia had been Moscow's closest ally in the Balkans, and the Bulgarian authorities were known to work closely with the Russian KGB. Zhivkov, the Bulgarian head of state, identified his country's friendship with the Soviet Union by saying that the two countries had "a single circulatory system." They also have closely related languages and both use the Cyrillic alphabet. Russian television has been sent directly to Bulgaria without translation.

Persecution of religion in the small country—half the size of Kansas—dates from the end of the Second World War. Religion's popular following was not as large and intense as in other areas of Eastern Europe, Poland and Romania, for example. Nor was Bulgarian nationalism as anti-Russian as in these two countries. The Orthodox Church had been a primary bearer of Bulgarian culture during centuries of Muslim political dominance, and Bulgaria had been part of the Ottoman Empire from 1396 to 1878, but only a few Bulgarians converted to Islam.[2]

Under Communist rule, dechristianization has been much greater than in many other places. The Orthodox hierarchy was tolerated and its historical role recognized, but it was controlled fully by the Communist authorities. Bulgarian bishops, for example, were forced to be spokesmen for the Communist peace movement at international conferences. The Communists still kept a few monasteries open for tourists but by and large this part of Eastern Orthodox Christianity was dismantled.

In 1985, the thirteenth centenary of Christianity in the country was celebrated with participation of Orthodox clergy but under strict state control. It was symbolic that 114 Communist party officials ranked ahead of Patriarch Maxim in the seating arrangements.[3] The Marxist leader of the country, Todor Zhivkov, mentioned the church only briefly and in a derogatory fashion.

Dechristianization has not been possible without persecution. As Communist rule set in, thousands of persons, laity and clergy alike, were sent to prison for religious belief. Three hundred and sixteen out of 2400 priests were imprisoned at the Belene Island concentration camp.[4] Metropolitan Stefan at first welcomed the new postwar regime. Bulgaria had fought on the German side in both world wars, and initially the Russians were seen as fellow Slavs and liberators. Soon, however, the Metropolitan recognized their Stalinist tactics which he opposed. Forced into retirement, he probably would have been executed except for his international reputation.

As hostilities came to an end after the Second World War, non-Communist democratic forces organized a Peasants' Party and in spite of harassment won a major block of votes in the nationwide election. Very soon, however, the Russians hanged its leader and totalitarian rule set in with an accompanying attack on religion.

Metropolitan Stefan's successor, Exarch Paisi, also was forced out of office because he opposed Communist strategies. Exarch Kiril, who followed him and became first Patriarch of Bulgaria in 1953, compromised but resisted effectively. By the early 1960s, however, the majority of the population had given up religious practice. A general amnesty for believers was announced in 1964, and the situation improved for all but the Muslims beginning in 1970. But legal restrictions against contact with the outside Christian world remained debilitating. As late as 1982 a gift of Bibles from abroad was refused out of fear, as it came from foreigners.[5] To the present, the majority of church buildings are either closed or in disrepair.

The people's revolution of 1989 was less dramatic than in the other satellite countries but none the less powerful in its impact on Bulgaria.[6] Zhivkov, the Communist party leader, had ruled the country as Moscow's regent since the end of the Second World War. On November 10, the day after the opening of the Berlin wall, he was removed from office. The myth that he had resigned voluntarily lasted only a few days. With his demise, the persecution of religion was abandoned.

The larger part of Bulgarian history has been Christian. Nationality and religion long have been associated. The Bulgars were a Slavic speaking Turko-Mongol tribe, and they were converted from paganism by Saints Cyril and Methodius in the ninth century. It was these missionaries who devised the Cyrillic alphabet. Christian loyalty remained strong down through intervening ages and only a few Bulgarians known as Pomaks changed loyalties to Islam. By the time of the Enlightenment in Western Europe the Orthodox Church however came to be dominated by unpopular

Greeks from Constantinople. In this situation, the church was unable to give as much moral or intellectual leadership to the nation as might have been expected after independence in 1878. Still its link with the monarchy was not simply negative. To his credit, for example, King Boris successfully defended the Jews against the Nazis, saving the lives of thousands.

Under the Communists, there was intense antireligious education and in less than two decades more decline of religion than elsewhere in Eastern Europe. Even after Zhivkov's fall, the Communist party remained in power. Subsequently, when it changed its name to the Bulgarian Socialist Party and allowed free elections, the old leadership won by a very narrow margin.[7] Reformed democratic sentiments were dominant in the capital and other major cities and they continued to be influential. But the opposition had been overconfident, too sure of victory. Still the wave of change which swept over Eastern Europe was not escaped. Former rulers were forced into coalition. The attempt to establish a free democratic political system and a market economy had begun.

In spite of forty years loss of political and religious freedom under the Communists, it must be said that some economic and social progress was made, especially initially. At the end of World War II, three-fourths of Bulgaria's population lived in villages and engaged in small-scale farming. Today about two-thirds of the population is urban and only one-fifth agricultural. Secularization has accompanied the movement from the countryside.

A legacy of backwardness dated from the century-long Turkish occupation. Now, after the Second World War, a significant middle class grew up, although without the entrepreneurship of a capitalist economy. Above all else it was perestroika in the USSR which was responsible for change in Bulgaria whose Communist regime fell into step only reluctantly. It was commonly said that "restructuring" more than openness was the order of the day. Restructuring had been perennial under the Zhivkov regime as part of its own political strategy to remain in power. It was the new developments in Russia that made possible organization of a variety of human rights and environmental groups.

Richard Crampton, writing in *The World Today* on "The Intelligentsia, the Ecology and the Opposition in Bulgaria," argues that Bulgarian intellectuals held strong feelings during the second half of the 1980s.[8] But, he claims, initially they had no unifying cause. It was, he maintains, the environmental issue which turned out to be crucial for them. As a result of perestroika in Russia, Bulgarians came to believe that "the gamekeeper had turned poacher." Bulgarian intelligentsia who "had eyes for the prized birds of openness and freedom" felt that at last the restraining fear had been removed.[9] Crampton argues that early in 1988 the Bulgarian intelligentsia closed ranks to save the planet.

A public exhibition in the Danubian city of Ruse made it clear for all to see that there was a large and dangerous amount of lung disease. It was undoubtedly caused by the discharge from a metallurgical plant located on the Romanian bank of the Danube. Periodically chlorine gas was being emitted. Simply put, Ruse was being poisoned. As this became well known, mass protests followed and a committee was organized. A popular article of February 17 observed that it was painful to live in Ruse. For not only was the natural environment unhealthy, but also the moral environment suffered, and these unhealthy changes were becoming increasingly serious. The population of the town, it was observed, was suffering from depression, and a feeling of hopelessness prevailed. It had lost its confidence in the future.[10]

Human rights issues and concern for the environment became joined together in a pattern somewhat similar to that in East Germany. Already, as early as November 1987 a number of Sofia University intellectuals, many of whom were Communist Party members, had organized the Discussion Group for the Support of Glasnost and Perestroika. Largely from its constituency the Independent Association for the Defense of Human Rights was organized in January of 1988. When the Ruse environmental committee was forcibly disbanded by the government, a number of its former members founded Ecoglasnost, a well organized national ecological association in March 1989.

A month earlier, in February, Zhivkov, as head of the communist state, had warned the intelligentsia that he would not tolerate national nihilism or negative attitudes toward the country or toward socialism. His warning was ignored. Meanwhile a Democratic League for the Defense of Human Rights in Bulgaria Against Assimilation had been organized, primarily for the defense of the Turkish minority. The Bulgarian authorities unwisely expelled a number of the league's leaders shortly before the May-June Paris Conference on Security and Cooperation in Eastern Europe. In France, they were lionized as guests, and Bulgarian communism's abuse of its Turkish minority came into full view.

In fact, the perversity and incompetence of the Communist regime was most evident from its persecution of its Muslim citizens. Islamic holidays, circumcision, and other traditional ceremonies were banned and Muslim women required to do military service along with men. Turks number about 800,000 in the country and Pomaks, descendants of Bulgarians who became Muslims in the Ottoman Empire, about 150,000. There are Tartars and Gypsies as well, in all about 1.2 million Muslims in the population. Their birth rate is higher than that of other citizens and estimates are that as many as sixty percent continue some religious practice. This is the case in spite of the fact that many copies of the Koran have been destroyed and whole Muslim villages sacked.

Pomaks were required to adopt Slavonic names in the early 1970s and in 1984 the Communists forced the same requirement on the Turks.[11] The regime's motivation seems to have been a combination of pathological revenge for earlier Ottoman oppression, fear of the present high Turkish birth rate, and the haunting spectre of militant Islam. Persecution of the Turkish minority apparently was decided upon in secret by the Party Central Committee. Moscow was not pleased but did not oppose the new measures openly. Neither did the government of Turkey, as it did not want to lose access to its main trunk line route to Europe. Finally though, Turkey did open its borders and some 300,000 Bulgarian Turks suddenly emigrated; later about 90,000 returned. The economic consequence was that the labor force in Bulgaria was depleted. Politically, the regime was shown to the world in all its antiminority bias.

Michael Shafir emphasizes the xenophobic character of communism in both Romania and Bulgaria. In each land there was deep fear of strangers, and reform became the chief target of the ruling regimes.[12] In principle, the outlook was the opposite of international socialism. In Romania, Shafir argues, the reaction and bias against Islam were overt; in Bulgaria xenophobic communistic attitudes were more covert.

In the eyes of the Bulgarian regime, the demonstrations which took place in the eastern part of the country in May and June, 1989 seemed to pose a threat comparable with the Polish Solidarity movement. In consequence, the protest was crushed brutally. The Bulgarian foreign minister admitted that seven persons were killed. Amnesty International listed eleven victims. In mid-August, there was again violence and more deaths.

Already as the first crisis had developed, Zhivkov, speaking on state television on May 29, accused foreign forces of instigating tensions and a slanderous campaign against Bulgaria. The regime organized rallies in late May and early June in Sofia and other cities against the Turks. Even the Bulgarian Orthodox Church was mobilized on the false charge that the building of the Bulgarian Church of Saint Ivan of Rila in Instanbul, for many Bulgarians one of their holiest shrines, had been stoned and damaged.

The shift in the attitudes of the Bulgarian Church against the Communists did come quickly. When prayers were held in St. Dimitar Cathedral for the opposition movement and in remembrance of Father Popieluszko, the recent Polish martyr, the committee organizing the memorial was rebuked by the Patriarch. Similiarly, the founder-initiator of the Independent Committee for the Defense of Religious Rights, Freedom of Conscience and Spiritual Values, the Orthodox priest, Christofor Sabev, who had been arrested for his defense of the Turkish and Muslim minorities, initially did not have the support of the Orthodox Church hierarchy and in fact he was reprimanded by Patriarch Maxim.

Several thousand citizens joined Sabev in a protest march in Sofia during December 1989 shortly after Zhivkov lost power.[13] The demonstrators called for legal guarantees of religious freedom, religious education in the schools, the viewing of worship services on television and freedom for clergy to work in hospitals. As the political situation allowed more openness, the Holy Synod of the Orthodox Church presented its own list of requests to the National Assembly. They included the end of state interference in the life of their church and the return of seized monasteries and churches along with their icons. New churches needed to be erected, the Synod argued, the theological seminary of Gara Cerepis must be returned, and the clergy's right to visit hospitals must be confirmed legally. In response to these demands, a new religious policy was formulated by the government after a roundtable discussion in which all religious groups participated. Bulgaria and the Vatican resumed diplomatic relations. (Unlike Romania and Russia, Roman Catholic Uniates in Bulgaria had not been forced to merge with the Orthodox.[14])

Overall, religious problems have not been as pressing or loyalties as intense as elsewhere in Eastern Europe. Certainly the Bulgarian intelligentsia has been more secular than the Russian. There can be little doubt that there was major dechristianization and that religious faith and practice declined under the Communists. And it appears now that nationalism has taken the place of communism without any popular religious revival. Still there is new freedom, the reopening of closed churches and opportunities for religious education and social service as well as foreign church inter-church contacts. How much will the opportunity be grasped? How much vitality will the church show?

While Western Europe was experiencing the Reformation, the Renaissance, and the Enlightenment, Bulgaria was still under Turkish rule. The Orthodox Church had a major role in preserving national identity throughout a long history of Muslim political dominance. However, it was seldom if ever a major force for democratic liberalization. In the post-World War II era, nationalist sentiment was not anti-Russian in Bulgaria as in Poland and Romania. Nor was it as much tied to religion. Now a largely nonviolent transition from bureaucratic Communist dictatorship toward pluralism, multiparty democracy, and a market economy has been made, and it offers new opportunities for religion. In appraising the future, it must not be forgotten that throughout a long past, "Bulgaria has continually produced Christians of high caliber with a remarkably open approach to those from other traditions."[15] In that inheritance, one may hope, lies the possibility of new developments, now that the heavy hand of state oppression has been lifted.

8

ALBANIA

"Some tourists in 1986 described the experience of visiting Albania as like being on another planet. The atmosphere of repression created a sense of emptiness and meaninglessness."[1] So reported Broun in *Conscience and Captivity* two years later and added: "No country in Europe today is more impenetrable in its self-imposed isolation, or more paranoid in its attitude toward the outside world, than Albania during and since the four-decade rule of Enver Hoxha."[2] Information was very difficult to obtain about conditions in the country. Albanians who attempted to cross the border were shot and tourism was minimal.

The reasons for this isolation are varied. For instance, the Albanian language is very difficult to learn for those to whom it is not native. Long a part of the Ottoman empire, in many respects the country has been the most backward in all of Europe. In mountain villages in the north, pagan beliefs persist to the present. The ancient Law of Lek prescribes rules for honor, loyalty, and vengeance.

Albanians are a single racial and linguistic group, although there have been two subdivisions, the Gegs and the Tosks. About half of the Albanian people live in Yugoslavia or elsewhere today. They are descendants of an Indo-european people who settled in the Balkan Peninsula about the end of the Bronze Age, perhaps as early as 1000 B.C.E. Known as the Illyrians, they had their own independent kingdom until they were conquered by the Roman Empire in 168 B.C.E.

The regime was not pleased when it became known in the West that in 1972 the 74-year-old priest, Father Stefen Kurti, was executed for secretly baptizing a fellow prisoner's baby at the mother's request.[3] Word also reached the outside world in 1977 that Father Fran Mark Gjoni was sentenced to twelve years in a labor camp when some Bibles and other religious literature were discovered in his attics.[4] He had found them in parks and on the seashore, he said. The latter is possible as outsiders have floated Bibles into Albania in plastic sacks.

The Albanian decree banning all religion was issued in 1967. By September of the year all churches, mosques and monasteries, some 2,169 in all, had been closed.[5] Denis R. Janz, Professor of history of Christianity at Loyola University in New Orleans describes "Rooting out Religion: The Albanian Experiment" as follows:

> Other countries' efforts to destroy religion look like child's play compared to the Albanian campaign. Nowhere else was the pressure on religion so brutal and sustained. Albania was in fact unique in outlawing all forms of religious practice and belief, and in officially proclaiming itself the first and only atheist state in the world. Here, the Party alleged, was the sole exemplar of a truly religionless society. Here alone was it claimed that the great post-Enlightenment dream of the death of religion had been fulfilled.[6]

A year after the overthrow of communism in the former satellite countries of Eastern Europe, revolutionary changes that observers had speculated would require decades to accomplish were taking place in a period of months. Easter was celebrated openly in Albania in the spring of 1991 for the first time in almost a quarter of a century. Bells rang from the towers of both Orthodox and Roman Catholic churches as each honored Christ's resurrection on its respective calendar.[7]

Mosques and churches were reopened slowly. The nation of some three million citizens on the mainland of the southern Adriatic coast is also the only one in Europe to have a Muslim majority. For the first time in twenty-three years, on January 18 in Tirana, Muslims held a worship service where hundreds of persons prayed together at the Etem Bey mosque in the ritual led by Mufti Ibrahim Bala, while fifteen thousand observers stood by.[8]

As in other areas of Eastern Europe, economic collapse facilitated religious change. A contributing cause was the drought which had slowed industry and left farms dry in 1990. Half-humorously and sometimes very seriously there was talk of divine retribution, although if this were the case no one seemed to know why it had been so long delayed. *The Economist* asked:

> Is Albania's the first revolution caused by global warming? A dry summer parched Albania's rivers, halting hydroplants which make most of its electricity. Chrome production, Albania's industrial staple, slowed. By the autumn factories in other industries were shutting down and food was scarce. Irreparable Chinese tractors rusted in the fields, and private gardens, though now legal, went dry. In December jobless workers joined fed-up students on the streets.[9]

Evident everywhere was the longtime cause of revolution: the backwardness and decline of the economy. Finally students and workers demonstrated; some protests included religiously motivated believers. Four days before Christmas the last statue of Stalin was torn down. In its place, there were requests for a statue of Fan S. Noli, the Orthodox Bishop who was the first democratic president of Albania after the first world war.[10] Earlier during the second week of December 1990, the Albanian army was called in to put down riots in several towns, and 160 rioters who had been arrested faced trial for illegal assembly.[11]

As early as January 11, 1990 at Shkodra in North Albania, thousands of persons had protested against the persecution of religion.[12] They asked in particular for the reopening of churches. Four hundred were arrested and 120 held over a period of time. A young Albanian had commented: "I place my hope in the young people of Shkodra. I pray every day that we will one day create the revolution." How much has the revolution become a reality? The end of Stalinism would mean the possibility of reform from within and an opening to outside.

In response to other protests as well (some of which we will note), Albania's President-Dictator, Ramiz Alia, announced free elections on short notice, and they were held at the end of March 1991.[13] Not unexpectedly, the Communists won, partly by intimidation and partly because of fear of change. But few if any problems had been solved by this strategy. Abortion had been banned and large families encouraged by the regime and the population is expected to reach four million by the year 2000.

New pressure was put on the government in mid-1990 as thousands of young people had crowded into Western European embassies in the capital city seeking asylum. After unsuccessful attempts to starve them out, some five thousand were bused out of the country secretly by night.[14] Early in 1991, there was mass flight by ship to Italy across the Adriatic Sea.[15] It was a small counterpart to the East German exodus to the West in 1989. The Italian government, unable to cope with the influx, attempted to send some of the dangerously overcrowded vessels on which the refugees had arrived back to Albania. The plight of the men, women and children on board was indeed pathetic. Many of the emigrants had travelled for days without food, water or medical supplies.

Meanwhile, in Albania, there was not even the remnant of an organized party of Christians able to help the victims, much less to direct revolution into humane channels. For decades this Stalinist land arrested citizens for the slightest religious gesture. Making the sign of the cross, for example, was punishable by three years of imprisonment.[16] Only a short while before the revolution a citizen was given a five-year sentence for wearing a crucifix, and another received ten years for being found in possession of a Bible. There were reports of emigrants to the West who said that they had been baptized but did not even know what the Bible is. A Muslim recounted that his father had often muttered behind a curtain, but his son did not know at the time that he was praying. Among Muslims, a pragmatic atheism persisted throughout the Communist tyranny, based on the principle of *taqiya*, which permits one to conceal or even deny faith under persecution.

At Skanderbeg Square in the heart of Tirana on February 20, 1991, a huge crowd chanted against the deceased dictator, "Hoxha Hitler." The tall gilded statue of the former head of state, dominating the square, was tumbled down with cables.[17] Hoxha, the Stalinist dictator who had ruled for four decades from the outset of communism until his death in 1985, was of Muslim descent.

Before the coming of the Communists, the Roman Catholic Church had been the best organized religious body in the nation. Albanians have a very long Christian history. St. Jerome was of Albanian descent, as is Mother Teresa. The bishopric of Durrachium (Durres) is reputed to have been established in 66 A.D. with seventy Christian families.[18] The Albanian, Bishop Astio, was one of the first Christian martyrs.

The checkered history of the land to the present has been strongly conditioned by its geography. The Albanians moved farther north when the region was invaded by the Goths and the Huns in the fourth century and the Bulgars in the fifth. It is remembered that an independent state was established by Prince Progon in 1190 and lasted until the middle of the thirteenth century. In the middle of the fourteenth century Albania was conquered by the Serbs.

It is only in the later period that Islam became predominant. The Ottoman Turks invaded at the end of the fourteenth century. Albanians waged a twenty-five-year-long war for their independence led by the freedom fighter, George Kastriota, called Skanderbeg who is still eulogized in Albania literature to the present. In the end, the Albanians lost, and in 1468 their land became a part of the Ottoman empire.

Only after the war which began in 1912 did they finally win renewed national freedom. Albania's independence was recognized by the great powers after the First World War, although nearly half of ethnic Albanians were assigned to the new Yugoslavia. In Albania proper, beginning in 1925, Ahmet Zogu reigned first as president and then from 1928 until 1939 as King Zog I. Although he cooperated with Mussolini's Fascist Italy out of economic necessity, in April 1939 he was overthrown by the Italians and the country annexed by them. Finally, after the Second World War, communism was installed. It is important for later developments that Albanian Communists conquered after the Second World War without Russian help; in this they were virtually unique.[19]

The Communist attack on religion initially did not meet as wide resistance as in Poland, for example. The new regime maneuvered to split Muslim leadership and Christian bishops and their clergy were imprisoned and executed. Before the Second World War, there were 220,000 Orthodox faithful in 200 parishes and 29 monasteries; Roman Catholics numbered 124,000 in 123 parishes.[20] The Orthodox Archbishop Kristofor Kissi was deposed in April 1949 and subsequently tortured to death. Another Orthodox archbishop, three bishops, and numerous priests disappeared. It is estimated that 30 Franciscans, 13 Jesuits, and 60 parish priests were executed or died in labor camps. Under the Communists, all Catholics were branded Fascists.

Limited tolerance was given by the regime when the church finally was legalized on July 30, 1951.[21] Religious activity was limited to worship services. Often Hoxha quoted the statement of a leading nineteenth-century Roman Catholic, Vaso Pashko, "The religion of Albanians is Albanianism."[22] Religious persons were publicly mocked and there were atheist mass meetings. Finally in 1967, inspired in part by Mao's Communist Cultural Revolution, all places of worship were closed, including 2,169 mosques.

Albanians have not been known as intensely, much less fanatically, religious, and Greek Orthodox and Roman Catholic Christians long have lived side by side with Muslims without major hostility. The Bketashis, a heretical Muslim sect known popularly as the Dervishes, has a significant following.[23] Charismatic and tolerant, Albanian culture mixes Christian and Muslim elements in a manner that appeals to Albanians. By contrast, Janz reports:

> When Stalin died in 1953, Hoxha knelt in tears before the statue in Tirana's city square and vowed his undying loyalty. It was not an empty gesture. . . . In Hoxha's view, religion was an embarrassing stain on the national life, and the country's first task was a merciless, life-and-death struggle to eliminate it.[24]

The semireligious character of the attack on Faith in God was evident enough. A ruthless and paranoid person, Hoxha boasted a pseudo-intellectualism that surpassed that of most other party bosses in Eastern Europe. Part of his Marxism had been learned in France where he lived for a few years before the Second World War. As a dogmatic Communist, he was fully convinced that religion only stood in the way of social progress and in 1967 it was completely forbidden.

Under Hoxha, Albania changed sides in the Communist movement a number of times. Against Yugoslavia, he was allied with the Russians for support. And when Khrushchev sought reconciliation with Tito, Hoxha switched to the Chinese. He became disillusioned with China when Mao received Nixon. Albania it seemed was to be the only pure Stalinist land. Now in need of economic aid, it seeks to rejoin Europe. But membership in the European community requires greater respect for freedom and human rights as well as tolerance for religion. And so in sudden and radical reversal, religion is again being allowed to function.

Albania did not sign the Helsinki Human Rights accords. In Stalinist style, its draconian measures led to some degree of modernization and change.[25] There has been economic development of heavy industry on the Eastern European Communist pattern. Almost universal literacy was achieved. Three quarters of a million persons were reported to be attending schools. As Stalinism receded, there was said to be lingering resentment against the antireligious policy but as was so often the case in Eastern

Europe no organized opposition was powerful enough to overthrow it until other conditions changed.

Typically, the Communist cadres became sterile and uncreative. Alia, Hoxha's self-designated successor, has sought to improve the situation without losing control, and other members of the ruling elite have supported him in working for moderate change. But following the demise of communism in other former satellite countries, street riots and the flight of refugees suddenly ran ahead of his strategy. While continuing to employ brutal police methods to stem the tide, he simultaneously looked for a broader base of popular support. Sigurimi, the secret police, has been reigned in and border guards in November halted the shooting of fugitives.

In December 1990, following protests at Tirana University, the regime allowed organization of an opposition democratic party headed by a professor of economics and a professor of cardiology.[26] Most of the party's senior members had to resign from the Communist Party in order to take on their new role. This much, along with religious freedom, was a necessary concession for the much sought after Western economic help. It is difficult to say how deeply the changes will penetrate.

In mid-August 1990, Mother Teresa came for three days to Tirana to visit graves of her sister, mother, and other near relatives. She was introduced to the president of the Albanian Red Cross, met the foreign minister, and even the widow of Hoxha. But she was not authorized to establish a house of her order The Missioners of Charity. Religion's future in the land, positively or negatively, will turn ultimately on Christian-Muslim relations.[27] Father Simon Jubani, who celebrated mass in Shkodra, is a leader in the organization of a Peoples' for Religious Unity, which includes members of all religious groups. The leading Muslim Mufti speaks optimistically about the new opportunities for religious instruction and the possibility of collecting and using funds for religious purposes. In the new Albanian constitution religious freedom is guaranteed by articles 53 and 55.

Again events have moved so quickly that it is difficult to sort out important and lasting trends from ephemeral occurrences.

9

RUSSIA

Filling a Religious and Moral Vacuum

On Sunday, June 17, 1990, the Russian Orthodox liturgy was celebrated in St. Isaac's cathedral in Leningrad for the first time in fifty years. Located near the Winter Palace (where the Russian Communist revolution began), it is the largest church in the city that was the capital of the nation from Peter the Great to Lenin. St. Isaac's cathedral can accommodate thirteen thousand worshipers. Constructed in the form of a cross and first dedicated in 1858, it was built to rival St. Peter's church in Rome. Many serfs either lost their lives or won their freedom by sharing in the work. Forty years were required for its completion.

RUSSIAN ORTHODOXY AND THE COLLAPSE OF COMMUNISM

In 1931, the Communist rulers of the country turned the former sanctuary into a state anti-religious museum. They hung a Foucault pendulum under its central dome. "No Soviet 'Museum of Atheism' was complete without one," symbolizing the victory of scientific discovery over religion and superstition.[1] The rotation of the earth (a modern scientific idea, compared to the traditional religious notion that the earth is steadfast) is illustrated by the pendulum; its great ball changes position as the planet moves.

The crowd inside and outside the church on June 17 was so large that traffic was stopped for several hours. Parts of the liturgy were shown on state television. Boris Yeltsin, president of the Russian federation, attended and commented that the event was "a tribute to what is being done [by the church] for the morality and purification of the people and that the state should work side by side with the Church for the sake of spiritual and moral values."[2]

What was going on needed to be understood in relation to two different attitudes, the long held Communist fear that religion would be a revolutionary force against the regime and the contemporary hope that it would be a revolutionary force rejuvenating civil society and national life. In fact, the fear of religion's potents for engendering revolution (although they were labelled "reactionary") goes far toward explaining why it was persecuted so relentlessly by the state in the USSR for seven decades.

During the period of persecution, the Communist state also turned the Orthodox Leningrad cathedral of Our Lady of Kazan, a building located prominently on Nevsky Prospect, with a gracious semicircular colonnade of Corinthian columns, into a museum of religion and atheism. Unlike St. Isaac's cathedral, it was not reopened for religious worship in 1990. A wide variety of often life-sized antireligious exhibitions long stood in the former sanctuary. More recently, the former church had been redesignated a museum of the history of religions and atheism. On the steps of Kazan cathedral in 1990, free-church Christians could be seen preaching openly and proclaiming their faith with enthusiasm.

There was a radical break with the Communist past. Beginning the year before the people's revolutions in the satellite countries, 1988, religion was given new freedom in the USSR. A year after the revolutions, 1990, this freedom was enacted into law in Russia itself.

It was all part of a growing religious scene. At the beginning of October 1990, the Supreme Soviet enacted, by a vote of 341 to 2, a new nationwide law on "Freedom of Conscience and Religious Organizations."[3] The statute guarantees every citizen's right to adopt, practice, and proselytize his faith or to profess no religion at all. The law also requires state officials to respond within a month to a request for the return of a church building seized by the Communists. The request need not be granted, but it must be considered. Patriarch Alexi II, the newly elected head of the Russian Orthodox church, especially commended the legalization of churches' charitable work and the authorization given for the religious education of children. "It's a major event in the spiritual life and renaissance of our society and its spiritual and moral education," he said.

The ideological collapse of communism had left an immense vacuum in Russian society—moral as well as religious. Could earlier Christian traditions now be called on to fill it? Some observers even argued that the Russian intelligentsia was less secularized than that of the West. Marxism had not supplied anything which could take the place of religion at a deep level. To be sure there was controversy among different religious groups. Churches earlier belonging to the Ukrainian Greek Catholic church, affiliated with Rome, had been handed over to the Orthodox church on Stalin's orders following the Second World War. Many of them were now being given back. It was a revolutionary step. A new policy was not put into effect simply as an expression of goodwill on the part of the state. Call for the return of the Greek Catholic Uniate churches—the circulation of petitions, large street demonstrations, and even hunger strikes—made clear that religion could be a dangerous revolutionary force if repressed.[4]

For the first time in fifty-six years, the full hierarchy of the Ukrainian Greek Catholic church (of the Eastern rite) was able to meet together openly. It did so in Rome on June 25–26, in audience with Pope John Paul II. Bishop Philemon of Lutsk (auxiliary of Lvov) was the spokesman.

The Bishop described the USSR as a society in moral collapse. From the earliest days of the revolution, there was an attack on the family, and now divorce has become a commonplace. . . . The unnatural economic system, Bishop Philemon continued, has destroyed basic ethics—since an honest worker could no longer expect honest pay. As a result, corruption, deceit, and dishonesty are everywhere. After so many years of demagoguery and abuse, people no longer have any respect for civil authority. In the villages, family life has been damaged and love for the land almost destroyed by forced collectivisation, so that the young people are leaving the villages in droves. Substance abuse is a mass phenomenon; there is no family which does not suffer from the results of alcoholism.[5]

Recognizing the moral crisis of the society, the state has decided to give religion a more positive role in public life. In short, the need for a moral revolution was recognized. Daily television carries scenes of churches and priests, mostly Orthodox, portraying them positively. What the future of religion will be, how powerful a force it will prove itself, is by no means clear. On September 23, 1990, the new patriarch presided over a worship service in Upensky cathedral, within the walls of the Kremlin in Moscow.[6] The mayor of Moscow, Gavriil Popov, attended. It was in this church—constructed before the discovery of America—that czars were crowned; conquered princes swore allegiance under its five onion-shaped domes. After the liturgy, thousands of people walked through the Kremlin's Trinity Gate to downtown Moscow and on to the Church of the Great Ascension. Some of the marchers carried banners with the slogan: "We are Russians. God is with us."

The banners made evident that nationalism and religion are joined in Russia, as they have been elsewhere in revolutionary power. If a strongly nationalist regime of the type advocated by Solzhenitsyn were to come to power, Orthodoxy might well supply its ideology. If a reform government continues, religious institutions at least can expect greater freedom.

On July 10, 1991, with Mikhail Gorbachev in attendance, Patriarch Alexi blessed Boris Yeltsin at his inauguration as President of the Russian Republic. The dramatic reversal of the fortunes of the Orthodox Church could hardly have been more graphically depicted by Cecil B. DeMille.

Among the population at large, there is religious revival. How large it is is debated. One of the best-informed specialists on religion in the USSR, Jane Ellis of Keston College, has written:

The reality is a slow, gradual, often painful process of people redis-covering their Christian roots. . . .

The return of large numbers of the intelligentsia to the Russian Orthodox Church is very remarkable. This is so not only because it is an outright rejection of decades of atheist propaganda and the whole of the future toward which the Communist Party of the Soviet Union is striving. The present-day Russian intelligentsia has a profound awareness of its own history and roots, and cannot be ignorant of the irony that its members are finding a path to the future in a church which their forebears dismissed with contempt a century ago.[7]

The extent of religious belief among citizens in general is not fully cer-tain. A public-opinion poll taken by the All-Union Public Opinion Research Center in Moscow reported that the number of persons declaring them-selves as Orthodox had increased from 19 percent to 33 percent from December 1989 to April 1990. The report, if correct, indicated the fluidity of the religious situation.[8]

The 1990 mid-June liturgy in St. Isaac's cathedral was celebrated to mark the departure of Metropolitan Alexi II (Ridiger) of Leningrad and Nov-gorod—now patriarch—from his old diocese. The head of the church was already a public figure. He had won election to the Congress of Peoples' Deputies a year earlier and made speeches to the congress fully robed. He was known internationally in religious circles and had presided as chairman of the European Council of Churches. Ten days earlier he had been elected to his new office by his fellow bishops who, together with laymen, met in synod at Zagorsk, outside Moscow. Following the death of the long-ailing Patriarch Pimen, clergy and laity alike looked for more active leadership free from state interference.

Why was so great emphasis placed on the office of patriarch? The answer is that it is central in Russian Orthodoxy. Heroic dissidents had protested the tyrannization of religion by the Russian Communist regime. Now they were no longer held in prison. What would be most effective as Orthodoxy reemerged in public life? Needed most of all was not simply individual prophetic witness, important as that remained. Only the renewal of the Church's institutional life, under responsible administration, could spread faith widely enough throughout the vast dechristianized land. The new leader's person would be crucial for his church.

The patriarch, as leader of his church, is comparable in rank only with a pope, the head of the Roman Catholic communion. His person and char-acter are of great importance. This new patriarch of the Russian Orthodox church is well-educated in his own tradition. After his seminary training, he did graduate work at the Orthodox Theological Academy in Leningrad. The main hallway of the academy is lined with portraits of past patriarchs, their heads covered with their own distinctive garb. Now Alexi II's picture will be among them. Past and present are joined with hopes for the future in the line of succession.

Alexi's choice tells much about the needs and problems of his church in a time of reconstruction. Born in Talin, Estonia, in 1929, he was ordained to the priesthood in 1950. He became a monk in 1961 and the same year was elected bishop of Talin and Estonia. When he took office in Leningrad in 1986, he continued to retain jurisdiction over the Estonian area of his church. Alexi's election as patriarch was not fully expected on all sides. Before it occurred, one of the most responsible Western commentators had remarked: "it is hard to observe the overwhelmingly Russian members of the church electing a non-Russian, particularly at a time when national passions in the USSR are running so high."[9] But the leaders of the synod did elect him, and he is a person with more than ordinary understanding of the highly inflammatory minorities question in the USSR.

Patriarch Alexi had long worked in the office of the Moscow Patriarchate. There he became acquainted with the difficult problem of relations with the Uniates who now seek to recover their churches, especially in the Ukraine, where they are most numerous. The new leader of the Russian Orthodox church has a good record in interfaith relations. Along with Roman Catholic Cardinal Martini, he chaired an ecumenical assembly at Basel in Switzerland in 1989. For years he was active in the international peace program sponsored by the Communist state.

Patriarch Alexi long has collaborated with the regime successfully. The Orthodox hierarchy has suppressed some of its most competent and idealistic priests at the state's command. Alexi was in office during the Khrushchev years, and it is charged that he not only worked with state's Council for Religious Affairs, providing information, but with the KGB as well.[10]

It would be hard to deny that the prospects for religion in Russia seem the best that they had been since the revolution in 1917. Under perestroika, some monasteries have been reopened. Churches were allowed social service activities. Mother Teresa opened communities in the country. Church buildings were being given back by the hundreds, indeed by the thousands for religious use. So many that church officials often lacked funds for refurbishing them, and there was a shortage of priests and choir directors. As we have already suggested, the government's new policy, inaugurated with celebration of the millennium of Christianity in 1988, could be justified in terms of expediency. As a member of the faculty at the Leningrad Theological Academy put the matter: "There are a half dozen revolutions going on in the country. The regime needs the Church!"

Advocates of perestroika in the church announced their own congress for the fall of 1990, to be led by persons such as the long disenfranchised and imprisoned priest and member of the Congress of the Russian Republic, Father Gleb Yakunin. At least five parties need to be considered in appraising the prospects for religion in the USSR in the near future. First there is the Russian Orthodox church under the patriarch and other Orthodox bodies such as those in the Ukraine, Georgia, and Armenia. Second, one cannot ignore the long-persecuted underground church. What it can accomplish, now that it has surfaced, remains to be seen.

Third, one must take note of the Orthodox bishops and clergy outside the USSR, many of whom have been opponents of the patriarchate. Internationally, there are power struggles and bitterly hostile divisions (engendered by the Soviet government's policy) in the Orthodox communion. Fourth, not to be overlooked are the Roman Catholics to whom we have already referred. They are now legally recognized (registered) and have been a subject of discussion between the Kremlin and the Vatican since diplomatic relations have been taken up between the two. Finally, there are Baptist and other free-church groups very active in areas where no Orthodox church buildings remain open, as in large parts of Siberia.

CAN ORTHODOXY BE A FORCE FOR SOCIETAL RENEWAL?

Religion's revolutionary potential in the USSR has been attested to by the militantly atheistic campaign that was directed against it for six decades. In spite of all the Communists' attempts to reduce it to obscurantism, they continued to fear it as the powerful social force that it has been throughout most of the nation's history. The name of the long-eulogized Russian hero Alexander Nevsky (1220?–1263), for whom one of the major churches is named in Leningrad, is remembered because he was a leader in settling new areas as well as fighting against national foes such as the German knights. Christianity was a major force not only in supporting and preserving national identity after the Mongol conquest, but it was the seedbed for renewal and revolution. Even if it has not always been a positive social force (and it has remained untouched by the Reformation or the Enlightenment) in Russian history, it has been nonetheless very powerful. Russian Orthodoxy, to say the least, has conveyed inclusive life-orienting symbols. Marxist interpreters labeled religious symbols, myths, and narratives as ideological. But even simply in terms of the history of ideas, such a description is truncated.[11]

From the last century, the Russian situation has had a curious relationship to Western European atheism. The West often was looked to uncritically by intellectuals before the 1917 revolution, and Western nihilism accepted and made a life stance. Granted that institutional religion was in a number of respects decadent and corrupt in the country and offered little or no social criticism or advocacy of reform. Still it was tied with national symbols and patriotism under the czars, in particular, the notion of the third Rome. Constantinople, the second Rome, had fallen to Muslim rule in 1453. Moscow remained true to Christianity, a new Rome, and was given a sense of manifest destiny. This myth (or ideology) continued in secular guise after the 1917 revolution: communism was to be preserved in the

Russian homeland against the rest of the world and eventually spread worldwide.

Today, the USSR is a land in transition and revolution. Communist dogmatism inspired neither work nor virtue. The Chernobyl catastrophe shattered utopian expectations about science. Finally something revolutionary had to be done, and change was initiated from above by Gorbachev. The cold war was brought to an end and religious tolerance begun.

Now the initial stage of perestroika is over. The Communist party has lost its exclusive control of cultural life, and the political situation has become polarized between left and right. Of course, it was perestroika which made possible the peoples' revolutions and new freedom of religion in the former Russian satellite states of Eastern Europe. The end of the oppression of religion in the USSR was contemporary with them.

Religion benefited from glasnost and perestroika in both the former Eastern European satellites and in the USSR itself. The struggle against belief in God had been at the center of Communist ideology for more than half a century. Atheists argued that it had to be restrained by the state because it was a barrier to progress. Marxism had envisaged a this-worldly utopia at the end of a period of revolutionary struggle. To achieve a classless society, violence and force could be used legitimately, Marx held, and they were. With his utopian view of human nature, he expected even the end of the state. It did not come to pass.

Of course, liberalization in the USSR did not take place in just the way that the regime had envisaged. In a change of form of government, Gorbachev became president and not just the secretary of the Communist party. But nationalism showed itself to be very much alive and a highly disruptive force. In the First World War, it had helped to destroy the Austro-Hungarian Empire. Now it threatened the breakup of the Communist Russian Empire. A number of the fifteen republics sought not only greater autonomy but independence. Ruling the USSR was more difficult because the Communist command economy was in crisis and declining.

Initially, when Gorbachev came to power there was talk of tightening the screws on religion. Soon, however, policy change in the opposite direction could be seen developing. As he was not lost in a world of ideology, the new party secretary's approach was more pragmatic than dogmatically antireligious. He knew that among intellectuals, the group in society most enthusiastic for his reform program, a positive interest in religion had been growing for at least two decades.

RELIGION AND THE STATE

The interrelations between religion and nationalism were complex. A considerable number of the religiously disposed nationalists were conservative and even reactionary. Gorbachev's strategy was to split the conservative opposition by a more favorable attitude toward religion. At the time, state estimates were that at least 20 to 25 percent of citizens had living religious interests. Why should so large a part of the nation, including many of the most genuinely patriotic persons, be alienated from the national ethos because of this outlook and loyalty? Should they not rather be enlisted for perestroika? Reliable statistics about religion were hard to obtain, but Orthodox bishops listed the annual rate of baptisms as at least two million, a level, it was claimed, that had held over a period of two decades.

Gorbachev and his Communist party colleagues were forced to make a policy decision on whether to support full continuation of the longstanding antireligious campaign or to give ground.

On July 30, 1986, a veteran anti-religious specialist and former activist in the League of Militant Godless, Iosif Kryvelev, published an article entitled "Flirting with Dear Little God" in Komsomol'skaya Pravda in which he assailed the inroads that "God-seeking" had been making among the creative intelligentsia. Kryvelev singled out three leading Soviet writers for attack: Kirgiz author Chingiz Aitmatov, Siberian prosaist Victor Astaf'yet, and Belorussian writer Vasil'Bykaw (Bykov). These three writers had made their respect for religion explicit and were undisputed leaders of the intelligentsia.[12]

Slowly it became clear that Kryvelev was the loser; the intellectual community simply was not on his side. Conveniently, the regime's choice was made easier by the hostility toward religion of some of the most determined opponents of change, notably Yegor Ligachev, party secretary for ideology until the fall of 1988. Freedom for religion would also be a great plus internationally. The change of direction was signaled first through the Council for Religious Affairs. Its spokesmen, more than before, were prepared to acknowledge past mistakes in the treatment of religion. Writers who were proreligion were allowed to challenge old abuses and continuing restrictions. Step-by-step restraints began to be relaxed. Overall, in terms of the nation, pitifully few churches were available in proportion to the population and its needs. Very many of them were concentrated in the Ukraine, especially in the Western Ukraine.

Control of religious institutions by officials of the Council for Religious Affairs had been thoroughgoing down to details. Bishops, when they came to their area of residence, brought gifts and tried to establish a positive relationship with local CRA bureaucrats. When bishops were not able to find rapport with them, clergy were greatly hampered in a variety of ways. Of course, some bishops more than others followed the state office directives, and when they did not, they were even put out of office. In short, terror was widespread. Clergy were required to pay unproportionately high income taxes. Money raised by the churches was taken in unproportionate amounts by the state, for example, for its peace program. There was harassment of active laity by party officials.

Quite abruptly, state interference and control was relaxed and even relinquished. Now the bureaucracy that had so long restricted religion was to serve it more positively. How long would the new policy last? it was asked. That would at last become clear when, after long legislative consideration, it was enacted into law in 1990.

The precedent for the state control of religion in Russia dates at least as far back as Czar Peter the Great.[13] It was Peter, an Enlightenment monarch, who copied the Western European Protestant model and replaced the patriarchate of the Russian Orthodox Church with a synod. In effect, religion was put under the czar's control and the church's policies and outlook regulated by his subordinates for the state's own ends. The Communists have carried on in the same way. To be sure, under monarchy the government was favorably disposed to Christianity and built churches. Under communism, the intention was to destroy religion and substitute materialism for belief in God. Churches were closed en masse.

It was the defeat of the First World War that put the Russian Church in immediate jeopardy. Its head, the czar, was executed. Even while the czar was still living just before the Communists took power, a reforming Orthodox Church council was called and met in the capital city. The church was in internal as well as external crisis, and the mode of its government was debated. Some church leaders favored a ruling synod. The majority decision, however, was to reestablish the patriarchate. Three candidates were nominated for the office of patriarch, and then lots were drawn following a New Testament tradition. The choice fell on Belavin Tikhon.

Taking office, the new patriarch soon was faced with an all-out attack on the church and its priests by the Communists. The reforming council came to a premature conclusion and could carry on no further, as church bank accounts were frozen by the new regime. The arrests of clergy multiplied. The Communists found a pretext for seizure of the church's precious objects. Large amounts of grain were destroyed in the civil war between the Whites and the Reds. The famine was real enough, and to pay for more food, the Communists ordered that chalices and crucifixes, adorned with jewels and gold and silver, should be sold to raise funds to feed the hungry populace. Lenin understood well the strategy. Although he argued that religion could not be destroyed by force alone, he despised it and urged that its adherents should be taught a lesson. Soon under Communist rule a more humane and scientific worldview would prevail, he promised. The superstition of religion would be done away with, and its end could be speeded by persecution.

Patriarch Tikhon, elected in 1917, long was pressured to submit to the Communist state and finally issued a declaration of loyalty to the regime. Imprisoned and then eventually released, he conformed to the government's wishes in a statement whose authenticity is still disputed; claims are even made that he was murdered. Patriarch Tikhon's successor, Sergi, received his office neither from a council nor appointment by his predecessor. Also imprisoned by the Communist revolutionaries, he eventually gave in to their demands and pledged loyalty to the Soviet regime as he was set free. The state had won control of the patriarchate. It was at this juncture that thousands of Orthodox Christians went underground.

In the early 1920s, the government promoted a rival religious group, the "Living Church." It was one of three major parties in the Renovationist schism. Even before the 1917 revolution, there had been dissatisfaction about Peter the Great's reforms. After the Communists came to power, the Renovationists separated themselves in schism from the patriarch. Indeed, attempts were made to defrock him while he was still in prison. Leaders of the Living Church urged cooperation with the Communist state. While the patriarch was detained by the state, they even managed to maneuver to have many major church sanctuaries turned over to them. The movement continued to have some influence until the Second World War. The Communists, however, lost interest in sponsoring it when they could control the patriarchate to which the majority of believers adhered. The Renovationists never achieved major allegiance.

Attacked by the Communists, Russian Christians had no long record of tolerance to which to appeal. Their own church's history with respect to tolerance was not a good one. Until the first decade of the twentieth century, no other branch of Christianity had been allowed in the nation, except among foreign nationalities residing in the land. In the early 1920s, as civil war subsided, the state seemed to favor ecclesiastical reform by supporting groups not associated with the patriarchate. The clergy associated with the Living Church movement and the Renovationist schism applauded the coming of Marxism and favored the new regime.[14] They were sincerely and positively disposed to socialism and communism and the new order. The difficulty was that the Living Church did not have mass appeal to the less-educated faithful; on the contrary, more than had been expected, they remained loyal to the patriarch.

It is important to note that in the period before the revolution, the majority of Russian intellectuals were secular and often cynical in regard to their religious orientation, uncritically accepting a wide range of ideas from Western Europe. Secularity reached even to the training of the clergy in church institutions; many were only nominal in their belief. The institutional church, overpowered by the regime, was in fact controlled by the state bureaucrats, a tradition that has continued under the Communists. A major change in the present period is that the Russian intelligentsia is much more interested in and even committed to Christianity than before the Communist revolution.

It was the legislation passed in 1929 which confirmed and established Stalin's policy toward institutional religion. It continued to set the pattern until the new 1990 legislation passed in the name of perestroika. For more than half a century, church activities were limited to the sanctuary. The religious education of children was outlawed. No social service, much less any political role, was allowed believers in God. Church property, taken over by the state, was rented to local parishes. The period of 1936 to 1939 was the time of maximum terror, and at last most clergy had been put out of their parishes. As few as only three bishops continued to function in office when Stalin decided on rapprochement with the church as the Nazis invaded the country.

As Stalin took over new territory at the time of the division of Poland with the Germans, before his own country was attacked, he did use the Russian Orthodox Church to help absorb the new groups of population and their religious institutions.[15] Then, when the Germans attacked Russia, the ruling patriarch spoke out against them, even before the dictator mustered courage to do so. Stalin, knowing that he needed church support, finally called in the high clergy. Friendly and cordial, even jovial, he made concessions. Schools and publications could be reactivated. The church had a respite from persecution and carried on significant reconstruction and renewal until Stalin's death. The agreement with him, however, was an informal one and never was put in legal form or enacted into law.

In historical perspective, as persecution was resumed under Khrushchev in 1959, it became clear that tolerance had been based only on a personal compact with Stalin. At the same time that the antireligion campaign was renewed again and more churches closed than left open, the regime under Khrushchev allowed the Russian churches to join the World Council of Churches. In its deliberations, the Orthodox high clergy lied and knew that they were lying, for example, about the absence of persecution. Legalization was used as a tool to close down services and dismiss priests in tricks without end. Priests unable to exercise their office openly often went into the "True Orthodox" and other underground movements. Patriarch Sergi's submission to the Communist regime was criticized and disavowed by many of them. The entire resources of the state were directed against the practice of religion and belief in God. Actually, the atheist campaign, supported by the state and imposed from above, was often counterproductive. The belief and practice of faithful laypeople was of key importance in keeping the church alive under overwhelming state pressure.

LINGERING EFFECTS OF PERSECUTION AND MARGINALIZATION

In the larger national arena, open and active protest against the official persecution dates from as far back as the letter sent to the patriarch by two Moscow priests, Father Nikolai Eshilman and Father Gleb Yakunin, on November 21, 1965. Long imprisoned, Yakunin has remained a leading spokesman for reform up to the present. Like a number of other candidates for the priesthood, he came to his sense of vocation while studying in a secular field; he graduated from an agricultural institute. Expelled from the seminary in Moscow, he nonetheless secured work in a church in the city. Not surprisingly, he became a target for the police.

Even after he had finished serving his sentence and was due for release in November 1979, Yakunin was taken to a Leningrad prison for further interrogation, and a new trial was scheduled. After it took place on August 25–28, 1980, he was sentenced to five years further imprisonment and a subsequent five years of internal exile. There are good reasons why such a person today does not look to the Orthodox metropolitans and bishops for renewal and reform, and they may still view him as potentially revolutionary!

An appendix to the letter that Fathers Yakunin and Eshilman sent to the patriarch, dated December 13, 1965, told in detail about the repressive measures being taken against religion by CROCA, the Council for Russian Orthodox Church Affairs. "The suffering church turns to you with hope. You have been invested with the staff of primatial authority."[16]

The letter continued:

> There is a growing desire in the Russian Church for purification from the disease which has been growing in it through the fault of the church authorities; there is an ever-increasing desire in the Church for true conciliar communion. . . .
>
> The supreme ecclesiastical authorities are now confronted with an unavoidable choice: they must either redeem their serious guilt before the Russian Church by definite actions or else completely join the enemy camp, for "no man can serve two masters."[17]

The response of the patriarch then was to ban the priests from exercising their ecclesiastical office.

During the fifth assembly of the World Council of Churches in Nairobi in November 1975, Father Yakunin, together with a layman, Lev Regelson, appealed by letter to that body for support. The World Council leadership felt obliged to evade the issue and referred it to a study commission. The official Russian delegates threatened to terminate their membership in the council should it support the complaints. For his trouble this time, Yakunin was jailed for more than a decade. Under perestroika he was not only released but elected a member of congress in the Russian Republic.

The Russian Orthodox Church hierarchy, long completely subservient to the state, now has the problem of overcoming the lingering Stalinist legacy in religious institutions. There has been a widespread lack of community. The Yakunin Report, one of the most reliable sources of information, recounts: "In the modern Orthodox parish, as in no other communities of no other denominations, the sense of Christian brotherhood is weakened. . . . People [who] have stood side by side in worship and have taken Communion from the same chalice for decades . . . turn out to be unacquainted with one another."[18]

There are a variety of reasons why "densely packed, united, devout congregations" are charged with coldness. Not the least has been the government (and the Orthodox hierarchy's) treatment of clergy. In daily life, they were denied any authority or leadership outside of cultic acts. Fear of KGB informers was widespread.[19] It was part of the persecution that religious communities—meaning churches—could not sponsor common projects, help members in time of need, hold prayer meetings for adults or classes for children and young people.

Individual local churches have been under the direction of a parish executive committee. Generally, such committees consist or two or three persons. They control not only finances but the appointment of priests to a locale. Their members need not necessarily be Christian. But this is not the end. In such a setting and limited by so many restrictions, priests easily become "prisoners of the rites." An émigré comments: "The priest sees thousands of unknown people process past. He becomes a mere dispenser of the liturgy, completely consumed, not only by the regular performance of the liturgy itself, but also by the interminable string of private ceremonies requested by the faithful (blessing of water, baptism, absolution, prayers for the dead)."[20]

A key problem is the training of clergy and their relation to parish life. The KGB's interference penetrated even into theological seminaries. Theo van der Voort of Holland studied in the Leningrad Theological Academy from 1974 to 1977. He himself converted to Orthodoxy, was ordained a priest, and now lives in the West. Van der Voort has written in detail about life at the Leningrad Academy, which he attended. He reports that some of the

> new students are sent to a room where a nice, friendly, fatherly person starts a talk with him, and asks how he likes the city, the museums and the academy, and how the study is going. When the student feels at ease, suddenly the question is put: "Are you a citizen of the Soviet Union?" As answering "No" cannot be recommended in these cases, the answer, "Yes, of course" is given. The friendly person continues by saying that therefore it is his duty to help his country. As he may know, the Soviet State has many enemies. ... If he happens to hear something, he should phone or write a report about it. If the student is not very careful, he'll leave that room with a phone number or address, and he is told a report is expected in a couple of weeks.[21]

Van der Voort estimates that as many as half the students may have been informants. How much has the situation changed under perestroika? Conclusive evidence is lacking to date; no doubt it has improved. Van der Voort's judgment was that in spite of all harassment, the majority of students seemed to have a sense of religious vocation.

Religion's association with nationalism is at the same time positive and dangerous. It is positive because it brings long-suppressed traditions to life, negative because Christianity in principle is a universal, not a national religion. As an example, the history of the Georgian Orthodox Church will be discussed: nationalism and religion have a century-long union in Georgia.[22] S. F. Jones, who teaches at Mount Holyoke College, lived for two years in Tbilisi and has written an account of "Soviet Religious Policy and the Georgian Orthodox Apostolic Church: From Khrushchev to Gorbachev."[23] He explains recent developments:

> Gorbachev hopes to gain the support of church leaders for *perestroika* and his religious reform package and to undermine those demanding more radical change. . . . The experience of the last two years, however, suggests that Gorbachev's policy has achieved the opposite results. Religious activists are not only expanding the influence of the churches in the community, but calling for democratization of their own organizations and the removal of compromised church leaders.[24]

Stalin himself was from Georgia (a theological student), and in the era between the world wars, Jones reports, "A combination of atheist propaganda, terror and rapid urbanization led to the virtual elimination of practising believers."[25] There was some respite from persecution during and after the Second World War, and then a renewed attack in the Khrushchev era. In the same period, as was the case with the larger Russian Orthodox body, in February of 1960 the Georgian Orthodox Church joined the World Council of Churches.

Zviad Gmasakhurdia, a Georgian human rights activist, recounted how Patriarch Epremi II told him, "when Moscow plays the piano, we must dance to its tune."[26] The patriarch endorsed the Communist program as "wonderful" and according to Gmasakhurdia himself, practised simony. Eduard Shevardnadze, later foreign minister, was made First Party Secretary for the Georgia region in September of 1982. He came with instructions from Moscow to clean up the widespread corruption which had reached even to religion. Gmasakhurdia and others had tried to set up a "Christian court" to investigate abuses. Editor of two samizdat journals, *The Georgian Messenger* and *The Golden Fleece*, he was the leading dissident in the area. For his efforts, Gmasakhurdia was arrested in April 1977 and sentenced to three years' imprisonment and two years' internal exile. Church leaders supported the government's attack on him, cooperating with the atheist state. In May 1991, Gmasakhurdia was elected president of the Republic of Georgia and promised to lead it to full independence from Moscow and the Soviet Union.

UNCERTAIN PROSPECTS FOR RELIGION

Now events have gone full circle. What was most feared by the Communist party has taken place—the fusion of religion and nationalism. On

April 9, 1989, twenty-one protestors were killed by Russian troops after mass demonstrations for freedom and national rights. Jones comments:

> Georgian nationalists, whose influence has escalated profoundly since the demonstrations of November 1988 and particularly since the tragic events of 9 April, see the church as playing a vital part in the struggle for national self-expression. ... The party has almost no support in Georgian society and the local leadership will probably be prepared to make major concessions to the church.[27]

It is reported that increasingly religion flourishes. Religious tolerance has not been fully accepted by the Orthodox in spite of the fact that it is now state policy. Even in the era of perestroika, a Hare Krishna congregation had remained unregistered in Tbilisi, the capital city.[28] Four Orthodox Christian members of the Georgian National Independence Party broke into its premises armed with sabres and daggers. One of the raiders told four Krishna devotees that an Orthodox priest had said that the movement should be driven out of Georgia. The next day their leader was forced to go to the theological academy, where his Hare Krishna garments were torn off. Later, when public protest was lodged, the Hare Krishnas were informed that persecution would cease if the rector of the theological academy ordered its end.

Roman Catholics and the Eastern Orthodox stand closer to each other than to the Protestants in the USSR. An International Theological Commission for Dialogue between the Roman Catholic Church and the Eastern Orthodox Churches has been at work since 1987, and has issued at least three public declarations. Practically, however, at the level of parish and congregational life, there are great tensions. The Uniate Church in the Ukraine dates from 1596. It was forcibly reunited with the Russian Orthodox Church at the Lvov Church Council in 1946. Both the legitimacy and the practical results of this council are now being challenged. Tensions show every promise of continuing. It is charged, for example, that Orthodox bishops forced the Uniates to give up Western ties and become part of the larger Russian body.

The Russian Orthodox Church is the larger body, and there is no reason to believe that it will not remain predominate in the country. In the modern period, the Eastern Churches have been much more isolated and on the defensive than the Roman Catholic and Protestant Churches in the West. Nothing at all comparable with the Second Vatican Council has been possible. (As we noted, a Russian Orthodox reform council was attempted just at the time the Communists came to power.) Eastern European Christendom has yet to come to terms with modern historiography, biblical criticism, and modern science. At this point, a positive relation with Roman Catholicism can be of great value and help. Actually, there was less tension between the churches of Moscow and Rome before the Uniates surfaced again in the period of perestroika.

Not just Roman Catholic influence from the Vatican but Protestant missionary zeal from the United States in particular now impinges on the Russian religious scene. The low-church Protestant movement came to Russia in the middle of the last century in a concern for personal religious experience and salvation which found its first focus in the interest of a noblewoman and her friends in St. Petersburg, the capital city. But it spread primarily to the lower classes of the population and has populist roots. For persons of this conviction, there has been full freedom of religion only for a few brief years at the beginning of the century. The czarist state long took the side of Orthodoxy against the "sects."

At the end of the Second World War, the government forced the organization of an All-Union Council of Evangelical Christians. This was the means by which low-church life and activity was to be controlled. It was state policy that no one was allowed to hold a religious meeting of any sort—to pray, preach, or sing publicly—without registration. In a strategy of harassment, new congregations (primarily but not exclusively Baptist) numbering in the hundreds found it impossible to register and obtain permission to carry on their activities. Unregistered Baptists were hunted down, imprisoned, and otherwise persecuted. In the early 1960s when persecution was renewed under Khrushchev, leaders of the All-Union Council of Evangelical Christians were issued special secret instructions by the government. In turn they passed the word on to their constituency. It was that

> congregations in the past had not heeded the Soviet laws on religion, and . . . Church activities that were expressly forbidden in the April 1929 Law were being carried on: "There have been cases of young people under eighteen being baptised, material assistance has been given out of Church funds, Bible evenings and other special gatherings have been held . . . there have been meetings for preachers and training of choir leaders. . . ." Children were no longer to be allowed to take part in the services.[29]

In effect, denominational officials were being called on—as in the case of the Orthodox hierarchy—to help stamp out religion. Opposition centered in an action group, the Initsiativniki, which in August 1961 issued its protest: "In our days Satan is dictating through the workers of the All-Union Council of Evangelical Christians and Baptists, and the Church accepts all their decisions which directly contradict the laws of God."[30] A considerable body of believers went underground, and the schism spread throughout the country. The schism between unregistered and registered Baptist groups in the USSR, engendered and intensified by the state, grew out of the pattern of persecution. The government did, however, increase the freedom of the registered Baptists to counteract the influence of unregistered ones.

To identify specifically what is happening under perestroika, there are reports from the forty-fourth congress of the Baptist Union, which met in late February 1990. The outgoing Union president, Yevgeni Logvinenko, noted subsequently that it was the first time in recent years, presumably since the late 1920s, that there was no interference by state officials. In fact, this was the first public admission of such interference behind the scenes. Congress sessions were held not in the cramped Moscow Baptist Church but at the Izmailov Conference Center.[31] Pressure was strong for greater organizational democracy and congregational autonomy from the over seven hundred delegates.

Numerically, what seemed clear was that the Baptists had an identifiable, relatively stable constituency. Often courageous people, they were not about to convert all their neighbors, much less the nation. Baptisms had increased to over 11,000 in 1989; 183 new congregations had been registered and sanctioned by the government. Still, since 42,000 Pentecostals had left to form their own separate denomination, there had been a net loss to the Baptist Union in the year that had passed. Baptist officials long have done their best to educate their members, using correspondence courses, but even enrollment in these was limited by the state. Now they are allowed to open a seminary.

There also continue to be groups of Lutherans and Mennonites in the USSR, but they do not spread throughout the population as much as the Baptists. The Baptists, with their doctrine of separation of church and state, stand sociologically at the opposite extreme of the church-state spectrum from Moslems living in the USSR. Of course, Islam has a potential for revolution, but this topic goes beyond the scope of this book. Buddhism, a much smaller religion in the USSR, apparently is not growing.

How much did Christians fit Toynbee's notion of a creative minority in a time of trouble? In many respects, religion and its traditional social structures were seen as a threat to the Communist Bolshevik regime and the values it represented. The attack against religion would not have succeeded without ruthlessness, lies, and violence. Stalin murdered millions of persons, and large groups of Christians were among his victims. At its best, religion was both a stabilizing and a creative force. As we noted earlier, at the outset of the great patriotic war, as the Russians called it, the patriarch spoke in defense of the nation even before Stalin recovered from the stunned silence that descended on him when the Nazis first attacked. Religion was on the side of nationalism and love of native land. Actually, in the areas of German occupation, religion had a mass rebirth with filled and overflowing churches, and Stalin had little choice but to cease persecuting it on his side of the battle lines. In spite of all that had been done against it, it remained alive and not far beneath the surface.

Could Christianity then supply the meaningful life symbols that communism lacked with power and effectiveness? One important question was how much its adherents had come into the modern world. Clearly a large part of the population knew very little about the faith. Religious education had been interdicted in entirety. The older abuses against which communism had protested were largely forgotten. The fact is that the question of how the church was to come into the modern world had haunted sensitive believers since before the revolution in 1917. Communism had attempted to hold it back, claiming alone the cause of modernity. One's own children could not be openly taught belief in God or even brought to worship services. Now at least this was allowed, along with church social work. Condescendingly it was said that since there was a lack of help in hospitals, Christians were to be given responsibility of caring for bedpans. Two goals of the 1917 reforming council long had been thwarted by Communist rule: more openness to the modern world and greater freedom from state control.

To say the least, the Marxists, in trying to control religion, had recognized its social power. But how much of religion remained after they had so long worked against it ought not to be overestimated. Still, it remained a link to history, and now it is sufficiently unknown and new enough to be appealing. It simply had not been on the side of the establishment and need not be rejected for this. Importantly, religion should not be linked to an earlier monarchism or just to nationalism in the USSR. New reformed, living religious symbols are needed.

Perestroika was not the result of Christian conviction, but it could not ignore religion. And perestroika was revolutionary. In a changed situation, religion was being dealt with more fairly. Of course, religion's persistence in the form of folk piety is remarkable. For decades, the struggle with Marxism had been fought from a position of bondage. Now as Marxist dogmatism receded and the old Marxist utopian dream collapsed, it became clear that secularity alone would not solve the issues. A balance between structure and creativity was imperative. Religion had roots and depth; either metaphor was useful. To be sure, if the Christian message was heard, Marxism could be drowned out. Urgent issues remained to be faced: peace, the end of the cold war, new world political structures, and most of all, the decline of the economy. With the relaxation of the antireligious campaign and its misplaced and often fanatical albeit forced zeal, religion could contribute to the renewal of society at large. As social structures are being changed in the country, both philosophical and religious issues are being raised. Not insignificantly, when President Gorbachev received Patriarch Pimen, a leading liberal philosopher sat with them.

BERDYAEV AND THE CHALLENGE TO RELIGIOUS HUMANISM

A theologian whom dissidents have read through the period of persecution is now being studied with renewed interest. Nicolas Berdyaev, exiled from the Soviet Union only a few years after the revolution, is again being discussed in his native country. From religious premises, he criticized both communism and capitalism, the latter for its isolated atomic individualism, which in his judgment was the antithesis of Christian personalism. One of the tragedies of communism is that Russia lost the presence of one of the most creative of the Orthodox intellectuals who went to live in Paris. He wrote of the Church:

> It must always be remembered that the Church bears two different meanings, and the confusion of these two meanings or the denial of one of them has fatal results. The Church is the mystical Body of Christ, a spiritual reality, continuing in history the life of Christ. ... But the Church is also a social phenomenon, a social institution ... as part of history, Äitü is sinful, liable to fall and to distort the eternal truth of Christianity.[32]

"The soul of the Russian people was molded by the Orthodox Church," Berdyaev is sure. Communists long have claimed to be able to understand religion best from the point of view of their own materialism. Berdyaev proposed the reverse: to understand communism from the point of view of religion—Russian religion! Communism in his country, he believed, was significantly different from Western European communism. "In the Russian revolution there were, incontestably, features which belong naturally to all revolutions, but it is also a unique distinctive revolution accomplished once for all."[33] This was the case in no small measure because traditional Russian messianism and apocalypticism, earlier associated with the Orthodox Church, were secularized but not abandoned.

Apocalypse, of course, is a religious idea. Scriptural apocalypses such as the books of Daniel and Revelation attempt to forecast history, often with a sense of doom. Communists claimed the end of an old era and believed that their revolution was the end of all revolutions. Berdyaev did not accept their claim to finality and attempted to appraise the larger historical pattern.

His conclusion was that the Communist revolution absorbed and transformed earlier epochs. In spite of its very un-Russian origin in Western Marxist thought, it took on an oriental style which in many respects resembled Slavophilism.[34] "The old consecrated Russian empire fell and a new one was formed, also a consecrated empire, an inverted theocracy." From exile, Berdyaev viewed what took place under communism as the death of both humanism and religion. "Stalinism, that is to say communism of the constructive period, is being imperceptibly transformed into a peculiar sort of Russian fascism."[35] The exile's judgment was that

> the militant anti-spiritual materialism of communism is a phenomenon of spirit, not of matter. It is a false orientation of spirit. ...
> It is the very religious character of communism, the very religion of communism, which makes it anti-religious and anti-Christian. A

communist society and state profess to be totalitarian, but only the Kingdom of God can be totalitarian; the kingdom of Caesar is always partial.[36]

Berdyaev reflected that a revolution can be understood from a variety of points of view: that of the people actively engaged in it — revolutionaries and counterrevolutionaries — or from a more objective, historical, and scientific point of view by others who appraise it more disinterestedly and have not been part of it, or from the point of view of people who have taken it into their inward experience. This latter point of view in Berdyaev's judgment is what appeared among Russian Marxists. Losing perspective, (paradoxically) they understood "the meaning of revolution" less than anybody.[37]

Communism did not just come from nowhere. Russia's defeat in a world war brought it to power, but it had long precursors. Berdyaev emphasizes that revolutionary fervor — calls for reform as well as disgust with the establishment — all were present on the Russian scene throughout the nineteenth century. An older sacred canopy was dissolving. Nihilism, anarchism, and even apocalypticism were widespread among intellectuals and were not unrelated to religion.

Neither the nobility nor the intellectuals trusted the czar or looked to him for leadership. The peasants, to be sure, lived in their own world and were conscious of being oppressed by landowners. The czar and empress had lost touch with the people; she, in particular, tried to reestablish it through the strange figure of Rasputin, the charismatic and dangerous holy man in whom she came to believe. The Orthodox Church itself was ruled by a reactionary procurator of the Holy Synod, K. P. Pobedonostzev — a condition which even no traditionalist wants to reproduce today.

It was into this potentially revolutionary setting that communism came as a foreign force. Berdyaev emphasizes that Lenin, narrow in outlook and without any capacity for contemplation, (mistakenly) lived in a world which was divided dramatically into black and white. In apocalyptic expectation of the revolution, any method that contributed to it was allowed. "Lenin was a revolutionary to the marrow, precisely because through his whole life he defended an integral totalitarian outlook of life and permitted no infringement of it whatever."[38]

The point to which Berdyaev is leading his reader is that it would be a mistake to regard the Russian revolutionary as a humanist. "Lenin did not believe in man.[39] He recognized in him no inward principle; he did not believe in spirit and the freedom of the spirit, but he had a boundless faith in the social regimentation of man." What Lenin did not understand was that revolution itself could become an end in itself as its leaders fought among themselves for power. Practically, he misjudged Stalin as he himself seems to have recognized just before his death.

But religion for Berdyaev offers no easy alternative. He finds a striking parallel to Lenin's outlook in a powerful church leader. "For twenty-five years the celebrated procurator of the Holy Synod, K. P. Pobedonostzev, ruled the Russian Church and in ideas the Russian State also. He was the spiritual leader of the old monarchist Russia during the period of its decline."[40] His world outlook was one of nihilism with a religious basis. Pobedonostzev had absolutely no faith in persons. The procurator was an outspoken reactionary, and his contemptuous disparaging attitude was carried over into relations with the bishops with whom he worked. In short, there was no transfer of belief in God to relations with men.

Berdyaev describes Lenin's attitude toward the world and persons as similarly nihilistic. "In Russian Marxist communism this process of dehumanization went even further and was conditioned by the whole set of circumstances in which Russian communism arose. There entered traditions not of Russian humanism, which had a Christian origin, but of Russian anti-humanism, deriving from Russian state absolutism, which always regarded man as a mere means to an end."[41]

Life in the world was vain for both the old reactionary and the new revolutionary. It had to be organized by coercion and force. Both Pobedonostzev and Lenin despised ecclesiastical hierarchy, and Lenin called for revolution against it. The outcome was fanaticism, intolerance, cruelty. From Berdyaev's point of view, both positions need to be overcome in a renewed Orthodox Christian humanism.

History would prove communism wrong, Berdyaev was sure, in the long run. The soul of a new humanity could not be formed out of negative emotions, hatred, revenge, and violence. "This is the demoniacal element of Marxism and it is called dialectic", Berdyaev writes. "Dialectically, evil passes over into good, darkness into light. The moral impulse in human life loses all independent significance, and that is undoubted dehumanization."[42]

Communism, in principle the antithesis of Christianity, considered evil as a pathway to good. A new society and a new humanity were to be born out of the growth of evil and darkness. But it did not come to pass. The world now waits to see if the present challenges will afford Russia and the Soviet Union an opportunity for rebirth.

10

ANATOMY OF THE REVOLUTIONS

Recovering Spiritual and Humanistic Traditions

A paradox became evident in the peoples' revolutions of 1989. From the Communists' point of view, they never should have taken place. The Communists' own proletarian revolution was to be the last and final revolution to end all revolutions. Judged on this premise, the 1989 revolts were "post-revolutionary revolutions." Most unexpected of all had been their suddenness. Of course there had been a long struggle, but the final change of power came swiftly. Neither churchmen not politicians had anticipated that the situation would become revolutionary so quickly.

William Echikson, the *Christian Science Monitor* reporter whom Havel described as "one of the few Western journalists . . . who cared and understood," speaks of "the heartfelt joy of Czechoslovakia, the heavy emotion of East Germany, the explosive rage of Romania" and "the cool, calculating logic of Poland and Hungary." He writes: "The Cold War began after the Soviet Union imposed its will on Eastern Europe. It ended because Eastern Europe is free."[1] The end of the cold war had worldwide implications influencing Africa, the Middle East, and Latin America.

Echikson emphasizes that it was not primarily Gorbachev or the West who effected the liberation of the former Russian satellite countries.[2] The Eastern Europeans themselves forced the Communists' hand and brought them down.

Freedom did not come to Eastern Europe as a gift from Moscow or Washington. It came from more than forty years of struggle — a daily, grinding struggle against a corrupt and evil system. . . . In Eastern Europe, the abstract notion of struggling for fundamental human rights and self-determination came alive. The issues are not about power and money. They are about right and wrong, truth and lies.[3]

Seen in their wider setting, the revolutions of the late twentieth century have an evident relation to what had happened earlier in two world wars. "The lamps are going out all over Europe; we shall not see them lit again in our lifetime."[4] So remarked British Foreign Secretary Sir Edward Grey when the First World War broke out in the summer of 1914. Are the lamps now being relighted in a common European house? The continuing struggle for reform in the USSR leaves the question open. Grey was right about this much: years of tragedy lay ahead. A century of relative peace that dated from the defeat of Napoleon and the Congress of Vienna was coming to an end. Members of all major confessions marched off to war in August 1914. They were supported by the prayers of their clergy: the Orthodox in Russia and Serbia, Anglicans in England, Lutherans in Germany, and Roman Catholics in the Hapsburg empire of Austria-Hungary.

No ruling dynasty or government could survive defeat in a major world war, argues Hannah Arendt.[5] The Russian Romanovs were replaced by communism and Stalinism. The German Kaiser abdicated, and his rule was followed by the Weimar Republic, which collapsed into Nazism. The centuries-long reign of the House of Hapsburg came to an end, along with its empire in Central Europe. The world was not made safe for democracy with the fall of these dynasties and their authoritarian union of throne and altar—as Americans led by Woodrow Wilson had hoped. On the contrary, the incredible era between the two world wars saw the birth of modern totalitarianisms that brought death to tens of millions of innocent citizens.

Earlier in the century not as much thought seems to have been given to the relationship between religion and statecraft, ethics and politics as later in the peoples' revolutions. An aristocratic pattern was taken for granted in 1914. The Christian churches were more often than not on the side of the establishment. Large bodies of workers had been lost to them through social protest that was often anticlerical. After the First World War the symbolism of monarchy lingered on in Romania, Yugoslavia, and Hungary. But it had little popular appeal and was replaced either by republican ideals or, when these faltered as in the Weimar Republic in Germany, eventually by totalitarianism. In the recent peoples' revolutions against communism, the question of the relation between spirituality and politics, religion and ethics, has been raised anew.

The nations of Central Europe, long caught between East and West, were seldom sure of themselves and their independence. In the early period following the Second World War, there was idealism about a new order— to be sure, amid oppression. National governments were reconstructed and industry began anew.

Echikson identifies what he calls communism's founding fathers in the Russian satellite countries. They included Erich Honecker in East Germany, Gustav Husák in Czechoslovakia, Janos Kádár in Hungary, and Nicolai Ceausescu in Romania. Each was in power for decades, and by the time of the peoples' revolutions, all of them were gray old men over seventy.

They had dominated their countries' postwar history for too long. Still, they were more than just apparatchiks. Most of them had come into the Communist movement while it was still being persecuted in their countries; they had been arrested and suffered for the Marxist cause.

> The Founding Fathers dominated their countries' entire post-war histories. The ideology they espoused once seemed attractive and worthy, not stagnant and corrupt. These communists joined the Party out of genuine commitment, to fight for a Brave New World. They were idealists, bony puritans with ascetic features. They were tough. They hoped. They dreamed. The world around them was filled with injustice, masses of impoverished workers and peasants groveling before a well-off few. These communists, who believed in a better world, sacrificed and suffered for their beliefs. But power corrupts.[6]

Other leaders, especially second-generation ones who joined the Communist party after the war, characteristically showed less idealism and more personal ambition. *Nomenklatura* (the list of persons approved for office) became endemic. Most of the individuals on the lists were careerists. Ideologically, they were conformists. Corrupt and privileged, they became rigid and wooden in style. As early as 1957, Milovan Djilas noted that the apparatchiks were ruining communism.[7]

Following the peoples' uprisings, it was evident that the hoped-for democratic future would depend very much on the nature of the structures — political, economic, ethical, and religious — which were to be built. (An English commentator cited the importance of the *Federalist Papers* in the early United States as a model of responsible planning for liberty under law.)[8]

We have noted that the major churches occupy a very different position than they did before the First or even the Second World War. They no longer stand on the side of established power (in Eastern Europe this position came to belong to the Communists) but of the disenfranchised and persecuted. Human rights had become a leading Christian project, championed by the Vatican and the World Council of Churches alike. After the revolutions, the problem is one of developing appropriate structures in something other than a restorationist pattern.

As has been indicated, the change was not motivated simply by idealism. Even the Communists could not ignore religion's positive moral influence in society, as well as its negative potentialities. The persecution in Russia was brought to an end in the revolution through perestroika imposed from above. By contrast, in the former Russian satellite countries of Eastern Europe, it has been populist revolt from below, not imposition from above, that has brought about renewed freedom. Even in the peoples' revolutions, however, there were elites who structured mass movements of protest; they were constituted significantly by churchmen as well as literary figures, even reform Communists. When such elites were lacking or proved ineffective, the results were tragic, as in Bucharest and Beijing.

What Echikson calls "a chiseling process"—the reconstruction of civil society—was the opposition's central idea during the 1970s and 1980s. It was a methodical, step-by-step strategy which fed off communism's failures.

> While communists emphasized the collective will, oppositionists con-centrated on the power of the individual. ... Eastern Europeans turned to Civil Society after realizing that traditional political activity was doomed to failure. ... One could not count on foreign help, on meaningful change initiated from within a ruling Communist Party, or on change from a popular uprising. Violence was ruled out, for both pragmatic and ethical reasons.[9]

Reflection about civil society could find justification in the writings of Thomas Paine, John Locke, Alexis de Tocqueville, and John Stuart Mill. Paine argued that development of civil society was the only way to check the despotism of paternalistic government. The spiritual father of the strat-egy was no other than Adam Michnik. Michnik correctly judged that the interests of the Russian and Polish governments, as well as those of the dissidents, converged more than was realized. No one wished violence or invasion. So what strategy should be employed? Dissidents should not do too much and provoke a crackdown. But they should do enough to pressure the state to accept independent institutions and expand the limits of free-dom. Even when Solidarity was outlawed, Michnik did not consider the chiseling strategy a failure. After Solidarity had won the first free and open Polish election since the Second World War in June of 1989, he exclaimed: "Either we continue along an evolutionary path toward parliamentary democracy, or we will become a Romania in economics, a Romania in politics—and an Afghanistan in the streets."[10]

It had long since become evident in Eastern Europe (in the era of the two world wars) that there were greater possibilities for evil than the believers in Enlightenment democracy (for example, that of the French Revolution) had suspected. Philosophers of the Frankfurt school spoke of "enlighten-ment about Enlightenment." Specifically, naive versions of the rightness of the popular will had proved dangerous; a large majority of Germans voted for Hitler at the height of his power. Arendt's analysis is that totalitarian regimes tried to destroy the moral and religious traditions which have grown up with civilization over the centuries—and they nearly did so!

One way to understand positively what happened in 1989 is in terms of a return to a common European tradition. The goal of return to a European home may appear to be too general to allow confirmation or specification. On the other hand, it can be argued that Stalinism, in particular, repre-sented a dismantling of any remaining common European house. Marx's materialism was a clear and conscious break with long-accepted philosoph-ical and religious traditions. His intention was not to explain the world but to change it by radical and even violent revolution, an outlook even less attractive in an era of atomic weapons. Marx himself saw as impediments the religious traditions with whose help Western European civilization had been built. He believed that their foundations had already been destroyed by Feuerbach's attack on theism. Stalin only simplified and dogmatized the more subtle analysis by Marx and Lenin.

The question of a return to a common European home assuredly is not simply one of religion. The larger issue is about the creative and sustaining bases of culture — whether social and political life can continue without symbolism of the sacred and ultimate concern. Throughout much of the European intellectual experience, the humanism inspired by Greek philosophy and Jewish-Christian claims for revelation have lived together in synthesis. How happily can be debated. Modern so-called secular humanists (often attempting to reduce religion to ethics) have sought to separate them in greater or lesser degree. They have come together again in the revolutions of the late twentieth century in something other than a simple restorationism.

Communism's attempted life without God simply has not worked out. Even in secular terms, something more than the victory of capitalism or the restoration of Enlightenment tolerance had been taking place before the peoples' revolution. What, besides economics and self-interest, would be the basis of the new civil order? The Judeo-Christian worldview and morality lived on with various degrees of intensity, but religion alone had not been able to overthrow tyranny. It had been joined with humanism in "courtesy toward God," to use Böll's phrase. Was this the answer? If Havel's outlook is taken as the model, it draws on ethical and religious symbols.

It can be argued that the Western intellectual tradition has profited from the skepticism that has been evident at least since the Renaissance; religious intolerance was challenged by liberalism. Communism had a different perspective: the belief that life without God is not only possible but necessary. A variety of thinkers inside and outside of Russia have been convinced that denial of deity is required for intellectual integrity. The issue raised by Marxism to the present is whether religion belongs rightfully to a common European house. A free and open critique of longstanding philosophical and religious traditions can be illuminating. Their unqualified rejection in atheism, however, is another matter. Many sociologists now hold that life without religious symbols is scarcely possible. Religious questions are perennial; at issue is only how they are to be viewed and evaluated.

Arendt argues that when the old status quo was threatened by totalitarianism, neither capitalism nor liberal rationalist conviction had the strength necessary to resist.[11] Religious leadership was forced into resistance by the very nature of the situation. It became related to both the workers and the students. Historically, one might speculate that religion does better in times of disfavor and some persecution by the state than in times of uncritical identification with the political status quo.

The workers that communism had claimed for itself remain the largest social class in Eastern Europe. Strikes became one of their few ways of showing dissatisfaction. When workers joined with intellectual dissidents, as in Solidarity in Poland or in Czechoslovakia in the Prague Spring, there was danger. The two-hour strike on November 23, 1989, was crucial in Czechoslovakia. Especially in Poland, it was in the church that workers and intellectuals made contact with each other.

Students were important almost everywhere. They were in the streets in Czechoslovakia and East Germany as well as Romania. Less careful and prudent than their parents, they took chances, and they also turned to religion. "When young people don't find answers in the official ideology anymore, they make room for God," said Václav Malý, the Czechoslovak priest forbidden to say Mass by the Communist state.[12]

In the peoples' revolutions, technology—radio, television, and video recordings—all were used to help spread the message of freedom. Not the least, broadcasts from Radio Free Europe brought separated individuals and peoples closer together. Contact and information from abroad made clear that it was possible to integrate life outside of communism—in a more moral and spiritual way. Another world existed, free of Communist terror. The communication revolution offers great promise for peaceful international understanding in the future. Will it have similarly revolutionary influence in the USSR? The course of reform in Russia has been directly related to that in the former satellite countries. Polish philosopher Kolakowski has described what took place:

> Nikita Khruschev announced to the Soviet Communist party, and soon to the whole world, that he who had been the leader of progressive humanity, the inspiration of the world, the father of the Soviet people, the master of science and learning, the supreme military genius, and altogether the greatest genius in history was in reality a paranoiac torturer, a mass murderer, and a military ignoramus who had brought the Soviet state to the verge of disaster.[13]

The retreat from Stalinism that began under Khrushchev and continued under Gorbachev required a wrenching change of collective memory. In the end, the issues were moral and religious, not just economic and political; they concerned the whole framework of value and meaning on which both public and private life are based. In spite of its totalitarianism, Stalinism had provided a unifying ideology. To be sure, Stalin's writings embodied a very crude form of communism whose acceptance was enforced by brute police power. Nonetheless, citizens stomped in dismay in Red Square when it became known that the dictator had died.

Khrushchev had not attacked the Communist party, only Stalin. It was Khrushchev who rejected reform communism in Hungary in 1956 and sent Russian troops to crush the revolution. Uncritically and naively Communist, he was too much of a loner to stay in power, and when he was replaced by Brezhnev, Stalin's abuses were covered up again. The Prague Spring was put down and invasion justified by the Brezhnev doctrine. Glasnost and perestroika under Gorbachev represented a recognition that something else was needed, as there was an acute crisis in the society—economic, political, and ideological. Moral and even religious issues remained unresolved (guilt and conscience).

In his January 1987 Plenum speech, Gorbachev spoke out as a reformer in criticism of the stagnation to which continuing Stalinism had led:

> Interest in the affairs of society slackened, manifestations of callousness and skepticism appeared and the role of moral incentives to work declined. The stratum of people, some of them young people, whose ultimate goal in life was material well-being and gain by any means, grew wider. Their cynical stand was acquiring more and more aggressive forms, poisoning the mentality of those around them. . . .
>
> Disregard for laws, report-padding, bribe-taking and encouragement of toadyism and adulation had a deleterious influence on the moral atmosphere in society. Real care for people, for the conditions of their life and work and for social well-being were often replaced with political flirtation—the mass distribution of awards, titles and prizes. An atmosphere of permissiveness was taking shape, exactingness, discipline and responsibility were declining.[14]

It was not without reason that Aleksandr Solzhenitsyn had observed: "Powerful and daring minds are now beginning to struggle upright, to find their way out from under heaps of antiquated rubbish. But even they still bear all the cruel marks of the branding iron, they are still cramped by the shackles into which they were forced half-grown."[15]

But the shackles remained. By mid-1990 the new democratic freedoms seemed to have spun out of control and Gorbachev was reversing course. Yuri Afanasyev identifies the pattern of change in terms of two interrelated processes: transition from empire to a commonwealth of independent states and from a centralized, planned economy to a market economy and private enterprise.[16] By the fall of 1990, it was clear that both were in crisis. On December 20, 1990, Eduard Shevardnadze resigned dramatically as foreign minister and spoke out: "Dictatorship is imminent. No one knows what sort of dictatorship it will be. . . . But I cannot reconcile myself to events that are occurring in our country, or to the sufferings that await our people."[17]

The change in the USSR evoked anxiety throughout the former satellite lands. Very soon after the people's revolution in East Germany, widespread concern had developed for establishing independence from Russia as soon as possible. It had resulted in reunification. There was little probability that Communist regimes would be re-established by popular will in Poland, Hungary, or Czechoslovakia. Still, the pattern of events in the USSR raised fears and uncertainties. Even if either the left or the right came to full power, it was unlikely that religion would be persecuted as before. The decline of Communist ideological dominance was accompanied by the rise of an intensive nationalism of such force as to threaten to pull the Russian empire apart. Nationalism was often reinforced by religious sentiment. The government strategy following celebration of the millennium of Christianity in Russia in 1988 was to reactivate religion and attempt to use it for stability in the midst of widespread nationalist unrest. Hedrick Smith judges that this was the primary reason that churches were reopened and renewed freedom given to Christians, as Stalin had done during the dark days of the Second World War.[18] The heritage of the Russian Orthodox church would enhance patriotism and public order.

Garadzha, director of the Russian Communist party's Institute of Scientific Atheism, had already given up identifying religion with obscurantism and superstition when he wrote in January 1989: "Atheists are losing out if they refuse the help and support of the clergy of various confessions in moral education, by exalting Communist morality over and above universal human values which are affirmed in the teachings of many religions, assimilated over thousands of years in the development of world civilization."[19]

Garadzha makes polemic against the view that there are two opposing forces in the spiritual domain of society, atheism and religion. Where one gains, the other loses. What kind of atheism is it, he asks, which presents itself as some kind of creed opposed to religion—an anti-religion? In his judgment, Marxism warns against such a view, which remains within the framework of religious consciousness. Its mistake is to attempt to replace religious intolerance with atheistic intolerance. Garadzha denies that Karl Marx put man in the place of God in an affirmation of humanism. This was Feuerbach's view, and Marx spoke against it.[20] Communism was to be brought about not by a denial of God but by the denial of the validity of private property.

> We have at last realized that religion is one of those phenomena which will be a fellow traveller on the road to restructuring of our society on the basis of genuine democracy, *glasnost,* and socialism. . . .
>
>   In the practicalities of daily life there is so much common ground between believers and atheists that it is unthinkable and harmful to seek to set up divisions between them.[21]

What has been taking place in the USSR in perestroika and glasnost (the background of the revolutions) is the rehabilitation of history, and religion has been included. In the peoples' revolutions, it was not simply that religious conviction moved out of the sanctuary into society at large. At least equally as often, if not more often, religious conviction was reawakened outside of the sanctuary and returned to express itself in and through institutions.

It needs to be recognized that Eastern Europe will not become as uniformly Christian as it was Communist! Christians ought to have no illusions on this point. Christianity is not totalitarian, as was communism. In a pluralistic, democratic society there is no centralized authority that can impose ideology from above. Citizens now live in a situation in which there is a diversity of conflicting cultural and religious options. Convinced believers should welcome the opportunity to argue their case in free and open discussion. Christian influence needs to be exercised from below, not from above, as in the era when it was allied with monarchy. It was Christians' willingness to be salt, a light on the hill, that gave them a revolutionary role. No simple restorationism will be adequate in the new postrevolutionary setting.

This much the peoples' revolutions of 1989 made clear: more than the Communists realized, religion can be liberating, both personally and with respect to community structures. But one ought not to be too hopeful about its new possibilities. Christianity lived in a ghetto in Eastern Europe, and there are lingering patterns of thought and organization from the Communist era. Now all the Western religious developments of the postwar period, including a wide range of theologies, are pouring in. Needless to say, there is resistance as well as accommodation. A multitude of so-called sects, both Christian and non-Christian (representatives of other world religions) are invading from the West, rich in funds and evangelistic zeal. Unfortunately, often their lack of political and social sophistication and understanding of culture limits their possible contribution to democratic reconstruction. Put simply, traditional churches fear the intrusion of "the cults."

Neubert emphasizes that atheism is not necessarily being replaced in all instances by religious faith. In East Germany, agnosticism can be another alternative. The situation is significantly postmodern. Granted that there is an important place for religious authority, in a pluralistic society any truth that it may bring clearly must make its own way by open communication and conviction, by argument and not imposition.

Very specific problems presented themselves immediately after the new opening for religion. Early in the spring of 1990, the World Council of Churches held a special consultation at its headquarters in Geneva. Representatives of major churches in Eastern Europe had been invited to consider a timely topic: what should be the status of persons and institutions that had cooperated and received support from the newly defunct Communist regimes? In most counties, bishops had been appointed with state permission and collaboration (but not in Germany or Poland). Many clergymen had received part or all of their salaries from the state.

It was easy enough to argue, if one lived safely in the West, that communism was wrong and clergy should in no way cooperate or consult with state authorities in Eastern Europe. Contact with state officials cannot be avoided fully, especially in totalitarian states, even by the most drastic individualism. It needs to be remembered that no one knew when circumstances might change and there would be freedom of religious practice in Eastern Europe. One of the most courageous German Lutheran bishops remarked realistically that even in the new situation of freedom, he did not expect to eliminate all compromise, only to control his compromises with care. The responsibility of institutional religion is not just one of prophetic judgment and conviction of sin, but continuity of institutional presence and ministry, even amid suffering and tyranny. The point is that even a prophetic role is not always as simple as it may first seem to be.

Circumstances were not always the same in different countries. In fact, Eastern Europeans, harassed by communism, actually showed surprisingly little interest in what was going on in one another's lands. In some settings (Poland and Germany were among the better ones) church hierarchies were more successful than others in preserving religion against the totalitarian state. (A celibate priesthood could help, as it made it more difficult to bring pressure against the families of clergy.) A Christian presence inspired strength in the face of apathy and cynicism — at times even when it was compromised with the state.

What is important about the pattern of events in Eastern Europe was that religion lived on in the belief and devotion of individual persons. Some of their folk piety had been little influenced by the Enlightenment. Intellectually, there were also critical rational theologies with a strong sense of modernity. But suddenly modernity was in crisis. Enlightenment rationalism, no more than earlier dogmatic and authoritarian versions of religion, seemed to speak to the situation. It had become more existentially radical.

A key test of religion's integrity in postcommunist Europe will be in the area of Jewish-Christian relations. Jews might well have played a greater visible role in the peoples' revolutions had there been more of them alive in the satellite countries. Tragically, most of the Jewish population was killed in the Nazi period. Many of the survivors (Romania had the largest number) had left for Israel. There still were outstanding Jewish leaders such as Walesa's advisor, Professor Bronislaw Geremek. However, the revolution for which he was providing ideas and guidance was primarily a Catholic Christian one.

Jews were still expelled from Poland as late as 1968 under the Communists. There were rumors of lingering anti-Semitism in Hungary, even after the change of regime. But there were as well responsible leaders who understood the tragedy of the Holocaust. The East German regime had avoided the guilt issue, not acknowledging any responsibility for what had happened. This was not the case in West Germany, and merger with it made possible more open discussion of the past and its evils. There was a renewed interest in Judaism among Jews in the 1980s, but their proportion in the population is not large. In Czechoslovakia there were just a few thousand left in the country, and even in Hungary there were only 80,000.

Millions of Jews remain in Russia, and many of them wish to go to Israel or the United States. (The situation is very different from that in the former satellite countries and is beyond the scope of this book.) Reports are that even in liberated Eastern Europe, many Jews remain fearful about the future.[22] On the other hand, their fears could now be expressed more openly to the world. Our interest has been primarily in Christianity—Roman Catholic, Protestant, and Orthodox—as these were the dominant forms of religion. There seems to be every probability that interest in interfaith dialogue will be greater than before and will include religions such as Buddhism and Hinduism as well as Islam and Judaism.

What Eastern Europe had needed practically, in the latter part of the twentieth century, was a larger input of scientific research and technological reason. But this did not stand alone. Moral wisdom was also imperative. No one saw this more clearly than Andreij Sakharov, the atomic physicist who championed human rights in the Soviet Union.[23] Science itself (or a successful modern economy) could not be commanded into being by a Stalin or his successors. The growth of scientific knowledge depended on personal honesty and freedom.

In its longer history and in spite of the tragedy of two world wars, Western European civilization had been immensely creative in science, the arts, statecraft, and religion. Its influence had extended worldwide, laying the basis for democratic civil society in the Americas, Australia, Africa, and Asia. Of course, evaluated critically, so-called Christendom had been a mixed blessing. It fell far short of the ideals of Christianity. When religious leaders in Eastern Europe called for peace, more was at stake than the alleged "utopian idealism" of Jesus' Sermon on the Mount. Nonviolence was no longer irrelevant since the invention of atomic and hydrogen weapons which could destroy civilization, if not all life on the planet.

Optimistically, it could be said that the people's revolutions opened up Europe for the twenty-first century. We noted at the beginning of this chapter how the empires which declared war on each other in 1914—beginning the tragic scenario of decades of chaos—were all sanctioned in their militarism by state churches. A religious vacuum became evident (one that Nietzsche had pointed to) as their sacred canopies—in Germany, Austro-Hungary, and Russia—dissolved. It would be a mistake to suppose that time is inevitably on the side of pluralistic democracy. A secularized progressive worldview often supposed that history is like an army marching forward. Two world wars have refuted such naïveté for most Eastern Europeans. A simply humanistic outlook does not reach to the depths of the problem of evil. There is ample evidence from the present century that history at times moves tragically backwards.

Historical research and reflection about the revolutions we have discussed is only beginning. Not all of the participants would accept a simply historical explanation. Many Christians felt that their church was preserved by God's providence against the Communists. This much is clear: Christianity proved to have a much more profound worldview than that which Marxism allowed. Simple pro- and anti-religion slogans did not say enough.

Christianity is not just a cosmology or philosophy but a faith.

Atheism as exemplified in communism was only one type of misconceived modernity, although an extreme type. Its basic premise was that human beings can control and master history; destiny is finally under their control. The Marxist view was supported and reinforced by utopianism, scientism, class struggle, and hatred. A whole variety of evils were perpetrated, allegedly to bring about a radically new order. Its appraisal of human autonomy as beyond any outside control, apart from the processes of history, proved too simple. A consciousness of contingency remained, a sense of existential loneliness and nihilism.

Viewed realistically, the new setting brings fresh opportunities; old compromises need to be overcome. Of course, religion in the populace does not change as much. The religious are religious still, the irreligious still irreligious. All the open problems of the noncommunist religious world, including tensions among churches, have begun to be imposed on Eastern Europe. Eastern Europe must confront and dialogue with "modernity," biblical higher criticism, pluralism, and ecumenism, together with continuing calls for peace and social justice. The encounter with world religions envisaged by the Second Vatican Council is only beginning to be felt. Old parochialisms and grievances remain barriers. Can Russian Orthodoxy emerge as a moral force, the Roman Catholic church transcend in measure its ties with nationalism, Protestants overcome at least some of their divisiveness?

Other forms of atheism and materialism remain, beside communism. Together they raise the question of the meaning of freedom and liberation. Christianity proclaims the kingdom of God, which transcends and judges all earthly orders. The kingdom of God is not just a philosophy, although it has multiple ethical and philosophical implications. In the Christian tradition it is tied historically to the figure of Jesus, whose person has seemed compelling to believers, even in the face of totalitarianism. They invoked his ethics of nonviolence toward their attackers.

Was Nietzsche wrong with his pessimism and skepticism? "God is dead," he proclaimed. Nietzsche believed that God never really was alive, although people once had believed in him. Nietzsche's claim that European civilization and Christendom were defunct seemed to have been confirmed (only a few decades after it was made) in the tragedy of two world wars. He knew the weakness of the European union of throne and altar, and spoke dramatically of "the last pope."

Nietzsche's prophecy of growing darkness and chaos brought on by the death of God seemed to have fulfillment in Eastern Europe and the tragedy of totalitarianism. In the late twentieth century, its version of history, of the self, ethics, and the meaning of life is receding in Eastern Europe. Communist atheism and revolt against God seem to have burned themselves out. It is not so much that the religious are still religious, the irreligious still irreligious. What is important is that in most countries Christianity had a significant role in opening the window to freedom.

NOTES

1. THE VARIED FACES OF REVOLUTION

1. Hannah Arendt, *On Revolution* (New York: Viking Press, 1963), 22, 40.
2. Franz König, paper presented in London, Spring 1990, 13.
3. Jan Vladislaw, ed., *Václav Havel: or Living in Truth* (London: Faber and Faber, 1987), 36.
4. Vladislaw, 44–45.
5. Vladislaw, 55.
6. Patrick Michel, *La société retrouvée, politique et religion dans l'Europe sovietisée* (Paris: Fayard, 1988), 11.
7. Michel, 10.
8. *See* Paul Tillich, *Systematic Theology,* vol. 3 (Chicago: University of Chicago Press, 1951), 369–72.
9. Adam Michnik, *Letters from Prison and other Essays,* trans. Maya Latynski (Berkeley, Calif.: University of California Press, 1986), 6–7.
10. Ibid., 11
11. Michnik, 3.
12. Michnik, 5.
13. Michnik, xxxii.
14. Michnik, xl.
15. Michnik, xl.
16. Adam Michnik, *L'église et la gauche, le dialogue polonais,* trans. Agnes Slonimski (Paris: Seuil, 1977), 7, 159.
17. König, 4.
18. Ibid.
19. Jerzy Holzer, "Solidarity's Adventures in Wonderland," in Stanislaw Gomulka and Antony Polonsky, eds., *Polish Paradoxes* (London: Routledge, 1990), 97.
20. König, 9.
21. Hannah Arendt, *The Origins of Totalitarianism* (New York: Harcourt Brace, 1951), 430.
22. Sir Ralf Gustav Dahrendorf, "Roads to Freedom: Democratization and its Problems in East Central Europe," *Uncaptive Minds* 3:2 (March–April 1990): 1.
23. Timothy Garton Ash, "Angry New Eastern Europe," *New York Review of Books* 37:13 (August 16, 1990): 51–58.
24. Ash, 52.
25. Ash, 56.
26. Helga Königdorm, *Das Argument* 32:3 (May/June 1990).
27. Dahrendorf, 2.

162   NOTES

28. Dahrendorf, 3.

29. *See* Alec Nove, *Glasnost in Action: Cultural Renaissance in Russia* (Boston: Unwin Hyman, 1989), 24.

30. Nove, 34.

31. Ibid.

32. Nove, 16–17.

33. Arendt, *Totalitarianism*, 391.

34. *Religion in Communist Lands* 18:1 (Spring 1990): 72–79.

35. Ibid., 73.

36. Ibid., 74.

37. Ibid., 75.

38. Ibid., 76.

39. *Religion in Communist Lands* 18:2 (Summer 1990): 111.

40. Arendt, *Totalitarianism*, 9.

41. Géza Németh, "Christianity's Answer to Nationalism," *Hungarian Observer* 3:5: 10–13.

42. Németh, 11.

43. Németh, 12.

44. Ibid.

45. Ibid.

2. GERMANY

1. *Glaube in der 2. Welt* 18:5 (1990): 26.

2. Nigel Hawkes, ed., *Tearing Down the Curtain* (London: Hodder & Stoughton, 1990), 63.

3. Hawkes, 68.

4. Hawkes, 65–66.

5. Helmut Halafter, "Brief aus Dresden," *Glaube in der 2. Welt* 18:5 (1990): 31.

6. Hawkes, 73.

7. Arvan Gordon, "Courtesy Toward God," *Religion in Communist Lands* 18:2 (Summer 1990): 146.

8. Janice Broun, *Conscience and Captivity: Religion in Eastern Europe* (Washington, D.C.: Ethics and Public Policy Center, 1988), 125.

9. Broun, 108.

10. Gordon, 145.

11. Broun, 116.

12. Gordon, 149–50.

13. Gordon, 154.

14. Ehrhart Neubert, *Gesellschaftliche Kommunikation im socialen Wandel* (Berlin-Treptow: Ev. Bekenntnisgemeinde, 1989); *Reproduktion von Religion in der DDR-Gesellschaft* (Frankfurt am Main: Evangelischer Pressedienst, 1989).

15. Gordon, 149.

16. Reinhold Niebuhr, *Children of Light and Children of Darkness* (New York: Scribners, 1957).

17. Kurt Nowak, "Der Protestantismus in der DDR-Erfahrungen und Schwierigkeiten auf dem Weg zur Democratie," *Zeitschrift für Evangelische Ethik* 34 (July–September 1990): 173.

18. Craig R. Whitney, "German President Calls for National Meditation," *Houston Chronicle*, October 4, 1980: 19A.

19. Jürgen Moltmann, *The Crucified God*, trans. R. A. Wilson and John Bowden (New York: Harper and Row, 1974), 8.

3. HUNGARY

1. Hawkes, *Tearing Down the Curtain*, 51–52.
2. Paul Lendvai, *Hungary: The Art of Survival*, trans. Noel Clark, (London: I. B. Tauris, 1988), 12.
3. *Die Presse*, June 30/July 1, 1990: 3.
4. Lendvai, 10.
5. Lendvai, 53.
6. Lendvai, 4.
7. Lendvai, 142. The Lakitelek meeting was held on September 27, 1987, and reported in *Magyar Nemset*, November 14, 1987.
8. Broun, *Conscience*, 329.
9. Broun, 327.
10. *Informationsdienst Osteuropaeisches Christentum* 2:10–11 (June 10, 1990): 7–8.
11. Trevor Beeson, *Discretion and Valor: Religious Conditions in Russia and Eastern Europe* (Glasgow: Collins, 1974), 244.
12. Broun, 142.
13. Broun, 325.
14. Michel, *La société retrouvée*, 46–49.
15. Lendvai, 56.
16. Broun, 328.
17. Hawkes, 40.
18. Hawkes, 52.
19. Broun, 323.
20. Beeson, 259.
21. Broun, 145.
22. Lendvai, 23.
23. Broun, 328.
24. Broun, 158.
25. Broun, 156–57.
26. Broun, 149.
27. Broun, 150.
28. *Informationsdienst Osteropaeisches Christentum* 10–11 (June 10, 1990): 21–23.

4. POLAND

1. Timothy Garton Ash, *The Polish Revolution: Solidarity* (New York: Scribners, 1983), 283.
2. Ash, 128.
3. Hawkes, *Tearing Down the Curtain*, 13.
4. These remarks were in a personal conversation with Bishop Dabrowski in Warsaw.
5. Broun, *Conscience*, 166.
6. Hawkes, 14.
7. Ibid.

8. Broun, 189.

9. *See* Leszek Kolakowski, "The Breakdown," *Main Currents of Marxism*, vol. 3 (Oxford: Clarendon Press, 1978).

10. Ash, 141.

11. Michel, *La société retrouvée*, 12.

12. Michel, 17.

13. Zbigniew Nosowski, "A New Opium for the People: or What has Really Happened in Eastern Europe," unpublished paper.

14. Broun, 186.

15. Nosowski, 11.

16. Michael T. Kaufman, *Mad Dreams and Saving Graces* (New York: Random House, 1989), 140–41.

17. Kaufman, 156–57.

18. Nosowski, 14.

19. *See* Jósef Tischner, *Marxism and Christianity: The Quarrel and the Dialogue in Poland*, trans. Marek Zaleski and Benjamin Fiore, S. J. (Washington, D.C.: Georgetown University Press, 1987) and Jósef Tischner, *The Spirit of Solidarity*, trans. Marek B. Zaleski and Benjamin Fiore, S. J. (San Francisco: Harper and Row, 1984).

20. Nosowski, 8.

21. Nosowski, 21.

22. Ibid.

23. Broun, 177.

24. Michel, 150.

25. Broun, 182.

26. Michel, 222.

27. Ash, 40.

28. Zbigniew Nosowski, "There is no Freedom without Solidarity," unpublished paper, 18.

29. Ash, 58, 205.

30. Nosowski, "There is no Freedom without Solidarity," 15.

5. CZECHOSLOVAKIA

1. Public statement issued by Civic Forum before the first election campaign after the revolution; mimeographed form obtained from their Prague office.

2. *Glaube in der 2. Welt* 18:2 (1990): 23.

3. Hawkes, *Tearing Down the Curtain*, 102.

4. Hawkes, 103.

5. Hawkes, 104.

6. *Spiegel* 48 (November 27, 1989): 167.

7. *Keston News Service* 345 (March 8, 1990): 18.

8. Statement of the Program Commission, drafted by Milos Zeman, dated March 7, 1990.

9. Hawkes, 108.

10. Program Commission statement.

11. Broun, *Conscience*, 309–10.

12. Mimeographed translation of the speech obtained from the Civic Forum office in Prague.

13. Václav Havel, *Power of the Powerless* (London: Hutchison, 1985), 69–70.

14. *Neue Zürcher Zeitung* 23 (April 24, 1990): 1.

15. Václav Havel, *Letters to Olga*, trans. Paul Wilson (New York: Holt, 1989), 236.

16. Gordon, "Courtesy Toward God," 100.

17. Broun, 375.

18. Broun, 19.

19. Beeson, *Discretion and Valor*, 190.

20. Broun, 307.

21. Broun, 70.

22. *Keston News Service* 339 (November 30, 1989): 13.

23. Beeson, 220–21.

24. *Glaube in der 2. Welt* 18:2 (1990): 17.

25. Broun, 99.

26. William Echikson, *Lighting the Night: Revolution in Eastern Europe* (New York: Morrow, 1990), 181.

27. Echikson, 181–82.

28. Broun, 319–22.

29. Broun, 91, 97.

30. Echikson, 183.

31. Echikson, 307.

32. Echikson, 308.

33. *Herder Korrespondenz* 7 (July 1990): 332–37.

34. Tomáš Masaryk, *Conversations with Karel Čapek: Masaryk on Thought and Life* (London: Allen and Unwin, 1944), 141ff.

35. Havel, 268. See Erazim Kohák, *Jan Patočka: Philosophy and Selected Writings* (Chicago: University of Chicago Press, 1989), 3.

36. Tomáš Masaryk, *Modern Man and Religion* 91, cited in Hanus J. Hajek, *T. G. Masaryk Revisited: A Critical Assessment* (Boulder: East European Monographs, distributed by Columbia University Press, 1983), 92.

37. Kohák, 15.

38. Kohák, 7.

39. Havel, *Letters to Olga*, 240–41.

40. Kohák, 130.

41. Havel, *Letters to Olga*, 375.

6. ROMANIA

1. Echikson, *Lighting the Night,* 184.

2. Hawkes, *Tearing Down the Curtain,* 132.

3. Broun, *Conscience,* 219.

4. Hawkes, 125.

5. Hawkes, 126.

6. *See* Dionisie Ghermani, "Der Sonderfall Romanien," *Herder Korrespondenz* 4 (April 1990): 188–92.

7. Hawkes, 144.

8. Hawkes, 125.

9. Broun, 203–204.

10. Broun, 203.

11. Broun, 209.

12. Broun, 219.

13. Broun, 341–43 gives the list of ALRC demands.

14. Broun, 212.

15. Broun, 214.

16. *Keston News Service* 356 (August 9, 1990): 10–11; Ibid. (August 20, 1990): 9.

17. Anneli Ute Gabanyi, *Die Unvollendete Revolution* (Munich: Piper, 1990), 214.

7. BULGARIA

1. Broun, *Conscience and Captivity*, 64.

2. Ibid., 47.

3. Ibid., 64.

4. Ibid., 49.

5. Ibid., 48.

6. John D. Bell, " 'Post-Communist' Bulgaria," *Current History* 89 (1990): 419.

7. Ibid., 428.

8. Richard Crampton, "The Intelligentsia, the Ecology and the Opposition in Bulgaria," *The World Today* 46 (February 1990): 23.

9. Ibid.

10. Ibid., 24.

11. Broun, *Conscience and Captivity*, 59.

12. Michael Shafir, "Xenophobic Communism—The Case of Bulgaria and Romania," *The World Today* 45 (December 1989): 208–09.

13. *Glaube in der 2. Welt* 19:1 (1991): 3.

14. Broun, *Conscience and Captivity*, 53.

15. Ibid., 63.

8. ALBANIA

1. Broun, *Conscience and Captivity*, 40.

2. Broun, 23.

3. Broun, 35.

4. Ibid.

5. Denis R. Janz, "Rooting Out Religion: The Albanian Experiment," *The Christian Century* (July 15-August 1, 1990): 701.

6. Ibid., 700.

7. *Glaube in der 2. Welt*, 19:2 (1991):17.

8. Ibid.

9. *The Economist* (December 22, 1990): 66.

10. *Glaube in der 2. Welt*, 19:2 (1191): 4.

11. Ibid.

12. Ibid., 1990/18:5 (1990): 3.

13. Ibid., 19:2 (1991): 4.

14. *Maclean's* (July 23, 1990): 30–31.

15. *Der Spiegel* (March 11, 1991): 180–181.

16. Broun, *Conscience and Captivity*, 35.

17. *The Economist* (March 20, 1991): 47.

18. Broun, *Conscience and Captivity*, 223.

19. Ibid., 26.

20. Ibid., 25.

21. Ibid., 31.

22. Ibid., 24.

23. Janz, "Rooting out Religion," 701.

24. Ibid.

25. *The Economist* (December 22, 1990): 66.

26. *Informationsdienst Osteuropaeisches Christentum* 2:22-23(1990): 2.

27. *Glaube in der 2. Welt* 19:2 (1991): 3.

9. RUSSIA

1. *Keston News Service* 353 (June 28, 1990): 3–4.

2. Ibid.: 3. The subsequent issue of *Keston News Service* 354 (July 12, 1990) reported that St. Isaac's cathedral had not yet been returned to the church for continuous use.

3. Scott Shane, "Supreme Soviet Approves Religious Freedom," *Houston Chronicle*, October 6, 1990, 23.

4. *Informationsdienst Osteuropaeisches Christentum* 2: 5-6 (March 21, 1990): 23 describes a hunger strike in Minsk.

5. *Keston News Service* 354 (July 12, 1990): 12–13.

6. *Houston Chronicle*, September 24, 1990, 9A.

7. Jane Ellis, *The Russian Orthodox Church: A Contemporary History* (London: Routledge, 1988), 287.

8. See *Informationsdienst Osteuropaeisches Christentum* 10-11 (June 10, 1990): 2, and *Keston News Service* 353 (June 28, 1990):15.

9. Jane Ellis, in *Keston News Service* 351 (May 31, 1990): 18.

10. See Gerhard Simon, *Church, State and Opposition in the U.S.S.R.* (Berkeley, Calif.: University of California Press, 1974), 86.

11. Dimitry Pospielovsky, *The Russian Church under the Soviet Regime, 1917-1982* (Crestwood, N.Y.: St. Vladimir's Seminary Press, 1984), I:43.

12. John B. Dunlop, "Gorbachev and Russian Orthodoxy," *Problems of Communism* 38 (July-August 1989): 102.

13. Ibid.

14. Pospielovsky, I: 43.

15. Ibid., I: 194.

16. Ellis, *The Russian Orthodox Church*, 292.

17. Beeson, op. cit., 71.

18. Ellis, 41.

19. Ibid.

20. Mikhail Meerson-Aksyonov; *see* Ellis, 79.

21. Ellis, op. cit., 113. Van der Voort was interviewed in Amsterdam by the author.

22. *Keston News Service* 350 (May 17, 1990): 12.

23. S. F. Jones, "Soviet Religious Policy and the Georgian Orthodox Apostolic Church: From Khrushchev to Gorbachev," *Religion in Communist Lands* 17:4 (Winter 1989): 290–312.

24. Ibid., 293.

25. Ibid., 294.

26. Ibid., 298.
27. Ibid., 310, 312.
28. *Keston News Service* 355 (July 1990): 3.
29. Simon, *Church, State and Opposition*, 156.
30. Ibid., 154.
31. *See* Rowe, "Soviet Baptists Engage in *Perestroika*," *Religion in Communist Lands* 18:2 (Summer 1990): 184–187.
32. Nicolas Berdyaev, *The Origin of Russian Communism*, trans. R. M. French (London: Geofrey Bles, 1937, 1955), 172.
33. Ibid., 132.
34. Ibid., 141.
35. Ibid., 147.
36. Ibid., 153–154.
37. Ibid., 130.
38. Ibid., 118.
39. Ibid., 127.
40. Ibid., 155.
41. Ibid., 183.
42. Ibid.

10. ANATOMY OF THE REVOLUTIONS

1. Echikson, *Lighting the Night,* 55.
2. Echikson, 60.
3. Echikson, 3.
4. *See The New Encyclopaedia Britannica*, vol. 5, 15th ed. (1986), 493.
5. Arendt, *Totalitarianism,* 391.
6. Echikson, 69.
7. Milovan Djilas, *The New Class: An Analysis of the Communist System* (New York: Praeger, 1957).
8. Dahrendorf, "Roads to Freedom," 5.
9. Echikson, 155-57.
10. Echikson, 173.
11. Arendt, *Totalitarianism,* 391.
12. Echikson, 147.
13. Vladamir Tismaneanu, *The Crisis of Marxist Ideology in Eastern Europe: The Poverty of Utopia* (London: Routledge, 1988), 124.
14. Tismaneanu, 199.
15. Tismaneanu, 121.
16. Yuri Afanasyev, "The Coming Dictatorship," *New York Review of Books* 38:33 (January 31, 1991), 36–39.
17. Peter Reddaway, "Empire on the Brink," *New York Review of Books* 38:33, 9.
18. Hedrick Smith, *The New Russians* (New York: Random House, 1990), 395.
19. Garadzha, 76.
20. Garadzha, 77.
21. Garadzha, 78–79.
22. Echikson, himself Jewish, includes an excellent section on Jews and the peoples' revolutions in his book, 240.
23. *See* Anne Herbst-Oltmans, "Das Gewissen der Nation: In Memoriam Andrej Sacharov," *Glaube in der 2. Welt* 1:18 (1990): 1819.

INDEX